DEVELOPMENTAL PSYCHOPATHOLOGY

From Infancy through Adolescence

DEVELOPMENTAL PSYCHOPATHOLOGY

From Infancy through Adolescence

THIRD EDITION

Charles Wenar

The Ohio State University

McGraw-Hill, Inc.

New York   St. Louis   San Francisco   Auckland   Bogotá   Caracas
Lisbon   London   Madrid   Mexico City   Milan   Montreal   New Delhi
San Juan   Singapore   Sydney   Tokyo   Toronto

This book was set in Palatino by Ruttle, Shaw & Wetherill, Inc.
The editors were Jane Vaicunas, Beth Kaufman, and Tom Holton;
the production supervisor was Elizabeth J. Strange.
The cover was designed by Joan Greenfield.
The photo editor was Debra Hershkowitz.
Arcata Graphics/Martinsburg was printer and binder.

DEVELOPMENTAL PSYCHOPATHOLOGY
From Infancy through Adolescence

Acknowledgments appear on pages 567–569, and on this page by reference.

 This book is printed on recycled, acid-free paper containing a minimum of 50% total recycled fiber with 10% postconsumer de-inked fiber.

1 2 3 4 5 6 7 8 9 0   AGM   AGM   9 0 9 8 7 6 5 4 3

ISBN 0-07-069286-6

Library of Congress Cataloging-in-Publication Data

Wenar, Charles, (date).
   Developmental Psychopathology: from infancy through adolescence /
Charles Wenar.—3rd ed.
      p.   cm.
   Includes bibliographical references and index.
   ISBN 0-07-069286-6
      1. Child psychopathology.   2. Adolescent psychopathology.
RJ499.W396   1994
618.92'89—dc20   93-36673

INTERNATIONAL EDITION

ABOUT THE AUTHOR

CHARLES WENAR is professor emeritus of psychology at The Ohio State University. He headed both the developmental area and the clinical child program in the department of psychology there. A graduate of Swarthmore College and State University of Iowa, Dr. Wenar was both a clinician and a researcher at Michael Reese Hospital, the Illinois Neuropsychiatric Institute, and the University of Pennsylvania. His two previous books and numerous articles, as well as his research on autism and on negativism in healthy toddlers, attest to his long-standing interest in both normal and disturbed children. In 1986, Dr. Wenar received the Distinguished Professional Contribution Award of the Section on Clinical Child Psychology of Division 12 of the American Psychological Association for his meritorious contribution to the advancement of knowledge and service to children.

To Johnerik and Leif, remembering the talks and the walks.

CONTENTS

PREFACE

PROGRESS IN DEVELOPMENTAL PSYCHOPATHOLOGY

It is gratifying to note how quickly the 1990 edition of *Developmental Psychopathology* has become dated. This is a sure sign of vitality. However, we are dealing with more than sheer energy—we are dealing with progress. This revised edition provides comprehensive coverage of these exciting new developments:

Developmental psychopathology—conceptual and empirical advances. The basic premise of the developmental approach to understanding childhood disorders was established as symbiotic relation between normal and abnormal development, each nourishing the other and neither being a comprehensive account of development without the other. Our own formulation of psychopathology as "normal development gone awry" epitomizes this interdependence. Once this basic idea was established, however, such phrases sounded too general to be satisfactory. What was needed was a more *differentiated conceptualization* of how the interdependence operated to result in normal development on the one hand, and psychopathology on the other. The concepts of *risk* and *protective factors* currently fill this need. It is the dynamic interplay between the two that determines whether development will follow a normal or deviant course and, in the latter case, if there will be a return to normality.

Empirically there is now sufficient data to chart the *developmental pathways* of a number of psychopathologies. Such pathways provide information as to which variables at which developmental periods deviate from their normal course as well as the nature of such deviations. Often there is also information concerning risk factors responsible for the deviations. Our knowledge of protective factors however is still limited.

Finally, there has been some progress in understanding the *models* that account for deviant development. *Precocity* has been added to the traditional psychopathologies of timing—fixations, lags, and regression—while the idea that deviant development is *qualitatively different* from normal development appears more frequently than before.

Multideterminism. The previous edition marked the shift from thinking in terms of a single cause for a given psychopathology to thinking in terms of multiple causes. All too often, however, this shift resulted in a mere listing of possible determinants as if such a list were a satisfactory solution to the etiological mystery. Currently, there are a number of attempts to *integrate* the data in terms of the relative importance of the etiological variables as well as the interaction among them. At times this integration is conceptual, at times statistical, and, in the ideal cases, a combination of the two.

Understanding specific disorders. As would be expected, this edition documents the conceptual and empirical progress in understanding specific disorders, e.g., the importance of *theory of mind* for autism, of *coercion theory* for conduct disorder, and for *attachment theory* for depression and abuse.

BROADENING THE SCOPE OF DEVELOPMENTAL PSYCHOPATHOLOGY

In addition to making progress, the scope of developmental psychopathology has been broadened. The following topics receive particular attention in the current edition.

Comorbidity. The co-occurrence of two or more psychopathologies was once regarded as an irritating methodological confound to be swept under the rug of research. Now investigators realize that comorbidity frequently occurs and needs to be understood in its own right. Because the realization came so recently, however, there is much to be learned about the nature and reasons for comorbidity.

Multiculturalism. The sheer number of ethnic minority children has forced clinical child psychologists to pay special attention to them and their mental health needs. Much of the literature concerns providing services congruent with their particular ethnic background. However, there is also a growing interest in the implications of cultural diversity for the question of what constitutes normal and deviant development.

Problem behavior. While not new, the trend of broadening clinical child psychology to include nonpsychopathological conditions continues. For example, *emotional maltreatment* has been added to physical and sexual abuse, and *depressed mothers* to the list of deviant parenting. While not falling within traditional diagnostic categories, the children are sufficiently distressed and dysfunctional to be of concern to the clinical child psychologist.

Assessment. Two major developments in assessment are the appearance of *DSM-IV*, providing criteria for diagnosing mental disorders in infants, children and adolescents, and the revised definition of *mental retardation* published by the American Association on Mental Retardation. (The former will be presented in terms of the DSM-IV Draft Criteria [3/1/93] since the DSM-IV itself was not yet published.)

FOR THE STUDENT

The goal of the present edition has not changed—namely, to enable the student to "think developmentally" about childhood psychopathologies. However, visual material has been added for the first time along with summary charts of particularly complex findings. Review articles are often cited so students can have access to more detailed presentations of research than is possible within a given chapter. Also there are references to literature on topics which, while important, had to be excluded because of space limitations.

ACKNOWLEDGMENTS

I would first like to express my thanks to my colleague Mike Vasey who combines a sharp intellect and a wealth of information with a generous spirit. I consulted him frequently and relied both on his knowledge and his judgment.

I am indebted to many individuals at McGraw-Hill. Beth Kaufman had the unenviable task of guiding me through the maze of reviews, revisions, and deadlines. All this she did while being unfailingly enthusiastic about the project. As sponsoring editor, Jane Vaicunas cut a number of what appeared to me to be Gordian knots so my work could proceed apace. Tom Holton, editing supervisor par excellence, shepherded the manuscript from word processor to printer. Martha Cameron disciplined my overly long sentences and saw to the myriad of details that is the lot of a copy editor. Safra Nimrod was responsible for the photographs that help enliven the text and Cheryl Besenjak saved me the aggravation of obtaining permissions. Marketing was in the capable hands of Jill Gordon.

Finally, I am grateful to the many reviewers of this edition. I was impressed by their thoughtfulness and thoroughness and profited greatly from their comments. In particular, I would like to thank the following individuals: Michael Alessandri, San Jose State University; Karen Bierman, The Pennsylvania State University; Ronda J. Carpenter, Roanoke College; Byron Egeland, University of Minnesota; Jon B. Ellis, East Tennessee State University; Per F. Gjerde, University of California at Santa Cruz; Sherryl Goodman, Emory University; Arthur C. Jones, University of Denver; Linda Koenig, Emory University; Alan J. Lipman, The George Washington University Medical Center; Robert J. McMahon, University of Washington; Sally Ozonoff, University of Utah; Andrew G. Renouf, Western Psychiatric Institute and Clinic, University of Pittsburgh; and Stephen R. Shirk, University of Denver.

And then there is Solveig, my loving helper, who is in a class by herself.

CHARLES WENAR

DEVELOPMENTAL PSYCHOPATHOLOGY
From Infancy through Adolescence

CHAPTER 1

THE DEVELOPMENTAL APPROACH

Chapter Outline

Overview
    A General Developmental Model
    Interaction
Specific Models of Childhood Psychopathology
    The Medical Model
    The Behavioral Model

    The Psychodynamic Model
    The Cognitive Models
    Developmental Psychopathology
Some Comments about Methodology
    The Naturalistic Tradition
    The Laboratory Tradition

You are a clinical child psychologist.[1] A mother telephones your office frantic over the sudden personality change in her boy. "He used to be so sweet and then, out of the clear blue sky, he started being sassy and sulky and throwing a fit if anybody asked him to do the least little thing. What really scared me was last night he got so mad at his brother, he ran at him and started hitting him with all his might. His brother was really hurt and started screaming, and my husband and I had to pull them apart. I don't know what would have happened if we hadn't been there. I just never saw anybody in a rage like that before."

---

[1] This and subsequent sections will concern the experiences of a hypothetical clinical child psychologist. However, the experiences themselves might apply to any professional who is involved with the mental health of children. All names are fictitious.

What is the first question you ask?

You are at a cocktail party and, after learning that you are a clinical child psychologist, a former star-quarterback-turned-successful-business-executive takes you aside. After some rambling about "believing in sexual equality as much as the next fellow," he comes to the point. "Last week my son turned to my wife and announced that when he got old enough, he was going to become a girl. When my wife asked him where he got a crazy idea like that, he said that he thought boys were too rough, and he liked to be with girls more. I know he's always been a 'mama's boy,' but I'll be damned if I want any son of mine to have one of those sex changes done on him."

What is the first question you ask?

You are a clinical child psychologist conducting an initial interview with a mother who has brought her daugh-

ter to a child guidance clinic. "She has always been a sensitive child and a loner, but I thought she was getting along all right—except that recently she has started having some really strange ideas. The other day we were driving on the highway to town, and she said, 'I could make all these cars wreck if I just raised my hand.' I thought she was joking, but she had a serious expression on her face and wasn't even looking at me. Then, another time she wanted to go outside when the weather was bad, and she got furious at me because I didn't make it stop raining. And now she's started pleading and pleading with me every night to look in on her after she has gone to sleep to be sure her leg isn't hanging over the side of the bed. She says there are some kind of crab creatures in the dark waiting to grab her if her foot touches the floor. What worries me is that she believes all these things can really happen. I don't know if she's crazy or watching too much TV or what's going on."

What is the first question you ask?

The first question is the same in all three cases: *How old is your child?*

OVERVIEW

Our general concern is with time—or, more precisely, with change over time.

Our specific charge is to understand psychopathological disturbances of childhood.

Our procedure will involve placing various psychopathologies within a developmental context and examining them as instances of *normal development gone awry.*

The three vignettes illustrate this procedure. Whether the described behaviors are regarded as normal or pathological depends upon when they occur in the developmental sequence. All three are to be expected in toddlers and preschoolers but would be suspect at later ages. It is not unusual for a docile infant to become a willful, negativistic, temperamental tyrant during the "terrible twos." If the child were 10, however, his attack on his brother may well represent a serious lapse in self-control. In a like manner it is not unusual for preschool boys to believe that they can

grow up to be women because they have not grasped the fact that sex remains constant throughout life. If an adolescent boy seriously contemplated a sex change, this would be cause for parental concern and professional attention. And finally, ideas of omnipotence and a failure to clearly separate fantasy from reality are part of normal cognitive development in toddlers and preschoolers; their presence from middle childhood on suggests the possibility of a serious thought disturbance and an ominous lack of reality contact.

The vignettes also provide us with our first clue to understanding child psychopathology as normal development gone awry: psychopathology is behavior which once was but no longer can be considered appropriate to the child's level of development. This was one of Freud's most brilliant and influential insights. The general thesis that adult disturbances have their roots in childhood continues to be a pervasive etiological hypothesis accepted even by those who reject all other aspects of Freudian theory. We shall make use of the same developmental hypothesis but apply it within childhood itself. As we examine various psychopathologies, we shall discover that there are many variations on this theme of psychopathology as developmentally inappropriate behavior; therefore we shall constantly be seeking the specific *developmental model* that best fits the data at hand. We shall also come across some unexpected exceptions for which the model itself does not seem to hold.

At the applied level, the developmental approach underlies the child clinician's deceptively simple statement, "There's nothing to worry about—most children act that way at this age, and your child will probably outgrow it"; or its more ominous version, "The behavior is unusual and should be attended to, since it might not be outgrown." A considerable amount of information concerning normal development must be mastered before one can judge whether the behavior at hand is age-appropriate, as well as whether a suspect behavior is likely to disappear in the course of a child's progress from infancy to adulthood. In addition, the child clinician must know which frankly psychopathological behaviors stand a good chance of being outgrown with or without therapeutic intervention and which are apt to persist.

Incidentally, to state that behavior is outgrown is not as much an explanation as a label for ignorance. While certain psychopathologies tend to disappear with time, exactly what happens developmentally to cause their disappearance is not known. In fact, the phenomenon has rarely been investigated. The best we can do is to recognize that "outgrown" is a nonexplanation.

Before we set out to understand child psychopathology as normal development gone awry, there are a number of preliminary matters to be attended to. First, we must present a *general developmental model* in order to examine various characteristics of development itself. Then we must select those *variables* that are particularly important to the understanding of childhood psychopathology and trace their normal developmental course. Our vignettes, for example, suggest that the variables of self-control, sexual identity, and cognition should be included in the list. We shall also have to select the *theories* that will contribute most to the developmental approach. Next, we shall turn to a descriptive account of the *behaviors comprising childhood psychopathology,* since these are the behaviors we must understand in terms of our developmental perspective. And, finally, we must examine *longitudinal studies* that have followed groups of normal and disturbed children into adulthood, since these studies will provide a general guide as to which psychopathologies are apt to persist and which are likely to be outgrown.

A General Developmental Model

Our general developmental model includes the time dimension along with intrapersonal, interpersonal, superordinate, and organic variables. These five categories will be referred to as *contexts.*

Time Since our general concern is with change over time, our task would be simpler if there were agreement as to how change should be conceptualized. There is not.

Some psychologists anchor change in chronological time. Gesell is a prime exemplar, since he links crucial behavioral changes to chronological age. In tracing the child's relation to the parents, for example, he describes age 6 as a time of high ambivalence toward the mother, cravings for affection being followed by tantrums and rebellion. Age 7 is calm and inward, the child being companionable, sympathetic, anxious to please. Age 8 is stormy again, with the child demanding the mother's attention while being exacting, rude, and "fresh," while 9 marks a return to self-sufficiency, eagerness to please, and affectionate behavior. And so it goes (Gesell et al., 1946).

A different way to conceptualize change is in terms of *stages* of development, Piaget's cognitive theory and Freud's psychosexual theory being two prominent examples. Stage theories are more concerned with change itself than with chronological age. Typically they make two assumptions: stages represent qualitative reorganizations of behavior rather than "more of the same"; and the sequence of stages is unalterable. Thus, something new emerges at each stage, and the order of emergence is fixed. For both Piaget and Freud, the question "How old is the child?" is not as important as "What stage is the child in?" Fortunately for the clinician, the stages they depict can be assigned chronological age guidelines.

The conceptualization of change over time

is of more than academic interest. A characteristic of stage theories is that they often regard the transition between stages as a time of increased tension, unrest, and even reversion to less mature behaviors. The psychosexual stages have this characteristic, while Piaget describes the child's return to immature ways of thinking during cognitive transitions. Even Gesell, whose maturational theory does not include specific stages, describes development in terms of periods of unstable expansion alternating with ones of stable consolidation. All such conceptualizations stand in contrast to radical environmentalism, which claims that stability or instability is primarily the consequence of the experiences the child is having. The important point for us is that normal development may entail built-in times of stress and upset; the transitions from infancy to the preschool period and from middle childhood to adolescence, for example, are two potentially stressful periods. Knowing when disturbed behavior is part of normal growth helps the clinician decide when to tell a parent, "Most children act like that, and yours is likely to outgrow it."

There is another aspect of the time dimension. Our developmental approach implies that in order to evaluate the meaning and import of an event in a child's life, it is essential to know not only *what* happened but also *when* it happened. To illustrate: a lengthy separation from the mother may have few adverse effects in early infancy before an attachment to her has developed but may trigger a dramatic reaction of protest and extreme withdrawal after an attachment has been formed. Being hospitalized becomes progressively less upsetting between 2 and 12 years of age and also may have different meanings, the younger children being distressed over separation, the 4- to 6-year-olds fearing mutilation or death or viewing hospitalization as punishment. Whether obese adults regard their body with disgust or not depends, among other things, on whether

they were obese during adolescence, a period when body consciousness is at a height.

It is also widely believed that events happening in the first few years of life have a more lasting effect on development than events happening subsequently. However, this so-called critical-period or sensitive-period hypothesis has not gone unchallenged and is viewed with a certain amount of skepticism (see Clarke and Clarke, 1977). While the controversy over the critical or sensitive period will play only a minor role in our presentations, we will not accept either hypothesis as a universally valid principle of human development. Rather, we prefer to test its validity in regard to the particular aspect of development under discussion.

The Intrapersonal Context The intrapersonal context will figure most prominently in our discussions of psychopathology, since it contains the greatest amount of developmental data. However, here, as with the context of time, we are confronted by the problem of how best to conceptualize the individual child. Once past the obvious variables of age and sex, in what direction should we go? Traditional behaviorists would persuade us to deal exclusively with manifest behavior and to avoid all mentalistic or inferential concepts; Freudians urge us to examine the child's ego strength and monitor the battles between id and superego; Piaget reminds us not to neglect egocentrism and the balancing act between assimilation and accommodation; Erikson points to the centrality of ego identity; and Werner insists on the importance of differentiation and hierarchical integration. (The technicalities of the various theories need not concern us here. However, it would be helpful to have the kind of general familiarity with the major developmental theories to be found in introductory texts in child development. See, for example, Berk, 1991.)

The choice among conceptualizations has

important clinical implications. The behavioral viewpoint leans toward a statistical and social approach to psychopathology. Since there is nothing in behavior itself which designates it as abnormal, the judgment must be based on its infrequency or on the fact that a given society chooses to label certain behaviors as psychopathological. In another society the same behavior might go unnoticed or even be regarded as a special gift.

The psychoanalysts, on the contrary, maintain that behavior is important only as it furnishes clues to the child's inner life; psychopathology is not a matter of behavior per se, but of the meaning of such behavior. The frequency of masturbation in adolescence, for example, is not as important as the stage-appropriateness of the fantasies which accompany masturbation.

Because our primary goal is to understand rather than to champion a particular conceptualization of the intrapersonal context, we shall utilize various theories only as they throw light on the psychopathology at hand. Such eclecticism assumes that no one theory offers a satisfactory account of all of childhood psychopathology, while various individual theories are apposite in accounting for specific disturbances.

The Interpersonal Context Interpersonal variables are concerned with interactions among individuals. Of all such interactions, the parent-child relationship will figure most prominently in our discussions since it is assumed to be the most important in determining normal or deviant development and has been most thoroughly investigated. We will be interested in different normal patterns of parenting and the children's behaviors associated with them as well as in such pathological extremes as neglect and physical and sexual abuse. Peer interactions also play a significant role in normal and deviant development, although their importance has only recently

been recognized. Here we will deal with such positive relations as popularity and friendship and their negative counterparts such as rejection and isolation. While sibling and teacher-child relationships fall within the interpersonal context, their relation to psychopathology has rarely been investigated.

The Superordinate Context Superordinate variables deal with aggregates of individuals taken as a unit, such as the family, the group, social class, culture. The study of the family as a unit, for example, has yielded a number of provocative hypotheses concerning the difference between normal and disturbed functioning. The group will concern us when we discuss the contribution of the gang to delinquent behavior and substance abuse. Cultural differences lie at the heart of our discussion of ethnic minorities and the stresses they must cope with. The role of social class in general and poverty in particular in producing psychopathology will also concern us.

The Organic Context The organic context involves various characteristics of the human body that are relevant to understanding deviant development: genetic material, variables involved in the body's structure and functioning with particular emphasis on the brain, and factors determining those innate individual differences called temperament.

The organic context should not be equated with the psychological representation or experience of the body; this belongs in the intrapersonal context. The two are clearly distinct: many physiological processes do not and cannot have any representation in consciousness; in the case of phantom limbs, pain is still felt in a toe that has been amputated; severe psychopathology may be marked by somatic delusions, such as believing that one's bowels are turning into stone.

The effects of psychological disturbances on

the organic body will be central to our examination of the eating disorders of bulimia and anorexia nervosa. Reversing the direction of influence, we will be concerned with the psychological consequences of physical illness and brain damage. We will also be concerned with the role genetic factors play in various psychopathologies and in various forms of mental retardation, one of which—Down syndrome—will be discussed in detail.

Interaction

We have been discussing the contexts as static entities. In reality, they are constantly interacting. The context of time interacts with all other contexts, which in turn interact with one another. Parents who are 25 years old when their daughter is born are not at the same stage in their development as they will be at 40 when she enters adolescence. In a like manner, the casual, improvised peer group of the preschool period differs from the adolescent clique, which vies with parents as the arbiter of taste in clothes, music, language, and social behavior. Being a member of the lower class in the socially stable 1950s had a different meaning than it did in the 1960s when riots and protests made the plight of the urban poor a matter of national concern. The social ferment of the 1960s has had other effects as well. The family as a social institution is being markedly changed by parents' willingness and need to place toddlers and preschoolers in day-care facilities, by the increasing number of working mothers, by the emphasis on negotiable rather than assigned parental roles, and by the increase in divorce and single-parent families. Our society has become increasingly tolerant of early sexual experiences and of couples living together without being married, while the emphasis on doing "your own thing" has broadened the spectrum of acceptable behavior. All these changes have an impact on what parents and professionals alike regard as normal or deviant development.

The changes described above are well known. Not so well known is the fact that the concept of childhood itself is changing. In the pioneer days, children were workers and miniature adults; since they were born into sin, their parents were advised—often by the clergy—to beat the devil out of them. Quite a different image from our present one, with its emphasis on the uniqueness of childhood and the importance of child-centeredness on the part of the parents. (For a more detailed account, see Abramowitz, 1976). To cite another example: in 1874 a brutally abused, starving, and mutilated child named Mary Ellen received legal protection from her parents only after she had been legally defined as an animal so that the laws against animal cruelty could be applied to her. This is a far cry from the current concern for children's rights; in Sweden, for example, corporal punishment is against the law and a child has the right to have a parent arrested for spanking him or her.

Just as the concept of childhood is changing, so is the concept of childhood psychopathology. Some changes have come from within the profession, such as Kanner's delineation of early infantile autism in 1943; others have resulted from social forces, such as the elimination of homosexuality as a psychiatric disturbance in 1974 which was spearheaded by pressure from gay activists groups, or the increasing interest in a multicultural perspective which was necessitated by the increasing number of minority children. The social ferment of the 1960s forced professionals to recognize that poverty vastly increases the risk of a variety of psychopathologies, thereby changing the course of the mental health movement from an individual to a community orientation. (See Chapter 17. For a comprehensive historical account, see H. E. Rie, 1971.) Thus, there is nothing final about the list of psychopathologies that will be introduced in Chapter 3. The list has changed and will continue to change in response both to theoretical and empirical progress within the profession and to social pressures and values outside the profession. In fact, a consistent application of our developmental model requires that this be so.

In sum, our model entails the interaction of variables both at a given point in time and over time. This continual and progressive interaction among variables is called the *transactional* approach (Sameroff and Chandler, 1975). The model itself is presented schematically in Figure 1.1.

SPECIFIC MODELS OF CHILDHOOD PSYCHOPATHOLOGY

The model we have presented is designed to be general and comprehensive. It is intended to serve as a means of organizing what might otherwise be a bewildering array of variables used to account for a given psychopathology. It also is sufficiently general to embrace the specific models of psychopathology that we are about to present.

There are, at present, a variety of models of childhood psychopathology. While having distinctive features, the models are not necessarily incompatible. Some share common features. Others are complementary or tangential. Still others represent irreconcilable differences. Each has merit; none is totally satisfactory. Moreover, few efforts have been made to integrate them all, as there is tacit agreement that such a unification lies far in the future. Therefore we must reconcile ourselves to living with diversity and partial truths. In our own presentation of models, we will concentrate on those features that will be relevant to our subsequent discussion of various psychopathologies. For a more comprehensive coverage of models of psychopathology than we shall give, see Bootzin, Acocella, and Alloy, 1993.)

The term ''model'' is best interpreted as a frame of reference, since it has little of the precision and explanatory potency of models in the physical sciences, such as a model for the

structure of the atom or the DNA molecule. Each model has its own concepts, often couched in terms of a specialized vocabulary, its own assumptions concerning which are relevant variables, its own view of etiology and remediation, and its own stand on the nature of scientific inquiry. In addition to its expected functions of organizing existing facts and generating new ones, a model of psychopathology must also serve the pragmatic function of being useful to the professionals concerned with understanding and remedying childhood disturbances.

The Medical Model

The medical model belongs in the organic context. Historically it was a step forward in the scientific study of psychopathology because it replaced the demonology of the Middle Ages. However, by its subsequent exclusion of all other etiological factors in the nineteenth century it became a roadblock to progress. Currently, the organic emphasis is more temperate and buttressed by a more substantial body of empirical findings than it was 100 years ago. The present-day medical model consists of two components. The first involves the general etiological hypothesis that certain psychopathologies result from organic dysfunctions. The second involves classifying and interpreting psychopathological behavior in the same way as physical diseases, namely, in terms of diagnostic entities.

Organic Etiology There is evidence that organic factors play a major role in certain kinds of adult schizophrenia and depression and in certain kinds of mental retardation and schizophrenia in children. Organic factors have also been implicated in the etiology of autism and in certain kinds of antisocial acting-out behaviors, hyperactivity, and learning disabilities in children, although the evidence varies in definitiveness. Thus, the list of psychopathologies having a possible organic etiology contin-

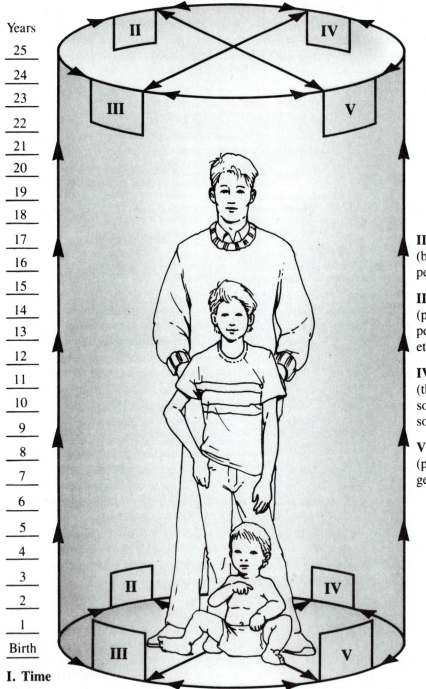

II. Intrapersonal
(behavior, cognitive,
personality variables)

III. Interpersonal
(parent—child, sibling,
peers, teacher—child,
etc.)

IV. Superordinate
(the family, the group,
socioeconomic status,
society, culture)

V. Organic
(physiological processes,
genes, etc.)

FIGURE 1.1
Contexts II to V interact at all points in time as well as over time.

ues to be impressive. Note the modifier "certain kinds of," however: a given psychopathology—adult depression, for example—may have an organic basis in some cases while being psychogenic in others.

There are three specific models of organic etiology. In the first, *genetic* factors are responsible for the appearance of a given psychopathology. Research has centered around three related areas of inquiry. The first of these concerns which psychopathologies have a significant genetic component; for example, there is compelling evidence for the inheritance of certain kinds of schizophrenia. The second area concerns the mode by which a genetic abnormality is transmitted. This involves tracing the path from gene to behavior and understanding all the mediators involved. The third area concerns the extent of heritability in a given psychopathology. Extremists maintain that genes per se determine the abnormal behavior; moderates counter that only vulnerability to a psychopathology is inherited, while its actual appearance depends on environmental conditions. For example, one child may become schizophrenic because of a genetic vulnerability interacting with a series of traumatic life experiences, while another child with the same genetic vulnerability may make an adequate adjustment because of a sympathetic, benign environment. (For the role of genetics in specific childhood psychopathologies and a discussion of misconceptions about genetic factors, see Rutter, 1991, and Rutter et al., 1990.)

Proponents of the *biochemical model* seek to discover the biochemical agents that may contribute to the etiology of psychopathological behavior. Again, schizophrenia has been the most frequently targeted disturbance, each new advance in medical science leading to new hope that the psychotoxic agent has been discovered. When bacteria were found to cause physical disease, it was also suggested that they were involved in mental illness; then

attention shifted to viruses and, most recently, to alterations in the metabolism of certain brain chemicals, or neurochemicals, particularly a group of naturally occurring neurochemical substances called monoamines. Despite promising leads, the gap between chemistry and behavior, as between genes and behavior, is far from closed—and the assumption of a direct causal relation is a highly oversimplified one.

The *neurophysiological model* assumes that abnormal behavior is due to inherited, congenital, or acquired brain pathology. Obviously, it overlaps with the genetic and biochemical models but includes other etiological agents such as intrauterine disease, premature birth, or traumatic brain insult. What this model does is make brain functioning the key to understanding psychopathological conditions.

At the most general level, the medical model is part of the quest to build a bridge between human behavior and human physiology. The quest is an ancient one and is currently being facilitated by astonishing advances in modern technology. However, to claim at this point that psychopathology is "nothing but" organic dysfunctioning would be as erroneous as to claim that it is "nothing but" a problem in adjustment. The organic context interacts with the intra- and interpersonal contexts, and knowledge of this interaction is necessary if progress is to be made in understanding the etiology of psychopathology. (For further details concerning the organic basis of psychopathological behavior, see Werry, 1986a.)

The Medical Model of Diagnosis At one level, diagnosis can be viewed as a variation on the age-old scientific exercise of classification. Psychopathologies, like insects and flowers, are so diverse that viewing each separately would be overwhelming. In order to simplify their task, therefore, investigators assume that there are classes in nature and that keen observation will reveal what these classes are.

To classify psychopathologies according to the medical model, we must first answer two basic questions. First, what is the rationale for regarding the behaviors as abnormal rather than normal? Second, are the specific classifications valid or true to nature? The first question establishes the general criteria for inclusion and exclusion and, among classifications utilizing the medical model, has been answered in a variety of ways. The least satisfactory answer is based on an analogy of mental health and illness to physical health and illness. An analogy is not an acceptable rationale and can be both incorrect and misleading. Yet it is the analogy which has crept into and dominates the very vocabulary we have used in dealing with psychopathology—mental illness, mental health, mental hygiene, syndrome, patient, treatment, cure, and, indeed, psychopathology itself all derive from medicine.

Whether a classification is really there in nature involves validation, with diverse professionals and investigators putting the classification to empirical and statistical tests which either affirm or cast doubt upon its soundness. As we shall see, some classifications, such as autism, have met the test of subsequent validation; others, such as minimal brain damage, have not.

But the medical model has always entailed more than a descriptive classification; the classifications themselves are called diagnoses, and these have both etiological and prognostic implications. It is the former which is most troublesome. Emil Kraepelin, who published the landmark classification of adult psychopathologies in 1833, set the stage by assuming an organic etiology for each class of psychopathology. While it is an erroneous overgeneralization, the equation "classification = diagnosis = organic etiology" lingers on, particularly in the ceaseless professional skirmishes between psychiatrists and other mental health professionals. The former claim that their medical background makes them the ultimate arbiters of diagnosis and therapy in mental as well as physical illness. Psychologists are particularly incensed by this stand, and heated legal battles are being fought over what constitutes the legitimate province of each professional.

There is another problem with medical terminology, involving the use of the word "symptom." To designate a given psychopathology, say, a phobia, as a symptom means that there is an underlying cause, just as in medicine a virus may be the underlying cause of the symptoms of the flu. The underlying cause need not be organic, however; it might just as well be psychological. Thus an 8-year-old boy may be obstreperous in class because he is afraid to express his defiance of his mother and displaces it onto the teacher. In this case the behavior in school is symptomatic of an underlying problem in the home. The issue of underlying causes is a complex and controversial one which will occupy us later. Suffice it to say at this point that the evidence is too inconclusive to resolve the controversies satisfactorily, but the word itself remains a bone of contention.

Since the term "medical model" has become so affect-laden among professionals, it is important to disentangle relevant from irrelevant issues. Purely as a classification system, one based on the medical model should stand or fall on the basis of proven validity and clinical utility—that is, on independent evidence that clusters of symptoms do, in fact, exist in nature, that etiology and prognosis are, in fact, what the system claims them to be, and on practitioners' reports of the fit between described classifications and observed behavior. Currently, there are two dangers. One is that classifications based on the medical model will be used as a vehicle for making unwarranted assumptions concerning organic etiology and for extending the province of psychiatrists into childhood disturbances which have little or nothing to do with medical training and expertise. The second danger is that nonmedical professionals and researchers will reject the classification out of hand because of the label "medical model," thus turning their backs on its empirical merits and clinical utility.

The Behavioral Model

Three characteristics distinguish behavioral psychology. First is the assertion that *observable behavior* comprises the basic data of a scientific psychology. The more radical theorists would limit psychology to the response organisms make to environmental stimuli, excluding all mentalistic and inferential variables such as thoughts, images, drives, and memory traces. More moderate theorists admit inferential concepts under two conditions: that such terms can be defined behaviorally and that their introduction facilitates the fundamental goals of predicting and controlling behavior. Next, behaviorists favor *research conducted under highly controlled conditions*, the laboratory experiment being the technique par excellence for establishing the necessary and sufficient conditions for producing the behavior being investigated. Measurement and quantification are highly valued as part of the overall emphasis on precision. Third, behaviorists assume that a limited number of *learning principles* can account for a wide array of behavior in animals and humans. True, there are other forces at work—genetic, instinctual, maturational, temperamental—but the acquisition, maintenance, change, or elimination of much behavior can be adequately and concisely accounted for in terms of learning principles.

Principles of Learning   The three principles of learning which form the basis of the behavioral approach are *classical conditioning* (also

called respondent or Pavlovian conditioning), *operant conditioning* (also called instrumental conditioning), and *imitation* (also called modeling or observational learning).

In classical conditioning a stimulus (the conditioned stimulus, or CS) which initially is incapable of eliciting a response (the unconditioned response, UR) is successively paired with a stimulus (the unconditioned stimulus, US) which is the UR's uniform or innate elicitor. After a given number of pairings, the previously neutral stimulus (the CS) comes to elicit the response (the UR) which is now known as the conditioned response, or CR. To vary the well-known example of a dog being conditioned to salivate to the sound of a bell, a tone (the CS) that is successively paired with a puff of air to the eyelid (the US)—a stimulus which naturally elicits a blinking response (the UR)—will, with time, itself come to elicit the blinking response (now called the CR), even when the air puff is omitted.

Two other principles derived from classical conditioning have proved useful in accounting for the development and elimination of psychopathological behavior. *Stimulus generalization* is the tendency for stimuli similar to the conditioned stimulus also to elicit the conditioned response; the greater the degree of similarity, the more vigorous the response. In the above example, the blinking response can be elicited by tones similar to the CR. The increase in efficiency is obvious since the organism does not have to learn to respond anew to each variation in the stimulus. *Discrimination learning* is the opposite of generalization in that it involves learning to distinguish among stimuli and to respond only to the appropriate one. Typically, the discrimination is established through nonreinforcement or punishment. Thus a preschooler who has learned that a dog is a woof-woof might label a number of animals woof-woof until the parent supplies another, more appropriate label.

In *operant conditioning* the organism operates upon or does something to the environment in order to achieve a given result. In essence, it is a process by which an organism learns to associate certain results with certain actions it has taken. These results may serve either to increase or decrease the likelihood of the behavior's being repeated. The term used to designate an increase in the likelihood of occurrence is reinforcement. Reinforcement can be positive or negative. In *positive reinforcement* behavior is followed by a reward; for example, the father of an 8-year-old treats his son's soccer team to ice cream after a victory. In *negative reinforcement* an aversive stimulus is removed; for example, a 10-year-old girl is excused from washing dishes for a week after improving her grade in history.

The two terms used to designate a decrease in the likelihood of a behavior's being repeated are extinction and punishment. In *extinction* the reinforcement maintaining a response is removed; for example, upon her therapist's advice, a mother no longer gives in to her 4-year-old's demands every time he has a temper tantrum, and the tantrums disappear. In *punishment* a response is followed by an aversive stimulus; for example, a 3-year-old's hand is slapped as she reaches out to touch a flame on the stove.

A distinction is also made between *primary* and *secondary reinforcers.* The first are unlearned, having a biological base: primary positive reinforcers include food, water, warmth, and sex, while primary negative reinforcers include pain, extremes of heat and cold, and intensely loud sounds. Most reinforcers are learned in association with primary reinforcers and are called secondary or conditioned reinforcers; the cuddly blanket which provided the infant with warmth becomes a security blanket during the toddler and preschool years, just as mother's harsh voice preceding punishment becomes feared in its own right. Subsequently words, the mere symbols of reinforcement, acquire great potency,

and much of the child's behavior is regulated by the value judgments of "good" and "bad."

One consequence of punishment is particularly relevant to our interest in psychopathology. Once exposed to an aversive stimulus, an organism will try in the future to avoid reexposure, a process which is called *avoidance learning.* Avoidance learning is a double-edged sword. It protects the organism from a repeated encounter with a possibly harmful situation; for example, once burned, a 2-year-old does not continually touch the burner of a stove. But avoidance learning can also lead to unrealistic avoidance of situations after they are no longer noxious; for example, an adult may be terrified of his reasonable, benevolent boss because, as a child, he was brutally beaten by his father. Thus avoidance prevents the individual from adopting new behaviors which are appropriate to changed circumstances.

The final concept which will be useful in subsequent discussions is *shaping.* Operant conditioning depends on the natural occurrence of the operant response. Yet, some of these responses have a very low rate of occurrence or, indeed, do not occur at all. In such instances the responses must be shaped by reinforcing successive approximations to the desired one; for example, young children are progressively taught to swim by first getting them accustomed to the water, teaching them to float, then to kick their legs or tread water while floating, and so on, until the basic skill of swimming has been mastered. (The most famous of the radical behaviorists is B. F. Skinner. For a general statement of his position, see *Science and Human Behavior,* 1953. The best-known statement of his environmental engineering is *Walden Two,* 1948.)

The third in the triad of learning principles is *imitation,* which involves learning a new behavior by observing and imitating another person's performance of that behavior. Thus, without any direct parental tutelage preschoolers will pretend to clean the house or hammer a nail as their parents do or will answer the phone with the exact words and intonation they have heard adults use. While learning theorists have devoted a good deal of attention to studying the possible mechanisms involved in imitation, their research and theorizing will not be relevant to our discussions.

Social-Learning and Social-Cognitive Theory It was the social-learning theorists who insisted that imitation or modeling be added to the list of basic learning principles. The thesis was defended by Miller and Dollard (1941) and subsequently by Bandura and Walters (1963). The learning theorists are "social" because they are primarily concerned with learning that takes place in a social context, such as between parent and child or among peers.

Among social-learning theorists, Bandura has been one of the most venturesome in making "private events," such as ideas, plans, wishes, and feelings, compatible with the scientific tenets of behaviorism. The study of private events, he argues, need not involve a return to the mentalism of the past, since these events can be operationally defined in terms of antecedents and consequences. The time-honored concept of a "mental" image, for example, can be anchored in behavioral antecedents, such as instructions to "Imagine you are lifting a weight," and measurable consequences, such as changes in muscle potential in the arms. Moreover, having the concept of an image accounts for the observed behavior better than if the concept were excluded. Thus the requirements of objective inquiry are satisfied. In general, Bandura argues that a host of cognitive variables, such as symbolic representations of experiences, expectancies, and problem solving, can be encompassed within the social-learning framework with no loss of rigor and with significant gains in explanatory scope. Rejecting Skinner's exclusive emphasis on observable antecedents and consequences,

Bandura maintains that external events affect behavior through intermediary cognitive processes which "partly determine which external events will be observed, how they will be perceived, whether they leave any lasting effects, what valence and efficacy they have, and how the information they convey will be organized for future use" (Bandura, 1977, p. 160).

Bandura also counters the charge that behaviorism makes the individual into a mere recipient of environmental events. He has his own version of initiative which he calls *self-efficacy*. In the initial stages, observing the differential effect of one's actions enables individuals to respond appropriately to various situations; for example, a preschool boy learns that playing in a day-care center will be rewarding and fighting will be punished, and behaves appropriately. Next, individuals come to anticipate not only that a given behavior will produce a given outcome, but more important, they also come to estimate whether they can successfully execute such a behavior. This conviction of success is called an efficacy expectation. Such an expectation of mastery affects both the initiation and persistence of coping behavior. Thus people fear and avoid situations they believe exceed their coping skills, and they behave assuredly in those situations which they believe themselves capable of handling. Therefore, self-efficacy influences both the choice of activities and persistence in the face of obstacles. It is important to note that Bandura's concept of self-efficacy is not merely speculative but also buttressed by empirical data (Bandura, 1986).

Normal and Abnormal Development The behaviorists' credo is that all behavior is one and—once allowance has been made for genetic, maturational, and temperamental factors—all behavior conforms to the basic principles of learning just described. Of course, one may divide behavior into categories, such as infant or adolescent, normal or abnormal, but this is done only to stake out territory of special interest to the investigator. The basic task is to discover how the principles of learning can be used to account for the special behaviors one has chosen.

The *developmental dimension* is introduced in terms of societal requirements for age-related behavioral changes. In our society, a child should be toilet-trained toward the end of the preschool period, should be able to cope with school by the beginning of middle childhood, and should function independent of parents by the end of adolescence, and so on. Other societies have different requirements and different timetables.

Some children grow up with the kinds of learning experiences that maximize their chances of making a successful adaptation to environmental demands, while others have experiences that minimize such an outcome. In the latter instance, behaviorists prefer to talk in terms of "maladaptive" rather than "abnormal" behavior to avoid any suspicion of a qualitatively different developmental outcome. Implicit in their stand is also a cultural relativism: what would be adaptive in one society may be maladaptive in another.

In addition to being cultural relativists, behaviorists have a penchant for quantification which leads them to define psychopathology as deviations in the frequency or intensity of behavior. Note A. O. Ross's definition of a psychological disorder as behavior which "deviates from an arbitrary and relative social norm in that it occurs with a frequency or intensity that authoritative adults . . . judge . . . to be either too high or too low" (Ross, 1980, p. 9).

According to such a definition, psychopathologies can be grouped in terms of behavioral deficit or excess. In *behavior deficit*, behaviors occur at a lower frequency or intensity than is expected within society, so the child's social, intellectual, or practical skills are impaired. Autism, learning disabilities, mental retarda-

tion, and even juvenile delinquency are examples, the last resulting from deficient behavioral controls. In *behavior excess*, behavior occurs at a higher frequency or intensity than is adaptive to the standards of society. The hyperactive child who is in a continual state of excitement, the compulsive child who repeatedly washes his hands, and the anxious child who is constantly terrified by real and imagined dangers all show signs of behavior excess.

However, other kinds of deviations are also recognized, one being the appropriateness of the stimulus-response relationships. In *inappropriate stimulus control*, either a response occurs in the absence of any appropriate stimulus, or a stimulus fails to elicit the appropriate response. A psychotic boy's delusion that his therapist will bite his head off if he enters the therapy room is an example, as is the anorectic girl's conviction that she is still too fat when she is on the verge of starving herself to death.

In addition to categorizing types of maladaptions, behaviorists have also conceptualized traditional psychopathologies in terms of learning principles. A phobia, for example, could readily be regarded as an example of maladaptive avoidance behavior, in which the child is too terrified to learn how harmless the feared object really is; depression may be interpreted as the result of extinction, in which significant positive reinforcements are withdrawn, and the person becomes passive and hopeless; while autism, with its imperviousness to the human environment, may result from a failure of parents to acquire secondary reinforcing value.

Behavior Therapies   One final development in the behavioral movement may prove the most significant in regard to the study of childhood psychopathology. It is the appearance of a cluster of remedial techniques called *behavior therapies*. The behavior therapies have taken a

number of behaviorists out of the rarefied atmosphere of the laboratory and challenged
them to apply their scientific principles to the
complexities of social interactions. In the process these therapies have firmly secured a
place for the behavioral movement in the clinical arena while raising searching issues concerning the adequacy of a simple learning
model to account for the therapeutic changes
that take place within individuals. (We shall
take up this thread in Chapter 17.)

The Psychodynamic Model

The psychodynamic school of thought was
founded by Freud and his followers, some of
whom subsequently rebelled against the
Freudian tenets of psychoanalysis. What they
all shared was an interest in discovering the
dynamics—the basic motives, the prime mov-
ers—of human behavior. This concern with intrapersonal forces immediately sets them
apart from the behaviorists, with their concern
for the environmental factors that shape behavior. As with the other two approaches discussed so far, our coverage of the psychodynamic approach will not be comprehensive;
instead, we shall concentrate on the two aspects of Freudian theory most relevant to understanding childhood psychopathology—the
structural and genetic theories. (For more extensive coverage, see Bootzin, Acocella, and
Alloy, 1993.)

The Structural Theory   Freud arrived at a tripartite conceptualization of the human psyche: the id, the ego, and the superego.

According to classical Freudian theory, the
id is the source of all psychic energy, which in
turn derives from biological drives. Among
these, the sexual drive is prepotent in its import for personality development. (Freud subsequently added the death instinct, which included aggression as the other primary
motivating force, but its conceptualization was

unsatisfactory and its status remains controversial.) The drives of the id are alogical, demanding immediate and complete satisfaction, or what Freud called discharge. Freud
coined the term *pleasure principle* for the id's
ceaseless striving for immediate discharge.
Ideation in the id is also at the service of the
pleasure principle, resembling the irrational
images and sequencing of events in dreams.
Freud called such ideation *primary process
thinking* to distinguish it from rational
thought. Developmentally speaking, the infant
is an id-dominated creature, concerned only
with reducing the tensions generated by physiological needs, having no capacity for delay
and no awareness of the realistic parameters
of the world he or she has entered.

In the classical formulation, the ego arises
from the id's need for maximal gratification.
Unlike the id, the ego is endowed with functions such as perception, memory, and reasoning which enable it to learn realistic means of
satisfying the id. A 2-year-old's ego may advise, "You can do anything you want with
your teddy bear when you're mad; but when
you get mad at your baby brother, better wait
until no one is around or else the pain of punishment will outweigh the pleasure of hitting
him." Thus the ego functions on what Freud
called the *reality principle;* he called the rational
thinking which is in tune with the parameters
of reality *secondary process thinking.* Note that
the ego requires the id to postpone immediate
gratification, although postponement is inimical to its nature, and that secondary process
thinking both delays and guides behavior.
Subsequently, the ego psychologists made a
major revision in the classical theory by postulating that the ego initially is endowed with
its own energy and can function autono-
mously rather than being subservient to the
id. Important as this change is, it will not bear
directly on our discussions.

The ego begins to emerge at about 6 months
of life, and the third structure, the superego,

comes into its own at about 5 to 6 years of age. It contains the moral standards of right and wrong which the preschooler takes over from his or her parents and which become an internalized judge of the moral rectitude of the child's behavior. In case of transgression, the superego punishes the child with guilt feelings. The superego is comparable to the conscience, but it is an absolutist, implacable conscience and demands continual obedience to its standard of proper behavior.

From middle childhood on, then, the ego must find ways of obtaining as much id gratification as reality will allow without arousing the superego, which in its way is as irrational in its demands as the id itself. The image of the beleaguered ego contending with inevitable conflict between irreconcilable intrapersonal forces has been regarded as stern and heroic by some, bleak and dour by others. It certainly has little of the behaviorist's belief in the malleability and therefore the potential perfectability of human behavior.

While Freud's structural theory is relevant to our concern with psychopathology, his genetic theory of psychosexual development will figure more prominently in subsequent discussions.

The Psychosexual Theory Freud's psychosexual theory assumes that eroticized intimacy exists throughout the life span, adult sexuality being only the culmination of a process begun in earliest infancy. Our bodies themselves are so constituted that stimulation of certain areas arouses exquisitely pleasurable sensations. Once having experienced them, we are forever driven to obtain the maximum bodily pleasures which society will allow. Freud called this biologically determined drive to obtain erotic bodily sensations *libido*. Furthermore, the body is constituted so that the mouth, the anus, and the genitals are particularly rich in erotic sensations when stimulated. Freud assumed that there is an inevitable progression,

whereby first the mouth, then the anus, and finally the genitals predominate as sources of pleasure. Equally important, each progression of libido is accompanied by a psychological change in the intimate relations with the parents or primary caretakers. The label "psychosexual" epitomizes the complementary relation between psychological and erotic development.

The three specific stages of psychosexual development are called the oral, the anal, and the phallic. These are true stages in that their sequencing is unalterable and each represents a qualitative change in personality. The Oedipus complex, which is the climax of the psychosexual stages, occurs toward the end of the preschool period. Finally, Freud stated that progression is never complete; even in normal development, residuals of prior stages can be found. Such residuals are called *fixations*. We will briefly describe both the stages themselves and their normal residuals.

In the *oral stage* the infant derives pleasure first from sucking and, after teeth appear, from biting. In the context of being fed, the first emotional attachment or, to use the Freudian term, the first *object relation* is formed. This initial intimacy is particularly potent in setting the tone for all future intimacies. Sensitive, loving caretaking engenders a positive image both of mother and of being mothered; caretaking marked by distress and frustration will engender an image in which love is mixed with anxiety and rage. And at a primitive level, being loved and being fed are forever equated.

Normal fixations include pleasure in sucking candy and chewing gum as well as smoking and kissing. In religion, the Madonna preserves the image of the all-loving, all-powerful mother figure, while in literature the witch epitomizes the angry, destructive mother, the poisoned apple or poison in general representing love contaminated by the destructiveness of hostility. "There's no apple pie like mother's apple pie'' and ''The way to a man's heart is through his stomach'' derive from the basic equation: being well loved equals being well fed.

In the *anal stage* the toddler achieves erotic gratification from retaining and evacuating feces or from manual manipulation of the anus. For the first time, the toddler also has control of the source of pleasure: whereas the infant is totally dependent on the caretaker for feeding, the toddler alone can decide when, where, and how to have a bowel movement. Toilet training requires the relinquishing of this pleasurable autonomy. For such a sacrifice the toddler should be adequately compensated by love. If training is punitive, unloving, or coercive, the toddler becomes rebellious and stubbornly resistive or anxious and overly compliant.

One normal residual of the anal stage is the cult of regularity; laxatives always sell well, and there are adults whose daily mood is contingent upon a daily evacuation. Preschoolers call one another ''you old BM'' or ''you old pooh-pooh,'' and adult cursing continues the tradition by substituting adult for childhood equivalents of feces. The preschooler's fascination with mud and clay derive from the earlier interest in feces. In addition, any number of behaviors can be categorized as being ''clean'' or ''dirty''—being personally clean, neat, orderly, being clean-minded and clean-living as contrasted with being messy and slovenly, being a dirty dealer, having a dirty mind, and telling dirty jokes, dirt being only a thin disguise for feces.

In the *phallic stage* masturbation and curiosity about anatomical differences are at their height, so the desire to peek and to show, to look and to exhibit, run high. The period is also marked by expansiveness, assertiveness, and an intoxicating sense of power as the child feels that he or she is now—or soon will be—''big'' and ''grown up.'' Normal residuals include an abiding interest in the human body,

sexual techniques, and intercourse evidenced in scholarly descriptions, pinup magazines, and pornography alike. The desire to show off also harks back to the phallic stage and is evident in the ''sex symbol,'' the muscle man on the beach, the actress who tries to captivate the audience, the physicist who tries to dazzle the scientific community, or even the conspicuous sufferer who proclaims that no one else has ever known such misery.

The *Oedipus complex* and *castration anxiety* climax early psychosexual development for boys, the girls experiencing a variation called the *Electra complex*. The preschool boy is incapable of feeling generous about his attachment to his mother; he feels possessive and jealous. In the exuberance of the phallic stage he wants to be the only person in his mother's life. This passionate attachment makes him his father's rival, which in turn leads to a wish that the father would disappear. The desire to possess the mother and destroy the father is called the Oedipus complex.

The Oedipus complex precipitates a crisis because of the boy's terrifying fantasy that the rivalrous, retaliatory father will cut off his penis. Freud claimed that castration anxiety is inevitable, even with the most benevolent of fathers, since it is essentially of the child's own making. As we will see when we discuss cognitive development, the 4- to 5-year-old is still in the egocentric stage of assuming that others feel as he does. Thus the boy reasons that if he wants to destroy the father, the father must have similar wishes toward him. It is the projection of his own hostility which makes castration anxiety inevitable. The typical resolution of the Oedipus conflict is for the boy to renounce his sexual feelings and his claim on the mother and identify with the powerful father. In essence he says, ''I am not your rival, I am like you.''

The boy's relations with the mother during this period set the tone of his future heterosexual strivings. If the relationship is positive, he will unconsciously seek to replicate it at the adult level; if the relationship is mixed with anxiety and/or anger, other kinds of relationships will prove attractive. Fear of physical injury, operations, or vigorous contact sports as well as a negative attitude toward same-sex competition may be a residual of castration anxiety. "I'm afraid to stick my neck out because someone will cut it off" is a thinly disguised expression of the preschooler's castration terror that assertiveness will lead to destruction by a powerful rival.

Freud regarded middle childhood as a period of diminished sexual activity caused by the repression that resolved the Oedipus complex along with an inherent decrease in the libidinal drive. Physiological maturation at puberty revives all the difficulties of psychosexual development in the first six years, which once again must be dealt with and mastered. However, Freud's contributions to understanding both the middle years and adolescence have been minor. More relevant to our subsequent discussion of homosexuality is the Freudian concept of normal and deviant sexuality in adulthood.

Adult sexuality remains a psychosexual development. Sexually, all the erotic elements of the first six years of life are revived as components of foreplay, except that oral, anal, and genital stimulation along with exhibition of the body serve the function of heightening the pleasure of the ultimate goal of mature sexuality, which is genital union. It may be that the idiosyncratic reactions of pleasure, indifference, and disgust in regard to specific aspects of foreplay are rooted in comparable experiences during the first three stages of psychosexual development. Sexual *perversions* result when elements of foreplay become goals in themselves; for example, the psychopathology called exhibitionism involves an irresistible desire to display one's genitals in public, while voyeurism involves Peeping Tom activities or the irresistible urge to view nude bodies. Both pathologies result from a failure to develop beyond the phallic period.

Mature sexuality is a psychological achievement as well. It too involves components of the early stages of psychological development: from the oral period comes the need for and ability to provide tender care, along with trust that the partner will be there in times of distress; from the anal period comes a willingness to negotiate the many areas of adult responsibility and decision making, such as how money will be spent, work loads apportioned, or discipline enforced; from the phallic period comes pride in those achievements that make the partner proud, whether it be a bowling trophy or a Ph.D.; from the oedipal period comes confidence that one is as good as the next person. However, maturity entails a mutuality, a givingness, and an appreciation of the partner's point of view which counteracts the basic egocentricism (using the term in the Freudian sense) of the early psychosexual stages.

And, just as is true of the sexual act, the psychological relationship is immature if any one of the initial psychosexual stages becomes a goal in itself—a woman who is primarily seeking someone to pamper and baby her, a man whose primary purpose is to impose his will and crush the autonomy of his partner, or an adult who only wants an audience to admire him or her for real or imagined achievements. Note that the psychosexual theory maintains that sexual maturity is only incidentally related to the performance of the sexual act. A man who has intercourse five times a week just to prove his prowess or three times a week because he read that this is the average for a person his age, is fixated or, quite literally, childlike in his behavior. Maturity is a matter of the psychological qualities one brings to the sexual experience itself and to the intimacy it entails.

Psychopathology The title of one of Freud's books, *The Psychopathology of Everyday Life,* (1938) succinctly states his thesis that normality imperceptibly blends into psychopathology. The difference between the two is quantitative rather than qualitative.

In structural terms, psychopathology is a matter of a significant imbalance between id, ego, and superego. If the id is excessively strong, either because of innate endowment or a weak ego and superego, the result is impulsive aggressive or sexual behavior. If the superego is excessively strong, the result is overly inhibited behavior in which the child is tortured by guilt feelings for the slightest transgression, real or imagined.

Psychosexual theory contains a rich source of clues as to both the nature and form of psychopathology. While fixations are normal, as we have seen, excessive fixations lay the groundwork for psychological disturbances, either because they hamper further development or because they increase the possibility that, having progressed, the child will return to the fixated, less mature stage. This latter process is called *regression.* The greater the fixation, the more vulnerable the child to regression. Excessive fixations can result either from inadequate libidinal gratification, such as inadequate love during the oral period, or excessive gratification, such as an oversolicitous, overprotective mother during the oedipal phase. The psychosexual stage of fixation determines both the severity and the kind of psychopathology. In general, the earlier the fixation, the more severe the psychopathology, so a child who is either fixated at or regresses to the oral stage is more disturbed than one who is fixated at or regresses to the anal stage. In addition, each stage is apt to produce a particular kind of disturbance: the Oedipus complex is associated with hysterical and phobic disturbances, the anal stage with obsessive-compulsive disorders, and the oral stage with psy-

chosis. (These classifications will be discussed in Chapter 3.) Thus, for example, the bizarre ideation of the schizophrenic, which is determined more by idiosyncratic needs, longings, and fears than by a desire to communicate intelligibly, marks a return to the primary process thinking of the id-dominated oral stage.

As a developmental theory of psychopathology, the psychodynamic model has no peer. Yet it is also mentalistic, inferential, exceedingly complex, peppered with contingencies, and lacking just those clear behavioral referents and accessibility to tightly controlled research which behaviorists claim are essential to a scientific psychology. It is also true that neither the preferred method of investigation, namely psychoanalysis or psychoanalytically oriented psychotherapy, nor the data it produces are available to the general scientific community. But to conclude, as some have done, that psychodynamic concepts are unscientific because they cannot be tested by the usual controlled procedures is unjustified. Psychodynamic theory has generated more research than any other personality theory, and while older reviews claimed that the theory was totally lacking in scientific credibility, a more recent review found it to be faring surprisingly well (Fisher and Greenberg, 1977). It is also true that a number of psychodynamic concepts are either taken for granted by the general scientific community or regarded as tenable hypotheses: that adult psychopathologies have their roots in early childhood; that anxiety may be conceptualized as the anticipation of pain, and that defense mechanisms are used to reduce it; that early conscience is the internalization of parental values by means of identification; that the infantile conscience is particularly absolutistic and punitive; that frustration is one of the conditions leading to aggression; that behavior may be determined by ideas and impulses which are unconscious; that there is a cognitive progression from irrational to rational thinking in the first eight years of life; that adequate maternal care during infancy is essential to subsequent healthy personality development; and even the once-shocking idea that sexuality is present throughout childhood. Like all other models, the psychodynamic one has its advantages and limitations, but the charge that it lies beyond the pale of science or that it has been discredited by controlled studies is false.

Subsequent Developments Freud himself was most interested in exploring the motivational aspects of his theory, in particular the sexual and aggressive drives and the workings of the unconscious. His followers, notably Heinz Hartman and Ernst Kris, expanded his concept of the ego or the reality-oriented, adaptive functions of the psyche (Hartman, 1964), the superego, or conscience (Jacobson, 1964), and the defense mechanisms (A. Freud, 1946), while enlarging the interpersonal context from the nuclear family to society (Erikson, 1950). The initial emphasis on a single trauma as the origin of neurosis concomitantly shifted to a consideration of the complex interaction among intra- and interpersonal variables. (For a more detailed account of the psychoanalytic movement, see Rie, 1971.)

More recently, interest has shifted to the interpersonal context of object relations and the affective bond that is established between individuals. The most important individual for our purposes is John Bowlby (1973), whose theory of *attachment* has had a powerful influence on the conceptualization of normal and deviant development and has generated considerable research. We will be referring to both in subsequent discussion.

Self-Psychology The shift to an emphasis on the ego brought with it an interest in exploring the self as exemplified by the works of Kohut. (Our presentation follows Maddi, 1980.) According to Kohut, the well-developed self

gives an individual a conscious appreciation of who and what he or she is while lending meaning and direction to behavior. The self has two core needs.

- *The need to be mirrored* is manifested in children's need to have their expressions and products recognized, approved of, and admired. Early mirroring experiences underlie *ambition*. The most important mirroring person in the child's life is the mother.
- *The need to idealize* is manifested in the child's admiration of and identification with a more powerful adult. Early idealizing experiences underlie *goals*. The most important idealized person is the father.

The nuclear self emerges during the second year of life. It is bipolar, including nuclear ambitions at one pole and nuclear goals at the other. The mother who has successfully mirrored the child and the father who has presented himself to be idealized produce an autonomous individual with self-esteem and self-confidence, whose talents and skills are developed and in the service of ambitions and goals.

If the parents do not serve their growth-promoting functions, for example, by being preoccupied or hostile or intrusive, a number of *narcissistic personality disorders* and *narcissistic behavior disorders* may develop. We will only sample a few. Among the personality disorders is the *understimulated self* resulting from lack of parental response. Such a person will do anything (engage in promiscuity, perversion, gambling, drug abuse, etc.) to create excitement and ward off feelings of deadness. The *overstimulated self*, resulting from excessive parental attention, shies away from creative and leadership activities for fear of being overwhelmed by unrealistic fantasies of greatness. Among behavior disorders is the *mirror-hungry personality* who, lacking parental mirroring, is famished for admiration and incessantly strives to get attention. The *ideal-hungry personality*, by contrast, is equally insatiable in the search for others to admire and look up to.

These types need not necessarily be psychopathological, although they may be. Kohut also maintains that certain people with schizophrenia and borderline states can best be understood within his framework of self-psychology.

Comment Note that each model we have presented has undergone its own development. The medical model no longer couches issues dichotomously as, for example, heredity versus environment. Rather there is a recognition that organisms develop in all the other contexts which interact with and affect organic variables. (See, for example, Scarr, 1992.) The psychoanalytic model has shifted from emphasizing the intrapersonal to exploring the interpersonal context, while the behavioral model has changed in the opposite direction. Freud was primarily concerned with drives, the unconscious, and mental events, while ego psychologists concentrate on adaptation to the social environment, and object relations theorists emphasize the primacy of interpersonal relations. Traditionally, behaviorists wanted to banish the intrapersonal context with all of its mentalistic baggage, substituting an environmentally oriented objective psychology. It remained for the social-learning theorists to reintroduce mental terms such as images, expectancies, and the self by putting them on a sound objective basis.

With all this shifting about there are more overlapping contexts among models and, consequently, more of a chance of a unified model emerging. However, as we have noted, such a model lies in the future.

The Cognitive Models

Strictly speaking, there is no cognitive model of childhood psychopathology. This is a puzzling state of affairs in light of the fact that since mid-century interest has shifted from motivation to cognition and Piaget has been the towering figure in developmental psychology. While a number of researchers have utilized Piagetian concepts to account for specific psychopathological phenomena, there has been no attempt to integrate all the relevant aspects of Piagetian theory with the psychopathological thinking and behavior of children. Consequently, the current situation resembles a patchwork more than a comprehensive frame of reference. However, we shall be referring to Piaget with sufficient frequency to justify a review of some of his major concepts.

General Remarks Newborns know practically nothing about the world they have entered. In particular, they do not know that they are individuals and that they are entering a world composed of animate and inanimate objects. All they know is the stream of sensations they are experiencing. There is nothing about the sensation of hunger which informs infants, "I am coming from your stomach"; there is nothing in two vaguely seen dots which says, "I am your mother's eyes"; nor does a sound announce itself as coming from a rattle. The infant must learn to distinguish experiences comprising "me" from those comprising "not-me," and among the latter he or she must learn to distinguish things from people. Depending upon what aspect of cognitive development one studies, evidence of this kind of learning can be found until middle childhood.

Cognitive development is not a simple matter of accumulating increasingly large pieces of correct information until a comprehensive understanding of the self and the environment is achieved. On the contrary, initial understandings are erroneous and must be revised in light of experience, and these revisions, in turn, must be further revised, until an accurate grasp of reality is achieved. Since erroneous understandings contain the seeds of psychopathology, it is essential that the child remain open to growth so that, by constant testing, erroneous beliefs can be revised and corrected.

Piaget's Stage Theory In addition to the above picture of cognitive development, Piaget makes the assumption that successive modifications in thinking occur in orderly, fixed stages. Each stage of cognitive development is qualitatively distinct, and no higher type of thinking can evolve until the child has gone through all the preceding stages. The timetable may differ from child to child, but the order can never vary. It is these stages and the significant cognitive advances within each which will concern us next. (One of the most succinct and clearest expositions of Piaget's theory is found in Chapters 1 and 2 of Piaget, 1967.)

The *sensorimotor stage* lasts for approximately the first two years of life and is so called because the vehicle for intellectual growth is the sensory and motor apparatus. Incapable of symbolization, except toward the end of the period, infants and toddlers must explore and learn by acting directly upon the environment motorically and by watching and listening.

For our purposes, the significant development in this period is that of the *object concept,* or *object permanence.* For the first few months, infants give no evidence of missing an object they can no longer see or hold. Thus the world exists only when they are acting upon it or perceiving it. Out of sight not only means out of mind but out of existence as well. Only gradually, through a succession of cognitive steps, do infants come to realize that objects exist regardless of their own actions or perceptions—objects exist "out there" as part of the environment, while actions exist "in here" as part of the self. Instead of being the center or even the creator of the universe, toddlers grasp the fact that they are only one of the many furnishings of the world. A giant step has been taken toward separating me from not-me.

The *preoperational stage* lasts from approximately 2 to 7 years of age and marks the appearance of symbolic functions. The most obvious but by no means the exclusive manifestation of symbolization is language, which develops rapidly in this period. However, the preschooler tends literally to believe what he or she sees. Consequently, something that looks different is different. Piaget's well-known documentation of this thesis dazzled the psychological world. If, before their very eyes water is poured from a wide squat glass into a tall narrow glass or a ball of clay is rolled out into an elongated snake, children will claim that there is now more water or more clay. It looks like more, so it must be more. Piaget calls such literal thinking *intuitive,* to contrast it with thinking based on reason.

The *concrete-operational stage* extends from approximately 7 to 11 years of age. The triumph of middle childhood is that children are capable of understanding the world in terms of reason rather than in terms of naive perception. They grasp the notion that an object remains the same despite perceptual variations. Piaget's term for this achievement is *conservation,* denoting that objects conserve or maintain their identity in the face of manifold changes in appearance. Although realistic, the child's thinking is still tied to concrete reality, however, and bound to the here and now.

The *formal-operational stage* begins around the twelfth year and lasts into adulthood. It is in this period that general ideas and abstract constructions flourish. The ability to draw conclusions from hypotheses rather than relying totally on actual observation is called *hypothetic-deductive thinking.* Adolescents can go wherever their thoughts lead them. They discuss, they write, they ruminate. They create a philosophy of life and explain the universe. They are also capable of being truly self-critical for the first time because they can reflect on and scrutinize their own ideas.

Piaget's theory has generated an impressive body of research that confirms some aspects and disconfirms other. More sophisticated experimental techniques show that Piaget underestimated the infant's cognitive capacities: object permanence is possible earlier than Piaget postulated. By the same token, altering tasks to make them more familiar can produce realistic rather than illogical thinking in the preschooler. Piaget's concept of stages is hotly debated. There are those who maintain that cognitive development is gradual and continuous rather than marked by qualitative advances, for example. Because of such shortcomings, alternative cognitive theories are gaining in popularity. One of these is *information processing,* which views the human mind as a complex, symbol-manipulating system operating much like a digital computer. There is also a group of neo-Piagetians who prefer to retain and modify the theory, which, they claim, contains too many valuable and valid insights to be discarded. (See Berk, 1991, for an extensive critique of Piaget as well as for a detailed presentation of information processing.)

Developmental Psychopathology

Developmental psychopathology has two basic requirements, one empirical, the other conceptual. Empirically, the temporal antecedents, characteristic manifestations, and subsequent course of a psychopathology, with and without intervention, must be delineated. Conceptually, the relation between normal and psychopathological development must be explicated. The most general assumption here is that all development is one in that the same principles apply to its normal and abnormal courses. The specific challenge is to understand why development takes one path rather

than the other in the case of a given disturbance. The unity of development also means that the choice of becoming a general developmentalist or a clinical child psychologist is a matter of how attractive one finds the subject matter; it is not a choice between two different conceptualizations of development.

A number of models can meet these two criteria, most notably the psychoanalytic and behavioral. Werner's (1948) organismic model could also be included but presenting it would take us too far afield at this point. [For an application of the organismic approach to childhood psychopathology, see Cicchetti and Schneider-Rosen, 1986.] It is not surprising that there is no single model of developmental psychopathology, since there is no comprehensive theory of development itself. Our own formulation—psychopathology is normal development gone awry—is purposely general enough to embrace more specific models. In this way, we are free to go where provocative ideas and relevant data lead us.

In contrast to our open-ended approach, a number of leaders in the developmental psychopathology movement have more specific ideas as to how it is best conceptualized and what its core issues are. (See Sroufe and Rutter, 1984.) It will be profitable for us to examine these ideas now.

Multideterminism and Interaction Developmental psychopathology endorses two currently popular ideas concerning etiology. The first is that the search for a single cause—for example, juvenile delinquency results from neglectful parents—is simplistic and futile. Rather, psychopathologies have multiple causes. Moreover, the causes interact with one another as well as changing over time. For example, a high-risk factor in the intrapersonal context might or might not result in psychopathology depending on what occurs in the interpersonal context and the child's stage of development. As we shall see, all the disturbances we will discuss will turn out to be multidetermined.

Unfortunately, all too often multideterminism results in a mere listing of contributing variables. Such a listing cannot be regarded as an adequate etiological account. Rather, the variables must be *integrated* into some kind of meaningful pattern. At times this integration takes place statistically, so we learn which are the most and least potent variables, which serve as catalysts, and which as confounds. The integration may also be conceptual; for example, variables are placed in categories to show how they are meaningfully related to the psychopathology at hand. In our presentations of different psychopathologies we will pay particular attention to such statistical and conceptual integrations where they exist.

An interaction model does not mean that every variable or every context makes a significant contribution to etiology. Thus, society's message, "Thin is beautiful" may play an important role in the etiology of anorexia nervosa, while societal messages play little or no role in the etiology of autism. Which variables and how many will prove adequate is an empirical matter. (See Pennington and Ozonoff, 1991, for a defense of simple etiological explanations.)

Multideterminism in etiology has its counterpart in interactionism in the interpersonal sphere in that it replaces a model which states that the direction of influence is only from parent to child. Again, this unidirectional model—like the single-cause model of etiology—is simplistic and inaccurate. To begin with it is based largely on correlational data, and correlations say nothing about direction of effect. More important, it makes the child nothing more than a passive recipient of parental behavior. On the contrary, an infant's sex, health, intellectual endowment, and temperament impact upon parental behavior; for example, mothers of infants who are temperamentally difficult to care for may become increasingly frustrated, irritable, and guilty. Moreover, children have their own preferences and goals and quickly learn techniques for getting their own way. [See Bell's (1968) discussion of bidirectional effects and Bandura's (1985) similar concept of reciprocal determinism.]

As was the case with multideterminism, the relative contribution of parent and child to the development of a particular psychopathology is an empirical question, and interactionism does not require that their contributions are comparable; for example, there is evidence that the child's contribution to physical abuse is less than the parent's.

Multideterminism and interpersonal interaction provide a general framework for thinking about developmental psychopathology. The current scene is also characterized by more specific concepts and issues. We will now turn to some of these.

Developmental Pathways A current way of conceptualizing developmental psychopathology is in terms of developmental pathways, which are also called trajectories or developmental tracks. The initial question in constructing a pathway is, At what point in time and for what reasons does development begin to be diverted from its normal course? In other words, at what point is the child *at risk* for becoming psychopathologically disturbed? But not all at-risk children become disturbed; therefore, both the factors that make children more vulnerable to risk and the factors that protect them from risk must be uncovered. In those cases in which protective factors are outweighed by risk and vulnerability, the question becomes, How do the latter two factors work their mischief over time in order to produce a full-blown psychopathology? Finally, since children grow out of disturbances as well as growing into them, charting developmental pathways involves understanding the factors leading to extinction as well as those leading to persistence of psychopathology. (See Loeber, 1991, for a more detailed presentation of developmental pathways and of methodologies for obtaining data.) The final challenge is to explain the data in terms of developmental principles and to understand the mechanisms and processes responsible for propelling the child from one step to the next along the path to a particular disorder (Cicchetti, 1989).

There are further questions that can be raised concerning pathways. (Our presentation follows Loeber, 1991.) First, there are questions as to whether and how a pathway is affected by traditional *demographic variables* such as sex, intelligence, and socioeconomic status. The next question concerns understanding varying *ages of onset* in psychopathologies. For example, there is evidence that children who have late-onset delinquency (i.e., at 13 years of age) are no more antisocial than nondisturbed children in middle childhood, whereas children who have early onset (i.e., at 7 years of age) are both more disturbed than those with late onset and also tend to be hyperactive. Then there is the question of the *nature of the progression* itself: Are the steps along the path discrete and interchangeable or is the order fixed and the effects cumulative? In regard to substance abuse, for example, the latter is the case. Here progression is from beer or wine, to marijuana, to other illicit drugs. While the majority of individuals advance in this fixed order the number becomes progressively thinner with each step, while those reaching the more advanced levels both retain behaviors typical of earlier levels and are more seriously disturbed.

The final question concerns why pathways cross to produce *comorbidity* or the co-occurrence of two psychopathologies. In the past, clinicians tended to focus on a single disturbance and researchers tried to study "pure" cases, regarding the existence of other psychopathologies as potential confounds. However, it has become increasingly clear that certain disturbances, such as anxiety and depression or conduct disorders and hyperactivity, frequently occur together. To ignore comorbidity for the sake of simplicity or neatness of research design would be to remain ignorant of the special conditions producing multiple disturbances while depriving clinicians of an understanding of an important group of clients.

The *clinical applications* of developmental pathways in terms of prevention and remediation are obvious. The more we learn about the earliest risk factors, the better able we will be to design effective preventive programs. And at least for those psychopathologies showing a progression in seriousness of disturbance, the earlier we can intervene the more effective treatment is apt to be.

One final complication: developmental pathways involve more than simply charting similar behaviors (see Sroufe, 1990b). For example, undersocialized aggressive behavior in childhood not only results in adult antisocial acting out but in alcoholism and schizophrenia as well. In certain instances, the changes in behavior involve what are called *transformations*. This means that there is continuity in an inferred psychological concept while the behavioral manifestations of this concept change over time. As we shall see when we discuss attachment (Chapter 2), an insecurely attached infant may be overly independent of the mother but in preschool may be overly dependent on the teacher. The inferred insecurity is the same but is expressed differently at different ages.

In our subsequent examination of specific psychopathologies we will be charting developmental pathways and will give a more detailed account of the examples cited above.

Risk, Vulnerability, and Protective Factors While risk, vulnerability, and protective factors are part of developmental pathways, they are sufficiently important to be discussed in their own right.

A *risk* is any condition or circumstance that increases the likelihood that a psychopathology will develop. (Sroufe, Cooper, and De-Hart, 1992, briefly summarize the literature on risk and protective factors, while Luthar and Zigler, 1991, discuss the methodological problems in defining and measuring stress and competence in risk research.) While there is no comprehensive agreed-upon list of risk factors, they span all contexts. In the organic context, risk may involve birth defects, neurological damage, inadequate nutrition or a parent who has a disorder with a known genetic component. In the intrapersonal context, it may be low intelligence, low self-esteem, or poor self-control. In the interpersonal context, it may be parental neglect or abuse or poor peer relations. In the superordinate context, it may be poverty. While single risks have limited predictive power, multiple risks have a cumulative effect; for example, children with two alcoholic parents are more than twice as likely to develop problems as are children with one alcoholic parent. Or again, in a longitudinal study of 1583 children from infancy to ages 4 and 5, Sanson et al. (1991) found that single measures such as difficult temperament, prematurity, problems in the mother-infant relationship, and low socioeconomic status were poor predictors of maladjustment while two or more risk factors increased predictability from two- to fourfold.

While risk may determine disturbances directly, *vulnerability* is the term used for factors that intensify the response to risk. Rutter (1990b) identifies a number of these factors. Sex is one; for example, while both sexes are adversely affected by parental discord, boys have a higher rate of disorder than girls. Temperament is another vulnerability factor; children who are difficult to care for are more often targets of parental irritability, criticism, and hostility than are easily managed children. Rutter's list also includes the absence of a good relationship to both parents in the case of marital discord, low planning ability and a lack of positive school experiences in the case of institutionally reared girls, and lack of affectionate care following parental death or separation.

Since not all children who are at risk become disturbed, the challenge for researchers is to discover the factors that promote or maintain healthy development. These are called *protective factors;* for example, the presence of one loving, dependable parent in the presence of three or more risk factors lowers the rate of problem behavior from 75 to 25 percent. Children who make a good adjustment in spite of being at high risk for becoming disturbed are called *resilient.* Research on resilience shows it is enhanced when children receive good and stable care or, in the case of older children, when they have a positive relationship with a competent adult, when they are are good learners and problem solvers, are engaging to others, and have areas of competence valued by themselves or society, whether they be academic, athletic, artistic, or mechanical. Institutions such as the school and church can serve as sources of support, for example, by being nurturing or offering role models. (A summary of the research on resilience can be found in Masten, Best, and Garmezy, 1990. The complexity of empirical findings is nicely illustrated by a study conducted by Masten et al., 1990.)

Rutter (1990b) is more interested in the mechanisms mediating protective processes than in a listing of protective variables. On the basis of empirical studies, he derives four such mechanisms. First is *reduction of risk impact.* For example, parents who strictly supervise and regulate peer group activities outside the home, who know where their children are and guide them in their choice of play and friendships, reduce the likelihood of delinquency in children reared in a high-risk environment.

Next is the *reduction of negative chain reactions.* Risks may be cumulative; for example, a defiant, negativistic boy not only has to cope with the stress of parental divorce but also with the fact that his parents tend to take out their hostility on him rather than his docile sister. Measures which prevent such an accumulation and perpetuation of risk factors will serve a protective function. Next, *self-esteem* and *self-efficacy,* or what we call initiative, help children feel they can cope successfully with life's problems. These qualities are enhanced by a secure and harmonious parent-child relationship and success in tasks that are important to the child. The final protective mechanism is *opening of opportunities.* Development involves "turning points," which offer a chance to reduce the impact of risk factors. Thus, adolescents who continue their education have more opportunities for vocational fulfillment than dropouts do, while moving away from the inner city or joining the army may reduce delinquency. (For a detailed presentation of concepts and research on risk and protective factors, see Rolf et al., 1990.)

Table 1.1 summarizes the risk, vulnerability, and protective factors and the protective mechanisms.

The concept of risk and protective factors has important implications for clinical practice. While clinical child psychologists must be concerned with pathogens, it is equally important for them to assess positive factors as well—a skill or talent in the child, a sympathetic grandfather in the family, a supportive coach or teacher, a youth organization in the community. These resources, in turn, will figure prominently in planning therapy or remedial measures.

Two Types of Risk Developmental psychopathology covers a broader spectrum of children than those who are psychopathologically disturbed; that is, those who fall within accepted diagnostic categories of psychopathol-

ogies. The standard diagnostic manual, DSM-IV Draft Criteria (3/1/93) has a category for "Other conditions that may be a focus of clinical attention" and distinguishes such *problem behaviors* from *disorders,* which is the general classification of psychopathologies. Among these problem behaviors one finds physical and sexual abuse, noncompliance with medical treatment, and acculturation difficulty. In a similar manner, Lewis and Miller's (1990) *Handbook of Developmental Psychopathology* has a chapter on child maltreatment, while Ollendick and Hersen's (1989) *Handbook of Child Psychopathology* has a number of chapters on physical disorders. These children fall somewhere between those with problems of normal development (such as the obstreperous toddler or the prankish adolescent who steals hubcaps) and psychopathologically disturbed ones. They are experiencing more than the normal amount of stress and distress and their behavior is sufficiently deviant to require professional attention.

Because there are two categories of childhood disturbances, there are also two categories of risk. The first one, as we have just seen, includes children who are at risk for developing one or more psychopathologies; the second includes children at risk for developing problem behaviors sufficiently serious to merit professional attention.

There is no agreed-upon list of risks for problem behaviors. The ones we have chosen illustrate different sources of such behaviors. Children with chronic illnesses and brain damage (Chapter 13) are at risk because of deviations from bodily intactness. Maltreated children and children of divorce (Chapter 14) are at risk because of the behavior of caretaking adults. Adolescents with a homosexual identity (Chapter 11) and ethnic minority children (Chapter 15) are at risk not because of any inherent disturbance but because of prejudicial treatment by society.

Being at risk for behavior problems may or

TABLE 1.1

Risks, Vulnerabilities, and Protective Factors

Organic	Intrapersonal	Interpersonal	Superordinate
		Risks	
Genetic Pre- and perinatal influences; neurological damage; inadequate nutrition; difficult temperament	Low intelligence; low self-esteem; low self-efficacy; low self-control; insecure attachment	Marital or familial disharmony; abuse or neglect; poor peer relations; large number of siblings	Poverty
		Vulnerabilities	
Difficult temperament	Sex; poor planning ability	Poor relations with both parents; lack of affectionate care; lack of positive school experiences	
		Protective factors	
Easy temperament	Average or above intelligence; competent; socially engaging	Positive, stable care; competent adult role models	
		Protective mechanisms*	
	Reducing risk impact Reducing negative chain reaction Promoting self-esteem and self-efficacy Opening up opportunities		

* Both intra- and interpersonal
Sources: Robins (1972); Rosenblith and Sims-Knight (1992); and Rutter (1990).

may not overlap with being at risk for psychopathologies. In the case of physical illness the overlap is small; in the case of child maltreatment, the overlap is larger. However, being at risk for developing a psychopathology is not of the essence; having serious behavior problems is.

The fact that both categories of children are designated by the same term—"risk" or "at risk"—raises the semantic issue of distinguishing them in future discussions. There is no acceptable substitute for the term and arbitrarily differentiating it by a device such as risk-1 and risk-2 is stylistically awkward. Our solution, which is not too satisfactory, is to flag the second meaning by using the term "risk"

to introduce the discussion, such as "the risk of . . .".

The Multicultural Approach The multiple cultural approach is congruent with the current emphasis on interaction and multideterminism. As we shall see in Chapter 15, cultural background is a superordinate variable that significantly affects the interpersonal, intrapersonal, and organic contexts, as well as the risk for becoming disturbed and the definition of psychopathology itself. Thus, a number of cultures traditionally emphasize the dominance of the male rather than equality of the sexes, while in others obedience and conformity in the children are valued over self-assertiveness and independence. In some cultures symptoms are internalized and somatized to a greater degree than in others while beliefs in malevolent spirits are more common and therefore regarded as less psychopathological. Thus a developmental psychopathology based primarily on Anglo-Americans cannot be assumed to apply to other cultures.

However, the main impetus for including various cultures has come from changes within society itself. It is estimated that by the turn of the century a third of the U.S. population will be members of ethnic minority groups. In order to evaluate and help minority children, clinical child psychologists must first understand them. Yet, in spite of the increased emphasis on the interpersonal and superordinate contexts, clinical child psychologists have been unaccountably reluctant to study minority children and to think through the implications of their diversity for clinical practice and for the concept of developmental psychopathology in general. While there is now enough literature to warrant a special discussion of the mental health of ethnic minorities, such literature has only begun to tap into the richness of the field itself.

SOME COMMENTS ABOUT METHODOLOGY

In discussing research, Meehl (1978) referred to the five "noble traditions" in clinical psychology that he speculates will be around long after current fads have faded: descriptive clinical psychiatry; psychometric assessment; behavior genetics; behavior modification (with its remarkable technical power); and psychoanalytic theory (with its unsurpassed level of interest). We shall have many encounters with all of these noble traditions, for they make up the rich and varied foundation on which clinical psychology rests.

Meehl's point concerning traditions is equally applicable to methodologies. The three

giants of psychology—Pavlov, Freud, and Piaget—utilized quite different research methodologies. Thus the progress of psychology as a science has taken place by means of diverse investigatory strategies. Note that we said "as a science." Science is defined as the search for knowledge. Different sciences have found different methodologies to be most fruitful in this quest: astronomy, the oldest science, advanced through observation of naturally occurring events, while physics and chemistry advanced through highly controlled laboratory experiments. Psychology, in contrast, has not settled on a method of choice. What is true of psychology in general is doubly true of developmental psychopathology, which owes as much to the Darwinian tradition of *natural observation* as it does to the *laboratory experiment*. The research of choice is the research which is clearly conceived and elegantly executed, regardless of the methodology.

Instead of looking at methodology in the abstract, we shall approach it through research that has actually advanced our understanding of childhood psychopathology. (For a more formal discussion, see Achenbach, 1978.) We shall use illustrations taken from studies that we shall discuss in detail in subsequent chapters.

The Naturalistic Tradition

The Clinical Eye In developmental psychopathology, the naturalistic tradition in pure culture is carried on by individuals with a clinical eye, which is at the opposite extreme from the innocent eye. "The Emperor's New Clothes" notwithstanding, inexperienced individuals quite literally see very little of the behavior occurring around them. As Piaget has taught us, current stimuli, in order to register, must be assimilated into organized bodies of meaningful concepts, which in turn have grown out of meaningful observations in the past. Thus the clinical eye requires, first, sensitive and disciplined observation with the intent of maximizing understanding. The challenge may well last a lifetime. But observation is not enough: the clinical eye must nourish a conceptualizing mind. A vast quantity of accumulated clinical wisdom goes no further than the application of past experience to present problems. To make the leap from the applied to the conceptual is rare among clinicians, but it marks the transition from personal experience to embryonic scientific knowledge.

Naturalistic observation aims at describing and understanding naturally occurring behavior. Developmental psychologists call this study of children in their natural environments *ecology* (see Bronfenbrenner, 1989a). It maximizes the chances of obtaining ecologically valid ("true to life") data and of capturing the multiplicity of variables which may be responsible for producing such behavior. By selecting comparative and contrasting populations and settings, the researcher takes a step toward disentangling relevant from irrelevant and confounding variables. However, there are practical limits to the extent to which such disentangling can be done. Limitations in the degree of control over the data should not be equated with a lessening of investigatory rigor. There is no reason to claim, for example, that Darwin and Piaget were less rigorous than Pavlov just because they chose to examine naturally occurring behavior rather than to work in a laboratory. Or in the research we are about to cite it would be unthinkable to view the investigators as lacking in rigor (see Shakow, 1953).

Our two examples of the use of the clinical eye represent two successive levels of understanding. Kanner's delineation of autism (Chapter 4) is a model of *descriptive classification*, in which the entity is clearly and accurately described in its own right while also being differentiated from other disturbances that resemble and therefore could be mistaken

for it. Redl (Chapter 9), through his keen observation of a small group of impulsive, acting-out boys, was able to analyze their behavior according to a number of separate psychological functions, such as memory, anticipation, and social perspective-taking, and to discover how each function deviated from normal.

Objective Procedures The clinical eye has undoubtedly made major contributions to our science. But like all research procedures, it has its disadvantages. What if one observer fails to verify what another has reported? What if two observers disagree as to what has occurred? Behavior such as guilt or anxiety is not objectively "out there" like a fossil or a plant. To correct for the possible error involved in individual observation, objective procedures have been devised. Such procedures have two advantages: their reliability can be tested, and they can be used by all members of the scientific community. In certain instances, naturally occurring behavior still comprises the basic data; for example, observers can be trained reliably to record the number of friendly overtures made to normally achieving and learning disabled fourth-graders during recess. In other instances, special instruments may be used that measure naturally occurring behavior indirectly: standardized interviews, behavioral checklists, and personality tests are examples. These instruments must be shown to be reliable and valid so that there is evidence that they do, indeed, measure the behavior they purport to evaluate.

We shall encounter studies that use objective procedures both for descriptive purposes and for hypothesis testing. Rutter is a master at testing hypotheses by means of objective measures of various naturally occurring events. In Chapter 9 we shall follow his line of reasoning as he attempts to tease out the relation between schooling on the one hand and conduct disorders on the other.

The Laboratory Tradition

While it is possible to introduce objective procedures and control of variables into naturalistic research, it takes considerable ingenuity (and often good luck) to do so (see Wenar, 1976). Both objectivity and control are built into laboratory studies. The instruments are objective and available to the scientific community, while the actual conduct of the research is explicitly described so others may replicate it. The investigators' control of the situation allows them systematically to manipulate the variable or variables being studied, while holding all others constant. The result is a powerful tool for disentangling crucial from confounding and tangential variables as well as for revealing processes responsible for the psychopathological behavior being investigated.

Of the many admirable examples of controlled studies we shall encounter, we shall select only three. A series of interrelated investigations provided evidence that mental retardation is not synonymous with a slow rate of learning but may be, in part, due to a failure to generate appropriate hypotheses for learning and remembering or—and this is the most intriguing puzzle—a failure to utilize potentially efficient strategies even when they are available (see Chapter 12). Controlled studies of autism are separating mental retardation as a confounding variable and isolating other variables that seem specific to the psychopathology: difficulty with processing patterned information and a deficiency in imitation being two of the most important (see Chapter 4). Finally, Douglas's elegant programmatic research is exploring hyperactivity as the product of a defect in sustaining attention. Douglas has also isolated a variable of impulsivity,

which undermines the hyperactive child's ability to stop, look, listen—and think (see Chapter 6).

Along with its many assets, the laboratory study has a potential disadvantage which is the mirror image of that of the naturalistic study—the maximizing of control may result in artificial data. Instead of being a paradigm of reality, the findings may have little ecological validity, being applicable only to the highly rarefied setting of the laboratory (see Bronfenbrenner, 1977).

In general, naturalistic studies rate high on ecological validity and, in certain instances, on objectivity of procedures, but controlling variables is exceedingly difficult. Laboratory studies rate high on objectivity and control but leave unanswered the question of ecological validity. In actuality, the uncontrolled naturalistic study has taught us as much about childhood psychopathology as the highly controlled, objective laboratory study. While particular psychologists may stoutly defend one methodology as being scientific, science itself is capricious. So far at least, it has no favorites.

In our presentations of the various psychopathologies, we will distinguish empirical evidence based on clinical observations from those using objective procedures and laboratory settings when such distinctions are not obvious.

Note: Because the developmental psychopathology literature is so extensive, it is not possible to present all of the topics or cover all of the research. In an attempt to partially compensate for omissions we will cite articles covering topics that we can only mention in passing; and whenever possible we will include research review articles in addition to individual studies.

In order to update coverage of topics or to pursue individual interests, it might be helpful to have a list of journals and annuals devoted to developmental psychopathology. The following list is selective rather than comprehensive.

Journals

Development and Psychopathology
Journal of Abnormal Child Psychology
Journal of the American Academy of Child and Adolescent Psychiatry
Journal of Clinical Child Psychology

Annuals

Advances in Clinical Child Psychology
Rochester Symposium on Developmental Psychopathology

Annual Progress in Child Psychiatry and Child Development

Having outlined our general developmental model, we are now ready to describe the normal development of the intra- and interpersonal variables that will have a bearing on our subsequent discussions of the various childhood psychopathologies. Then, in Chapter 3, we will be able to build a bridge to the psychopathologies themselves and learn which ones tend to persist and which ones tend to disappear with time.

NORMAL DEVELOPMENT

W e are now in something of a quandary. If we are to understand childhood psychopath-

ology as normal development gone awry, obviously we must first chart normal development. But having decided not to follow any one of the current models and instead favor a looser, more inclusive framework, we still need a conceptual guide for selecting variables to discuss. Fortunately, it is still possible to draw up a list of variables crucial to a child's well-being so that, if anything goes radically wrong with any one of them, we can seriously consider the possibility that the child is disturbed.

First there is a group of variables binding the child to the human environment. Prominent in this group is the bond of love that develops between infant and mother in the first year of life, which is called *attachment*. Throughout childhood and throughout life the ability to feel deeply about and become attached to another individual lies at the core of the human experience. Attachments may become erotic, resulting in *sexual* relationships, or at a more moderate and diffuse level, the human bond may be expressed in friendships and companionableness, which we shall call *social relations*. If something goes radically awry with any of these bonds—if, for example, the loving overtures of a parent are met with rage or profound indifference, if sexual intimacy is a source of terror rather than pleasure, if the child is socially isolated and friendless— we would rightfully be concerned.

Another basic variable involves *initiative* or self-reliant expansiveness. The bright-eyed infant scanning the environment for new and interesting sights epitomizes this urge to explore and to master. In many of their ventures children are free to follow their own interests; but increasingly with age they are required to stay with a task whether or not they want to. We shall call this combination of initiative and necessity *work*, the special setting for work during childhood being the classroom. If, instead of having initiative and the capacity for work, the child is apathetic or distracted or fearful of any kind of venturing out, or if there is a persistent, self-defeating rebelliousness at

being told what to do no matter how benign and reasonable, again we have cause to be concerned about the child.

Perhaps the most obvious variable for us to examine is *self-control*, the control of *aggression* looming particularly large in the public mind. Socializing children often involves curbing their preferred behaviors; with time, children take over this monitoring, controlling function themselves, eventually adding another mechanism specifically concerned with judging the moral content of behavior, the *conscience*. Self-control also involves the generation of *anxiety*, which serves as one of the principle deterrents to performing socially disapproved actions. Having "everything under control" is a sign of healthy growth, while both excessive and deficient control are deviations; the child who is plagued by anxiety and guilt as well as the violently destructive child concern parent and clinician alike.

Finally, it is essential for the child to understand the physical and social environment as well as him- or herself, a variable we shall call *cognition*. Reality can be distorted by magical ideas in the first few years of life because of cognitive immaturity. Therefore it is essential that these distortions be replaced by realistic understanding; the persistence of bizarre, magical ideas, such as a 10-year-old believing he can hear through his "belly button" and can control television pictures by merely thinking about them, is generally recognized as a sign of disturbed development.

In sum, the ten variables we have selected in our developmental approach to childhood psychopathology are attachment, initiative, self-control, conscience, cognition, anxiety, sex, aggression, social relations, and work. (For an extensive coverage of the variables, see Berk, 1991.)

ATTACHMENT

The bond of love between parents and child is one of the pivotal variables determining the course of development throughout childhood. We shall refer to it in many of our discussions of psychopathology—the failure of the bond to develop in infancy, the rupture of the bond by death or divorce, the contamination of the bond with excessive anger or anxiety, the atrophy of the bond through neglect. It is essential, therefore, to understand how this bond is established in infancy and how it develops throughout childhood. While labeled differently in various theories, we shall call the bond *attachment*. (For a discussion of various conceptualizations, see Ainsworth, 1969.)

The Formation of Attachment

Human beings have the longest period of helpless infancy of any species. In order to survive they must be cared for by more mature human beings for many years. Thus attachment takes place in the caretaking situation; the kind of care infants receive determines, to a significant degree, the kind of attachment they form. While most of our information comes from the infant's attachment to the mother, psychologists have begun to recognize and investigate the importance of father-infant attachment as well. (For a summary of research on mother-infant attachment, see Rosenblith and Sims-Knight, 1992.)

The development of attachment to the mother or primary caretaker (for convenience, the two terms will be used synonymously) follows a reasonably predictable course. Neonates are initially programmed to respond to stimuli emanating from other people. By 2 weeks of age they prefer the human voice over other sounds, and by 4 weeks, prefer the mother's voice over other human voices. In the second month, eye contact is established. Between the third and fourth months, these precursors of attachment reach a cognitive and emotional climax: the pattern of stimuli comprising the human face is perceived with sufficient cohesiveness and detail to be distinguished from other patterns of stimuli and, equally important, is a source of special delight. The percept "people" and the affect "pleasure" are fused into what is called the *social smile*. The social smile is indiscriminate and hedonistic: infants light up when anyone hits upon that combination of grimacing and vocalizing and bouncing and tickling which delights them. On their part, adults will go through all kinds of absurd antics to elicit such a smile. The simple fact that delighting the infant is highly rewarding to the adult is one of the strongest guarantees that an attachment will be formed.

Between the sixth and ninth month, indiscriminate responsiveness gives way to selectivity as infants show a strong preference for the mother and other special caretakers. This inner circle of caretakers can elicit greater delight than anyone else and can most readily comfort the infant in times of distress. In addition, two negative affects come to the fore. The first is *separation anxiety* when the mother leaves. Despite the label, the distress is not akin to fear, as are most anxieties, but is better described as anguish—that painful blend of protest and despair which wells up when a crucial source of pleasure disappears and one is helpless to bring it back. Thus separation anguish is more closely related to depression than to terror. *Stranger anxiety,* or the fear of unfamiliar persons, is not as prevalent as it was once believed to be. However, the indiscriminate pleasure that marked the era of the social smile is replaced with a more cautious, wary response to unfamiliar adults.

Separation anxiety has implications for many aspects of normal and deviant development. First, intense anxiety is part of normal development. Indeed, there are those who claim that the absence of such anxiety is suggestive of deviate development; for example, some children reared in impersonal institutions will subsequently respond to anyone who shows them affection (like the infant during the stage of the indiscriminate social smile) while failing to form an enduring relationship and being unaffected by loss (see Chapter 14). We also learn that, from the beginning, intense affection and intense anguish over loss go hand in hand. Dare I love deeply and risk abandonment? is a question that comes up throughout life and that each individual must answer in his or her own way. Certain delinquents are difficult to help because they fear that if they let themselves become emotionally attached to their therapist, the therapist will desert them as other adults have done in the past.

Hostility is also a consequence of attachment, although it has received less attention than anxiety. In reunions after separations, such as hospitalization, it is not unusual for infants and toddlers first to ignore their parents and then become unusually angry and touchy for the next few days or even weeks. Infants and toddlers are cognitively incapable of grasping the reality of the situation, such as the fact that the separation was for good reason and unavoidable; all they can understand is that they needed the mother and she was not there. In their eyes she becomes a "bad" mother and the target for anger (see Bowlby, 1973).

Thus we see that attachment, even in its normal manifestations, is never purely positive; it is inevitably a mixture of love and anguish and fear and anger. It is when the negative components begin to dominate that the chances for deviant development are increased.

Caretaking

A few comments concerning *caretaking* are relevant to the discussions to come. The traditional image has been that of the mother caring for a totally helpless, passive infant. However, there is now convincing evidence that infants from the beginning are actively taking in and trying to cope with their environment (see Appleton, Clifton, and Goldberg, 1975). They also have their special temperament—their individualized tempo and activity level, their characteristic mood and adaptability, their special set of vulnerabilities and resiliencies, their preferences and dislikes (see Bates, 1987). Psychologists have verified what mothers have known for many years—namely, that certain infants are temperamentally easy to care for while others are difficult, regardless of the kind of care they receive. Thus caretaking is now viewed as an interaction between mother and infant in which each has to accommodate to the other. If all goes well, the result is a

Sensitive caretaking involves stimulation as well as comforting.

mutual enhancement of development in which not only the infant grows but also the mother in terms of her caretaking skills, feelings of competence, and sources of gratification.

Caretaking itself is conceptualized as a combination of *comforting* and *stimulation.* Comforting and relieving the infant's distress has been the traditional view of mothering. More recently, attention has turned to the mother as stimulator. The very fact that she is human means she is a source of fascinating and delightful visual and auditory stimuli. The mother is also a mediator of stimulation, bringing the infant in contact with a variety of interesting sights and sounds such as rattles and rings and mobiles. Her sensitivity to the infant's needs and the promptness and appropriateness with which she responds to them are more important than the sheer amount of time she spends with the infant. And through her comforting and stimulation, the mother provides both the emotional security and the varied environmental input necessary to normal development.

Caretaking determines the kind of attachment that will develop. If the mother is sensitive in her caretaking, if she is alert to the infant's needs and reacts quickly and appropriately, the infant will develop a secure attachment. Securely attached infants respond positively to the mother and, because of her consistency, are confident she will be there when needed. Thus they develop a loving, trusting relationship. Closeness does not result in dependency and clinging, however; on the contrary, securely attached infants explore the environment confidently.

There are three patterns of insecure attachment. If the mother is intrusive, infants will be *resistant* or ambivalent toward her, demanding attention and affection but petulant when receiving it. The distant and angry mother has an *avoidant* infant who ignores her in a kind of psychological armed truce. A mother who is an inconsistent mixture of neglect and rejection produces a *disorganized-disoriented* attachment evidenced by contradictory responses, such as approaching the mother with flat or depressed affect, looking away while being held, or exhibiting a dazed expression. The majority of infants are securely attached, while the disorganized-disoriented attachment is both the most disturbed and the rarest form.

Cognitively, the different kinds of attachments result in what are called *internal working models* that not only are the infants' mental representations of attachment-related experiences and feelings but also serve as a kind of template or set of expectations for subsequent attachment-relevant experiences. (see Main, Kaplan, and Cassidy, 1985). Thus, a secure attachment prepares infants to view future closeness in terms of love and trust; they can subsequently reveal intimate thoughts and feelings without fear of betrayal, and they know that their cry for help will be answered, however this cry may be expressed.

Well-cared-for infants are also apt to develop a positive self-image and confidence in their ability to cope successfully with problems as they arise. There is evidence, for example, that the securely attached infant becomes the effective problem solver as a toddler and the flexible, resourceful, and curious preschooler who is enthusiastically involved with school tasks and peers (Bretherton, 1987).

Insecurely attached infants make a different kind of adjustment as preschoolers. Resistant attachment tends to be related to impulsivity and ineptness with peers or passivity and dependency. Avoidant attachment tends to be related to hostility, antisocial behavior, and social isolation. Both groups are more dependent on the teacher and have lower self-esteem. (Sroufe, 1989, has a more detailed presentation of conceptual issues and empirical studies.) Finally, similar differences between securely and insecurely attached infants were observed when they were 10 years of age, the former being more socially competent, flexible, and adaptable, the latter being more dependent on adults (Urban et al., 1991). We will return to the topic of secure-insecure attachment when we discuss the extremes of deviant caretaking represented by physical abuse and neglect in Chapter 14.

Another reason why attachment is important is that it is a prerequisite for successful *socialization*. Infants and toddlers have no natural desire to be neat and clean or to respect property; quite to the contrary, they want to explore and mess and possess at will. Why, then, should they ever give up the pleasure of immediate gratification? Because the love of the parents is at stake. The behavior that the parents regard as good is rewarded with love; the behavior that they regard as bad is punished by the withdrawal of love. In normal development, toddlers and preschoolers for the most part acquiesce, because the love they receive compensates for the autonomy they lose. But already we can sense the possibilities for abuse of parental love. Suppose parental demands are excessive and entail total subjugation, as may have happened during childhood in someone who became anorectic (see Chapter 11)? Or suppose demands are made with inadequate compensations of love, as may have happened during the childhood of someone who became a juvenile delinquent (see Chapter 9)? We would rightly suspect that chances of deviant development would be increased.

Finally, attachment is linked with *exploration*. Securely attached infants explore the environment confidently because they are venturing out "from a secure base." Insecurely attached infants are either hesitant and uncertain or must defensively block the mother out, thereby depriving themselves of what should be her growth-promoting mediations. Thus, attachment sets the stage for the self-reliant expansiveness that we call *initiative*, which, as we shall soon see, is the pivotal development of the toddler period.

Subsequent Developments

According to Ainsworth (1991), the *preschooler's* increased ability to use language and to understand the mother's point of view results in increased communication and negotiation with her in order to arrive at mutually acceptable plans for action. Ainsworth also speculates that attachment—specifically, the need to maintain proximity, distress upon separation, joy at reunion, grief at loss, and security seeking—is an important component of all subsequent affectional ties, although there obviously are other components as well. Attachment plays a part in friendship, especially the close ones of adolescents, and is also present in the bonds with siblings and other kin. Finally, it is a central feature of adult sexual partnerships. (See Vormbrock, 1993.)

However, the descriptive picture of attachment in *middle childhood* grows dim, Gesell's previously summarized account of the relationship of the 6- to 9-year-old child to the parents being one of the most complete (see Chapter 1). In adolescence, the issue of attachment again comes to the fore. Adolescence is a time of major revolutions: a biological revolution brought about by sexual maturation, an interpersonal revolution involving a shift away from the family and toward the peer group, an identity revolution involving a search for a fulfilling adult role. While we now know that the picture of adolescence as necessarily a time of "storm and stress" is exaggerated, the cultural expectation of independence still marks the period as a time of significant change in the relation between parent and child. Attachment is caught up in this change. Parental expressions of affection become an embarrassment, offers of comfort and help are apt to be met with the standard outcry, "I'm not a baby any more!" If the adolescent is having problems with growing up and becoming independent, however, parents are also having problems with growing older and no longer being needed. A change in status and function is occurring in all parties involved in the interaction, as the interpersonal context of our developmental model would indicate.

While adolescence can go relatively smoothly, it still stands as a time of increased vulnerability for those whose relations with their parents make the challenge of independence an exceptionally threatening one. In examining anorexia nervosa, for example, we shall be dealing with an instance in which the stresses cannot be managed and contribute to the production of a psychological breakdown (Chapter 11).

INITIATIVE

If attachment is central in the first year of life, initiative is central in the second. Toddlers literally and figuratively stand on their own two feet and turn their backs on their mothers. Intoxication with a newfound sense of power propels them into a stage of willfulness and negativism. The selfsame 2-year-old who, a few months ago, was terrified at the mother's departure, now counters her every request with an imperious "No!" For her part, the mother finds that she must increasingly restrict her child, who is into everything and all over the place. Thus begins the conflict between freedom to do what one wants and conformity to the requirements of society, a conflict that will last a lifetime (see Figure 2.1). We will take a closer look at the toddler's self-reliant venturing forth, which we call *initiative*, tracing its roots in infancy and commenting further on some of its manifestations during the "terrible twos."

Origins and Nature

Initiative in the toddler period has a number of roots in infancy, the primary ones being curiosity and exploration. The old image of the infant's life as totally dominated by physiological needs such as hunger, thirst, and sleep is erroneous. (The landmark article is White, 1959.) As soon as there are periods of alert wakefulness, neonates begin exploring their environment. Their searching eyes and receptive ears lead the way, followed increasingly by motoric exploration as they outgrow their body's initial clumsiness. In the first month of life exploratory behaviors are remarkably mature, characterized by orientation, concentration, perseverance, gratification with success, or annoyance at failure. Infants are as hungry for stimulation as they are for food, their endless fascination undergirding the giant steps taken in comprehending their environment in the first year (Appleton, Clifton, and Goldberg, 1975).

But infants not only want to take in the environment; they want actively to control it as well. When 8-week-old infants who were placed in a specially designed crib discovered they could make a mobile move by turning their head, they repeatedly did so with great glee (Watson and Ramey, 1972). Around 20 weeks of age infants begin to take the initiative in establishing, sustaining, and renewing contact and interaction with the mother, lifting their arms in greeting her, clinging to her, following her when they are able to crawl. By the end of the first year they may be so adept and insistent in their demands for attention that some mothers become resentful (Sander, 1964). Other evidence of an early need to control are the many "battles" between mother and infant: 8-month-olds who have had the experience of holding the bottle, thereby taking feeding "into their own hands," may strongly resist attempts to make them drink from a cup (Spock, 1963). The "battle of the bottle" is subsequently replaced by the "battle of the spoon," as 1-year-olds insist on feeding themselves, although their ineptness results in bringing the oatmeal to their nose or ear or hair as often as to their mouth. The mother

FIGURE 2.1
The other side of the "helpless child" story. (*Source:* Calvin and Hobbes copyright 1985 by Bill Watterson. Dist. by Universal Press Syndicate. Reprinted with permission. All rights reserved.)

who cannot stand the ensuing mess and tries to take the spoon away by sheer force might be met with a tenacious determination to hold onto it and a rage reaction when the infant is over-powered. Just over the horizon—during the toddler period—lies the "battle of the potty."

There is an important cognitive component to this desire to control the environment. Neonates are too immature cognitively to grasp the relation between their actions and environmental events. By the middle of the first year the connection has been established, but—and this is the important point—it is an unrealistic, magical one. After discovering that their vigorous, jerky movements can make a mobile on their crib dance, they proceed to repeat these movements and look at the television set or the clock or other familiar objects, expecting them to dance also. Again, infants whose attentive mothers come when they cry initially believe that their cry actually produces the mother's presence. But how could it be otherwise? How could infants grasp the reality of the sequence—that the mother was in another room, that she heard the cry, that she could decide to ignore it or come to the infant, and that she chose the latter? While unable to grasp

reality, infants can make sense of their immediate experience, which is, "I make jerky movements, objects dance; I cry, mother appears; *ergo* my actions alone cause environmental events to happen." In short, infants have an *omnipotent* concept of causality. While such thinking would be a sign of severe psychopathology in adolescence, it is not only developmentally appropriate in infants but represents a significant advance over the prior period, when the notion of causality itself was not grasped (see Piaget, 1967).

The desire to venture out in infancy continues into the toddler period, locomotion opening up a whole new world for the toddler to explore and master. It is important to underscore the spontaneous, *intrinsically rewarding* nature of this exploration, in contrast to the socializing parents' directives and prohibitions, many of which go against the grain. Also, as toddlers explore they continue to develop the concept of the *self-as-agent,* and as their explorations are successful and pleasurable, they develop *self-confidence* and a healthy self-pride. This self-reliant venturing out, which we call initiative, has variously been labeled autonomy, mastery, competence, and independence by others. While the definitions may vary, all the terms share an emphasis on the self-as-agent and on expansiveness.

We now have a better appreciation of why anything that impedes the toddler's self-reliant exploration is apt to be resented and resisted. Typically such resistance takes the form of negativism, which may be an active noncompliance (shouting "I won't" or throwing a tantrum) or a passive noncompliance (ignoring the parent or doing nothing). Evidence indicates that the toddler will bridle no matter how sweetly reasonable the parent is (Wenar, 1982). Just as the self-centered infant knew only, "Mother is not here when I need her," the self-centered toddler knows only, "My parents are preventing me from doing what I want to do." The terrible twos are, by and large, of the toddler's own making. By the same token, exasperated parents can take comfort in the fact that, while nothing they do will prevent or shorten its reign, negativism is usually "outgrown" in a couple of years.

We have emphasized the toddler's physical venturing forth because it sets the stage for the conflict between compliance and defiance which will figure so prominently in our discussion of psychopathology. However, not all initiative is physical. Producing varied sounds seems to have an intrinsic appeal, and the toddler soon learns that certain sounds, made either fortuitously or in imitation of adult speech, have the magical property of eliciting responses of great delight from parents. "Baby's first word" typically becomes the occasion for rejoicing. The toddler also learns that words as well as gestures can be used to communicate, subsequently realizing that they are also more versatile and require less effort. In addition to their communicative value, words and language play an important role in self-control and cognition. Subsequently, when we turn to the psychopathologies, we shall learn that the absence or breakdown of communicative speech plays a crucial role in two of

the most severe childhood disturbances—autism and schizophrenia (see Chapters 4 and 10).

Developmental Course of Initiative

The toddler's fascination with objects continues throughout childhood. "What is it?" and "How does it work?"—questions first asked about ordinary household objects—are asked about objects in the wider physical environment and, eventually, in outer space. In the realm of tools, the toy hammer is replaced by the tool kit, the blunt scissors by the sewing machine; ahead lies the computer. The 10-word vocabulary of the 19-month-old increases to the 80,000-word vocabulary of the first-year high school student. In the social realm, playing house with the preschoolers next door develops into the complex gangs and cliques of adolescence.

We could go on, but we are not as interested in areas of self-reliant expansions as in certain consequences of initiative for the self. First, discovering what one can do plays a central role in *self-definition*. The 3-year-old who announces excitedly, "I can jump" and the high school sophomore who says, "I was elected class treasurer," have defined themselves through their various ventures.

Children who succeed in their ventures are accruing a sense of *self-worth* and pride. Such healthy self-love can be as important as a healthy love relation with another person. Objective studies of self-worth or self-esteem provide us with an account of its development in terms of progressive *differentiation* (see Harter, 1990b). Before middle childhood, children cannot verbalize a general self-esteem, although they do differentiate two separate kinds, one deriving from being socially acceptable, the other from being competent. They fail to differentiate specific sources of self-esteem within these categories, however, so being good at schoolwork, for example, is fused with being good at sports.

By middle childhood a global sense of self-worth begins to emerge along with three specific areas of competence—academic, physical power, and social. Adolescence brings the additional areas of close friendship, romantic appeal, and job competence. However, these areas have different import or *salience;* making all A's or being beautiful may mean everything to one child but be a matter of indifference to another. Thus, salience is closely linked with self-worth; children with high self-worth are competent in areas that are important to them, while children with low self-worth are not competent in areas that are important to them (Harter, 1986). From middle childhood on, self-evaluation is also closely related to behavior: academic self-esteem predicts school achievement, curiosity, and motivation to take on challenges while social self-esteem is related to being liked by peers.

Finally, enterprising individuals are developing a sense of being in charge of their own destinies, which psychologists have studied under the heading of *locus of control.* Individuals who perceive events as contingent on their own behavior or some characteristic of themselves have an *internal* locus of control; individuals who believe that events are the result of factors other than themselves, such as luck or chance or fate, have an *external* locus of control. Thus initiative affects the individual's perception of personal responsibility for events. Such perceptions have been shown to be significantly correlated with academic achievement; for example, children who believe that education does not matter because they will never have a chance to make anything of themselves do poorly compared to children who believe they can use education to make a difference to their future (Phares, 1976).

Adolescence may be a period that presents special problems in regard to initiative. The adolescent must negotiate the transition from dependent child to independent adult, a transition made difficult by conflicts at many levels. Parents, for their part, want their adolescent to take on responsibilities, earn money, date, and be popular, but they also want to retain their role as guides to proper conduct and as decision makers. And adolescents themselves are ambivalent about independence. Physically, sexually, and intellectually they are young adults, not children; they have the capacity to work and devote themselves to an ideal; they are socially sensitive and can form meaningful friendships. Yet they also sense that they might lack the experience, judgment, and psychological maturity to use such assets appropriately. Finding a niche in a complex society and mastering the intricacies of vocational and sexual relations are often a matter of trial and error. Setbacks are apt to bruise their egos and remind them that, if they are no longer children, they are also not quite adults. When all the conflicts within and between family members boil over, the last of the normal battles of childhood is fought—the battle of the generations. The adolescent is viewed as wild, disrespectful, and amoral, the parents are seen as old-fashioned, self-centered, and lacking in understanding.

Like attachment, initiative is fundamental to normal development. A significant diminution of initiative is an ominous sign, while a lack of initiative, as evidenced in autism, indicates severe psychopathology. Curiosity, which lies at the heart of initiative from earliest infancy, requires the ability to focus attention on interesting stimuli or the task at hand. When there is a deficit in this ability to pay attention, healthy initiative is replaced by the scattered behavior of the hyperactive child (Chapter 6). Bleak institutional settings can crush initiative so that normal infants and mentally retarded children are no longer motivated to use their abilities and skills (Chapters 14 and 12). A special kind of loss of initiative called learned helplessness may underlie the defeatist attitude that characterizes depression (Chapter 7). Both the normal negativism of the terrible twos and the normal transitional problems of adolescence can become exaggerated to the point where they block further growth (Chapter 5) or, in the case of adolescence, eventuate in drug use and abuse (Chapter 11).

SELF-CONTROL

In a number of psychopathologies, self-control figures more prominently than any other single variable. In early childhood, control of bodily functions is a basic aspect of self-control. Toddlers may fail to learn to control their bladders and continue to wet their beds at night or, less frequently, their pants during the day. Eating may get out of control, leading to obesity at one extreme or self-starvation even to the point of death at the other (Chapters 5 and 11). When self-control is excessive in middle childhood, the groundwork for certain internalizing disorders is laid; when self-control is weak, acting-out behavior such as aggression and juvenile delinquency may result (Chapters 8 and 9). Therefore, it is essential that we understand the development of self-control from infancy to adulthood and the factors that enable the child to achieve normal self-control.

Factors Involved in Self-Control

While neonates have some capacity for regulating physiological tension and for self-soothing, they are readily overwhelmed by distress and must rely on caretakers to protect them. As we have seen, sensitive caretaking builds up a trusting expectation that relief will be forthcoming; this, in turn, counteracts helplessness and increases tolerance for distress. In addition, by 4 to 6 months of age, infants have a number of capabilities for regulating exter-

nal stimulation, one of the most important being attention. Thus, they can turn away from something unpleasant or can prevent an interpersonal exchange from becoming too exciting by temporarily looking away. The sensitive caretaker responds to such cues by moderating stimulation, thereby facilitating the infant's sense of self-control (Sroufe, 1990a). As we will see, failure to effectively regulate excitation is involved in hyperactivity (Chapter 6) and possibly in autism (Chapter 4). While self-regulation is undoubtedly important, socially engendered requirements for self-control have received the most attention. It is these requirements that we will examine now.

Descriptively, the situation could not be simpler. The exploring toddler reaches for a vase on the living room table. Her mother rushes in, says "No," and slaps her hand. She withdraws. She may reach again, and again be punished. The pattern is repeated many times. Eventually, however, as the toddler approaches the vase and begins reaching for it, she suddenly stops, shakes her head, and even slaps her own hand. Then she withdraws. She never again reaches for the forbidden vase. She has achieved self-control. However, teasing out the factors involved in this achievement and understanding how they work is far from simple. Let us examine certain important ingredients. (See Kopp, 1982, for a description of the path from situational compliance in the toddler to self-regulation in the young preschooler.)

As our example suggests, there is *reward and punishment*. These may be physical: a toddler who puts his toy away at mother's request may get to lick the chocolate-pudding bowl, while another toddler who pokes a finger into the light socket may get slapped or spanked. Rewards and punishments may also be psychological. As we have just seen, attachment enables parents to bestow love for conformity to their directives; it also enables them to withdraw love when disobeyed, thus creating a situation akin to separation anguish in the child. Thus the child's concern about being love-worthy is a major force in the motivation to seek parental approval and avoid parental disapproval by complying with socializing directives.

In rewarding and punishing the child, parents convey more meaning than they intend, since they are also serving as a model of either controlled or uncontrolled behavior. Children are adept imitators. A parent can be taken aback on hearing a toddler, during a pretend telephone conversation, turn around and shout, "Be quiet! Can't you see I'm on the phone?" in an exact duplication of the parent's own words and tone of voice. In certain instances, *modeling* or *imitation* may serve to undermine socialization; a father who punishes aggression by losing his temper and beating the child is simultaneously serving as a model of uncontrolled behavior.

A host of *cognitive* variables are involved in self-control. At the simplest level, toddlers must be able to grasp cause-and-effect relations and remember what behavior leads to reward or punishment; only then will they be able to apply past experiences to the situation at hand. They must then be able to integrate fragmentary experiences into guiding principles of behavior in such a way that "I should not take that toy" will eventually become "I should not take anything that belongs to somebody else." Words play a pivotal role in this process of achieving higher levels of self-control. The simple "No" becomes, "Mustn't touch," and then, "That's Jimmy's truck, not yours," and finally, "You shouldn't take other people's things without asking them first." As the directives become increasingly complex, they guide behavior in an increasingly wide variety of situations. And as the cognitively developing child can both verbalize these directives and grasp their meaning, built-in controls become increasingly effective (Vaughn, Kopp,

and Krakow, 1984). Since, "saying things to oneself" is one aspect of thinking, we can see why *thinking* is regarded as the ally of control: the very fact that the child must stop and think serves to check immediate action, while the content of the thought itself serves to guide behavior into socially acceptable channels. As thinking serves its *delaying* and *guiding* functions, control is enhanced.

However, thought is not the only aid to counteracting impulsivity; interpersonal *trust* is equally important. Socialization consists not only of prohibitions but also of delayed gratification. The child's capacity to wait is enhanced if the promised rewards are consistently forthcoming. If parents are unreliable or if the environment is disorganized and unpredictable, children are less likely to tolerate the tensions of delay and more apt to seize upon the pleasures of the moment. Finally, the availability of *substitute gratifications* or *distractions* (Mischel and Baker, 1975) helps the child master the frustration of being forbidden to pursue a desired goal. The sensitive parent who has prohibited a toddler from touching a treasured vase may then present the child with a favorite set of pots and pans to play with. As children grow older, they become increasingly capable of redirecting their own activities into acceptable substitutes (Toner and Smith, 1977). Note that some substitutes involve the relinquishing of the original goal, as with our toddler. Others provide alternative, socially acceptable ways of achieving or partially achieving the goal; a boy who is forbidden to fight with a peer can defeat him in athletics, for example. One function of play and fantasy is to provide safe substitutes for achieving forbidden goals; the girl recently punished by her mother can spank her doll for being a "mean old mommy," while adults continue to fantasize victories and glories in situations too threatening to undertake in real life (Mischel, 1974). Our discussion of a group of impulse-ridden boys will illustrate what happens when many of these factors involved in self-control fail to develop adequately (Chapter 9).

Parental Discipline

There are three dimensions to parental discipline. First is the specific technique used, or what the parent does. Next is the affect accompanying the technique, such as warmth, anger, or coldness. Finally, there is the degree of control the parent exerts, which can range from total neglect to total domination. Ideally, we should know the effects on children of all possible combinations of these three variables, but we do not. What we do know can be summarized as follows.

Some techniques have been conceptualized as *love-oriented* in that they involve either praise and reasoning (*induction*) or the threat of *love withdrawal*. Induction involves explanation together with appeals to pride, to a desire to grow up, and to a concern for others. It tends to produce children who are responsible, cooperative, concerned with their own role in events, introspective, and guilty. In the preschool period, induction often must be accompanied by some intense affect or forcefulness for it to be effective because the children are still too young to respond to sweet reason alone. In love withdrawal, the parent conveys the implicit message, "If you do X, I temporarily will not love you." The children tend to comply immediately, but also to become anxious and conforming and to have low self-esteem.

The *authoritarian* or power-oriented parent is demanding, controlling, and unreasoning. The implicit message is, "Do what I say because I say so." If parents discipline in a punitive, rejecting manner, their children tend to become aggressive, uncooperative, fearful of punishment, and prone to blame others. They are low on initiative, self-esteem, and compe-

Induction: reasoning about breaking a dish.

tence with peers. Authoritarian parents do not have to be punitive, however; they can discipline out of concern and respect for the child. Unfortunately, this kind of stern but fair parent has not been studied.

The *permissive* parent can be either indulgent or neglectful. In the former instance the parent is undemanding, accepting, and child-centered and makes few attempts to control. The result is a selfish, dependent, irresponsible, aggressive, "spoiled" child. The neglectful parent is indifferent, uninvolved, or self-centered. Lax, unconcerned parenting is the breeding ground for antisocial aggression and juvenile delinquency. Self-centeredness on the parents' part is associated with self-centeredness in the children, along with impulsivity, moodiness, truancy, lack of long-term goals, and early drinking and smoking.

Authoritative parents set standards of mature behavior and expect the child to comply, but they are also highly involved, consistent, loving, communicative, willing to listen to the child, and respectful of the child's point of view. Their children tend to be self-reliant, self-controlled, secure, popular, and inquisitive. (For a comprehensive review of parental discipline, see Maccoby and Martin, 1983.)

The literature on parental discipline furnishes several leads as to which kinds are detrimental. Extremes of rejection, brutality, neglect, and permissiveness should be avoided. An inconsistent alternation between neglect and harsh punishment is apt to result in antisocial behavior; the child receives no love to make self-control worthwhile, while parental punitiveness foments rebellion and serves as a model of impulsive hostility. Excessive indulgence with few restrictions is apt to produce children who are impudent, demanding, disrespectful tyrants at home, are bossy and uncooperative with peers, and have few friends.

There is no one discipline ideally suited to all children, because healthy growth itself can take many forms. One parent may value assertiveness and creativity, another conformity and docility; a sensitive, introspective child may have advantages in certain settings, a tough-skinned scrapper in another. In other words, there are stylistic differences in normal development which are not a matter of healthy versus unhealthy adjustment. If there is no absolute answer to the question which discipline is best, such absolutism does not seem necessary in light of the diversity of healthy personality development itself.

Developmental Trends

To tell infants to wait a minute when they cry or to punish them for having a bowel movement makes no sense. It is only in the toddler period that requirements for self-control begin to be developmentally appropriate. Such requirements are apt to precipitate the angry storms, the temper tempests, and shouts of defiance of the terrible twos and threes. Gradually, however, the storm subsides. Not only are controls being strengthened but affective investments are being diversified, the intense involvement with parents and siblings now being supplemented by extrafamilial adults and peers. Diversification aids modulation, so the preschooler is increasingly capable of managing feelings that are becoming increasingly manageable.

The period between 6 and 9 years of age is the high point of self-control. The early anxieties and jealousies within the nuclear family, the accommodation to peer groups, and the transition from home to school have all been weathered, and no comparably dramatic new adjustments need to be made. Children of this age are variously described as conforming, practical, industrious, self-motivated, and self-controlled. They have more insight into their own behavior and the behavior of others than they did formerly and are more orderly, organized, and persistent. They are less aggressive and possessive than before, while the tendencies to blame and ridicule, to be greedy and possessive, or to snatch and steal are all on the wane. There is also a general tendency to be more inward rather than acting on the feelings and impulses of the moment.

The calm of middle childhood is shattered by the physiological changes and explosive growth of puberty. The period between 12 and 14 years of age may be marked by turmoil: some preadolescents are confused, touchy, negativistic and solitary, aggressive, deliberately provocative, and resistant to authority. Little wonder that some developmentalists have seen a similarity between this period and the terrible twos, even while recognizing that the preadolescent is vastly more complex. Adolescence itself is not so dramatically unstable, although, as we have seen, the many problems involved in the transition to adulthood still make it a time of vulnerability rather than stability in regard to self-control (see Sanford et al., 1943).

CONSCIENCE

Self-control evolves from parental prohibitions epitomized by "No" and "Wait." Conscience develops from parental evaluations typified by "good boy" or "good girl," "bad boy" or "bad girl." It is this added element of evaluation which makes conscience a special kind of control mechanism. Because conscience is a complex psychological creation, we had best describe it before discussing its development.

Description

Conscience grows out of evaluations of the child's behavior. "Evaluation" suggests that conscience is intimately connected with *values*. Typically we think of moral values as residing in the conscience and rightfully so. But the human conscience contains values from many other sources: some, such as success, achievement, and self-reliance, are cultural values; some, such as cleanliness and an unwillingness to waste food, derive from the family's style of living and parental idiosyncrasies; some, such as fair play and cooperativeness, come from peers. To various degrees, such values exist in harmony, conflict, and isolation. Their psychological potency is not determined by their moral weight; a man who is unconcerned about beating his children may suffer a pang of conscience over having forgotten to send his mother a birthday card.

Next, conscience involves *thinking, feeling,* and *behaving*—understanding what is morally right or wrong, feeling appropriate satisfaction or guilt, and acting in a moral manner. But this is the description of the ideal, integrated conscience. In reality, one element can

overshadow the other two: the Devil can quote scripture, people can feel righteous or guilty over acts that have nothing to do with morality, and moral behavior can serve immoral or amoral ends.

A special word should be said about the feelings originating in the conscience. Interestingly, we have a ready label for the negative affect accompanying transgressions, which is *guilt;* but we have no such label for the positive affect accompanying obedience, so we will arbitrarily call it *self-satisfaction.* Both affects derive from the parental evaluations "good boy" or "good girl," "bad boy" or "bad girl"; the former implies that the child is worthy of love, the latter that he or she is not. Because of the bond of love, being love-worthy is a source of one of the greatest pleasures of early childhood, while not being love-worthy subjects the child to intense anguish. As toddlers and preschoolers develop, they begin to internalize these two judgments; they judge their own behavior as good or bad. And as they say "good boy" or "good girl," "bad boy" or "bad girl" to themselves, they also experience the same pleasure and anguish that accompanied parental evaluations. The pleasure becomes self-satisfaction, the anguish becomes guilt.

Already we can sense the importance and potential dangers of guilt. Certainly guilt is essential to normal development, but the preschooler's negative self-judgment enters the scene long before it can be employed judiciously. This raises the possibility of all kinds of problems. It is time for us to look at the developmental picture and find out why.

The Development of Conscience

Freud, in trying to understand the childhood origins of adult psychopathology, and Piaget, in trying to understand the cognitive development of children, arrived at a similar picture of the early conscience as an absolutistic, punitive, irrational tyrant. While they hypothesized different reasons why early conscience was such a monster, they both believed that it is the child's own creation and not necessarily a reflection of rigid, punitive socialization on the parents' part.

Piaget (1932) provided the richest documentation of the cognitive distortions that characterize moral judgment in the preschool period and the beginning of middle childhood. He demonstrated that the seriousness of a transgression is judged by its physical consequences; breaking five cups is worse than breaking one cup, for example, even if the former event was accidental and the latter intentional. Wrongdoing must be punished unconditionally, and in certain cases, the more severe the punishment the better. Punishment is an end in itself, and there is little concern that it fit the crime or help the child avoid similar misdeeds in the future.

The next stage in the development of conscience is marked by an inflexible egalitarianism: the child believes in "an eye for an eye" in regard to retaliation and, in regard to altruism, believes that one does something nice for someone else so that he or she will do something nice in return! In short, the absolutistic, unconditional, punitive nature of the child's thinking is clear. It is only during the latter part of middle childhood that children begin to take intentions into account and consider degrees of punishment which match the seriousness of the transgression. Punishment itself serves a constructive purpose. Children begin to realize that people in authority can be wrong, that rules exist for social regulation and can be altered by common consent, and that fairness requires that an issue be considered from the points of view of all parties involved.

Piaget (1932) calls the early stages of thinking *moral realism*, which might seem a strange term except that by realism Piaget means literalness rather than rationality. Preschoolers literally believe what they see and hear. They can see a broken cup, but they cannot see an intention, so naughtiness is manifested by its physical consequences. A father can carry a toolbox that his son cannot budge, a mother can read books that do not even have pictures: How could such omnipotent and omniscient parents be wrong? Parents unwittingly cater to the child's literalism. When they tell their toddler or preschooler that he is a "bad boy" or that she is a "bad girl," they have two perspectives that the child lacks: they know that what their child is doing is no worse than what other children his or her age do and that the behavior is only temporary. The child however, is incapable of thinking, "This is just a phase and I will outgrow it"; instead, "bad" takes on an absolute connotation.

Elaborating and expanding on Piaget, Kohlberg (1976) reconstructs the stages of moral development in the following manner. At the *preconventional* level, children evaluate actions in terms of whether they lead to pleasure or punishment. Those resulting in rewards are good; those resulting in punishment are bad. During the *conventional morality* stage, the child adopts the conventional standards of "good boy" or "good girl" behavior to maintain the approval of others or conform to some moral authority such as religion. In the *postconventional or principled stage*, children judge behavior in terms of the morality of contract and democratically accepted law, of universal principles of ethics and justice, and of individual conscience, holding themselves personally accountable for moral decisions. Between 6 and 16, the preconventional level gradually declines while the other two levels increase, although only about one-quarter of 16-year-olds have achieved the highest level.

Although we know that the tyrannical conscience changes, we do not know why. Piaget emphasized the importance of the cognitive give-and-take during peer interaction as counteracting the rigid authoritarianism of early moral reasoning, but the evidence has not been clearly supportive. The parent who confronts the child with such simply stated challenges as, "How would you feel if someone did that to you?" may help the child think of transgressions in terms of all the parties involved. Dramatic play requiring children to assume various roles, such as those involved in playing house or grocery store or space travel, may also help the child realize that the same situation can be seen from different perspectives depending on the individual's role, thus counteracting the rigidity of absolutist thinking. Social-learning theorists emphasize the importance of parents as models of moral behavior, of their reinforcing moral behavior in their children, and of their combining punishment with reasoning, very much as is done in inductive disciplining. When the mystery concerning the agents of change has been solved, we will be in a better position than we are now to insure that normal children "outgrow" their primitive conscience and to help disturbed children who continue to suffer needlessly from its tyranny.

This would be a good place to emphasize a point that has come up in previous sections: there is a significant gap between reality and the young child's understanding of reality. Separation anxiety is an unrealistic fear in most instances, as is the infant's anger with the mother for not being there when needed regardless of the reason for her absence; the toddler can throw a tantrum in response to the most reasonable request from the most loving mother; and now we see a conscience developing that has little resemblance to the values the parent is trying to teach, no matter how simply those values are presented and how patiently they are explained. One implication is that good parenting cannot protect the child from the inevitable distresses and distortions of early childhood; however, good parenting can prevent such distresses and distortions from being magnified and, equally important, can maximize the corrective forces inherent in

continued growth. For the child clinician, the implication is that the child's view of family and friends and school is just that, rather than an accurate report of reality; age-appropriate distortions can result in an attentive mother being perceived as a "mean old witch," while a competent father may be seen as a destructive giant. Especially before middle childhood, the child is capable of creating a chamber of horrors out of personal needs and cognitive distortions.

To return to conscience: up to this point we have been dealing with the thinking aspect of conscience, not with feeling or acting. Children show guilt as early as 3 years of age, but we know little about it in the preschool period. We do know that the conditions eliciting it change during middle childhood. Young school-age children are concerned primarily with punishment rather than with guilt over transgressions. Thus they have an *externally oriented* conscience. Subsequently the theme of confession increases and is a kind of halfway house between externally oriented fear of punishment and internally oriented guilt. Children are inwardly troubled and driven to confession, even if they could get away with the transgression, because of what others might think of them (Thompson and Hoffman, 1980). However, confession can also be used manipulatively by children learning the trick of saying "I'm sorry" in order to forestall punishment. It is only in the preadolescent period that true guilt in the sense of an *internal judgment* and self-criticism appears. Punishment or even the love and opinion of others are not central; rather, preadolescents are concerned with the damage done to their own self-image and self-respect (Graham, Doubleday, and Guarino, 1984).

Conscience, like self-control, can be either too strong or too weak. Excessive guilt has been implicated particularly in the obsessive-compulsive neurosis and in depression, while antisocial children with acting-out behavior may have an externally oriented conscience concerned only with getting caught and being punished. We shall deal with these deviations in Chapters 7, 8, and 9.

COGNITION

The aspect of cognitive development most pertinent to understanding the relation between normal and psychopathological development is the separation of the self from the social and physical environment—what has been called the separation of the me from the not-me. Within this general domain, we shall explore the development of causal thinking and the concept of egocentrism, both of which will figure in future discussions.

Causality

An adolescent girl who will not speak for fear that feces would come out of her mouth, or a young man who always sleeps on his back in the belief that, if he did not, he would turn into a woman, would be regarded as psychopathologically disturbed, because they are convinced that they can cause events which, in reality, are beyond their control. This magical notion is called *omnipotence*. Yet omnipotence is not the creation of the mature mind— many concepts of causality are initially magical. Piaget tells us that, between 5 and 8 months of age, the infant is beginning to grasp the idea that events, rather than being discrete, are related to one another: if A happens, then B is likely to follow. Yet infants mistakenly believe causal relations are dependent on their own activity. We have already seen two examples of such omnipotent thinking: infants who believe their cries produce the mother's presence and those who believe their bodily movements can cause any object in the room to jiggle and dance.

While infants correct such omnipotent ideas through subsequent experience, they reappear

in the preschool period; once again, children believe they cause things to happen in the physical and social environment that in reality are independent of them. Again, such faulty ideas must be corrected by subsequent experiences during middle childhood.

Let us now consider the implications of magical thinking for early development. The first six years are unmatched in terms of intense affect and fateful beginnings: attachment brings with it anxieties over loss; socialization requires the control of initiative, anger, and sexual behavior; evaluations in terms of good and bad are internalized and become sources of self-satisfaction and guilt; and as we shall soon see, peers place their special demands on social participation. All of these momentous events occur at a time when the child is cognitively incapable of fully understanding the reality of what is happening. Distortions are likely to occur. If, for example, a 5-year-old girl's parents are going through a stormy period in their marriage marked by quarreling and accusations, the child might not understand the reality of the situation (indeed, how could she?) but instead distort it in terms of her own "badness" causing the disharmony. Thus omnipotence can create fears and guilts that have no basis in reality. As we shall see in Chapter 14, physically abused children can blame themselves for the pain inflicted upon them, while, according to psychoanalytic theory, cognitive distortions of reality lie at the hearts of neurosis (Chapter 8).

Egocentrism

Piaget defines egocentrism as conceiving the physical and social world exclusively from one's own point of view. Consequently, characteristics of the self are used to define or interpret characteristics of the objective environment: the me is confused with the not-me.

Egocentric thinking appears at all stages of cognitive development. The infant believes the very existence of objects depends on its actions. For preschoolers, egocentrism has an important social consequence in that it prevents them from understanding that other people have their own point of view. The ability to view the same situation from multiple vantage points—for example, to see an episode of classroom cheating from the viewpoint of the boy who cheated, the boy who was pressured into helping him cheat, and the teacher responsible for disciplining the classroom—represents a giant step forward in cooperative social interactions. In fact, a lively research interest has sprung up around what is called *social perspective taking* and its consequences for social behavior.

Social perspective taking has its own progressive stages; for example, 3- to 6-year-olds seldom acknowledge that another person can interpret the same situation differently from themselves, while 7- to 12-year-olds can view their own ideas, feelings, and behaviors from another person's point of view and realize that other persons can do the same in regard to them (see Selman, 1980). However, as was true of conscience, there is a gap between cognition and behavior, and psychologists are trying to tease out the variables responsible for translating social perspective taking into prosocial functioning (see Selman, Schultz, and Yeates, 1991). As we shall see, social perspective taking will enter into the discussion of a number of psychopathologies, particularly conduct disorders and juvenile delinquency (Chapter 9).

Egocentrism makes its last childhood stand in early adolescence. Piaget assumed that times of cognitive transition are times when primitive modes of thought are apt to reappear. One aspect of egocentrism may be expressed as self-consciousness; if someone laughs on the bus while the adolescent boy is fumbling to find the correct change for the fare, he is certain that he is being laughed at. Another aspect of the adolescent's egocentrism is the belief that ideas alone will win the

day and that their ideas hold the key to solving the world's problems—if only the world would listen!

Recent research has cast doubt on many of Piaget's findings concerning egocentrism. It has been shown, for example, that preschoolers will adjust their language according to whether they are speaking to younger or older children. (For an extensive critique, see Gelman and Baillargeon, 1983.) Thus they are not as locked in to egocentric thinking as Piaget would have us believe; rather, they shift back and forth, at times being able to see a situation from the viewpoint of others, at times not.

However, in most studies contradicting Piaget's findings, the task has been simplified so as to make it more congruent with the child's cognitive level. Life itself does not treat children so sensitively. Rather, children are confronted with perplexing and disturbing questions regardless of their ability to understand them: Why did mother die? Why do I suffer a painful illness? Why do my parents yell at each other all the time? Why am I beaten brutally, or neglected, or seduced? We can speculate that, under such conditions, children's thinking might show the kind of irrationality Piaget describes so well.

Reality Testing

No one knows for certain how cognitive growth takes place. However, many theories postulate a progressive change as the child tests faulty ideas against reality. The psychoanalysts in fact call this process *reality testing.* When faulty ideas fail to serve their function as guides to realistic behavior, they are modified to bring them in line with reality. Healthy growth requires that reality testing be kept vigorously alive. If not, stagnation with the possibility of deviant development may occur.

Failure to correct irrational thinking is not the only source of irrational behavior, however. Another source is anxiety, the topic that will concern us next.

Information Processing

As we have noted, information processing is an alternative model of cognition to Piaget's. It is concerned with analyzing the processes by which information is gathered and used to solve problems. In keeping with its analogy to computers, the model has two components corresponding to computer hardware and software. The first traces the intervening steps between environmental stimulus and behavioral response. The stimulus input initially impinges on the *sensory register,* such as vision or audition, and then goes to *short-term memory.* This is working memory and is the setting for active information processing. From here information goes to *long-term memory* for more permanent storage as memory traces. The second component contains the *control processes* that are involved in selecting, monitoring, evaluating, and revising information so that it can be appropriate to the problem at hand (see Shiffrin and Atkinson, 1969). We shall explore this information-processing model in more detail when we discuss mental retardation in Chapter 12. Three control processes that will be of special importance are *rehearsal* and *clustering* as aids to memory and *retrieval strategies* for retrieving information from long-term memory (see Figure 2.2).

Dodge (1986) adopted the information-processing model specifically to social situations and *social problem solving.* Here the sequence runs as follows: encoding social cues, forming mental representations of and interpreting those cues, searching for possible responses and deciding on a particular response from those generated, and, finally, acting on that response. The second step of cue interpretation involves the important psychological process of *attribution.* An attribution is an inference about the causes of behavior. Dodge's thesis is that, in disturbed children, the cog-

nitive process is either distorted or deficient. Aggressive children, for example, attribute hostile intent to others even when their behavior is benign or accidental; they generate more aggressive responses, and expect aggression to be effective in obtaining rewards and increasing self-esteem (Quiggle et al., 1992). We will return to social information processing when we discuss aggression and depression in Chapters 9 and 7, respectively.

ANXIETY

While anxiety has diverse definitions, its conceptualization as anticipation of pain is most relevant for our purposes. The concept itself originated with Freud, who used the term *signal anxiety* to designate the moderately painful anticipation of a noxious situation which warns, "Danger ahead!" Forewarned, the child can take steps to avoid reexposure to the situation. As we have seen in our discussion of self-control, anxiety lies at the heart of socialization, the child forgoing various pleasures to avoid the pain of parental discipline.

The Developmental Picture

We will be discussing the development of fear in detail in Chapter 8, so we will only outline it here (see Wenar, 1989). Certain fears, such as fear of loud noise and of unexpected movement, seem to be innate, while the fear of strangeness enters the picture in the second half of the first year. Such primitive fears decline in the preschool period as other, experientially based ones appear. Here we find the fear of doing "bad" things and of failure, of traffic accidents and fires. However, unrealistic fears, such as of imaginary animals and characters, also appear for the first time.

In middle childhood the trend toward realistic fears continues; fear of bodily injury and failure increases while fear of ghosts declines. However, irrational fears—such as fear of snakes and mice, of nightmares and fictional

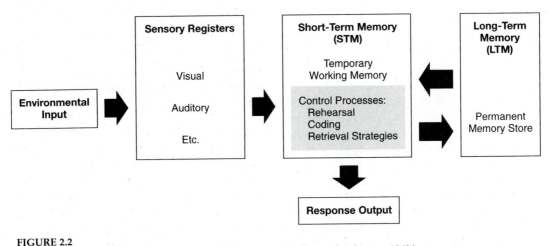

FIGURE 2.2
An information-processing model. (*Source:* Adapted from Shiffrin and Atkinson, 1969.)

characters—are still present. Adolescence brings with it new, age-appropriate fears, such as sexual fears, concerns over money and work, and concerns over war. The fear of failure is heightened, again as would be expected. Irrational fears are now infrequent but do not altogether disappear; adolescents can be afraid of the dark, of storms, of mice and snakes, or of cemeteries.

In sum, the development of fears reflects the increased realism of children's thinking and their developmentally appropriate concerns along with the gradual decline in irrationality, although the latter never completely releases its hold.

Defense Mechanisms

The major features of defense mechanisms are so well known that they need be only briefly reviewed. Freud stated that signal anxiety can itself become so painful that certain maneuvers are undertaken to defend the individual against it. The basic defense is *repression,* in which both the dangerous impulse and the ideas and fantasies associated with it are banished from consciousness. In essence, the child says, "What I am not aware of does not exist";

for example, a girl who is frightened of being angry with her mother no longer is aware of such ideas and feelings after repression. If repression is insufficient, *reaction formation* might be called into play; the child thinks and feels in a manner diametrically opposed to the anxiety-provoking impulse. Continuing our example, the girl now feels particularly loving toward her mother and would not dream of being angry. In *projection,* the forbidden impulse is both repressed and attributed to others; the little girl might be upset that "all of the other girls" she knows are so sassy and disrespectful of their mothers. In *displacement,* the impulse is allowed expression but is directed toward a different object; for example, our little girl becomes angry with her older sister or with a teacher.

We would like to call attention to certain *cognitive* and *developmental* implications of defense mechanisms. Defense mechanisms inevitably persuade the individual that a distorted image of reality is an accurate reflection. The child who claims to have no hostility toward her parents on the basis of repression is as convinced as if, in reality, the relationship were an unusually congenial one. The point illustrates the Freudian thesis that if affect is sufficiently intense, it can readily twist reason into endless distortions, which are then mistaken for the truth.

But also recall that, in discussing cognition, we stressed the importance of continual reality testing in order for development to proceed along acceptable lines. If defense mechanisms prevent reality testing by protecting the child from facing his or her fears, are they not pathogenic by their very nature? In answering this question we must rely on the clinical observations of Anna Freud (1965).

While acknowledging their potential danger, Anna Freud sees no inherent incompatibility between defense mechanisms and the general goals of socialization. Neatness and orderliness, which might be a reaction formation against the messiness of the toddler period, can be an adaptive, serviceable defense through adulthood; a political activist who is displacing anger toward parents onto anger toward entrenched political corruption still has a useful and meaningful direction to his life. In addition, the healthy child can use defenses flexibly, relying on them to manage a particularly painful episode in development but discarding them when they are no longer needed. It is when defenses become rigid, pervasive, and extreme and when the child's repertoire of defenses becomes unduly narrow that they are in danger of jeopardizing future growth. (For a comprehensive discussion of defense mechanisms, see Cramer, 1991.)

The Dual Nature of Anxiety

Anxiety, like other variables we have discussed, can either promote or block development. On the positive side, it prevents constant reexposure to painful and destructive situations; it raises the level of motivation, enabling the child to make maximal use of abilities; and it engenders defenses that may be socially adaptive and growth promoting. However, anxiety can also perpetuate inappropriate, self-defeating defenses and can bizarrely distort both thought and action. Consequently, anxiety will figure prominently in our discussions of psychopathologies and of psychotherapies as well (Chapter 17).

SEX

Sexuality has been approached from a learning-cognitive point of view and from an affective point of view; both will be relevant to the subsequent exploration of homosexuality (Chapter 11). Infants, lacking innate knowledge, must learn to classify themselves as "boys" or "girls." This sex classification is called *gender identity*. In addition, society prescribes which behaviors and feelings are appropriate to boys and which to girls, and children must learn such appropriate *sex-role behavior*. Finally, sexuality involves intense *erotic pleasures* which, at the very least, must be controlled through socialization or which, if psychoanalytic theory is correct, form the leading edge of major personality developments and changes in interpersonal relations.

Gender Identity

The typical 2- to 3-year-old male child has grasped the idea that "boy" applies to him and can correctly answer the question, "Are you a boy or a girl?" However, he does not comprehend the real meaning of the label, nor has he grasped the principle of categorizing people by sex, relying instead on external cues of size, clothing, and hairstyle. Remember that the preschooler is still cognitively in the preoperational stage, literally believing what he sees, so his categorizations by sex are on the basis of manifest differences. Because children this age are incapable of conservation (understanding that objects remain the same even when their appearance changes), they also believe that as appearances change so do essences—things that look different are different. Consequently, it is perfectly possible that boys change into girls and vice versa just by altering their clothes, hairstyle, and behavior to that of the opposite sex (see Marcus and Overton, 1978). And, referring to our vignette in Chapter 1, it is perfectly possible for a child to grow up to be a "mommy" or a "daddy" regardless of his or her present status. It is only around 6 or 7, when conservation is cognitively possible, that children grasp the idea that gender is permanent and immutable. They also come to realize that the genitals are the crucial factor determining gender. (For a critique of this cognitive theory, see Bem, 1989.)

Sex Role

Every society prescribes behaviors and feelings appropriate and inappropriate to each sex. Traditionally in our society, boys should be dominant, aggressive, unsentimental, stoic in the face of pain, pragmatic, and work-oriented; girls should be nurturing, sociable, nonaggressive, emotionally expressive, and concerned with domestic and child-care pursuits. The message is inescapable: parents know it, advertisers know it, television directors know it, gym teachers and car sales people know it. Now that there is a strong movement afoot to change the traditional stereotypes and foster equality between the sexes, the same social forces are being mobilized to send the new message. Society is never subtle about an issue so important as sex role. Along with the image go rewards for conforming to and punishments for deviation from the prescribed role. In fact, it was society's punitiveness toward women who deviated from their traditionally prescribed role which eventually led to the rebellion against the narrowness of the prescriptions themselves.

In spite of the feminist movement, sexual stereotypes have remained remarkably consistent over the past three decades, however (Ruble, 1988). Children as young as 3 years of age can classify toys, clothes, household objects, and games according to social stereotypes, and preschoolers do the same with adult occupations (Weinraub et al., 1984). As thinking becomes less concrete and more inferential in middle childhood, psychological characteristics such as assertiveness and nurturance are added to the list. While awareness of stereotypes increases, acceptance declines, as can be seen in adolescents' pursuit of gender atypical vocations (Carter and Patterson, 1982).

So far we have been dealing primarily with knowledge of stereotypes. Very early in development there is also a preference for sex stereotypical behavior. Children aged 2 to 3 prefer sexually stereotyped toys (trucks for boys, dolls for girls) and would rather play with same-sex peers (O'Brien and Huston, 1985). In middle childhood boys increasingly prefer sex-typed behavior and attitudes, while girls shift to more masculine activities and traits. This is just one of many examples of boys being more narrowly sex-typed than girls. "Sissies" are teased; "tomboys" are tolerated.

Social learning theorists point to the many ways culturally prescribed behavior according to gender is reinforced. While the role of women has changed dramatically since the 1960s, parents' differing expectations of their sons and daughters have remained essentially the same, as has their behavior. Fathers play more vigorously with their infant sons than with their infant daughters. In the toddler and preschool periods boys receive more physical punishment, are rewarded for playing with sex-typed toys, and are encouraged to manipulate objects and to climb. In middle childhood parents interact more with the same-sex child, boys are reinforced for investigating the community and being independent, while girls are supervised more and rewarded for being compliant. In general fathers are more narrowly stereotyped in their behavior than are mothers, which is one reason boys are punished for deviations more than girls are (see Block, 1983). Finally, both teachers and peers, in numerous obvious and subtle ways, exert pressure for conformity to social stereotypes.

Another reason boys' behavior is narrowly prescribed is that social stereotypes change slowly. The feminist movement has not altered the image of masculine superiority, which is part of Western culture and which is still present in the media and advertisements. Nor has it changed our society's differential monetary rewards for men and women. Thus there is no mystery about the fact that girls wish to be boys more frequently than boys wish to be girls.

Erotic Pleasure

In addition to learning gender and sex roles, children also have erotic experiences of intense pleasure when stimulating their genitals and are curious about anatomic differences and intercourse. Having already discussed psychosexual development (see Chapter 1), we shall focus here on the literature describing the development of erotic pleasure.

The infant's erect penis unmistakably points to the presence of at least one precursor of adult sexuality in the first year of life. The toddler may derive sporadic pleasure from genital stimulation, and by the preschool period the child is frequently practicing masturbation as a source of pleasurable sensations, looking at the genitals of adults and peers, and asking questions concerning anatomic sex differences and the origin of babies. Erotic feelings may be aroused by the tickling and teasing and generally pleasurable excitement of caretaking during the toddler period. A mother may become concerned when her preschooler wants to masturbate while lying in bed with her, or a father may realize that his

little girl is becoming too excited by "riding horsey" on his foot (Gesell and Ilg, 1949).

While informed parents no longer react to sexual behavior with threats to cut the boy's penis off or with terrifying visions of the insanity and depravity that will be his certain fate, even the most enlightened ones must inevitably require a certain amount of self-control. Typically, the parent wants to curb socially disapproved expressions of sexual behavior without alienating the child from natural feelings and curiosities. Instead of judging the child as bad, the parent conveys the message that there is a proper time and place for sexual behavior. Without such socialization, there might well be an increase in heterosexual activity throughout middle childhood, as there is in cultures with different sexual taboos. As it is, boys during middle childhood talk and joke about sex in their gangs, sometimes experimenting with mutual masturbation, while girls talk more about love and have powerful sexual fantasies, although engaging less in actual experimentation. Sexual curiosity is evidenced by an interest in peeking, seeking pornographic or sex-education books, and exchanging sex information with same-sex friends (Gesell and Ilg, 1949). Middle childhood is also the time of sex cleavage between boys and girls in regard to peer relations, such cleavage being a function of variables such as activity (sports versus a classroom art project), adult behavior in separating the sexes, and the risk of being teased when interacting with the opposite sex group (Thorne, 1986).

Puberty ushers in physiological maturity, the period extending from around 8 to 18 years of age for girls and from around $9\frac{1}{2}$ to 18 years of age for boys (Tanner, 1962). The complexities of sexuality now clearly occupy the center of the stage. At the simplest level, there is the matter of obtaining accurate information. Because society rarely provides ready access to factual material, the adolescent is apt to accumulate both correct and incorrect information and to have areas of uncertainty and ignorance. In the search for personally gratifying sexual techniques, however, instructions in lovemaking are of limited value, each partner having idiosyncratic sources of erotic arousal and having to adapt to those of the other partner. Thus adolescents are dealing not merely with the awkwardness of inexperience but also with individual differences that make the same technique exquisitely pleasurable to one partner and deeply repugnant to another. And because intense pleasures are at stake, frustration readily becomes rage, insensitivity touches off anxiety or disgust. In addition, each sexual venture involves the question, What kind of sexual being am I? Adolescents know that society will judge them, and they in turn will judge themselves in terms of the success or failure of their ventures. Most important of all, sexuality is part of the questions, "Whom can I love?" and "With whom can I share my life?" Such questions transcend those of information, technique, and social criteria of adequacy. In sum, the adolescent is searching for a physically and psychologically fulfilling relationship with another person under the pressure of imperious demands for periodic sexual gratification.

AGGRESSION

While there has been a notable relaxation of controls on sexual behavior, as evidenced by earlier sexual experiences for both boys and girls and the increase in unmarried couples living together, concern over the control of aggression may well have increased. It is not clear whether there has been a quantitative increase in violence, but certainly the potential for homicide and mass destruction has accelerated while uncontrolled aggression is a much more serious problem from a prognostic

point of view than is excessive inhibition (Chapter 9).

As with sex, there is no consensus concerning the definition of aggression. It is defined here as behavior that has injury or destruction as its goal, and anger or hatred as its accompanying affect.

The Developmental Picture

Infancy Anger can be differentiated from general distress in the 6-month-old baby and is marked by crying, random and overall body movements such as kicking, flailing of arms and legs, and arching of the back.

The Toddler Preschool Period The period between 1 and 4 years of age is the high-water mark for unvarnished expressions of rage, the developmental trend being from explosive, undirected outbursts of temper to directed attacks, and from physical violence to symbolic expression of aggression (Goodenough, 1931). Thus temper tantrums that include kicking, biting, striking, and screaming peak around $3^1/_2$ years of age and gradually decline. The more directed expressions of aggression, such as retaliation, are negligible in the first year but increase, until about one-third of the outbursts of 4- and 5-year-old children are of this nature. Concomitantly, verbal forms of aggression such as name calling, arguing, and refusals also increase.

The descriptive picture makes sense in light of what we have learned about development. The infant cannot be angry *at* anyone because the independent existence of others has not been grasped; directed anger becomes possible only after the object concept is understood. While the toddler can intend to aggress, the idea that an attack actually hurts does not register until around the third year of life. Thus only from 3 years of age on is the child capable of meeting all the criteria of our definition of

Anger.

aggression. Subsequently, attack becomes less physical and more verbal and "psychological." While it would be comforting to believe the transition from physical to verbal aggression represents an intrinsic diminution in aggression rather than merely a change in form, this does not appear to be the case. A blow to self-esteem can be as painful as a blow to the face; a humiliation can be more destructive than a beating.

The situations likely to evoke aggression also follow a developmentally meaningful trend: frustrations in relation to feeding, sleeping, and receiving attention in the first year; toileting in the second year, particularly being forced to remain on the toilet when the toddler is ready to leave. Thwarting of initiative, either by an authoritarian caretaker's refusal to permit an activity or, to a much less extent, by the child's own ineptness in achieving a goal, also begins to trigger aggression in the toddler period and continues to do so through the preschool period. Anger over having to share or not being able to appropriate an object belonging to another child peaks in the 3- to 4-year-old (Goodenough, 1931). Typically, aggressive episodes are brief, preschool quarrels lasting less than half a minute.

The meaning of aggressive behavior itself changes according to the intra- and interpersonal context. In certain emotionally unstable children, extremes of aggression alternate with extremes of withdrawal and fearfulness (Macfarlane, Allen, and Honzik, 1954). On the other hand, vigorous social participation and the formation of mutual friendships also increase the incidence of aggressive behavior. Thus while aggression solely as a desire to harm and destroy may be undesirable and aggression accompanied by withdrawal and fearfulness may be part of a general emotional instability, aggression that results from a high level of sociability may be regarded as innocuous or even healthy.

Middle Childhood After the preschool period, aggression in the form of a crude physical attack in reaction to the immediate situation declines, and children's behavior becomes progressively more intentional, retaliatory, and symbolic (Hartup, 1974). Children are concerned with getting even and paying back in kind, while their aggressive repertoire proliferates: bickering, quarreling, teasing, and swearing abound, along with bullying, prejudice, and cruelty. Their increased cognitive sophistication enables them to differentiate intentional from accidental provocations and respond less aggressively to the latter. In keeping with the development of conscience, children now can be troubled by their outbursts. To counterbalance this gain, their increased time perspective also enables them to hold a grudge and have both more delayed and sustained aggression than was possible in the preschool period.

The situations provoking anger continue to reflect the situations that are of concern to the child. Anger over other children's cheating, lying, teasing, and bossing as well as over adults' lecturing, unjust punishment, and neglect, along with anger over their own ineptness and poor grades in school reflect children's concern with strict justice, their growing desire for independence, their need to be valued in their own right, and resentment over being ignored. On the other hand, their pride dictates that they should not be pushed around or mocked or treated as less than they are. From the earlier period they retain irritation over their own shortcomings and jealousy of siblings, especially when siblings take their property and when parents hold them up as models.

In general, then, anger is developmentally appropriate in middle childhood, unlike anxiety, which is a mixture of realistic and unrealistic fears. Thus the developmentally oriented clinician knows it is "normal" for an 8- or 9-year-old boy to have an unrealistic fear of nightmares, but it is not normal for him to have a tantrum when his mother continues talking on the phone after he asks her a question.

Adolescence The early phase of adolescence, often called preadolescence, is a generally unstable time. The more infantile modes of expressing anger, such as stamping feet, throwing objects, and crying, may reappear for a while and disappear subsequently. In adolescence verbal expressions of anger predominate, such as sarcasm, name calling, swearing, ridiculing, and humiliating. Sulking frequently follows an angry outburst. The situations evoking anger resemble those of middle-childhood—unfair treatment, encroachment on rights, refusal of privileges, being treated as a child, and being incapable of achieving a goal. (For a more detailed account of the research on aggression, see Parke and Slaby, 1983).

Further Characteristics of Aggression

Societies and classes within societies differ in the amount and kinds of aggressive behavior they consider acceptable. In our society, boys are uniformly more aggressive and more physically aggressive than girls, who rely more on verbal aggression (Maccoby and Jacklin, 1980). We have already discussed two other sources of aggression: parental discipline and the attribution of hostile intent, which, in turn, is used to justify aggression. Finally, a child is more likely to behave aggressively in a crowded playroom than in an uncrowded one and when ill and tired rather than when well and rested. Thus variables ranging from societal to situation-specific all have an effect on aggression.

More important for our purposes are the multiform variations of aggressive behavior. First, let us consider the effect of certain defense mechanisms on the expression of aggression. In *displacement,* changing the object of anger reduces the fear of retaliation. The familiar example is the parent who, after failing to get a raise at work, comes home and punishes his child for leaving his tricycle in the driveway.

Next, aggression can be *sublimated;* that is, both the affect and the destructive intent are sufficiently modified so as to become socially acceptable. Competitive athletics are a prime example: anger is sublimated into a "fighting spirit," and the intent to destroy becomes a determination to defeat; the cheerleaders shout, "Yea, team, fight, fight, fight!" and the following day, sportswriters describe the home team as having been "slaughtered" or "annihilated."

Aggression can assume *passive* disguises. Dawdling, or complying with parental demands in slow motion, is an exquisite form of revenge that both exasperates the parents and robs them of their right to punish the child for open defiance. Underachievement in school may represent a child's unconscious retaliation against parents who have demanded too much intellectually and given too little emotionally. In general, the clinician must be aware of the possibility that an unrealistic ineptness in an area highly valued by parents (such as physical awkwardness in a healthy boy whose father wants him to be an outstanding athlete) may at least be partly motivated by unconscious hostility.

Finally, aggressive behavior itself can serve nonaggressive goals. The toddler who realizes that her genuine temper tantrum always monopolizes parental attention may soon learn to use anger as a highly effective manipulative behavior. The adolescent, experiencing the loneliness of becoming independent of the family, may adopt the face-saving tactic of maintaining contact through contrived confrontations. Certain acting-out children—toddlers and juvenile delinquents alike—are not so much angry as in desperate need of being loved and valued; despairing of that, they settle for getting attention. "It is better to be wanted for murder than not be wanted at all."

The many disguises and uses of aggression give us our first taste of the complexity that lies ahead. Aggression may or may not appear as aggressive behavior, may or may not be appropriate to the target, may motivate constructive as well as destructive behavior, and may be serving needs in addition to the one to destroy. Yet complexities such as these are inherent in human behavior, and oversimplifi-

cation would lead to distortion of the very psychopathologies we are trying to understand.

The Management of Aggression

Generally, parents should be affectionate and serve as models of self-control. Love-oriented discipline and reasoning along with consistently prescribed standards of behavior favor control of aggression, while punitiveness, rejection, neglect, and inconsistency undermine it. The heightened arousal characterizing aggression should be channeled into alternative, constructive behaviors; it can motivate the sprinter, the satirist, the social reformer, as well as the delinquent. Attention should be paid to the problems underlying aggressive behavior—the feeling of being unloved, the humiliating sense of insignificance, the self-loathing. The aggressive child, in turn, should be helped to find constructive ways of coping with anger and to focus on its source (Berkowitz, 1973). We will have more to say about aggression when we discuss its pathological extremes in Chapter 9.

We have now finished our discussion of self-control and the major behaviors the child is required to control. However, we have not exhausted our list of important developmental variables. In concentrating on socialization and on the socializing parents we have neglected peer relations as well as school, work, and occupational choice. These are the topics that will concern us next.

SOCIAL RELATIONS

Peer relations are a potent predictor of subsequent psychopathology. In our discussion we shall distinguish a general interest in peers, which we shall call *sociability*, from *friendship*, which represents a more intense involvement with particular peers—both of which differ from *groups*, which are organizations of individuals possessing norms or values regulating the behavior of the individual. In interpreting the significance of social relations we shall refer to Sullivan (1953), one of the few authorities on child development who fully appreciated their significance. (For a more empirically oriented review and evaluation, see Hartup, 1983.)

The Early Years

There is no lack of dramatic developments in the first six years, but we shall treat such developments summarily, because they have yet to be linked with psychopathology. Two-month-old infants are interested in looking at one another, and by 10 months of age there is a more varied and sustained reaction expressed in mimicking, patting, hitting, and imitation of laughing. By 15 months of age affection appears, and by 2 years there is participation in games, although the toddler's short attention span and limited ability to communicate and to control the behavior of others gives sociability a fleeting, improvisational quality. However, toddlers have been observed to select one member of the group to be an object of attention, concern, or affection, the relationship suggesting the intensity and focus of a friendship, except that it is often not reciprocated (see Bridges, 1932, and Vandell and Mueller, 1980).

Clearly, all early social behaviors are less stable and intense than attachments, and for good reason. Peers have no interest in assuming the caretaking role of relieving distress and providing stimulation; nor do they have the caretaker's skill in responding quickly and appropriately to needs. However, they have one inherent advantage over adults in that, being at comparable developmental levels, they are naturally attracted to one another's activities. A parent may love a child for what he or she is; peer attraction is based on interest. Peer

relations are important not because they represent diluted versions of attachment, but because they add a new dimension to development.

A number of changes take place in the preschool period. Positive exchanges such as attention and approval increase, although sharing and sympathy do not. Competition and rivalry are also on the rise, while quarrels are fewer but longer. More important, immature or inefficient social actions are becoming more skilled; for example, there is greater speaker-listener accommodation so that the child begins to talk *to* rather than *at* another child, while collaboration begins to emerge in social problem solving (see Hartup, 1983). Cooperativeness, respect for property, constructiveness, and adaptability are the basis of general social attraction; the child who is highly aggressive, quarrelsome, or dictatorial, who refuses to play with others or is dependent on adults for attention and affection rates low on attractiveness and sociability (Dodge, 1983).

Friendships now have that combination of sharing and quarreling which will characterize them throughout childhood. They are unrelated to general sociability, as will also be true into adulthood. Finally, under special circumstances, such as having no adult caretaker in a concentration camp, preschoolers can form remarkably cohesive groups, caring for one another with great warmth and sharing responsibilities with a total lack of the jealousy, possessiveness, and competition that so often mark peer and sibling relations (Freud and Dann, 1951).

Friendship

According to Sullivan (1953), friendships in middle childhood and adolescence are essential for the transition from the egocentrism of the preschool period to the mutuality, sharing, and concern for the partner which mark mature sexual relations. We can see the beginnings of that shift in middle childhood. Anger does not lead to disruption of the relationship as it did in the preschool years, but friendship is now sufficiently important to be sustained in the face of difficulties. The child is also beginning to want his or her friend to be happy and is concerned about the friend's attitude toward himself or herself. Thus the concept of a friend as an independent individual is beginning to register. What is more, being with a friend is rewarding in its own right, whereas formerly the pleasure of friendship was limited to sharing specific activities. However, the readiness with which friends are shifted and the dependence of friendship on propinquity, along with a tendency to make a public show of friendship, attest to the superficiality of the relationship.

In adolescence friendships become even more sustained and personalized. Being together rather than doing together is now paramount and is apt to involve the sharing of forbidden and disturbing feelings, especially sexual feelings and problems with parents. In the process, the friend can gain support, relieve guilt, and check reality with a trusted confidante. However, adolescents are also more frank and critical of their friends than they were as children or than they will be as adults. Anyone who knows adolescents is aware of their ability to be pitiless critics, to epitomize faults with a nickname, while all the virtues and extenuations, all the overlooking and covering up of shortcomings vanish. Finally, friendship teaches the adolescent the responsibility and respect of intimacy—tolerance of others, a balance of giving and receiving, knowing the limits to expression and confession. (For a detailed account of the levels of friendship, see Damon, 1977. For a longitudinal study, see Keller and Wood, 1989.)

Such a developmental progression through middle childhood and adolescence fits nicely with Sullivan's concept of friendship as a prelude to adult intimacy, in which sexuality is united with mutuality, sharing, intimate exchange, concern for the partner, and steadfastness. Finally, Sullivan states that friendship increases self-knowledge. The critical confrontations in adolescence are particularly valuable because parents have difficulty with playing the role of critic or are either too involved with or too isolated from their adolescent to play the role constructively.

Sociability

The qualities making for sociability in the preschool years continue to hold sway in middle childhood. (See Newcomb, Bukowski, and Pattee, 1993, for a comprehensive review of research.) The child who is accepted by others is resourceful, intelligent, emotionally stable, dependable, cooperative, and sensitive to the feelings of others (Coie, Dodge, and Coppotelli, 1982). Rejected children are aggressive, distractable, and socially inept in addition to being unhappy and alienated. Moreover, they are at risk for being school dropouts and for having serious psychological difficulties in adolescence and adulthood (Parker and Asher, 1987). Neglected children, who are neither liked nor disliked by peers, tend to be well adjusted especially if they are socially competent but merely prefer solitary activities to peer interaction (Carlson, Lahey, and Neeper, 1984).

Among the many determinants of sociability two social-cognitive and one affective variable will figure in our future discussions. We have already dealt with the role of *social perspective taking* in countering the rigid authoritarianism of the early conscience, and it is easy to see how it would also facilitate sociability by countering self-centeredness. The second social-cognitive variable is *social problem solv-*

ing, which is concerned with conflict resolution. As we have seen, it involves a number of social-cognitive skills: encoding and accurately interpreting social cues, generating possible problem-solving strategies and evaluating their probable effectiveness, and, finally, enacting the chosen strategy. Young children's strategies are impulsive and designed to meet their own needs, such as grabbing, pushing, and ordering other children about. Older children take the needs of others into account and are inclined toward persuasion and compromise (Selman and Demorest, 1984). *Empathy,* the affective component of sociability, involves both an awareness of the feelings of others and a vicarious affective response to those feelings. Toddlers have been observed to respond empathetically to the distress of others, for example, by giving a crying child a favorite toy (Thompson, 1987). Empathic responses increase with age and in the range of eliciting stimuli, broadening eventually to include general life conditions rather than immediate distress, as in concern for the poor or the sick. As for the psychological significance of peer relations, Sullivan claims that the shift from "me" to "we" is highly unlikely in the parent-child relationship and highly likely among peers. The child literally and figuratively looks up to parents as the source of love and of socializing directives that must be obeyed because of parental authority. By contrast, the child can look peers in the eye, literally and figuratively. The word "peer" itself means "equal." Consequently, the possibility of mutuality is greatly enhanced. In this context of sharing, children learn what Sullivan calls *accommodation:* instead of thinking of themselves as unique or special, as they might at home, they begin to learn how to get along with others.

There is another important dimension that sociability adds to the child's development. At home the child has to be *love-worthy* because affection and obedience lie at the heart of the parent-child relationship. With peers the child must be *respect-worthy,* which is a matter of proven competence. Children must expose themselves to comparisons with other children in regard to athletic ability, manual skills, resourcefulness in suggesting and implementing interesting activities, and so on. They are valued in terms of their actual contributions to the activities that peers themselves value.

In sum, sociability prepares the child to live in the adult world of peers, just as friendship is preparation for adult sexuality.

The Group

Middle Childhood The insubstantial, play-oriented groups of the preschool period become the middle childhood *gang,* which, by the time children are 8 to 10 years of age, is sufficiently potent to compete with the family in terms of interest, loyalty, and emotional involvement. The child begins to subordinate personal interests to the goals of the group, tries to live up to group standards, and criticizes those who do not. Thus, "we" becomes more important than "I." The gang no longer needs to rely on stereotyped games and activities such as hopscotch or jump rope but is sufficiently autonomous to respond to general suggestions such as, "Let's make a club-house," or "Let's give a party." Names, insignia, and secret passwords help give the gang a special identity. In addition to being identifiable social units, gangs traditionally have been segregated by sex, boys being action-oriented, girls being sociable in their interests.

Just as friendship advances mutuality, the gang advances the sense of belonging. It offers training in interdependent behavior, ventures out further than the individual could go alone, and through its cohesiveness buttresses the individual member's self-control. Sullivan notes that by being able to test one's feelings against those of the group, the individual is less apt to exaggerate them, either positively or negatively.

Adolescence Group involvement reaches a high point in adolescence. The adolescent group is an autonomous social organization with purposes, values, standards of behaviors, and means of enforcing them. In its stability and differentiation it resembles adult groups rather than those of middle childhood. Conformity peaks in 11- to 13-year-olds and gradually declines; it is greatest in those adolescents low in status among their peers and high in self-blame.

Adolescent groups vary in structure and nature. There is the small, close-knit *clique* whose members are bound together by a high degree of personal compatibility and mutual admiration. The *crowd* is a larger aggregate than the clique, is concerned with social activities such as parties and dances, and does not demand the same high personal involvement. Crowds vary in status; being a member of a high-status crowd is one of the surest ways of gaining popularity. An important function is that of providing a transition from unisexual to heterosexual relations. The gang still survives and requires more loyalty than the crowd. It is often hostile to adult society and has a specific goal—sexual, athletic, delinquent. It retains its emphasis on adventure and excitement as well as on the formal trappings of organization, such as name, dress, and initiation ritual.

These groups serve as the adolescent's primary bridge to the future. They provide a sense of belonging, which is especially important during this period of transition between being a child and being an adult. They help adolescents master uncertainty by prescribing behavior, right down to what clothes to wear, what music to listen to, and what language to use. They provide both provocation and protection in changing from a same-sex to a heterosexual orientation. Finally, they support individuals in their opposition to their parents. This does not imply that the majority of adolescents are rebellious and alienated; the battle of the generations is fought only fitfully and the values of the group, such as cooperation, self-control, and dependability, are congruent with or even reflections of parental values (Coleman, 1980).

What mars adolescent groups is their rigidity and demands for conformity. Adolescence is a high-water mark for group prejudice, when caste and class lines are sharply drawn, and inclusions and exclusions are absolute. For all their rebelliousness against adult society, adolescents are more slavishly conforming to the group than they have been before or will be in the future. In short, in middle childhood and especially in adolescence there is a narrow group-centeredness, which is the counterpart of the child's earlier egocentrism. Perspective and flexibility, evaluation of individuals in terms of personal worth, loyalty without chauvinism, social commitments that transcend immediate group interests—all these lie in the future. (See Hartup, 1983, for a review of the research on groups.)

As we shall see, peer relations play an important role in both juvenile delinquency and drug abuse. However, there is a question whether they play a leading etiological role. Does the juvenile gang force its members to defy the law whether they want to or not or do angry, defiant youths seek out juvenile gangs? Does peer pressure cause drug abuse or are adolescents who become addicted those who are particularly disturbed to begin with? We will return to these questions in Chapters 9 and 11.

WORK

Why discuss work? Work is what adults do. It is important to the adult's self-esteem and self-definition, the question, Who is X? usually being answered in terms of what X does. Work both expresses and shapes personal values while playing a central role in determining friends, social activities, and conduct. The decision to enter the labor market on a full-time basis marks the end of childhood as much as any single decision can. What children do is play. So why not discuss play? The principal reason is that while there are no psychopathologies of play, there are psychopathologies of work as it is conceptualized here (Wenar, 1971).

Work and Requiredness in Middle Childhood

Work derives from initiative. Watch toddlers exploring the environment and you will see embryonic workers. They are totally absorbed in what they are doing, distracted neither by extraneous inner needs nor by external events; they experiment, construct, and solve problems within the limits of their intelligence and skill; they persist in the face of frustration. Note that we have described an embryonic worker, not a miniature one. A host of developments lies ahead. The one that concerns us now is *requiredness.*

Initiative in pure culture is the toddlers' paradise. They can do what they want just because they want to do it. As we have seen, socialization, with its "no," "wait," "good boy" and "bad girl," is an intrusion, although sensitive parents try to preserve initiative while requiring self-control. The next major development in regard to initiative is school. As with socialization, children cannot choose *not* to go to school, nor can they choose not to learn what they are supposed to. With the introduction of requiredness, initiative takes on an important characteristic of adult work—work is something you do whether you want to or not. Ideally, work will be intrinsically rewarding and pleasurable, but these are not of the essence.

Interestingly, disagreements among educators concerning requiredness echo disagreements among parents concerning socialization. Some educators, like some parents, favor giving the child's spontaneous interests free rein, capitalizing on natural curiosity and the ability to learn through discovery. Other educators, like other kinds of parents, emphasize formal instruction, along with the adult's ability to guide wisely and to serve as models of disciplined thinking. Good teachers from both camps share a concern with keeping spontaneous curiosity alive while enabling children to master the content of their intellectual heritage. And good teachers are concerned when children fail to live up to their potential. A special group of such children, the learning disabled, will be discussed in Chapter 6.

There are other aspects of school which make it a halfway house between the free exercise of initiative and the constraints of adult occupation. School is often the child's first encounter with an extrafamilial organization empowered to make significant decisions concerning the regulation of his or her daily life. The boy entering kindergarten, for example, is among children he has not chosen to be with; he is also with an adult on whom he has no special claim and who may feel obliged to show him no favoritism. His physiological needs cannot be gratified at will since neither the refrigerator nor the toilet is available on demand. Rather, there are schedules and rules that apply to all. Thus school is an *impersonal* environment compared to home.

What is more, the products of children's efforts are valued as never before. Children are with an adult whose principle function is to scrutinize what they do and help them do even better. Grades introduce an element of public evaluation; not only the teacher but parents and peers as well have knowledge of the quality of the children's products. "Right" and "wrong" enter the picture and take a place alongside "good" and "bad" as preconditions for adult approval or disapproval. In sum, school is *product-oriented*. Schoolchildren add "student" to the list of self-characterizations, and their success or failure in this new role contributes significantly to their self-esteem. (For a review of literature on school as socializing agent, see Minuchin and Shapiro, 1983.)

School failure figures prominently in discussions of psychopathology. Both the future delinquent and the future schizophrenic might be variously described as disruptive and inattentive in class, defiant and a truant, for example, while the devaluing of achievement in school is an important factor determining drug use in adolescence (see Chapters 10, and 11).

Thus the ability to harness and direct initiative into the work-oriented demands of school takes its place alongside other facets of self-control as a determinant of normality or psychopathology.

Vocational Choice and Identity in Adolescence

In addition to being students, adolescents begin to think of themselves as potential workers. The complexities of vocational choice are such that exploring them will continue into young adulthood. The job market itself is complicated and constantly changing, and today's adolescents probably are as poorly prepared for a vocation as they are for mature sexual behavior. The world of work has its own structure of class- and sex-appropriate occupations, its hierarchy of prestige, its requirements for occupational preparation. But work is not only doing a job; it is relating to others as well. In fact, more jobs are lost for interpersonal reasons than for lack of skill and inadequate preparation. Fellow workers have different needs—to dominate and protect, to destroy and seduce, to expand and conserve, to placate and manipulate. Finding a congenial interpersonal setting introduces an unpredictable element into the adolescent quest because there

is no sure way of knowing how their idiosyncratic needs will mesh with those of fellow workers.

Along with interpersonal factors, intrapersonal factors are important in choosing a vocation. Ideally, adolescents' interests, values, and talents should all find full expression in the work they choose. Yet development itself decreases the probability of such a harmonious outcome. Vocational self-knowledge lags behind other cognitive developments, and most high school seniors make important choices concerning education or work on the basis of little accurate information concerning their aptitudes. Fortunately, they have progressed in other areas, so the unrealistic idealism of middle childhood, such as an airy dedication to "helping others," has been replaced by a realistic set of vocational values.

In sum, adolescents must engage in a long period of trying to define their vocational as well as sexual selves. In a special form of reality testing, they set out to discover the most rewarding fit between their peculiar set of ideals, values, and talents and the world of work. Because the work they do will be an important aspect of self-definition and self-esteem, more is at stake than just finding a "good job." (For a fuller discussion of adolescent vocational choice and work, see Santrock, 1990.)

Interestingly, the adolescent's search for a vocation in the broad sense has much in common with Erikson's (1968) well-known concept of the adolescent *search for identity* (see also Marcia, 1980). For Erikson, the adolescent's question, Who am I? is closely related to the question, What can I do that will be fulfilling? Similar intra- and interpersonal variables are involved. Adolescents bring with them a unique constellation of aptitudes, interests, values, and personality traits, which are their heritage from the past. Their occupation must offer an opportunity to continue and fulfill this special heritage so that what they value most will be valued by others, whether such "others" are the nation, an industry, the neighborhood, or a handful of close friends.

The instability of the adolescent period makes this search for identity a difficult period of trial and error with two inherent dangers: at one extreme there may be premature occupational choice, the adolescent latching on to a stereotyped image of the "successful executive" or "prestigious doctor" only to be trapped in meaningless activities. At the other extreme, uncertainty becomes pervasive and immobilizing, so the adolescent bogs down in what Erikson calls role diffusion. However, such untoward outcomes need not be discussed now. In successful vocational choice, as in successful socialization, the individual wants to do what is required by maturity. If he or she can no longer live in the toddler's paradise, it does not matter; finding fulfillment in the adult world is far better.

There are also important *cognitive* changes in adolescent identity. Ask schoolchildren, "Who are you?" and they are apt to answer in concrete terms, such as their address, physical appearance ("I'm tall"), play activities ("I'm good at baseball"), or possessions ("I have a bike"). Adolescents, by contrast, are more abstract ("I'm ambitious"), future-oriented ("I want to be a doctor"), interpersonal ("I like people"), and concerned with psychological traits ("I'm all mixed up") and ideologies ("I'm a liberal"). The development here is not an additive process in the sense that complex, abstract ideas are added on to simple, concrete ones. Rather, adolescents conceive of themselves differently, with prior descriptions either dropping out or integrated into a more complex picture (see Montemayor and Eisen, 1977).

While we have introduced the concept of identity in relation to vocational choice, it is important to many other topics we have discussed, such as self-control, sex, and relations to parents and peers. In fact, it will be the central organizing concept when we examine the risks and psychopathologies of the adolescent transition in Chapter 11, and the special problems African-American adolescents face in achieving a positive identity (Chapter 15).

LESSONS FROM NORMAL DEVELOPMENT

This review of normal development has taught us a number of lessons that will stand us in good stead as we discuss childhood psychopathology.

First, we have seen the importance of *context* to the understanding of behavior. The context of time is essential; *when* a behavior or an event occurs is as vital to understanding it as *what* it is (see Chapter 1). The contexts of intra- and interpersonal behaviors are equally important. We saw, for example, that aggressive behavior may alienate a preschooler from the group or might be part of sociability and friendship. Other examples anticipate the discussion of psychopathology: juvenile delinquency can represent an impulsive lashing out at society, a desperate bid to be noticed, or a need to be accepted by a delinquent gang.

The superordinate context of culture, as discussed in Chapter 1, alerts us to the fact that all we have described as normal development applies primarily to Anglo-Americans. How universal it is remains to be seen. There is evidence for example that while a secure attachment is usual in other cultures, Western European infants show more avoidant attachment, perhaps because parents encourage nonclinging and independence, while Japanese infants show more resistant attachment, perhaps because they are rarely separated from their mothers (see van IJzendoorn and Kroonenberg, 1988). As we shall see when we discuss minorities (Chapter 15), other cultures place greater emphasis on conformity, obedience, and masculine dominance; this emphasis may, in turn, affect what is considered normal and deviant. Awareness of cultural differences protects us from assuming that "our" way is "the" way, while raising the searching question, What is the best way?

Next, we have seen the *complexity of growth patterns* characterizing normal development. Some patterns conform to a simple incremental model: just as children become taller and heavier, they become more intelligent with age. Other variables follow different patterns. Self-control is low during the terrible twos, increases to a high point during middle childhood, declines dramatically during preadolescence, and recovers again during adolescence, although still remaining on the unstable side. Piagetian egocentrism is conquered during the first eighteen months of life but reappears in the preschool period to distort the verbalized concepts of causality, and returns again in the self-referent thinking of the adolescent. Negativism peaks in the early preschool period, only to vanish from the developmental scene, except for a brief return during preadolescence.

As was noted in Chapter 1, the professional must be mindful of the many complexities of development in making a judgment concerning the possibility of psychopathology. But even more is needed. Knowledge of norms does not in and of itself tell us whether a child's behavior is pathological. Knowing that most children behave in such and such a way does not mean that this particular child is developing normally, and the child clinician is typically concerned with a given child. To return to the opening clinical vignettes in Chapter 1: if the child is a toddler or preschooler rather than an adolescent, it is significantly more likely that the child's furious attack on a sibling or desire to change sex or magical thinking is normal. However, the possibility still remains that this particular toddler or preschooler is severely disturbed. The conscientious clinician proceeds to examine the context variables of history, general personality,

interpersonal relations, and physiological intactness before coming to a final decision.

INTEGRATION

Figure 2.3 integrates what we learned about developmental pathways in Chapter 1 with our ten developmental variables. It represents the behavior of a hypothetical boy, Zack. As we describe his behavior we will show how it would be represented on the figure.

When Zack was 8 years of age (T-1), he experienced an increase in familial disharmony when his parents began arguing violently. However, his good relation with his father enabled him to take the stress in stride ($P > R + V$).

When he was 10 years old (T-2), Zack's parents divorced and he was placed in his mother's custody. At this point, a number of behavior problems soon began to develop ($R + V > P$). The principal behavior was angry outbursts and fighting, which adversely affected all of his important interpersonal relations. (Aggression is shown by a totally dark bar, indicating a complete, severe deviation.) He began to be regarded as a hothead by peers, and his popularity rapidly declined (dark area of Social Relations indicating severe deviation). However, he did have two good friends who formed a special group of outsiders (white area of Social Relations, indicating normal development). With his mother he was chronically sullen (light area of Attachment, indicating moderate deviation), although there were outbursts of temper tantrums and name calling, especially after he came home from visits with his father (dark area of Attachment, indicating severe deviation). His angry outbursts were usually overreactions to ordinary frustrations of everyday life; he was not spoiling for a fight by imagining everyone else was against him (Cognition is normal, since there was no distortion in regard to attribution). He went from being a B

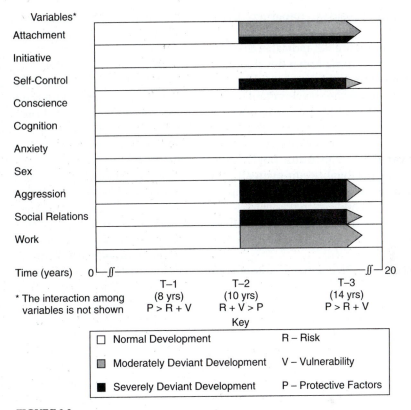

FIGURE 2.3
A developmental pathway.

to being a C student at school, and, while he acted bored and sardonic, he was not a behavior problem (light area of Work, indicating a moderate disturbance). Rather than doing homework, he concentrating on building elaborate model railroads (a hobby he had shared with his father), becoming quite skilled and covertly enjoying being praised when displaying them (Initiative is normal, since the decline at school was compensated for by an increase in hobbies). He and his friends talked about "wet dreams," masturbation, and other pubertal changes, and, while wary of girls, he was no more so than a number of other shy pre-adolescent boys (Sex developing normally).

He was properly but not excessively troubled (Conscience) over his outbursts and was not excessively anxious (Anxiety). Finally, while his self-control had declined significantly, it had not collapsed altogether. He was not an impulse-ridden boy, driven to strike out with violent, antisocial behavior at the slightest provocation; rather, he was "basically a good kid" in the grips of a problem too big for him to handle (Self-Control partly dark, partly white).

When he was 14 years old his mother remarried, and, with time, the boy established a good relationship with his stepfather (P>R + V). His problem behaviors gradually moderated and subsided (tapering light-shaded areas).

To generalize: Figure 2.3 indicates that the degree of deviation from normal development is a function of how *severe* the disturbance is both *within and across* the developmental variables and the *duration* of the disturbance. It is also a function of the *balance* between risk, vulnerability, and protective factors. The figure also shows that a disturbance does not envelop all of the child's personality—or even all of a given variable. As we have noted, it is important for the clinical child psychologist to assess areas of intactness and resources as well as deviations especially when planning remedial measures.

Our challenge in the coming chapters is to construct developmental pathways for the various classifications of childhood psychopathologies. First, we need to discover which of the ten variables have been adversely affected and to what degree of severity. Then, we need to discover both the balance between risk, vulnerability, and protective factors that produces psychopathology and the balance that enables the child to "outgrow" the disturbance.

Before doing this, we need to become acquainted with the psychopathologies themselves and we need to have a general overview as to which are apt to continue into adulthood and which are apt to be "outgrown." These are the matters that will occupy us next.

THE BRIDGE
TO THE
PSYCHOPATHOLOGIES

We now have a general developmental model and a working knowledge of the variables we will use in understanding psychopathology as normal development gone awry. It is time to focus on the psychopathologies themselves. First, we will discuss the way normality shades gradually into psychopathology both conceptually and empirically; then the major psychopathologies of childhood will be described; finally, longitudinal studies of normal and disturbed children will be summarized so that we can learn which psychopathologies tend to persist and which tend to be outgrown. Then, in Chapters 4 to 12 selected psychopathologies will be explored.

THE CONCEPTUAL BRIDGE

Time and again in our previous discussion we have seen that the same variables that facilitate development have the potential to impede its course. Attachment goes hand in hand with separation anxiety, which, if exaggerated, may undermine the preschooler's self-reliant expansiveness; initiative can become a self-defeating noncompliance in which the child strikes out at all authorities, even those who can be genuinely helpful; self-control can become a prison and conscience a punitive inquisitor; realistic anxiety can become unrealistic terror; peer groups can mercilessly torment the outsider; schoolwork can become drudgery. This affinity between growth and failure to grow is our first, tentative support for viewing psychopathology as normal development gone awry. Note the word "tentative," since we have yet to put the view to the test in regard to specific psychopathologies.

In fact, one of the major unresolved issues in the study of psychopathology concerns the continuity or discontinuity between normal and disturbed behavior, which at times is referred to as the *quantity versus quality* debate. Is all pathological behavior on a continuum with normal behavior? For example, is a phobia just an exaggeration of normal fearfulness, is delinquency just an exaggeration of minor antisocial acts (such as the mischievous stealing of hubcaps), or is the sexual perversion of exhibitionism just an exaggeration of "streaking"? Or do we find, particularly among the severe psychopathologies, certain kinds of behaviors or certain patterns of development that have little or no counterpart in normal behavior and normal development? We are in no position to debate the issue now, but we should keep it in mind as we examine specific psychopathologies.

THE DIAGNOSTIC BRIDGE

There is no agreed-upon classification of childhood psychopathologies. Some derive from a single theory (such as the psychoanalytic or behavioral); others are in the psychiatric tra-

dition of accurate descriptions of symptoms; others stress the statistical manipulation of readily observed behaviors, while still others are a grab bag from sundry traditions. However, there are characteristics that all classification systems should share. There should be a *rationale* for regarding behaviors as psychopathological rather than normal, and the rationale should be appropriate to the population being studied. There should be a reason for including bed-wetting as a psychopathology, for example, while excluding unpopularity. The classifications should be more than variations of adult categories because, as we have seen, pathological adult behavior can be developmentally appropriate in children, while a number of childhood psychopathologies, such as autism, enuresis, learning disabilities, truancy, and certain types of hyperactivity, have little or no counterpart in adulthood.

Next, the range of psychopathologies should be *comprehensive;* each category should be *clearly delineated* in terms of its behavioral characteristics and *differentiated* from other categories it may resemble. Ironically, at present, there is an inverse relation between a detailed coverage of the various psychopathologies and the reliability of the categories themselves: specific disturbances such as school phobias or compulsions tend to have low reliability as measured by agreement among experts as to diagnosis, while broad-gauged classifications, such as neurotic versus psychotic behavior, fare better.

One purpose classification systems serves is to parcel an unwieldy mass of information into meaningful and manageable units. However, they do more than help place a given child in a given category: they are points of departure for exploring *etiology* on the one hand, *prognosis* on the other. Thus the diagnosis of adolescent schizophrenia should carry with it implications as to causative factors and prognosis, both in regard to the chances of outgrowing the disturbance and the effectiveness of therapeutic intervention. At present, we are far from realizing such an ideal goal.

While classification may be essential, children rarely fit neatly into a single diagnostic category. Consequently, *multiple diagnoses* are often preferable to a single diagnostic label. The clinician should take into account *acuteness* or *chronicity* based on the history of the disturbance, evaluate the *severity* of disturbance, specify the *developmental period* the child is in, and describe the *specific behaviors* that comprise the psychopathology. Thus a child's diagnosis might read: a severe, acute reactive disorder of middle childhood, with phobic and compulsive features, manifested by persistent restlessness, irritability, fitful sleep, along with occasional panic while waiting for the school bus and a frequent need to retrace his paper route to make sure each paper was properly delivered.

In many classifications the categories themselves carry connotations concerning severity of disturbance. Reactive disorders are regarded as the least severe because of their close relation to realistic events. Severity increases as the disturbance becomes progressively more internalized, that is, more self-perpetuating and independent of reality, more pervasive and more disruptive of normal functioning. Anxiety disorders are regarded as more serious than reactive disorders because the problem is internalized to a greater degree; for example, an adolescent girl may realize that her bus phobia is irrational, since there is little chance of her being killed in an accident, yet the terror persists. A personality disorder is more serious still, since the problem affects a wider range of behavior than is affected in anxiety disorders. Psychotic disorders represent the extreme of disturbance because the behavior is more bizarre and further removed from normal functioning than in the other classifications.

Most classifications differentiate distur-

bances that are psychological, or—to use the technical term—*functional,* in origin from those that are *organic* in origin. In "pure cases" of brain syndrome, for example, organic brain pathology is established and affects behavior in characteristic ways; in "pure cases" of psychophysiological disorders, an otherwise healthy body begins to malfunction because of some psychological distress. In actuality, pure cases are all too rare; a number of disorders may have an organic and a functional component. Mental retardation is a case in point: organic and functional factors, either singly or in combination, may play a major etiological role, while subnormal intellectual functioning itself may place a child at risk for developing psychological problems.

Finally, a number of specific psychopathologies can be ordered along a dimension of *internalization-externalization* of children's problems. When children themselves suffer, they are regarded as internalizers. Anxious children, for example, generally are well behaved but are tormented by fears or guilt. Delinquents, on the other hand, engage in antisocial behavior; the form their disturbance takes differs from that of internalizers in that they act out their problems in relation to society. Thus they are called externalizers. Internalization-externalization is a dimension of behavior, not a typology; while a certain percent of children fall at either extreme, many of them are mixtures of both elements; that is, they can be both anxious and aggressive or have a "nervous stomach" and steal.

The current scene in regard to classifying childhood psychopathologies is a lively one. The appearance of a revision of a widely used diagnostic manual has occasioned a rethinking of the traditional questions: What are the basic requirements of a diagnostic system that relies on clinical observation? How well does the present revision meet such requirements? At the same time, a classification based on the statistical manipulation of discrete behavioral items is coming into prominence and promises to be an alternative to traditional clinical diagnosis. It is worthwhile to examine both of these developments in detail.

THE TRADITIONAL APPROACH: DSM

The various editions of *The Diagnostic and Statistical Manual of Mental Disorders* (DSM) are in the tradition of classification based on naturalistic observation. The tradition has primarily been carried on by psychiatrists and relies heavily on the observational skills of the clinician for its implementation. The third edition of the manual, known as DSM-III (American Psychiatric Association, 1980), appeared in 1980, and its revision, DSM-III-R (American Psychiatric Association, 1987), was published in 1987. While DSM-IV was not published in time to be included here, we do have access to the DSM-IV Draft Criteria (American Psychiatric Association, 1993). When we come to describing the various disorders of infancy, childhood, and adolescence, we will be using the DSM-IV Draft Criteria. However, other information concerning DSM-IV—critical evaluations by authorities in the field, reliability and validity studies, and research findings—will not be available. For these we will be forced to fall back on DSM-III and DSM-III-R. (See Cantwell, 1980; Spitzer and Cantwell, 1987; and Rutter, 1988.)

Goals

The highest priority of DSM-IV is to be a useful guide to clinical practice by providing brief, clear, and explicit statements of the criteria defining diagnostic categories. Additional goals are to facilitate research, improve communication among clinicians and researchers, and provide an educational tool for the teaching of psychopathology.

Evaluation

We shall now present five standards for evaluating diagnostic classifications and see how DSM-IV has fared.

Rationale   The rationale for singling out behavior as abnormal is typically embodied in a definition of psychopathology. In reality, there is no generally accepted definition, as our survey of models has shown. The authors of DSM-IV do not pretend to resolve the knotty issue of conceptualizing psychopathology but settle for stating their own criteria. A mental disorder is a behavioral or psychological syndrome that is associated with present *distress* or *disability* (that is, impairment in one or more important areas of functioning) or with increased *risk* of suffering death, pain, disability, or loss of freedom.

There is one other point worth noting. The authors are careful to state that disorders, not individuals, are being classified. Thus, the manual never refers to "a schizophrenic" or "an alcoholic," as if the psychopathology were the person; instead it uses "a child with schizophrenia" or "an adult with alcoholic dependency." The point itself is simple but basic and easily lost sight of.

Objectivity of Description   The diagnostic categories should be objectively described and operationally defined. There is now convincing evidence that reliability is directly related to behavioral specificity and declines as terms become more general, more inferential, and more theoretical. Thus, "Fights more frequently than age-mates" is more satisfactory than "Is aggressive" or "Has destructive impulses." In respect to objectivity, DSM-IV is behavior-specific in its criteria. To take only one example, Separation Anxiety Disorder is defined in terms of ten behavioral criteria, such as unrealistic worry about possible harm befalling major attachment figures, repeated nightmares involving the theme of separation, persistent reluctance or refusal to go to school in order to stay with major attachment figures.

Reliability Reliability refers to the consistency of results obtained from using a diagnostic instrument. An instrument that would place the same child in different categories when used by two different clinicians would not be very useful. One criterion of reliability is the consistency with which a diagnostic instrument functions at two points in time, or *test-retest reliability*. More frequently, however, diagnostic systems use *interobserver agreement*, in which two experts are asked to evaluate the same child at the same point in time.

In his review of studies of reliability of DSM-III, Cantwell (1988) concludes: "One has to be disappointed both in the number of studies and in their results, particularly in the area of reliability" (p. 32). While it is true that some diagnoses are more reliable than others, much work remains to be done before the entire instrument is satisfactory. However, there are flaws in some of the studies themselves. In one study the judges were first- and second-year fellows in child psychiatry with no experience in DSM-III. None of the studies followed the usual procedure of having an initial training session in which judges' diagnoses are compared with those of experts so that sources of misinterpretation and error can be found and corrected. Moreover, when experienced clinicians do the diagnosing, half of them rely on global clinical impressions and ignore the DSM-III criteria. Such methodological shortcomings lead one to wonder how much the unreliability of DSM-III is due to the instrument itself and how much is due to flawed studies.

Validity *Validity* is the extent to which a test measures what it claims to measure or, in this case, the extent to which a diagnostic system does, in fact, correctly classify disturbed children. The concept has proved a troublesome one and has spawned a variety of definitions. There is *content* or *face* validity, which is the degree to which the content of a diagnostic category has an obvious relation to what is being evaluated. In the case of Separation Anxiety Disorder, the three behavioral criteria mentioned make sense on the face of it. Ideally, the criteria should also be analyzed statistically to test whether they do, in fact, cluster together. *Predictive* validity compares current evaluations with some future criterion; for example, children diagnosed as schizophrenic in middle childhood should continue to be more disturbed as young adults than children diagnosed as having a school phobia. *Concurrent* validity compares the current evaluation with some other contemporary criterion; the diagnosis of a reading disability based on parental report could be compared with scores on a reading achievement test, for example. Note that the difference between predictive and concurrent validity concerns whether the outside criterion lies in the future or is current. *Construct* validity is the relationship between a diagnostic category and other variables that should be related to it theoretically; for example, children classified as violently antisocial should do poorly on measures of self-control, such as the ability to delay gratification. And, finally, *discriminative* validity is the extent to which clinical features are unique to the disorder in question and differentiate it from other similar disorders. It corresponds to the traditional clinical task of differential diagnosis.

Admittedly, DSM-III has primarily face validity. (Again we follow Cantwell's 1988 review of studies.) One reason for this is that there are few independent criteria that can be used for predictive or concurrent validation studies, and many of the relations between diagnostic categories and other variables either have not been investigated or have yielded controversial findings. However, the picture is not totally bleak. For example, research has shown that the three kinds of childhood depression described in DSM-III—Major Depression, Dysthymia, and Adjustment Disorder with Depressed Mood—have a different age of onset, course, and recovery. Next, as we shall see when we discuss the multivariate statistical approach, a number of categories derived from objective procedures overlap with those in DSM-III, thus providing evidence of concurrent validity.

Comprehensiveness A diagnostic system should be comprehensive in its coverage of psychopathologies. In this respect DSM-IV is satisfactory. In addition, it supplies information concerning a host of characteristics of a given disorder where such information is available; for example, prevalence, age of onset, course, predisposing factors, differential diagnosis, laboratory findings, and specific age- or cultural- or gender-related features.

Multiaxial Classification

A significant departure from the past is the use of a *multiaxial* classification system. Instead of being assessed only in terms of the presenting problem, the child is evaluated in terms of five dimensions, thereby insuring a more comprehensive picture of the disturbance.

Axis I: Clinical Syndromes. This axis contains all the disorders we will be concerned with.

Axis II: Personality Disorders. Since these apply primarily to adults, we will not discuss them.

Axis III: General Medical Conditions. This axis includes general medical conditions that are potentially relevant to the under-

standing or management of cases: for example, injuries and infectious diseases, diseases of the nervous system or digestive system, and complications of pregnancy and childbirth.

Axis IV: Psychosocial and Environmental Problems. This axis includes the negative life events, familial or other interpersonal stresses, inadequacy of social support, and environmental deficiencies or difficulties that comprise the milieu within which the child's problems developed. (See Table 3.1 for a summary of relevant categories.)

Axis V: Global Assessment of Functioning. This is the clinician's judgment of overall level of functioning. Such information is useful in planning treatment and measuring its impact. The judgment is made in terms of a Global Assessment of Functioning (GAF) Scale, which goes from superior functioning (100 points) to persistent danger of hurting self or others or persistent inability to maintain minimal personal hygiene (1 to 10 points). (See Table 3.2 for a condensed version of the GAF.)

A multiaxial evaluation might look like this:

Axis I: Major Depressive Disorder; Reading Disorder

Axis II: No diagnosis

Axis III: Hypothyroidism

Axis IV: Parent-child problem (neglect of child)

Axis V: GAF = 35

Two Special Features

DSM-IV has two features that distinguish it from other editions. More than any other current nomenclature of mental disorders, DSM-IV is grounded in *empirical evidence* concerning diagnosis. This evidence was obtained from a comprehensive review of published literature,

TABLE 3.1

Examples of Axis IV: Psychosocial and Environmental Problems

Problems with Primary Support Group. These include: death of a family member; health problems in family; disruption of family by separation, divorce, or estrangement; removal from the home; remarriage of parent; sexual or physical abuse; parental overprotection; neglect of child; inadequate discipline; discord with siblings; birth of a sibling.

Problems Related to the Social Environment. These include: death or loss of friend; social isolation; living alone; difficulty with acculturation; discrimination.

Educational Problems. These include: illiteracy; academic problems; discord with teachers or classmates; inadequate school environment.

Occupational Problems. These include: unemployment; threat of job loss; stressful work schedule; difficult work condition; job dissatisfaction; job change; discord with boss or coworkers.

Housing Problems. These include: homelessness; inadequate housing; unsafe neighborhood.

Economic Problems. These include: extreme poverty; inadequate finances; insufficient welfare support.

Problems with Access to Health Care Services. These include: inadequate health care services; transportation to health care facilities unavailable; inadequate health insurance.

Problems Related to Interaction with the Legal System/Crime. These include: arrest; incarceration; victim of crime.

Other Psychosocial Problems. These include: exposure to disasters, war, other hostilities; discord with non-family caregivers (e.g., counselor, social worker, physician); unavailability of social service agencies.

Source: Adapted from DSM-IV Draft Criteria (3/1/93). Copyright 1993 American Psychiatric Association.

from reanalysis of projects containing information concerning diagnosis, and from field trials in which data on 6000 subjects were analyzed in terms of reliability and validity of diagnostic criteria. The resulting five-volume DSM-IV sourcebook provides documentation of the decisions reached concerning the classifications and their behavioral components.

Next, DSM-IV explicitly deals with *multicultural* considerations. First, there is a new section describing culturally specific symptom patterns, preferred idioms for describing distress, and prevalence; for example, in certain cultures depressive disorders are character-ized by a preponderance of somatic symptoms rather than by sadness. Next, there is an index of culture-bound syndromes that are found in one or only a few of the world's societies. The index includes the name of the condition, the cultures in which it is found, a brief description of the psychopathology, and a list of possibly related DSM-IV disorders.

The Developmental Dimension

In many ways, DSM-IV represents an impressive accomplishment. One shortcoming, however, is its failure to acknowledge the de-

TABLE 3.2

**Selected Levels of the Global Assessment of Functioning
(GAF) Scale**

Code (Note: Use intermediate codes when appropriate, e.g., 45, 68, 72.)

100 | 91	Superior functioning in a wide range of activities, life's problems never seem to get out of hand, is sought out by others because of his many positive qualities. No symptoms.
80 | 71	If symptoms are present, they are transient and expectable reactions to psychosocial stressors (e.g., difficulty concentrating after family argument); no more than slight impairment in social, occupational, or school functioning (e.g., temporarily falling behind in school work).
60 | 51	Moderate symptoms (e.g., flat affect and circumstantial speech, occasional panic attacks) OR moderate difficulty in social, occupational, or school functioning (e.g., no friends, unable to keep a job).
40 | 31	Some impairment in reality testing or communication (e.g., speech is at times illogical, obscure, or irrelevant) OR major impairment in several areas, such as work or school, family relations, judgment, thinking, or mood (e.g., child frequently beats up younger children, is defiant at home, and is failing at school).
20 | 11	Some danger of hurting self or others (e.g., suicide attempts without clear expectation of death, frequently violent, manic excitement) OR occasionally fails to maintain minimal personal hygiene (e.g., smears feces) OR gross impairment in communication (e.g., largely incoherent or mute).
10 | 1	Persistent danger of severely hurting self or others (e.g., recurrent violence) OR persistent inability to maintain minimal personal hygiene OR serious suicidal act with clear expectation of death.

Source: DSM-IV Draft Criteria (3/1/93). Copyright 1993 American Psychiatric Association.

velopmental dimension within disorders. Preliminary evidence indicates that the symptom picture of a disorder changes with age; for example, in Separation Anxiety Disorder younger children worry excessively about separation or harm befalling the attachment figure and have nightmares associated with such possible separation, while older children primarily have physical complaints on school days and are reluctant to go to school (Ollendick and King, 1991). Or again, motor disturbances are more characteristic of younger boys with Attention-Deficit/Hyperactivity Disor-

der, while older boys are characterized by inattention (Holmbeck and Kendall, 1991).

THE MULTIVARIATE STATISTICAL APPROACH: CBCL

Until recently there has been a perfect inverse relation between reliability and utility in classification. The traditional diagnostic systems had low reliabilities, while the reliable categories, such as internalizer versus externalizer or neurotic versus psychotic, were too gross to be useful to the clinician. However, just as the authors of DSM-III have been concerned with improving the precision of their diagnostic categories, advocates of precision have devised a more finely differentiated set of classifications.

Progress in science, so the argument goes, often involves a change from description to measurement and quantification. In the realm of diagnosis, quantification has often involved a multivariate statistical approach. (For a review of the studies, see Quay, 1986.) The basic format is simple. Collect specific behaviors used in describing psychopathologically disturbed children, eliminate the infrequent, redundant, and obscure ones, and subject the rest to statistical techniques designed to determine which are highly related. The statistical technique frequently employed is called *factor analysis* and the related behavioral items are called factors. After examining the content of the interrelated items, the investigator assigns each factor a label. Such labels may resemble those used in traditional diagnosis, such as delinquent or hyperactive; however, they should not be regarded as equivalent until empirical evidence has shown them to be.

Another general issue concerns whether a taxonomy should consist of *categories* of disturbances, as in the DSM, or *dimensions* of disturbances, such as those derived from a multivariate statistical approach. One objection to categories is their all-or-none quality; for example, a child either is or is not depressed, and if he is, the clinician must decide whether the degree of disturbance is mild, moderate, or severe. The dimensional approach assumes continuity within disorders, the number of symptoms being a measure of severity. For example, it can tell whether a given child is more depressed than the normal population and yield a precise measure of the degree of disturbance. (See Quay, 1986. For a comprehensive review of taxonomy, see Achenbach, 1988.)

To illustrate the multivariate statistical approach we shall concentrate on the work of Achenbach, who is currently advancing it further than his predecessors (Achenbach, 1979; Achenbach, 1991; Edelbrock and Achenbach, 1980). Achenbach's first step was to collect descriptions of pathological behavior from psychiatric case histories and from the literature. Through a series of preliminary studies these were reduced to 118 items that formed the Child Behavior Checklist (CBCL). Examples of items are: the child argues a lot, complains of loneliness, does not eat well, runs away from home, has strange ideas. Another set of items dealt with competencies and were used to construct additional scales, but they will not concern us now.

Next the CBCL was filled out by parents of 1800 children referred for mental health services, and the results were factor-analyzed. The analyses yielded both *wide-band* and *narrow-band* factors. Wide-band factors included the now familiar categories of externalizing and internalizing behaviors, or conflicts with the environment and problems with the self. The narrow-band factors included specific syndromes or behavior problems, such as depressed, obsessive-compulsive, somatic complaints, hyperactive, aggressive, and delinquent.

To give two illustrations of narrow-band syndromes: the Schizoid scale contained the behavioral items of clinging to adults, fretting, fear of school, auditory and visual hallucinations, nightmares, shy and timid, while the Delinquent scale contained the behavioral items of destroys own and others' things, disobedient in school, has bad friends, lies, cheats, runs away, sets fires, steals, truants, and swears. As so often happens in multivariate studies, the majority of the narrow-band scales could be subsumed under either the internalizing or externalizing scales.

The data were analyzed separately for boys and girls and for the age groups 4 to 5 years, 6 to 11 years, and 12 to 16 years so that sex and age differences in syndromes could be detected. It was found, for example, that, while 6- to 11-year-old boys and girls shared the syndromes of Delinquent, Aggressive, and Hyperactive, the girls had the additional syndromes of Sex Problems and Cruel; 12- to 16-year-olds shared the syndromes of Somatic Complaint and Schizoid, with the boys having the added syndromes of Uncommunicative, Immature, and Obsessive-Compulsive, and the girls having the added syndromes of Anxious-Obsessive and Depressed Withdrawal.

To obtain norms, the CBCL was next administered to 1400 nonclinical children matched for age, sex, race, and socioeconomic status with the clinical population, and percentiles were calculated for the scores in the various narrow- and wide-band syndromes. With data from the normal and clinical populations it was possible to determine cutoff scores, below which the child would be considered within the normal range and above which the child would be considered disturbed. These cutoff scores were at the ninety-eighth percentile of scores for the total population. Thus a boy with a score of 1 on the Schizoid scale would be at a point equivalent to 69 percent of the population and therefore within normal limits; however, the same boy's score of 26 on the Aggressive scale would be higher than 99 percent of the population and might well be cause for concern. After scoring all eight or nine narrow-band scales (the number depending on the child's age and sex), one can obtain a profile indicating which scales are within normal limits and which exceed them. A hypothetical child might be within the normal limits for the internalizing scales of Schizoid, Depressed, Uncommunicative, Obsessive-Compulsive, and Somatic Complaint, while exceeding the norm in the externalizing scales of Delinquent, Aggressive, and Hyperactive. (Figure 3.1 presents the profile of a 15 year-old boy using self-report version of the CBCL.)

Because using computers to generate syndromes is quite different from using clinicians, it is interesting to compare Achenbach's (1980) factors with the diagnostic categories of DSM-III. Using a correlation technique, Edelbrock and Costello (1988) found considerable overlap between the factors derived from the CBCL (here called profile scales) and the DSM-III categories. Table 3.3 summarizes their findings. DSM-III is more differentiated; for example, it distinguishes two degrees of depression (Major Depression and Dysthymia) and has a special diagnosis for Separation Anxiety. It also contains diagnoses not found among Achenbach's syndromes, most notably Autism, Anorexia Nervosa and Bulimia Nervosa, and specific learning disabilities. Thus, the DSM-III is probably the more clinically useful of the techniques. Incidentally, the omission of Autism illustrates the difficulty statistical techniques have in capturing rare but important disturbances.

It is easy to understand the appeal of the statistical approach for those who value precision. Test-retest reliabilities are characteristically satisfactory, while the behavioral nature of the basic data gives them a palpability the more inferential diagnostic systems lack. As an added bonus, the CBCL and similar instruments are great time-savers compared with the traditional diagnostic procedures.

Yet one should not make the mistake of assuming that the combination of behavioral specificity and statistical manipulation guarantees precision. To begin with, objectivity in behavioral evaluation is a matter of degree. While it is true that the statement "Is disobedient at home" is more objective than "Has a problem with authority figures," the former still requires a judgment. Thus the same behavior a mother might regard as disobedient in her son might be dismissed by the father as "just the way boys are." Behavioral ratings depend on who does the rating and the situation in which the behavior occurs: parents, teachers, and professionals may all disagree in

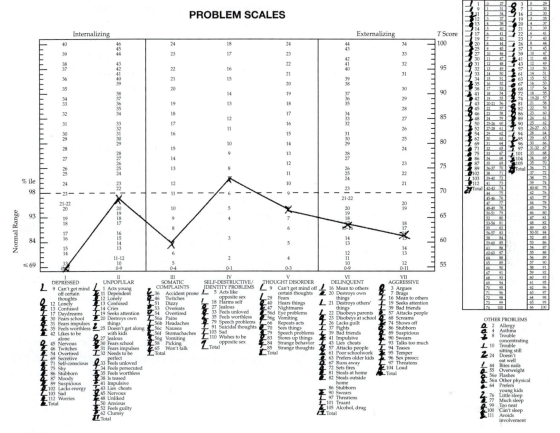

FIGURE 3.1

Problem scales of a hand-scored YSR profile completed for 15-year-old Robert. (*Source:* Achenbach, 1982.)

rating a particular child either because they evaluate the same behavior differently or observe the child in different settings, or because of a combination of both factors. In point of fact, Achenbach, McConaughy, and Howell (1987) found that, while agreement within the same category of informants—specifically, parents, teachers, mental health workers, peers, and the children themselves—was reasonably high, agreement among these categories of informants was low. To cite one example, the mean correlation between parents was

.59, but the mean correlation between parents and teachers, mental health workers, peers, and the children's self-ratings ranged from .24 to .27. While the latter correlations were statistically significant, they were too low to have clinical utility.

In an attempt to integrate assessment data from parents, teachers, and the children themselves, Achenbach (1991) has devised what he calls a *taxonomic decision tree*. The initial screening question asks if any scale is in the clinical range. If the answer is no, then there is no

TABLE 3.3

Summary of Relations Between Child Behavior Profile Scales and DSM-III Diagnoses*

Scale	DSM-III diagnosis
Aggressive[1,2,3,4]	Conduct disorder
Anxious-obsessive[4]	Overanxious disorder
Cruel[3,4]	Conduct disorder
Depressed withdrawal[4]	Major depression Dysthymia
Delinquent[1,2,3,4]	Conduct disorder
Depressed[1,3]	Major depression Dysthymia
Hostile withdrawal[2]	Attention deficit disorder Oppositional disorder
Hyperactive[1,2,3]	Attention deficit disorder
Immature[2]	Attention deficit disorder Separation anxiety
Immature-hyperactive[4]	Attention deficit disorder
Schizoid[2,4]	Overanxious disorder
Schizoid or anxious[1]	Separation anxiety Overanxious disorder
Social withdrawal[1,3]	Avoidant disorder Major depression Dysthymia
Somatic complaints[1,2,3,4]	Overanxious disorder
Uncommunicative[1,2]	Overanxious disorder Major depression Dysthymia

* Superscripts indicates sex and age groups for which the scale is scored: 1 = boys aged 6–11, 2 = boys aged 12–16, 3 = girls aged 6–11, 4 = girls aged 12–16.

Source: Edelbrock and Costello, 1988.

evidence of clinical deviancy. If there are deviant scores, the next question is whether deviance is confined to the same syndrome in all sources. If so, the child can be regarded as having a single problem such as aggressive-

ness. Next, there is the possibility that different sources agree that a child has multiple syndromes, such as an attentional deficit and a delinquency problem. It is when different sources yield different deviant behaviors that one must conclude either that the child's behavior actually differs among settings or that observers in these settings may be biased. In the former case, treatment should be setting-oriented; in the latter, treatment is targeted at changing the biased evaluation of the child.

The problem involved in discrepant views of the same child is not confined to multivariate statistical assessment but is present in all assessment procedures that rely on multiple sources of information. While we have a few leads as to what sources would be most valid for what particular psychopathologies, there are no general rules concerning sources of information for all childhood psychopathologies (Routh, 1990). There is some evidence that parents and teachers are better informants in regard to disruptive symptoms of hyperactivity, inattentiveness, and oppositional-defiant disorders than are boys, who tend to underreport them. On the other hand, child reports are more informative about subjective symptoms such as anxiety and depression. But when dealing with groups of children, as is done in research, there is no evidence that weighting one group of informants increases diagnostic accuracy over treating all informants as equal. This may be because, for large samples, unequal weightings average out to near-equal weighting. (see Piacentini, Cohen, and Cohen, 1992. For a specific study, see Bird, Gould, and Staghezza, 1991.)

In discussing *clinical applications*, Achenbach and McConaughy (1987) recommend that the CBCL and its different adaptations for parents, teachers, and peers be used in conjunction with an interview designed to provide historical and current information relevant to the child's disturbance, and with results from intelligence tests and other tests which would aid the clinician in understanding the child's problems and in making appropriate treatment recommendations.

THE CLASSIFICATIONS: HEALTH AND NORMAL PROBLEM BEHAVIOR

If we are to treat psychopathology as normal development gone awry, we need to anchor our thinking in a definition of normality. Moreover, we need to have an idea of the problems and problem behaviors inherent in normal development, since normality never means problem-free.

Healthy Development

Since the various DSMs do not define healthy development, we must rely on another classification, the so-called GAP Report (Group for the Advancement of Psychiatry, 1966).

The GAP Report states that there is no single criterion for health; rather, a number of functions are involved. In *intellectual* functioning, health involves "adequate use of capacity, intact memory, reality-testing ability, age-appropriate thought processes, some degree of inquisitiveness, alertness, and imagination" (p. 220). Healthy *social functioning* involves an adequate balance between dependence on others and autonomy, a reasonably comfortable and appropriately loving relation with adults and other children, and an age-appropriate capacity to share and empathize with peers. Healthy *emotional functioning* involves an adequate degree of emotional stability, some capacity for self-perspective, some degree of frustration tolerance and sublimation potential, along with some capacity to master anxiety and cope with conflicting emotions. Healthy *personal and adaptive functioning* requires a degree of flexibility, a drive toward mastery, an integrative capacity, a degree of

self-awareness, the existence of a self-concept, and the capacity to use fantasy in play constructively.

Note that the definition makes frequent use of the qualifying phrases "a certain degree of" or "some capacity for." As clinicians we would prefer more exact statements so that our evaluations would be less subjective. Such objective criteria for health lie in the future; the definition reflects current reality. On the positive side, the GAP Report does not present an idealized picture of the "normal, well-rounded child," with the implication that any deviation from such an ideal is suspect. Indeed, what is impressive about normal children is how much "deviance" they can take in stride!

Finally, the GAP Report emphasizes the importance of stage appropriateness—which they prefer to age appropriateness—of development. There should also be a general "smoothness" of development, as contrasted with alternating periods of exceptionally slow and rapid growth. And finally, there should not be excessive discrepancies in growth among the components of health, as is seen in the pseudomature 6-year-old whose adult behavior effectively blocks peer participation.

Normal Problems and Normal Problem Behavior

Normal development involves both problems and problem behaviors. To take one example of the latter: one study found that about half the children in kindergarten through grade 2 were described as restless, while another study found a similar percent of 6- to 12-year-olds were described as overactive (Campbell, 1989). While both of these behaviors are part of the syndrome of hyperactivity, it would be incorrect to assume that half the children were hyperactive since they have neither the clustering nor the intensity and chronicity of problems that would interfere with adaptive functioning. On the other hand, it would be equally foolish to deny that restlessness and overactivity constitute a problem both at home and in the school.

Campbell (1989) describes some typical nonpsychopathological developmental problems during the infancy and preschool period:

The "difficult" infant. Studies of individual differences in infants, or infant temperament, have shown that some are easy to care for while others are difficult. The latter tend to be irritable, slow to adapt to change in routine, intense and negative in their reactions, and irregular in their biological functioning. If cared for sensitively, infants can "outgrow" this difficult phase; however, if caretakers are impatient and intolerant, or change routines abruptly and often, the chances of behavior problems in the toddler period are increased.

Insecure attachment. We have already described the concept of secure and insecure attachment and reviewed the evidence that the insecurely attached infant may be at risk for problems in the area of initiative and social relations. However, such problems are not inevitable and can be minimized by sensitive caretaking.

The defiant toddler. Disciplinary problems and uncertainty as to when and how to set limits are the major concerns of parents of toddlers. In most instances the problems are stage-specific, leaving no residue. However, parental mismanagement, say, in the form of overcontrol, may increase the likelihood that problems will develop and persist.

Aggression and withdrawal in preschoolers. Aggressive behavior toward peers is a common complaint of parents and teachers of preschoolers, boys being more aggressive than girls. However, as with other behavior problems, there is no need to read ominous portents into such aggressiveness unless it

is coupled with mismanagement by parents or a discordant family situation. Social withdrawal, unlike aggression, is relatively rare and has not been satisfactorily studied. There is tentative evidence that the shy, quiet child is less at risk for developing behavior problems than is the disruptive one, but such risk may be increased in extreme cases when combined with other internalizing problems such as separation anxiety or dysphoric mood.

Rather than describing normal problems, Dunn (1989) explored the factors involved in either successful or unsuccessful *coping* with the normative life events of beginning school, moving, and the birth of a sibling. She found that protective or risk factors resided in the children themselves, in the family relations, and in relationships outside of the family. To use the birth of a sibling as an example: children who reacted with persistent fears and with sleep and feeding problems were temperamentally worriers. A highly conflicted relationship with the mother before the birth of the sibling led to increased conflicts and confrontations subsequently; however, such conflicts could be lessened if the child had a close relation with the father. In general, the balance between resilience and vulnerability holds the key to understanding whether ordinary life events will be successfully mastered or not.

THE CLASSIFICATIONS: THE PSYCHOPATHOLOGIES

For this overview we will follow the classifications in the DSM-IV Draft Criteria, concentrating on those psychopathologies that will subsequently be discussed in detail. Our descriptions will be in summary form. Those wishing an account of the entire field of childhood psychopathology and a complete description of the disorders are referred to the DSM-IV Draft Criteria itself.

Adjustment Disorder Adjustment Disorder will be described first because it forms a link between the normal problems just described and the more serious psychopathologies to come. In an Adjustment Disorder there is an identifiable psychosocial stressor which produces the symptoms. Either the distress or the social or academic impairment is in excess of what would be expected from exposure to the stressor; for example, there may be temporary work paralysis or suicidal thoughts. However, such symptoms do not persist longer than six months after the termination of the stressor.

Disorders of Infancy, Childhood, or Adolescence

As for the more serious psychopathologies, the DSM-IV Draft Criteria distinguish between disturbances which are specific to children and those which are essentially the same for children and adults. We will deal with the former first.

Mental Retardation Mental Retardation is defined as significantly subaverage intellectual functioning (i.e., an IQ of 70 or below) and concurrent deficits in adaptive functioning such as self-care, social skills, and personal independence.

Learning Disorders (Academic Skills Disorders) These include *Reading Disorder, Mathematics Disorder*, and *Disorder of Written Expression*. In each instance, the academic ability is substantially below that expected given the child's chronological age, measured intelligence, or age-appropriate education.

Pervasive Developmental Disorders The primary disorder here is *Autistic Disorder* marked by a qualitative impairment in social interaction (e.g., lack of social or emotional reciprocity, impaired use of nonverbal behavior such as eye contact and gestures to regulate social interaction), gross and sustained impairment in communication (e.g., delayed or total absence of spoken language, stereotyped language, absence of imaginative play) along with restricted, repetitive, and stereotyped patterns of behavior, interests, and activities.

Disruptive Behavior and Attention-deficit Disorders The disorders included here were formerly listed under separate categories. They have been subsumed under a single classification because of the frequency with which they overlap. We will be concerned with the following specific disorders:

- *Attention-deficit/Hyperactivity Disorder* is characterized by a number of inattentive behaviors (e.g., being easily distracted, having difficulty in following through on instructions, frequent shifting from one uncompleted activity to another), and hyperactivity-impulsivity (e.g., acting before thinking, inappropriate running and climbing, fidgeting, having difficulty waiting in line or taking turns).
- *Conduct Disorder* is characterized by repetitive and persistent patterns of behavior in which either the basic rights of others or major age-appropriate societal norms or rules are violated (e.g., initiating fights, using weapons that can cause serious physical harm, stealing, fire setting, truanting).
- *Oppositional Defiant Disorder* is marked by a pattern of negativistic, hostile, defiant behavior (e.g., loses temper, argues with adults and defies their requests, deliberately annoys others, lies and bullies).

Feeding and Eating Disorders of Infancy or Early Childhood In this category we will be concerned with a persistent failure to eat adequately that is not due to a medical condition.

Elimination Disorders Here we will only be concerned with *Functional Enuresis* which is defined as repeated voiding of urine into bed or clothes at a chronological age of at least 5 years.

Separation Anxiety Disorder This disorder is characterized by excessive anxiety concerning separation from those to whom the child is attached: for example, unrealistic worry about harm befalling an attachment figure, refusal to go to school in order to stay with an attachment figure, refusal to go to sleep without being near an attachment figure.

Reactive Attachment Disorder of Infancy or Early Childhood This disorder is characterized by disturbed social relatedness (e.g., excessive inhibition or ambivalence, or diffuse attachments manifested by indiscriminate sociability with relative strangers). Grossly pathogenic care, such as neglect or frequent change of caretakers, may also be present.

Disorders of Both Children and Adults

The following disorders either have the same manifestations in children as in adults or can be made applicable to children with a few specific modifications.

Substance-related Disorders Here we will be concerned with dependence and abuse.

- *Substance Dependence* is a maladaptive pattern of substance use leading to clinically significant impairment or distress. Among its various manifestations are a need for markedly increased amounts of the substance to achieve the desired effect, a characteristic withdrawal syndrome for the substance, and an inability to fulfill major role obligations at work, school, or home.
- *Substance Abuse*, while still leading to impairment or distress, involves fewer symptoms; for example, increased tolerance and withdrawal reactions are not included. It is, therefore, a less severe disorder.

Schizophrenia This is a severe, pervasive disturbance consisting of delusions, hallucinations, disorganized speech, bizarre behaviors, and the so-called negative symptoms of flat affect, avolition, and alogia. Among the different types of schizophrenia are the *Paranoid Type,* marked by delusions or hallucinations; the *Disorganized Type,* marked by disorganized speech, behavior, and inappropriate affect; and the *Catatonic Type,* marked by motor immobility or extreme agitation, negativism or mutism, or peculiar posturing, stereotyped movements, or grimacing.

Mood Disorders Here we will be concerned with two kinds of *depressive disorders.* A *Major Depressive Disorder* is defined in terms of a depressed mood, weight loss, insomnia, psychomotor agitation or retardation, feelings of worthlessness or guilt, indecisiveness, recurrent thoughts of death, and markedly diminished interest or pleasure in activities. It occurs in single or repeated episodes. *Dysthymic Disorder* designates a chronic state of depression lasting at least one year.

Anxiety Disorders Among the many anxiety disorders, we will be concerned with the following:

- *Panic Attack* is characterized by a number of physical symptoms such as shortness of breath, dizziness, palpitations, trembling, and sweating, along with a fear of dying or going insane.
- *Specific Phobia* is a fear cued by the presence or anticipation of a specific object or situation (e.g., flying, heights, animals). The phobic stimulus is avoided or endured with marked distress. While adults recognize the unreasonable nature of the fear, this is not true of children. We will be particularly concerned with *School Phobia.*
- *Obsessive-Compulsive Disorder* is characterized either by obsessions, defined as recurrent thoughts, impulses, or images which are intrusive and inappropriate and cause

marked anxiety or distress, or compulsions, defined as ritualistic behaviors (e.g., hand-washing) or mental acts (e.g., counting, repeating words silently) that a person feels driven to perform in response to an obsession or according to rigidly applied rules.

- *Posttraumatic Stress Disorder* results when a person has experienced an event involving actual or threatened death or injury to the self or others. Among the many symptoms are persistent reexperiencing of the traumatic event (e.g., through recurrent, intrusive, distressing recollections), persistent avoidance of stimuli associated with the trauma (e.g., inability to recall aspects of the trauma or a diminished range of interests or activities), and persistent symptoms of increased arousal (e.g., difficulty falling asleep, irritability, difficulty concentrating).
- *Generalized Anxiety Disorder* (including Overanxious Disorder of Childhood) is defined as excessive anxiety and worry out of proportion to the likelihood or impact of the feared event.
- *Social Phobia* is characterized by a persistent fear of unfamiliar social situations, self-consciousness, and restricted social relationships, although the child is capable of social relationships with familiar people.

Gender Identity Disorder   This is evidenced by a strong, persistent cross-gender identification such as a repeatedly stated desire to be, or insistence that he or she is, the opposite sex, preference for cross-dressing and cross-sex roles in fantasy play, a strong preference for playmates of the opposite sex, and an intense desire to participate in games of the opposite sex.

Eating Disorders   We will be concerned with the following:

- *Anorexia Nervosa* is an intense fear of gaining weight even though the subject is underweight, an undue influence of body weight

on self-evaluation or denial of the seriousness of current low body weight, and a body weight less than 85 percent of that expected. There are two specific types: the *Binge Eating/Purging* type, in which the person engages in recurrent episodes of binge eating and purging, and the *Restricting* type, in which the person does not engage in episodes of binge eating.
- *Bulimia Nervosa* is marked by recurrent episodes of binge eating along with a sense of lack of control over eating during the episode. Self-evaluation is unduly influenced by body shape and weight. Weight is often normal. In the *Purging* type, a person regularly engages in self-induced vomiting or the use of laxatives or diuretics. In the *Nonpurging* type there is strict dieting, fasting, or vigorous exercise but no regular purging.

Table 3.4 relates the various psychopathologies to normal developments.

LONGITUDINAL STUDIES

The Continuity of Behavior

The issue of the persistence of psychopathology is one aspect of the general problem of continuity of behavior, which lies at the heart of developmental psychology. The discussion of personality variables in Chapter 2 demonstrates that continuity is not a simple matter of the constant recurrence of a specific behavior. Developmental forces reshape manifestations of the same variable; for example, the toddler's temper tantrum becomes the highly organized vengeance of rival street gangs. At the very least, manifest behaviors must be organized into *categories* relevant to psychopathology, and the developmental course of these categories charted.

Such a model is still too simple, however, because it only allows room for categories of pathological behavior to continue or to disappear over time. In reality, one kind of psychopathology may be replaced by another: an

Chronological time	The Context of Time				Attachment	Initiative and work	Self-control
	Developmental periods	Piagetian stages	Freudian stages	Eriksonian stages			
Birth	Infancy: 0–12 months	Sensorimotor: 0–2 years	Oral	Trust *vs.* mistrust	Social smile, 3–4 months Attachment: separation anxiety, hostility, 6–9 months	Exploration; self-as-agent; battle of bottle and spoon	Not required Regulates excitation; 4–6 months
1 year	Toddlerhood: 1–2½ years				Secure *vs.* insecure		
2 years		Preoperational: 2–6 years	Anal	Autonomy *vs.* shame, doubt		Willful, negativistic; battle of the potty	Low: "terrible twos"
3 years	Preschool age: 2½–6 years					Expansion of skills	Increasing
4 years						Concrete self	
5 years			Phallic Oedipal	Industry *vs.* inferiority			
6 years	Middle childhood: 6–11 years	Concrete operations: 6–11 years	Latency	Initiative *vs.* guilt	Fluctuation	School: requiredness, impersonality, product orientation	High
7 years							
8 years						Psychological self	
9 years							
10 years							
11 years	Preadolescence: 11–13 years	Formal operations: 11 years on			Vigorous denial		Low
12 years							
13 years	Adolescence: 13–18 years		Genital	Identity *vs.* role diffusion	Emancipation	Vocational choice; identity	Increasing
14 years						Abstract, future-oriented self	
15 years							
16 years							
17 years							
18 years	Young adulthood: 18–20 years			Intimacy *vs.* isolation	Rapprochement		High
19 years							
20 years							

Personality Variables*

Conscience		Cognition		Anxiety	Sex		
Cognitive	Affective	Causality	Social, self		Gender	Erotic feelings	Psychosexual developments
		Omnipotence of action		Innate			Mouth libidinized; object relation
							Anus libidinized; autonomy
			Egocentrism	Innate declines			
...oral realism: ...solute, rigid, ...eral; ...econventional ...vel	Guilt (Freudian theory)	Omnipotence of words; precausal thinking		Dark, imaginary creatures, etc.; defense mechanisms (timetable uncertain)	Determined by external clues; changeable	Masturbation; sexual curiosity	Genitals libidinized; exhibitionism; castration anxiety; Oedipus complex
...orality of ...ooperation; ...onventional ...orality	Punishment is sole concern		Social perspective taking; cooperation; communication; reflection	Realistic and imaginary, supernatural dangers	Determined by genitals; immutable		Diminution of sexuality
	Troubled; confesses; others' reactions are important		Social problem solving				
...elf-accepted ...oral principles	Guilt: self-oriented regardless of others	Realistic grasp of physical causality		Age-appropriate: prestige, sex, responsibility, etc. Some unrealistic fears		Central concerns: information, techniques, adequacy, love	Revival of earlier conflicts
							Integration of previous stages into mature love

*Each entry marks the *beginning* of a continuous developmental process.

Chronological time	Personality Variables (continued)*			
	Aggression	Social Relations		
		Sociability	Friendship	Groups
Birth	Rage differentiated from distress (6 months)	Interest in peers		
1 year	Peak for uncontrolled aggression; age-appropriate provocations		Unreciprocated "friendships"	
2 years		Empathy		
3 years	Intentional attack, tantrums, retaliation			
4 years		Cooperative play	Insubstantial, activity oriented	Insubstantial play groups
5 years				
6 years	Increasingly verbal-symbolic, intentional, retaliatory; age-appropriate provocations	Accommodation to others; respectworthiness	More sustained, other oriented; superficial	Gangs: identifiable units
7 years				
8 years				
9 years				
10 years				
11 years	Immature modes reappear, e.g., tantrums			
12 years				
13 years	Verbal expressions predominate: name calling, sarcasm, etc.; age-appropriate provocations		Sustained; personalized; sharing, frank, critical	Stable groups with potent control: clique, crowd, gang
14 years				
15 years				
16 years				
17 years				
18 years				
19 years				
20 years				

*Each entry marks the *beginning* of a continuous developmental process.

Onset of Psychopathologies[†]

m: prior to age 3

Depression: any age
Brain syndrome: any age
Mental retardation: any age
Posttraumatic stress
  disorder: any age
Adjustment disorder: any age

ng disorder: —————— Reactive
cy thru early   attachment
hood   disorders of
ation deficit/   infancy and early
ractivity disorder: _____ childhood
  age seven

ration anxiety disorder: — Oppositional defiant disorders: — Conduct disorder: ————————— Gender identity disorder ———
hool period   3 years; more common in middle   preschool through   Separation anxiety disorder:
                           childhood and adolescence   adolescence   preschool thru middle childhood

tional enuresis: 5 years ——

                                                                                        — Phobias: childhood thru ———
                           Learning disorders: adolescence
                           beginning school years
ol phobia: 7 years ——————— Obsessive-compulsive   Schizophrenia: childhood onset
                           disorder: middle child-
                           hood thru adolescence

———————————————————————————————— Substance related disorders: ————————————
                                                early adolescence

                         ——Suicide: increases in ————————————
                           adolescence

                                                                                        — Schizophrenia: adolescent ———
                                                                                          onset

rexia nervosa: ——————— Bulimia nervosa: adolescence ————————
escence

[†]Age of onset not given for all psychopathologies.

enuretic preschooler may become a depressed underachiever in middle childhood; a truant from school may turn to drug abuse; or a psychotic adolescent may pull together and become an adequately functioning obsessive-compulsive neurotic. Thus we must be on the lookout for *systematic relationships* among psychopathologies within the developmental context and, if possible, evaluate how such relationships affect the child's prognosis in terms of making it more favorable or unfavorable.

Finally, continuity must be evaluated with and without *therapeutic intervention.* As we shall see, certain psychopathologies are responsive to remedial measures, while others are not. Understandably, the more severe the disturbance, the more difficult it is to alter its course.

Before reviewing longitudinal studies of the continuity of psychopathological behavior, it will be necessary to discuss the methodological issues involved in conducting longitudinal research (see Farrington, 1991, and Verhulst and Koot, 1991).

Research Strategies

The Retrospective Strategy   A time-honored method of gathering developmental data is the *interview* in which a disturbed adult or the parents of a disturbed child are systematically questioned for historical information; the origins of the psychopathology are subsequently reconstructed from such data. Despite its popularity among clinicians and researchers alike, many retrospective data are of questionable reliability and validity. In order for a parent to be a satisfactory informant, he or she must accurately observe the behaviors a clinician will deem important (without foreknowledge of what behaviors these might be), preserve the observations in memory over a considerable period of time, and recall them intact on being questioned. Such an image befits a computer better than it does a human being, who is apt to distort information at all three stages even when the parent and child are psychologically sound—let alone if they are disturbed. While *retrospective data* may contain initial leads as to which intra- and interpersonal variables may be fruitful to study, they are currently considered an inadequate basis for understanding the origins and developmental course of childhood psychopathologies (Yarrow, Campbell, and Burton, 1970).

The reaction against retrospective data has spurred an interest in techniques that evaluate the child at two different points in time, Time 1 and Time 2. The interval should be sufficient to capture general developmental trends, while the evaluations should be independently conducted by individuals who are more objective than parents. Three of the most popular strategies are the *follow-back,* the *follow-up,* and the *cross-sectional* model, all of which eliminate a number of the deficiencies of retrospective data, although they have limitations of their own.

The Follow-Back Strategy   Like the retrospective approach, the follow-back study begins with a population of disturbed children or adults but obtains Time 1 data from records kept by observers other than parents: school records, teachers' assessments, child guidance case studies, court records, and so forth. A control group should also be selected, say, from the next name in the list of classmates or clinic patients, in order to narrow the variables relevant to the psychopathology being studied. For example, one might find that parental death, while hypothetically an important precursor of a given pathology, occurred no more frequently in disturbed children than in a control group.

In the follow-back study, not only can the investigator immediately focus on the target population, but also the strategy has a flexibility that allows the pursuit of new etiologic leads as they emerge. As we shall soon see, the follow-up strategy has neither advantage. However, the follow-back strategy has a number of limitations. The *data* may be uneven in quality, some being comprehensive and reflecting a high degree of professional competence, others being skimpy and distorted by conceptual or personality biases. The data also tend to be gross—for example, number of arrests, decline in school grades, intact or broken family, number of job changes—lacking both the detail and the interrelatedness of variables found in an in-depth evaluation.

Other problems concern design and *population bias* in particular. Clinical populations may not be representative of disturbed children in general. To take one example: parents who seek professional help for a child with a school phobia may be different from those who do not, so findings from a clinical population cannot be generalized to all parents of phobic children. Or again, children who are arrested may not be a representative sample of all youthful offenders, because police officers have their own biases as to whom they arrest and whom they let go.

More important, reliance on child guidance and court records bias the data in terms of accentuating pathology and exaggerating relationships found at Time 1 and Time 2. To illustrate: one follow-back study indicated that 75 percent of alcoholics had been truants, compared with 26 percent of healthy individuals—a highly significant difference; yet, a follow-up study revealed that only 11 percent of truants become alcoholics, compared with 8 percent of the nontruant population that became alcoholic. Thus truancy can have a variety of outcomes, its particular association with alcoholism being too weak for predictive purposes. In general, follow-up studies, which capture the variability of development, show fewer relations among Time 1 and Time 2 variables than do follow-back studies, which select especially disturbed individuals.

The Follow-Up Strategy What could be a more ideal method of charting children's development than the follow-up strategy? The resulting longitudinal data should reveal which children develop what psychopathologies, together with the fate of the population with and without intervention. The children may be evaluated at Time 1 and Time 2 only, or at regular intervals. Instead of being at the mercy of extant records as with follow-back studies, the investigator can insure that data will be gathered by well-trained investigators using the best available evaluative techniques.

Yet the follow-up study has a number of disadvantages. It is extremely *costly* in terms of time, money, and expenditure of effort. Investigators are bedeviled with the problem of *attrition;* not only do they lose track of subjects, but they also may do so selectively, the most disturbed, unstable families or children tending to move around, move away, or be uncooperative. Thus researchers may be faced with a dwindling number of people in the very population they are most interested in studying. Population *selectivity* is another problem. Because most psychopathologies are rare, large numbers of children must be evaluated at Time 1 to insure a reasonable number of disturbed ones at Time 2. As one solution, many investigators begin with a disturbed population or with a population at risk for developing a given psychopathology, such as infants of schizophrenic mothers, who have a greater likelihood of becoming schizophrenic than do infants from an unselected population. However, such selectivity may introduce the same population bias we noted in the follow-back design.

Moreover, the follow-up study is *rigid.* Once having selected variables to study, the design does not allow the investigator to drop some and add others as results from relevant studies come in or as new theories and concepts come to the fore. Moreover, new measurement techniques may be devised which are superior to the ones in use but cannot be substituted for them.

One final problem with the follow-up studies is the so-called *cohort effect*; one cannot assume that groups born at different times are equivalent, since the time of birth may significantly affect development. Children born in times of war or depression are not necessarily comparable to those born in times of peace and prosperity, just as children born before television or the sexual revolution or the feminist movement grew up in a different environment than those born afterward. Thus the results of a twenty-year longitudinal study may or may not be applicable to the current population of children.

The Cross-Sectional Strategy   The cohort effect may also confound the *cross-sectional* approach to gathering developmental data, which consists of studying different age groups at one point in time. Although these groups may be equated for all the variables thought to be important, they cannot be equated for differential experiences which they might have had because of their time of birth. For example, the parent-child relationship of a group of 14-year-old boys who grew up during the Vietnam war might differ significantly from a group of 7-year-old boys who grew up after the war. Thus age and environmental events are confounded.

One solution to the confounding of developmental with cohort effects is the so-called *longitudinal, cross-sectional approach*. In this design children at different ages are studied as in the cross-sectional approach but are subsequently followed until the children in the younger groups are the same age as those in the next older groups; for example, groups of 3-, 6-, and 9-year-olds can be followed for three years, so that the 3-year-olds are now 6 and the 6-year-olds are 9. Such a design allows one to compare the age trends obtained cross-sectionally with longitudinal data. The saving in time is obvious; a longitudinal study that would have had to follow the 3-year-olds for six years can now be accomplished in half the time. As with any design, this one is not foolproof, because problems in equating groups and in selective loss of subjects remain. (For an example of the longitudinal, cross-sectional study, see Klausmeier and Allen, 1978.)

Evaluation   While the follow-up and follow-back strategies are an improvement over the retrospective approach, neither is a panacea. Because of its flexibility, the follow-back strategy is most suited to generating hypotheses. Leads as to possible significant antecedents can subsequently be accepted or rejected as they are put to further tests. However, follow-up studies, because of their ability to monitor the child's development while it actually occurs, provide the most convincing data concerning change. This strategy also comes closest to testing causal relations among variables, although because it is basically naturalistic rather than experimental, it cannot provide the kind of manipulation and control of variables essential to the establishment of causation.

One final cautionary note: the designs of follow-up and follow-back studies have only recently received the attention they deserve. Consequently, our review of longitudinal research will include studies of varying degrees of methodological sophistication and results with varying degrees of conclusiveness. While containing the most important leads as to the developmental course of childhood psychopathology, the findings reviewed should be regarded as tentative.

The Findings

In our subsequent presentations we will explore longitudinal studies of specific psychopathologies. At this point we will present an overview of findings. First, the *continuities* among psychopathologies will be examined, including those that are behaviorally consistent within categories of behavior and those that change from one classification of psychopathology to another. Then the *discontinuities,* or the psychopathologies which the child "grows out of" or "grows into" by adulthood, will be presented. The primary concern will be with long-range predictions from childhood into adulthood, although occasionally developmental trends within childhood itself will be dealt with. (This presentation is based on Gelfand, Jenson, and Drew, 1988, and Robins, 1979.) Finally, we will examine *risk* factors and *resilience.*

The Continuities   The three deviations with the greatest degree of continuity from childhood to adulthood are the psychotic disorders, undersocialized, aggressive behavior, and severe mental retardation.

The *psychoses* of infancy and early childhood, which include autism and schizophrenia, have a gloomy prognosis, although even here one-quarter to one-third of the children make an adequate adult adjustment with or without treatment. The deviant behavior of those who do not recover may change while still remaining in the psychotic category; for example, an autistic preschooler may no longer evidence the classic signs as an adult, but may be diagnosed as a simple or undifferentiated schizophrenic. More provocative is the finding that around one-quarter of the psychotics who fail to recover develop clear evidence of organic brain pathology, even though none was discerned earlier. Finally, the prognosis for schizophrenia in adolescence is as poor as it is for the early psychoses.

Undersocialized, aggressive behavior after 6 years of age becomes predictive of subsequent aggressive-antisocial behavior in the adolescent period; specifically, disobeying the teacher, cheating, unpopularity because of fighting and quarreling, poor school work, and truanting are predictive of what is popularly called juvenile delinquency. Neurotic symptoms such as "nervousness," nail biting, bed-wetting, and thumb sucking are unrelated but not incompatible with becoming a delinquent; some delinquents rate high on the anxiety-withdrawal dimension.

Undersocialized, aggressive behavior in adolescence, in turn, is predictive of a host of acting-out behaviors affecting every area of the adult's life—criminality, vagrancy, excessive drinking, marital friction, promiscuity, and gambling. About half the children evidencing undersocialized, aggressive behavior will continue such behaviors into adulthood, although there is no way of predicting which children will do so. Robins (1979) concludes that "if one could successfully treat the antisocial behavior of childhood, the problems of adult crime, alcoholism, divorce, and chronic unemployment might be significantly diminished" (p. 509). The implicit irony is that until recently there has been relatively little interest in or funding for helping undersocialized, aggressive children.

An interesting example of continuity of disturbance but discontinuity of behavior is *adult schizophrenia,* which is characterized by emotional withdrawal, anxiety, and thought disturbances in the form of delusions and hallucinations. None of the characteristics are found in children destined to become schizophrenic as adults. The prevalent belief to the contrary, there is no evidence that the shy, withdrawn child is apt to develop schizophrenia—or any other adult psychopathology. On the contrary, the at-risk child evidences both acting-out and withdrawal behaviors and is characterized as unstable, irritable, aggressive, resistant to authority, seclusive, friendless, and given to daydreaming. The conceptual bridge between such behaviors and adult schizophrenia remains to be built (Ledingham, 1981).

School adjustment, which includes both academic achievement and attendance, is moderately related to adult adjustment, although, obviously, the specific behaviors involved are different. On the positive side, absence of both underachievement and serious truancy predicts a high level of adult success in slum-dwelling children; on the negative side, the presence of these problems in similar populations predicts problems with the police, sexual misbehavior, and problem drinking. Sadly, truancy in both sexes predicts having children who will also be truant.

The limited data on *sexual behavior* present a mixed picture in regard to the continuity-discontinuity dimension. There is no evidence that the sexually deviant boy will grow up to become the adult who engages in sex crimes. Thus there is discontinuity in regard to specific sexual behavior. However, to the extent that sexually deviant behavior is evidence of poor self-control and a tendency to act out, it is predictive of adult antisocial behaviors, which may include sex crimes along with other criminal, irresponsible behavior (Kohlberg, LaCrosse, and Ricks, 1972). Thus self-control rather than sexuality per se becomes the predictive variable. The same findings hold true of girls, except that in addition to antisocial behavior the sexually deviant girl is also likely to become the hysterical woman. This relation between sexual problems and hysterically determined body dysfunctions has been noted from the time of the Greeks to Freud.

Finally, there is a relation between the sheer quantity of problems and subsequent disturbance even if each problem taken alone is not sufficiently potent to be predictive. Thus, if children have nine or more specific problems, they are at risk for developing some form of psychopathology in the future.

The Discontinuities   Aside from the early psychoses and severe mental retardation, problem behavior in the toddler and preschool period tends not to be a good prognosticator

of subsequent disturbances, although the evidence is not wholly consistent on this point. Such unpredictability is congruent with the fluidity of early development. Around 6 or 7 years of age predictability increases, children with many symptoms at one age tending to have many symptoms later as well.

In contrast with undersocialized, aggressive behavior, a wide range of *anxiety disturbances* tends to be "outgrown" by adulthood, since anxiety-withdrawal disorders have a good prognosis. Not only is the shy, withdrawn, inhibited child unlikely to become a neurotic adult, but adult adjustment is likely to be as good as that of a random sample of the normal population. Other behaviors that tend not to persist are nervous habits such as nail biting, sleep disturbances, and eating problems such as food pickiness and refusal to eat (but not obesity and anorexia). The only cloud in this sunny picture is the finding that preadolescent boys (aged 11 to 13) who are introverted, shy, and somber and preadolescent girls who are excessively modest, dependent, and finicky eaters tend to be maladjusted adults.

The findings from a follow-up study of 200 adults seen ten to fifteen years earlier at a child guidance clinic underscore and elaborate on the summary just presented. Except for the extreme deviation of psychoses and excessive antisocial behavior, there was little continuity between child and adult disturbances. Childhood neurosis, which comprised the largest category of children, did not portend severe maladjustment in adulthood, with or without therapy. It was easier to predict health than maladjustment, since the healthier children were likely to continue to be so while children with severe problems might either remain disturbed or improve. Severity of disturbance, social class, and IQ were significantly related to the degree of adult maladjustment. Sex was another predictive variable, withdrawn girls and aggressive, antisocial boys rating low on adult adjustment. In regard to age, the data indicated that problems in the preadolescent period (11- to 12-year-olds) and very early in life (before age 5) foreshadowed later maladjustment. In general, children receiving outpatient therapy failed to show a better social adjustment than those equally disturbed children who received no therapy. (For further details and an extensive discussion of the problems involved in follow-up research, see Cass and Thomas, 1979).

Normal Children Even psychotic and antisocial, aggressive children who have the gloomiest prognosis are not all fated to become disturbed adults. But if disturbed children can "outgrow" their psychopathology, can normal children "grow into" disturbances as adults? The evidence suggests that this possibility exists. While the Berkeley Growth Study did not specifically address the issue of psychopathology, it was concerned with the kind of adjustment children made as adults. One investigator found that a group of able, confident, well-adjusted children turned out to be brittle, restless, puzzled adults (Macfarlane, 1964). A more statistically elegant analysis of the same data uncovered a type of gregarious, vigorous, cheerful adolescent boy who became a tense, touchy, hostile man, as well as a type of bright, driving, relatively mature adolescent girl who grew to be an isolated, rigid, pushy, depressive woman (Block and Haan, 1971). When aggressive behavior is discussed in Chapter 9, data will be presented indicating that children rated as extremely high on adjustment in early childhood can be rated very aggressive or withdrawn a few years later.

The thought that certain well-functioning children are at risk for becoming disturbed is a tantalizing one. Just what are the telltale signs indicating that all is not as well as it appears to be? And even if we know these signs, what are the implications of informing the parents that such a child is at risk and needs help, as our concern with prevention would require? Such questions are so far from being answered as to be almost hypothetical.

However, the developmental approach requires an equal concern with "growing into" as with "outgrowing" psychopathology.

Incidence versus Duration Robins (1979) makes an important distinction between variables that predict the incidence or likelihood of occurrence of various childhood psychopathologies and those that predict their duration. Let us take a brief look at the former.

Low socioeconomic status and broken homes have frequently been found to be associated with the now familiar constellation of antisocial, aggressive behavior and underachievement in school, although they are not related to anxiety, psychoneurosis, and psychophysiological (psychosomatic) symptoms. Closer scrutiny has revealed that it is parental behavior rather than socioeconomic status or broken homes per se which is highly correlated with psychopathology. Specifically, *antisocial parents* who quarrel, separate, and work at low-level occupations when they work at all are apt to have acting-out, low-achieving children. Such parents are more frequently found in the lower classes and in broken homes. Finally, having a large number of siblings has also been found to be associated with both antisocial behavior and poor school achievement and adjustment.

Psychiatric illness in parents increases the incidence of psychopathology in children. While it is difficult to disentangle the contribution of genetic from environmental factors, the passing on of problems from one generation to the next occurs at a rate well beyond chance for hyperactivity, school problems, delinquency, schizophrenia, and mental retardation. Genetic factors have been most clearly established in the cases of the last two disturbances. However, the generational picture is complicated by the fact that disorders other than the one exhibited by the parents also appear in their children more frequently than in the general population. A schizophrenic mother, for example, is more apt to have not only a schizophrenic child but one with various kinds of antisocial, acting-out behaviors such as convictions for felony, alcoholism, and drug abuse. Why this should be is not clear.

The above information concerning incidence or likelihood of occurrence is essential to the clinician and researcher concerned with *prevention* of psychopathology. However, the variables predicting incidence do not predict the duration of the psychopathology once it has occurred. Information concerning duration of psychopathology is crucial to the issue of *treatment* when a decision must be reached regarding whether therapeutic intervention is warranted and, if so, what measures can be taken to shorten the natural course of the psychopathology.

Resilience Werner and Smith (1992) evaluated 505 subjects in infancy, early and middle childhood, late adolescence, and early adulthood. True to the interactive model, they conceptualized resilience as the balance between risk and protective factors. Risk factors included poverty, perinatal stress, and parental psychopathology or discord. Most of the low-risk subjects became competent, confident, caring adults while two-thirds of the high-risk subjects had delinquency records, mental health or severe marital problems, or were divorced. However, the authors were particularly interested in the remaining third of the high-risk group; this group became competent, confident, caring adults, although they did pay a price in terms of a certain aloofness in interpersonal relations and stress-related health problems.

The authors were able to isolate three clusters of *protective factors:* (1) at least average intelligence and attributes that elicited positive responses from family members and other adults, such as robustness, vigor, and a sociable temperament; (2) affectional ties with parent substitutes such as grandparents or older siblings, which encouraged trust, autonomy, and initiative; and (3) an external support system in church, youth groups, or school, which rewarded competence. In regard to parental protective factors, education was particularly important and maternal confidence and indulgence of their sons in infancy.

The authors were also able to chart the complex *interactions* among protective variables at a given point in time and the ways in which these interactions set the stage for subsequent developments. We can only sample their findings. Active, sociable, temperamentally easy-to-care-for infants elicited more positive responses from their mothers at age 1 and from alternative caregivers at age 2 and had a wider network of caring adults in middle childhood. In addition, positive parental interactions with the infant were related to greater autonomy and social maturity at age 2 and with greater scholastic competence at age 10. Scholastic competence at 10, in turn, was positively linked with a sense of self-efficacy at age 18 and to less distress for adult men and a greater number of sources of emotional support for adult women including spouse or mate. Scholastic competence at 10 was also positively related to parental education. Incidentally, this interaction of intra- and interpersonal variables over time nicely fits our general developmental model in Chapter 1.

Finally, the authors were able to determine the relative weight of risk and protective factors in contributing to the favorable outcome in the high-risk group. Overall, rearing conditions were a more potent determinant of outcome than prenatal and perinatal complications, while the intrapersonal qualities of competence, self-esteem, self-efficacy, and temperamental dispositions were more important than the interpersonal variables of parental competence and sources of support within and outside the family. These intrapersonal qualities, which we call *initiative*, enabled the subjects to take advantage of the opportunities for growth life offered them at various turning points, such as joining the military in order to gain educational skills or becoming an active member of the religious community in adolescence. While manifested in different ways at different developmental periods, initiative itself was continuously present from infancy until adulthood.

CONCLUDING REMARKS

This overview of diagnostic categories and longitudinal studies helps us appreciate the special fund of information a professional must have to make knowledgeable statements concerning *diagnosis* and *prognosis* epitomized by the statement, "Most children act like this and your child will outgrow it," or its more ominous version, "The behavior is unusual and your child should receive special help." We now have at least a working idea of what the psychopathologies are, when they are apt to appear, and the chances of their continuing, changing into other psychopathologies, or disappearing with time.

We have also ventured in a preliminary way into the realm of *prevention* and *treatment*. The longitudinal data suggest that special efforts should be directed toward eliminating or ameliorating the early psychoses, severe acting-out behavior, and mental retardation. Ironically, these are the very disturbances that are only fitfully responsive to even the most heroic therapeutic efforts and can be prevented only in special instances.

Equally as troublesome as the inadequacy of therapeutic techniques for children who need help most is the ethical issue of providing psychotherapy for that large group of anxious-withdrawn children who are apt to "outgrow" such behavior without treatment. Certainly the conscientious professional cannot recommend remedial measures on the basis that they will forestall even greater and more intractable trouble in the future—one of the bedrock reasons for treating children. Rather, the clinician must find other grounds for recommending treatment, such as a humanitarian concern that

children should not suffer unduly, even if such suffering is temporary. Parents also have the right to be informed before treatment that the chances are in favor of the child's outgrowing his or her disturbance. They should also know that a probability statement is not a guarantee because there is always the possibility that a particular child will continue to be disturbed. With such information parents can make an informed decision whether to agree to treatment for their child.

The longitudinal overview has also dispelled any notion we might have had that children are easier to treat than adults. As with adults, some children respond readily to treatment, while others are highly resistive. The decision to become a professional helper should be made on the basis of wanting to help children and finding such help intrinsically rewarding, not on the basis of an expectation that somehow the task will be an easy one.

We are now ready for a detailed exploration of selected psychopathologies. As much as possible we will take them in chronological order. However, since depression and schizophrenia may appear at different points in development, we have located them to reflect the concentration of research in the infancy to middle-childhood period in the case of depression, and the concentration of research in the middle-childhood period in the case of schizophrenia. In all cases we will use the information about normal development provided in Chapter 2 to answer the question, How can this psychopathology be understood in terms of normal development gone awry? How deviations from normality at one point in time affect future development will also be discussed. This dual concern requires reconstructing the natural history of the psychopathology. Finally, the issue of the efficacy of psychotherapeutic measures in curtailing further deviance will be addressed. However, a systematic examination of psychotherapy will come only after our exploration of the psychopathologies is concluded.

AUTISM: A SEVERE DEVIATION IN INFANCY

What lies at the heart of human development in the first two years of life? The establishment of the bond of love, surely, and curiosity, and symbolic communication culminating in speech. And what if all were wrenched from their normal course? One would rightly predict severe psychopathology.

One such psychopathology will be discussed here: autism. First, its behavioral manifestations and effects on subsequent development will be outlined. Then, the knotty and unanswered etiologic question will be discussed, namely, What causes these deviant behaviors?

You are a clinical child psychologist approaching a group of disturbed preschoolers in a play yard. From a distance they look surprisingly like any healthy, intelligent youngsters. You particularly notice a little girl on a swing. Her face is pensive. She has an ethereal beauty. You go up to greet her and start a friendly conversation. She does not look at you, nor does she look away. Rather, she looks through you as if you did not exist. You are face to face, and she looks through you. If you were to put her on your lap, her body would not accommodate to yours, but she would sit as if you were a chair. If she needed you to do something, say, open a door, she would take your hand (rather than taking you by the hand) and bring it in contact with the doorknob. As a person you would not exist.

CHARACTERISTICS AND EPIDEMIOLOGY

The initial encounter with autistic children can be a shattering experience. Other disturbed children might ignore you or defy you or call you names or strike out or kick and bite, all of which are forms of relating. But to be impervious is different; it runs counter to the basic responsiveness of one human being to another.

In his classic paper, Kanner (1943) delineated the three essential features of early infantile autism. The first is *extreme isolation* and an inability to relate to people, as we have just seen. The second is a pathological *need for sameness.* This need applies both to the child's own behavior and to the environment. Often the child's activities are simple, such as sitting on the floor and rocking back and forth for long periods of time, or twirling his or her shoelaces, or running up and down a hall. Sometimes the activities resemble complex rituals, such as a 5½-year-old who takes a toy truck, turns it on its side, spins a wheel while making a humming noise, goes over to the window, looks out while drumming his fingers on the sill, and then returns to the truck, only to repeat the exact same sequence over and over. The need for environmental sameness can be expressed in a number of ways; for example, the child must have the exact same food and plate and utensils, or wear the same article of clothing, or have the same ar-

rangement of furniture. The intensity of the need is evidenced not only by the rigidity of the behavior but also by the child's panic and rage when attempts are made to alter the environment even in minor ways, such as providing a different food or moving a chair to a different part of the room. (For an example of such rigidity in a laboratory study, see Ferster and DeMyer, 1962.)

The third characteristic of autism is either *mutism or noncommunicative speech.* The latter may include echolalia, phrases or sentences that are irrelevant to the situation (for example, while repeatedly flushing the toilet, an autistic girl suddenly said, "The hamburgers are in the refrigerator!"), extreme literalness (e.g., when taught to say "Please" to get a cookie, an autistic boy would use the word only when he wanted a cookie, as if "please" and "cookie" had become inseparably linked), and personal-pronoun reversals, typically the child referring to himself as "you." Kanner (1946–1947) presents evidence that, in certain instances, seemingly irrelevant remarks are meaningful from the child's point of view. A 5-year-old would frequently say "Fifty-five," which seemed nonsensical until it was learned that his favorite grandmother was 55 years old and the number was his way of referring to her. Another autistic child said, "Don't throw the dog off the balcony," which again was seemingly irrelevant but referred to the fact that, three years previously, his mother had angrily said this when he was throwing a toy dog off the balcony. The first child was recalling a loving image that represented comfort to him; the second child was checking an impulse to throw something. Neither child was communicating because, instead of taking their listeners into account, they were living in and expressing a world of private meanings.

There are other behaviors that may be present in the autistic child, but not necessarily. Autistic children are frequently healthy and appear intelligent, judging by their facial ex-

Kanner's 1943 paper is a prime example of the *naturalistic tradition* as implemented by means of the *clinical eye*. The descriptions remain vivid and fresh and can be read with profit many decades after they were written. As any good naturalist should, Kanner also took care to differentiate infantile autism from other conditions that might resemble it, schizophrenia in particular. But many clinicians share Kanner's keen eye for detail; what distinguishes him is his ability to organize these richly detailed clinical pictures into categories of behavior that de-

fine the psychopathology. Thus the clinical eye nourished a conceptualizing intellect. If today we can say, "of course" there is aloneness, sameness, and mutism, it is because Kanner opened our eyes to the "obvious." After all, autism has probably been in existence for centuries and had gone unnoticed, just as the cognitive developments in the sensorimotor stage had before Piaget. Kanner's *descriptive classification* of early infantile autism remains a scientific achievement of the first order.

pression. They also may have excellent rote memory and may perform remarkable feats of remembering names or tunes or pictures. Finally, they are at home and content in the world of physical objects rather than in the interpersonal world.

The DSM-IV Draft Criteria summarizes the current view of the basic diagnostic features of autism as follows:

1. Qualitative impairment in social interaction, as manifested by at least two of the following:
   a. marked impairment in the use of multiple nonverbal behaviors such as eye-to-eye gaze, facial expression, body postures, and gestures to regulate social interaction
   b. failure to develop peer relationships appropriate to developmental level
   c. markedly impaired expression of pleasure in other people's happiness
   d. lack of social or emotional reciprocity
2. Qualitative impairments in communication as manifested by at least one of the following:
   a. delay in, or total lack of, the development of spoken language (not accompanied by an attempt to compensate through alternative modes of communication such as gesture or mime)
   b. in individuals with adequate speech,

marked impairment in the ability to initiate or sustain a conversation with others
   c. stereotyped and repetitive use of language or idiosyncratic language
   d. lack of varied spontaneous make-believe play or social imitative play appropriate to developmental level
3. Restricted repetitive and *stereotyped patterns of behavior, interests, and activities,* as manifested by at least one of the following:
   a. encompassing preoccupation with one or more stereotyped and restricted patterns of interest that is abnormal either in intensity or focus
   b. apparently compulsive adherence to specific, nonfunctional routines or rituals
   c. stereotyped and repetitive motor mannerisms (e.g., hand or finger flapping or twisting, or complex whole body movements)
   d. persistent preoccupation with parts of objects

Subsequent research has added important new information concerning autism while generally confirming Kanner's three defining characteristics (Prior and Werry, 1986). Although autistic behavior may be noted in early infancy, it can also appear after a period of up to thirty months of normal development.

The social imperviousness and manneristic behavior of the autistic child.

Oddly enough, its appearance is not necessarily associated with any particular precipitating event. The clinical impression of average or above average intelligence, based on the child's facial expression and feats of memory, has not been confirmed. Initially it was thought that the child's unrelatedness prevented the utilization of innate intelligence, but subsequent research found that retardation tends to persist over time when progress is made in social relations. Only one-fifth to one-quarter of autistic children have normal to borderline intelligence, the majority being moderately to severely retarded (Prior and Werry, 1986).

While it was also initially thought that autism existed only in the middle class and was not inherited, subsequent studies showed it is found in all classes (Gillberg, 1990) and that there is a genetic component probably not for autism per se but rather for some language or sociability abnormality that interacts with other factors to produce autism (Folstein and Rutter, 1988).

Finally, autism can coexist with known or-

ganic brain pathologies. Out of 243 children who had been infected with congenital rubella (German measles) in utero, 10 had symptoms of autism along with organic defects such as visual, auditory, and neurological handicaps (Chess, 1971). In addition, both grand mal and psychomotor seizures develop in about one-third of the population, the first few years of life and adolescence being peak times (Gillberg, 1988).

That autism can coexist with both mental retardation and known organic brain pathologies complicates, rather than solves, the task of understanding etiology. It would be unwarranted to claim that either one causes autism, because the majority of mentally retarded and organically damaged children do not evidence the full-blown syndrome described by Kanner (although individual behaviors that constitute the syndrome—such as social isolation—might appear separately in specific cases). The discovery of coexisting pathology means we must understand not only the etiology of "pure" cases of autism but also the special role mental deficiency and organic brain damage play in producing autism in given instances.

It was previously believed that the frequency of autism was low, ranging from 4 to 6 per 10,000 children. More recent studies place the frequency between 6.6 to 13.6 per 10,000 children (Gillberg, 1990). Differences in findings may be due, in part, to how narrow or wide a definition of autism is used (Vicker and Monahan, 1988). There is an excess of boys over girls, the ratios ranging from 2.6:1 to 5.7:1 when Kanner's criteria are used (Gillberg, 1990).

DEVELOPMENTAL PATHWAY

One would correctly predict that so severe and pervasive a disturbance occurring so early in life would have ominous implications for future development. Slightly less than 10 percent will do well in adult life, holding jobs and, in a few cases, marrying and having families. Fully 60 percent will be completely dependent in all aspects of life. No communicative speech by 5 years of age and an IQ below 60 are poor prognostic signs, along with early seizure onset and possibly seizure onset in adolescence (Gillberg, 1991). Those who achieve communicative speech by 5 years of age and have average intelligence have a 50-50 chance of making an adequate adjustment (Rutter and Garmezy, 1983). Thus, the prognosis is poor under the most favorable of conditions, and the overall prognosis is worse than that of other severe childhood disturbances, such as borderline psychosis or mental deficiency.

It is also possible to sketch a more differentiated developmental picture than is found in outcome studies (Miller, 1974; Paul, 1987). Based on retrospective accounts of *infancy*, the following behaviors are absent, delayed, or qualitatively impaired: eye contact, posturing anticipatory to being picked up, smiling in recognition of a familiar person, vocalization, stranger anxiety, interest in early games such as peekaboo, pointing, and response to sound. The infant's body may be rigid and therefore difficult to cuddle, or flaccid to the point of "collapsing" or "melting" into the mother's body. Many of these retrospective descriptions have been validated by an ingenious research technique involving analysis of home movies of infants who subsequently turned out to be autistic (Adrien et al., 1991).

Autistic *toddlers* and *preschoolers* show few positive social responses. They do not follow or greet parents, or kiss and cuddle, or go to parents for comfort when hurt; but neither do they physically withdraw and avoid. Rather, they seem profoundly detached. Not only is language delayed, but babbling may also lack the richness and variety found in normal development. Understanding of language is also impaired; the child may follow a simple command if it is accompanied by a gesture, but not one that contains two ideas such as, "Go to your room and get your toy." There is no delight in "chatting" or in give-and-take conversation, and there is no infatuation with the magic of verbal communication. The child is deficient in social imitation (for example, waving bye-bye), in meaningful exploration of objects (being content to spin a wheel on a toy car or mouth it, for example), and in dramatic play such as "house" or "tea party." Play patterns tend to be limited and rigidly repeated.

In *middle childhood* the lack of social relatedness abates somewhat, but the children tend to be friendless, noncooperative, and lacking in empathy. While no longer impervious, their social responses are odd and inappropriate. Those who speak do so in a non-communicative way, talking *at* a person rather than *with* them. What they say is often confined to the immediate situation. Those with adequate intelligence perform up to grade level, although many may be placed in special classes because of problems in social adjustment. Activities continue to be ritualistic, with adherence to strict routines and marked distress at slight deviations. Special preoccupations might appear, such as memorizing timetables.

Adolescence is a time of dramatic developments. Seizures appear in about one-quarter to one-third of the children, predominantly those with IQ scores below 65. At the other extreme, Kanner, Rodriguez, and Ashenden (1972) found that the period could be one of significant improvement. Certain adolescents seem to realize that their behavior is deviant and make a conscious effort to act in an appropriate manner. Between 5 and 15 percent of autistic children achieve a satisfactory social and occupational adjustment, with or without therapy (Lotter, 1978). Typically, they cope with life by scrupulously sticking to the rules of acceptable behavior. Their speech, for example, may resemble that of certain foreigners who use flawless English but still sound rather stilted. Work and play have the same quality of being learned by rote without the freedom to vary and improvise which comes with full understanding. Adequately functioning *adults* know the letter of the law, but the spirit eludes them. They can be devoid of empathy and, significantly, seem generally indifferent to sexuality. On the positive side, their slavish devotion to rules and regulations can fit nicely into the demands of a bureaucratic society.

One final point: while the majority of autistic children continue to be severely disturbed, they do not become classically schizophrenic in the sense of having delusions and hallucinations. Whether there is a basic difference between autism and schizophrenia is a hotly debated issue to which we shall return.

SPECIFIC DELAYS AND DEVIATIONS

There is a simple way to understand the primary features of autism: the major pleasures and interests of normal infants are aversive to autistic ones. In the first weeks of life a multitude of factors conspire to make the adult human the most attractive and pleasurable stimulus for the normal infant. For example, the human voice quickly becomes preferred over all other sounds, and the patterning of the face, particularly the eyes, holds a special fascination; moreover the infant learns to adjust his or her body to that of the caretaker when held and to anticipate relief from distress when the caretaker comes into view. In addition, the need for variable stimulation lies at the heart of exploration of the environment, the infant being nicely constituted to seek ever more complex challenges as the simple ones are mastered. In autism, the very basis of cognitive and affective development is undermined, so avoidance and repetition replace approach and expansion.

In a most general way we have accounted for autism. Yet scientists are rarely satisfied with such generalities and continue to ask, "Yes, but why?" What has gone wrong to produce this negative image of normal development? At present the answers are legion, everything from blood platelets to social class being implicated. (For a detailed presentation, see Dawson, 1989.)

In our research review we will be interested in discovering which psychological functions are *age-appropriate*, which are shared with children at comparable levels of mental retardation and therefore represent a *developmental delay*, and which are *developmentally deviant*, in that they cannot be accounted for in terms of the autistic child's mental age level. Only developmentally deviant behavior is regarded as *specific to autism*, although developmental delays can play an important role in producing the defining features of autism.

In organizing the literature we have followed the tradition of going from basic to higher-order processes; that is, from perception to higher-order thinking and social relations. However, only imitation, language, social relations, and restricted repertoire of behavior (here called executive function) define autistic behavior. The other categories are associated processes that may contribute to but are not part of autistic symptomtology.

Quantitative versus Qualitative Difference

Whether psychopathology represents a quantitative or a qualitative difference from normality is a perennial question. Generally speaking, the quantitative view is more prevalent: phobias are regarded as extremes of normal fears, delinquency is viewed as an exaggeration of normal adolescent rebelliousness. The three major developmental models of psychopathology—fixation, regression, and developmental delay—are quantitative. Yet DSM-IV Draft Criteria describes autism in terms of *qualitative* impairments. This could mean that autistic behavior has no counterpart even in the behavior of younger, normal children and that the developmental sequencing of behavior does not follow that charted for normal children.

To evaluate the quantitative versus qualitative issue, Wenar et al. (1986) compared the development of 41 autistic children between 5 and 11 years of age with that of 195 normal children between 3 months and 5 years of age, using a standardized observational technique called the Behavior Rating Instrument for Autistic and other Atypical Children (BRIAAC). The investigators found that severely autistic children's obliviousness to caretaking adults, their minimal expressiveness, their disinterest in or fleeting exploration of objects, their unresponsiveness or negative reaction to sound, and their indifference to social demands all indicated an imperviousness to the social and physical environment that had little counterpart in normal behavior and development. However, such qualitative differences were present only in the most severely disturbed autistic children; less disturbed ones and normal 2- to 3-year-olds shared the same developmental sequence but progressed at different rates. Hence autism could be regarded as "normal development in slow motion."

While not dealing with the issue of severity, Dawson's (1991) discussion of early socioemotional development, also concludes that in certain cases, "both the surface behavior and the function or need it fulfills may be unique to the autistic child and parallels in normal developmental patterns may be difficult to find" (p. 227). Already we see that we must enlarge our models of deviations to include qualitatively different behavior.

Finally, Burack and Volkmar (1992), in their objective study, found no difference between high- and low-functioning autistic children and nonautistic, developmentally disabled children in regard to the development of receptive and expressive communication (e.g., understanding commands, using words). However, they did find a difference in the patterning of behavioral domains that constitute adaptive behavior (e.g., daily living skills, social coping skills, communication, and play). Here the variability was greater in the autistic group, and greater for low-functioning than high-functioning autistic children. This finding alerts us to the possibility that the *patterning* of components of a given psychological variable may be another way in which disturbed children differ from normal ones. Moreover, if this patterning is unique, it might be considered a qualitative difference. We will return to these points later.

Perception, Attention, and Arousal

While autistic children might show disturbances in vision and audition, these are not specific to their psychopathology but can be found in mentally retarded children (Prior and Werry, 1986). They are also capable of sustained attention. However, autistic children do deviate in certain respects. They prefer a higher level of sound, including music and speech, than do matched retarded children (Frith and Baron-Cohen, 1987), while novel

Laboratory studies of etiology provide some of the best illustrations of the advantage of the *control of relevant variables* inherent in this research methodology. The discovery that a considerable number of autistic children might also be mentally retarded casts doubt on previous research by raising the question, Which aspects of these children's behavior are the result of autism per se and which are shared with the general population of mentally retarded children? The question, in turn, is part of the quest to find the psychological defects or deficiencies specific to autism. It can be answered by adding a control group of nonautistic retarded children matched for mental age with the low-functioning autistic children. A further question can also be raised: To what extent is the behavior of low-functioning autistic children shared with a younger, normal population? In other words, does the observed behavior of the autistic group represent developmental delay or fixation, or does it represent a qualitatively distinct behavior having no counterpart in normal development? This question can be answered by adding a control group of normal children whose chronological age is matched with the mental age of the autistic children. Thus a study might be designed as shown in Table 4.1.

One such study was conducted by Hermelin (1976), using 10- to 15-year-old autistic children with a mental age of about 5 years, matched with mentally retarded children with similar chronological and mental ages, and with normally developing

TABLE 4.1

Research Design Comparing Autistic, Mentally Retarded, and Normal Children

	Autistic children	Mentally retarded children	Normal children
Chronological age	8	8	5
Mental age	5	5	5

5-year-olds. In the first experiment, the children were presented with a card on which were two black rectangles, one large and one small. Then they were presented with a series of cue cards with either a large or small rectangle of the same size as the ones on the original card. The task was to match the rectangle on the cue card with the one on the original card. In this task the autistic children performed as well as the mentally retarded and normal children. Even when the cue card was first shown, then removed, so that the children had to match from memory, the autistic children performed as well as the normals and were superior to the retarded children. Therefore there is nothing deviant in their basic ability to discriminate size. However, when a series of five black rectangles of differing sizes were presented in random order and the children were asked to arrange them from smallest to largest, the autistic children's performance was inferior to that of both other groups. This is only one

and unpredictable stimuli may elicit aversive responses rather than an adaptive orienting response. For example, whereas repeated presentation of a novel stimulus will lead to slowing of heart rate and habituation in normal infants, in autistic children it results in an acceleration in heart rate and a failure to habituate. (See Dawson, 1991, for a summary of objective studies.)

Unlike normal toddlers, who can modulate their responses to environmental stimulation, autistic children may be *extreme* and *erratic* in their reactions. As infants they may be hyper-

irritable or too placid; as toddlers their bodies may be excessively rigid and their actions may have a driven quality, or they may be limp and inert like a sack of flour. They may scream in distress when a vacuum cleaner goes on, but then at another time prefer a louder sound than a normal child. They may be impervious to the speech of the adult standing next to them while listening intensely to the sound of a garbage truck two blocks away.

Some authors conceptualize this responsiveness in terms of a faulty *arousal mechanism.* Others prefer to theorize in terms of an *imbal-*

of many instances in which the autistic child is capable of responding appropriately to simple stimuli but is hamstrung when dealing with complex patterning or ordering of stimuli.

The control the laboratory affords also allows the kind of highly refined exploration of a given psychological function that would be next to impossible using any other research methodology. Let us take memory, for example, since one could hypothesize that the autistic children's difficulty in coping with the physical and social environment might be owing to a memory defect. The laboratory approach allows the investigator systematically to vary many parameters of memory: the kind of material to be remembered, such as meaningful or nonsense; the interval of time for remembering the material, from immediate recall to varying periods of delay; and the mode of presentation of the material to be remembered, such as visual or auditory. Even more important, a laboratory approach can separate a memory defect from a defect in the initial intake of information; for example, an apparent deficiency in the recall of a list of words may be because the autistic children were able to take in fewer words than the other groups. Only when there is evidence that the groups are similar in the amount of information they can initially process can one properly attribute an inferior recall to a memory deficiency.

Prior and Chen's study (1976) illustrates this last point. The investigators made sure the autistic, mentally retarded, and normal groups were equally adept in the acquisition phase of the task before testing for recall. The study involved nine children in each group, all of whom had mental ages between 4$\frac{1}{2}$ and 5 years of age, with the autistic and retarded groups being approximately 10 years of age, the normal children around 4 years of age. The test material consisted of hollow blocks of various sizes, shapes, and colors. The blocks were presented two at a time, and the children were to guess which was the "correct" one. (The "correct" choice was arbitrarily determined beforehand by the researchers.) If they succeeded, they would receive a bit of candy hidden in the hollow. To illustrate: for a given child a small white pyramid might be the correct choice. This block would be paired with other blocks, such as a large white cube or a small black cylinder. Each child had to solve a number of such puzzles. In the initial phase of their research, the investigators demonstrated that the autistic children were as adept as the other children in learning the correct choices. Only then did the researchers vary the time between presentation of pairs from 30 to 60 to 120 seconds to test the effect of the length of interval on memory. They found that, while delay did significantly affect performance—the longer time intervals making it more difficult for the children to remember the correct responses—it affected all groups of children equally. Mental age rather than autism was the significant determiner of memory.

ance between excitation and inhibition in the brain. The insufficiently aroused child is comfortable assimilating only a small portion of available stimulation and gravitates toward simple activities that do not tax the meager supply of energy. If arousal or excitation is excessive, the child is readily overwhelmed by novel and complex stimuli; as a protection, many of the sights and sounds of the everyday environment are defensively blotted out through inattention or through clinging to the safety of simple repetitive activities. The latter hypothesis of hypersensitivity is the more popular one. (For a detailed presentation of objective studies, see Dawson and Levy, 1989.)

Memory

Autistic children's short-term memory is intact, with regard to both visual and auditory material; for example, their ability to repeat a series of digits is age-appropriate. The picture in regard to long-term memory is not clear. A case has been made that studies controlling for mental retardation indicate a developmental delay rather than a autism-specific deviation

(Prior and Werry, 1986). However, there are also studies yielding conflicting findings. (See Boucher and Lewis, 1989.) Therefore the issue cannot be decided with certainty at present.

Learning

There is evidence that autistic children respond to reward and punishment, success and failure in operant conditioning experiments as do normal children. They also become noncompliant or withdrawn as tasks become too difficult. However, their failure to generalize beyond the immediate learning situation may be even greater than that of retarded children. Consequently, although autistic children do respond to operant techniques, their resistance to new learning is a pervasive one (Prior and Werry, 1986).

The research evidence clearly points to a deficit in *imitation* in autistic children regardless of their mental age level. Lovaas, Koegel, and Schreibman (1979) vividly describe autistic children's failure to imitate even after each child had 1000 trials of hearing a teacher say "phone" and observing a model pick up the phone. The children would learn only part of the response, such as merely touching the phone, or they would pick it up regardless of when the teacher gave the command.

Ohta's (1987) study found that autistic children could imitate simple hand gestures such as a "V" or a "bull horn," but they had difficulty with more complex gestures such as making a T sign using both hands. Like Lovaas, Ohta noted that they made strange partial imitations such as holding one hand palm up rather than down. Finally, Dawson and Levy (1989) found that autistic children's level of imitation was similar to that of 1- to 4-month-old infants. Reversing the situation, adult imitation of the autistic child increased general social responsiveness as measured by gaze, vocalization, touch, and gestures, while decreasing perseveration in exploration and play. A similar facilitating effect is found when adults imitate normal infants (See these same authors for an example of using imitation as a therapeutic tool with autistic children.)

Higher-Order Thinking

When level of intelligence is controlled, autistic children have no specific deficiency in knowledge of *object permanence*. They not only achieve this differentiation but also can use mental representation of objects to solve problems as opposed to using trial-and-error behavior. Autistic children can also *categorize* objects as evidenced by their ability to sort by color or shape or classification, such as food or vehicle (see Sigman et al., 1987).

On the other hand, a number of deficiencies in higher-order thinking have been documented, and various hypotheses have been generated to account for them. Since an overall integration has not been forthcoming, we can do no more than list the diverse deficiencies and hypotheses.

One hypothesis is that these children can take in information but cannot relate it to past experience; to use Piaget's term they cannot *assimilate*. Autistic children tend to echo rather than understand. One consequence is that thinking is concrete and situation-specific; for example, once a girl has learned that "ride" means leaving the house and getting into a particular car, she will be unable to grasp the idea that "going for a ride" can mean leaving from any place in any car.

Another deficiency concerns comprehending verbal and nonverbal *symbols* and using them to communicate. One important function of symbolization is to release the child from his or her reliance on action; for example, the act of walking upstairs can be represented by the thought, "I can walk upstairs." Symbols can replace trial-and-error behavior as well; for example, the child can think, "My ball is not in the kitchen or the playroom but upstairs in my room, so I will go upstairs to get it," thus saving himself the necessity of going from one room to the next. Finally, symbols open the door to abstractions that have no specific referent in concrete reality, such as "right" and "wrong," "good" and "bad." For the autistic child, however, the basic idea that a sound or gesture can represent an object or activity is not fully grasped. Recall that the autistic infant will not imitate bye-bye gestures, the autistic toddler does not pretend to sweep the floor and set the table, and finally, symbolic play is impoverished in the autistic child's preschool period (see Miller, 1974).

Another specific problem autistic children have is in *coding* and *organizing* stimuli in terms of patterns and rules. The amount of information from the social and physical environment impinging on any individual at any given time is prodigious. What prevents normal children from being overwhelmed is the fact that the information is not random, but patterned and meaningfully organized. While normal children are particularly adept at reducing information to manageable proportions by organizing it according to patterns and classes of events, autistic children are deficient in this respect. One can speculate that their repetitious, stereotyped behavior is an attempt to establish islands of predictability and stability in a potentially overwhelming environment. (Frith & Baron-Cohen, 1987).

Language Acquisition

Many of the perceptual, cognitive, and social deficiencies we have explored converge in the autistic child's acquisition and use of language, which is one reason it is so potent prognostically. In addition, autistic children do more poorly in certain aspects of language development than do retarded children, suggesting that something more than a cognitive delay is involved. Autistic children may go about mastering the various components of

language in idiosyncratic ways, and these components may also be acquired in a disjointed manner, rather than in the synchronistic manner observed in normal children.

Using an information processing framework to integrate objective studies, Dawson (1991), claims that, while autistic children are capable of detecting novelty, *processing of novel information* is abnormal. For example, while normal children are apt to exhibit greater left-than right-hemisphere activiation while processing linguistic information, the pattern is reversed in autistic children; by contrast, hemispheric activation is normal during nonverbal, visual spatial tasks. Dawson speculates that the reason autistic children do well with tasks involving physical objects and develop the concept of object permanence is that the physical world is stable and predictable; however, language is relatively variable and unpredictable, thus exceeding the limited range of information autistic children can process. (For a detailed account of autistic language as normal development gone awry, see Schopler and Mesibov, 1985. Unless otherwise noted, our presentation will follow summaries of objective studies found in this volume. For a succinct account of objective studies of autistic language, see Tager-Flusberg, 1989.)

Prosody, according to linguists, is the melody of speech. Normal infants make remarkable progress in discriminating and imitating speech sounds. They may be innately programmed to discriminate human speech from other sounds, and their subsequent babbling will have the rhythm and melody of speech, even though the content is meaningless. Moreover, prosody provides valuable clues to phrases and sentence boundaries, both of which are signaled by a fall-and-rise pattern in fundamental frequencies. The structure of language would be much more difficult for infants and toddlers to grasp if we spoke in a monotonous, robotlike fashion with each word intoned exactly as the preceding one.

Prosody also helps direct attention to the most important elements of an utterance and signals the speaker's attitudes and mood.

While not all autistic children are deficient in the use of prosody, and while such an abnormality in itself would not undercut language development, a number of autistic children do have a deficiency that, when taken in conjunction with other deficiencies, can make language difficult to comprehend. Lacking the clues for analyzing speech into meaningful units, some autistic children are forced to learn whole phrases that are used in a rigid, echolalic manner. The lack of discrimination of units also blocks the flexible recombining of such units into new ways to express new meanings. (For a detailed presentation of prosodic development in normal and autistic children, see Baltaxe and Simmons, 1985.)

Syntax is the way words are combined to produce meaningful sentences. The evidence indicates that while autistic children may lag behind normal children, they are no different from children at a comparable intellectual level. In both production and understanding, autistic children display mastery of a variety of grammatical rules. The girl who said, "The hamburgers are in the refrigerator" while flushing the toilet repeatedly was not communicating, but her sentence was grammatically correct (see Tager-Flusberg, 1989).

Moreover, autistic children follow the same developmental path in the acquisition of syntax as normal children (Tager-Flusberg et al., 1990). However, they may deviate in the way they use such grammatical rules. For example, they use the past tense appropriately in connection with ongoing activities but not in talking of events outside the context of ongoing activities.

Semantics involves the meaning of words and sentences, and it is here that the autistic flaws appear. When dealing with concrete objects, autistic children may be developmen-

tally delayed, but no more so than a comparable group of retarded children. For example, they know that the category "fish" includes a bluefish and a shark, might include a seahorse, but would not include a padlock. Thus autistic children do not acquire idiosyncratic word meanings, but show the same pattern of generalization of meaning as children at a comparable developmental level (Tager-Flusberg, 1985). However, words that are not anchored in concrete reality present difficulties. While the normal toddler's vocabulary contains a wide range of experimental and social terms, such as "bye-bye," "all gone," "up," and "dirty," the autistic child's vocabulary typically relates to static aspects of the environment such as inanimate objects and food.

This general difficulty with words that do not refer to concrete objects and the attendant specific difficulty with relational words continues throughout childhood. While the normal preschooler masters such relational words as "big" and "small," the autistic child has great difficulty, tending to treat them as absolute qualities, so "big" becomes as much a characteristic of a given object as its shape. By the same token, active verbs that refer to some clearly perceived ongoing event, such as eating, are more easily grasped than ones that have no specific physical referent, such as "want," "like," and "believe." While autistic children use the present tense as frequently as normal children do, their use of the past tense is significantly depressed. Prepositions such as "beside" or "in" are troublesome because they are not characteristics of objects but denote relations among objects. "I" and "you" present special problems because they have shifting referents depending on the speaker rather than consistently designating a single person. Even high-functioning autistic children have difficulty in double classifications, which involve two people doing two different things at the same time; for example, "I have a ball and am sitting down; you have a bat and are standing up." Each idea can be grasped separately but cannot be entertained simultaneously.

Thus we can see progressively complex steps in learning language. The simplest rule is this: one word, such as "chair," stands for one object. Relational words, such as "on" or "I," are difficult because they do not refer to a single object or person. Multiple classifications of a single object are baffling (for example, a "white chair" presents problems because other objects may be white without being chairs and chairs need not be white), while double classifications are more baffling still. The patterning of words to produce sentences, the ordering of phrases within sentences, and the relations among sentences produce even greater obstacles in terms of analyzing and integrating information (Menyuk, 1978). Finally, it follows that holding a conversation, which requires a constant shift of perspective from self to others, presents extreme difficulties to an autistic child. (For a detailed presentation of semantic problems in autistic children, see Menyuk and Quill, 1985, and Tager-Flusberg, 1989).

Communication

Speaking is more than understanding and ordering verbal symbols, however; it is communication as well. Normal infants are quick to grasp the notion of communication via expressive sounds. Within the first three months they can take turns vocalizing with their caretaker and, by the end of the first year, they can vocalize to indicate needs and feelings as well as to socialize. The socially isolated autistic child has no such need to communicate. It has been noted, for example, that autistic children are impoverished in their use of gestures to communicate even when such gestures are within their repertoire (Prior and Werry,

1986). Thus the cognitive problem of symbolization is compounded by a motivational problem of disinterest. Moreover, even when children have mastered the basic rules of combining words into meaningful sentences, they still may have trouble with *pragmatics,* the social context of language, which involves learning when to say what to whom in order to communicate effectively and to achieve an underlying objective. In fact, pragmatic deficits are found even in high-functioning autistic children, suggesting that they are specific to the disturbance; autistic children have been described as talking *at* others rather than talking *with* them in the sense of engaging in reciprocal exchanges; also, they do not explain matters well, often failing to fill in all the information that the listener needs to follow them. Thus, they may launch into a topic which interests them at the moment, without finding out whether the listener shares that interest or even is familiar with the topic (Volkmar, 1987). In fact, Tager-Flusberg (1989) concludes that the language deficit in autism results from a profound problem with key aspects of intentional communication, especially those that are exclusively social-interactional. In this respect they differ from mentally retarded children who have no such specific difficulty in communication but demonstrate deficits across the board.

What is specific to autism—what sets it apart from retardation and language impairments—is a mismatch between syntax and semantics or between syntax and pragmatics. The "echo-box" quality of autistic children's speech means they store in memory and later repeat in syntactic structures that have little or no meaning to them. Here syntax is unrelated to semantics. Autistic children also produce sentences that are grammatically impeccable but that have no relation to the social context, such as "Don't throw the dog off the balcony." Such disjointed development is very much at odds with the progression of normal speech, which is characterized by synchrony among the various components, children knowing the meaning of what they say and knowing the rules for using words to communicate to others (Swisher and Demetras, 1985).

Language Comprehension

Like communication and pragmatics, language comprehension in the first few years depends heavily on social interaction. In normal 8- to 12-month-olds, such comprehension grows out of social exchanges between caretaker and infant. Commands such as "Give me the spoon" are given typically when the infant is handing the parent the spoon, while parents frequently call for attention by saying "Look" and "See" when the child is already attending. When the caretaker names the objects the infant is exploring, he or she uses accompanying gestures and physical manipulation; thus visual attention is as important for the infant as listening. Language comprehension is initially a kind of overlay on already meaningful social behavior. Autistic children, with their social isolation and odd interests, make it difficult for caretakers even to set the stage for language comprehension. This difficulty continues into the toddler and early preschool period since language comprehension continues to be closely tied to the social context. (For an account of the subsequent development of language comprehension, see Lord, 1985.)

Summary

An integrative review will be helpful at this point. Table 4.2 shows a detailed summary of research findings. Autistic children's basic psychological functions of seeing, hearing, attending, and remembering are generally commensurate with their level of mental retardation, although certain peculiarities may well be specific to autism. The higher-level functions of object permanence and categorizing objects are also in keeping with their mental age level. While they can be conditioned by operant techniques at an age-appropriate level, their deficits in imitation and their failure to generalize what they have learned may well be specific.

It is in the realm of higher-order thinking and in language that their deviations are most clearly in evidence. Here the children's thinking tends to be concrete, situation-specific, literal, and inflexible. Ideas anchored in concrete reality can be grasped readily, but relationships, patterns, abstractions, and double and multiple classifications are difficult for them to understand. Their concreteness hampers their ability to use symbols in general and language in particular. They can grasp syntax to the point of using grammatically correct sentences and can understand concrete words, but abstract words and ideas often elude them. They have only limited ability to use language to communicate. The disjointed nature of language development is as distinguishing a feature of autism as the specific deviations themselves, the discrepancy between syntactic and lexical aspects on the one hand and pragmatic functioning on the other being particularly striking.

The Developmental Model We have encountered two new models of normal development gone awry. The first is a *qualitative* one in which the behavior of autistic children has little or no counterpart in normal development. In the second, deviance lies in the relationships between variables rather than within a single variable itself. We will call this deviation *asynchrony*. Progress among variables is disjointed, some proceeding at a normal pace while others lag or follow an idiosyncratic course. While asynchrony has been noted in the clinical literature (see A. Freud, 1965), it is now being verified in objective studies such as language development and, to a lesser extent, adaptive behavior in autistic children.

TABLE 4.2

Specific Delays and Deviations in the Functioning of Autistic Children

Function	Age appropriate	Developmentally delayed*	Developmentally deviant†	Below normal‡
Perception				
Hearing and vision		●		
Auditory preference for high levels			●	
Size discrimination		●		
Extreme, erratic responsiveness				●
Attention				
Sustained attention		●		
Attention to novel, unpredictable tasks				●
Memory				
Short-term memory	●			
Long-term memory§		●		
Learning				
Operant conditioning	●			
Generalization			●	
Imitation			●	
Higher-order thinking				
Object permanence		●		
Ordering stimuli			●	
Categorization		●		
Symbol comprehension, both verbal and gestured			●	
Grasping codes and rules			●	
Language				
Prosody (in some children)¶			●	
Syntax		●		
Semantics				
Concrete words		●		
Abstract, relational words, prepositions			●	
Multiple classifications			●	
Pragmatics			●	
Intentional communication			●	
Synchrony of elements			●	
Comprehension			●	

* Behavior is appropriate to subnormal mental age.
† Behavior is deviant even when controlled for mental age; specific to autism.
‡ Behavior is below normal but there is no control for mental age.
§ Classification is controversial.
¶ Language-delayed (aphasic) children often used as controls.

DELAYS AND DEVIATIONS IN SOCIAL RELATIONS

Autistic children's deviant transaction with their human environment is one of the most striking features of their psychopathology. Since we have already described the developmental course of social relations we will now examine them in detail, citing clinical and objective studies and presenting explanations purporting to account for the data. (For a detailed presentation see Volkmar, 1987.)

The Infant and Toddler Period

The relation to the caregiver is central in this period. In the case of autism a number of factors conspire to divert development from its normal course. (Except when noted, our presentation follows Dawson and Galpert, 1986.)

Gaze Patterns While normal neonates are not capable of establishing eye contact until the end of the first month of life, the ability to do so is an important step in the bonding process, mothers typically reacting with pleasure and saying that the infant now knows her. By 6 months the infant will initiate social contact through gaze, while infant and caregiver engage in coordinated patterns of engagement and looking away. Toddlers use gaze to signal the completion of their own vocalization and to invite the partner to speak (Volkmar and Mayes, 1990). Thus gaze plays an important role in a number of social interactions.

Autistic children's gaze is deviant. In extreme cases they look through or past the adult, thus preventing the development of interactional patterns mediated by gaze. Studies of older children who have established eye contact find that it lacks the nice complementarity of normal glance exchange. For example, autistic children are more likely than mentally retarded ones to look elsewhere rather than at adults and to look less at adults during one-

to-one interactions (Volkmar and Mayes, 1990; and Buitelaar et al., 1991. For a summary of the literature see Volkmar, 1987.)

Affect The social smile appears around $2^{1}/_{2}$ to 3 months of age in normal infants and plays a major role in binding the infant and caregiver in mutually pleasurable exchanges. In severely disturbed autistic children the social smile is conspicuously absent. Even when they begin to relate, they react to the caregiver warily, only gradually being able to tolerate closeness (Wenar et al., 1986). Moreover, while 30- to 70-month-old autistic children look and smile at their mother as frequently as do normal children, they do not combine smiling with eye contact in a single act and they are less likely to smile in response to the mother's smile. Thus they are not deficient in the quantitative expression of affect but in its communication. This baffling uncoupling of affect and gaze may account for the fact that their mothers smile less at them than do mothers of normal children (Dawson et al., 1990).

Vocalization The human voice is innately attractive to the neonate and, by 2 to 4 months of age, infants and their mothers engage in patterns of simultaneous and alternating vocal exchanges that may be the precursor of later verbal communication. While there are few studies of autistic children, their characteristic mutism, evidenced by lack of babbling, blocks this avenue of social interaction.

Imitation Early imitation again attests to the attractiveness of the social environment for normal infants, while autistic infants' deficiency in this area means that observed human behavior is not sufficiently compelling to be incorporated into their own repertoire.

Initiative and Reciprocity When responded to contingently by sensitive caregivers, normal infants soon begin to take the initiative in eliciting responses. This, in turn, can lead to simple back-and-forth sequences which mark the beginning of reciprocity. For example, when the mother who has delighted her infant daughter by tickling her tummy after diapering pauses, the infant might flail her arms and legs, signaling that she wants more. In this way a sequence of pleasure-pause-signal-pleasure is established which continues until mother or infant tires. The most direct evidence concerning reciprocity in autism comes from a study of home movies of eight infants who subsequently became autistic. There was a decline in social play in the second year, the children being passive recipients of adults' playful overtures rather than actively interacting with them (Losche, 1990).

There is a precursor of reciprocity called *joint attention behavior,* which has been of considerable interest to researchers. Toward the end of the first year of life, the normal infant starts pointing to an object when a caregiver is present or holding an object up for the caregiver to see or signaling by looking from the object to the caregiver. Rather than attending to an object alone the infant now tries to attract the adult's attention so that the interest can be shared. Note that the infant is assuming the initiative and the goal is sharing. The infant is not signaling in order to get an adult to do something the infant cannot do such as bringing a toy which is out of reach.

Research has shown that autistic children display joint attention behaviors less often than mentally retarded or language-disabled children (Mundy and Sigman, 1989a). The behavior is not only autism-specific, but it may also be one of the earliest manifestations of a social deficit to be studied objectively. There is also evidence that when joint attention behavior occurs, it is not accompanied by the sharing of positive affect as it is in normal and Down syndrome children (Kasari et al., 1990). There is more at stake here than a specific social gesture, since joint attention behavior is concur-

rently associated with language development and is a significant predictor of language acquisition among autistic children (Mundy, Sigman, and Kasari, 1990)

Attachment Rogers, Ozonoff, and Maslin-Cole (1991) found no difference in the attachment behaviors of seventeen autistic preschoolers and a matched group of children with other developmental or psychiatric disorders; that is, they showed the same amount of proximity seeking, contact maintenance, proximity avoidance, and contact resistance in relation to the mother. However, so many methodological changes had to be made in order to accommodate to the unusual behaviors of the children that it was impossible to compare the findings to those of normal infants.

While these results are unexpected, Rogers and Pennington (1991) are careful to point out that they only mean that the behaviors indicative of attachment security or insecurity are no different in autistic and retarded or severely disturbed children. The speculation is that attachment has been so critical to the survival of the human species that certain behaviors are programmed to appear by evolution. It is doubtful whether such behaviors indicate the kind of intense and complex interpersonal relation that characterize attachment in normal infants.

Play Among developmental psychologists there is general agreement that pretend play is one of the most important settings in which children learn the give-and-take and mutual adaptation which defines reciprocal relationships. Games such as "house" or "store" not only require children to take on roles alien to their realistic selves but also to continually accommodate to one another as the game progresses. If the "Mommie" asks the "storekeeper" for a pound of coffee, the "storekeeper" must respond in terms of coffee rather than cookies and whether he says he does or does not have the coffee will determine the "Mommie's" response. And on it goes until the drama is completed.

Researchers have found that there is an orderly progression in play leading up to pretend, or what is called *symbolic*, play. Around 9 months of age *relationship* play appears in which there is the simultaneous association of two or more objects in a nonfunctional manner; for example, stacking blocks or using one block to push another. At the end of the first year *functional* play appears in which realistic toys are used in a functional or conventional manner, such as using a spoon to feed a doll, dialing a telephone and bringing the receiver to the ear. Symbolic play appears between 13 and 22 months of age.

A study comparing autistic, retarded, and normal children with mental ages of 25 to 26 months found that autistic children had the same range of play activities as the other two groups but spent more time on the less sophisticated and stereotypic relational play. In the mentally retarded and normal groups functional and symbolic play tended to dominate or replace the simpler forms. Moreover, the autistic children tended to produce fewer sequences of related acts than did the mentally retarded group, attesting to their difficulty with reciprocal relationships at the symbolic level. There was also evidence that the lower level of play in the autistic groups was not a result of their language deficits (see Sigman et al., 1987).

Compliance and Negativism There is evidence that autistic children are compliant to requests if such requests are within their intellectual grasp. Thus, they respond appropriately when in a predictable, highly contingent, structured environment. Also, in spite of the fact that they have been described as being excessively negativistic, there is no evidence to support such a claim (Volkmar, 1986).

The Self While speculations concerning what the autistic child's self must be like abound, objective data are meager. However, there have been a cluster of studies concerning self-recognition as operationalized by the ability to discriminate a change in one's mirror image. The procedure is to put a small amount of rouge on the end of the infant's nose and watch for reactions to the mirror image, such as touching the nose or smiling. Autistic children recognize their images as well as retarded children do. However, their affective response is different since they evidence less smiling or coyness (Mundy and Sigman, 1989b). For the most part, however, the autistic self remains uncharted territory in terms of objective studies.

Table 4.3 summarizes the findings for the infancy and toddler period.

The Preschool and Middle-Childhood Period

After around 5 years of age the more extreme manifestations of social isolation moderate, although the general picture is still one of significant deviation. After touching on motivational-affective factors we will concentrate on reciprocity, which lies at the heart of normal social interaction. Finally, we will briefly describe research on autistic children's pathological need for sameness.

Motivational-Affective Factors The motivation to be an active participant in the social environment, which is so strong in normal children, is weak in autistic children. Parents report that they have less interest in other children and do not join in play or imitate them (Stone and Lemanek, 1990b). One consequence of this isolation is that autistic children are deprived of opportunities to learn about the social environment—what it is like, how to adapt to and master it. Thus, even those who

TABLE 4.3

Delays and Deviations in Social Behavior and in Self-concept
The Infancy and Toddler Period

	Developmentally delayed*	Developmentally deviant†	Below normal‡
Social behavior			
Imperviousness to social environment		●	
Gaze		●	
Positive affect		●	
Vocalization§		●	
Imitation		●	
Initiative			●
Reciprocity:			
Joint attention behavior		●	
Shared affect		●	
Attachment	●		
Play		●	
Compliance and negativism	●		
Self-concept			
Self-recognition	●		
Positive affect or coyness			●

* Behavior is appropriate to subnormal mental age.
† Behavior is deviant even when controlled for mental age; autism-specific.
‡ Behavior is below normal, but there is no control for mental age.
§ Data are sparse.

become interested in peers might find that they lack the skills necessary for entering and sustaining a relationship, their awkward overtures tending to antagonize rather than attract others (Howlin, 1986).

On the affective side, clinicians have described autistic children as lacking in *empathy,* defined as the process by which a person responds affectively to another as if he or she were experiencing the same affect. In normal development, empathy has been observed in preschoolers (Hoffman, 1978), although it might appear even earlier. In one of the few objective studies, Yirmiya and colleagues (1992) found that even nonretarded autistic children between 9 and 16 years of age performed less well than normal controls on empathy-related measures. This deficiency in empathy deprives autistic children of that immediate understanding of the feelings of others which plays such an important role in many interpersonal interactions. Case histories on adults who are no longer autistic note that this deficiency persists; for example, at times they may be bewildered when trying to understand how others feel, or they may be socially gauche, failing to realize when a tactful glossing over of a painful truth is preferable to embarrassing honesty.

Reciprocity Reciprocity requires a finely tuned give-and-take between individuals. Senders must adjust their messages to what they infer to be the receivers' level of comprehension, while receivers must be able to grasp the message which has been sent. Moreover, each subsequent message must be adjusted to the content of the previous one. The messages themselves can be both verbal and nonverbal, the latter including gestures, tone of voice, and body language. Already we can sense how reciprocity, which begins so early in life that it becomes automatic much of the time in normal children, presents major obstacles to autistic ones. In fact, an inability to fully participate in age-appropriate reciprocal social interaction may persist throughout their lives (Baron-Cohen, 1988). Since we have already covered the difficulties with verbal messages in the sections on language comprehension and communication, we shall concentrate on the literature concerning the *nonverbal aspects* of social interactions.

Receptive Difficulties Just as autistic children can grasp object permanence in the physical environment, they know that people exist independently of them. They also understand that people are agents of action in regard to physical objects; for example, they understand that people can cook food and drive cars (Rogers and Pennington, 1991). But can they understanding the feelings of others? Most of the studies in this area involve recognition of facial expressions of emotions as depicted either in photographs or drawings.

Hobson, Ouston, and Lee (1988) found that autistic adolescents were able to sort photographs of faces according to mood (e.g., "happy" or "sad") just as well as a group of mentally retarded children. However, the autistic children's criteria used for sorting the expressions were unusual; e.g., when given the choice of sorting according to expression or according to the type of hat worn by the people in the photographs, they chose the hat more often than did the retarded children, suggesting that they found expression less salient.

In everyday life, emotions are not expressed by a face in isolation from the rest of the body, and it is this integration of information from diverse sources which proves so difficult for many autistic children. The basic studies were done by Hobson (1986a, 1986b), who found that autistic children were inferior to mentally retarded children in matching facial expressions of various emotions to the appropriate vocal and bodily expressions. Thus, the fact that people look and sound and act in special ways when displaying the basic emotions of happiness, sadness, anger, and fear is not readily grasped. Finally, there is evidence that high-functioning autistic adults are less adept than normal adults in recognizing emotional cues in facial and vocal modalities (Macdonald et al., 1989).

Before leaving this topic it should be noted that there are a sufficient number of negative findings for some investigators to question whether recognition of affect is a primary deficit rather than a result of a general cognitive lag (Ozonoff, Pennington, and Rogers, 1990). For example, Tager-Flusberg (1992) found no dearth of affective words in the spontaneous speech of 3- to 7-year-old autistic children when compared with a control group of Down syndrome children. However, it is not clear whether findings discrepant from Hobson's are due to procedural differences in the studies. (For an exhaustive presentation of methodological problems in doing research on perception and understanding of emotions, see Hobson, 1991.)

On the positive side, Baron-Cohen (1991) found that autistic children understand the causes of emotions, at least at a simple level; for example, they understand the relation between situations and affect—one feels happy at a birthday party and unhappy when one falls down. They also understand that desires cause emotions in that their fulfillment leads to positive affect, their frustration to negative affect. Thus, a child who wants candy and is given some is happy; a child who cannot find her mother is sad. However, they are inferior to matched mentally retarded children in situations requiring an advanced cognitive ability called false beliefs, which we shall soon discuss under the topic of perspective taking.

Turning now to the understanding of gestures, what little objective data there are indicate that autistic children do as well as Down syndrome children in recognizing simple instrumental gestures such as pointing, moving the finger to indicate "come here," or putting the finger to the lips to convey "be quiet" (Attwood, Frith, and Hermelin, 1988).

Expressive Difficulties   Clinical observations suggest that, while preschool autistic children evidence the basic affective reactions of pleasure, wariness, and rage, they lack the more highly developed ones such as shame, affection, and guilt, which are usually present by 2 to 3 years of age in normal children (Dawson and Galpert, 1986). In the interpersonal realm, 2- to 4-year-old autistic children display less positive affect interacting with adults than developmentally delayed children (Mundy and Sigman, 1989b). Subsequently, this dearth of facial expression, poverty of bodily gestures, and lack of modulation in expressive aspect of voice give an impression of woodenness (Attwood, Frith, and Hermelin, 1988). A similar decrease in affective expressiveness can be found even in well-functioning autistic adults (Macdonald et al., 1989).

In an objective study, Attwood, Frith, and Hermelin (1988) found that autistic adolescents were no different from normal and retarded children matched for mental age in regard to using instrumental or action-oriented gestures (just as they were no different in understanding such gestures, as we have just seen). However, they never used expressive gestures—gestures deliberately expressing feelings concerning the self or others. Among these would be hugging and kissing another child, putting an arm around another to console or as a sign of friendship, putting the hand over the face to express embarrassment. Such social gestures, unlike instrumental ones, re-

quire knowledge of how another person feels along with an expression of one's own feelings and desires. There is some evidence that the discrepancy between instrumental and social understanding lasts through adolescence. In an objective observational study, Loveland and Tunali (1991) had the experimenter relate an unhappy personal experience during snack time—that his wallet had been stolen or his pet had died. The Down syndrome control children expressed the socially acceptable concern over the loss, while the autistic children commented on the snacks.

Table 4.4 summarizes the findings for the preschool and middle-childhood period.

Looking back, we can see how the autistic children's social problems are compounded. As receivers, they have difficulty making sense of verbal messages and nonverbal gestures that are being sent by others. As senders, their limited repertoire of messages tend to make others shy away from them. This, in turn, narrows their social experience, further impairing the development of social skills. While they are adept at nonverbal instrumental communications, most of them either use others as a means of satisfying their own needs or issue simple commands to be obeyed, neither of which is conducive to reciprocal exchanges.

Explanations

First we will discuss two cognitive explanations of the deviations in social relations in autism: *perspective taking* and the overlapping but broader concept of *theory of mind*.

Perspective Taking   Piaget claimed that the infant views the physical and social environment in terms of the self, a phenomenon he calls *egocentrism*. Gradually, however, the developing child is able to view the environment from the perspective of others, to see the world through other people's eyes. This ability is

TABLE 4.4
Delays and Deviations in Social Behavior
The Preschool and Middle-Childhood Period

	Developmentally delayed*	Developmentally deviant†	Below normal‡
Motivation: Social initiative			●
Affect: Empathy§		●	
Reciprocity: Receptive difficulties in understanding others			
Understanding others as action agents	●		
Understanding feelings of others§		●	
Understanding causes of emotions	●		
Understanding instrumental (action) gestures	●		
Reciprocity: Expressive difficulties			
Variety of affective cues		●	
Using instrumental (action) gestures	●		
Using expressive (affective) gestures		●	

* Behavior is appropriate to subnormal mental age.
† Behavior is deviant even when controlled for mental age; autism-specific.
‡ Behavior is below normal, but there is no control for mental age.
§ Classification is controversial.
¶ Nonretarded autistic children used in certain studies.

called perspective taking and is crucial to the ability to communicate and engage in reciprocal social interactions.

There is evidence that autistic children have unevenly developed perspective-taking ability. Reed and Peterson (1990) compared 12-year-old autistic children with a group of normal and retarded children matched for mental age on two kinds of perspective-taking tasks, one perceptual, the other cognitive. The *perceptual* task required the child to imagine what another person could see when looking at an object from that person's vantage point. For example, there were various toy animals on a turntable and the experimenter, who was sitting across from the child, requested to see parts of the animals' bodies such as their nose or tail. To comply correctly, the child had to rotate the turntable until the animal was in the correct position in terms of the experimenter's perspective.

The *cognitive* task required the ability to assess the mental state of another, such as that person's knowledge, ignorance, or belief. The situation used here is called *false belief* and requires the child to infer what another person knows and does not know. In this particular setup the experimenter had dolls act out the following sequence: Doll A hides a marble and leaves the room; doll B transfers the marble to another hiding place; doll A returns. The experimenter then asks the child the crucial question: Where will doll A look for the marble? The child must understand that doll A will act on her belief even though it is no longer valid. A correct answer indicates that the child has distinguished what he or she knows from what the doll knows.

In this study, the autistic children performed as well as the two control groups on the perceptual tasks but not as well on the cognitive ones. In all probability perceptual perspective taking has only limited applicability to social situations, whereas the autistic children's problem with cognitive perspective taking would hamper communication and social interaction in general.

Theory of Mind   While developmental psychologists have extensively explored children's understanding of their physical and social environment, they have only recently turned their attention to studying children's understanding of the content and function of mental life, such as what perception or memory or intentions or dreams are and how they function. The term used for this study of the understanding of mental phenomena is *theory of mind*.

According to Wellman (1988), a theory of mind has three characteristics. First is the recognition that mind has a *special domain*— namely, mental states and activities—which is different from other domains such as the physical or interpersonal. Next, mind consists of a coherent *interconnected body of concepts*. Beliefs, desires, and intentions are not isolated realms but are interrelated; for example, a belief that children should not be abused leads to a desire to help them and an interest in becoming a clinical child psychologist. Finally, mental activity is *causally related to behavior*; for example, going to the grocery store is causally related to a desire to have a home-cooked meal. Included in the theory of mind is both the ability to conceive of mental states and activities in oneself and to infer them in others.

Wellman (1988) claims that preschoolers between 3 and 5 years of age can have a theory of mind in which all three elements are present. However, the theory is a simple one which should not be equated with an adult's understanding of mental life. Thus, the preschooler's picture of the mind is like that of a passive container of images, belief, dreams, and so forth. The mind as an active agent which organizes information from the world, hypoth-

esizes, reasons—in short, the notion of the mind as an intermediary that interprets and directs all perception and action—is beyond the preschooler's grasp. (See Johnson, 1988, for a more technical discussion of the limitation of the preschooler's theory of mind.)

How does the theory of mind relate to autism? Let us start at the most general level. One of the main distinctions between people and physical objects is that people have a mental life while objects do not. If the child does not fully grasp the idea that others have a mental life, he or she will tend to treat them as if they were things. Recall that this is exactly what severely disturbed autistic children do, for example, when they take a person's hand and bring it to a doorknob when they want the door to be opened.

Researchers have explored certain aspects of the theory of mind in autistic children. We have already discussed false belief, which involves knowing what others do and do not know. This can be viewed either in terms of perspective taking or theory of mind, since the two concepts overlap. Now let us see how such knowledge affects *communication*. The study was done by Perner and coworkers (1989) using autistic children with a chronological age (CA) of 13 years 6 months and a mental age (MA) of 6 years 2 months. The procedure involved an experimenter, two collaborators, A and B, and a toy bee which could make flying motions and nod its head. The experimenter demonstrated the flying motions to the child while A but not B was in the room. Then A left on some pretext, and the experimenter demonstrated the bee nodding to the child. B has seen neither demonstration. Then A and B entered the room and asked the child what the bee can do. The crucial issue is whether the child answers the question differently on the basis of the fact that A and B have different knowledge of the bee; for A an answer in terms of flying would be redundant while either answer would be appropriate for

B. Only 12.5 percent of the autistic children mentioned nodding first to A as compared with the majority of 3 year olds. This weakened ability to adjust communication to the knowledge of the receiver probably is an important element in autistic children's weakness in pragmatics.

The next study, done by Perner and colleagues (1989) addresses the more basic issue of *knowledge acquisition* itself. In this study the child must distinguish what another person knows or does not know, given what the person has or has not seen. Most autistic children grasp the nature of seeing itself; namely, that at least one eye must be open and there must be an unobstructed line of vision between the eye and the object seen (Baron-Cohen, 1989a). In normal children this ability is present as early as 2 years of age. However, such understanding only involves the relation between physical objects and human bodies. It does not require any inference as to what is going on in another person's mind. In tasks requiring such an inference, autistic children do significantly more poorly than normal ones. In this particular study, experimenter A allowed either the autistic child or another experimenter B to peek into a cup and see what was hidden there. In both instances the experimenter emphasized the fact that one individual was allowed to see the object while the other one was not. Afterward, the autistic children were asked what was in the cup and whether B knew what was in the cup. The children were also asked to justify their response. About two-thirds of the autistic children had difficulty making knowledge attributions and justifying them both in terms of themselves and in terms of another person. In normal children this ability develops between 3 and 4 years of age.

The Role of Affect   Since cognitive explanations such as perspective taking and theory of mind have captured the interest of developmentalists, the role of affect has been relatively neglected. Yet we have seen a number of examples of affective blunting in social situations: the absence of the social smile and of delight in joint attention behavior in the first years of life and the subsequent poverty of or deviations in affective expression. Because social interactions lack the positive affective charge they normally have, the motivation to become socially involved is reduced. At the same time autistic children are more difficult to "read" and relate to because of decreased affective cues. (For a theory of the role of affect in autism, see Hobson, 1989.)

Summary

First, an overview. Autistic children's understanding of the physical environment contrasts with their transactions with the social environment. They function adequately in dealing with the former and also with the readily perceived manifestations of the latter. Thus, for example, they can see the connection between a happy expression and a birthday party. However, they are deficient in the more inferential aspects of social understanding—that the birthday girl feels happy as well as looking happy, and that she has her own fantasies, expectations, and thoughts about the party. In fact, autistic children have been humorously described as pure behaviorists, going no further than their perceptions of human behavior will lead them. (For specific objective studies, see Baron-Cohen, 1989a.)

As for the details, autistic children's knowledge of others is satisfactory or appropriate to their MA when such knowledge is derived from external cues alone (Ungerer, 1989). Thus they recognize the independent physical existence of people (just as they understand object permanence) and know that others can initiate actions; they understand what others can and cannot see and can also grasp the relation between situation and affect. At a more inferential level they can assume the perspective of others in regard to viewing the physical environment. However, higher-order inferences—those concerning what other people know and believe and feel—present difficulties even when allowing for autistic children's mental and linguistic deficiencies. For example, while autistic children can understand people as agents of actions who can do things for them or give them pleasure, they are deficient in inferring what other people do and do not know. Or again, they can understand and use instrumental gestures involving action such as "Come here," or gestures involving their own need satisfaction such as "Get me that," but they do not use expressive gestures involving their own or other people's feelings. Their understanding of other people's expressions of affect presents a mixed picture. Autistic children can categorize basic facial expressions correctly, but the integration of face with vocal and bodily cues presents difficulties. In contrast to this difficulty in integrating complex external cues, autistic children can successfully infer the relation between desire and affect, although not between belief and affect. To complete our summary, autistic children do not clearly grasp the relation between perceiving and acquiring knowledge.

A number of factors act as obstacles to developing reciprocal interactions. In the infant and toddler period, the autistic children's deviant gaze, vocalization, and imitation hamper the development of early social exchanges with the caregiver. The lack of sharing for the pleasure of sharing is indicated by the meager number of joint attention behaviors—for example the rare occurrence of simple interactive activities such as peekaboo. In subsequent years, when symbolic activities become increasingly important, the problem with language, particularly pragmatics, has already been covered. To this we should add the infrequency of pretend or symbolic play. Finally, autistic children's affective life is deviant. There is very little of the delight in social ex-

changes seen in the first year of normal development; thus, a potent incentive to engage in such exchanges is missing. The social smile is either rare or detached from its communicative function. Autistic children are also deficient in empathy, which, in normal children, provides a direct access to the feelings of others. On the positive side, autistic children comply with requests which are appropriate to their mental development and are no more negativistic than MA-matched normal children.

Executive Function   Autistic children's pathological need for sameness has been almost totally neglected as far as objective studies are concerned. Such studies typically go under the heading of *executive functioning*. Using a group of 12-year-old autistic children, Ozonoff, Pennington, and Rogers (1991) defined executive functioning in terms of planning ability and flexibility of thought, among other qualities. They measured *planning ability* by the Tower of Hanoi task in which a tower must be built on the first peg by transferring graduated disks from two other pegs without putting a larger disk on top of a smaller one. *Flexibility* was measured by first having the children learn one code for sorting cards and then shifting the code. The investigators found that not only were the autistic children inferior to a matched clinical control group, but their deficiency was more pronounced than in the areas of theory of mind and emotional perception. Such striking findings should encourage more studies of this important characteristic.

COMMENTS ON RESEARCH

Now that we have presented a number of studies of autistic children, let us return to the general issue of research on this population. As we have seen, the finding that a majority of them were retarded forced the inclusion of a control group of nonautistic retarded children. Other studies have added a language-impaired group to control for the factor of noncommunicative speech. Yet a number of problems remain.

To begin with, when one studies any severely disturbed group of children, securing their interest and cooperation is a challenge. This challenge is particularly daunting with severely disturbed autistic children because of their basic difficulty in relating to others. Consequently, the *reliability* of the obtained data is always a concern. For example, Perner and colleagues (1989), in their study of communication described above, found upon retesting the children in a comparable setup, that only three of the eleven children who gave the correct response the first time gave it on retest, while seven of the thirteen who gave an incorrect response initially gave a correct one. Low reliability, in turn, goes hand in hand with low *replicability*. For example, Prior, Dahlstrom and Tracie-Lee (1990) could not replicate either the findings concerning understanding expressions of affect or those involving false belief, leading them to conclude that the deficits were not autism-specific but a result of retardation. Thus, the nature of autism itself introduces an element of tentativeness to research findings.

Next, discrepant findings result when autism is viewed in an all-or-none manner, that is, as a disturbance which a child either does or does not have. In reality, autism has its own developmental dimensions (Rogers and Pennington, 1991). Its manifestations are modified by chronological age and mental age, as well as by the severity of the disturbance itself. Thus, contradictory findings may be due to the fact that the populations differed significantly, say, in severity of disturbance, even though both were correctly diagnosed. The conclusion that all autistic children were deficient in categorizing objects, for example, was based on low-functioning children. Subsequent research on higher-functioning ones showed

that no such deficiency existed (Tager-Flusberg, 1989). Or again, the attachment behaviors found by Rogers, Ozonoff, and Maslin-Cole (1991) were not observed by Wenar et al. (1986) in a special subgroup of severely autistic children. Thus, results might appear inconsistent, when, in reality, the autistic populations involved differed in their stage of development and in the degree of disturbance.

In sum, discrepant findings from different studies may be due to the unreliability of the data or the failure to take into account the degree of disturbance. Fortunately, these problems can be reduced by the recent development of a number of reliable assessment instruments which can provide objective data concerning the comparability of populations across different studies (See Volkmar and Cohen, 1988).

One final comment: As we have stated, we are particularly interested in attempts to *integrate* rather than merely to list research findings. While such attempts are being made in regard to autism (see, for example, Dawson, 1991), they are highly speculative and would take us too far afield. There is also a debate over whether the basic deficit in autism is affective or cognitive and an attempt to explain research findings in terms of one or the other. (Wicks-Nelson and Israel, 1991, summarize this controversy.) This search to find the single key to unlock the mystery of autism seems misguided. In normal development one would never maintain that attachment, exploration, and communication were all due to the operation of a single psychological variable. In a pervasive disturbance like autism the single variable approach seems equally unlikely.

THE DEVELOPMENTAL MODEL

A number of models of deviant development are needed to account for the research findings. First there is *fixation*; for example, the imitation of the autistic child is like that of a 1- to 4-month-old infant. Then there is *developmental delay* or a significantly slow rate of development seen in the finding that autistic children have the same repertiore of play activities as normal controls but concentrate on the less advanced kinds of play. Then there are two new models. In the *qualitatively different* model, typical autistic behavior has little or no counterpart in normal development, such as the obliviousness to the caretaker, minimal affective responsiveness, and disinterest in exploration seen in severely disturbed children. Then there is *asynchrony* marked by a disjointed progression among components of a particular variable; for example, while the interpersonal gaze develops normally, it is only weakly associated with its usual communicative and affective elements. Or again, affective blunting robs self-recognition and joint attention behavior of their positive emotional charge.

One final point which concerns the use of mentally retarded children as a control group. When autistic children perform at the same level as comparably retarded children, the usual assumption is that we are dealing with a developmental delay or a fixation. This assumption is warranted, however, only if mental retardation itself can be conceptualized as "normal development in slow motion." As we shall see in Chapter 12, this assumption may or may not be warranted, introducing a certain element of ambiguity as to the proper developmental model.

INTERPERSONAL HYPOTHESES

Many hypotheses in this area concern the mother who, for a variety of reasons, cannot provide the infant with warm, sensitive care (Miller, 1974). She may be cold, obsessive, and intellectual, or she herself may be disturbed—psychotic, depressed, or immature.

On the whole, the hypothesis of mother-engendered autism has not fared well when evaluated by objective studies because such mothers are not significantly different in their personality characteristics and attitudes toward their children from mothers of children with handicaps other than autism (McAdoo and DeMyer, 1978). One consequence of the decline in popularity of the theory of interpersonal relations as a cause of autism is that parents in general and mothers in particular no longer have to blame themselves for their children's psychopathology. Caring for an autistic child is difficult enough without the additional weight of undeserved guilt.

ORGANIC HYPOTHESES

"If we deliberately set out to make a healthy infant autistic, we would not know how to do it." This statement by a psychoanalyst who devoted his professional life to studying and helping autistic children is his way of saying that the origins of autism do not lie in the interpersonal context. Brutally abuse or neglect infants and they will become disturbed but not autistic. Therefore we must shift our focus to the organic context, where the challenge becomes that of finding the connection between the manifestations of autism and organic variables.

In general, while many abnormalities have been found, none is specific to autism; the bridge from the organic to the behavioral abnormality remains to be built (Rutter and Garmezy, 1983). And, while the technological advances in physiological and biochemical research are impressive, such advances prove nothing if the basic requirements of a well-designed study have not been met. Specifically, the autistic population must be well defined and clearly differentiated from other disturbed populations, the factor of mental retardation must be controlled for, the reliability of the assessment instrument must be well established, and normative developmental data should be available. Because a number of studies of organic etiology have not been sufficiently rigorous, results are equivocal or fail to be replicated.

There is one other obstacle, this time in the intrapersonal context. It would be easier to know what to look for in the organic context if one knew exactly what the *basic* defects were in autism. At present, this is just what we do not know. Certain deviations, such as pragmatic speech, probably are not basic but are a consequence of a general difficulty with social relations. But what other aspects of autism can be accounted for by other, more basic processes which have gone awry? Is the autistic child's deficiency in imitation basic or the result of social imperviousness? Or is this imperviousness itself the result of some more basic cognitive or affective deviation? These questions remain to be answered.

Genetic Factors

Both familial and twin studies indicate that genetic factors play an important role in the etiology of autism. In regard to the former, many more families than would be expected by chance have two autistic offspring, while, in regard to the latter, concordance for autism is higher in identical than in fraternal twins (Ritvo et al., 1985). Among genetic anomalies, the fragile X chromosome may be a contributing factor in 5 to 16 percent of the cases (Gillberg, 1988), although the data vary a good deal (Folstein and Rutter, 1988). What remains to be determined is exactly what aspects of autism are inherited and the mechanisms by which the genetic material is translated into autistic behavior.

Neurological Factors

Autopsies on autistic children have found either no neuropathology or no consistent pattern of neuropathology in the brains of autistic children. The most sophisticated computer-assisted tomography (CT scan), which uses computer-controlled x-rays to produce views of successive layers of brain tissue, indicate abnormalities in the cerebellum and major brain tissue damage (Gillberg, 1988). However, the findings are preliminary and the neural circuitries that need to be dysfunctional for autism to occur have not been identified. While there is also an increased incidence of abnormal EEGs in autistic children, the significance of this finding for autistic behavior again has not been established (Schreibman and Charlop, 1989).

Impairment of *cerebral lateralization* has recently come into prominence as an etiologic explanation because of the interest in hemispheric specialization. The left hemisphere deals with verbal material while the right hemisphere deals with spatial and other nonverbal material. Because autistic children have a language deficit while their spatial abilities are less impaired, it was logical to hypothesize a left-hemisphere defect. After reviewing the evidence, Fein et al. (1984) concluded that not only is the left-hemisphere hypothesis inadequate to account for many of the cardinal features of autism, but also the heterogeneity in form and severity of major autistic symptoms reflects a corresponding heterogeneity in the timing, locus, and severity of central nervous system insult. While left-hemisphere deficits may contribute to specific language problems in individual cases, such deficits should not be regarded as the key that unlocks the etiologic mystery of autism.

Neurochemical Factors

Recently interest has shifted to neurochemical factors, particularly the cerebral neurotransmitter serotonin. This is one of the "chemical messengers" responsible for communication among nerve cells. In normal development there is a decline in serotonin levels, whereas a subgroup of autistic children fail to show this decline. The finding has been interpreted as indicating the relative immaturity of the neurological system. It also is relevant only for a subgroup of autistic children rather than to the group as a whole (Schreibman and Charlop, 1989).

Pregnancy and Birth

Perinatal *brain injury* has been implicated in autism; for example, neonatal convulsions and other biological hazards carrying the risk of brain damage differentiate autistic children from their nonautistic twins, and unfavorable perinatal factors have been found more frequently in autistic children than in their siblings or in controls. However, no single event or combination of events can account for many cases of autism, nor is there an explanation for why autism should develop rather than, say, mental retardation or cerebral palsy, which also may be due to the same prenatal hazards. Also, in one of the few studies using matched mentally retarded children instead of normal children as controls, Levy, Zoltak, and Saelens (1988) found that the autistic children had fewer obstetrical complications.

TREATMENT

The prognostic picture for autism is only slightly altered by psychotherapy. However, significant improvements are possible even though heroic efforts are required to achieve them, progress is slow and fragile, and gains are easily lost. Even the majority of behaviorally oriented therapists, who have been most vigorous and versatile in their remedial efforts—reporting successes in the areas of teaching language, increasing appropriate self-help and social behavior, and decreasing inappropriate behaviors such as self-mutilation and tantrums—write primarily in terms

of improving the level of functioning rather than of "curing" autism in the sense of producing a child whose behavior falls within the normal range.

The usual way of presenting therapy with autistic children is to discuss and compare specific kinds of treatment, such as psychotherapy, behavior therapy, or medication. By contrast, Rutter (1985) maps out an integrated goal-directed approach based on what has been learned about autism and then locates specific treatments within this overall model. His approach has the obvious advantages of being comprehensive and empirically based. Rutter's approach also assumes that, just as there is no one etiologic key to understanding such a pervasive disturbance as autism, there is no one kind of therapy that should be regarded as a treatment of choice.

For overall goals of therapy, Rutter (1985) lists (1) fostering normal cognitive, language, and social development, (2) promoting learning, (3) reducing rigidity and stereotypes, (4) eliminating nonspecific maladaptive behaviors such as tantrums and self-injury, and (5) alleviating family distress. Because of its relevance to our presentation of the basic deficiencies in autism, the first goal will be discussed in greatest detail.

In promoting *language* development, Rutter (1985) emphasizes the social, communicative aspects as well as the purely linguistic components of speech. (See Table 4.5.) In regard to the former, he recommends that parents have a half-hour period each day of uninterrupted play and conversation with their autistic child, when any and all kinds of communication are encouraged, not just speech per se. The goal is to enhance the social usage of language. Direct teaching must be geared to the child's developmental level because there are important individual differences among autistic children.

Although not specifically mentioned by Rutter, one of the most impressive language training programs has been conducted by Lo-

TABLE 4.5
Aim: Promotion of Language Development

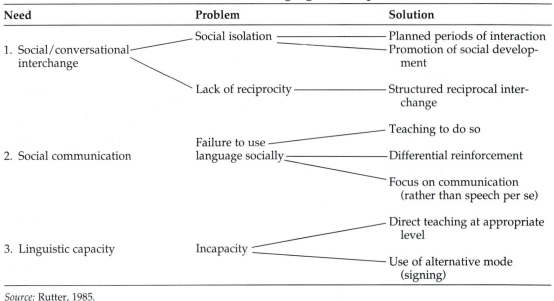

Need	Problem	Solution
1. Social/conversational interchange	Social isolation	Planned periods of interaction Promotion of social development
	Lack of reciprocity	Structured reciprocal interchange
2. Social communication	Failure to use language socially	Teaching to do so Differential reinforcement Focus on communication (rather than speech per se)
3. Linguistic capacity	Incapacity	Direct teaching at appropriate level Use of alternative mode (signing)

Source: Rutter, 1985.

vaas (1977), who uses an operant conditioning model. In children with deficits in observational learning, imitation must be taught through reinforcements. When this is accomplished, the therapist may begin uttering sounds for the child to copy. After being rewarded for vocalizations, the child is reinforced for closer and closer approximations of the therapist's verbal stimuli. Next, through the therapist's modeling and reinforcing of words and phrases, the child gradually acquires a repertoire of language. The meaningful use of language is accomplished by two of Lovaas's programs. In *expressive discrimination* the child is reinforced for making a verbal response to an object, such as correctly labeling a cup when it is presented. In *receptive discrimination* the stimulus is verbal and response nonverbal, such as correctly responding to "Give me the cup." Sequences are carefully graded so that new ones are based on mastered material. Ideally, language itself becomes self-rewarding and external reinforcers and prompts are eliminated. (Newsom and Rincover (1989) discuss behavioral treatment in detail.) As often happens, impressive initial reports of improvement led to overoptimism that subsequently had to be tempered. As has been noted, regardless of technique, improvement is painfully slow and fragile.

Other remedial programs, such as TEACCH, are based more on the principles of normal language development than is the behavioral approach. (For a detailed account, see Watson et al., 1989.) TEACCH views remediation within the context of the many factors that impede language development in autistic children: the impaired social relations, the odd and repetitious involvement in objects which limits the basis for communication, the failure to generalize from one situation to another, the use of nonverbal rather than verbal demands to get another person to do something, along with the language-specific impediments. The motivational, social, and pragmatic aspects of language receive as much attention as developing specific linguistic skills.

Because autistic children vary widely in their language ability, TEACCH requires a detailed assessment of each child. It also involves setting specific goals that are congruent with the child's present level of functioning and that are realistic in terms of what is known about autistic children's openness to learning. The remedial program itself includes a number of teaching strategies and activities. The motivational aspect of teaching is handled by making language relevant to the children's own interests and showing them that words are powerful means for getting people to act in a desired way; for example, "ride" is taught not as a label to a picture, recognition of which is rewarded with candy, but as a means of obtaining a favored tricycle. While teaching begins in a highly structured situation, every effort is made to transfer what is learned to the children's everyday environment. For example, the child who has learned the request "open" is presented with many objects, such as locked closets and peanut butter jars, which require him or her to use this command. Comprehension is aided by teachers simplifying their language and supplementing it with gestures. And, as is done in the case of normal children, language is integrated into ongoing activities and is supported by as many contextual cues as possible, rather than being taught as an isolated skill.

Although the behavioral and linguistic approaches seem quite different, they have a good deal in common. The linguistic approach uses contingent reinforcement because this is the most effective means of altering the behavior of severely autistic children, while the behavioral approach has become increasingly concerned with the pragmatics of language as shown by Lovaas's (1977) advanced training in expressive and receptive discrimination. In fact, this is only one example of the many instances in which therapeutic approaches that seem different turn out to have a number of common features.

In regard to promoting language, all studies reveal striking individual differences in outcome, the most positive results being achieved when there is evidence of some limited language skills, such as understanding speech or speechlike babbling and echoing of words, before treatment begins. For the mute autistic child, lacking in prelinguistic and linguistic skills, speech training is ineffective (Rutter, 1985).

With regard to *social* development, autistic children need both intensive personal interaction and facilitation of social cognitive capacity. Rutter (1985) recommends deliberate intrusion on the children's solitary pursuits with activities that are pleasurable, individualized, and structured so that they can readily become reciprocal. Ruttenberg (1971), using a psychodynamic framework, describes a therapeutic program whose primary goal is that of establishing a close relationship to a single caretaker. These child-care workers have a high degree of "motherliness," that is, they give the children sensitive attention and care and comfort them, but also participate in and facilitate reciprocal and constructive play beginning with patty cake and finger play and advancing to assembling puzzles and coloring. The program does not include promoting social cognition, for example, through direct teaching of social skills, but even Rutter (1985) acknowledges that little is known about this aspect of helping autistic children.

Reducing rigidity and stereotypy may be accomplished through a series of small steps, each of which is acceptable to the child. Stereotyped behaviors may also be reduced by introduction of activities that are incompatible or compete with them. Because there is evidence that stereotyped behaviors are maximized in barren, bleak environments, it is important that the child be provided with toys and activities. Too frequently a vicious cycle is set up whereby the unresponsiveness or peculiarities of autistic behavior discourage adults from interaction; this lack of interaction, in turn, increases the undesirable behavior.

Rutter's (1985) advice concerning *pharmacological interventions* is particularly important because such interventions are regarded as facilitators of a general therapeutic program rather than as a "cure" for autism. He states that while no drug is specific to autism, some drugs may be useful for controlling particular behaviors; for example, tranquilizers may reduce agitation and tension. Fenfluramine, a drug that lowers blood serotonin, was originally thought to be an effective treatment for autism, but subsequent studies showed it was only effective in reducing certain types of behaviors in some individuals. Currently, the safest and most effective drug is haloperidol, a dopamine receptor-blocker that decreases the level of a number of autistic symptoms. (See Gadow, 1992, for a review of the psychopharmacotherapy literature.)

Alleviating family distress has two components. The first is helping parents cope with feelings of guilt and anger, as well as with the burden of having to care for a child who often is unresponsive and unrewarding to be with. It is just as important for parents to understand what they can do to be helpful as it is for them to understand the realistic limitations of help. The idea of parents becoming cotherapists is gaining in popularity. Behavioral therapists, in particular, have advocated parental involvement not only to counteract parental feelings of helpless frustration, but also to extend the therapeutic program to the home setting, thereby maximizing chances of generalization to a number of naturalistic settings.

Unlike Rutter, whose comprehensive program involves a variety of treatment approaches, therapists are prone to search for a treatment of choice. Currently, behavioral techniques occupy that position because of their objective documentation of progress. Other psychotherapies too often rely on therapists' narrative accounts of success which are subject to biases and methodological flaws.

A Comprehensive Behavioral Program

Unlike therapies that target specific behaviors, Lovaas's treatment (Lovaas, 1987; Lovaas and Smith, 1988) provided a comprehensive behavioral program in a total therapeutic environment. His subjects were nineteen autistic children between 40 and 46 months of age, nine of whom were in the average to moderately retarded range of intelligence, the rest being severely retarded. The subjects were matched for diagnosis, age, and intelligence with forty control subjects who received either less intensive or no treatment.

The basis of treatment was reinforcement (operant) theory. Each subject was assigned well-trained student therapists who worked in the subject's home, school, and community for an average of forty hours per week for two or more years. Extensively trained parents also implemented treatment procedures, so treatment could take place during all the subjects' waking hours year around. Various behaviors were targeted, and separate programs were designed for them. For example, high rates of aggression and self-stimulation behaviors were reduced by being ignored, by the use of time out, by shaping of alternative, socially acceptable forms of behavior, and, as a last resort, by a loud "No!" or a slap on the thigh.

The results were impressive. When the treated subjects began school, 47 percent successfully passed the first grade in a regular class and obtained average or above average scores on IQ tests, as compared with 2 percent of the control group; 42 percent passed a special class for aphasics and were mildly retarded, as compared with 45 percent of the control group; while only 10 percent were placed in classes for autistic and retarded children and scored in the profoundly retarded range on the IQ test, as compared with 53 percent of the control group. In a follow-up study when the children were 13 years of age, eight of the nineteen were indistinguishable from a comparison group of nondisturbed children in measures of intelligence, personality, and adaptive functioning (Lovaas, Smith, and McEachin, 1989). (For a critical evaluation of Lovaas's study see Schopler, Short, and Mesibov, 1989, and for his defense, see Lovaas, Smith, and McEachin, 1989).

Whether Lovaas's program would be equally successful with older autistic children is not known since there is evidence that preschoolers make significantly more progress than children in middle childhood when a variety of therapeutic techniques are used (Wenar and Ruttenberg, 1976). Regardless of the issue of general applicability, the fact that almost half of the younger autistic children achieved normal functioning is heartening indeed. However, there is a question regarding the role of Lovaas's behavioral technique in effecting the change. One of the few studies to compare therapeutic approaches using a standardized instrument and objective observers was done by Wenar and Ruttenberg (1976), who found that treatment was better than custodial care but that no one type of treatment had an advantage if it was sensitively and expertly implemented. This generalization applied to psychoanalytically oriented psychotherapy, behavior modification, educational therapy, and activity therapy. Thus, the specific therapeutic technique used may not be as important as how well and how extensively it is used. (For a single case study, see Kaufmann and Kaufman, 1976, the story of parents who devoted their lives to helping their autistic son

initially by imitating his behaviors rather than using reinforcement.)

Obstacles to Progress

The obstacles to therapeutic progress in severely disturbed autistic children are formidable. Most psychotherapies require at least a minimum of cooperation, while therapeutic progress necessitates change. Yet the very nature of their psychopathology renders autistic children impervious or resistant to responding to the therapist, while causing them to react to any variation in the status quo with panic and rage. In addition, the concreteness of autistic children's thinking results in their learning only what they are specifically taught. They do not *generalize* readily, nor do they *grasp rules*. Teach an autistic boy that a block may be yellow or blue, and you may have to continue teaching him that it can also be red or green or black or white. The idea that a block can be any color comes slowly. To make the point in a different way: in treating less disturbed children, the therapist can be reasonably sure that the progress such children make during the session will generalize to home or school; with the autistic child such a transfer is far less likely to happen. To compound the problem, there is evidence that what the child learns does not really become part of the self but has to be constantly maintained by environmental stimulation and rewards. In technical terms, the child does not *internalize* advances the way a less disturbed child does.

One of the greatest impediments to therapy is the autistic child's lack of *initiative*. In charting the progress of a large number of autistic children, there is evidence of a predictable sequence: imperviousness and resistance followed by acceptance until the children finally begin to do things on their own. This sequence applies to their relationship to significant adults, their exploration of physical objects, and their learning of social skills (Ruttenberg et al., 1978). It is often the shift from recipient to agent, from willingness to be taught to wanting to learn, that marks a crucial turning point in therapy and that is so difficult to achieve. Lovaas (1977), for example, after citing impressive evidence that mute autistic children can be taught to speak in simple sentences, goes on to state that a major stumbling block is their lack of motivation to practice on their own—so unlike normal toddlers, who are infatuated with talking and practicing not only with others but also by themselves.

Such obstacles not only help us understand the slow progress of autistic children but also sensitize us to the importance of generaliza-

tion, grasping rules, internalization, and initiative to normal development, all of which happen so naturally that we tend to take them for granted. Thus psychopathology can illuminate normal development as well as the other way around.

While we have now finished our presentation of autism, this is not the last time we will be discussing a massively crippling psychopathology. Schizophrenia is just such a disturbance and the comparison between it and autism will be illuminating. However, since it is not anchored in any one particular developmental period, we must postpone our presentation so we can continue to the toddler period and its psychopathologies.

CHAPTER 5

DEVIATIONS IN INITIATIVE AND EARLY SOCIALIZATION

The toddler and preschool period is a time of increased expansiveness on the child's part and increased restrictions on the part of the socializing adults. It is natural that these two should go hand in hand: toddlers who are now physically able to explore vast new regions of the environment inadvertently damage valued household items and personal possessions, leave chaos in their wake, and occasionally endanger themselves. Unfettered initiative must be limited by "No" and "Don't." Socializing parents want to teach their toddlers control of unacceptable behavior, while the enterprising toddlers brazenly assert their autonomy. The ensuing battles are fought over the issue, Who is going to control whom? If all goes well, the toddlers will emerge as socialized preschoolers who can both control themselves and be assured of their autonomy. In short, they are both self-controlled and self-reliant.

In this chapter we will discuss certain pathological deviations from this normal development. The healthy need for self-assertion evidenced in *negativism* can be carried to an extreme of *oppositional-defiant behavior*, which disrupts relations with caretaking adults, while blocking the child's own growth.

While the requirements for self-control affect many aspects of the toddler's life, they are keenly felt when they intrude upon bodily functions. The young child lives close to his or her body, eating and elimination holding special pleasures and special fascinations. The socializing parents' demands can, therefore, trigger some of the most intense conflicts of early childhood. Such disturbances are sometimes referred to as habit disorders. We shall discuss three such disturbances—*feeding disorders, obesity,* and *enuresis.*

OPPOSITIONAL-DEFIANT DISORDER

Oppositional behavior, which also has been called negativism and noncompliance, is intentional noncompliance with adult requests, directives, and prohibitions (Wenar, 1982; for a review of oppositional behavior, see Gard and Berry, 1986). The element of intentionality is essential because a child may not comply for reasons other than opposing authority, such as being absorbed in a game; therefore noncompliance is too broad a term to epitomize this behavior. Oppositional behavior and negativism are synonymous terms, the latter being found in the older, classical writings on the topic. In the following presentation, the term *negativism* will be used when dealing with normal behavior, *oppositional,* or *oppositional-defiant behavior* when dealing with a clinical entity.

Schachar and Wachsmuth's (1991) study of 7- to 11-year-old boys shows that the distinction is a valid one. They found that, in many ways, boys with an oppositional-defiant disorder differed from normal boys; they had more problems with peer and sibling relations and came from families in which there was a greater amount of paternal psychopathology, marital fighting, and general family dysfunction.

Oppositional-defiant behavior can range from focal opposition expressed in a single symptom to a generalized oppositional character disorder. It also spans the developmental periods from toddlerhood through adolescence. Levy (1955), for example, writes about therapy with oppositional 2-year-olds, while other clinicians describe it in middle childhood and especially in adolescence.

According to the DSM-IV Draft Criteria, its manifestations involve outbursts of temper; arguing; defying and deliberately annoying others; blaming others for their own mistakes; being touchy, angry, and spiteful (see Table 5.1). However, unlike conduct disorders, there are no violations of the basic rights of others or of major societal norms and rules, such as persistent lying, aggressiveness, and theft. While its exact prevalence is not known, oppositional-defiant behavior is one of the most frequently reported problems of children referred to the clinic.

In regard to *comorbidity* oppositional-defiant disorder can be accompanied by other psychopathologies, particularly aggressive, antisocial conduct disorders, but learning disabilities and mental retardation may be present as well. In fact, Schachar and Wachsmuth (1991) found so much overlap between boys with oppositional-defiant disorders (ODD) and conduct disorders (CD) that they recommended regarding the former as a variation of the latter rather than as an independent psychopathology.

Our preference is for keeping the diagnoses separate for a number of reasons. While difficult, it is possible to find ODD children who do not also have CD (Schachar and Wachsmuth, 1991). The fact that ODD children do not violate the basic rights of others or major societal norms, and Schachar and Wachsmuth's finding that ODD children, unlike CD children, have an affectional bond with others, define two variables that are sufficiently important to justify the continued differentiation of the groups. Third, autonomy plays a central

Oppositional-defiant behavior.

role in accounting for negativism and oppositional-defiant behavior, while it is rarely mentioned in discussions of CD. Since the same behaviors can have different meanings in terms of motivations, cognition, past experience, and so on, behavioral overlap between groups cannot be regarded as the ultimate criterion for deciding whether they are similar or not. The most important consideration is that oppositional-defiant behavior has not generated the kind of intensive empirical scrutiny that would allow for a judicious decision regarding its independent status.

Developmental Pathway

Infancy, Toddler, and Preschooler Period Much of the information concerning the *intrapersonal context* during this early period comes from clinical observations (see Wenar, 1982).

The precursors of negativism in normal development can be seen in the first few months of life when infants resist being fed before they are ready by clamping their jaws and lips together. Similar resistance to being weaned to a cup and, later, to being spoon-fed have humorously been called the "battle of the cup" and the "battle of the spoon." Negativism flourishes in the toddler period, which is aptly described as the "terrible twos." Even at this tender age, toddlers show great versatility in their techniques, according to Levy (1955). Some are manifestly willful. "I *should* move my bowels, but I *won't*," as one toddler put it; or, from the exasperated mother's viewpoint, "I can't talk him out of anything; no matter what I do, he persists in having his own way." But direct confrontations can be alloyed with passive maneuvers; food refusals can become pickiness or dawdling. Finally, there are purely passive techniques, such as mutism or

TABLE 5.1
DSM-IV Draft Criteria for Oppositional-Defiant Disorder

A. A pattern of negativistic, hostile, and defiant behavior lasting at least six months, during which at least four of the following are present:

- Often loses temper
- Often argues with adults
- Often actively defies or refuses to comply with adults' requests or rules
- Often deliberately does things that annoy other people
- Often blames others for his or her mistakes or misbehavior
- Is often touchy or easily annoyed by others
- Is often angry and resentful
- Is often spiteful or vindictive

B. The disturbance in behavior causes significant impairment in social, academic, or occupational functioning.

Source: American Psychiatric Association, 1993.

pretending not to hear or to understand parental directions.

In their objective longitudinal study of toddlers and preschoolers, Kuczynski and Kochanska (1990) conceptualize negativistic behavior as a social strategy. Direct defiance is the least skillful strategy because of its openness and aversiveness to parents. Passive noncompliance is also considered unskillful but not so aversive to parents. Simple refusal is an intermediate category in terms of skill because it is direct but not aversive. Negotiation, which attempts to persuade parents to modify their demands, is relatively indirect and nonaversive, so it is the most skillful. The investigators found that direct defiance and passive noncompliance decreased with age, while simple refusal and negotiation increased, reflecting a more active and adroit way of expressing resistance to parental requests (see Table 5.2). Of particularly interest to us is the finding that only the least skillful forms of resistance were predictive of externalizing problem behaviors at 5 years of age.

In the *interpersonal context* research has primarily been concerned with the parent-child relationship, which has been viewed in three different ways. The first describes *global* characteristics of parents and of the interaction. Mothers of oppositional children have been described clinically as overcontrolling and aggressive, while fathers have been described as passive, peripheral, and distant. Objective studies show that these mothers are more negative toward and more critical of their children than are mothers of normal children and that they engage in more threatening, angry, and nagging behaviors. Both parents give their children significantly more commands and instructions while not allowing enough time for the child to comply. (See Gard and Berry, 1986, for a summary of the research.)

Social-learning theorists believe it is more fruitful to examine *specific conditions* that elicit and maintain noncompliant behavior than to deal with general characteristics of parents and interactions. An example of this approach is the work of Forehand (1977) and his colleagues. They found that noncompliant behavior is maintained by parental attention, which serves as a reinforcer even though such attention often takes the form of anger and punitiveness. In addition, they discovered the types of parental commands which are apt to elicit noncompliance. The so-called alpha commands are specific and clear. They include commands that have a clearly designated, explicitly stated objective, questions that involve a motoric response, and instructions to stop an ongoing behavior or not to begin a behavior that is about to take place. The so-called beta commands are vague and interrupted. They are difficult or impossible to obey, either because of their ambiguity or because the parent issues a new command before the child has a chance to comply. Beta commands are more characteristic of parents of noncompliant children than are alpha commands.

Westerman (1990) regards the social-learning approach as too static, preferring to study

TABLE 5.2

Longitudinal Comparison of Children's Response to Maternal Control Attempts From Time 1 (Toddler Age) to Time 2 (Age 5)

Children's response	Time 1		Time 2	
	M	SD	M	SD
Compliance	.57	.12	.61	.12
Passive noncompliance	.37	.15	.16	.12
Direct defiance	.07	.08	.03	.05
Simple refusal	.07	.05	.16	.13
Negotiation	.07	.06	.21	.10

Source: Kuczynski and Kochanska, 1990.

the ongoing *process of interaction.* In his research he videotaped and subsequently analyzed the behavior of mothers and their 3- to 4¹/₂-year-old sons aged as they did various tasks. He found that mothers of the healthy group coordinated their behavior with that of their sons, becoming more specific in their directives when their children failed and less specific when they succeeded. By contrast, mother of compliance-problem children had less of this ability to regulate their directives according to their children's activities. Thus, the crucial variable was not so much the amount and kind of directives as the mother's sensitivity to ongoing behavior. One might infer that this sensitivity makes the difference between the child perceiving the mother as being "with" him or as imposing her directives upon him.

Middle Childhood and Adolescence   In *middle childhood,* school plays a special role in negativism, as would be expected from our developmental model. The toddler's "I won't" may become "I won't learn." Clinical observation suggests that if negativism is pushed to the extreme of oppositional-defiant behavior, the result may be underachievement and school failure. Often in such cases academic achievement is overly valued by parents, who set high standards for the child; school failure represents the child's revenge. Levy (1955) ob-

serves that such parents need not be coldly intellectual; they can be quite warm and child-centered. Note that now a social institution—the school—has become the arena for acting out problems originating in the home. However, it is also possible that certain teachers or methods of teaching or even pervasive school atmospheres may provoke negativism independent of the home situation.

Adolescence is another period of heightened negativism because, as in the toddler period, the issue of autonomy comes to the fore and negativism becomes part of the adolescent's angry reproach: "I'm not a baby anymore."

In adolescence, or even in middle childhood, the law becomes the coercive force and law enforcers become the coercive adults, especially for children of lower socioeconomic status. For those who are labeled juvenile delinquents, the court is now the arena for acting out oppositional encounters. However, because the law becomes the new opponent, this does not mean that the old ones fade away. A vivid picture of oppositional behavior from every developmental level is presented by D. C. Ross (1964) under the label of the "negatively organized child." A 15-year-old boy was brought to the clinic because he threatened to shoot his girlfriend's father after the father had forbidden her to see the boy. This was the climax of innumerable stormy oppositions to people in authority. At home no issue was too large or too small to become a battle of the wills—the tie he wore, the food he ate, the music he enjoyed, his disorderly clothes closet, his poor dental hygiene, his choice of friends and leisure-time activities. His parents relentlessly nagged, exhorted, pleaded, and scolded, which only succeeded in exasperating the boy. Despite superior intelligence, he was failing in school, probably in retaliation against his intellectually ambitious parents. Home life was unbearable, and he spent as little time at home as possible. Fortunately, he excelled in athletics and enjoyed working on a friend's farm, where he could do as he pleased. Aside from this, his response to most of the demands placed on him was a defiant "I won't."

Negativism and Oppositional-Defiant Disorder

Negativism is part of the normal development of the self-as-agent. Levy (1955) adds that it protects the child against submissiveness; for example, when he asked a negativistic boy, "What would happen if you gave in to your mother just once?" the boy replied that the mother would make him do everything her way and would never let him do anything on his own. Thus negativism can both enhance and protect the autonomy of the self.

While not originally aggressive, negativism can subsequently be used as a safer form of aggression than angry outbursts and direct attack either by children who are submissive and fearful or by children having to deal with strongly authoritarian adults. The passive forms of negativism, such as dawdling, pretending not to hear, mutism, and inattention, are favored by these children (Levy, 1955).

The literature lacks a full-dressed discussion of the difference between negativism and oppositional-defiant behavior. Levy (1955) distinguishes the two in terms of the excessiveness of the reaction—psychopathology is an *exaggeration* of normal behavior. Exaggera-

tion, in turn, consists of intensity, pervasiveness, and persistence. Equally important, such exaggeration tends to block future development. Thus Levy writes of the rigidity of personality and of the social isolation resulting from oppositional behavior, both of which cut the child off from growth-promoting experiences with socializing adults and peers. Forehand's research also implies that a quantitative difference in the ratio of alpha to beta commands helps tip the scale in favor of normality or psychopathology.

Note that the psychopathology as exaggeration is not the same as psychopathology as age-inappropriate behavior. While an oppositional-defiant disorder may be age-inappropriate (for example, when an 8-year-old "acts like a 2-year-old"), it is also found both in the toddler and adolescent period, where negativism is age-appropriate. Consequently, the clinical child psychologist's job of distinguishing normality from psychopathology in these two periods is a particularly difficult one.

Finally, there is evidence from Crockenberg and Litman's (1990) objective study that as early as 2 years of age, defiance and self-assertion are independent behaviors, the first involving the adult ("No, I won't!"), the second involving the self ("I'll do it my way"). Self-assertion is associated with competence, while defiance is not. We have also seen from Kuczynski and Kochanska's (1990) study that defiance is the most unskillful form of negativism, predicting subsequent externalizing problems. Such studies suggest that opposition may be not merely an exaggeration of normal negativism; within the general category of noncompliant behaviors, we can begin to distinguish those that are growth-promoting and those that place the child at risk for developing a behavior disorder.

Kuczynski and Kochanska (1990) also make a point concerning compliance which clinical child psychologists should note. Normatively, children's most frequent response to parental requests is compliance. If this were not so, socialization would not be possible. However, extremes of compliance are dangerous. A rigid and compulsive form of compliance develops among infants of abusive parents and, in their own study, overly compliant boys were perceived as having an increase in internalizing problems.

Treatment

Based on research findings, Haswell, Hock, and Wenar (1982) suggest the following techniques to prevent negativism from escalating into oppositional behavior. Because a rapid series of intrusive directives is the surest way to incite opposition, the caretaker should alert the toddler or preschooler that a transition is in the offing ("In a few minutes you will have to put your toys away"), wait until she has the child's attention or gently capture it before issuing a directive, and then give the child time to comply. In the face of noncompliance, a brief period of "time out" in which the parent does not attend to the child is better than continued pressure.

Predictably, psychodynamically oriented therapists prefer to explore the child's conscious and unconscious feelings toward family members, while atheoretical practitioners follow the commonsense advice of telling parents not to nag and coax, and to avoid being dictatorial, overprotective, overcorrecting and putting the child into a "give in or lose" situation (Bakwin and Bakwin, 1972).

In order to alter both the elicitors and reinforcers of oppositional behavior, Forehand (1977) taught parents to replace their vague, interrupted beta commands with specific alpha ones; to shift from punishing noncompliant behavior to rewarding compliance with praise, approval, and positive physical attention; and to employ a "time-out" procedure of isolating the child for a brief period after noncompliance. It is also helpful to teach parents the general principles of operant learning rather than providing them solely with techniques for handling specific problems. While the successes in the home do not generalize to the school, they do affect other behaviors within the home; for example, one girl who was reinforced for picking up her toys spontaneously began to keep her clothes tidy. Successful treatment also reduces other undesirable behaviors such as tantrums, aggression, and crying. Moreover, there is evidence that the compliance of untreated siblings undergoes the same positive change, since the mother alters her behavior to them as well (Humphreys et al., 1978). Finally, there is evidence that gains made in middle childhood are sustained in adolescence. (For details of Forehand's parent-training technique, see Forehand, 1990. For a review of studies of effectiveness, see McMahon and Wells, 1989.)

FEEDING DISORDERS

You know, I was 32 years old before it dawned on me that I didn't have to eat everything on my plate! I was alone in a restaurant, staring at a pile of turkey and dressing with gloppy brown gravy wondering how in heaven's name I was going to get all that food into my stomach. Then it hit me. This is just a lot of damned foolishness. I've been a good girl long enough. Now it's time to grow up.

On a more serious note, a young bachelor underwent psychoanalysis because of a number of fears, one being panic when eating out with a woman. He could tolerate business lunches but only felt really safe when cooking his meals and eating alone in his apartment. During therapy the following repressed material was uncovered:

My mother sat at the head of the table and served the family. (His father had died when he was 5 years old.) I remember that she would say to me, "Tell me when I've given you enough potatoes or peas," or something. But when I said, "That's fine," she would always take just a little more and plop it on my plate. It would make me furious, but I never could say anything to her.

He also reported the following dream:

Mother and I were sitting on a pier overlooking a marina of some sort and she was sewing. Suddenly, she put the needle through my eyelid and pulled it closed with the thread. I didn't dare move because that would tear my eyelid off. When I woke up I still felt terrified.

We will return to this young man's memory and his dream after discussing early feeding disorders.

As adults, most of us would not regard eating as the emotional high point of the day. It has its minor irritations and pleasures, which are quickly forgotten. Consequently, we tend to underestimate the significance of hunger and feeding in the life of the infant and toddler. We need the psychoanalysts to remind us of the importance of eating and of the interplay between somatic, psychic, and intimate interpersonal relations which it engenders. Physiological distress and relief from such distress are the most highly charged experiences of early infancy. The first ego, so the psychoanalysts maintain, is a body ego: the first dim notion of the self as good or bad depends on the ratio of bodily pleasures to bodily distress. Similarly, the first view of intimacy as pleasurable and trustworthy or noxious and untrustworthy depends on the sensitivity and reliability of relieving physiological distress and maximizing physiological pleasures.

The Infantile Period

Now let us focus specifically on eating, using Anna Freud's clinical observations (1965) as a guide to our conceptualization. One of the earliest conflicts between the infant and the socializing caretaker centers on feeding. In the 1920s and 1930s, C. M. Davis (1929, 1935) conducted a series of studies to determine what infants would do if given complete freedom to choose the kind and quantity of nourishment they wished. One-week-old infants could choose among four formulas and orange juice throughout the nursing period, while 6-month-olds were presented with a wide variety of foods for periods of six months to a year. The results were both enlightening and amusing. All the children were healthy and well-nourished at the end of the study, and there were no digestive disorders owing to the self-selection of food. However, there was a wide variation in the quantity eaten, including unpredictable food jags—three to four bananas at one meal, five to seven servings of potatoes, a full quart of milk in addition to a complete meal! Thus infants "naturally" have strong but shifting food preferences and vary widely in the amount needed to satisfy them at any given feeding. Such variability is a far cry from the adult caretaker's concern that the infant eat a given quantity of food and a balanced diet. The erratic nature of the infant's hunger also conflicts with the adult's need for regularity and intrudes on the adult's realistic commitments to activities other than feeding. A certain amount of disharmony between infant and caretaker is inevitable and, Anna Freud notes, normal. If the mother is reasonably sensitive and flexible and the infant reasonably tractable and resilient, they manage to accommodate one another.

But many things can go wrong. The mother may be insensitive, depressed, inconsistent, neglectful, burdened by realistic problems; temperamentally the infant may be erratic, hypersensitive to distress, or difficult to divert; or the infant may transmit behavioral signals that are weak, undifferentiated, and difficult to read. Consequently, infants are frequently in a high state of distress. Note that, at this stage, infants react directly to the mother as her behavior impinges upon them, since they have not yet evolved a mental representation that can be sustained in her absence. Note also that their reactions to distress are primitive—crying, vomiting, unmodulated rage, refusal to eat, apathetic withdrawal—since the more sophisticated defenses and socially attuned coping devices have yet to develop.

As for objective studies, Ainsworth and Bell (1969) found that feeding was the single most important caregiving activity determining the security or insecurity of the infant. Mothers who fed sensitively, who were aware of the infant's hunger signals and responded to them promptly and appropriately, tended to have secure infants; insensitive mothers who were oblivious to or ignored such signals, or responded capriciously and irregularly, tended to have insecure infants.

The Toddler and Preschool Period

Based on clinical observations, Kanner (1977) estimates that a quarter of all toddlers and preschoolers have feeding difficulties, typically not eating enough, eating too slowly, being picky eaters, or eating nutritionally undesirable foods from the mother's point of view. He believes the majority of problems are caused by parents who rigidly try to force the "correct diet" on the toddler or who are obsessively and coercively overprotective. Toddlers, in turn, may respond in a number of ways. At the most primitive level, they may gag and vomit or complain of stomachaches; at a more sophisticated level they may dawdle or become picky eaters; the more manipulative ones use eating to monopolize the parent's attention and dominate them, say, by insisting on certain foods prepared in a given way or by intentionally provoking and upsetting the parents.

Kanner's observation that toddlers will continue provocations on their own points to a significant advance over the infantile period. Not only are toddlers differentiated from the mother; they are also aware of her vulnerabilities and can intentionally set about to defy, subvert, and upset her. Such social sensitivity and intentional behavior is in striking contrast to the infant's primitive repertoire of reactions. The confrontation is still between caretaker and child; it is the technique for managing the confrontation which has changed.

However, the toddler has not developed to the point of internalizing the requirements of socialization so that the requirements become self-perpetuating, as in the case of the 32-year-old woman and the young bachelor, whose eating problems introduced our discussion. Let us take a second look at these vignettes in light of what we have learned.

In the first vignette, the mother's mandate, "Eat everything on your plate," created anxiety and guilt over disobedience so strong that the woman resisted critical evaluation of the mandate until adulthood. Yet the conflict between doing what she wanted or obeying her mother was readily available to the woman's consciousness, and the price paid for obedience was relatively minor.

The young man faced a more serious dilemma. His rage is understandable. On the one hand, the mother implicitly said, "You are the decision maker, I will do what you say," but then she added, "What you decide does not matter; the ultimate power is mine." He felt betrayed. But why did he not protest? For fear of losing the mother's love, symbolized, so the psychoanalysts would claim, by food. As his dream indicated, any attempt to break away from the mother's control would be self-destructive. There is both a binding and a blinding—he could not face the mother's subversive control, and he could not break away and become independent of her. The impasse continued into adulthood, where the demands for independence reactivated it and its attendant anxiety. We can also see that the young man's anxiety involved both kinds of eating problems we have discussed—the conflict over autonomy in the toddler period and the infantile equating of being fed with being cared for and protected against the terror of isolation and helplessness.

The two examples also teach us something about the developmental model of psychopathology. Eating disturbances may represent exaggerations of developmentally normal disharmonies between caretaker and child, as Anna Freud claims. The damage that eating disturbances cause may be undone by subsequent experience. Alternatively, they may persist but only cause minor discomforts, or they can serve as the nucleus of a crippling anxiety.

On the basis of objective studies, Birch (1990) views food preferences as the result of intrinsic physiological factors—such as hunger, satiety, and the positive or negative consequences of ingesting certain substances—and extrinsic, social factors typically those associated with the socializing parent. Social factors, particularly the affect generated by the social context of feeding, operate through classical conditioning, imitation, and the child's acquisition of information regarding acceptable and unacceptable food (see also Rozin, 1990). There is evidence that internal factors can be a serviceable guide to food intake; for example, toddlers eat more following low caloric intake than following high. However, Birch's own research (Birch et al., 1987) showed external factors are more potent by the preschool period. In this study, one group was allowed to eat snacks ad lib, while another was given extrinsic rewards such as a toy if they ate everything on their plate. Extrinsic rewards increased consumption significantly while they were in effect. However, when they were withdrawn, both the preference for and consumption of food declined below the level it was at before being rewarded. While admitting the preliminary nature of the evidence, Birch concludes that the imposition of rigid external controls can impede the development of adequate internal controls. This conclusion is significant for us because, as we shall see later, one of the factors involved in obesity and anorexia nervosa is a decreased responsiveness to internal cues concerning hunger and satiety.

Middle Childhood and Adolescence

In the realm of normal development, the Berkeley Growth Study (Macfarlane, Allen, and Honzik, 1954) uncovered two peak ages for food finickiness: between the first and sixth year of life, when 30 to 40 percent of the children evidenced the problem, and again around 12 years of age, when it was evidenced by approximately 20 percent of the children. In the early years, the finicky eaters came from disharmonious homes in which conflict and tensions between parents were high. However, it was not related to a variety of personality variables. In 12-year-old boys, by contrast, finicky eating was related to irritability, overdependence, attention demanding, temper tantrums, lying, and poor appetite; in girls, finicky eating was only related to insufficient appetite. The authors speculate that the 12-year-old boys were highly conflicted over their dependency on the mother, wanting very much to break away and assert their masculinity but not being sufficiently secure to do so. Consequently, they vacillated between clinging and angry rejection. At a more general level, the study indicates significant sex differences in intrapersonal variables and, more important, it suggests that the same behavior problem might have different meanings depending on the developmental status of the child.

In a prospective study of 800 children beginning when the children were 6 years old, Marchi and Cohen (1990) found that problems at mealtime in this early period lead to increased food avoidance in adolescence, that is, to avoidance of two or more of the common food groups. One can speculate that the coerciveness described by Birch and colleagues (1987), in which the child had to eat a nonpreferred food to get a reward, had the long-run effect of reducing the range and intake of consumed foods. As to more serious disturbances, the authors found that digestive problems and, to a lesser extent, pickiness in the early period were related to symptoms of anorexia nervosa in adolescence. Early digestive problems were also related to adolescent bulimia, along with pica (eating inedible substances such as sand, paint chips, and paper). (Both anorexia and bulimia will be discussed in Chapter 11.)

Costanzo and Woody (1985), in a retrospective study, found that female college students who worried about weight, who were guilty about eating, and who were self-restrained and guilt prone in general recalled having parents who were highly controlling and concerned about eating. The parents were achievement-oriented, the father and siblings dieted, eating occurred under conditions of negative arousal, and the parents used eating and weight as the basis of general approval or disapproval of the children.

The Developmental Model

While meager, the evidence nicely illustrates how the meaning of the same behavior—in this case, eating—changes with development. In infancy it is intimately connected with attachment; in the toddler period, with negativism; and in preadolescent males, with conflicts over dependency. By implication, the same behavior can represent different degrees of disturbance depending on its age appropriateness. A 12-year-old boy who is a problem eater because of a desire to become independent of the mother is less disturbed than one whose eating problem is due to the infantile fear of being helpless if the mother should leave him. The data also illustrate the change from being directly reactive to the environment to reacting to mental representations of events. The

infant and toddler develop feeding problems through direct interaction with the caretaker; the college student who is no longer living at home is able to represent interpersonal difficulties over food in memory and continues to be affected by such memories.

Finally, the consequences of feeding problems may be relatively benign, as in the case of restricted food preferences in adolescence, or serious, as in the case of the maladjustment in middle childhood or excessive dieting and bingeing in adolescence. The specific developmental model suggested by the data is either fixation or regression since problems at an earlier period either persist or are reactivated in a subsequent period.

OBESITY

Our understanding of obesity is neither as definitive nor as detailed as we might wish. Inconclusive research findings might be due to unresolved problems in assessing obesity (see Linscheid, Tarnowski, and Richmond, 1988) and to the complexity of obesity itself. While defined simplistically as an excess in weight, or more specifically as body weight greater than 20 percent of normal for height and weight, obesity varies in degree and chronicity. Thus a chronically and grossly obese child may be different in many respects from a child whose obesity is moderate and developing or remitting (Werry, 1986b). One difficulty in research on obese children, therefore, may be that generalizations are not warranted in light of the distinctions among the children themselves.

Prevalence

It is estimated that 5 to 10 percent of preschoolers are obese (Woolston and Forsyth, 1989). The prevalence rises to 9.2 percent in middle childhood and 14.8 percent in adolescence (Leon and Dinklage, 1989).

Obesity tends to persist rather than being "outgrown." The older the child, the stronger the relation to subsequent weight. Only 35 percent of obese 5-year-olds will be of normal weight at 15 years. Fully 80 percent of 10- to 13-year-olds become obese adults, while the odds are 28 to 1 that obese adolescents will become obese adults. Finally, there is evidence of a strong relation to socioeconomic status; 40 percent of lower SES children being obese, while only 25 percent of upper class children are. (For specific studies, see Foreyt and Goodrick, 1988.)

Risks

Obesity puts the child at risk for a number of physical and psychological difficulties, although the evidence for the latter is somewhat contradictory. Among the physical difficulties are orthopedic problems, hypertension, and cardiovascular disease (Foreyt and Goodrick, 1988). Obese children have also been described as having low self-esteem and poor self-image and as being depressed. There is some evidence that peers view obesity more negatively than physical handicaps, and it is reasonable to infer that ridicule and social isolation contribute significantly to the obese child's problems (Leon and Dinklage, 1983). One of the better studies of adjustment, in the sense that it used objective measurements, found that obese children had significantly more problems than children in the general population, but that such problems were not as severe as those of children being seen in a clinic for behavioral disorders (Israel and Shapiro, 1985).

However, findings concerning social stigma and psychological problems come almost exclusively from populations seeking medically supervised weight reduction. While there is evidence that children prefer a mesomorph (athletic) build and that this preference increases with age, there is no convincing evidence of a negative stereotype of an obese body build or of discrimination against obese children (Jarvie et al., 1983). There is also no evidence for a decrease in self-esteem in the population as a whole (Wadden et al., 1984).

Such contradictory research findings suggest that clinical child psychologists should avoid stereotyping obese children as having low self-esteem and a poor self-image because of social stigma. Such problems are most likely to be found in a special group of children who are sufficiently dissatisfied with their weight to seek professional help in reducing it.

Etiology

Obesity can be due to a number of factors. In the organic context, heredity accounts for around 10 percent of the variance in weight. It can also be caused by medical conditions such as hypothyroidism and Klinefelter's syndrome (Woolston and Forsyth, 1989). The set point theory, based on the observation that weight fluctuates within very small limits and that weight once lost is readily gained, postulates a kind of biological homeostasis regulating input and output to maintain a given individual at a given weight. Presumably, obese children have higher set points than nonobese ones (see Linscheid, Tarnowski, and Richmond, 1988).

At the interpersonal level, infantile obesity can be caused by mothers who overfeed as the result of misinformation or cultural practices or, more ominously, by traumatic separation from the primary caretaker or severe family disorganization in which the child's needs are ignored or misperceived (Woolston and Forsyth, 1989).

Social-learning theorists emphasize the crucial role obese parents play in reinforcing and serving as models of eating behavior. For example, Klesges, Malott, Boschee, and Weber's (1986) observational study of 30-month-olds during and after supper found that parental directives to eat were positively correlated to the percent of time spent eating and to the child's relative weight; directives to exercise were positively related to extremes of activity and negatively to relative weight.

Foreyt and Goodrick (1988), in their comprehensive model, discuss obesity as an imbalance whereby energy intake via eating exceeds energy output by exercise, documenting their formula with objective evidence. On the intake side, for example, there is little evidence for the common belief that obese children eat more or different foods than do their peers (Werry, 1986b). Nor do they differ in eating styles, such as "wolfing" their food down (Israel, Weinstein, and Prince, 1985). However, the authors cite evidence for increased inactivity and consequently decreased energy expenditure. Even when obese children engage in activities such as sports, they tend to be far less vigorous than their normal-weight peers.

Foreyt and Goodrick (1988) elaborate the many factors affecting both sides of the energy equation. Factors controlling eating behavior

are environmental ones, such as food availability at home, in the neighborhood, and school; family and peer eating behavior; and parental knowledge and attitudes regarding food. Intrapersonal factors, such as the child's knowledge of nutrition and perception of overeating and hunger, also affected intake. Environmental and intrapersonal factors also control exercise behavior: the availability of exercise facilities, adult models and family exercise patterns, and peer behavior; the child's attitudes toward and perceptions of exercise, and the reward value of active versus sedentary behavior. (The model is presented schematically in Figure 5.1.)

By contrast, Bruch (1973) developed her more limited etiological theory on the basis of clinical observations. To begin with, Bruch delineates two psychogenic causes. The first is reactive obesity, in which the child eats excessively after experiencing a trauma such as the death of a parent. Such cases are rare in childhood and typically represent an attempt to ward off depression. Next, there is develop-

FIGURE 5.1

A comprehensive model of childhood obesity. (Adapted from Foreyt and Goodrick, 1988.)

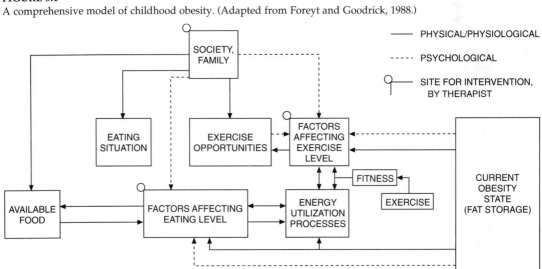

mental obesity, which is intimately linked with the child's personality. This category is of greater interest here.

Numerous specific problems are included within the category of developmental obesity. While Bruch does not do so, it is possible to order many of the problems developmentally. The symbolic meaning of food as love and autonomy in the infant and toddler period has already been discussed. In addition, food may symbolize the girl's wish to be a man and possess a penis, her wish to become pregnant, or her fear of pregnancy during the oedipal stage (if one holds to the psychosexual theory) or the preschooler's conflict over her sex-role identity (if one holds to the social-learning theory). Such problems may resurface in adolescence when eating may also serve as a substitute for sexual gratification and a way to avoid adult responsibilities. Other meanings of food seem to span the entire developmental age range: eating as an expression of rage and hatred or as a way of gaining a sense of power and self-aggrandizement.

If a variety of developmental conflicts underlie obesity, how do certain children "choose" to overeat rather than evidencing other kinds of deviant behaviors? Bruch (1973) feels that the choice is made much as we learn about the external environment—specifically, by feedback. The infant learns to differentiate a rattle from a string of beads partly because each responds differentially to exploratory behaviors such as shaking and mouthing. Analogously, the infant learns to differentiate inner drives and affects by the differential responses of the caretaker. The sensitive mother is constantly on the alert for specific cues from the infant. She learns to interpret his behavior: "That's his hungry cry," "She's just fussy and needs her nap," or "He's really mad." As she responds appropriately—now feeding, now soothing, now diverting—the infant comes to distinguish more clearly among inner states of arousal.

But suppose the mother interprets all distress as hunger. Perhaps she is overindulgent, perhaps she cannot tolerate negative affect, perhaps she is rejecting and pops a bottle into the baby's mouth in the hope that the infant will be quiet and quit bothering her. When verbal labeling enters the developmental picture, such mothers continue the pattern by responding to all signs of distress with, "Oh, he's just hungry." Consequently, the child will fail to differentiate inner states, so a variety of needs and affects are regarded as hunger. Instead of being angry or bored or frightened or sexually aroused, the child feels hungry and eats. The self is similarly impoverished. Instead of learning, "I am a person who has a rich variety of sensations, needs, and affects," the infant learns, "I am a person who is hungry."

Bruch claims there is a further complication. As the self is impoverished, initiative suffers. By imposing her interpretations and insisting on them, the mother robs the child of the desire to explore and experiment independently. Bruch cites the case of a 14-year-old whose mother went down on her knees to tie his shoes during the interview, answered all questions directed to him, and hovered anxiously over him. While such children may well learn techniques for tyrannizing their mothers or the entire family, they feel helpless in meeting the developmental demands outside the family circle. Characteristically, they are sedentary, avoiding self-assertive, competitive, and aggressive activities which require motoric involvement. In fact, physical inactivity seems as important as food intake in contributing to obesity. The father also contributes to the child's difficulties, at times being passively subservient to his wife, at times demanding that the child look and act and achieve in accordance with the father's own standards. Thus both parents in their own ways try to impose their own needs and images on the child.

In sum, a diffuse body- and self-awareness plus a crippled sense of effectiveness are the psychological conditions underlying developmental obesity.

In a general way, Bruch's conceptualizations are supported by objective studies; as we saw in our discussion of eating problems, all aspects of eating can be affected by interpersonal influences, while a certain subgroup of obese children have been found to have low self-esteem and a poor self-image. Yet Bruch's unique contributions in terms of maternal behavior and its consequences for the child remain in the realm of clinical observations.

Treatment

Because of the concern over fitness in our present-day society there is a plethora of diet and exercise programs available to the obese individual. Among psychological approaches, individual, family, and group therapies have been tried, behavior therapists being particularly ingenious in devising programs for children and parents. (See Linscheid, Tarnowski, and Richmond, 1988, for a detailed account of behavior therapies.) There is evidence that behavioral programs that include parent training are more effective than those centering only on the child (Israel, Stolmaker, and Andrian, 1985). Training sessions typically cover information about food intake and activity, cues which identify external and internal stimuli associated with overeating or inactivity, and the importance of rewarding desired behaviors. Homework is assigned for both parents and children which implements the specific suggestions presented in the sessions. (See also Foreyt and Goodrick, 1988, for a comprehensive treatment plan based on their etiological model described above.)

In summarizing treatment of childhood obesity, Israel (1990) concludes that multifaceted behavior programs—that is, ones involving both parent and child in the many aspects

of controlling food intake and increasing exercise—are the most effective. However, they do not produce weight loss in all children; in many cases, the amount of weight loss does not result in a nonobese status, and, most important, posttreatment levels often are not maintained over long periods of time. As everyone who has dieted knows, taking off weight is easy; the hard part is keeping it off.

ENURESIS

You are a clinical child psychologist visiting an Israeli kibbutz. The client is a 5-year-old boy who wets his bed at night. In Berkeley, California, where you practice, only 20 percent of children continue to wet their beds and at this age bed-wetting ceases to be part of normal development, becoming instead the psychopathology of enuresis. But you also know a number of other facts. While toilet training is benign and child-centered on the kibbutz, bed-wetting is twice as prevalent here as in Berkeley. Finally, the client, like other kibbutz children, is psychologically healthier than his Berkeley counterpart in that he rarely has tantrums or fears or eating and sleeping problems.

What do you decide? That the little fellow is generally coming along all right, that bed-wetting at his age is not all that deviant in the kibbutz, and that paying undue attention might prolong it? Or is bed-wetting one way 5-year-olds have of saying "Something's troubling me!" and indeed, at this age, is deviant behavior the only way 5-year-olds can send such a message? If so, you would want to investigate the situation further to find what has gone wrong.

Such decisions are never easy. Fortunately, you know one more fact that will help you decide. We will discuss it in time, but right now we will use the example to illustrate the child clinician's problem of shifting criteria of disturbance to fit different social contexts. As enuresis becomes more prevalent, does it lose its status as a symptom? Surely we would not say that of malnutrition, illiteracy, or gang violence, all of which are very prevalent in certain cultures and classes. But is bed-wetting as serious as those conditions? At what point do we say, "This is just the way these children are brought up," and at what point do we say, "This is deviant development"? The problem of distinguishing differences from deviations is central for clinicians who choose to work with inner-city African Americans or Native Americans or Chicanos, as well as those who go to foreign countries.

The Nature of Enuresis

There are several different ways of classifying enuresis. *Diurnal enuresis* refers to daytime wetting; children are considered enuretic if they wet beyond the age of 3 or 4. *Nocturnal enuresis* refers to nighttime bed-wetting and is typically diagnosed when children are 5 years of age. However, there is variability in the age criteria, some preferring to locate diurnal en-

uresis as late as 5 to 6 years, nocturnal enuresis as late as 6 to 7 years. Approximately twice as many boys as girls are bed-wetters. Nocturnal enuresis declines from about 20 percent of 5-year-olds to 5 percent of 12- to 14-year-olds. The percentages vary with varying definitions (Figure 5.2). The figures on diurnal enuresis are 3 percent of 6-year-olds and 1 percent of 7- to 17-year-olds. The spontaneous remission rate for untreated enuresis is about 15 percent each year, a figure which is important when evaluating whether treatment is more effective than no treatment. (For a detailed account of the research, see Fielding and Doleys, 1988, and Walker, Milling, and Bonner, 1988.)

Primary enuresis refers to the child who has never been trained to be dry at night; *secondary enuresis* refers to the child who relapses after a year or more of dryness. The two types represent two kinds of developmental deviation, one in which development fails to take place (fixation), and the other in which development

FIGURE 5.2
Nighttime dryness based on 859 children (adjusted for race, sex, and prematurity) by three criteria: (A) percent dry by age of first attaining dryness; (B) percent dry by age of finally attaining dryness without further relapse; and (C) percent dry at specific age. Vertical axis: percent. Horizontal axis: age in years. (*Source:* Oppel, Harper, and Rider, 1968.)

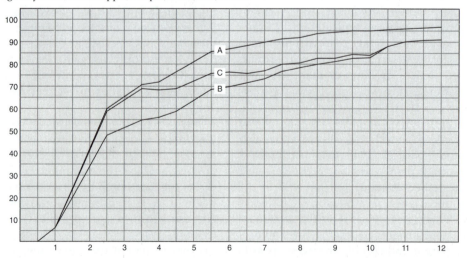

occurs but the child returns to a previous stage (regression).

Etiology

In the *organic context,* enuresis can be caused by a number of factors such as insufficiency of the sphincter muscle or chronic diseases such as diabetes mellitus. The incidence of urinary infection is elevated among children with nocturnal enuresis. Other organic hypotheses state that enuresis is caused by a delay in the development of the neuromuscular system, since achieving bladder control has a strong neural component, or by organic brain pathology, since some studies have found a higher incidence of EEG abnormalities. However, the evidence for both hypotheses has been contradictory or inconclusive. Enuresis has also been regarded as a sleep disorder presumably because children sleep too deeply to respond to the signals of a full bladder. However, the evidence is not confirmatory since enuresis occurs in light sleepers. Finally, the fact that enuresis runs in families suggests a genetic component, although the mechanism of transmission is not known.

Turning to the *superordinate context,* there is evidence that the incidence of enuresis varies from country to country and among racial and ethnic groups; in this country, it is more prevalent among lower socioeconomic groups. In the *interpersonal context,* there is no clear evidence supporting the idea that enuresis is related to strict or lax training methods or to the age training is begun. In the *intrapersonal context,* there is some evidence that the incidence of behavior problems increases among enuretic children, particularly among girls. However, the majority of children do not have additional problems, and for those who do, it is impossible to determine whether they caused or were caused by the enuresis. (For details of the research, see Fielding and Doleys, 1988.)

A Developmental Study

The kibbutz example that opened the discussion of enuresis is based on one of the few longitudinal studies of enuresis (Kaffman and Elizur, 1977). In the kibbutz, four to six infants are cared for by a trained caretaker, or *meta-pelet* (plural, *metaplot*) in a communal children's house. Each child spends four hours daily with his or her parents. Generally speaking, the children's development and the parent-child relationships are similar to those in traditional Western families. From the standpoint of research, the advantage of the kibbutz is that the *metaplot* rather than parents have the responsibility for toilet training, which, as has been noted, is generally benign and child-centered. In the study reported by Kaffman and Elizur, 153 children were assessed on a number of physiological, interpersonal, and intrapersonal variables from infancy to 8 years of age. They regard enuresis as beginning at 4 rather than 5 years of age.

While the investigators found the usual genetic and physiological predisposing factors in the 4-year-old enuretics (enuretic siblings, smaller functional bladder capacity, impaired motor coordination), the personality and interpersonal factors are of greater interest. The enuretic children had a significantly greater number of behavior symptoms than the nonenuretic ones, suggesting that they were generally more disturbed. Within this general context, two high-risk personality patterns could be distinguished. Around 30 percent of the children were "hyperactive," aggressive, and negativistic in response to discipline, had low frustration tolerance, and resisted adjusting to new situations. How difficult it must have been for these children to sit or stand still when being potty-trained! A smaller group of enuretics were dependent and unassertive, had low achievement and mastery motivation, and masturbated frequently, perhaps to compensate for their lack of realistic pleasures. In contrast, the nonenuretic children were self-reliant, independent, and adaptable, and they had a high level of achievement motivation. They also showed a negative response to wetness and urine contact, in contrast to their enuretic counterparts, who showed no such reaction. The authors note that the two sets of high-risk traits did not characterize all enuretics; like obesity, bed-wetting can be a single symptom, part of a personality pattern, or one element in a picture of severe emotional disturbance.

In the interpersonal sphere, the clearest relation was between parental disinterest and enuresis; while there was some correlation with both emotional coldness and indulgent infantilization, it was not statistically significant. In addition, temporary separation from the parents was the only stress related to increased bed-wetting, for the kibbutz children took in stride the stresses of a sibling's birth, hospitalization, and even war. Interestingly, absence of the *metapelet* produced no such reaction, suggesting that the parent-child relationship was central. While not statistically significant, a relationship between bed-wetting and the *metapelet's* behavior was suggested; permissiveness, low achievement demands, and insecurity on the part of the *metapelet* tended to be related to enuresis, whereas structured, directive, and goal-oriented toilet training in the context of a loving relationship enhanced early bladder control.

The authors draw some general conclusions from the data. For low-risk children the timing of toilet training does not matter. In the high-risk group, delayed training increases the likelihood of enuresis. The motorically active, resistive, and aggressive infant is difficult enough to socialize, but the difficulties are compounded during the terrible twos and threes. In the interpersonal realm, a permissive attitude, combined with noninvolvement or uncertainty, tends to perpetuate bed-wetting

since there is neither sufficient challenge nor sufficient support for the child to take this particular step toward maturity. Such a finding is congruent with studies of normal development that show that a child's competence is maximized when parental affection is combined with challenges and an expectation of achievement. Overall, the children's personality characteristics were more highly correlated with enuresis than were interpersonal variables.

The Problem of Prognosis

Let us now return to the decision concerning whether to recommend therapy for the 5-year-old Israeli boy. In their longitudinal study, Kaffman and Elizur found that 50 percent of enuretic children were identified as "problem children" when they were 6 to 8 years of age, in contrast to 12 percent of nonenuretics. Learning problems and scholastic underachievement were the most frequent symptoms, although some of the children also lacked self-confidence and felt ashamed, guilty, or depressed. While some children "outgrow" enuresis, the behavior problems of others increase (Essen and Peckham, 1976). The importance of the point cannot be overemphasized. Looking at a graph showing the progressive decline of enuresis, one would opt for the prediction that the child would "outgrow" his problem. But longitudinal studies that include intrapersonal and interpersonal variables alert the clinician to the possibility that enuresis in some 4-year-olds may be the first sign of problems that will persist and perhaps escalate.

Unfortunately, Kaffman and Elizur did not analyze their data to discover why certain enuretic children are at risk. The kind of shaming which might well be responsible for their negative self-image in this country is minimal in the kibbutz, where the attitude is one of acceptance of bed-wetting. It may be that the child's aggressiveness or dependence and the uneasy permissiveness of caretakers continue to hamper the child in subsequent socialization and in achievement of the self-discipline necessary for making a successful school adjustment.

There is one final point to be made concerning the relation between psychopathology and development. The children who were not enuretic at 4 years of age evidenced a significant amount of fearfulness at 3 years of age. They showed diverse fears during the day and were especially frightened about going to sleep or would awaken crying for their caretakers. It is possible that such behaviors were a sign of the stress of toilet training, and that even in a benign setting the conflict between autonomy and losing parental love can take its toll on healthy children. The finding also underscores the limitations of using the symptom approach exclusively when defining psychopathology. A child clinician must decide when a disturbance is part of healthy growth (as in the fearful 3-year-old) and when it is the first sign of trouble to come (as in the enuretic 5-year-old). Longitudinal studies are all too rare in this regard. Until more data have accumulated, the clinician has no choice other than to evaluate the various etiological variables along with the child's general development and rely on the guidelines resulting from accumulated experience.

Treatment

Among *drug treatments,* the antidiuretic hormone desmopressin is effective and has negligible side effects. The main disadvantage is the likelihood of relapse when medication is discontinued, although gradual tapering of the dose reduces the probability of this happening (see Gadow, 1992). Support and encouragement along with periodic awakening of the child during the night to urinate have had some success. Restricting fluids before bed has not, nor has psychotherapy.

On the other hand, the urine alarm, or *pad-and-bell method,* has a proven record of effectiveness and of superiority to the treatments just mentioned. A urine-sensitive pad is placed in the child's bed. It activates a bell or buzzer when the child wets, thereby awakening the child, who then goes to the bathroom to finish voiding. Eventually the response of awakening becomes anticipatory, allowing the child to get up before urinating. Studies have shown the technique to be effective in 70 to 95 percent of the cases, although a 41 percent relapse rate within 6 months of treatment has been a problem. Two methods have been successful in solving this problem. The first is overlearning. After achieving dryness, children increase their intake of liquid before bedtime and continue to use the alarm. Theoretically, the increased liquid intake generalizes control to levels of greater bladder fullness. The second method is intermittent reinforcement such as using the buzzer only 70 percent of the time. According to operant learning principles, conditioning is more resistant to extinction with intermittent than with continuous reinforcement. While this method takes longer to achieve dryness, it significantly lowers the relapse rate. (See Walker, Milling, and Bonner, 1988, for a more detailed account of treatment.)

Another procedure of proven effectiveness is dry-bed training (DBT), an omnibus approach involving, among other things, reinforcement for inhibiting urination, practice of appropriate voiding, overlearning, retention-control training, nighttime awakening, mild punishment, family encouragement, and a urine alarm. Studies of the relative contribution of the various components of DBT indicate that the urine alarm is the single most effective element, with other procedures making a unique contribution to overall effectiveness. Thus, DBT may represent a significant advance over the urine alarm alone.

THE DEVELOPMENTAL MODEL

We have learned a number of clinically useful lessons about the importance of contexts in understanding psychopathological behavior. First there is the *organic* context, which includes the genetic and physiological factors in enuresis and obesity. The *intrapersonal* context alerts us to the fact that the same disturbance can play different roles in the child's overall functioning. Thus, enuresis may be a reaction to a specific trauma, or the primary psychopathology, or one manifestation of another psychopathology such as antisocial acting out or depression. Failure to take these different roles into account can result in inappropriate recommendations for therapy and is responsible for a good deal of confusion in the research literature. In the *interpersonal* context, parental behavior has consistently emerged as a potent determinant of psychopathology; only in enuresis is there a suggestion that it may be less influential than the child's temperament.

The *superordinate* context of socioeconomic status and culture holds some surprises: enuresis flourishes among both disadvantaged American slum children and well-cared for children in the kibbutz. The formula "poverty engenders psychopathology" proves too simple to account for the psychopathology of toddlers—as it will again in the case of delinquents.

Then there is the all-important context of *time*. The same psychopathological behavior may have different meanings depending on when it occurs in the developmental sequence: witness the changing meanings of eating from infancy through the preschool period. Time poses the knottiest questions for the clinician: When is a disturbance temporary (as in the fearful 3-year-old who will be dry during the night a year later), and when is it the first sign of trouble to come (as in the enuretic 4-year-old)? Or again, when is disturbed behavior age-appropriate (such as the 5-year-old who gorges herself because of some unrealistic sexual anxiety), and when is it a regression to a previous developmental stage (such as the 5-year-old who gorges himself because of a sudden terror over being separated from his mother)? Research furnishes far too few guides to answering these questions; much of the time the clinician must rely on skill and experience.

We have also learned about different *models* of deviant development. One model involves failure to progress as expected: for example, control of bladder is not achieved. This, of course, is the *fixation* model of psychopathology. Another model involves an *exaggeration* of normal development—oppositional-defiant behavior and feeding problems being the prime examples—if such exaggerations are prolonged and block further growth. The final model is *regression,* the clearest example being secondary enuresis.

Our presentation of various psychopathologies will continue to examine initiative, but not the self-reliant expansiveness we have just discussed. Rather, the focus will shift to curiosity and exploration, which require the ability to pay attention and to work up to one's potential. Both can go awry, producing hyperactivity on the one hand and learning disabilities on the other.

CHAPTER 6

EARLY DEVIATIONS IN CURIOSITY AND TASK ORIENTATION

As we have just seen, initiative can go awry in the toddler period by becoming excessive and producing an oppositional disorder. However, initiative involves not only self-reliance and autonomy but curiosity and exploration as well. As Piaget has taught us, even infants are problem solvers, implicitly asking, What is that? and How does it work? until, by the end of the first year, they are actively experimenting with the physical and social environment. In a like manner, toddlers have a remarkable ability to give their undivided attention to the tasks involved in exploration. Subsequently, school adds an element of re-

quiredness to intrinsic curiosity which, in turn, is transformed into the work of learning specific subjects.

Yet this ability to concentrate on the task at hand in the toddler and preschool periods can be seriously curtailed by an *attention deficit*, which prevents children from keeping their minds on a particular task and which also results in *hyperactivity*. In middle childhood a different deviation appears in intelligent, motivated children who are unable to achieve at an appropriate level in one or another academic subject such as reading or arithmetic. This deviation is called *learning disabilities*

(LD). In both instances, the inability to concentrate on and master increasingly complex tasks diverts initiative from its normal course.

ATTENTION-DEFICIT HYPERACTIVITY DISORDER

Hyperactive behavior has been the problem child among child psychopathologies. No one is quite sure where it belongs, while some authorities claim it should not exist! For a while, hyperactivity was thought to result from a subtle form of brain malfunction called minimal brain dysfunction, or MBD (see Chapter 13), which produced poorly controlled motor behavior. As the condition was better understood, emphasis shifted from motor behavior to cognition, and hyperactivity was considered to result from a basic defect in attention. Thus, DSM-III lists attention deficit with and without hyperactivity. Subsequently, DSM-III-R simplified the dual diagnoses into the single Attention-Deficit Hyperactivity Disorder (ADHD). Attention-deficit without hyperactivity was relegated to a residual category, Undifferentiated Attention-Deficit Disorder. The DSM-IV Draft Criteria allow for a predominantly inattentive type, a predominately hyperactive-impulsive type, as well as a type that combines inattention with hyperactivity-impulsivity. To further complicate matters, the centrality of attention deficit itself is currently being questioned, although a satisfactory substitute explanation has not been found. In the meantime, MDB withered away as an etiologic agent from lack of empirical support, although ADHD is still regarded as resulting from some yet to be discovered brain malfunction.

Whether this restless diagnosis has finally found its proper home remains to be seen. Meanwhile, we will take the characteristic behaviors at face value in order to locate hyperactivity among our basic variables. The most obvious feature of hyperactive children is their poor concentration and impulsivity, along

Hyperactive behavior.

with their overactivity (see Table 6.1). Beginning in the toddler and preschool period they lack the task orientation so characteristic of normal development. This weakened task orientation affects *initiative* in regard to their ability to work at a problem and get it done, and their venturing out confidently and mastering various social and academic challenges.

The best prevalence estimate is around 5 percent of school-aged youngsters, making ADHD a common disturbance. Three to six times as many males as females are identified (see Whalen, 1989).

Before examining ADHD in greater detail, we shall first review the many assessment and diagnostic problems it has presented.

T A B L E   6 . 1

DSM-IV Draft Criteria for Attention-Deficit Hyperactivity Disorder

A. Either (1) or (2):

   (1) *Inattention:* At least six of the following symptoms of inattention have persisted for at least six months to a degree that is maladaptive and inconsistent with developmental level:

   - Often fails to give close attention to details or makes careless mistakes in schoolwork, work, or other activities
   - Often has difficulty sustaining attention in tasks or play activities
   - Often does not seem to listen to what is being said to him or her
   - Often does not follow through on instructions and fails to finish schoolwork, chores, or duties in the workplace (not due to oppositional behavior or failure to understand instructions)
   - Often has difficulties organizing tasks and activities
   - Often avoids or strongly dislikes tasks (such as schoolwork or homework) that require sustained mental effort
   - Often loses things necessary for tasks or activities (e.g., school assignments, pencils, books, tools, or toys)
   - Is often easily distracted by extraneous stimuli
   - Often forgetful in daily activities

   (2) *Hyperactivity-Impulsivity:* At least four of the following symptoms of hyperactivity-impulsivity have persisted for at least six months to a degree that is maladaptive and inconsistent with developmental level:

   Hyperactivity
   - Often fidgets with hands or feet or squirms in seat
   - Leaves seat in classroom or in other situations in which remaining seated is expected
   - Often runs about or climbs excessively in situations where it is inappropriate (in adolescents or adults, may be limited to subjective feelings of restlessness)
   - Often has difficulty playing or engaging in leisure activities quietly

   Impulsivity
   - Often blurts out answers to questions before the questions have been completed
   - Often has difficulty waiting in lines or awaiting turn in games or group situations

B. Onset no later than 7 years of age

C. Symptoms must be present in two or more situations (e.g., at school, work, and at home)

Source: American Psychiatric Association, 1993.

Problems in Assessment

Hyperactivity, in the form of fidgeting, impulsivity, and distractibility, is not only one of the most visible of behavioral constellations but also among the most frequent complaints parents and teachers make about supposedly normal children. It is ironic, then, that assessment has proved so difficult.

In part the problem is one that bedevils

much of psychological assessment; namely, different measures of the same variable do not correlate very highly. Hyperactivity can be measured by mechanical devices that record the actual amount of body movement, by direct observation, or by interview ratings and questionnaire scores. In a way, a certain amount of disagreement among techniques is to be expected. The measurement of the sheer amount of bodily activity says nothing of how appropriate or inappropriate that activity is, while it is the quality of inappropriateness which lies at the heart of adults' evaluation of children's behavior as being hyperactive. Or again, behavioral observations in a given setting might be expected to differ from the kind of overall evaluations often tapped by interviews and questionnaires.

However, the problem in assessment goes deeper than variability among instruments. For various assessments to be highly correlated, the behavior itself must be reasonably consistent in different settings. There is evidence that this is not the case with hyperactivity, which increases in familiar, structured, task-oriented settings such as the classroom and decreases in informal or high-energy-expenditure settings such as the playground. Consequently, an inexperienced clinical child psychologist may brace himself or herself for assessing a hyperactive preschooler who is described as a "holy terror" at home only to find that the child is a model of cooperativeness in the unfamiliar, gamelike testing situation.

Because the classroom is usually regarded as the acid test of hyperactivity, teachers' evaluations are often regarded as the most central in detecting it. But does it matter whether hyperactivity is *situational* or *pervasive*? Apparently it does. In their summary of objective studies, Costello, Loeber, and Stouthamer-Loeber (1991) concluded that, compared to situationally hyperactive children, pervasively hyperactive children showed more symptoms of the disorder, had more symptoms of dis-

ruptive behaviors and more internalizing symptoms of anxiety and depression, functioned at a lower level at home and school, and were more likely to come from disadvantaged families. Pervasively hyperactive children also have a worse prognosis than situational hyperactive children who, at least in middle childhood, turn out to be no different from normal controls (Campbell, Endman, and Bernfield, 1977; Rutter and Garmezy, 1983).

As a final assessment problem, Barkley (1991) points out that the laboratory methods used to measure inattention, impulsivity, and overactivity have only low to moderate ecological validity; that is, they do not correlate highly with such behaviors in natural settings. As a remedy, Barkley suggests either more reliance on assessment in natural settings or combining several procedures into a battery. Such a battery might include parent and teacher rating scales, a laboratory task to evaluate inattention and impulsivity, and an analogue situation such as observing free play in a laboratory play room.

Problems in Diagnosis

Because the behaviors comprising the hyperactive syndrome are commonly found in a number of other disturbances, the independence of the diagnosis has been questioned. Prior and Sanson (1986) claim that ADHD has no unique diagnostic status because it is found in children with conduct disorders, learning disabilities, and other psychopathologies. Moreover, it has neither a specific, unique etiology nor a specific response to treatment.

There is also evidence for diagnostic independence, however. Many factor-analytic studies show that hyperactivity emerges as a factor separate from *conduct disorders* both in the general population and in clinical samples. For example, Fergusson, Horwood, and Lloyd

(1991), in a factor-analytic study of 9- and 10-year-olds, found two distinct but highly correlated factors of attention deficit and conduct disorder.

Other studies have shown that it is possible to separate purely hyperactive, inattentive children and purely aggressive, conduct-disordered children from those who have both disturbances provided that adequate measures are used. Children with ADHD have more cognitive and achievement deficits while aggressive, conduct-disordered children have more antisocial parents and family hostility and are more often from a low socioeconomic status. Moreover, ADHD children are frequently off task in classroom and playroom situations, which is not true of aggressive, conduct-disordered children. Not only do the children in this latter group have better control of their behavior, but their social skills may also be better because the group may have some popular as well as some rejected children while ADHD children are rarely popular. Finally, the prognosis for aggressive, conduct-disordered children is ominous, while that of ADHD children is relatively benign, especially for situational hyperactivity. Children who have both ADHD and a conduct disorder tend to have the worst features of both disturbances. They have lower academic attainment and more school expulsions along with antisocial behavior, substance abuse, and poor occupational attainment and adjustment; in addition, their parents tend to be hostile and delinquent. In regard to etiology, the organic context plays a prominent role in ADHD, while adverse family factors are prominent in conduct disorders (see Hinshaw, 1987). Finally, there is an overlap between ADHD and oppositional-defiant disorder; this is to be expected in light of the strong affinity between ODD and conduct disorder (see Chapter 5).

The overlap of ADHD with *learning disabilities* is also to be expected because inattention is apt to interfere with learning, while the stress of academic failure may result in restless, inattentive behavior. However, the degree of overlap may well have been exaggerated in certain studies which had an overly liberal definition of learning disability, such as generally low academic achievement. When rigorous criteria are applied, the percent of learning disabilities among ADHD children ranges from 17 to 33 percent (Semrud-Clikeman et al., 1992).

Research evidence for a difference between ADHD and LD children comes from a study by Tarnowski, Prinz, and Nay (1986). They compared ADHD, LD, ADHD-LD children, and a normal control group on measures of sustained attention, selective attention, and span of apprehension. They found unique patterns of attentional deficits associated with each diagnostic group. The most important finding for our purposes was that the ADHD group evidenced deficits in sustaining attention, which, as we shall soon see, is one of the core features of this disorder. The LD group was characterized by difficulties with selective attention, while attentional deficits were most pervasive in the combined ADHD-LD group.

In sum, objective studies indicate that ADHD should be retained as a diagnostic entity. However, there is considerable *comorbidity* with conduct disorder and, to a lesser extent, with learning disabilities.

Within the diagnosis itself, there is a debate over whether the distinction of attention deficit with and without hyperactivity is justified. In their comprehensive review of objective studies, Goodyear and Hynd (1992) concluded that children with attention deficit disorder (ADD) with hyperactivity are more likely to have more behavior problems, to be less popular, to be more self-destructive and impulsive on tasks of attention, and to be more likely to have a codiagnosis of conduct disorder. Children with attention deficit disorder without hyperactivity are more socially withdrawn, have a slower cognitive tempo, are more self-

ADHD

Situational vs.	Pervasive
ADHD	ADHD
	More symptoms
	More disruptive behaviors
	More internalizing disorders
	Lower level of functioning
	Disadvantaged families
	Poorer prognosis

ADD with H vs.	ADD without H
More behavior problems	Socially withdrawn
Less popular	Slower cognitive tempo
More self-destructive	More self-conscious
More impulsive	More likely to be LD
More likely to have CD	

ADHD, Conduct Disorder (CD), and Learning Disabilities (LD) Compared

ADHD vs.	CD	ADHD + CD*
More cognitive	More antisocial	Lower academic
deficits	parents	attainment
More achievement	More family hostility	More school expulsions
deficits	Lower SES	More antisocial behavior
More off-task	More social skills	More substance abuse
behavior	Worse prognosis	Poorer occupational
More prominent		adjustment
organic etiology		More parental hostility
		More parental
		delinquency

ADHD vs.	LD	ADHD + LD*
More deficits	More deficits	Most pervasive
in sustained	in selective	attentional
attention	attention	deficits

*Compared to the other groups individually

FIGURE 6.1
Summary of findings concerning ADHD.

conscious, and have a higher incidence of learning disorders.

Figure 6.1 summarizes the descriptive findings concerning ADHD.

Implications for Research

This is not the first time we shall make this point nor will it be the last: unless researchers are able to study pure cases of a given diagnostic category, or unless they are able to control for possible confounds (as in the case of controlling for IQ when studying autism), there is no way of knowing whether the obtained results apply to this category. The point is nowhere more important than in the case of ADHD children. As we have seen, there is a good deal of overlap between this category and conduct disorders. Unless researchers are careful to eliminate conduct-disordered chil-

dren from their ADHD population, or unless they have a comparison group of conduct-disordered children, there is no way of knowing whether the results are specific to ADHD, to conduct disorders, or to children who have both disturbances. The same principle applies to learning disabilities and to situational versus generalized hyperactivity.

Unfortunately, past investigators have not been as scrupulous in selecting subjects and controls as they might have been. In part this is due to certain assessment instruments which include features of different diagnostic categories in a single instrument. In part it is due to the difficulty in locating pure cases because these are rarer than mixed ones. Whatever the reasons, research results often are confounded, and all too often one must rely on few well-designed and executed studies. We should keep this caution in mind as we examine the nature, etiology, and developmental causes of ADHD. (For a summary of empirical findings, see Schachar, 1991.)

Core Characteristics

The core characteristics of ADHD are typically inattention, impulsivity, and hyperactivity.

Inattention   ADHD children have difficulty sustaining attention in tasks or play activities. This deficit affects a wide range of tasks from simple reaction time to complex problem solving requiring self-directed and self-sustained effort. In discussing ADHD children's attentional deficit, we shall rely on the research of Douglas and her colleagues (1983), who have conducted an extensive series of studies on this topic.

Attention is not a simple process. On the contrary it is multifaceted, and so it is logical to ask what aspects have gone awry in the case of ADHD children. Douglas disagrees with the idea that such children are distractible in the sense that their attention is readily "captured" by every extraneous stimulus in the environment. Studies that have introduced various kinds of distractions show that ADHD children perform as well as normals. In one study, for example, the children were required to read with a telephone ringing, lights flashing, and the sound of a calculating machine. To express this idea in more formal terms, ADHD children are not deficient in the *selective* aspect of attention, that is, in the ability to filter out irrelevant environmental stimuli in order to focus on stimuli specifically relevant to the task at hand.

The evidence in regard to distractibility is not totally consistent, however. Some studies have shown that highly interesting or salient stimuli embedded within the target stimuli will impair performance. Even though there may be some exceptions, the overall finding is

that poor performance of ADHD children is not due to an inability to filter out or ignore irrelevant environmental events (Campbell and Werry, 1986).

Research does show, however, that ADHD children have a basic deficit in *sustaining* attention. Two of the purest measures of sustained attention are *reaction time tests,* in which a warning signal (such as a buzzer) is followed by a preparatory interval terminated by a stimulus (such as a light) to which the subject has been instructed to respond as quickly as possible (for example, by pressing a lever); and *continuous-performance tests,* in which letters appear on a screen one at a time, the child having been instructed to respond to a given letter (such as X) only when another letter (such as A) precedes it. Not only are hyperactive children generally inferior to normal controls on these simple tasks, but their performance also deteriorates with time.

Unfortunately, Douglas's findings concerning sustained attention have not proved to be as robust as one would like, since other investigators have not uniformly confirmed them. (See, for example, van der Meere, Wekking, and Sergeant, 1991.) Rather, deficiencies in sustained attention turn out to be both context-dependent and task-dependent; for example, attention improves if the task is interesting, if the child is fined for errors, if the task is self-paced rather than experimenter-paced, and if the experimenter is present rather than absent—all of which suggest a motivational problem rather than a basic attentional deficit (Barkley, 1990). In addition, Halperin and colleagues (1992) found that, while inattention differentiated ADHD from normal controls, it was not diagnosis-specific since it was found in children with other disturbances.

Whether failures to replicate are due to a flaw in the idea itself or to methodological differences among studies is impossible to say at present. Seidel and Joschko (1990) point to the many variations in methodology: different diagnostic criteria and demographic characteristics such as age and IQ have been used; instructions, kinds of stimuli presented, rates of presentation, and measurement of change all differ. Their own study showed that differences in sustained attention are demonstrable but depend on the particular measurement used. Yet, one might argue that a basic explanatory variable should be sufficiently robust to override methodological variations among studies, and certain psychologists are casting about for other explanations.

Barkley (1990) prefers an explanation in terms of *rule-governed behavior*. Rules are defined behaviorally as relationships among behavior, antecedents, and consequences. Barkley hypothesizes that ADHD children are deficient in learning such rules. This, in turn, may be the result of neurologically determined insensitivity to consequences of behavior. As a result, the rewards and punishments which are normally employed to condition or train children only weakly control their subsequent behavior, so that ADHD children rapidly satiate and become bored with the task at hand. Their failure to comply with the instructions in the continuous-performance test is just one instance of a general weakness in complying with directions and sustaining compliance over time. The evidence for Barkley's explanation is admittedly suggestive rather than definitive, so its soundness awaits the results of future investigations.

Impulsivity Another core characteristic of ADHD children is impulsivity. In ordinary terms, they "act before they think." When confronted with a complex task, for example, they may accept the first solution that comes to mind, never challenging themselves to consider whether it is the best or most appropriate. They may blurt out incorrect answers in class or have difficulty taking turns in orga-

nized play, again because of a weakened ability to control the impulse to action. It is not by accident that we tell a child to *stop* and think; in fact, Douglas epitomizes the basic defect in ADHD children as an inability to stop, look, listen—and think.

A number of studies support the observation that ADHD children are impulsive (Douglas, 1983). On the Continuous-Performance Task, for example, they respond to the preceding letter rather than to the target letter, or they respond to nonsignificant letters. On more complex tasks, ADHD children make not only very rapid responses but irrelevant and inappropriate ones as well, which suggests that they tend to respond carelessly and impulsively.

While ADHD children do not lack search strategies, they are deficient in them compared with normal children. This deficiency is evidenced in solving both perceptual and logical problems. In the Matching Familiar Figures Test, for example, the child is required to choose from a group of similar pictures the one that is identical to a standard picture, such as a man or a house. ADHD children perform in an impulsive manner, failing to systematically compare the standard with the entire array of pictures or failing to check back and forth between the standard and the array. Thus their basic weakness in attentional and inhibitional skills makes them respond prematurely and incorrectly. Finally, Schachar and Logan (1990), using a reaction time setup, compared ADHD and normal children in their ability to obey a signal to inhibit responding interspersed among signals to respond. They found that the ability to inhibit peaked after the second grade in the normal control group but that pervasively hyperactive children had a severe inhibitory deficit.

Not only do ADHD children have inefficient strategies, but the advantage of having a strategy to begin with also does not occur to many of them. Tutors may complain that the children are unaware of their own role as problem solvers; they do not realize that they must make a deliberate effort instead of having the solution "just come" to them.

Hyperactivity While it seems counterintuitive, motor overactivity is a far less robust dimension of ADHD than is inattention (Campbell and Werry, 1986). There is some evidence that ADHD children are more active on a twenty-four-hour basis (including sleep) than are normal control children and that they show greater restlessness in the form of task-irrelevant movements, squirming in their seats, and out-of-seat behavior than do normal controls. However, the differences are most marked with younger children and tend to decrease with age. Also, as we have seen, differences may depend on the situation. Even when group differences exist, they are not striking since many children diagnosed as ADHD do not have a higher than normal activity level. Finally, activity level does not clearly differentiate ADHD from other disturbances; for example, evidence of a significantly higher activity level than that found in conduct-disordered children is inconsistent.

Factor-analytic studies indicate that hyperactivity is not distinct from impulsivity since the behaviors defining them cluster together. (See, for example, Bauermeister et al., 1992.) This suggests that both may be signs of a more global problem in poor regulation and inhibition of behavior. In addition, impulsive errors and excessive activity discriminate ADHD from non-ADHD children better than inattention, suggesting that they may constitute the core problem (Barkley, 1990).

Cognitive and Academic Correlates

Because the ability to sustain attention and inhibit disruptive impulses is basic to all cogni-

tive processes, one would expect the deficiencies found in ADHD to have far-reaching effects. We will now examine the evidence concerning a number of these effects.

IQ and Academic Achievement ADHD children score 7 to 15 points below normal controls on standard intelligence tests. However, it is not clear how much this discrepancy is due to lower intellectual ability and how much is due to deficiencies in test-taking skills, with inattention and impulsivity preventing the children from doing their best. Generally speaking, ADHD children vary widely in their intellectual functioning, covering the entire spectrum of intelligence (Barkley, 1990).

There is no doubt that ADHD children do poorly in school. They repeat more grades, receive lower marks in academic subjects, and score lower on standard measures of reading, spelling, vocabulary, and mathematics than normal children. In addition, academic performance tends to deteriorate with time.

While the data are meager and unsatisfactory, they suggest that there is no qualitatively distinct pattern of cognitive deficits associated with ADHD and LD. In addition, longitudinal studies suggest that LD precedes ADHD; for example, there is no evidence that hyperactivity in the preschool period predicts subsequent LD, while children with a reading disability have an increase in ADHD between 5 and 13 years of age (McGee and Share, 1988).

The reasons for poor academic achievement remain a matter of speculation. Some authorities favor a cognitive etiology, arguing that the core difficulties prevent the development of the problem-solving strategies and higher-level conceptualizations essential to academic success. Others stress motivational factors, school failures lowering self-esteem and progressively undermining the desire to achieve as the child grows older. Of course, there is no reason both processes cannot be taking place at the same time (Campbell and Werry, 1986).

Memory Evaluating memory in ADHD children is difficult because it is necessary to distinguish an inability to remember from a failure to attend to the material in the first place. However, it does seem that ADHD children's memory is intact as long as the list of stimuli is relatively short or as long as the stimuli can be grouped together in a meaningful way. However, memory deteriorates as the number of stimuli to be remembered increases. There is some evidence that this is so because ADHD children, instead of increasing their effort as the task becomes more difficult, actually expend less effort and use less efficient memory strategies (Campbell and Werry, 1986).

Higher-Order Processes The picture here is similar to that found in memory; adequate performance on simple tasks but deficient performance as the task increases in complexity. Again we follow Campbell and Werry's (1986) integration of objective studies. In a study of word knowledge, for example, ADHD children performed as well as controls when choosing between two alternatives, but more poorly when confronted with five. In general, ADHD children do poorly on concept formation tasks, which require careful attention to and effortful processing of relatively large amounts of information.

The ADHD children's poor performance on tasks requiring higher-order thinking seems to be due, in large part, to their general approach to the task and their choice of inefficient problem-solving strategies. In their approach they tend to be careless and casual, investing the minimal effort and readily engaging in task-irrelevant behaviors. In their strategies they tend to be rather haphazard and capricious rather than thoughtful and organized. In a task requiring the scanning of an array of stimuli

they are apt to skip around, focusing on novel or striking ones instead of systematically examining them all, thereby failing to process all the relevant information. For example, when presented with pictures of flowers varying in two aspects of four dimensions (three or five petals, straight or curved stem, with or without leaves, and set in a square or round background) and asked to find out which one the experimenter was thinking about by asking questions that could be answered either yes or no, the ADHD children's scattered attention prevented them from examining all the pictures in order to discover the basic dimensions and from solving the problem with the fewest questions.

The above findings raise an intriguing question. Suppose that, by some means such as medication or therapy or enticing rewards, one could get the ADHD child to become genuinely task-oriented. Would the cognitive deficiencies remain? This question may be formulated in terms of *performance versus competence* and concerns whether a particular deficiency reflects a basic lack of ability (competence) or whether the ability is there but obscured by other factors such as indifference or fear or a reluctance to become deeply involved (performance). On this point of performance versus competence the evidence is mixed. Some data indicate that, even when told about a more effective strategy for solving a problem, the ADHD children did not recognize it as such, which suggests a competence deficit. However, other studies find that performance improved as the task became more interesting and that concept learning was equal to that of normal controls provided that every correct response was positively reinforced. Such findings suggest a performance deficit with intact cognitive abilities. In light of the limited data, answering the basic question of performance versus competence lies far in the future.

Response to Reinforcement ADHD children have their own special way of responding to reinforcement. As we have just seen, their performance will improve if every correct response is positively reinforced. What is unusual is that their performance actually deteriorates when reinforcement appears only after every second correct response or at regular intervals. The withdrawal of expected rewards can interfere with performance, even on simple tasks. Such a pattern of response to reinforcement has led Douglas (1983) to hypothesize that ADHD children have an exceptionally strong need for immediate gratification. In fact, they tend to invest more energy and interest in obtaining a reward than in meeting the demands of solving a particular problem. Instead of being task-oriented, they work with one eye on the rewarding adult, as it were. Consequently, withdrawal of rewards is particularly upsetting. Douglas (1983) regards this need to have immediate gratification as being so important that she places it among the core characteristics of ADHD children.

Developmental Pathway

First we will view ADHD within the framework of normal development gone awry. Campbell (1990), addressing herself primarily to the period from infancy to middle childhood, makes the point that normal development shades imperceptibly into deviance. This means that the clinical child psychologist will often have difficulty deciding whether a given child is disturbed or not. In addition, the fluidity of early development will make it difficult to predict if a child will "outgrow" the problem behavior. In general, both decisions will become easier to make as the child approaches middle childhood, since standards for sustaining attention, task orientation, and

cooperation become more clearly delineated and patterns of behavior become more stable.

In fleshing out this overview with empirical data, we will continue to follow Campbell (1990) unless otherwise noted.

Infancy The picture in infancy is sketchy. There is evidence that infants who are temperamentally difficult to care for because of their high activity level, irritability, unpredictability, and unconsolability, are at risk for developing subsequent problems, including hyperactivity. However, the relation is sufficiently tenuous that it is not possible to predict subsequent ADHD from temperament. There is also preliminary evidence that intrusive caretaking in infancy predicts hyperactivity in kindergarten children more effectively than a host of intrapersonal measures, including temperament (Jacobitz and Sroufe, 1987). Sroufe (1990) conceptualizes the findings in terms of the caretaker's role in helping the infant learn to control and modulate arousal and attention. Sensitive caretakers are helpful; intrusive ones are not. At the anecdotal level there are accounts of advanced motor activity such as climbing out of the crib and wearing out the mattress with constant rocking and of mothers' difficulty in nursing her squirming, wriggling child (Ross and Ross, 1976).

The Toddler Period The normal toddler is "all over the place and into everything," while the need for autonomy results in noncompliance with parental requests. Consequently, it may be difficult to tell a vigorous toddler with a high activity level and low threshold for anger from one with ADHD. In addition, parents differ in their tolerance for motoric exploration and defiance: some will regard such normal behavior as disturbed. The toddler whose exploration has a frenzied quality which interferes with problem solving and mastery, whose inability to sustain attention leads to flitting from one object to another without becoming involved in any one, and whose opposition is expressed in frequent temper tantrums is more likely to have ADHD.

The Preschool Period Preschoolers are expected to be sufficiently task-oriented to complete what they start and monitor the correctness of their behavior, along with being sufficiently cooperative to accept tasks set by others and participate in peer activities. As in the toddler period, deviations from expectation may be part of normal development, perhaps because of temporary difficulties in adjustment or temperament or unrealistic adult requirements. The main clues to disturbance lie in the severity, frequency, pervasiveness, and chronicity of the problem behaviors.

ADHD preschoolers are described as restless, acting as if driven by a motor, their impulsiveness and thoughtlessness leading to increased risk for injury and poisoning. Some are also moody, demanding of attention, defiant, and noncompliant. Anecdotal accounts picture them as unresponsive to physical punishment, reasoning, and persuasion when with adults, aggressive and destructive in peer interactions (Ross and Ross, 1976). For their part, mothers of ADHD preschoolers report that their life is more stressful than mothers of normal children or mothers of older ADHD children. When placed in day care the children may be noisy and talkative, wandering around the classroom inappropriately and disrupting the play of other children. The more active and aggressive ones may be shunted from one preschool to another in the hope of finding a setting that will tolerate their behavior (Barkley, 1990).

Around 40 percent of 4-year-olds have sufficient problems with inattention to be of concern to parents and teachers. Yet the majority of these concerns will no longer be present within three to six months. Even among preschoolers diagnosed as ADHD, only 48 percent will have the same diagnosis by later childhood or early adolescence. Chronicity is the key to persistence: preschoolers whose problems persist for a year are more likely to have behavior problems and be considered ADHD in middle childhood (Campbell, 1990).

Middle Childhood By middle childhood the standards for self-control, task orientation, self-monitoring of appropriate and inappropriate behavior, and cooperation in the family and peer group are sufficiently clear that the difference between normal variability of behavior and ADHD is more readily apparent. Thus a persistent constellation of behaviors—disorganization and inability to follow routines at home and school, disruptive behavior in the classroom and with peers—raise serious questions of psychopathology. Note that even here individual behaviors in isolation, such as rebellion against routines at home and fighting at school, may represent nothing more than glitches in the normal development of the child.

At home parents complain of failure to accept responsibility, of having to supervise self-help activities such as dressing and bathing, of temper tantrums, and a general pattern of immaturity. However, it is school with its requirements to sit still and listen, obey and follow through on instructions, and organize work, which is the source of greatest distress to ADHD children. (For specific objective studies, see Campbell, 1990.) The 20 to 25 percent of ADHD children with a reading disability are doubly handicapped, as are those with math and writing disabilities. Moreover, their erratic performance—some days performing well, other days failing—leads to the accusation that they could do well "if they really tried." Half the ADHD children will experience social rejection because of their intrusive, inept social behavior. While some may develop feelings of low self-esteem, others will blame their peers because of limited self-awareness.

Between 30 and 50 percent of children ages 7 to 10 are likely to develop symptoms of conduct disorder, the most common being lying and petty thievery, while a quarter or more will have problems with fighting. ADHD children who have not developed some comorbid psychopathology, either conduct disorder or learning disability, are in the minority. Those with only ADHD will have the best adolescent outcomes, experiencing problems primarily with academic performance and eventual educational attainment. Finally, the majority of ADHD children will be placed on stimulant medication, over half will have some type of individual and family therapy, while around one-third will receive special educational assistance (Barkley, 1990).

Adolescence The idea that ADHD is "outgrown" in adolescence has proved to be incorrect. The ADHD adolescent must face the normal challenges of physiological changes, sexual adjustment, peer acceptance, and vocational choice burdened by the multiple problems arising from past developmental periods. Klein and Mannuzza (1991), in their review of longitudinal studies, concluded that there is a continuation of childhood symptoms; one study found that 70 percent of the adolescents evidenced the full syndrome of ADHD. In addition, a substantial subgroup (25 percent) engaged in antisocial activities such as stealing and fire setting. Between 56 and 70 percent were likely to repeat grades, and the group as a whole was over eight times as likely to be expelled or drop out of school, as compared with normal controls (Barkley, 1990). In the interpersonal context, Barkley and colleagues (1992) found that it was the comorbidity of ADHD and oppositional-defiant disorder that

was associated with greater than normal risk for negative communication patterns between adolescent and parent, angry familial exchanges and conflicts, and unreasonable beliefs. The comorbidity was also associated with greater maternal distress and hostility.

Adulthood Longitudinal studies of ADHD children indicate that, as adults, they have more ADHD, conduct or antisocial disorders, and substance abuse than do normal control adults; for example, one study reported 31 percent versus 3 percent for ADHD, 27 percent versus 8 percent for conduct disorder, and 16 percent versus 3 percent for substance abuse. (Our presentation follows Klein and Mannuzza's 1991 review.) There was no increase in other disorders such as anxiety and depression. Conduct disorder and substance abuse tended to aggregate in the same individual, the former developing before the latter.

While the risk for criminal behavior increases in adulthood, this holds only for those with conduct disorders and other antisocial behaviors; there is no direct connection between ADHD and criminality. Most studies of criminal behavior have failed to take into account the high percent of ADHD children who also have conduct disorders; therefore, their results are open to question (Lilienfeld and Waldman, 1990). Farrington, Loeber, and Van Kammen's (1990) well-designed study of 411 males 8 to 9 years old, corrected this confound by dividing their population into groups who only had ADHD or CD or a combination of the two. They were subsequently evaluated for adult criminal behavior. Only 8 percent of the ADHD-only group had adult convictions as compared with 25 percent of the CD-only group and 32.3 percent of the group with both disturbances. While CD alone predicted subsequent adult convictions, ADHD did not.

While no cognitive deficits have been documented in adults, academic achievement and educational history both suffer (Klein and Mannuzza, 1991). Most of the studies concern males, but what little data there are suggest a lack of sex differences in the adult picture. Finally, while a number of variables from middle childhood have been studied, none is a good predictor of adult outcome.

The Developmental Model

As we have seen, parents and teachers frequently complain that normal preschoolers are inattentive, restless, and distractible. This suggests that ADHD may be an *exaggeration* of developmentally appropriate characteristics, just as oppositional behavior may be an exaggeration of the developmentally appropriate negativism of the toddler period. Evidence supporting this speculation comes from Barkley (1982), who found that while 40 to 97 percent of hyperactive children displayed hyperactive behavior in fourteen home settings (such as mealtime, bedtime, playing alone), between 0 and 33 percent of normal children evidenced the same behavior. The difference, then, is a quantitative one of frequency.

There are also some relevant developmental data on the core components of ADHD. Levy (1980) found that between 3 and 7 years of age, both the total number of errors and the reaction time decreased on the Continuous-Performance Task. He interprets these results as indicating a progressive increase in the ability to sustain attention and to inhibit irrelevant responses. A complementary finding is that the deterioration of performance over time in the Continuous-Performance Task declines between 6 and 10 years of age (Seidel and Joschko, 1990). The Draw a Line Slowly Test, which measures motor inhibition, did not change between 3 and 4 years of age; however, there was a significant increase in time between 4 and 7 years of age, indicating an increasing ability consciously to inhibit motor

behavior in normal children. Because both the capacity for sustained attention and motor inhibition increase during the preschool period, we can assume that this normal developmental trend failed to exert its full influence on ADHD preschoolers, who may be considered either *fixated* or *developmentally delayed*.

Turning to higher-order processes, there is evidence that 4- to 5-year-olds displayed no systematic pattern of scanning when trying to determine whether two objects are the same, with the result that their judgments may be inaccurate. In contrast, children over $6\frac{1}{2}$ years of age proceeded slowly and systematically, looking back and forth at the corresponding features of each pair of stimuli. Thus they were able to detect both obvious and subtle differences which enabled them to make accurate judgments (see Figure 6.2). The ADHD children's unsystematic and partial scanning strategies, therefore, suggest a *fixation* or *developmental delay* in this particular cognitive skill.

In the noncognitive realm, a study by Buss, Block, and Block (1980) found that not only was activity level fairly stable between 3 and 7 years of age, but that the personality characteristics that were correlated with it were also stable. As might be expected, the highly active children were described as more energetic, restless, and fidgety and less inhibited and physically cautious. The personality correlates are more interesting. The highly active children were more self-assertive, aggressive, competitive, and manipulative and less obedient, compliant, shy, and reserved. For our purposes the basic question is: Do ADHD preschoolers have these same characteristics, only raised to the *n*th degree? If so, we could be sure we are dealing with an *exaggeration* of normal development.

Thus, most behavioral and personality characteristics of ADHD may represent an *exaggeration* of normal development, while problems with sustaining attention, motor inhibi-

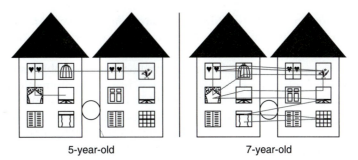

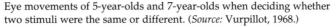

5-year-old   7-year-old

FIGURE 6.2
Eye movements of 5-year-olds and 7-year-olds when deciding whether two stimuli were the same or different. (*Source:* Vurpillot, 1968.)

tion, and problem-solving strategies may represent *fixations* or *developmental lags*.

The Organic Context

While brain damage is no longer regarded as the primary cause of ADHD, the psychopathology is still considered organic rather than psychogenic in nature. A number of possible etiologies have been explored.

Arousal Level   Perhaps the most obvious inference about ADHD children is that their behavior results from a chronic state of hyperarousal. However, as was the case with activity level, the obvious inference turns out not to be the correct one. While many studies have produced conflicting results, the evidence points to underarousal.

Peripheral measures of arousal such as heart rate and skin conductance or galvanic skin response indicate there is no difference between ADHD and normal control children in a resting state. However, ADHD children are somewhat less responsive than controls to specific stimuli or task demands. Central measures of arousal have typically employed the EEG. Here the results are less consistent than with peripheral measures but they suggest that, at least in a subgroup of children, under-

arousal is the more common pattern (Campbell and Werry, 1986).

Drug Response   One of the most frequently cited pieces of evidence for an organic etiology for ADHD is the response to *stimulant medication,* which has the effect of increasing attention and task orientation. However, the case is far from being airtight (Rutter and Garmezy, 1983). While it is true that ADHD children respond favorably to medication in the short run, it is not clear whether the medication merely provides symptomatic relief or whether it corrects a basic biological dysfunction, especially because many children continue to progress after the medication has been discontinued. Also, for the organic hypothesis to be convincing, the effects of the stimulant drugs should be specific to ADHD. However, these drugs have the same effect on normal and enuretic children and on normal adults. In sum, while the response of ADHD children to stimulant drugs is both interesting and important, it cannot be taken as proving the organic hypothesis in the case of this disturbance.

Neurological and Pathological Findings
There is no evidence of major neurological

damage or dysfunction in ADHD children; less than 5 percent have brain damage due to infection, trauma, or injury. However, in certain children there is an increase in the so-called *soft signs* (see Chapter 13) of central nervous system dysfunction. These consist of developmental delays in functions such as speech and motor coordination, nystagmus, and asymmetries of reflex. Not only is the concept of soft signs controversial, but there is also no evidence that they are specific to ADHD since they are found in other disturbances and in impaired intelligence. The same conclusion holds true for *minor physical anomalies.* These are subtle physical defects such as misshapen ears, widely spaced eyes, curved fifth finger, third toe larger than second, and very fine hair that cannot be combed. These anomalies were initially thought to be related to ADHD, but subsequently turned out to be characteristic of a wide variety of disturbances including conduct disorders, autism, and retardation (Barkley, 1991).

The frontal and frontal-limbic areas have been implicated in the central nervous system dysfunction in ADHD, since there is evidence of a decreased blood flow and decreased EEG activity in the frontal lobes, more so in the right than in the left hemisphere. In biochemical investigations, norepinephrine, dopamine, and serotonin have been the neurotransmitters most frequently studied in an effort to identify CNS abnormalities. Each system is usually hypothesized as being underactive. However, to date, no clear-cut *biochemical* abnormality has emerged. (For a detailed account of the biochemical literature, see Deutsch and Kinsbourne, 1990).

Other Factors   The fact that parents and siblings of ADHD children themselves show a higher-than-expected rate of this disorder suggests that there is a genetic component. The limited number of adoption and twin studies comparing identical and fraternal twins support the genetic hypothesis. However, no study has successfully solved the complex methodological problems of separating hereditary from environmental influences, so the evidence cannot be regarded as definitive. (Deutsch and Kinsbourne, 1990, have a succinct account of the methodological problems.)

Both smoking and alcohol consumption have been implicated as etiological factors. Streissguth and colleagues (1984), in a well-controlled longitudinal study, found that drinking and smoking during pregnancy were correlated with the kind of attentional deficit characteristic of ADHD children when the children were 4 years of age. However, since the children were not ADHD at that time, the crucial link to the psychopathology has yet to be established. On the other hand, prenatal and perinatal complications and adversities have not been found to be related to ADHD.

Various *toxic factors* have been implicated in the etiology of ADHD, but most have not withstood the test of replication and rigorously controlled research. For example, lead toxicity can account for only a small group of ADHD children. Food additives were popular culprits for a while, resulting in a number of children being placed on diets which reduce these additives. While a few children may have a special sensitivity to such additives, there is no evidence that it is characteristic of the population as a whole. Sugar consumption was another widely publicized villain that subsequent research showed to be an innocent bystander (Barkley, 1991).

Evaluation   The search for the specific organic factors responsible for ADHD has been characterized more by false starts than by breakthroughs. In part, the search has been hampered by the intrinsic difficulty of building a bridge from physiology to behavior, especially deviant behavior. The search has also been needlessly hampered by poorly designed and controlled studies. In spite of the impressive number of studies, the organic etiology of ADHD remains a mystery.

The Interpersonal Context

While the etiology of ADHD may lie in the organic context, the children develop in a social environment. The nature of their interactions with parents and peers can play a significant role in compounding or ameliorating the difficulties inherent in the disturbance itself.

Parent-Child Relations There is evidence that for ADHD children a negative, controlling mother-child interaction begins when the children are as young as 2 to 3 years of age, the children playing more aggressively, the mothers reprimanding them and redirecting their activities more than is the case for normal controls (Campbell and Werry, 1986). The pattern persists into middle childhood, although it becomes less negative. It is also less negative in undemanding, unstructured situations such as free play, which minimize the children's deviant behavior. Interestingly, as the children's behavior improves with stimulant medication, so does the interaction, suggesting that the mother's controlling behavior may be a response to the intense, inappropriate, exasperating behavior of the children, to a certain extent.

Mothers report feeling drained by the stress of caring for their ADHD children, as well as socially isolated and distressed. There is also an increased amount of distress and disorganization in the families of ADHD children, although it is impossible to tell whether the children's behavior is a response to or a cause of the family picture (Campbell and Werry, 1986). It is not clear whether maternal distress, along with family disharmony and divorce, are different from that found in other populations of disturbed rather than normal chil-

dren. Moreover, there is evidence that a positive family environment, marked by firmness, support, consistency and love, is no guarantee that a child will "outgrow" his or her disturbance. Some will, while others will continue to have problems (Campbell, 1990).

In all probability, there is an interaction between family and child: family factors probably do not cause ADHD but exacerbate and maintain it in vulnerable children, while the children's deviant behavior increases family discord and disruption.

Peer Relations In normal peer relations children learn to share, negotiate, modulate aggression, attend to the needs of others, wait, and take turns. The impulsive, intense, motorically active, and impatient ADHD child has difficulty learning all these lessons even though they are basically social. (Our presentation follows Campbell, 1990.) Negative peer relations have been observed early in development, ADHD kindergartners being more disruptive of peers' play and rejected by them than normal controls. By middle childhood, ADHD children are talkative, aggressive, disruptive, and noncompliant and engage in more negative verbal interactions such as teasing and name calling.

ADHD children perceive themselves as unpopular and are, in turn, actually rejected and less likely to be regarded as popular or chosen as a friend. Moreover, ADHD children can be rejected after a single session in a play group. Somewhat paradoxically, ADHD children are able to see situations from the viewpoint of their peers in hypothetical situations, a cognitive ability called *perspective taking,* which is typically a facilitator of positive peer interaction. For example, Whalen, Henker, and Granger (1990) found that in a task requiring subjects to evaluate filmed behavior of unknown peers as good or bad, ADHD children were no different from normal controls. The authors concluded that faulty social information processing is not the basis for ADHD children's unsatisfactory peer relations.

Treatment

Pharmacotherapy Stimulants are the treatment of choice for ADHD children. The three major groups are amphetamines (Dexedrine), methylphenidate (Ritalin), and pemoline (Cylert). Untoward side effects can be controlled by changing the dosage. Treatment is equally effective for both sexes (see Whalen and Henker, 1991). Stimulants are more effective in middle childhood through adolescence than in the preschool period. Tricyclic antidepressants have been used with some success with those children who do not respond to stimulant medication or with children who exhibit marked symptoms of anxiety or depression. A review of stimulant treatment shows that approximately 75 percent of the children improved (except where noted, our review follows DuPaul and Barkley, 1990). However, it is important to note the kinds of behaviors that changed, as well as those that were not affected.

In line with the view that hyperactivity is the result of an attentional defect, many of the positive results concern a normalization of attention-concentration and impulse control. In a laboratory setting, children were less impulsive and more planful on tasks requiring deliberation, made fewer errors of omission in tasks requiring sustained attention, evidenced fewer task-irrelevant behaviors, and in general were more goal-directed, more coordinated, and less impulsive when medicated. Their reaction time also decreased when rapid responses were required. Among cognitive functions, perception, memory, concept attainment, and cognitive style were also improved. In the classroom, teachers rated children as less noisy and disruptive, more task-oriented, and more appropriate in their social behavior.

On the playground, there was an increase in appropriate activity. As we have already noted, the mother-child interaction also improves. Rather than either "speeding up" or "slowing down" behavior, therefore, the overall effect of the drugs is one of making behavior more appropriate to the situation. It is as if the child's self-regulating, adaptive mechanisms could come to the fore once he or she was no longer buffeted about by the reaction of the moment. Generally, an elevated positive mood accompanies medication, although negative affects such as depression, fearfulness, and withdrawal have also been observed.

A number of important variables are not affected by stimulants, however, the most important being academic achievement. While there are short-term improvements in performance on complex cognitive and academic tasks, long-term effectiveness has not been established. Stimulants make hyperactive children more amenable to learning, but they obviously cannot provide the academic knowledge the children have failed to acquire, nor can they magically raise the overall level of their thinking. There is also no evidence that medication in and of itself significantly improves the long-term prognosis. Thus, stimulants serve an important purpose by setting the stage for the therapeutic work that may still have to be done.

In sum, stimulants are remarkably effective in ameliorating many of the most troublesome behaviors of ADHD children, both in terms of task orientation and social adjustment. The most important single exception to this generally positive picture is academic achievement. However, stimulants cannot be regarded as a "cure" because, even with prolonged use, children will continue to have academic problems and may develop antisocial behavior patterns. Despite these limitations, the efficacy of stimulants is more firmly established than that of any other form of treatment (Gittelman, 1983a).

This summary of the advantages and limitations of medication also serves as a useful background for understanding the reservations certain professionals have voiced concerning the use of drugs with hyperactive children. Like any treatment, pharmacotherapy should be administered with a high degree of professional competence. The child's problems should be carefully evaluated, while the kind and dosage of medication should be constantly monitored. Similarly, the decision to discontinue medication should be made only after comprehensive assessment of the child's functioning at home, in the school, and with peers. Since there are few objective guides, all these decisions are a matter of clinical judgment. (See Kinsbourne and Caplan, 1979; hyperactivity is discussed under the heading Impulsive Extremes.) There is often a temptation to cut short this time-consuming procedure. At its worst, medication can be regarded as a quick cure-all or as a means of making the child more tractable and less burdensome to parents and teachers. Thus medication can be overprescribed or wrongly prescribed, while compliant behavior on the child's part can be equated with cure. The illusion that life's problems can be solved by taking a pill is a seductive one, and one that can operate to the disadvantage of the child who is its victim. (For a detailed discussion of medication, see DuPaul and Barkley, 1990).

Behavioral Approaches *Behavior therapists* have been the most versatile in applying their techniques to remedying many of the problems attendant upon hyperactivity and in documenting their successes. The techniques themselves have varied greatly: the traditional ones emphasize reinforcing desirable behavior while ignoring or punishing undesirable behavior, whereas the newer, cognitively based ones emphasize self-instruction in order to increase self-control (Douglas, 1980). Not only teachers but parents as well have been instructed in the use of behavioral techniques to increase the scope of the child's therapeutic environment. Behavior therapy has been successfully used to induce children to sit still and pay attention, to reduce their disruptive behaviors in class, and to improve performance on a variety of school tasks. They also have been employed to deal with behavior problems in the home. While reports of success are impressive, most involve short-term management. The problems of generalizing success across settings and sustaining it over time remain to be solved.

Behavioral techniques have been successfully adapted to *classroom management*. While praising appropriate behavior and ignoring inappropriate behavior is the basic ingredient, ADHD children need frequent and powerful incentives such as tangible or token rewards as well as prudent reminders backed up by loss of privileges or time out for disruptive behavior. Peer-administered consequences may be especially useful. Success depends on the teacher's ability to monitor the children's behavior frequently and provide immediate feedback. Integrating school and home programs is important for consistency.

Social-skills training has been adapted to helping ADHD children with their problems in peer interaction. Training covers techniques for entering into a group, conversing with peers, resolving conflicts, and controlling anger (Guevremont, 1990).

Cognitive-behavioral interventions have also been tried in an attempt to solve the problem of maintaining therapeutic effects over time. One example is self-instruction in which the children are trained to use self-directed speech in order to define and focus on the task, suggest solutions and monitor their behavior in achieving a stated goal. Such self statements are modeled on those of the therapist; for example, "It looks like I have to copy that square." "I went too fast and did not make that corner right." While a few studies have yielded impressive results, the techniques in general do not have a substantial record of success (Abikoff, 1991; Dush, Hirt, and Schroeder, 1989).

Medication versus Behavior Modification

A number of studies have addressed the issue of the relative effectiveness of medication and behavior modification. The literature is not totally consistent on the issue. Gittelman (1983a), for example, claims that there is no area of functioning, whether cognitive, academic, or social, that shows the superiority of behavior therapy over drug therapy, while Gadow (1985) finds evidence of the superiority of be-

havioral methods in regard to academic performance. Nor is there agreement as to whether combining drug and behavior techniques is more effective than either one alone.

The issue of comparative effectiveness. Whalen and Henker (1991) list a number of variables—or what they call "abilities"—that must be taken into account in deciding on a particular therapy (see Table 6.2). The list is worth keeping in mind any time the issue of the relative effectiveness of treatment arises. We can elaborate on only a few of their variables. In regard to *applicability*, stimulant treatment (ST) is more effective than behavior therapy (BT, excluding cognitive behavior therapy) over a

TABLE 6.2

Comparing and Contrasting Treatment Modalities: An Array of Therapeutic "Abilities"

Applicability: What is the bandwidth or scope of problems that can be treated, and what is the developmental range of effectiveness?

Adaptability: How readily can the treatment be tuned or tailored to meet particular clinical and developmental requirements?

Communicability/teachability: How readily can the basic therapeutic skills and ingredients be identified and taught?

Availability: Once the initial research and demonstration projects conclude, how readily can the treatment be provided by community practitioners under real-life conditions?

Controllability: How readily can standards of delivery be ensured across administratively, philosophically, and geographically diverse treatment settings?

Compatibility: How readily can the treatment be combined with other necessary or desirable interventions?

Durability: What is the stability or predictability of improvement during the course of treatment, and how long are treatment-generated gains maintained once treatment is discontinued?

Generalizability: How well do positive outcomes generalize beyond the treatment targets and settings? What is the range and quality of positive emanative effects?

Constrainability: How widespread and serious are the unintended side effects and undesirable emanative effects of the treatment?

Feasibility: How manageable is the sum total of temporal, psychological, economic, and other burdens imposed on the child and his or her significant others?

Visibility: How likely is the child to be stigmatized because of his or her participation in treatment?

Palatability: How good is the match between client goals, values, and proclivities and therapeutic philosophies and tactics?

Source: Whalen and Henker, 1991.

wider range of domains, although the latter may be more effective in improving specific skills. ST is also more effective over a broader age range, although each has a different span of maximal effectiveness—preschool to middle childhood for BT, middle childhood to adulthood for ST. *Communicability and trainability* are obviously less of an issue for ST than for BT. *Durability,* or sustaining change once improvement has occurred, is more problematic for BT than ST as long as medication is continued. Both techniques arouse concerns in regard to side effects, or *constrainability:* that the child will become dependent on a pill and initiative will suffer in the case of ST, or that reinforcement will decrease intrinsic motivation to perform on tasks in the case of BT. ST is at a disadvantage in regard to *visibility*, as taking a "hyper pill" runs the risk of stigmatizing the child as different and deficient, especially with peers. Note that we have only listed variables. The relative weight they should be assigned may well vary from case to case; for example, stigmatizing may be so potent as to outweigh the advantages of ST.

Other Treatment Approaches *Parent counseling* is employed to educate parents concerning the nature of hyperactivity, to relieve the guilt they often feel, as well as to deal with their frustrations and disappointment. *Parental training* instructs parents in the specific behavioral skills of observation, pinpointing behaviors to be changed, data taking, and devising strategies of reinforcement, punishment, and extinction. The advantages of parental training are that the therapeutic principles can be readily grasped, the parents can immediately become involved in changing specific behaviors, while the charting of these changes provides concrete evidence of change, thereby reinforcing the parent as well as the child. If behavioral techniques are also being used at school, parental training has the additional advantage of providing parent and teacher with a common language and a common base for coordinating their remedial efforts. (For a detailed account of parent counseling and training, see Anastopoulos and Barkley, 1990.)

Family therapy has been used not directly to remedy the hyperactivity but to work through the problems that might have been generated by having a hyperactive child. Such children may have become a "scapegoat" on whom family members displace many of their own problems, or they may be used as a "negative bond" to hold a wavering marriage together. Helping families become aware of and change such patterns of interaction relieves the hyperactive member of the burden of rejection and discrimination.

Multiple Interventions Because ADHD has multiple etiologies and may involve disturbances in a number of intra- and interpersonal areas, multimodal treatment tailored to the needs of the individual child seems the most appropriate approach to remediation. Medication, behavioral treatment, remedial education, parental counseling, and family therapy all should be used as needed. Consequently, the proper treatment of the ADHD child requires a special cooperative effort on the part of the pediatrician, the school, and the mental health professional (Kenny and Burka, 1980).

You are a clinical child psychologist. A pediatrician has referred an ADHD 8-year-old, and you have completed your evaluation. You are now planning your treatment strategy. The mother has told you that the pediatrician has placed her child on a special diet rather than on medication to control his hyperactivity. You know that research shows this diet to be ineffective, but bringing this up with the mother would put her in a conflict between the two professionals responsible for helping her child. You might discuss the decision with the pediatrician at some later date when both of you have more time—if indeed such a day ever comes. Your immediate concern is with informing the pediatrician of your findings and of the treatment program you have in mind.

You next make an appointment to see the mother again in order to explain the findings and treatment plans to her. You also will start working on the family problems centering around having a hyperactive 8-year-old and three younger siblings. While well intentioned, the parents have become increasingly exasperated with the boy and have escalated their punitive behavior. Your initial conference will center around the two great principles of behavioral therapy—ignore the negative and reward the positive (thus reversing the present family pattern) and focus on specific behaviors (which will immediately involve the parents in the constructive task of observing and recording the child's behavior and its social consequences).

You know the psychologist at the boy's grammar school. She is young, unsure of herself, and overworked. While conscientious, she does not seem particularly resourceful. Since the mother took the boy to the pediatrician initially because the school had found him "unmanageable," you suspect that his teacher has also reached the end of her rope. Yet you will contact the school psychologist and see what can be done. The fact that other professionals are now involved might be a relief to the teacher and serve as an opening wedge to exploring other ways of dealing with the boy's management problems.

Because the boy is significantly below grade level in reading, he definitely will need more help in this area than is available in the schools. You know an excellent woman in remedial reading, but she is something of a prima donna who does not "believe in medication," regards special diets as "a hoax," and resents the "MDs who have no business making all the decisions and all the money off of children with educational problems." While she is infinitely patient with children, she is difficult and confronting with her colleagues. It would be easier on you to refer the child to a less talented but more cooperative reading specialist. For the moment you do not know which to choose.

You now have three names on your calendar and a question mark for the fourth. All will require a lengthy contact just to devise the remedial program. Implementing the program will require additional contacts in the future. All of this will take time, and time is always precious. Then there is the matter of billing. To charge the parents for all the time you will have to spend on the phone would confront them with a bill that would work a real hardship on their family budget. But you yourself cannot afford to charge them only for their direct contacts with you. You decide on a compromise—to charge for

some of your time but not all, knowing the decision will mean a financial sacrifice on your part.

While the ideal of skilled specialists meeting the multiple needs of the ADHD child is an attractive one, its realization is exceedingly difficult. The sheer logistics of communication among specialists, as well as the added time involved, are problems in their own right. In addition, professionals differ in their degree of skill as well as in their willingness to cooperate with other professionals. They may be divided on the issue of medication and of behavioral therapy, each of which is apt to be strongly championed by some and equally strongly opposed by others. And the question of who has the ultimate responsibility for the child's welfare—which is the question of ultimate authority and power—can be a touchy one. Professionals are people with their own vested interests, vanities, personal and financial aspirations. To weld them into a cooperative team is a major undertaking.

LEARNING DISABILITIES

You are a clinical child psychologist. It has been a rough day. The climax was a phone call to the principal of Wyckwyre Junior High School. It is the kind of suburban school in which children from two-swimming-pool families do not speak to children from one-swimming-pool families. The call had been about Jon Hastings, a 16-year-old with a long history of school failures. The intelligence test showed him to be bright enough to do college work, and yet he is only in the eighth grade. He is articulate, has a talent for making miniature rockets and speedboats, and a real flair for drawing cartoons. Yet the written word is Jon's nemesis. He reads laboriously one word at a time, while his writing is even more painfully slow. Because of repeated failures and because he is now a social misfit with peers, he has begun cutting up in class and talking back to the teacher.

You had phoned the principal to suggest ways of bypassing Jon's reading disability. Since he is sufficiently bright to absorb most of the lecture material, could he be given oral examinations every now and then? If he were taught how to type, could he type instead of writing his examinations? Would the principal consider introducing special classes for all the learning-disabled children?

The principal was suave and ingratiating and a compendium of the resistances you have run up against in the past. He "understood your concern" but asked that you "look at the situation from my point of view." The school had "tried everything possible to no avail," "the boy is incorrigible," "you can't help a child unless the child wants help," and finally—you could feel this one coming, since you had heard it so often—"I can't give one student a favor without giving a favor to all of them. I'd have half the mothers in my office next day demanding something extra to pull their child's grades up." You had always doubted the validity of this "special-favor" objection but had never found an effective way of countering it. Stalling for time you had asked if you could come and talk with the principal. He was most gracious. He would be happy to tell you about the school and have a student show you around—which was not at all what you had in mind.

A few years back an insightful but poorly educated mother had remarked, "When I get frustrations I come here and bring them to you. When you get frustrations, where do you put them?" The question comes back at times like these.

In Chapter 2 on normal development, we saw how the inherently curious infant becomes the academically achieving student. While the drive to explore is potent, curiosity thrives on stimulation from the social and physical environment during infancy and the preschool period, verbal stimulation being particularly important in our present concern with learning disabilities. With school comes the requirement to learn and the beginning of the child-as-worker. Parental values concerning the importance of education and achievement will encourage maximization of the child's potential. Teachers wrestle with the problem of whether traditional or progressive education will best enhance the child's desire to master academic material. Peers serve to reinforce academic learning, although the study of their influences has been relatively neglected. Progress will also be affected by work habits and freedom from distracting anxieties and angers.

What can go wrong with this development? In the most extreme cases, biological and/or environmental factors render some children incapable of understanding the world in all its complexity, and they find academic subjects particularly perplexing. These children, the mentally retarded, do not learn at a normal rate because they lack the necessary intellectual endowment (see Chapter 12). Other children suffer from being members of a social outgroup and from the physiological and psychological effects of poverty. Such children are not necessarily retarded but have spent their early years in an environment whose very fabric makes it difficult for them to adapt successfully to the requirements of middle-class education.

The third case is the *learning-disabled* child, who is intelligent enough to do better, whose family and cultural background are congruent with academic achievement, who has no gross physiological defect that would obviously impede learning, and who is reasonably free from crippling psychological problems arising from sources outside the learning situation. Yet the child does poorly, perhaps in reading or in spelling or in arithmetic or in all three. Why?

Definitions and Operationalization

At the outset we encounter perplexities in regard to the two questions basic to understanding any psychopathology: How should it be defined? And how should the definition be operationalized?

In the Education for All Handicapped Children Act of 1977 (PL 94-142), learning disability is defined as a disorder in one or more of the basic psychological processes involved in understanding or using spoken or written language. It may manifest itself in a severe discrepancy between age and ability levels in one or more of the following areas of academic achievement: oral expression, listening comprehension, reading, writing, or arithmetic. According to this definition, LD does not include children who have learning problems that are primarily the result of visual, hearing, or motor handicaps; mental retardation; emotional disturbances; cultural or economic disadvantage; or limited educational opportunities.

One practical problem with this definition is that the "basic psychological processes" are not specified or operationalized. In fact, a comprehensive, satisfactory list of such processes is yet to be devised. In addition, there is no statement as to what constitutes a severe discrepancy and how academic achievement is to be assessed. The exclusion of a number of other groups of disturbed and deprived children has been criticized as being potentially prejudicial to them particularly in regard to receiving help. However, this criticism does not seem justified. The definition does not deny that other deviations can coexist with LD, and other programs are available to remedy the learning problems brought on by such conditions.

Other definitions avoid the issue of "basic processes" by defining LD as a discrepancy between at least average intellectual ability or expected grade level and level of achievement. However, this definition has its own problems (see Taylor, 1988a).

One consequence of the disagreement concerning definition and operationalization is that children are selected for research according to diverse criteria. This raises the possibility that the same label is applied to children with different disturbances or different severities of disturbance. For example, a child deficient in the psychological processes involved in reading may have little in common cognitively with one whose achievement in arithmetic is significantly below grade expectations. Labeling them both as LD may well lead to inconsistent research findings and failure to replicate studies.

With all its shortcomings, the concept of LD has had a number of positive consequences. It has called attention to a population of children who are neither "stupid" nor "lazy" in regard to school work, as they tended to be regarded in the past, while relieving teachers of the accusation of being incompetent. It has also stimulated research into cognitive skills and processes involved in learning specific subjects, the possible biological roots of such skills and processes, and the consequences of LD for general adjustment.

How General? How Specific?

While the category of LD can be defended, the results of research have been dismaying. The number of deficits uncovered makes one wonder how such children could learn to write their names, let alone do well in many academic subjects. Children with reading disability alone, for example, were found to be deficient in speech perception, phonemic awareness, phonological coding in short-term memory, availability and use of memory strategies, syntactic knowledge, use of text comprehension strategies, and metacognitive functioning (Stanovich, 1987)! Even allowing for the complexity of reading, such a list is "punishingly complex to interpret and integrate" (Ceci and Baker, 1987: 103).

Currently, many investigators believe that the chaotic nature of the research findings is due to the fact that LD embraces a heterogeneous group of children. Increased methodological sophistication is not the answer to this problem; dividing LD into *meaningful subtypes* is. Once this solution is agreed upon, the question becomes how best to go about discovering meaningful subtypes and what standards to use in judging their goodness.

Researchers are answering the first question with customary vigor, so there are now a plethora of subtypes. (For a detailed description, see Taylor, 1988a.) The majority are in the cognitive domain. Many of them are *clinically based*, in that they are defined by the investigator rather than being derived statistically, and they are often based on a significant discrepancy between language and perceptual abilities. At its simplest, this subtype consists of children who do well on one part of the WISC, say, the Verbal Scale, but poorly on another part, say, the Performance Scale.

Other subtypes have been derived by *statistically clustering* various test results. The so-called neuropsychological tests, for example, include sensory and motor skills (e.g., motor coordination, left-right orientation), language and auditory processing (e.g., verbal fluency and speech discrimination), and visual-spatial and construction skills (e.g., block construction and design copying). While their relation to neurological dysfunctions is often uncertain, they do distinguish LD from non-LD children (Taylor, 1988b).

Another kind of subtype is derived from analyzing patterns of dysfunction among or within *academic skills*. An example of the former would be children deficient in reading and spelling but not in arithmetic (Morris, 1988). An example of the latter would involve breaking down reading into a number of component skills such as whole-word decoding strategies or the ability to relate printed and spoken words. Finally, the *social functioning* of LD children has been organized in terms of subtypes. Fuerst, Fisk, and Rourke (1989), for example, found that 42 percent of LD children were normally adjusted, 15 percent had internalizing problems, 18 percent had externalizing problems, while the rest fell into no particular category.

The Developmental Dimension Subtypes cannot be assumed to resemble traits that are stable over time. What little evidence there is indicates that they change significantly. Between kindergarten and fifth grade, one subtype rapidly went from below to above average in visual-spatial abilities, while language abilities remained consistently impaired (Morris, 1988). Similarly, Spreen's (1988a) nine-year longitudinal study indicated that clusters changed significantly from adolescence to adulthood.

Which Subtype Is Best? Few subtypes successfully meet the statistical criteria of acceptability, and none has emerged as the clear choice. Variables used to establish subtypes are often unreliable (Forness, 1990). Moreover, depending on the method, different clusters can be derived from the same data. And finally, clusters do not adequately account for the population since between 25 and 38 percent of LD children fall outside of the major subtypes (Forness, 1990).

While certain subtypes have advanced understanding and enriched treatment, this has been more the exception than the rule. More typically, a single study is done and positive findings rationalized on an ex post facto basis. There is not the kind of integrated program that we saw in Douglas's research on ADHD children, for example. In regard to producing effective treatments, subtypes have yet to result in well-substantiated classroom applications. In a meta-analysis of studies of effectiveness, the overall impact was small at best and tended to disappear when better-designed studies were included. (For a detailed documentation of the above points, see Forness, 1990. See Kavale, 1990a, for a further discussion of the subtyping issue.)

The Organic Context

Since LD was first described, it has been assumed that organic factors play a major role in its etiology. Yet, as with ADHD, the specific organic factors responsible for the disabilities have yet to be discovered. There is a good deal of supportive indirect evidence, on the other hand. How else can one account for an inability to learn a specific academic subject in children who are intelligent, well taught, well adjusted, and encouraged to achieve academically by parents? The fact that there is a greater frequency of learning problems in natural parents and other blood relatives suggests a genetic component. A history of increased prenatal and perinatal complications, developmental delays, the presence of neurological soft signs, and electrophysiological abnormalities also raise the suspicion of lack of organic intactness. Finally, as we will soon see, the presence of neurological damage significantly affects prognosis. (See Taylor, 1988b, for specific research findings.)

Because of its centrality among etiological factors, the organic context will be examined in some detail.

Some learning disabilities are due to *central nervous system dysfunctions*. Children with cerebral palsy and epilepsy show an elevated rate of reading disability even when they are of normal intelligence. Children who have sustained a localized head injury, especially in the left cerebral hemisphere, are also likely to have difficulty reading (Yule and Rutter, 1985). Such cases are relatively rare, however.

A time-honored organic hypothesis concerns faulty cerebral dominance, or *cerebral laterality*. As early as 1925, Orton speculated that *dyslexia* resulted from a failure to establish hemispheric dominance between the two halves of the brain, a hypothesis that has been revived and revised in light of recent research on laterality. (Our presentation follows Kinsbourne and Hiscock, 1978, and Naylor, 1980.)

Research on brain-damaged patients and on normal subjects has indicated that the left cerebral hemisphere is functionally specialized for certain kinds of language processing, such as letters, syllables, numbers, and words, while the right cerebral hemisphere is specialized for nonverbal, visual-spatial processing, such as face recognition, as well as for nonverbal stimuli such as music, emotional tone, and intonation patterns. The *progressive later-*

alization hypothesis makes the reasonable assumption that, as the highly complex language of the adult develops from a nonlinguistic neonatal state, the cerebrum undergoes a similar development from functional symmetry to left-hemisphere specialization. The failure to develop lateralization constitutes the neurological basis for dyslexia.

A traditional index of lateralization has been hand preference in performing tasks, because each hand is controlled by the opposite cerebral hemisphere. In fact, a number of investigators reported a high incidence of left-handedness or ambidexterity in dyslexic children. Eye and foot preferences have also been used as indices of lateralization. A more recent technique called *dichotic listening* involves the simultaneous presentation of competing sounds in the two ears. Superiority in detecting right-ear sound is presumed to reflect left-hemisphere representation of language.

Despite the plausibility of and initial empirical support for the lateralization hypothesis, the bulk of the research shows that there are no important differences between normal and reading-disabled children in regard to handedness or eye preference. Dichotic listening studies have similarly failed to yield confirmatory data. In part, the contradictory findings have been due to methodological problems along with situational and experiential factors which can alter asymmetry of perception. (See Kinsbourne and Hiscock, 1978, for details.)

Nor has the developmental hypothesis fared any better. Far from being functionally equipotential, current research indicates that the infant's cerebral hemispheres are specialized. Anatomically, the neonate's temporal speech region is usually larger on the left side than on the right; patterns of electrical activity recorded off the infant's brain indicate asymmetries in response to speech and music; a right-handed preference has been shown in 3-month-old babies (infants retaining objects in the right hand significantly longer than in the left, for example); and there is right-ear advantage for speech and left-ear advantage for music in infants as young as fifty days old. Thus, it appears that brain functions are lateralized from birth and that language does not become increasingly lateralized as the child matures.

Direct studies of brain morphology have primarily involved computer tomography (CT), magnetic resonance imaging (MRI), and postmortem studies of the brains of dyslexics. These studies hypothesized that there would be symmetry in the brains of the reading disabled, thus deviating from the normal pattern of asymmetry. While certain studies did find such symmetry, others did not. Even in supportive studies, the results were compared with normal controls instead of groups of children with other deviations such as ADHD or conduct problems. Thus there is no way of knowing whether the pattern is unique to reading-disabled children. In their review of the evidence, Hynd and Semrud-Clikeman (1989) concluded that it is sufficiently suggestive to warrant further, better-controlled studies of brain symmetry, however.

The fact that learning problems tend to run in families suggests a genetic etiology. Since environmental influences are also present, the task becomes one of disentangling the two. (Pennington, 1990, provides a detailed account of conducting genetic research on reading disabilities.) After examining the evidence, Snowling (1991) concluded that a significant proportion of the variance in reading is attributable to genetic effects. Such effects can be both general and specific. There is evidence of a 40 percent risk to a son whose father is reading-disabled and a 35 percent risk if the mother is reading-disabled. In daughters, the risk of having an affected parent of either sex is around 17 percent. There is also suggestive evidence of a significant heritability for reading recognition, phonological coding, and spelling but not for reading comprehension or

for the reading-related skill of digit span. Finally, there seems to be a stronger heritability factor to spelling than to reading. In all cases, the mode of genetic transmission is not clear.

The Intrapersonal Context

Recognizing that a given psychopathology results from organic variables does not exempt psychologists from investigating other contexts. There are at least two reasons for this. First, an organically deviant child is still a child and all the variables in all the contexts will impact upon that child and shape his or her development. Second, the chances of bridging the gap between the organic and intrapersonal contexts are enhanced by increased precision on both sides; thus, the remarkable technological advances in studying the brain can be related to increasingly precise accounts of the nature of the psychopathology under consideration.

Reading Disability   We shall discuss reading disability, or dyslexia, because research has begun to uncover the factors responsible for the disorder. Reading involves a host of skills, from the ability to distinguish letters at the perceptual level to the ability to comprehend meaning. We shall concentrate on *phonological skills* and their relation to early reading because this relationship illustrates our general thesis that reading disability is normal learning to read gone awry, as well as our specific thesis that the earmark of a good idea is its ability to generate a body of interrelated studies.

First, a hypothetical situation. Suppose a friend shows you a sentence in arabic and challenges you to find the name David, which is pronounced "Da oód" in the Arabic language. (See Figure 6.3). Confronted with a swirl of graceful lines, dashes, dots and curlicues, how would you go about it? One way is to assume that Arabic uses a phonetic alphabet

لما كنا في كندا قابلنا داوود في شلالات نياغرا.

FIGURE 6.3
Find the name David.

as does English. Atomizing the sound of the word you note that it begins and ends with the same sound—"dah." Next, you assume that the written Arabic reflects the sounds of the oral language on a one-to-one basis. Consequently, you look for a visual pattern which begins and ends with the same "squiggle," with a different "squiggle" in between. Of course any or all of your assumptions may be wrong, but that is beside the point. What you are doing is proceeding from the known oral word to the unknown written representation of that word and trying to "break the code" of the latter. ("Dah-oo-dah" are the letters of the word on the far right.)

There are those who regard breaking the code as an essential first step in learning to read. Preschoolers have already broken the code of spoken language. In the first year or so of life the infant grasped the fact that those sounds coming from people's mouths were not just interesting auditory patterns but conveyed actual meaning; some sounds stood for mother or milk or father. Later the toddler began learning the rules for ordering these meaningful sounds or words into sequences or sentences in order to convey more complex ideas. Now the preschooler must break the graphic code by finding the relation between the unknown visual patterns and the known auditory patterns of words and sentences.

There are many problems in breaking the written code, the major one being that spoken words are directly perceived as units; for example, "cat," when spoken, registers whole. The fact that "cat" is really made up of three separate sounds, or *phonemes*, does not naturally occur to children. Written language is different. Written words do not register whole.

Even the convention of separating words by a space must be learned. More important, understanding that individual words are composed of units—the letters—and understanding that different letters represent different phonemes is crucial to learning how to read. The technical name for the awareness of and access to the sound structure of language is called *phonological awareness*, which, stated simply, is the awareness that words are made up of phonemes. Identification of the individual phonemes in words is called *phonological analysis* while combining a sequence of isolated speech sounds in order to produce a recognizable word is *phonological synthesis*. The attempt to understand the relation between these phonological skills and the early ability to read has produced an interesting body of research. (Our presentations follows Torgesen and Morgan, 1990, unless otherwise indicated.)

Developmentally, there is evidence that synthesizing skills increase from 7 percent of 3- to 4-year-olds to 98 percent of 9- to 10-year-olds. One measure of synthesizing skills is a word-blending task which consists of presenting individual phonemes at half-second intervals and asking the child to pronounce the word as a whole. Phonemic analysis shows a similar developmental trend. One way of measuring this skill involves orally presenting children with words containing two to five blended phonemes and asking them to tap out the number of phonemic segments.

There is strong correlational evidence indicating a positive relation between good performance on both types of phonological tasks and success in early reading. However, it is equally plausible to argue that reading instruction improves phonemic skills. A longitudinal study addressed this issue by assessing children at four points from the beginning to the end of the first grade. The results showed that phonological skills predicted subsequent reading performance but not the reverse. The specific finding was that synthesis skills facilitated reading acquisition, while phonological analysis seemed to emerge as a consequence of reading skill acquisition. Other studies showed that knowledge of letter sounds by itself does not aid learning to read words containing those letters. Only when letter sound training is preceded by instruction on an auditory blending task is there improvement. In all studies, intelligence was controlled to make sure the results were not due to general intellectual ability, even though evidence suggest only a low correlation between IQ and phonetic blending.

Mann and Brady (1988) present evidence that disabled readers have problems with phonological awareness. Poor readers tend to be correct about the pronunciation of the first letter in the word but have increasing difficulty with subsequent letters, indicating a lack of awareness of phonological segments within words. Poor readers also have difficulty on tasks requiring spoken words to be broken down into phonemes and syllables. Reading-disabled 10-year-olds performed significantly worse on a phoneme awareness task than a group of 6-year-old skilled readers even though the former group had been given considerable more reading instruction than the latter. The same holds true of functionally illiterate adults who have had years of instruction and may be high school graduates. Finally, Mann and Liberman (1984) found a deficit in short-term phonetic memory in kindergarten children who became poor readers in the first grade.

Additional Findings While differences in definition have resulted in estimates of *preva-lence* of LD ranging from 1 to 40 percent of the population, better-designed studies yield figures ranging between 10 and 15 percent, with boys outnumbering girls in a ratio ranging from 2:1 to 5:1 (Taylor, 1988a).

In regard to *general adjustment*, there is no significant difference in the self-concept of LD children and their peers when proper control groups are used. Their self-perceptions are also surprisingly accurate: LD children see themselves as being relatively intelligent but as having difficulty in some academic areas, while their physical appearance, anxiety level, popularity, happiness, and overall feeling of self-worth are like that of their peers. Finally, unlike low-achieving students, they do not become more negative about themselves as they grow older. (For specific studies, see Vaughn and Hogan, 1990.)

In contrast to the positive findings regarding self-evaluation, research indicates that only one-third to one-half of LD children adjust well, their problems ranging from mild to severe. There is no unitary pattern of emotional disturbance, but there is preliminary evidence that subtypes of LD children are differentially vulnerable to various disturbances. Children who have a nonverbal learning disability and do poorly in arithmetic are apt to have internalizing disturbances. By contrast, children with deficits in psycholinguistic skills and do poorly in reading and spelling are less prone to having problems and do not have a specific kind of problem. (For details of the research, see Rourke, 1988.) There is also some evidence that anxious-withdrawn behavior is more characteristic of low-achieving children in general, and not a specific consequence of LD (La Greca and Stone, 1990). In their classroom behavior, elementary school LD children tend to be externalizers, "hyperactivity" in the form of off-task behavior being characteristic (Bryan and Bryan, 1990). However, such behavior is not noted in secondary students (Vaughn and Hogan, 1990). Attentional problems have been found in kindergarten children who subsequently became learning-disabled, indicating that LD cannot be attributed solely to features of formal learning in the classroom (Bryan and Bryan, 1990; Vaughn and Hogan, 1990).

The Interpersonal Context

There is clear evidence from objective studies that LD children are perceived by peers, teachers, parents, and even strangers as less desirable social partners than their nondisabled classmates. (Our presentation of research findings follows Vaughn and Hogan, 1990, unless otherwise noted.) While a certain subgroup is popular, there are more rejected LD students and fewer popular ones than in non-LD populations. Girls are at greater risk for rejection and low peer acceptance than boys.

In their attempts to discover the reasons for poor peer relations, researchers have focused on *communicative behavior* in social interactions. Results indicate that LD children do not make appropriate modifications in their language to accommodate their listeners, have a more egocentric communication style, and are generally less appropriately responsive to peers. One reason for the sex difference in LD children's peer relations may be that verbal interaction is more important to female friendship than to male. Among males, those whose verbal scores are lower than their performance scores are particularly at risk for having deficient peer relations. By contrast, the prosocial behavior of LD children is no different from that of their peers; they interact as frequently, are equally sharing and helping, and may even have a greater than usual willingness to go along with others. There is some evidence that their naiveté and tendency to take others literally make LD adolescents easy prey for those who want to lure them into delinquent behavior (Pearl and Bryan, 1990).

The explanation for the empirical findings is still a matter of speculation.

The Classroom Context   The classroom plays an important role in aggravating or moderating the LD children's emotional problems. There is evidence that such children receive more criticism from teachers than do nondisabled children, that their initiatives are more likely to be ignored, and that teachers are less likely to involve them in nonacademic interactions. This differential treatment may affect the LD children's self-perception and, equally important, may be communicated to other children in the class who model their behavior on the teacher's by expressing similar negative feelings (Bruck, 1987). The physical environment of the school, such as seating arrangement or lighting, does not influence the behaviors of the LD children as was once believed (Kasik, Sabatino, and Spoentgen, 1987).

The Developmental Dimension

Empirical Findings   Let us recap and then expand on the developmental findings. There is evidence that certain of the markings of an LD student are present in kindergarten before formal classwork begins: the difficulty with phonetic representation in short-term memory, and attentional problems. We also found that cognitive functions tend to be fluid rather than traitlike from childhood to adulthood. This should not be interpreted as meaning that academic performance changes or that LD is outgrown. Just the opposite is true. Academic deficiencies tend to persist and may even worsen over time. Only a small percentage of children catch up with their peers, and for most disabled learners, improvement comes with great difficulty. Even adults who become functionally literate may read slowly, have difficulty with comprehension, and make many errors in syntax, punctuation, and logical ordering in their writing. (For details of the research, see Taylor, 1988a.)

One of the most comprehensive longitudinal studies was conducted by Spreen (1988a). A total of 203 LD children were first evaluated when they were between 8 and 12 years of age. They were then divided into three groups: Group 1 had clear neurological indices of brain damage; Group 2 had soft (i.e., subtle) signs of brain damage; and Group 3 had no signs. The groups were evaluated at a mean age of 19 years and again in their mid-twenties. In general, the more severe the neurological impairment, the worse the outcome. Learning problems were not overcome, adults of 25 functioning at levels between grades 5 and 9 in arithmetic, spelling, and reading comprehension. They held less-skilled jobs with lower incomes than those in the control group. They had greater external (impulsive, temper outbursts, hyperactive) and internal (quiet, taciturn) problems than the control group. While problems increased with neurological involvement, they were still not sufficiently severe to classify the population as being clinically disturbed. For example, the adults did not commit the kinds of offenses or have the kind of police record that would justify diagnosing them as delinquent. Rather they were troubled, frustrated, and unfulfilled. Women had more personality, social, and health problems than men.

Not all studies agree with Spreen's rather gloomy findings (Spreen, 1988b.) Some, for example, find no difference from controls or siblings in terms of occupational status; others find up to 50 percent of the LD group to be well-adjusted. Undoubtedly, outcome varies with the many factors determining LD. The advantage of Spreen's study is that he systematically explores the effects of one such factor, namely, neurological impairment.

The Developmental Model What we have covered so far is a descriptive account of the development of LD. What about our concern with viewing LD as normal learning gone awry and our search for models of deviation? Pellegrino and Goldman (1990) found that, at least in regard to simple calculations, arithmetic disability can be regarded as a *develop-*

mental delay rather than a qualitatively different way of solving problems. Thus, while employing the same strategies as non-LD children in simple addition, LD children more frequently used the slower, less accurate methods, such as counting both numbers on their fingers, rather than the more advanced methods, such as starting with the larger number and counting an amount equal to the smaller.

Snowling (1991) reached a similar conclusion in regard to the early stages of learning to read. The initial stage is visual in that children rely on letters to clue them in to words. Consequently, they make visual errors because they remember words according to features like the first letter, (reading "water" for "wish," for example), or by the length of the word, (reading "grandmother" for "gentleman," for example). The second stage is the one familiar to us in that it involves knowledge of letter-sound correspondence. There is evidence that phonological difficulties arrest children at the visual stage, although Snowling does not specify whether this is a fixation or a developmental lag.

In sum, either fixation or a developmental lag is an appropriate model for early reading and arithmetic disabilities. In light of the paucity of developmental studies, such a conclusion is tentative.

Treatment

Lyon and Moats (1988) evaluate the effectiveness of different treatments after first placing them in the framework of their models of LD (see also Kavale, 1990b).

Medically oriented models regard LD as an overt manifestation of an underlying biological pathology affecting perceptual systems, perceptual-motor functioning, neurological organization, and oculomotor functioning. Remediation involves training on visual discrimination, fine motor skills, and eye movements. The *psychoeducational model* focuses on weaknesses in auditory and visual processes related to academic functioning. Remedial programs advocate teaching academic skills on the basis of modality preference, such as visual, auditory, or kinesthetic; on the verbal or nonverbal nature of the subject matter; and on the oral or written nature of the response. *Neuropsychological models*, which relate learning strengths and weaknesses to efficient and inefficient brain regions, employ techniques that will bypass areas of dysfunction. Such areas might include sensory and motor skills, such as left-right orientation and motor coordination; language and auditory processing, such as verbal fluency and speech discrimination; and visual-spatial skills, such as copying designs.

There is little solid evidence that treatment based on either the medical or psychoeducational models has been successful. The neuropsychological model has fared better in terms of documented success, but because of the many methodological problems with such reports, it would be premature to regard the treatment procedures as having proven validity.

The picture is unclear in regard to *stimulant medication,* Gadow (1992) claiming that it is not effective, Kavale (1990b) claiming it is. One source of disagreement may be the fact that studies do not uniformly report whether ADHD was controlled for or not.

Behavior models eschew the idea of physiological and underlying psychological process malfunctioning, concentrating instead on identifying academic-skill deficits and modifying them by techniques derived from learning theory. Lovitt (1978), for example, advocates observing the children in order to discover the precise behaviors that are faulty, such as spelling "ie" words or adding two digits. Change is brought about by reinforcing correct behavior—for example, by praise or granting additional recess time—and by modeling, informing, using mnemonic devices, and cuing or telling children in advance what

is to be done. While behavioral techniques have increased attention and academic performance, successes are often limited to isolated, narrowly defined skills. In addition, the initial behavioral observations are often not practical in large classes, while the individualized procedures may not be cost-efficient.

There are a number of *linguistic models* of treatment. Some target the phonological deficiencies in processing and remembering linguistic material which are related to poor reading and spelling. LD students are taught to analyze the sound structure of words, to associate and use sound-symbol relations, and, at a higher level, to analyze text structure. While there are encouraging preliminary results the supporting research evidence is still thin.

Other linguistic treatments focus on (1) re-

A fourth-grader with a learning disability receiving special help with writing.

ception, or the ability to understand simple spoken sentences or gestures; (2) association, such as seeing that a picture of a dog and a bone go together better than a picture of a dog and an umbrella; and (3) expression, such as verbal fluency. While training on reception yields few benefits, training on association and expression produces somewhat better results (Kavale, 1990b).

Cognitive models are concerned with the specific strategies one employs when learning rather than being concerned with the learned content itself—with the "how" rather than the "what" of learning. Deshler and Schumaker's (1986) program, for example, involves improving the strategies high school students use for extracting information from a textbook. He has students read a chapter two to three times in order to become familiar with its major ideas, specific information, and organization. Students are trained to formulate questions about and paraphrase the main ideas and important details and to use visual images or associations as aids to comprehension and memory. The general cognitive model has been applied to reading comprehension, arithmetic problem solving, written language skills, and study skills, with documented success. However, such success depends on the teacher's accurate assessment of the child's content-specific knowledge as well as the teacher's own expertise with the subject matter.

In the interpersonal context, *parent training* therapies report successes, but their efficacy has not been properly evaluated by objective studies (Anastopoulos, DuPaul, and Barkley, 1991). While *social-skills training* has also been tried, there is no evidence that it increases peer acceptance (McIntosh, Vaughn, and Zaragoza, 1991). Finally, there is evidence that special class placement results in some modest improvement in LD children's academic performance, provided that they are correctly eval-

uated and are not also mentally retarded (Kavale, 1990b).

In general, treatments are most successful when they are directly related to academic content and rely on well-established principles of learning, such as cognitive, behavioral, and linguistic ones. Treatment based on underlying physiological or psychological processes, such as those based on the medical, psycho-educational, and neuropsychological approaches, have yet to establish their effectiveness. This does nothing to discredit the etiological validity of those three approaches, since etiological soundness and therapeutic effectiveness are two separate issues that may or may not be related.

Two final cautions (here we follow Kavale, 1990b). No matter what treatment is used, the gains are modest. Using 1 as a yardstick for a year's achievement in a particular content area for the average student in a given grade, most interventions fall below .50, or one-half year's worth of schooling, while something as simple as reducing class size improves achievement by about one-third of a year.

Next, the effectiveness of any intervention varies widely from one setting to another. Moreover, this variability is not related to age, sex, IQ, SES, or severity of disturbance. Practically speaking, there is no way of knowing ahead of time whether a treatment will produce significant improvement or none at all.

While the onset of many psychopathologies can be reasonably well located within broad developmental periods as we have been doing, such is not the case with depression. Not only can it originate in any period from infancy through adolescence, but its etiology and certain descriptive characteristics can also change with time. Exploring this disturbance and the related one of adolescent suicide will occupy us next.

CHAPTER 7

DEPRESSION, SUICIDE, AND THE CONSEQUENCES OF LOSS

Development would be easy to understand—but far less interesting—if it were linear or a matter of "more of the same": if children became progressively more intelligent, self-controlled, conforming, empathetic, and so on, just as they become taller and heavier. In the first chapter, however, we saw that such a linear model does not fit all the facts of development; instead, there are normal progressions and regressions, appearances, disappearances, and reappearances, as well as seemingly magical transformations.

What we discussed abstractly in the beginning can be concretely illustrated by the development of depression. Depression has been most extensively studied in two different periods—infancy and middle childhood—with little attempt to integrate the findings. Therefore it is not clear whether we are dealing with continuity, transformation, or two unrelated clinical entities.

We shall maintain that the key to understanding both periods is to regard depression as a reaction to loss but to two different kinds of loss: namely, the *loss of a loved person* in the infant-toddler period and the *loss of self-worth* subsequently. As we shall see, each kind of loss has a distinctly different origin in normal development, and in both cases psychopathological depression can be viewed as an exaggeration of the normal pattern of response. Thus loss serves to integrate conceptually what might otherwise be a bifurcated set of data.

However, this conceptual integration is too simple to encompass the complexity of etiological factors. To begin with, there are different kinds of loss of a loved caretaker. Lengthy separation and death will concern us here while loss through divorce will be treated in Chapter 14. Next, we do not mean to imply that depression is the only response to loss. As we shall soon see, depression is closely associated with both anger and anxiety. And, finally, we do not mean to imply that depression results exclusively from loss since it may have multiple roots. One possibility is that having a depressed mother puts the child at risk for becoming depressed. We will review the literature concerning this possibility.

First, however, we will present relevant descriptive information concerning depression in middle childhood and adolescence before turning to infancy and the concept of loss.

DEPRESSION IN MIDDLE CHILDHOOD

Characteristics

Depression, like anxiety and anger, is a normal phenomenon experienced by most people. Some individuals are moody "by nature," having a generally gloomy outlook on life. Dejection and despair, loss of appetite and fatigue, viewing oneself as worthless and life as futile are expected reactions to situations such as failure to achieve a crucial goal or loss of a loved one. Thus psychopathology is a matter

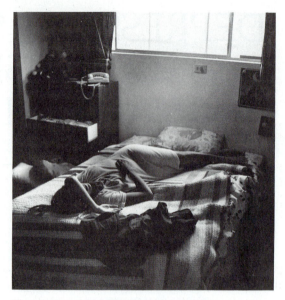

The inertia and hopelessness of depression.

of intensity, persistence, and poor prognosis in the milder cases along with inappropriate and bizarre behavior in extreme instances. Keep in mind that sadness or depressed affect as a single *symptom* should be distinguished from depression as a *syndrome,* which is a complex of symptoms having a specific etiology, course, outcome, and response to treatment, along with characteristic psychological, familial, and biological correlates.

The syndrome of childhood depression is modeled on that of adults. It involves changes in four areas: affect, motivation, physical and motor functioning, and cognition. (For a detailed picture, see Kazdin, 1990.) Kovacs and Beck (1977), conclude that many of the behaviors indicative of adult depression are present in children: emotional (feels sad, cries, looks tearful); motivational (schoolwork declines, shows no interest in play); physical (loss of appetite, vague somatic complaints); and cognitive (anticipates failure, says, "I'm no good") (see Table 7.1).

TABLE 7.1
DSM-IV Draft Criteria of Major Depression

At least five of the following symptoms have been present during the same two-week period and represent a change from previous functioning; at least one of the symptoms is either (1) depressed mood or (2) loss of interest or pleasure.

- Depressed mood most of the day, nearly every day, as indicated by either subjective report (e.g., feels sad or empty) or observation made by others (e.g., appears tearful). Note: in children and adolescents, can be irritable mood.
- Markedly diminished interest or pleasure in all, or almost all, activities most of the day, nearly every day (as indicated either by subjective account or observation made by others)
- Significant weight loss or weight gain when not dieting (e.g., more than 5 percent of body weight in a month), or decrease or increase in appetite nearly every day. Note: in children, consider failure to make expected weight gains.
- Insomnia or hypersomnia nearly every day
- Psychomotor agitation or retardation nearly every day (observable by others, not merely subjective feelings of restlessness or being slowed down)
- Fatigue or loss of energy nearly every day
- Feelings of worthlessness or excessive or inappropriate guilt (which may be delusional) nearly every day (not merely self-reproach or guilt about being sick)
- Diminished ability to think or concentrate, or indecisiveness, nearly every day (either by subjective account or as observed by others)
- Recurrent thoughts of death (not just fear of dying), recurrent suicidal ideation without a specific plan, or a suicide attempt or a specific plan for committing suicide.

Source: American Psychiatric Association, 1993.

There is evidence that the constellation of symptoms defining depression are *organized differently* depending on age and sex. Suicidal talk, for example, is associated with other depressive symptoms in 6- to 11-year-old boys but not in 4- to 5-year-old boys. In a like manner, 6- to 11-year-old girls feel persecuted and anxious along with being depressed while such symptoms are not present in 4- to 5-year-old girls. In older children symptoms are more severe, there is a greater possibility of suicide and greater loss of interest or pleasure (anhedonia) (see Kazdin, 1989a, 1990).

Research also indicates that depression in middle childhood has the same *temporal diversity* as adult depression. Thus depression that

is part of an adjustment reaction, (i.e., a reaction to an identifiable stress such as a divorce), major or severe depression, and dysthymic or mild but chronic depression differ in course and prognosis (Kovacs et al., 1984). Depression with an adjustment disorder and major depression are acute conditions in that their appearance and disappearance are relatively sudden, while dysthymia has an earlier onset and a protracted course. Despite this difference in course, major depressions and dysthymia are alike in that early onset is a poor prognosticator. The rate of "spontaneous" remissions is high in all conditions, but there are differences among the types of depression. Major depressions and dysthymia put children at risk for future depression; adjustment reaction with depression does not. Finally, children with dysthymia are at risk for recurrent major depressive episodes, the course of dysthymia being punctuated by superimposed attacks of major depression during the first five years of the psychopathology. Such findings suggest significant differences among depressed children even though they have the same symptoms. As we shall see when discussing other psychopathologies, treating a heterogeneous group as if it were homogeneous because the children have the same diagnostic label can create and perpetuate confusion.

There is a question as to whether depression in middle childhood can be regarded as the same as that in adults or whether the child's developmental status necessitates modifications and, if modifications are in order, what kinds and how extensive. (See Carlson and Garber, 1986, for a detailed presentation.) At one extreme there are those who point to the behavioral similarities in the manifestations of depression in children and adults as evidence that depression is essentially the same. A middle-ground position acknowledges the similarities but claims that symptoms such as aggression, negativism, conduct problems, separation anxiety, and school phobias may be uniquely characteristic or more characteristic of children than adults. The lack of sex differences in middle childhood also differs from the adult picture, where depression is more frequent in women than men, while adolescents differ from adults in their response to antidepressants.

At the other extreme are those who maintain that, while there are behavioral similarities, the child's cognitive, linguistic, and affective status is so different from that of an adult that the syndrome in children is distinct. While a depressed 8-year-old boy and a 30-year-old man may both say, "The future looks hopeless," for example, they mean something quite

different because their concept of future time differs, the boy's extending only to the next few months while the man's includes the rest of his life. In general, investigators accept the moderate view of significant similarities between adult and childhood depression with children having certain unique characteristics.

Prevalence estimates vary widely, depending not only on the age and sex of the child but, even more important, on the criteria and assessment instruments used. (See, for example, Kazdin, 1989b.) In nonclinical populations the prevalence rates vary between 2 and 5 percent, while in clinical populations they vary between 10 and 20 percent. (See Petti, 1989, for a detailed account of prevalence studies. Kazdin, 1990, describes and evaluates assessment techniques.)

Course

Depressive disorders are quite rare in the preschool period and somewhat more frequent in middle childhood, with no sex differences in incidence. During adolescence there is a dramatic increase, with girls accelerating twice as fast as boys; by age 16, girls are twice as likely as boys to have depressive symptomatology. Somewhat surprisingly, the change in rate is not due to the biological changes that come with puberty, this organic factor being the most obvious choice of an etiological agent (Angold and Rutter, 1992).

In one of the few prospective studies, Block and Gjerde (1990) found a striking sex difference in 18-year-olds with depressive symptoms (who were not necessarily pathologically disturbed). At 14 years of age, girls were ego-brittle, vulnerable, anxious, somatizing, and concerned with their adequacy; they felt a lack of personal meaning in their lives. By contrast, 14-year-old boys were antisocial and hostile, self-indulgent, deceitful and manipulative, sensitive to criticism, unpredictable, and basically mistrustful of others. Sex differences in precursors, while few in numbers, were in evidence as early as the preschool period.

Depressive feelings increase significantly in adolescence; for example, while 10 to 15 percent of children 10 to 11 years old evidence depressed mood, more than 40 percent of adolescents report substantial feelings of misery. The rise seems to be a function of puberty in boys (there are no data on girls) rather than of chronological age (Rutter, 1986a).

Shame enters the developmental picture in the toddler period, although it is not sufficiently stable to be part of the depressive picture until middle childhood, when it may accompany low self-esteem and excessive self-criticism. Guilt as a failure to live up to internalized standards also is not sufficiently stable to play a role in depression until the latter part of middle childhood (see Izard and Schultz, 1989).

The pattern of depressive emotions in normal and disturbed children and adolescents is similar, suggesting that psychopathology is a matter of degree. More important, depression in these two periods is a *complex pattern* of emotions as it was in earlier developmental periods. For all age groups from middle childhood to adulthood and regardless of severity of depression, the predominant affect is sadness, indicating that dejection, discouragement, and loneliness are the central features of the depressive experience. However, there are important age and sex differences in regard to the patterning of affects. In childhood anger plays a prominent role in depression, but not in adolescence and adulthood, and among children, boys evidence more hostility than girls, who in turn are more similar to adolescents and adults in their pattern. Finally, guilt is more prominent in adolescence than in childhood (Izard and Schwartz, 1986).

Adult Outcome The prognostic picture is similar for adults and children, the recovery rate being high but the risk of relapse also being high. Of those children with depression who go on to be disturbed, the great majority show depression as part of the adult disorder. However, in depressed children and adults, nondepressive symptoms are usually also present. Therefore it is not clear what role depression plays—whether it is primarily responsible for the other symptoms or merely one element in a complex of other disturbances (Rutter and Garmezy, 1983). When depression coexists with a conduct disorder, however, there is less of a risk for adult depression but a greater risk for adult criminality. In fact, the risk is as high as it is in children with only a conduct disorder and no depression (Harrington et al., 1991).

The Organic Context

Research with children has been modeled on studies of adults, where the evidence that organic factors play an important etiological role in depression is more extensive and definitive. (Our presentation follows Bootzen, Acocella, and Alloy, 1993, and Burke and Puig-Antich, 1990, unless otherwise noted.)

Family history studies of depressed children and adolescents and studies of offspring of depressed adults show a *genetic* component similar to that found in adults; for example, children of depressed adults are at considerable risk for developing depression themselves. Unlike research on adults, neither twin studies nor adoption studies have been reported, both of which are better able to disentangle the relative influence of heredity and environment than are family studies. In the former, monozygotic and dizygotic twins are compared for the incidence of depression, and, in the latter, the correlation between depression in the biological and adoptive parents is compared. In adults, the risk of depression is higher in monozygotic twin pairs, while adoptive studies support the importance of both genetic and environmental factors. In sum, data on children strongly suggest a genetic component to depression, but its strength and extensiveness remain to be discovered.

Biochemical research with adults indicates a hormonal imbalance as an etiological agent. Since hormone production regulates mood, appetite, and sexual interests, all of which are adversely affected by depression, such a relation is to be expected. The particular imbalance involves the hypersecretion of the hormone cortisol. Evidence for hypersecretion comes from the dexamethasone suppression test (DST). Dexamethasone is a drug that, in normal adults, suppresses the secretion of cortisol for at least 24 hours. Depressed individuals, however, resist the drug's effect, their cortisol returning to high levels within a 24-hour period. However, the DST response may be variable and not specific to depression, since it is found in people with schizophrenia and obsessive-compulsive and eating disorders.

The picture with depressed children is different. The percent of hypersecretion of cortisol is significantly less, as low as 8 percent of depressed children compared with 40 percent of depressed adults in one study. The findings suggest a positive correlation between cortisol hypersecretion and age. The DST response, on the other hand, is similar to that in adults in that depressed children vary in their sensitivity to the test; and as with adults, the test response is not specific to depression, but occurs in children and adolescents with separation anxiety, conduct disorder, and schizophrenia.

There are other differences between depressed children and adults in the organic context. *EEG sleep abnormalities* occur in depressed adults, but none of the changes have been found in children. However, such changes do appear in adolescence, indicating a linear relation between EEG abnormalities and age. By contrast, the relation to the antidepressant imipramine seems to be curvilinear: there is a positive response before puberty and in middle age and a weak response during adolescence and young adulthood. It is hypothesized that the increase in sex hormones during puberty and young adulthood may have a negative effect on the antidepressant action of imipramine.

Comorbidity

Half of depressed children and adolescents have at least one other disorder as well, typically anxiety or antisocial acting out. Measures of anxiety and depression are highly correlated, while 16 to 62 percent of children identified as anxious or depressed have comorbid depressive or anxiety disorders. (Our presentation follows Brady and Kendall's 1992 review of objective studies.) However, the two syndromes are sufficiently distinct to justify classifying children as one or the other or a combination of the two. Children with both depression and anxiety tend to be older, more generally disturbed, and more severely depressed than children with a single diagnosis, with anxiety symptoms typically predating the depressive ones. The relation between depression and aggression especially in boys has already been noted. In addition, Capaldi (1991) found that depressed mood and conduct problems occurred together in 45 percent of early adolescents.

Quiggle et al. (1992), using a social information processing framework, studied 220 nonclinically referred children in grades 3 to 6 who exhibited symptoms of aggression, depression, or both. The data consisted of reactions to hypothetical situations in which the children were rejected or ridiculed by the group or experienced an academic failure. The comorbid group had characteristics of both of the other groups. All three groups were likely to attribute hostile intent to others in a negative situation. Like the aggressive group, the comorbid children were likely to engage in aggressive behavior and indicated aggression would be easy for them. Like the depressed group, the comorbid children were also more liable to attribute the negative situations to internal causes, were less likely to use assertive responses, and expected such assertion to lead to more negative outcomes. While such findings might seem incompatible, contradictions are not unusual in actuality. It may be, for example, that the comorbid group is emotionally unstable, swinging back and forth between externalizing and internalizing behaviors. Other possibilities are also suggested by the authors.

Two short-term prospective studies throw light on the relationship between depression, aggression, and conduct disorders, although neither study used pathologically disturbed children. Panak and Garber (1992), studying children in grades 3 to 5, found that an increase in aggression predated perceived peer rejection, which, in turn, predicted an increase in depression. A second predictor was a tendency toward self-blame. Capaldi (1992), studying boys in grades 6 to 8, divided her group into conduct problems (CD), depressed mood (D), a cooccurrence of both (CO-OC-CUR) and neither problem (LO-LO). She found that, while depression and adjustment problems ameliorated in the D group, no such improvement occurred in the two other disturbed groups. In fact, the combination of school failure, being generally disliked by parents and peers, and low self-esteem in the CO-OCCUR group increased suicidal ideation. In general, conduct problems were more stable than depressed mood. As in the Panak and Garber study, antisocial behavior increased the risk of subsequently having a depressive mood. Parent indifference and lack of involvement was a second risk factor. Capaldi conceptualized the process leading from CD to D as follows: CD results in noxious behavior that alienates parents, peers, and teachers, and produces poor skill development, both of which result in profound social problems and school

failures. Parental rejection, in turn, produces low self-esteem. The impact of peer rejection, low academic skills, and low self-esteem becomes increasingly serious in adolescence, resulting in depressive symptoms (see Figure 7.1). (A detailed exposition of this model can be found in Patterson and Capaldi, 1990. See also Patterson and Stoolmiller, 1991, for a further test of its applicability.)

Two Types of Depression

A review of studies of adult depression by Blatt and Zuroff (1992) will serve as a bridge to our discussion of the relation between childhood depression and two types of loss. The authors point out that, in normal development, there are two basic tendencies, one toward relatedness and the other toward self-definition. In terms of our variables, these would be attachment and the self-reliant component of initiative. However, excessive preoccupation with either can lead to depression. In the former case, depression is due to a disruption of interpersonal relations; in the latter case, it is due to a threat to self-esteem. In the first instance, the individual is dependent and needs to be loved and cared for. In the second instance, the individual is self-critical, concerned with self-control and desires respect and admiration. The first individual fears abandonment and loss of love; the second fears disapproval, failure, and loss of autonomy. Negative feelings for the first individual consist of helplessness and weakness; for the second, inferiority, guilt, and worthlessness.

Extensive preoccupation with either one or the other tendency is due to deviant parenting in the first two years of life where attachment and individuation (or, in our terms, initiative) are core issues. In terms of our model of deviation, therefore, the conceptualization involves *exaggeration* and *fixation*. Finally, the actual occurrence of depression is due to life stressors that play into the specific fears and

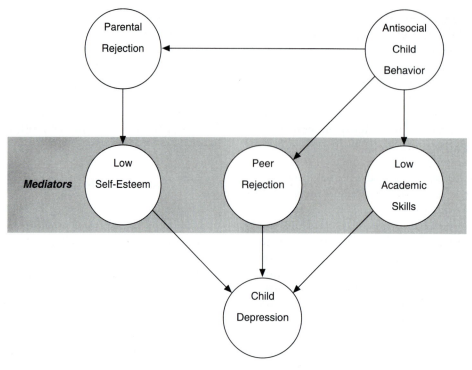

FIGURE 7.1
Mediators for effect of family and child, variables on child depression. (*Source:* Adapted from Patterson and Capaldi, 1990.)

vulnerabilities of the two basic types. (Blatt and Homann's [1992] conceptual integration of the two types of depression differs from ours by emphasizing their roots in insecure attachment rather than in loss.) Tentative support for the dual nature of depression comes from Harter's (1990b) study, which found two groups of depressed children and adolescents. In the larger group depression was due to low self-esteem, while in the smaller group it was due to the loss of a significant person.

We are now ready to explore the special threat posed by the loss of a loved one—specifically, deprivation in the infant-toddler period and death in later childhood. We will then turn to loss of self-esteem.

PARENTAL LOSS

Maternal Deprivation in Infancy

We have seen that adequate mothering in infancy is not a sentimental luxury but an absolute necessity for optimal physiological and psychological development. Being deprived of mothering after the bond of love is forged results in dramatically deviant behavior.

The classical studies of *maternal deprivation* were conducted by Spitz (1946) and Bowlby (1960). From the beginning, depression was observed as a response to a prolonged loss of contact with the mother. Typically, the infants were studied in settings such as hospitals, orphanages, or foundling homes that lacked adequate substitute mothering, even though the infant's physiological needs might have been adequately met.

The descriptive picture of the infant's reaction to maternal deprivation is important to our understanding of depression. Bowlby's (1980) descriptions are based on observations of hospitalized infants. He labels the first stage *protest*. The infant is severely distressed, cries loudly, searches the surrounding area for the mother, shakes the bed, and rejects all substitute caretakers. Agitation and anxiety are both prominent. There may also be generalized anger evidenced by striking out at substitute caretakers, temper tantrums, and destruction of objects. The next phase Bowlby labels *despair*. The infant becomes withdrawn and inactive—for example, lying in bed with face averted, ignoring adults. Attempts to initiate contact produce panic and screaming. Loss of appetite and weight as well as insomnia are present. The facial expression resembles that of a depressed adult. The term used for these behaviors is *anaclitic depression*. The final phase Bowlby labels *detachment*. The infant once again responds to caretakers, to food, and to toys. However, the infant no longer acts as if he or she were attached to the mother, treating her like any other friendly stranger. Relationships are socially acceptable, but lack depth of feeling.

Bowlby's (1980) conceptualization of the above pattern of responses is based on his theory of *attachment* in infancy. In brief, attachment in the first year of life involves the formation of an affectionate and secure relationship to the caretaker. The temporary loss of the caretaker is marked by separation anxiety and anger, while a more prolonged loss is met by sadness and anger. The specific components of the reaction to loss can be meaningfully related to various aspects of attachment. The painful yearning of protest, with its search for the sight and sound of the caretaker, is regarded as an effort to recover her and reestablish the bond of love. The confused agitation, distractability, and overactivity result from the frustration brought on by bond disruption; the innumerable behaviors that constitute attachment continue to be activated but cannot be properly consummated in the absence of the caretaker. Anger in the protest phase is basically directed toward the loved caretaker for not being there when needed, but is displaced onto other people and physical objects in an essentially indiscriminate manner.

During the protest phase the child still has hope that the loved caretaker will return. The phase of despair represents the abandoning of such hope as evidenced by grief, apathy, withdrawal, and somatic symptoms. In the final phase, detachment, the child protects himself from reexperiencing the pain of loss by denying the existence of the bond of attachment.

Bowlby (1980) claims that the basic pattern of yearning for the lost caretaker, anger, agitation, sadness, and defensive indifference are reactions to loss which can be documented from the toddler period through adolescence, although he also acknowledges that the evidence is meager. We shall return to this claim when we attempt a developmental integration of all the data on depression.

One final point pertains to the conceptualization of anaclitic depression. While the typical explanation is in terms of the rupture of the affective bond between mother and infant, Bibring (1953) regards depression as an expression of *helplessness*. It is the awareness that the heroic efforts to regain the mother during the protest phase are of no avail. In the past such efforts have been effective and now they are not; the ensuing helplessness lies at the heart of despair.

Short-Term Effects   Spitz and Bowlby's original descriptions of reactions to maternal deprivation have stood the test of time and are still regarded as valid. (Our presentation follows Rutter, 1972, 1979b.) The characteristic behaviors appear if separation occurs after the child is around 6 months old, because this is when attachment has developed; the behaviors continue to appear upon separation throughout the first three years of life. Not all infants show such behaviors after separation, though, perhaps because of temperamental differences, perhaps because of prior experiences with separation. Many other factors influence the responses to loss of mother. If the separation is of short duration, if the mother or other familiar figures can be with the infant periodically, if sensitive substitute care is available, then the distress-depression reaction is minimal; it is the extended stay in a strange, bleak, or socially insensitive environment with little or no contact with the mother or other familiar figures that is so devastating. Interestingly, the effect of the prior mother-infant relationship upon reactions to separation is uncertain; some investigators find that a good relationship enables the infant to tolerate the separation reasonably well, while others find that a poor relationship produces less disturbance, presumably because the infant has already experienced various forms of aversive or neglectful caretaking at home.

In sum, the effects of maternal deprivation depend upon the total interpersonal, intrapersonal, and temporal context (Etaugh, 1980). Intense, prolonged distress and despair appear only under special circumstances and can be avoided under others.

Long-Term Effects In a comprehensive review Rutter (1972, 1979b) finds no evidence that deprivation, uncomplicated by other stresses, is related to subsequent psychopathology. While hospitalization may produce anaclitic depression in infancy, in and of itself it is not the prelude to psychological disturbances in later childhood. There is a relation between antisocial behavior and broken homes, but the rise in such behavior is greater in homes broken by divorce rather than in homes broken by death, the latter representing the more severe disruption of the affective tie to the parent. In sum, Rutter concludes that the evidence suggests that it is a disturbed relationship between parent and child rather than a bond disruption per se which is related to the subsequent development of psychopathology.

Parental Loss in Middle Childhood

Historically, professionals thought depression did not exist in middle childhood because of the wide range of nondepressive responses to parental death, such as rebelliousness, restlessness, and somatic symptoms. (The clinical observations are summarized by Bakwin, 1972, and Malmquist, 1980.) Such behaviors were thought to be masking an underlying depression. While the concept of masked depression was subsequently discredited, the clinical observation that loss can produce a variety of responses other than or in addition to depression is a valid one. What is interesting is that if one juxtaposes the clinical descriptions of depression and masked depression in middle childhood with Bowlby's (1980) expanded description of reactions to loss of a loved caretaker in the first five years of life, the overlap is striking, especially when viewed in a developmental context (see Table 7.2).

Dysphoric Reactions Dysphoric responses form the affective core of bereavement at all ages.

Crying, Grief, and Apathy Violent or hysterical crying—which Bowlby (1980) calls protest, or the pain of yearning—has been observed from infancy through the preschool period, appearing as tearfulness in adolescence. The affect is constant but the quantity and degree of control change, as would be expected. For example,

TABLE 7.2
Reactions to Loss of Loved Parent

	Dysphoric reactions		Response to other caretakers		Externalizing reactions	
	Pain and despair	Self-comforting	Dependency	Fear of loss	Anger	Restlessness
Infancy	Anguished crying, grief, apathy	Thumb sucking, cuddling toys	Clinging	Separation anxiety	Indiscriminate tantrums	Agitation
Toddler/pre-schooler	Crying (but decreasing), sadness, withdrawal	Masturbation	Clinging, desire to be nursed	Separation anxiety	Playing out anger, tantrums (but decreasing)	Agitation
Middle childhood	Crying (but decreasing), sadness		Clinging, whining, baby talk; independence	School phobias	Disobedience, cheating, truancy, delinquency	Restlessness, schoolwork declines
Adolescence	Tearfulness, sadness, listlessness			School phobias	Rebelliousness, fighting, rudeness, drug abuse, drinking, running away, sexual acting out	Restlessness, schoolwork declines

Achenbach and Edelbrock (1981) found that crying, as part of a depressive syndrome, declines significantly between 4 and 16 years of age. The grief and total apathy of the infant-toddler period also moderate, older children being described as sad, withdrawn, listless, and moody. The overall developmental trend is from intense, pervasive expressions of affect to moderation and control.

Self-Comforting Thumb and finger sucking along with cuddling toys serve as solace from infancy through the preschool period, with masturbation appearing in preschoolers. Once again, the change from oral to genital stimulation is developmentally appropriate. Whether such behaviors disappear subsequently, or whether school-aged children and adolescents are more reluctant to admit to them, is an unanswered question. It would not be unreasonable to assume that masturbation would continue, especially in boys.

Response to Other Caretakers Loss of a loved parent affects the child's relation to the surviving parent and to other caretakers.

Dependency The infant-toddler period is characterized by clinging to the surviving caretakers and a regressive desire to be nursed again. Clinging, whining, and baby talk reappear as regressive behaviors in middle childhood, along with the more socially appropriate behavior of exaggerated independence, which may well represent a protection against the vulnerability of reexperiencing loss. One would not expect obvious manifestations of dependency in adolescents, who are striving for independence, although an exaggeration of this striving, similar to that observed in middle childhood, might be present.

Fear of Loss Fear of loss seems closely related to dependency: the more one needs the surviving caretakers, the more one is fearful of losing them. Separation anxiety has been noted from infancy through the preschool period and is supplemented by a fear of losing loved pets in preschoolers. While separation anxiety per se disappears from middle childhood through adolescence, school phobias appear. While there are diverse causes for school phobias, in those instances in which separation is critical, they represent an age-appropriate transfer of the fear of loss from home to school.

Externalizing Reactions Anger and agitation frequently accompany loss, although the form they take changes as the child develops.

Angry Reactions A number of behaviors can be conceptualized in terms of anger and follow the well-known developmental progression from intense, raw expressions of affect to more controlled, diverse, and disguised expressions. The arena for expressing anger also expands from home to school to community, as one would expect from a developmental perspective.

In the infant-toddler period one finds temper tantrums and violent temper outbursts. Preschoolers begin to harness such outbursts and express their anger symbolically through words and play. In middle childhood there are many signs of defiance of authority, such as disobedience, delinquent acts, cheating, or truanting from school. While the affective intensity has been tamed, the target has expanded to include not only home but school and society in general. This same trend continues into adolescence, a period in which rebelliousness, fighting, quarrelsomeness, rudeness, and negativism have been noted. Finally, there is a cluster of behaviors specific to adolescence which, while potentially arising from many different motivations, may well represent angry, defiant gestures directed toward authority, the implicit message being, "Nobody is going to tell me how to behave." This constellation includes running away from home, sexual acting out, drug abuse, and drinking.

Agitation A high state of manifest agitation has been observed from infancy through the preschool period, while school-aged children and adolescents are described as being restless. The primary development here, as it was in anger, is an increase in control, which moderates the expression of the reaction. Decline in the level of schoolwork in middle childhood and adolescence may be due, in given instances, to the difficulty in concentration which accompanies restlessness, although, as has been noted, the decline may also be due to anger directed toward authority figures.

Research Research on response to parental death in children is meager and consists primarily of clinical observations. There are few well-designed studies using objective measures. An exception to this generalization is Weller and colleagues' (1991) study of 38 bereaved children between 5 and 12 years of age. The researchers found that 37 percent of the children met the DSM-III-R criteria for a major depressive episode, although they were not as disturbed as a group of children hospitalized for depression. The bereaved group did not feel as guilty or worthless as the depressed one; unlike the depressed group, they had not attempted suicide, although they did have suicidal thoughts. Factors associated with depression in the bereaved group were mother as the surviving parent, a preexisting untreated psychiatric disorder in the child along with a family history of depression, and high socioeconomic status.

This single study highlights how little we know about the difference between normal bereavement and psychopathological depression and the conditions that produce one rather than the other.

Developmental Trends and Principles The developments just described conform to general trends and principles. First, there is increased control of affect, seen in the moderation of crying, apathy, agitation, and rage.

There is a trend toward expanding the psychological environment from home to school to community, seen in the change from separation anxiety to school phobias and from anger at caretakers to disobedience at school to breaking laws. The change from thumb sucking to masturbation represents an age-appropriate progression from oral to genital auto-eroticism. Finally, there is an overall change in terms of increasing differentiation. The protest-despair reaction is a comparatively global one occurring in a short period of time. With development, elements of the pattern become singled out or differentiated, just as the infant comes to use arms, legs, hands, and fingers as independent units of the body. With differentiation comes independence, so that by middle childhood reactions to loss can contain single elements or any combination of elements.

Adult Consequences

In the past, researchers made the mistake of relating parental death directly to adult disturbances while ignoring all intervening events. Predictably, the result was conflicting findings. By contrast, Brown, Harris, and Bifulco (1986) have developed a model that takes such intervening events into account, although in their research, they deal not only with death but also with a significant period of separation from the mother. In its simplest form the model assumes that a depressive episode is due to current adversities, or what the investigators call *provoking events,* such as a major disappointment. Next, the chance of such experiences bringing about depression is greatly influenced by the presence of *vulnerability factors* such as lack of social support, lack of intimate ties with a spouse, or having three or more children under the age of 14 living at home.

Brown, Harris, and Bifulco (1986), using an interviewing technique, found that loss of the mother before the age of 11, whether by death or separation, was clearly associated with subsequent depression for adult women in the general population and, to a lesser extent, for women diagnosed as being depressed. Thus it could be considered a vulnerability factor. Loss had no effect in the absence of a provoking agent, however. Incidentally, loss of a father before 11 years of age had no effect on depression regardless of whether there was a provoking agent. Brown, Harris, and Bifulco further reasoned that because working-class women experience more provoking agents and vulnerability factors, the relation between loss of mother and depression should be more common in this class. Analysis of the data showed this to be so.

A subsequent study by the same authors illustrates how complex the pattern of intervening events can be. The subjects were adult women who lost their mothers before the age of 17 either through death or through a separation of a year or more. One initial finding was that the rate of depression was twice as high in women who had experienced aberrant or traumatic separations, such as being neglected, abused, or abandoned, than it was in women separated by death or by socially accepted causes such as maternal illness, employment, or divorce.

Depression significantly increased if the child was placed in an institution after the death or separation, although this held only for lower-class subjects. Lack of care in the form of indifference or lax control following the loss or separation also increased the incidence of depression. Finally, a general feeling of helplessness in coping with life's stresses significantly increased depression. Overall, predictors were more potent in the lower than in the middle class. Of all the variables, the interpersonal one of lack of care was the most crucial; the intraindividual variable of helplessness was also important, but to a lesser degree.

In a more recent study, Bifulco, Harris, and Brown (1992) found that the rate of adult depression was particularly high in women

whose mother died before they were 6 years old and even greater if death occurred before they were 3 years old. Maternal death was followed by feelings of helplessness in childhood, which, in turn, was a precursor of depression. However, it was not the early timing of the death per se that was important. Rather, it was the fact that the death came at the end of a long sickness, which, the authors infer, prevented the development of a secure attachment. In sum, the developmental line is from insecure attachment (owing to maternal illness) to death before the child was 6 years of age, to middle-childhood helplessness, to being vulnerable to adult depression.

The following picture emerges when we integrate the two studies just described. Childhood helplessness, which is a vulnerability factor for adult depression, has roots in two different developmental periods. The first is maternal death before the child is 6 years old, if the death is preceded by inadequate maternal care. The second is separation from the mother for a variety of reasons, such as abandonment, in the general context of lack of care not only from the mother but also from all adults responsible for such care. This second root is not limited to the child's first six years but can happen at any point in development.

The findings concerning *father loss* in middle childhood and adolescence have a familiar ring (Herzog and Sudia, 1973). There is no evidence that paternal death is the prelude to subsequent psychopathology. While paternal loss owing to divorce, desertion, and separation does have adverse consequences, such losses are complicated by many added stresses, and there is no evidence that loss per se is prepotent. In fact, the same stresses in intact families are equally likely to produce subsequent psychological disturbances.

The lesson is clear. Both in infancy and middle childhood, the idea that maternal deprivation per se leads to depression is simplistic and inaccurate. Rather, depression is contingent upon the interaction of a host of intrapersonal (such as helplessness), interpersonal (such as lack of social support), and superordinate (such as socioeconomic level) factors, including the developmental factor of the child's age. The task of investigators is to tease out the interactions among variables and the ways such interactions might change as loss occurs at different points in development.

LOSS OF SELF-WORTH OR SELF-ESTEEM

Currently, research is concerned with loss of self-worth rather than loss of a loved caretaker. It centers on the *cognitive triad* of worthlessness ("I am no good"), helplessness ("There is nothing I can do about myself"), and hopelessness ("I will always be this way"). Note that it is not low self-esteem alone that leads to depression; it must be intensified by the ideas that the individual cannot change the state of affairs, which, in turn, will continue indefinitely. The original conceptualization of the cognitive triad was intended to account for adult depression and was subsequently applied to middle childhood. (Haaga, Dyck, and Ernst, 1991, review the conceptualization and objective studies of adults.) A summary of research on children will enrich our understanding of the triad as well as informing us as to how well it applies to children. (Unless otherwise noted, our presentation follows Hammen, 1990.)

There is good evidence of a correlation between childhood depression and low *self-esteem*. Moreover, the children's negative view of the self leads to a biased interpretation of information so as to "confirm" the belief in their inadequacy. For example, dysphoric children recalled more negative trait descriptions of the self in a memory test, while nondepressed children recalled more positive adjectives. However, this tendency is no longer evident when depression lifts.

Seligman's (1975) concept of *learned helplessness* has proven to be a particularly fruitful

behavioral translation of the helplessness dimension. The original data came from laboratory studies of dogs. In one study a dog was strapped into a hammock and administered sixty-four electric shocks from which there was no escape. Twenty-four hours later he was put into a box and again shocked, except now he could escape by jumping over a barrier into an adjacent box. Dogs with no previous experience with inescapable shock quickly learn to jump the barrier to safety. However, approximately two-thirds of the dogs who had been shocked failed to escape. After an initial reaction of running around frantically, they lay down and whined, passively accepting the pain. The behavior is not limited to dogs: it has been found in cats, rats, fish, nonhuman primates, and people.

In all the studies subjects learn that noxious events occur independent of their own responses. Therefore, they no longer respond with an effort to avoid pain. Such nonresponsiveness is called learned helplessness. It has a complementary cognitive and motivational component. Cognitively, the individual learns that responding is futile, and this knowledge concomitantly reduces the motivation to respond. In terms of self-conceptualization, the individual is no longer an agent but the recipient of whatever pain happens to come along.

In a subsequent reformulation the variable of *causal attribution* was added to Seligman's learned-helplessness model (Abramson, Seligman, and Teasdale, 1978). Three dimensions are involved: attribution must be *internal, stable,* and *global* in order to lead to depression. If uncontrollable events are attributed to characteristics of the individual, rather than to external agents, self-esteem will diminish as helplessness increases. If the uncontrollable events are attributed to factors that persist over time, then helplessness is stable. And if uncontrollability is attributed to causes present in a variety of situations, helplessness is global. Depression results from this attributional style in the individual interacting with uncontrollable bad events. Neither style nor uncontrollable events alone result in depression.

Studies of children's attribution styles have produced mixed rather than confirmatory results, however. (Again we follow Hammen, 1990.) There is also a question as to whether attribution styles are specific to depression rather than characteristic of psychopathology in general. The limited longitudinal evidence indicates that it is not predictive of depression.

Attribution style is similar to *locus of control:* the perception of being in control of one's life (internal locus of control) or of being controlled by external agents (external locus of control). The latter may be an element in helplessness. The few studies that have been done offer limited but not strong support for a relation between locus of control and depression.

In regard to *hopelessness,* there is evidence from a handful of studies that depression is related to high scores on an instrument designed to measure this variable.

While the cognitive triad is concerned with the intrapersonal context, it also recognizes the importance of *life stressors.* Depression, so the reasoning goes, is precipitated not by stressors in general but by stressors that impinge on the specific areas of an individual's vulnerabilities and incompetencies. While there is some evidence that this is true of adults, research on children has shown that they become depressed only in relation to interpersonal vulnerabilities rather than to other ones such as achievement.

Finally, Hammen (1990) cautions that most of the studies have been conducted on mildly rather than clinically depressed children; that depressive cognitions appear to be state-dependent, coming and going as depression waxes and wanes, rather than being an underlying trait that would serve as a "marker" of vulnerability; that the issue of specificity to depression is unresolved; and that there is much to be learned about how the depressive triad is acquired.

Developmental Reconstruction

Unlike the reactions to loss of a loved parent, the cognitive triad of worthlessness, helplessness, and hopelessness cannot exist in infancy. As we did before, we must once again turn to research on normal development. The most relevant data involve the development of the self-concept in general and of self-esteem in particular, as well as data on the development of affect in general and dysphoric affect and guilt in particular. The data summarized here come from more detailed presentations by Cicchetti and Schneider-Rosen (1986), Digdon and Gotlib (1985), Dweck and Slaby (1983), Kovacs (1986), and Garmezy (1986).

The basic question we must ask is not, At what point do the components of childhood depression appear on the developmental scene? but, At what point do the components of childhood depression become sufficiently stable and potent to produce the characteristic symptom picture? The literature on normal development indicates that depression is not possible in the preschool period but is possible in middle childhood. Even within this latter span, there is suggestive evidence that depression becomes increasingly possible as one moves from 7 to 11 years of age. More specifically, a sustained negative self-image, along with a self-sustained feeling of helplessness and a dysphoric mood, are not consolidated until middle childhood, while hopelessness and guilt do not become firmly established until the preadolescent period. Thus the components comprising the syndrome of depression become stabilized at different points in middle childhood, some appearing early, others not until preadolescence.

The following is a summary of relevant literature (see Table 7.3).

TABLE 7.3

Self-Esteem: Cognitive and Affective Components

	Preschool	Middle childhood	Adolescence
Self-concept ("I am")	Physical self: actions, body, possessions	Psychological self: traits, characteristics	Adult form: integration of components, stable characteristics, time perspective
Self-evaluation: worthy or worthless	Absolute "good" or "bad" Inconsistent, inaccurate Vacillates with context Knows others are proud or ashamed of him/her	Stable evaluations based on: evaluations of others, self-evaluation Negative self-evaluation, ideas of worthlessness	Adult stability achieved Persistent feelings of worthlessness
Self-evaluation: competent or helpless (especially cognitive competence)	Can set goals, take actions to achieve, evaluate outcome, feel satisfied or dissatisfied No explicit self-evaluation, no relating outcome to personal attributes May overestimate self, underestimate difficulty Attributes reasons capriciously	Evaluations based on: teachers' judgments, comparison with peers Realistic self-evaluation Pervasive feelings of helplessness possible	Accurate self-evaluation Persistent feelings of helplessness
Self-evaluation: hopeful or hopeless	Limited grasp of time, lives primarily in present	Understanding of time increases	Past and future grasped Hopelessness possible
Affect:			
Cognition	In others: distinguishes affects, identifies causes In self: physicalistic identification of situation, body	Distinguishes affects in self Sadness increasingly attributed to internal factors	Accurate grasp
Mood	Context-dependent and changeable	Sadness increasingly prolonged and sustained	Intense, persistent dysphoric mood possible
Guilt	Temporary guilt over accidental as well as intentional acts	Intentionality necessary	Intense, persistent guilt possible

The Self-Concept The preschooler has a physicalistic idea of the self. He is his body or his possessions or the things he does. In response to the question, "Who are you?" he is apt to reply, "I have a baseball and I go to playschool." Such an image is subject to frequent change. Only in middle childhood is the self defined in terms of psychological characteristics and traits, thereby achieving stability and continuity. For example, the child might say of himself, "I'm friendly and have a good sense of humor." However, it is not until adolescence that true self-reflection is possible in the sense of an integration of the components of the self into stable characteristics that can be viewed in terms of both past and future.

Self-Evaluation as Worthy or Worthless Preschoolers judge themselves absolutely and globally as "good" or "bad." However, such judgments are inaccurate and vacillate with the situation because they are based on the physicalistic "me." Thus the all-good-me can turn into the all-bad-me as the child behaves now one way and now the other. However, children are aware that others are proud or ashamed of them. In middle childhood the physicalistic "I" gives way to the conceptual "I," as has already been noted. This increased realism is accompanied by more stable personal evaluations and children can have sustained feelings of being proud or ashamed of themselves. Thus they can feel either worthy or worthless and unloved, these feelings being due to social evaluations, success or failure in living up to their own standards, or a combination. In adolescence, the judgment of worthlessness is comparable in stability and potency to that found in adults.

Self-Evaluation as Competent or Helpless A good deal of the literature here concerns intellectual achievement. On the positive side, preschoolers have developed to the point where they can set goals, take action to achieve them, evaluate the achievement against inner standards, and feel such positive and negative affects as pride and shame. However, they do not explicitly engage in self-evaluation or relate outcomes to personal attributes. For example, they do not ask what they did right when they succeed or wrong when they fail. Moreover, they may overevaluate themselves ("I am the best") and underestimate task difficulty while maintaining high expectations of success in the face of failure. Thus their view of achievement is unrealistically sunny. Finally, they always find reasons for success or failure no matter how farfetched, such as, "These dumb things [pieces of a puzzle] don't want to fit together."

Learned helplessness may not be possible in the preschool period. Preschoolers are much too optimistic, much too unconcerned with their own role in success and failure, much too capricious in improvising explanations for bad things happening, for them to make internal, stable, and global attributions no matter how uncontrollable events are. (For a review of the developmental data on learned helplessness, see Fincham and Cain, 1986.)

Two developments take place in middle childhood. The more important of these is school attendance, which introduces positive and negative evaluations by powerful others, the teacher in particular but peers as well. Next, social comparisons are used to evaluate competence, and these social standards are increasingly employed as criteria for success. Thus a realistic, objectively based self-evaluation replaces the former unrealistic optimism. A realistic awareness of reasons for success and failure also makes its appearance. The change in self-appraisal and awareness of one's personal role in success and failure may lead to feelings of helplessness when children are in situations of repeated failure ("No matter what I do, nothing ever works"). One finds a gradual increase in pervasive feelings of helplessness between 7 and 12 years of age.

Hopelessness The meager evidence indicates that preschoolers are incapable of hopelessness because they live primarily in the here and now. They can neither abstract a general theme of hopelessness from life nor project it into the future. There is little information concerning middle childhood, but the literature suggests that only the adolescent has a sufficiently realistic grasp of time to make a truly hopeless view of the future possible.

Affect: Cognitive Aspects Preschoolers distinguish the basic emotions in others and can even identify their causes, but they cannot bring the same cognitive sophistication to their own emotions. Instead, they are as physicalistic here as they are in regard to their self, identifying emotions by situational and bodily cues. For example, sadness is bruising a knee; happiness is having a birthday party. Thus others can be sad, but not oneself. School-aged children, by contrast, can distinguish emotions in the self. More specifically, the 7-year-old begins to attribute sadness to emotional factors such as failure, although an external orientation still persists. By 12 years of age, internality is prevalent and stable. As can be expected, adolescents accurately grasp the inner, mentalistic nature of emotions; for example, one can act in a way that is different from one's feelings.

Affect: Mood The preschooler's mood is context-dependent and changeable. There is also some evidence that the prevalent mood is positive. Seven-year-olds can have periods of sadness, but sustained sadness is generally possible only toward the end of middle childhood. The adolescent is capable of sustained dysphoric moods, which increase in frequency during this period and which must be distinguished from abnormal depressions.

Affect: Guilt The preschooler tends to be guilty over accidental and uncontrolled events. In middle childhood, intentionality is necessary for guilt. However, only the adoles-

cent is capable of experiencing intense and prolonged guilt.

Developmental Trends and Principles As was the case with loss of a loved caretaker, changes in the components of self-esteem follow well-established developmental trends and principles. One trend is from concrete to abstract thinking as exemplified by the change from a physicalistic understanding of the self and its affects to a more abstract conceptualization of both. Abstract thinking, in turn, brings a stability that contrasts with the more environmentally contingent concreteness of the preschool period. A parallel progression is from action to reflection upon action to explicit self-awareness; for example, from a self that consists only of ongoing behavior to monitoring and judging actions to explicit self-characterizations such as "I am worthless." Certain developmental trends and principles are common to both kinds of loss, the expansion in time noted in loss of a loved one, for example, being expressed here in an increased ability to envision a hopeless future.

Why the Triad? Understanding when the depressive triad *can* develop is different from understanding why it develops. Here data thin out and speculation expands to fill the vacuum. Some of the best clues come from Harter's research (Chapter 2). She found that self-esteem becomes more differentiated with age and that the competencies upon which self-esteem depends have different saliency for different children. Harter (1987) further found a strong relation between self-worth and mood, the correlations running between .67 and .82 in children 8 to 15 years of age. Furthermore, Harter (1986) found that 80 percent of fourth-graders with high self-esteem were able to discount their areas of low competence, while only 50 percent of children with low self-esteem were able to do so. The tendency to continually aspire to success in areas of weakness or the discrepancy between aspiration and achievement may be one precursor of feelings of despair.

A second source of depressive mood is the evaluation of significant others, not only parents but, as our review of research informs us, peers and teachers as well, all of whom can implicitly send the message, "You are no good." Parents, for example, may be hypercritical or disapproving or may set impossibly high standards for the child (Blatt and Homann, 1992). Peers can also be relentless in their taunting of the socially inept child.

While Harter (1990b) describes two different sources of low self-esteem—failure in one's own eyes and the negative evaluations of others—the two are obviously interrelated. Yet, the nature of this interrelationship remains to be clarified both conceptually and empirically. Relevant to this issue of interrelatedness, it is important to note that research on the cognitive triad requires the use and understanding of language, which, in turn, constrains it to the late-preschool and middle-childhood periods. Yet a host of significant events may have happened in the preceding years that children cannot verbalize. Clinical observation and speculation suggest that parents, especially intrusive ones, may undermine self-reliance; this, in turn, serves as a precursor of a sense of failure and depression. (See, for example, Blatt and Homann, 1992.) Documenting such clinical observations with objective data remains largely a task for the future.

CHILDREN OF DEPRESSED MOTHERS

One possible source of childhood depression is being cared for by a depressed mother.[*] Here, depression has nothing to do with loss.

------

[*] Since the point of departure here is the mother rather than the child, this topic belongs in Chapter 14, which deals with risk factors in the interpersonal context. It is placed here because of its affinity with the foregoing material on childhood depression.

Since children raised by depressed mothers are at increased risk of becoming depressed themselves (Dodge, 1990b), studying the mother-child relation would seem an ideal way to explore this particular root of depression. However, many factors conspire to entangle researchers in confounding complexities. (Unless otherwise noted, our presentation follows Downey and Coyne's 1990 review and evaluation of objective studies.)

To begin with, depression in mothers is apt to occur in conjunction with other psychological disturbances (anxiety and personality disturbances) and interpersonal difficulties (marital conflict and divorce). Moreover, depressed women tend to marry men with psychiatric illnesses, which increases the likelihood of family disturbances. Consequently, children are exposed not only to maternal depression but to other forms of psychopathology, marital conflict, and adverse living conditions. Next, as we already know, depression in children is apt to occur with other disturbances. In this welter of potentially confounding and pathogenic variables, homing in on the one specific to childhood depression is a daunting task. Yet, the task seems worthwhile since there is evidence that maternal depression is differentially important: depression is the only diagnosis that children of depressed mothers receive more often than children in a control group.

One final complication: children of schizophrenic mothers are also at increased risk for depression. This is a problem we will meet again, namely, the lack of *specificity* of research findings once one controls for the degree of disturbance. All one can conclude is that, in general, disturbed mothers have depressed children—and this does not tell us what we want to know.

The clearest examples of the effects of maternal depression come from studies of infants, where the situation is still relatively simple compared with what it will become. In reviewing the research, Field (1992) concludes that infants of depressed mothers develop a depressive mood style as early as 8 months of age, that this style generalizes to interactions with nondepressed women, that if it persists over a year it adversely affects growth and intellectual development. However, the findings hold only if the mother continues to be depressed. If she recovers, so does the infant, suggesting the contingent nature of the depressive mood. Also, the relation between infancy and the subsequent development of depression is yet to be made.

After infancy, the scent grows faint. By the preschool period, Lovejoy (1991) found that while depressed mothers exhibited more negative behavior than nondepressed controls in observed interactions, such behavior did not characterize the majority, who were undistinguishable from the controls in may ways. Or again, Politano, Stapleton, and Correll (1992) found that, while maternal depression was related to lower self-esteem in 8-year-olds, the strongest relation was with persistent anxiety. Whether this is the anxiety that serves as a prelude to depression is impossible to determine. On a more positive note, Radke-Yarrow and colleagues (1992), in their longitudinal study, found that maternal depression influenced the course of children's depression, increasing it from early to middle childhood but not from then on.

Because interest in children of depressed mothers runs high, ingenious researchers may well find a way to control for or eliminate confounds, allowing a clearer picture of the relation to childhood depression to emerge.

Explanations In regard to explanations, the situation is equally unclear. Evidence indicates that *genetic transmission* is weaker than it is in adults, while the effects of genetic and environmental mediation have not been clearly separated (Rutter et al., 1990).

The next most likely explanation is in terms of *parenting*. Here one must first translate symptoms of depression into parenting behavior, always keeping in mind that such behaviors may have a different impact on children of different ages. [Sigel and Blechman (1990) discuss the problem of translating symptoms into parenting behaviors, while Yarrow (1990) presents one solution.] Depressed mothers respond less frequently, less quickly and contingently, and with less positive affect than do nondepressed mothers, perhaps because of decreased energy and increased self-absorption. Next, there is an increased hostility and negativity toward the child, discipline being marked by coercion rather than negotiation, which requires more patience and willingness to see the child's viewpoint than the mothers are capable of. However, there are two problems here. The first is that similar patterns of parenting are found in nondepressed mothers who are experiencing stressors in the family (such as marital conflict), in the environment (such as poverty), and in the mother herself (such as physical or other psychiatric illnesses) (Downey and Coyne, 1990). Next, the specific links between mothering and depression have not been made, nor are the processes responsible for the linkage understood.

TREATMENT

Pharmacotherapy

Many of the medications for adults have been applied to children. The most widely studied are tricyclic antidepressants such as imipramine. As with adults, the medication reduces depressive symptoms in children, but its effectiveness is mediated by the child's plasma level and is reduced in children with psychotic symptoms. Imipramine has only limited effectiveness with adolescents, perhaps because the sex hormones during this period interfere with its antidepressant effects. While other medications reduce depressive symptoms, they are also suspected of having undesirable features such as adversely affecting growth, intelligence, and nonsymptomatic behavior. (For details, see Kazdin, 1990.) In addition, medications must show that they are more effective than placebos, which also relieve symptoms in depressed children.

Psychotherapy

Few methodologically sound studies of the outcome of psychotherapy have been done. Sample size has been small; children have not met DSM-III-R criteria for major depression; control or comparison groups or follow-up evaluations have been lacking. In their comprehensive search, Weisz et al. (1992) could locate only six methodologically sound controlled-treatment studies. However, their findings concerning *effectiveness* were encouraging. A meta-analysis of the data indicated that subjects receiving therapy were better off than 69 percent of the control subjects seven weeks after termination. Adolescents improved significantly more than did children, perhaps because treatment was modeled on that with adults.

The better-designed studies often draw upon the *cognitive behavioral* models and have an attention-placebo group in which, for example, discussion concerns a teacher rather than depression-related topics, or a no-treatment control group. Treatment includes role playing to teach interpersonal and problem-solving techniques, cognitive restructuring to decrease maladaptive cognitions such as "Nothing ever turns out right for me," and a number of self-evaluation and self-reinforcement techniques. Some studies also include training in relaxation. In general, the results show that treatment tends to be more effective than no treatment and produces change lasting several weeks. However, different cognitive behavioral therapies do not result in any significant difference. *Social-skills training* may also be effective in reducing depression, although the evidence comes mostly from single-case reports.

Weisz and colleagues (1992) argue persua-

sively that effectiveness could be improved if treatment were integrated with what is known about the development of cognition and competence, two variables that figure prominently in therapy. For example, negative beliefs about social competence would be particularly important therapeutic targets during early adolescence in light of the increased centrality of peer groups in this period. (For details concerning treatment, see Kazdin, 1990.)

DEPRESSION IN ADOLESCENCE

There is general agreement that adolescents have developed to the point where they can become depressed as adults do. Emotionally, they are capable of experiencing intense sadness and of sustaining this experience over time. Cognitively, they can think in terms of generalizations and can project into the future. They can consciously evaluate the self and judge it as helpless or inept. In fact, moderate versions of the classical signs of depression may appear in adolescence as part of the expected turmoil of the period. The question is no longer, Can an adolescent be depressed? but, How can one tell normal from pathological depression? This diagnostic task of the clinician need not concern us here, however.

The *reasons* for depression in adolescence are not new, since they involve actual or fantasied loss of a significant personal relation or of self-esteem (Weiner, 1980). However, the developmental context is different from what it was in middle childhood. In middle childhood, children have the basic security of knowing they are an integral part of the family unit. By contrast, adolescents are faced with the task of giving up their place within the family and developing a new status as an independent adult. Even in healthy adolescence, therefore, one might expect some temporary depressive states when closeness to the family is taboo but mature sources of love have not yet been found. Temporary loss of self-confidence might also be expected during the search for a vocation that would utilize the adolescent's competencies. Thus depression may be an exaggeration of normal developments in adolescence. (For a comprehensive account of adolescent depression see Weiner, 1992.)

ADOLESCENT SUICIDE

Epidemiology

Suicide is the third leading cause of death among 15- to 24-year-old adolescents, after accidents and homicides. According to Berman and Jobes (1991), whose presentation we follow unless otherwise noted, these three forms of violent death, taken together, account for the majority of all deaths in the United States of persons up to the age of 39. The suicide rate more than tripled between 1957 and 1977, from 4.0 per 100,000 adolescents to a peak of 13.3, subsequently dropping to 12.9 in 1987. This leveling off masks the fact that suicide among 15- to 19-year-olds increased while the

rate for 20- to 24-year-olds declined (Figure 7.2). While the rates for whites have always been higher than for blacks, the rate for blacks almost tripled between 1960 and 1987. The rates for Latinos and Native Americans showed a similar increase. Males have always outnumbered females by a ratio of approximately 5 to 1. Most suicides (70 percent) occur in the home. Firearms and explosives are the most frequent method used for both males and females (59 percent), followed by hanging for males and drug ingestion for females.

Suicide attempters are different from those who succeed in ending their lives. The typical attempter is a young female who ingests drugs at home after an argument, thus engaging in what is called low-lethality behavior. This is in contrast with the typical completer, two-thirds of whom are male gunshot-wound victims. The estimated number of attempters is between 50,000 and 500,000 per year. Their attempts should not be dismissed as mere attention-getting behavior since they are at risk for future and more serious attempts and possible completions.

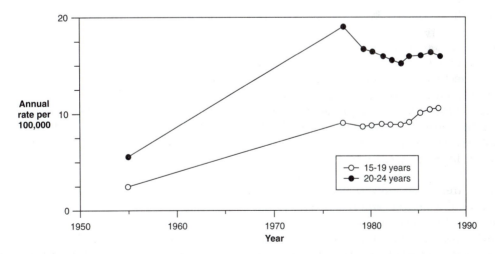

FIGURE 7.2
U.S. youth suicide rates, 1955–1987 for 15- to 19-year-olds and 20- to 24-year-olds. (*Source:* "Letter to the editor" by L. A. Fingerhut and J. C. Kleinman, 1988, *Journal of the American Medical Association, 259*, p. 356.)

Both suicide and attempted suicide are rare but not unknown in children under 12, and there are even clinical reports of repeated and apparently serious attempts at suicide among preschoolers (Rosenthal and Rosenthal, 1984).

Developmental Pathway

A classic reconstructive study was conducted by Jacobs (1971), who investigated fifty 14- to 16-year-olds who attempted suicide. A control population of thirty-one subjects, matched for age, race, sex, and level of mother's education was obtained from a local high school. Through an intensive, multitechnique investigation, Jacobs was able to reconstruct a five-step model of suicidal attempts.

1. A long-standing history of problems from early childhood to the onset of adolescence. Such problems included parental divorce, death of a family member, serious illness, parental alcoholism, and school failure. Subsequent research has shown that it is a high level of intrafamilial conflict and instability along with a lack of support for the child that is the risk factor, not a particular family constellation such as divorce or a single-parent family (Weiner, 1992).
2. An acceleration of problems in adolescence. Far more important than earlier childhood problems was the frequency of distressing events occurring within the last five years for the suicidal subjects; for example, 45 percent of the experimental subjects experienced a broken home, while only 6 percent of the control group did. Termination of a serious romance was also much higher among the suicidal group, as were arrests and jail sentences.
3. The progressive failure to cope with the increase in problems leading to isolation from meaningful social relationships. Among coping mechanisms, the suicidal and control groups were equally rebellious in terms

of becoming disobedient, sassy, and defiant. However, the suicidal adolescents engaged in much more withdrawal behavior, such as running away, long periods of silence, and a depressed mood. The isolation in regard to talking with parents was particularly striking; for example, while 70 percent of all suicide attempts took place in the home, only 20 percent of those who reported the attempt reported it to their parents. In one instance, an adolescent telephoned a friend who lived miles away, and he, in turn, telephoned the parents, who were in the next room!

4. A dissolution of social relationships in the days and weeks preceding the attempt, leading to the feeling of hopelessness.
5. A justification of the suicidal act, giving the adolescent permission to make the attempt. This justification was reconstructed from 112 suicide notes of adolescents and adults attempting and completing suicide. The notes contain certain recurring themes; for example, the problems are seen as not of the adolescent's making but long-standing and insolvable, so death seems like the only solution. The authors of such notes also state that they know what they are doing, are sorry for their act, and beg indulgence. The motif of isolation and subsequent hopelessness is obvious.

Subsequent research has helped flesh out Jacobs' (1971) picture of the development of suicide. (Our presentation follows Berman and Jobes, 1991, unless otherwise indicated. See also Weiner, 1992.)

Suicide Completers

The Intrapersonal Context A suicide completer is a youth with a high degree of intention to die who uses a highly lethal method to accomplish this end.

Comorbidity The majority of such adolescents have either a diagnosable psychopathology or symptoms. The three most prominent psychopathologies are depression, substance abuse, and conduct disorders. While the majority of depressed youths are not suicidal, 83 percent of youths with suicidal ideation show signs of depression. Drug and alcohol use and abuse have been found in 15 to 33 percent of completers, the "wish to die" increasing after the onset of substance use. Such abuse is also related to the lethality of the method used. Around 70 percent of completers exhibit antisocial behavior, ranging from shoplifting to drug selling to prostitution. In fact, conduct disorders may play an even greater role than depression in suicidal behavior (Capaldi, 1992).

Psychological characteristics. The primary risk factor is *impulsivity*, which is seen not only in angry, aggressive behavior but in low frustration tolerance and lack of planning as well. In fact, most completed suicides are impulsive; only one in four showing evidence of planning. There are also difficulties in school such as disciplinary problems, underachievement, and poor school performance.

Another characteristic is social isolation and *alienation*, adolescents reporting that they have no friends and feel lonely. In the cognitive realm, suicidal children and adolescents are deficient in problem-solving skills, particularly in regard to generating alternative solutions to situations involving interpersonal conflict. They feel they have less control over their environment, which, in turn, leads to rigid rather than flexible thinking. In certain extreme cases, they may display psychotic distortions of reality.

Finally, *imitation* plays a role in suicidal behavior. Exposure to the suicidal behavior of another person in the social network or in the family of completers is more common in suicidal adolescents than in controls. Such exposure should be regarded as accelerating the risk factors already present rather than being a sufficient cause of suicide. Suicides can also occur in clusters, which is another example of imitation. In spite of widely publicized reports, however, there is no conclusive evidence of imitative effects of television presentations on suicide. The evidence in regard to fictional presentations of suicide is even less conclusive.

The Interpersonal Context Suicidal adolescents report having poor family relationships and receiving little affection. They do not enjoy the time they spend with their families and hold negative views of their parents. There is a significantly higher level of turmoil in families of completers, including violence, suicidal tendencies and behaviors, and depression.

Suicide Attempters

Spirito and colleagues (1989) summarize research findings on suicide attempters. Most attempters take an overdose of a low-lethality drug in response to problems with parents, boyfriend or girlfriend, or school. The most important variable is hopelessness, which is more consistently related to suicide ideation and attempts than is depression. Moreover, the correlation of suicide intent and depression is accounted for by their common association with hopelessness (Kazdin et al., 1983).

There is evidence of a significant degree of overt conflict and disturbed communication in the families of attempters. Being from a home without a father is another risk factor (Andrews and Lewinsohn, 1992). Imitation of others who have committed suicide plays a small role in the attempt. There is also preliminary evidence of a deficit in interpersonal problem solving.

Finally, the authors point out the areas in which suicide attempters are no different from other disturbed adolescents. These include depression and substance abuse, sexual abuse and separation, divorce and psychiatric disturbances in the family.

A study of 3000 youths attending a free medical clinic provides information as to the feelings preceding and reasons for suicide attempts (Adolinks, 1987).

The feelings preceding the attempted suicide were, in order, anger, feeling lonely and unwanted, feeling worried about the future, being sorry or ashamed, along with the already mentioned hopelessness. Older adolescents were more worried about the future than were younger ones. The reasons adolescents gave for attempting suicide were, in order, relief from an intolerable state of mind or escape from an impossible situation, making people understand how desperate they feel, making people worry for the way they have been treated or getting back at someone, trying to influence someone to change his or her mind, showing how much they loved someone or finding out whether someone really loved them, and seeking help. Often several reasons were given rather than a single one.

Only around half of the adolescents said they wanted to die, 40 percent saying they did not care if they lived or died. Typically the attempt was made with little premeditation, although there may have been prior rehearsal either in general terms ("I hope I won't wake up in the morning") or in terms of a specific act. In many cases the act was done where it would be readily discovered, such as in the room next to one with people in it, although there were exceptions.

The majority of attempters improve within one month. However, about one-third subsequently experience major difficulties in the form of increased psychological and physical disorders, poor marital adjustment, and increased criminal behavior. One in ten will repeat the attempt, boys succeeding more often than girls. The risk for future disturbances is particularly strong in teenage males. The more

disturbed the adolescent before the attempt, the more likely that he or she will be disturbed subsequently (Hawton, 1986).

An Integrative Model

While we have learned a fair amount about suicide and attempted suicide, the data lie like an unassembled jigsaw puzzle. There is no dearth of theories—sociological, psychodynamic, behavioral, biological—but they are too removed from the data to be compared and evaluated. (See Berman and Jobes, 1991, for a discussion of such theories.) Nor has the developmental question—why adolescence?—been satisfactorily answered.

An exception to this unsatisfactory state of affairs is Harter's integration of data from her own research and the research of others (Harter, Marold, and Whitesell, 1992). Her model reconstructs the successive steps that ultimately eventuate in suicidal ideation in a normative sample of 12- to 15-year-olds.

Immediately preceding and highly related to suicidal ideation is what Harter calls the *depressive composite,* which is made up of three interrelated variables: global self-worth, affect, and general hopelessness. The first two are highly correlated: the lower the perceived self-worth, the greater the feelings of depression.

Moreover, the depressive composite is rooted both in the adolescents' feelings of lack of competence and in their lack of support from family and friends. These two variables of competence and support are, in turn, related in a special way. In regard to competence, physical appearance, peer likability, and athletic ability are related to peer support, while scholarly achievement and behavioral conduct are related to parental support. Finally, adolescents identify more strongly with peer-related competencies, the others being regarded as more important to parents than to themselves.

Path analysis of the research data showed

that competence and support was related to the depressive composite in the following manner. The path containing peer-related competencies and support was more strongly related to the depressive composite than parental-related competencies and support, perhaps because the former are more closely connected with the adolescents' own self-concept. However, parental competencies and support were important in differentiating the adolescents who were only depressed from those who were depressed and had suicidal ideation.

Among the competencies, appearance had the strongest relation to the depressive composite, followed by scholastic achievement, conduct, likeability, and athletic ability. One comment on this finding: in the search for risk factors, researchers tend to overlook the importance of physical appearance in adolescence in favor of more "psychological" variables. This finding, along with those concerning eating disorders, shows the centrality of the body percept during this period.

Turning to support per se, both parents and peers were equally linked to the depressive composite. However, the quality of support was crucial. Regardless of the level, if adolescents perceived they were acting only to please parents or peers, their self-esteem decreased while depression and hopelessness increased. It was unconditional support that helped adolescents minimize the depressive composite. Figure 7.3 summarizes Harter's model of suicidal ideation.

In regard to the question of which came first, lowered self-worth or depression, the data indicate that causation can go in either direction. Some adolescents become depressed when they experience lowered self-worth,

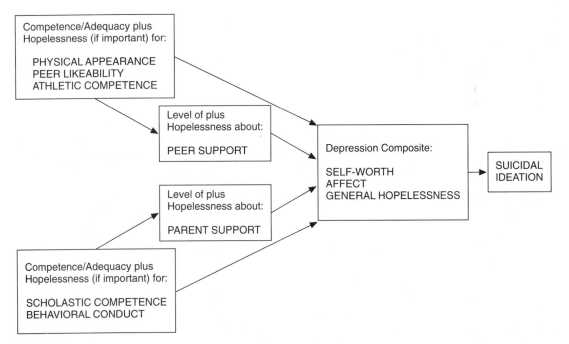

FIGURE 7.3
General model of risk factors. (*Source:* Harter, Marold, and Whitesell, 1992.)

while others become depressed over other occurrences such as rejection or conflict, which in turn lower self-worth.

To answer the question, Why adolescence? the authors marshal a number of findings concerning this period. In adolescence, self-awareness, self-consciousness, introspection, and preoccupation with self-image increase dramatically, while self-esteem becomes more vulnerable. Peer support becomes significantly more salient, although adolescents still struggle to remain connected with parents. For the first time, the adolescent can grasp the full cognitive meaning of hopelessness, while affectively there is an increase in depressive symptomatology. Suicidal ideation is viewed as an effort to cope with or escape from the painful cognitions and affects of the depressive composite.

Prevention and Treatment

The vast majority of suicidal adolescents provide clues as to their imminent behavior; one study found that 83 percent of completers told others of their suicidal intentions in the week prior to their death. (Our presentation follows Berman and Jobes, 1991.) Most of the time such threats are made to family members or friends, who do not take them seriously, try to deny them, or do not understand their importance. Friends, for example, might regard reporting the threats as a betrayal of trust. Thus, not only do adolescents themselves not seek professional help, but those in whom they confide also might delay or resist getting help. Consequently, an important goal of prevention is educating parents and peers concerning risk signs through various suicide prevention programs implemented in schools or the media.

Once an adolescent comes for professional help, the therapist must overcome resistance on the part of both the adolescent and the family. The adolescent is likely to feel humiliated by having to see a "shrink," along with mistrusting adults in general and regarding the

situation as hopeless. Parents may fear they will be exposed as being "bad" or afraid of losing control of their child. Thus, the therapist must be skilled in establishing a working relationship, often by being warm, sympathetic, forthright, and explicit in regard to the treatment plan.

The immediate therapeutic task is to protect the adolescent from self-harm through *crisis intervention* and to decrease real and perceived stressors. This might involve restricting access to the means of committing suicide, such as removing a gun from the house or pills from the medicine cabinet; a "nonsuicide agreement" in which the adolescent agrees not to hurt himself or herself for an explicit time-limited period; decreasing isolation by having sympathetic family members or friends with the adolescent at all times; giving medication to reduce agitation or depression; or, in extreme cases, hospitalization.

The crux of crisis intervention is problem-solving therapy, which involves a collaborative effort between therapist and adolescent in defining the problem, generating alternative solutions, and trying them out until a resolution is found. After the crisis is past, the therapist may use a number of different therapeutic techniques, such as individual psychotherapy or various behavioral techniques, depending on the adolescent's needs. Family or group therapy is also an option.

SUMMARY

From the beginning love and anguish are joined. One sign of infant attachment to the mother is an anxious protest as she leaves. Anaclitic depression is the pathologically extreme reaction when separation is prolonged and no adequate substitute care is provided. Certain infants are immune for some unknown reason, but others succumb. The behavioral hallmarks are agitation, anger, and anxiety followed by extreme withdrawal and despair.

The infant response to loss of the loved

adult is global because infants are still relatively undifferentiated psychologically. Their needs are few—for pleasurable and interesting stimulation and for relief from distress—although such needs are consuming. Infants are also at the mercy of the environment because they are neither practiced nor versatile enough to satisfy their need for interesting activities, and they are incapable of relieving physiological distress. Cognitively, they are trapped in the present, knowing only, "I need my loved caretaker and she or he is not here." They cannot understand the multiple reasons for the absence or its temporal limits when such limits exist, such as "Mommy can see you in a week." One way they cope with despair is by denying the bond of love; the parent is treated as just another adult, so that the anguish of prolonged separation may be bypassed.

In middle childhood children still suffer from the loss of the beloved caretaker, but their reaction is no longer global, because they are more differentiated. The bond of love itself has been elaborated, the parent now being a source of approval and disapproval of good and bad behavior, an appreciative audience for acquired skills, a recipient of affectionate overtures, and a guide to managing interpersonal problems. Children also have a varied set of meaningful relationships with others, peers in particular, but also distant relatives and extrafamilial adults. They are more practiced and resourceful in pursuing their own activities and have a repertoire of coping devices and defense mechanisms at their disposal. Cognitively, they can grasp the nature of concrete reality. While the affective core of the response to loss remains constant, its expression becomes more moderate and age-appropriate: anguish and despair become sadness and crying; indiscriminate tantrums become disobedience and delinquency; agitation becomes restlessness and difficulty in concentrating on school work.

In middle childhood both the self and the affects associated with self-worth have developed to the point that they can serve as a new source of painful loss when normal development goes awry. Specifically, the self is conceptualized in terms of stable psychological characteristics rather than being defined physically in terms of actions, possessions, or the body. This development makes possible stable evaluations of the self as worthy or worthless, competent or helpless, while an increased ability to conceptualize time adds the possibility of being hopeful or hopeless about one's future. Concomitantly, children are more sophisticated in their understanding of affect and capable of sustaining affective states longer than was possible in the preschool period. When there is a devastating loss of self-esteem, therefore, the child is developmentally capable of experiencing depression marked by the cognitive triad of worthlessness, helplessness, and hopelessness. He or she is also capable of a sustained mood of sadness, which is at the core of depression, along with anger and anxiety, which often accompany it. In sum, children have developed to the point that loss of a feeling of basic self-worth can be as devastating as loss of the love of a parent through death or other separations. While the conditions producing loss of self-esteem are still somewhat speculative, they include derogatory labels by significant adults, an overinvestment in unrealistically high standards, too great a discrepancy between experienced success and perceived potential, and noncontingent reinforcement, which may produce learned helplessness.

While loss of love is painful throughout development, its total impact, as well as its effects on future development, are a function of context factors. It seems safe to assume that the same holds true for loss of self-esteem. Clearly, it is simplistic and inaccurate to assume that if children lose a parent through death or long separation, then they will subsequently be psychologically disturbed. A great deal depends on the quality of care children receive after the loss.

Finally, our exploration of depression illustrates our thesis that psychopathology in childhood can best be understood within the framework of normal development. Moreover, the constant interplay between normal and deviant development enriches the understanding of both. Spitz's and Bowlby's research on anaclitic depression and maternal deprivation was a major force in stimulating the study of mothering and the development of attachment in normal infants, while the findings of researchers investigating the development of self and self-esteem in normal populations provided the crucial evidence for solving the mystery of the two sources of depression in disturbed children.

Recall that, in Chapter 5 we dealt with the issue of control in the toddler-preschool period—control of excessive negativism and control of the bodily functions of eating and urination. We will now return to this theme of control but in the middle childhood period. Here we will examine two extremes—excessive control, which is an important element in anxiety disorders, and inadequate self-control, which lies at the heart of conduct disorders.

ANXIETY DISORDER AND EXCESSIVE SELF-CONTROL

In the course of being psychoanalyzed, a middle-aged man recalls, "When I acted up as a kid my grandmother would scold me, saying, 'You're too young to have nerves!' For a long time after that I kept wondering, 'Am I old enough now?'—like having nerves was one of the signs of being grown up."

Grandmother, unknowingly, was a good Freudian. According to psychoanalytic theory, psychoneurosis or neurosis is a developmental achievement. Not that infants and preschoolers cannot suffer—as we have seen, they can; but they are not sufficiently sophisticated psychologically to have a classical neurosis until middle childhood.

However, Freud's concept of neurosis has always been a controversial one. His ideas concerning unconscious motivation, infantile sexuality, and the relation between adult psychopathology and childhood trauma were greeted with incredulity, shock, and derision by members of the professional community. While many of his concepts are now regarded as plausible or obvious, the psychoanalytic formulation of neurosis is currently under attack from two directions. As could be expected, behaviorally oriented psychologists regard the formulation as both incorrect and needlessly complex. In addition, DSM-III dropped the classification of neurosis completely, preferring diagnoses that are purely descriptive and have no etiologic connotations. Unfortunately, conceptually and developmentally oriented research have been in the doldrums until recently, so we are confronted with conceptualizations that lack sufficient objective data and objective data that are primarily descriptive.

We will proceed as follows. We will first briefly review the diagnostic situation, then deal with characteristics of the anxiety disorders as a whole and the two major etiological theories, and finally discuss each disorder individually.

THE DIAGNOSTIC CONTROVERSY

As discussed in Chapter 3, there is no agreement as to the optimal way of classifying childhood psychopathologies. Some of the current classifications are descriptive, others are tied closely to theories, while still others rely on statistical techniques to generate behavioral categories.

The controversy concerning the etiology of neuroses affected the classification of the psychopathology itself. Because of the pervasive Freudian influence, neurosis had come to be identified not only with the behavioral manifestations of the psychopathology but also with the psychoanalytic interpretation. As this interpretation increasingly came to be questioned and as other etiologic accounts—particularly the behavioral—gained in popularity, various attempts have been made to find a classification that would be strictly descriptive.

The solution of DSM-III was to discard the term *neurosis* altogether and substitute the more neutral term *disorder*. Thus a phobic neurosis becomes a phobic disorder, an obsessive-compulsive neurosis becomes an obsessive-compulsive disorder, and so on. The emphasis is on purely descriptive characteristics. No longer united by an etiologic account, the traditional neurotic subtypes are no longer joined in a single category but are dispersed among other categories. Thus neurotic depression becomes absorbed into the general category of Affective Disorders, while phobias and obsessive-compulsive disturbances are considered two varieties of Anxiety Disorder.

In light of the uncertain etiology of all childhood psychopathologies, there is a clear advantage to having DSM-III confine itself to the descriptive approach. In this way a number of possible etiologies can be included, while there is no danger that its users will confuse the soundness of a clinical description with the validity of a particular etiologic theory. The descriptions themselves can also serve as a common behavioral base from which research—both theoretical and atheoretical—can emanate.

THE ANXIETY DISORDERS

General Characteristics

Anxiety disorders have certain characteristics in common: the presence of anxiety; the unacceptable, alien nature of the symptoms to the individual; the relative intactness of reality testing; the enduring nature of the disturbance; and the fact that symptoms do not actively violate social norms. Descriptively, Freud was correct in locating anxiety disorders in middle childhood for the most part (see Table 3.1).

According to the DSM-IV Draft Criteria, two

classifications of anxiety disorders are specific to childhood: separation anxiety disorder, and overanxious disorder. The classifications that children share with adults are phobic disorders, obsessive-compulsive disorder, panic disorder, and posttraumatic stress disorder. While phobias might be the same regardless of age, school phobia is specific to childhood. (For a summary of objective studies of anxiety disorders, see Bernstein and Borchardt, 1991.)

Prevalence and Course Anxiety disorders are among the most common, if not the most common, childhood and adolescent disorders; various studies show that they are found in 8 to 9 percent of the general population (Bernstein and Borchardt, 1991). They also are quite prevalent among adult psychopathologies and are more frequent than depression and alcoholism. Approximately half of the adult symptoms originate before the age of 15 (Miller, Boyer, and Rodoletz, 1990). By the same token, anxiety disorders in childhood increase the risk of subsequent psychiatric difficulties. Waldron (1976), for example, found that 21 percent of neurotic children had a diagnosis of neurosis as adults, 14 percent had a diagnosis of personality disorders, and 5 percent were diagnosed psychotic. While there is continuity of anxiety between children and adults, the relation between specific disturbances is not clear; this is the case, for example, with the relation between separation anxiety in childhood and adult panic disorders (Klein and Last, 1989).

The Organic Context Anxiety disorders tend to run in families. For example, one study showed that children of parents with anxiety disorders are seven times as likely to be diagnosed as having an anxiety disorder as normal controls and twice as likely as children of depressed mothers (Bernstein and Borchardt, 1991). Panic, phobic, and obsessive-compulsive disorders seem to be influenced by *genetic*

factors, while the genetic component in other anxiety disorders has not been established (Klein and Last, 1989).

Evidence of *neurological* involvement comes from a longitudinal study by Shaffer and co-workers (1985). They found that the presence of two or more "soft" or subtle signs of neurological damage when the children were 7 years of age was a potent predictor of subsequent anxious-withdrawal behavior in adolescence. (The study is described in detail in Chapter 13.)

One of the most promising studies of *temperament* involves "behavioral inhibition to the unfamiliar," which is manifested by a tendency to be shy, timid, and constrained in novel situations. The longitudinal study by Hirshfeld and colleagues (1992) of children at 21 months, 4 years, $5\frac{1}{2}$ years, and $7\frac{1}{2}$ years of age found that those children who were consistently inhibited over the three preceding periods had higher rates of anxiety than children who were not consistently inhibited. Moreover, the parents had higher rates of anxiety disorders from childhood into adulthood. Since only 12 children were in the consistently inhibited group, the results are preliminary.

The Intrapersonal Context: Internalization In anxiety disorders suffering is turned inward. This characteristic has been amply demonstrated by factor-analytic studies of psychopathological behavior in children. Typical of such studies is Achenbach's factor analysis of a 91-item symptom checklist using 600 male and female psychiatric patients as subjects (Achenbach, 1966; Achenbach et al., 1989). The first principal factor was a bipolar one, which he labeled internalization-externalization. Among internalizing symptoms he included phobias, worrying, stomachaches, withdrawal, nausea, vomiting, compulsions, insomnia, seclusiveness, depression, crying—all indicating a distressed child (see Figure 8.1). Externalizing symptoms included disobedi-

FIGURE 8.1
An internalizer: worried, depressed, obsessing, and an insomniac. (*Source:* © 1993 United Feature Syndicate, Inc.)

ence, stealing, lying, fighting, destructiveness, inadequate guilt feelings, swearing, temper tantrums, running away, and vandalism—all indicating a child in conflict with the environment. Indirectly the data support the thesis that anxiety disorders are signs of excessive-self-control.

The Interpersonal Context: The Family   The meager research on families has yielded reasonably good evidence that separation anxiety or school phobias occur with overinvolved parents and overdependent children. Overprotection can be manifested in several ways: restrictive control, intrusion into psychological and physical privacy, reinforcement of dependency, and exclusion of outside influence. Marital conflict, while related to aggressive, acting-out behavior, has not been found in anxiety-withdrawal disorders. Instead, there is a complex interaction whereby marital conflict accompanied by opposite-sex parent dominance puts the child at risk. Thus, for example, if a dominating father disparages a weak and whining mother, the son is not apt to develop anxiety or withdrawal disorders, but the daughter is. (For details see Hetherington and Martin, 1986.)

Comorbidity   As we saw in Chapter 7, there is a close association between anxiety disorders and depression. There is also an association between anxiety disorders and attention deficit hyperactive disorder. Finally, there is comorbidity among specific types of anxiety disorders. Children with overanxious disorder are more likely to have simple phobias, panic disorder, social phobia, and avoidant disorder, while one-third of the children with a primary diagnosis of separation anxiety have a diagnosis of overanxious disorder (Bernstein and Borchardt, 1991).

There are a number of possible explanations for comorbidity. One disturbance may serve as a risk factor for another; two disturbances may have overlapping symptoms while being distinct entities; or two disturbances may share a common underlying agent or agents and be, in fact, different expressions of the same basic abnormality. Which explanation applies to anxiety disorders is not known at present.

Assessment   Anxiety is typically conceptualized as involving three components: behavioral, subjective, and physiological. Assessment usually deals with the first two, physiological reactions such as heart rate and sweaty palms being too difficult to measure in most clinical settings.

Information concerning anxious *behavior* can be obtained in structured diagnostic interviews where parents or teachers are specifically questioned about the child's fears: how general, intense, and persistent they are; what situations elicit them; when and why did they begin. Next, behavior rating instruments have been devised consisting of items such as, "Compared to children your child's age, how fearful or timid or shy is your child?" or "How upset is your child when you have to leave or when he or she has to go to school?" The score obtained by summing the individual items is compared with norms for the general population, which in turn, provides information as to how anxious a given child is. Finally, the child's anxious behavior can be directly observed in response to a feared object such as a snake or a dog. Trained observers use predetermined categories to record the child's behavior. They may also make an overall rating of the degree of anxiety the child displayed.

The *subjective* component of anxiety is evaluated by various self-report instruments. These may involve a global rating of how anxious children feel they are (e.g., "I am afraid of a lot of things" or "I feel nervous a lot of the time") or they may tap into specific fears such as fears of animals, physical injury, or monsters.

A perennial problem in doing research on anxiety is that the measures of the three components tend not to be highly correlated, and this is true for children as well as adults. In addition children report many more fears than do their parents. (For a detailed discussion of assessment, see Klein and Last, 1989, and Miller, Boyer, and Rodoletz, 1990.)

Treatment   There is a lively interest in devising ways of treating the various anxiety dis-

orders, and we will be describing a number of such programs. At this point we will make a few cautionary remarks concerning methodology. Many of the reported studies consist of a single case, there are often no control groups, the samples treated tend to be inadequately described, and objective measures of outcome tend to be used infrequently. While a variety of behavioral techniques have been used with reported success, further research is needed to determine the treatment of choice (Klein and Last, 1989). Pharmacological treatment is also marked by promising leads but poorly designed studies (Bernstein and Borchardt, 1991).

Etiologic Theories

Psychoanalytic Theory of Neurosis   *Conflict* lies at the heart of the psychoanalytic theory of neurosis—conflict between what infants, toddlers, and preschoolers want to do and what socializing adults require them to do. (Our presentation follows Nagera, 1966, and Shapiro, 1973.) The specific content of the conflict is determined by the psychosexual stages of development, described in Chapter 2.

The next component of neurosis is *anxiety*. Affect, like conflict, lies at the heart of psychoanalytic theory. It is the threat of parental punishment and withdrawal of parental love that provide an affective charge sufficiently strong to lead to the inhibition of socially unacceptable behavior. Anxiety is not only a deterrent; if sufficiently strong, it is exceedingly painful and can set into motion a whole array of maneuvers designed to protect the child from experiencing its distress. These maneuvers are called *defense mechanisms*, such as repression, projection, and reaction formation (see Chapter 2).

Finally, psychoanalytic theory states that neurotic symptoms have a *symbolic meaning*, which differs from the manifest content of the behavior. For example, let us take the case of a 7-year-old girl who was terrified of spiders, which she feared would bite her. Psychoanalytically oriented play therapy revealed that the basic neurotic conflict was between a desire to express anger toward her mother and her primitive conscience's mandate that she be a good girl. Her self-condemnation as "bad" engendered anxiety, and—as is typical of phobias—a triple defense was set into play. First came repression, so that the girl could banish the angry thoughts and feelings from consciousness. Next came projection, in which the mother was seen as angry at the girl. Finally, came displacement, in which a relatively innocuous object was invested with exaggerated destructive powers. Why a spider? There is never a pat answer to questions of symbolization, since the meaning can be highly idiosyncratic. In this instance the girl, having heard of the deadly bite of the black widow spider, equated both the quality of hostile attack and blackness with her mother, who made a great deal over the versatility of her "basic black" dress.

The Oedipus complex and the anal stage are the source of two prominent groups of symptoms—phobic and obsessive-compulsive. The content of the phobia represents variations on the oedipal themes of sex and aggression, the variations being legion—biting animals, automobile accidents, and fires can be feared because of their violence, for instance, while "slimy" snakes, and the physical closeness of a confined space can be feared because of their sexual connotations.

In the obsessive-compulsive neurosis the child regresses to the anal level. Recall that the conflict here is between conformity and rebellious self-assertion, and that in normal development the defense of reaction formation enables the child to make the transition from fascination with feces, dirt, and messiness to cleanliness, orderliness, and obedience. In the neurotic schoolage child, the anal conflict re-turns in a highly charged repetitive manner. In a hand-washing compulsion, for example, the child can never dispel the nagging feeling that his or her hands are not absolutely and totally clean; rituals to insure safety, such as checking locks on doors at night, can never satisfy the child that the house is absolutely burglarproof.

While the difference between *normal and pathological development* is a quantitative one, whether children go one way or the other depends on a variety of factors. Classical psychoanalytic theory states that too much or too little gratification tends to fixate a child at a particular stage and makes him or her vulnerable to regression. Subsequently, Anna Freud (1965) added the concept of the *balance of forces* making for progress or regression. The concept itself is similar to the now familiar one stating that a developmental path is the result of the balance between vulnerabilities and protective factors (see Chapter 2).

Some sources of vulnerability are *constitutional* in that certain infants have more intense reactions of anxiety and rage than others and are persistently disrupted by their effects. Other vulnerabilities are *experiential,* failure to receive sensitive care in infancy being particularly important.

As for assets—constitution and maturation can be aligned on the side of health as well as on the side of vulnerabilities. Certain infants are innately rugged and resilient, either experiencing less intense anxiety or readily taking it in stride. Growth-promoting experiences are legion: sensitive mothering in infancy, the development of friendships, achievement in school, positive relations with teachers, coaches, and other adult models. Even a neurotic conflict can itself become a constructive force in the child's developing personality: the boy who handles his hostility toward a younger sibling by the reaction formation of being especially concerned with the plight of relatively weak and helpless youngsters can eventually have a successful vocation in one of the helping professions. As Anna Freud (1965) puts it, one can never be sure whether a therapist is eliminating a neurosis or "nipping a future physicist in the bud."

The Behavioral Theory Behaviorists regard anxiety-flight as an adaptive response when it is a reaction to a realistic threat; when the response is inappropriate, however—when no real danger exists—the behaviorists regard it as psychopathological.

Traditional learning principles can account for the various ways in which innocuous and inappropriate stimuli come to elicit aversive emotional responses. The most familiar principle is *aversive classical conditioning*, and the most familiar case is of 11-month-old Albert who, after being exposed to a number of pairings of a white rat (CS) with a loud, frightening noise (US), became frightened by the sight of the rat alone (CR). A variation in this same model is higher-order conditioning in which a stimulus, once conditioned, serves as the basis for further aversive conditioning when paired with neutral stimuli. Thus, a child who hears that sex is "dirty" may develop a disgust for sexual behavior even without engaging in it.

A negative affective response may also be acquired by *observational learning* or *modeling*. Here the mere observing of another person responding with pain or anxiety to a previously innocuous stimulus—say a buzzer that always preceded a shock—will subsequently produce an aversive response in the observer when the innocuous stimulus is presented. On this basis a girl whose parents are afraid of being burglarized can come to fear every creak of the stairs after bedtime, as her parents do.

Once established, inappropriate behavior can spread by *stimulus generalization*. The classical example is, once again, little Albert, who after being conditioned to fear a white rat, subsequently was afraid of a number of white, furry objects. However, stimulus generaliza-

tion in an 11-year-old is bound to be more complex than it is in an 11-month-old. Semantically related cues can take precedence over the sheer physical similarity of words; for example, subjects conditioned to "hare" will generalize to "rabbit" rather than to "hair." Generalization can also occur to categories of objects; for example, a subject who receives an electric shock when a rural word such as "barn" is presented will also have an aversive reaction to other rural words.

The final component in the behavioral explanation of neurosis is the *reinforcement* of responses that enable the individual to avoid the conditioned aversive stimuli. Like psychoanalysts, behavioral theorists regard anxiety as an unusually potent motivator; any behavior that reduces or eliminates it will be reinforced. A wide array of such behaviors can be conceptualized as avoidance responses. One of the most important of these is "response inhibition," in which the child avoids both doing and thinking about doing a forbidden act. This, of course, is exactly the same process as repression. The difference is that behaviorists regard as superfluous the psychoanalytic assumption that the "ego" represses the forbidden idea into the "unconscious," where it continues to exist and press for expression.

The behaviorist's etiologic account of *phobias* is the most convincing; the mechanisms of aversive and vicarious classical conditioning are well supported by laboratory studies on both animals and humans (Bandura, 1968). Behaviorists add that, once learned, the reaction of the social environment is a potent factor perpetuating the phobia. While a child might originally develop a fear of insects by modeling a parent, the subsequent attention received from the parent, either positive or negative, may further reinforce the phobic response.

Compulsive rituals can result from symbolic mediation. To illustrate: during toilet training, "dirty" may become a stimulus whose aversive consequences can be reduced by washing one's hand. On learning that sex is also "dirty," an adolescent may reduce the anxiety engendered by sexual thoughts and activities by taking a shower. (A detailed account of the behavioral theory can be found in Bandura, 1968.)

A number of criticisms of the behaviorists' account of the development and maintenance of fears have been raised. Some attempts at classical conditioning of fear have not been successful, while the conditioned response in humans, unlike fears, are quickly extinguished. Moreover, some unconditioned stimuli elicit fear more readily than others; for example, it is difficult to condition fear to a wooden block or a mushroom. This difference in conditionability has lead to the idea of *preparedness*, which states that we are genetically programmed to respond with fear to some stimuli and not to others. Next, certain fears, such as the fear of being alone or the fear of the toilet, are difficult to explain on the basis of observational learning. And finally, parental reinforcement seems to account more adequately for the maintenance of fears than for their origins. Many of these criticisms have been rebutted, however, as stemming from methodological flaws in the research and conceptual limitations (Delprato, 1980).

In order to enhance the explanatory potency of their point of view, certain behaviorists are adding cognitive variables such as information processing. Kendall and Ronan (1990) have proposed a *cognitive-behavioral model* of fears and phobias. Their conceptualization centers upon the cognitive representation of the self, or the *self schema*, and the cognitive representation of others, or the *other schema*. The self schema of anxious individuals contains a high level of content specific to anxiety; for example, anxious subjects recall more anxious-content adjectives in a list of words than do nonanxious subjects. In their other schema, anxious individuals focus on others'

potentially hurtful judgments or harmful reactions. Another aspect of distorted thinking is an excessive self-focused attention and an inability to shift to a more external focus; for example, a girl who has to give a speech in class focuses on her own fears and her imagined critical attitudes of others to such a degree that she cannot concentrate on the speech itself and is overwhelmed by anxiety. Or again, when asked to "think aloud" into a tape recorder for two minutes before taking a stressful math test, anxious subjects were significantly more preoccupied with their negative expectations ("I'm no good in math") and negative affect ("I feel sort of scared") than nonanxious ones. (Vasey [1993] adds a developmental dimension to this model.)

FEARS AND PHOBIAS

Fear is usually defined as a normal reaction to an environmental threat. It is adaptive and even essential to survival because it warns the individual that a situation may be physically or psychologically harmful. Phobias are distinguished from fears on the basis of their intensity, which is out of proportion to the situation, their maladaptiveness, and their persistence. Phobias are also beyond voluntary control and cannot be explained or reasoned away. As we shall soon see, placing these definitions within a developmental context will make them less clear-cut than they now appear to be. But first we shall summarize some relevant evidence. Unfortunately for our purposes, most of the literature concerns fears rather than phobias. (For a general discussion of fears and phobias, see Miller, Boyer, and Rodoletz, 1990.)

General Characteristics

Incidence and Persistence It is estimated that 3 to 8 percent of children have excessive fears. In addition, fears reported by American,

Australian, and British children are almost identical (Ollendick, Yule, and Ollier, 1991). While most fears are transient—around half disappear in three months—some may be durable. There is also suggestive evidence that fearful preschoolers are predisposed to developing neurotic disorders five years later and that anxious 11-year-olds are at risk of developing anxiety and depressive problems in adolescence.

Phobias occur in 2.4 percent of children and 3.6 percent of adolescents (Bernstein and Borchardt, 1991). While phobias are more tenacious than fears, most of them will improve in two to three years with or without therapy, although psychotherapy can hasten the recovery. However, there is sufficient variability in prognosis not to assume that a given child will "outgrow" his or her phobia. Adult phobias are more intractable; only 20 to 30 percent show full recovery. Phobic children have a variety of other problems, and there is a close association between phobia and depression. A few childhood phobias, such as animal phobias, fear of physical injury, and psychic stress, may persist as adult problems. Childhood phobias also may lead to nonphobic adult disturbance, although there is no evidence that they lead to conduct disorders. (For a detailed account of phobias, see King, Hamilton, and Ollendick, 1988.)

Etiology   The etiology of phobias remains a mystery. While they may be due to a terrifying experience or to imitation, in many instances they are not. For example, a frightening experience such as being in an automobile accident can fail to produce a lasting fear or a phobia, while an intense fear of spiders may develop in a child who has neither been bitten by one nor observed a phobic reaction in others.

Stimulus Charting   Since the number of fears and phobias is legion, investigators have de-vised ways of organizing the eliciting stimuli into categories, typically through factor analysis. Ollendick, King, and Frary (1989), for example, found that fears clustered around five factors: failure and criticism; the unknown (e.g., ghosts, dark rooms); minor injuries and small animals; danger and death; and medical fears. Other researchers, such as King and colleagues (1989), have added a developmental dimension by grouping the categories in terms of age spans (see Table 8.1).

Such stimulus charting does not meet our criteria for a developmental approach because it fails to integrate the data with changes in normal development, especially changes in the self, in cognition, in social relations, and in affect itself. To take one example: both a 5-year-old and a 15-year-old may be afraid of robbers; however, there is no evidence that preschoolers are concerned over loss of property as adolescents are, so a robber may well mean a strange, evil, intrusive individual more akin to a ghost than a real person.

Stimulus charting is also unsatisfactory because fear reactions and phobias both tend to be inconsistent in childhood. For example, Miller, Barrett, and Hampe (1974) cited the example of a child who was terrified of riding an escalator with his mother, but who readily rode it with a friendly researcher who was there to observe the phobic behavior. Moreover, fear is not an absolute response to a stimulus but a contingent one, especially in the early years; for example, a 9-month-old may react to a stranger with interest while sitting on the mother's lap but react with terror if sitting a few feet away from the mother. Whether a stimulus will elicit fear depends on the child's general security, which often is affected by the familiarity or unfamiliarity of the social and physical setting; the level of cognitive development, which determines whether an event will be classified as familiar or strange; the child's immediate state of well-

TABLE 8.1
Common Fears across Age

8- to 10-year-olds		11- to 13-year-olds		14- to 16-year-olds	
Item	% Endorsement	Item	% Endorsement	Item	% Endorsement
Nuclear war	68	Nuclear war	80	Nuclear war	69
Being hit by a car	72	Not being able to breathe	62	Not being able to breathe	55
Not being able to breathe	68	Being hit by a car or truck	62	Bombing attacks—being invaded	53
Bombing attacks—being invaded	65	Bombing attacks—being invaded	62	Being hit by a car or truck	50
Earthquakes	62	Earthquakes	51	Fire—getting burned	48
Falling from high places	58	Fire—getting burned	51	Falling from high places	42
A burglar breaking into our house	56	A burglar breaking into our house	47	A burglar breaking into our house	39
Fire—getting burned	52	Falling from high places	46	Snakes	39
Being sent to the principal	47	Snakes	40	Spiders	36
Getting lost in a strange place	46	Death or dead people	39	Earthquakes	35

Source: Adapted from King et al., 1989.

being; and more long-term temperamental characteristics, such as being tough and resilient or sensitive and easily frightened (Sroufe, Waters, and Matas, 1974).

Definitions Reconsidered By most definitions, fears have been considered adaptive, phobias maladaptive. The distinction may be appropriate for adults who, for example, recognize that their fear of sitting in the front row of a class is an irrational one. However, the distinction runs into difficulties when viewed developmentally. Many of the earliest fears, such as the fear of loud noises or sudden movement, are intense, persistent, and maladaptive in the sense that in the vast majority of instances there is nothing dangerous in the environment. Thus by adult criteria they should be regarded as phobias, whereas in reality they are part of normal development. Because of the importance of the developmental dimension a number of clinical child psychologists have added *age-inappropriate* to the list of criteria for phobias.

Developmental Pathway

Unless otherwise noted, our presentation relies on the research of Jersild and Holmes (1935), who, although working more than fifty years ago, are among the few who have explored the development of fears in its complexity. Because they did not "chunk" their findings by factor analysis, they provide the richest data for a developmental reconstruction. We will supplement their data with more recent findings from child development.

The Infancy-Preschool Period In early *infancy* fear reactions might be regarded as innate because they appear early in development with no evidence of their being learned. Among stimuli that elicit such fear are loud noise, pain, falling, and sudden, unexpected movement. It is worth noting that such stimuli require little cognitive elaboration, the fear appearing and vanishing with the stimulus itself. Strangeness or unfamiliarity, whether in regard to people, objects, or situations, elicits fear in the latter half of the first year. The evaluation of a stimulus as "familiar" or "strange" requires a cognitive elaboration that is not necessary with innate stimuli. Moreover, such an elaboration is not possible in the earliest months of life. Neonates know little about the world into which they are born. They require time to become sufficiently acquainted with their new environment to begin regarding people, objects, and situations as familiar and recognizable or as unfamiliar and strange (see Campbell, 1986). In the early *toddler* period animals begin to elicit fear. In certain instances fear may be in response to the noise and sudden, unexpected movement characteristic of animals. However, even quiet animals may be effective stimuli, perhaps because of their unfamiliarity, although Jersild and Holmes (1935) speculate that there may be an innate fear of animals.

The change from toddler to the *preschool* period is marked by a decline in the primitive fears of noise, falling, sudden movement, and strangeness, although fear of pain and of animals have an irregular upward trend. Memory makes fear less a situational response by strengthening anticipation, so children now respond to the threat or the danger of bodily injury and, subsequently, to warnings that are part of socialization. Thus children increasingly fear traffic accidents and fires in response to parental punishment and other fear-inducing techniques; subsequently, they come to fear doing things parents regard as "bad." Fear of imaginary animals and characters and fear of nightmares also become developmentally possible as the early preschooler comes to differentiate reality from fantasy and recognizes the latter as a special realm of cognitive activity.

Finally, the end of the preschool period witnesses the appearance of fear of personal inadequacy, failure, and ridicule, the examples cited by Jersild and Holmes (1935) involving learning the academic skills of numbers and writing, or fear of other school-related functions. Such fears indicate the development of the concept of an achieving self to the point that anticipation of failure is a source of concern.

Middle Childhood By middle childhood, the cognitive distortions that characterize earlier periods have been corrected by and large, and the child's basic grasp of the social and physical environment resembles that of the adult. Fears follow this trend toward realism: fears of bodily injury, say, from traffic accidents or fires, increase; fears of ghosts and imaginary creatures decline. (Campbell, 1986, summarizes the objective studies.) Fear of failure increases, although it is never high in comparison with other fears. The old, primitive fear of sudden movement, falling, and strange people all vanish, although the fear of noise persists in response to thunder.

However, the tilt toward realism is not all-encompassing. While the fear of remote animals such as lions and tigers declines, fear of harmless animals such as rats and mice ranks high, while the fear of snakes far outstrips their actual danger. Fear of the dark and of nightmares also continues. A decline in fear of ghosts is compensated for by an increase in fear of fictional characters from stories, movies, and television. The finding is plausible. Imagination, by its very nature, is tangential to reality since it does not conform to the same rules as those governing the social and physical environment. Thus imaginary characters can retain their affective charge in the face of an increased cognitive realism.

In sum, middle childhood, like all other developmental periods throughout the life span, is marked by a mixture of realistic and unrealistic fear; only the proportions have changed.

Adolescence Adolescence brings with it new, age-appropriate fears. Sexual fears and concerns over money and work enter the developmental picture, as would be expected. Their increased cognitive ability enables adolescents to grasp and be concerned about a social context broader than home and school, as well as making it possible for them to project themselves into the future. Thus fears centering around war and peace make their appearance and dramatically increase between 14 and 18 years of age, along with more personal concerns about growing up and being able to cope with problems that lie ahead.

Adolescence also witnesses an increase in fears that are present only to a minor degree in middle childhood. The striking example is fear of failure or personal inadequacy, expressed primarily in the large number of school-related fears present throughout the entire period. Such fears may be due partly to the increased emphasis on achievement in high school, but they are also due to the ado-lescent's own increased ability to generate relatively stable standards and to be concerned over living up to them. As peer relations take on greater importance in adolescence, concerns over popularity and having friends begin to rise, especially for girls. And the increased self-consciousness of the adolescent is accompanied by an increased fear of looking foolish.

Finally, irrational fears, while infrequent, persist—for example, fear of the dark, of storms and noise, or mice and snakes. Fear of the supernatural is infrequent, but adolescence may bring with it new irrational fears, such as fear of cemeteries and of water (i.e., swimming alone, boating, deep water), which are rarely reported in middle childhood.

In sum, fears at this stage, as in previous ones, continue to reflect significant developments in the self, in social expectations and relationships, in cognition, and in physical maturation. Adolescence may also represent a further diminution of irrational fears, although they are not completely exorcised. (For details of the reconstruction, see Wenar, 1989.)

Overcoming Fears According to Jersild and Holmes (1935), mothers used a variety of techniques aimed at helping their children overcome fears: explanation and reassurance, setting an example (such as walking into a dark room or petting a feared dog), providing the child with coping techniques (such as letting a fearful child turn off the lights himself at night), graduating the approach to a feared object, using distractions or counterstimuli (such as having a child ride horsey on a vacuum cleaner when the frightening motor is not running), and forewarning the child in preparation for a potentially frightening experience (such as getting a shot from a doctor). Not only were the mothers ingenious, but their techniques have a surprisingly contemporary ring as well. However, they succeeded only fitfully. More typically, children overcame fears on their own; children's increased understanding of their environment and their increased ability to manipulate and explore were their greatest assets in achieving mastery. Using our own terminology, fears are overcome by *initiative*.

Why Phobias?

The literature is least satisfactory when it comes to determining the relation between fears and phobias. It would seem reasonable to assume that fears shade imperceptibly into phobias. For example, Ollendick, Yule, and Ollier (1991) found a substantial relation between fear and anxiety in 8- to 10-year-olds. Even so, it would still leave unanswered the basic question, Why do fears become so intense and persistent that the factors responsible for openness to change, such as initiative, fail to serve their growth-promoting function? One might expect that animal phobias would be the most amenable to the corrective influence of increasing cognitive and emotional maturity, yet just the opposite is the case. To compound the problems, what empirical data there are often blur the distinction between fears and phobias, so it is impossible to tell whether what is termed an intense or a clinical fear is the equivalent of a formally defined phobia. Consequently, any discussion of the relation between the two is bound to be tentative.

While disclaiming any intent of unraveling the etiologic mystery of phobias, Jersild and Holmes (1935) obtained data on sixteen preschoolers representing the extremes of a marked lack of fearfulness on the one hand and unusually high levels of fearfulness on the other. They found that both groups were in good physical condition, that there was no difference in the stability and security of the home atmosphere or in the mothers' understanding of the children's needs, and no difference in general friendliness and enjoyment of peer relations. However, there was a difference in certain personality traits: the fearful children were more frequently described as dependent on adults for help, easily upset emotionally, timid, shy, and insecure, and unable to stand up for their rights on the playground, while the least fearful children were described in the opposite terms. Such observations and inferences make sense in light of the previous hypothesis that self-confident exploration and the ability to test out the reality of fears is one of the major reasons they are mastered. Lack of confidence and a sense of personal ineffectuality or helplessness may exaggerate and perpetuate fears. Yet all of this is speculative and seems more relevant to disturbances in general rather than being specific to phobias. After almost sixty years, studies illuminating the relation between fears and phobias still remain to be done.

Relative Effectiveness of Different Therapies

With diverse therapies claiming to cure phobias, the question naturally arises, Which is the most effective? One study addressing this question is also a model of research on relative effectiveness. The children were evaluated objectively by individuals other than the therapist, thus eliminating the unconscious biases which creep in when therapists evaluate their own work. The groups of children receiving different treatment were carefully matched at the beginning to ensure that one was not better adjusted, more intelligent, and so forth than the other. Even more important, the therapists themselves were matched in terms of skill so that the outcomes would reflect the kind of therapy rather than the expertness with which it was implemented. The therapeutic goals were agreed upon so that improvement in both groups would conform to the same behavioral criteria and therefore be comparable. Finally, the test of therapeutic effectiveness was made at the end of a follow-up period, since there is evidence that immediate improvement tends to wash out with time.

The study was conducted by Miller and colleagues (1972), who compared the relative effectiveness of a behavioral therapy (reciprocal inhibition), a psychoanalytically oriented play therapy, and a control group of children on a waiting list who received no therapy. All sixty-seven subjects were phobic, the ones in treatment receiving one-hour sessions three times a week for eight weeks. All children were evaluated at the end of a six-week follow-up period. There was no evidence that either therapy was more effective, which might have been, in part, because the actual behavior of the therapists from the two different schools was quite similar! There was a diminution of symptoms in all three groups. Whether the two therapy groups improved more than the nontreated control group depended on who evaluated them; parents of the treated groups reported significantly greater improvement, while a noninvolved clinician found no differences among the three groups. Age proved to be a significant variable; 6- to 10-year-olds showed greater improvement with therapy than the controls, while 11- to 15-year-olds failed to show such a difference. Similar results concerning the relative effectiveness of behavioral and psychoanalytically oriented psychotherapy have been found with adults (Sloane et al., 1975).

In light of the fact that poorly designed studies of therapeutic effectiveness have been misleading in the past, our preference is to conclude that, at present, there is no treatment of choice for anxiety disorders (see Barrios and Hartman, 1988).

Behavioral Treatment

While therapists of many different orientations have reported success in treating childhood phobias, the greatest number of controlled studies have been done by the behavior therapists. (For a comprehensive account, see Barrios and O'Dell, 1989, and King, 1993.)

Systematic desensitization involves substituting the incompatible response of relaxation for the response of anxiety. (See Chapter 17 for details.) The therapist obtains a gradient of anxiety from the most intense (e.g., riding on a bus) to the least (e.g., walking along the street where the bus stop is). After being trained to relax, the children are instructed to relax after they imagine each successive step in the gradient until they eventually can do so at the point of highest anxiety. When practical considerations allow, the procedure can also be done using the actual feared object or situation, such as a dog or a dark room. In such cases, the procedure is called in vivo desensitization.

Prolonged exposure takes the opposite tack from progressive desensitization by exposing children to the full intensity of the feared stimulus and reinforcing them for remaining in its presence for a prolonged period of time. This "flooding" with anxiety prevents children from being reinforced by escape and also triggers a physiological reaction involving a return to normal functioning. The exposure itself can be imaginary or in vivo.

In *modeling* the child observes another person interacting adaptively with the feared object. More effective is *participatory modeling* in which the child, after the observation period, joins the model in gradually approaching the feared object.

Cognitive self-management strategies emphasize "self-talk" to counteract the effects of phobic ideation. There is some evidence that self-statements emphasizing competence (e.g., "I am brave and can take care of myself") are more effective than those countering the fear-producing properties of the stimulus (e.g., "Riding on the bus is lots of fun"). This finding raises the more general question as to whether the effective mechanism in treatment is reduction of anxiety or an increase in feelings of mastery or both.

SCHOOL PHOBIA

A youngster with a school phobia is a pitiful sight. On a school morning, a boy might sit at the breakfast table pale and silent, his eyes tearful, listlessly pushing a spoon around his bowl of oatmeal. If he forces himself to eat a spoonful and take a gulp of milk in response to parental coaxing, it is with great effort. Soon he says he has to go to the bathroom either to throw up or to have a bowel movement, which he might or might not do. As the time approaches for him to catch the school bus, he becomes increasingly agitated, pleading, crying, or shouting accusations at his mother. In no way can such distress be mistaken for ma-

lingering or attention getting; rather, it has all the behavioral and physiological characteristics of intense fear. However, if the child is allowed to stay at home, he is relieved and may resume his usual activities.

Two Forms of Disturbance

School phobia, also called *school refusal*, is defined as an irrational dread of some aspect of the school situation accompanied by physiological symptoms of anxiety or panic when attendance is imminent and resulting in a partial or total inability to go to school.

A school phobia may be due either to a fear of some aspect of the school environment, which might be regarded as a *true school phobia*, or to a fear of separating from the caretaker, which appears to be a specific form of *separation anxiety disorder* (Last and Strauss, 1990).

School phobias can be a fear of separation.

For example, the most frequently expressed fear of children with school refusal is that harm will befall the mother in the children's absence; this is followed by the fear of being ridiculed and the fear of failure in school.

While there can be overlap, the two are distinct disturbances. Children with a separation anxiety disorder are generally female, prepubertal, and from families of low socioeconomic status, whereas children with a true school phobia tend to be male, postpubertal, and of a high socioeconomic status. The mean age of onset for children with true school phobia is 14.2 years, while that for children with a separation anxiety disorder is 9.4 years. Children with a separation anxiety disorder are more severely disturbed in that they have more additional psychopathologies and symptoms other than fear of school; a true school phobic is less disturbed and a fear of school is the defining symptom. There is evidence that mothers of children with a separation anxiety disorder are also more disturbed, particularly exhibiting an increase in depression. Children with a separation anxiety disorder always remain at home with an attachment figure when not in school, whereas the school-phobic children are comfortable in many settings other than the school (Last and Francis, 1988).

Descriptive Characteristics

In regard to *prevalence,* school refusals are estimated to occur in 0.4 to 1.5 percent of the general population, and in 3 to 8 percent of clinically referred children (Last and Strauss, 1990). Common *precipitating events* are change of schools, parental illness or death, and a stay at home because of accidents or illness (King, Hamilton, and Ollendick, 1988), although in many cases there is no obvious reason for onset. While there has been some effort to explore the difference between younger and older school-phobic children (i.e., younger or older than 10 years of age) and between acute and chronic cases, the research has been limited and inconclusive.

The Interpersonal Context

Studies of the interpersonal context often have failed to differentiate the two kinds of school phobias.

The diverse interpersonal relations have been organized into three patterns: (1) an overindulgent mother and an inadequate father, dominated by a willful, stubborn, demanding child at home who is timid and inhibited in social situations away from home; (2) a strict, controlling, demanding mother, a passive father, and a passive, obedient child at home who is often timid and fearful away from home but who may become stubborn and rebellious at puberty; and (3) a firm, controlling father and an overindulgent mother closely bound to and dominated by a willful, demanding child who is alert, friendly, and outgoing away from home (Hersov, 1960).

One can speculate that the first two patterns are characteristic of a separation anxiety disorder and the third of a true school phobia. (Recall that the latter child is comfortable in a nonschool setting.) Even allowing for the validity of this speculation, it leaves unanswered the question of how the patterns of parental behavior produce the particular disturbances in the children.

Relation to Other Anxiety Disorders

Again we must deal with data that fail to divide the school-phobia population into two subgroups. In one of the few comparative studies, Waldron and coworkers (1975) found that the school-phobia group had more separation anxiety, were more dependent and depressed, and had a greater amount of unreal-

TABLE 8.2
Summary of Findings Concerning School Phobia

School phobia or school refusal		
	True School Phobia	**Separation Anxiety Disorder**
Sex:	Male > female	Female > male
Onset:	14.3 years	9.4 years
SES:	High	Low
Severity:	Few additional symptoms	More additional symptoms
		Remains at home
	OK in nonschool settings	(?) Dependent, depressed
Reasons:	Ridicule or failure in school	Harm to mother in absence
Parents:	(?) Firm father: overprotective mother	Mother: depressed
		(?) Overindulgent mother: inadequate father
		(?) Controlling mother: passive father

Vs. other anxiety disorders
More separation anxiety, dependent, depressed, unrealistically high self-expectations
More disturbance in parents and child

(?) = extrapolated from data

istically high self-expectation than did the children with other anxiety disorders. Both parents and children had more signs of disturbance than were found in the comparison group of neurotics. (Table 8.2 summarizes findings in school phobia.)

The Developmental Dimension

Few attempts have been made to place school phobia within a *developmental context*. As we have seen, there is evidence that separation anxiety predominates in younger children, while in older children the problem is specific to school and is characterized more by depression and withdrawal (Kelly, 1973). Such a pro-gression would make sense developmentally in terms of the increasing autonomy and self-evaluation of the school-age period. One can speculate that the same parental overdependence underlying separation anxiety in the younger child might subsequently produce feelings of personal inadequacy in meeting the demands of school as school itself increasingly comes to resemble the adult world in terms of its work requirements and peer orientation. Older children may suffer either from a chronic sense of inadequacy or an overvalua-tion of their abilities, an unrealistically high standard of achievement rendering them vul-nerable to overreacting to ordinary failures and setbacks.

Prognosis

Many prognostic studies have been done on hospitalized children with school phobias who probably represent a particularly severely disturbed subgroup. In these studies 22 to 100 percent of the children were found to have anxiety along with other neurotic symptoms or personality problems two to eighteen years after discharge from treatment. However, their functioning was satisfactory in terms of mood, work attendance, and interpersonal relations with friends (Miller, Boyer, and Rodoletz, 1990). The meager evidence on school-phobic children seen in outpatient clinics suggests a more favorable outcome. Flakierska, Lindstrom, and Gillberg (1988), who conducted a fifteen- to twenty-year follow-up study of thirty-five 7- to 12-year-olds, found that they were no different from normal controls in terms of completing school and contact with social authorities such as mental health clinics and the police, although they did have more outpatient treatment. Roberts' (1975) study was less optimistic, finding that 25 percent of children with school phobias subsequently had symptoms that created difficulties in attaining a reasonably stable and age-appropriate adjustment. The remaining adults, while not symptom-free, were making adequate adjustments. Attempts to identify predictors of later functioning, such as age of onset or return to school during therapy, have been inconclusive (Miller, Boyer, and Rodoletz, 1990).

Treatment

Studies of the effectiveness of *pharmacological treatment* are inconclusive. (Bernstein and Borchardt, 1991, summarize the literature.) For example, one study using the antidepressant imipramine found it facilitated school attendance and reduced depression, maternal dependence, and physical complaints. However, the children were receiving psychotherapy along with the medication and a large number of children on a placebo also returned to school. By contrast, another study using both imipramine and the antianxiety drug alprazolam did not find either medication superior to a placebo, although the authors admitted that problems in design may have attenuated the drug effect (see Gadow, 1992).

The literature on *psychotherapy* with school-phobic children is replete with reports of successful outcomes using a wide range of techniques from psychoanalysis to behavior modification. However, few reports meet criteria for methodological soundness, and only two compare relative effectiveness of different approaches (Klein and Last, 1989). In 1984 Miller and colleagues' (1972) study, which we have already presented, the majority of children were school phobics. Blagg and Yule (1984) found that 93 percent of the children in behavioral treatment began attending school with no or minor problems at the end of treatment; this contrasts with only 37 percent of children hospitalized for treating their condition and 10 percent of children who were treated at home. Moreover, behavioral treatment averaged two-and-a-half weeks in contrast to forty-five and seventy-two weeks for the other techniques.

Kearney and Silverman (1990) took a novel approach to treatment. They reasoned that therapy should be tailored to the variety of disturbances covered by the single diagnosis of school refusal. Because of their behavioral orientation, they translated these disturbances into behavioral terms. Only three of their four categories will concern us. Category 1 was avoidance of specific fears related to the school setting, such as the teacher or the school bus, and was treated with desensitization. Category 2 involved escape from aversive social situations, such as unsatisfactory peer relations, and was treated with modeling procedures to increase levels of social skills and with cognitive restructuring, such as substituting positive statements for ones like "Everyone will laugh at me when I make a mistake." Category 3 involved behaviors such as tantrums or physical complaints designed to keep the child at home and was treated by instructing parents to ignore the child, make him stay in his room, and give him the option of avoiding this negative home environment by attending school. Six of the seven subjects returned to school on a full-time basis at the end of treatment, maintaining their gains in a six-month follow-up. Such results are promising, but whether they can generalize to a larger group of children remains to be seen.

A controversial issue cutting across specific psychotherapies concerns the amount of pressure placed on the child to return to school. Some therapists regard an immediate return as essential even if some force must be applied, while others recommend timing the return in keeping with therapeutic progress. There is some evidence that while both procedures are successful, a graduated approach in conjunction with behavioral techniques circumvents the dropout problem that frequently occurs when the child is immediately returned to school (Klein and Last, 1989). However, there is general agreement that the child should return as soon as possible, even if only for a brief period.

SEPARATION ANXIETY DISORDER

As we have seen, the development of the bond of love to the caretaker and the fear of loss of the loved one go hand in hand in normal infant development. A number of factors are responsible for the mastery of this separation anxiety in the toddler period. Cognitively, the toddler is capable of holding the image of the caregiver in mind and of realizing that she continues to exist even after vanishing from sight. The upsurge of initiative attendant upon the ability to crawl and walk counteracts the infantile feeling of helplessness at the caregiver's departure, while expanding interests and relationships somewhat remove the caregiver from center stage.

Yet, for unknown reasons, the panic over separation can return from the preschool period through adolescence, producing two kinds of disturbance: separation anxiety and the special form of school phobia which is motivated by fear of being away from the caregiver. In both instances the developmental model is that of *regression*.

The core characteristic of separation anxiety disorder (SAD) is excessive anxiety over separation from people to whom the child is attached, typically the parents. Younger children may cling to or shadow the adult or have tantrums and cry or plead when the parent leaves. Older children may become upset over spending the night away from home or become distressed when away and need to call home frequently. Other symptoms include unrealistic, persistent worry about harm befalling the attachment figure, refusing to go to sleep without the attachment figure being near, complaints of physical symptoms such as headaches and stomachaches when separation is anticipated, and reluctance or refusal to go to school in order to be near the attachment figure. While not uncommon, the *prevalence* rate of SAD is uncertain.

Little is known concerning *etiology*. While separation anxiety is increased by insecure attachment, by unpredictable and uncontrolled separations, and perhaps by a temperamental vulnerability to anxiety in infancy, we do not know whether such variables are operative in disturbed children. Frequently, there is a stressor such as the loss or illness of a loved caretaker, but the condition can also appear for no obvious reason in well-functioning children. Generally speaking, much research needs to

TABLE 8.3

DSM-IV Draft Criteria for Obsessive-Compulsive Disorder

A. Either obsessions or compulsions:

Obsessions as defined by (1), (2), (3), and (4):

(1) Recurrent and persistent thoughts, impulses, or images that are experienced, at some time during the disturbance, as intrusive and inappropriate, and cause marked anxiety or distress

(2) The thoughts, impulses, or images are not simply excessive worries about real-life problems

(3) The person attempts to ignore or suppress such thoughts or impulses or to neutralize them with some other thoughts or action

(4) The person recognizes that the obsessional thoughts, impulses, or images are a product of his or her mind (not imposed from without as in thought insertion)

Compulsions as defined by (1) and (2):

(1) Repetitive behaviors (e.g., handwashing, ordering, checking) or mental acts (e.g., praying, counting, repeating words silently) that the person feels driven to perform in response to an obsession, or according to rules that must be applied rigidly

(2) The behaviors or mental acts are aimed at preventing or reducing distress or preventing some dreaded event or situation; however these behaviors or mental acts either are not connected in a realistic way with what they are designed to neutralize or prevent, or are clearly excessive

B. At some point during the course of the disorder, the person has recognized that the obsessions or compulsions are excessive or unreasonable. Note: this does not apply to children.

C. The obsessions or compulsions cause marked distress; are time-consuming (take more than an hour a day); or significantly interfere with the person's normal routine, occupational functioning, or usual social activities or relationships with others.

Source: American Psychiatric Association, 1993.

be done before we understand why normal anxiety becomes maladaptive (Bell-Dolan, Last, and Strauss, 1990). The families tend to be caring and close and the incidence seems to be higher in mothers who have a panic disorder (Crowell and Waters, 1990). Separation anxiety is also one of the few disturbances in which there is no sex difference in incidence.

Finally, there is evidence of a developmental trend whereby separation anxiety is more prevalent than overanxious disorder in pre-pubertal children followed by a high percent of dual diagnoses in the transition phase and a reversal after puberty in which overanxious disorder is dominant over separation anxiety (Miller, Boyer, and Rodoletz, 1990). What is not known is whether separation anxiety places the child at risk for developing an overanxious disorder or whether it becomes less frequent as it becomes more age-inappropriate (Bernstein and Borchardt, 1991, summarize objective studies.)

OBSESSIVE-COMPULSIVE DISORDER

Description

Obsessive-compulsive disorder is marked by intrusive ideas (obsessions) and impulses (compulsions) that (1) arise from sources over which the child has no control, (2) are irresistible, and (3) are often recognized as irrational (see Table 8.3). The disorder may appear to be an exaggeration of the normal ritualistic behavior of childhood; however, unlike those behaviors, these engender intense anxiety or guilt when interfered with as well as consuming an inordinate amount of time. While handwashing is the most familiar example, other behaviors concern safety (such as continually checking the doors to make sure they are locked), a preoccupation with orderliness, and repeatedly counting to a particular number or touching objects a given number of times. The most frequent obsessions involve fear of contamination and the thought of harm to the self or familiar figures (Bernstein and Borchardt, 1991).

It is not unusual for a child to combine a number of rituals. An 11-year-old boy who was terrified of germs used his "magic number" 4 for protection in a variety of ways: he touched his fork four times before eating, counted to 4 when entering the locker room in the school gym, got in and out of bed four times before going to sleep, lined up his perfectly sharpened pencils in groups of four. When he became worried that a ritual might not have worked, he repeated it four times.

In regard to *prevalence,* incidence rates between 0.2 and 1 percent have been reported in clinical populations, although this might be an underestimation. Boys outnumber girls by a ratio of 2:1 to 3:1.

The child and adult forms of the disorder are practically identical, one-third to one-half of adult cases having a childhood onset. The childhood form is not associated with depression as it is in adults. However it is associated with anorexia nervosa; anorectic females have obsessive symptoms independent of their preoccupation with food. It may also be associated with motor tics and conduct disorders (see Rapoport, 1986).

The age of onset can be from 9 to 16 years of age. An unexpected research finding is that the onset, while usually gradual, can be sudden or over a few months with no evidence of prior obsessive or compulsive traits such as fastidiousness, superstitiousness, or ritualistic behavior. For example, one teenager suddenly began getting up early in the morning and washing the walls of the room a few days each week.

In regard to *general characteristics,* children with obsessive-compulsive disorder tend to be of above-average intelligence, to have a rigid moral code accompanied by marked guilt feelings, and to have an active fantasy life. Problems such as fears and aggression toward parents are also present, along with an increased incidence of physical illness (Schwartz and Johnson, 1985).

Etiology

The etiology of obsessive-compulsive disorder remains a mystery. At a speculative level, compulsions are viewed as exaggerations of ritualistic behavior that is part of normal development, such as avoiding lines and cracks on the sidewalk or making sure special toys are lined up in a prescribed order before bedtime.

Leonard and coworkers (1990) explored this speculation by comparing a group of teenaged children with obsessive-compulsive disorder with a normal control group. From their review of the descriptive literature, supplemented by their own data, they outlined the similarities and differences between normal and deviant rituals. The similarities included the need to have things just so, counting (such as is done in jump rope and games like "Onepotato, two-potato"), the use of "lucky" numbers, and the occurrence of rituals at bedtime, leave taking, and periods of stress. But obsessive-compulsive rituals differ in that they come later in development (normal rituals fade around 8 years of age, while their deviant counterparts do not); the child is markedly distressed if the rituals are not performed; they are viewed as unwanted but beyond the child's control; and they interfere with socialization and healthy mastery of anxiety. While important, these data leave unanswered the basic question of how normal rituals become abnormal ones.

Recently, interest in etiology has shifted to the *organic* context. There is evidence from family studies of a genetic component (Swedo et al., 1989). Furthermore, an association between obsessive-compulsive symptoms and certain neurological disorders suggests a link to the basic ganglion, the structures of the brain under the cerebral cortex (Swedo et al., 1989).

Treatment

There are case reports of the successful use of behavioral intervention called *response prevention* in which ritualistic behavior is prevented from occurring. Like the prolonged-exposure technique, this one involves confronting the child with the anxiety released when a compulsive ritual is prevented from occurring. Like desensitization, the least upsetting ritual is prevented first, and after it is mastered, ones of increasing seriousness follow. Parent training is an important component of the treatment since response prevention is often done by the parents (Steketee and Cleere, 1990).

Psychotherapeutic drugs have been used with obsessive-compulsive disorder with some degree of success. The antidepressant clomipramine was superior to a placebo in controlling symptoms in one study of children and adolescents, although the responders did not fully

recover and there was a return of symptoms after drug withdrawal. Another antidepressant, fluoxetine, has also been used with positive results, although the results are preliminary (Gadow, 1992).

OTHER ANXIETY DISORDERS

Avoidant Disorder

Avoidant disorder is defined as an excessive shrinking from contact with unfamiliar persons in spite of a generally satisfactory relation with family members and familiar figures. There is self-consciousness, embarrassment, or overconcern about the appropriateness of behavior when interacting with unfamiliar people, and while children have at least one age-appropriate friendship, peer relations are restricted. In a new or forced social situation, the child's distress is marked by crying, muteness, or withdrawal. The onset is typically in the early school years, although it may also be seen as early as the toddler period after the normal wariness of strangers (also called "stranger anxiety") has disappeared. Whether it is in fact a regression to the normal wariness of strangers is not known. Avoidant disorder may significantly hamper the development of normal peer relations, thus making the child more vulnerable to both internalizing and externalizing disorders.

No data are available on prevalence of avoidant disorder in the general population, but preliminary findings suggest that it is less common than separation anxiety or overanxious disorder in a clinical population. (Our presentation follows Klein and Last, 1989.) Females are overrepresented in the clinical population. The children have a long history of difficulties with self-confidence and assertiveness which they do not "outgrow," the avoidant disorder being triggered by stress or developmental transitions. No data are currently available on prognosis.

Overanxious Disorder

This disorder is characterized by excessive or unrealistic worry over a six-month period or more. The worry may concern future events; current social, academic, or athletic competence; or past behavior. The disorder is characterized by marked self-consciousness, somatic complaints with no physical basis, feelings of tension, and a need for reassurance.

Overanxious disorder is found in about 2 to 4 percent of the population. (Our presentation follows Werry's 1991 summary of objective studies.) It may begin at any age in childhood, but there is conflicting evidence concerning its course. The sparse data suggest that its symptoms disappear or become subclinical within two years, although an unknown minority of cases run a chronic course. The sex ratio is equal until adolescence, after which females predominate. About half the children with overanxious disorder have at least one other disorder, most often another anxiety or mood disorder.

The evidence concerning etiology is contradictory. Studies suggest a link to parental psychopathology as various anxiety, mood, and alcohol disorders have been implicated. However, no study has demonstrated a specific relation between parental anxiety disorder (rather than other anxiety disorders) and overanxious disorders in the children. Longitudinal studies suggest that mood disorders, avoidant disorder, and disruptive disorders all may precede overanxious disorder. The reasons for the relationships are not known.

Posttraumatic Stress Disorder

This disorder follows an unusually distressing experience such as a serious threat to one's life, a natural disaster (e.g., an earthquake), or a violent incident (e.g., seeing another person seriously injured or killed). The traumatic event may be reexperienced in a number of ways; for example, there may be an intrusive recollection of the event or flashbacks of the experience. Next, events associated with the trauma are avoided or there is a general numbing of responsiveness expressed as a diminished interest in significant activities, being unable to feel love, or a feeling of detachment from others. Finally, there are persistent symptoms of hyperarousal, such as irritability, difficulty in concentrating, and an exaggerated startle response. The most obvious exemplars of posttraumatic stress disorders are combat veterans.

Since the classification is new, there is a question as to how appropriate it is for children. (Our presentation follows Davidson and Baum, 1990, unless otherwise noted.) Undoubtedly, children experience traumatic events which adversely affect their functioning and development. Yet it is not clear how such events should be conceptualized. While experiencing war or natural disasters or kidnapping seem logical candidates for inclusion, should physical and sexual abuse, divorce, and parental death also be added? The list of traumatic events may change with age since what is traumatic for a 2-year-old may not be traumatic at 12 years of age. On the response side, there is evidence that severely traumatized children experience the full range of symptoms. However, preschoolers do not become amnesic for the traumatic events, evidence psychic numbing, or experience sudden intrusive flashbacks. Unlike adults, they commonly engage in posttraumatic play and reenactment behavior and show more distortion in the sense of time (Bernstein and Borchardt, 1991).

In general, researchers have found that younger children have the most difficulty and require the most help in assimilating a traumatic event. This may well be because they have fewer coping devices than older children. Studies of sex differences have yielded contradictory findings. As a rule, disturbances are often minimal and short-lived, and children are less affected than adults.

Not unexpectedly, parents play an important role in children's reactions. On the positive side, children showed few adverse reactions to bombings if parents remained relatively calm. On the negative side, children can identify with parents' reactions; for example, some children of Vietnam war veterans exhibited posttraumatic stress responses including guilt, sleep disturbances, anxiety, and preoccupation with their parents' trauma.

The Developmental Dimension The kinds of symptoms children manifest after being exposed to traumatic events vary with age. *Young children* may regress to a previous level of functioning, such as losing bowel and bladder control, becoming irritable and crying frequently, sucking their thumbs, and developing fears and eating problems. They are apt to reenact the traumatic event though play, such behavior being unique to children. The play itself has a compulsive, repetitive quality that fails to relieve the accompanying anxiety. For example, a 5-year-old girl who was attacked and bitten by a monkey at the zoo would repeatedly return to this theme, although the play did nothing to help her master her fright.

For *school-aged children* fears and anxieties are the predominant symptoms. The children also complain of headaches and visual and hearing problems, are inattentive at school, fight with or withdraw from peers, and have sleep disturbances such as nightmares and bed-wetting. Like younger children, they engage in elaborate reenactments of the traumatic event.

Preadolescents and adolescents, like school-age children, may develop various physical complaints, become withdrawn, suffer from loss of appetite and sleep, and become disruptive or fail at school. They may also have suicidal ideation. Unlike younger children, they do not reenact the traumatic event.

Panic Disorder

The core criterion of panic disorder is discrete, recurring periods of intense, unexpected fear. The fear itself is not triggered by an anxiety-arousing situation. The symptoms include shortness of breath, dizziness, sweating, palpitations, chest pains, nausea, fear of dying, or fear of going crazy. While present in middle childhood, adolescence is the peak period for the beginning of the disorder, although it may be overdiagnosed in this period (Kearney and Silverman, 1992). Panic disorder is found more frequently in girls than boys. It is closely related to separation anxiety and commonly coexists with depression. The triad of panic disorder, separation anxiety disorder, and depression have been shown to cluster together statistically as internalizing disorders and all respond to antidepressants (Black and Robbins, 1990).

CHAPTER 9

CONDUCT DISORDERS AND INADEQUATE SELF-CONTROL

You are a clinical child psychologist. You arrive at your office at eight in the morning. Mark Redfleish is already waiting. He says, "Hi, Doc! Dad dropped me off on his way to work." He is a lively, assured 11-year-old, nice looking, well built but small for his age. An all-Ameri- *can-type boy. Except that, for the past two years, he has been breaking into, ransacking, and robbing houses in the wealthy suburb where he lives. At first he threw the stolen silverware and hi-fi sets into a nearby lake. Then he established connections with a man who bought the*

243

loot with no questions asked. After a robbery was discovered, Mark would show up and offer to help put the house back in order. His manner was one of sincere concern, and he asked for no favors in return. He was finally caught because a careless remark revealed that he knew an item had been stolen before the owner had mentioned it to anyone outside the family.

Mark is bright, enterprising, and capable beyond his years. But he is also a daredevil and a loner. He loves to ride his motorbike at full speed over a downhill path through the woods, making it jump over small crevices and creeks, doing a "pop-a-wheely" by riding only on the back wheel, turning sharply at the end of the ride in a cloud of dust. At school he was the youngest boy to smoke marijuana and drink alcohol. He charmed his way into being taught how to drive a car and then bribed the caretaker's son into letting him use the jeep to ride on the back roads on the far side of the lake. Yet he is not a show-off or a braggart, nor is he responding to dares. Rather he is obeying an inner restlessness.

Other boys are sporadically attracted to Mark's daring and helpfulness, but friendships are short-lived. He enjoys luring younger boys into joining him in venturing into forbidden places—a beer-and-wine carryout, an adult bookstore, an abandoned quarry—because he likes being in command. In school he is restless and inattentive, except in shop, where his interests and skills make him the top student. He is a master of the sincere lie—looking the teacher straight in the face. One of them said, "I just can't reach him with anything. I could beat him or plead with him or take him on my lap and cuddle him, and it just wouldn't matter."

Mark's father, a successful surgeon, has little time for his family during the week but enjoys being with his son on weekends, going hunting and ice-skating in the winter, fishing and sailing in the summer. In his eyes, Mark could do no wrong. Even the robberies were extenuated: "Wild colts make good horses," was what he told you. Mark's mother is basically a kind and loving woman but lacking in resources. Early on she perceived Mark's disregard for her prohibitions concerning dangerous objects and activities, and she did not know what to do about his constant lying. But more than anything else, his sheer energy exhausted her patience. Affection and reasoning gave way to angry shouts and finally to whippings with a strap. Mark was determined not to cry; he sensed that if she could not hurt him, she would be powerless.

At ten o'clock you see Angelo Ruccio, another 11-year-old, for the second time. He will be brought by his parole officer, since the judge has said that either he gets psychological help or he will be confined in the juvenile correctional center. "That's like playing tennis with both hands tied behind your back," you think, but it is far better than having the boy sent to a punitive, ineptly run institution. The judge was lenient because Angie was the only member of his gang to get caught breaking into and robbing a corner grocery store. He was caught because he was obviously a not-too-bright follower who was doing what he was told.

Yet his loyalty to the gang far outweighs any sense of wrongdoing. And for good reason. School has been an endless series of humiliations and failures. He was passed primarily because he was not a troublemaker, and his teachers became tired of yelling at him for making mistakes and handing in sloppy homework. His family is large and poor, and while they fight a good deal, they also have a sense of loyalty. The father is a laborer who is hired and fired according to the state of the economy. He is a bitter man who demands respect from his children but sees no reason for them to be good citizens in a society which has treated him so shabbily. To his mother—a meek, careworn woman—Angie is another mouth to feed, and while she prays to the Virgin every night to help her children, she wonders where she will get the strength to see her through another day.

So it is the gang that gives Angie a sense of belonging, of sharing, of being valued. While his slowness makes him the goat, the leader has taken a liking to him, and Angie's fondest dream is one day to become a leader himself. That will be a tough dream to shatter, and right now you do not know what you can put in its place.

TYPES OF CONDUCT DISORDERS

The lesson is familiar—the same pathological behavior may have different origins. In this case, the lesson is particularly important in light of the consequences of antisocial behavior, as we shall see.

While there is agreement in regard to the behaviors that define a conduct disorder, these behaviors have been clustered in somewhat different ways. Statistical analyses have produced two clusters of behaviors. The first includes fighting, disobedience, temper tantrums, destructiveness, uncooperativeness, impertinence, and restlessness. It has been labeled *undersocialized aggressive* or *aggressive* be-havior. The second cluster includes having bad companions, truancy from home and school, stealing with others, loyalty to delin-quent friends, lying, and setting fires. It has been labeled *socialized aggression* or *delinquent.* Representing a clinical-descriptive approach, DSM-III-R has two major types: the *solitary ag-gressive* type, characterized by aggressive physical behavior initiated by the person and not as a group activity, and the *group* type, where conduct problems occur as a group ac-tivity that may or may not include aggressive physical behavior. There is also a residual cat-egory of undifferentiated type. The DSM-IV Draft Criteria opt for a single category of Con-duct Disorder (Table 9.1). (See Baum, 1989, for a more detailed presentation and comparison of the various approaches to classification.)

In all classifications the variable of sociali-zation plays an important role. In socialized conduct disorders the children have been so-cialized with a deviant set of values. Typically they come from a lower-class home in a dete-riorated urban area. As was the case of Angelo, they have little chance to learn the accepted values of society. The gang—with its emphasis on physical prowess and ability to outwit others, its rebelliousness toward authority, and its desire for excitement—becomes central in their lives. Unlike their undersocialized counterparts, these children are fiercely loyal

---

TABLE 9.1

DSM-IV Draft Criteria for Conduct Disorder

A repetitive and persistent pattern of behavior in which either the basic rights of others or major age-appropriate societal norms or rules are violated, lasting at least six months, during which at least three of the following are present:

(1) Often bullies, threatens, or intimidates others
(2) Often initiates physical fights
(3) Has used a weapon that can cause serious physical harm to others (e.g., a bat, brick, broken bottle, knife, gun)
(4) Has stolen with confrontation with a victim (e.g., mugging, purse snatching, extortion, armed robbery)
(5) Has been physically cruel to people
(6) Has been physically cruel to animals
(7) Has forced someone into sexual activity
(8) Often lies or breaks promises to obtain goods or favors or to avoid obli-gations (i.e., "cons" others)
(9) Often stays out at night despite parental prohibitions, beginning before 13 years of age
(10) Has stolen items of nontrivial value without confrontation with the vic-tim either within the home or outside the home (e.g., shoplifting, bur-glary, forgery)
(11) Has deliberately engaged in fire setting with the intention of causing serious damage
(12) Has deliberately destroyed others' property (other than by fire setting)
(13) Has run away from home overnight at least twice while living in paren-tal or parental surrogate home (or once without returning for a lengthy period)
(14) Often truant from school, beginning before 13 years of age (for em-ployed person, absent from work)
(15) Has broken into someone else's house, building, or car

Source: American Psychiatric Association, 1993.

to peers; while they are relatively unconcerned about their antisocial acts, failure to live up to the standards of the gang produces guilt. Thus, unlike the impulsive-aggressive type, they are deficient neither in control nor in feelings for others.

Mark does not have problems with control, nor does his antisocial behavior spring from group membership. With his disregard for social and moral values, unconcern for the feelings of others, absence of guilt, and inability to form close relations to others, all masked by a social adroitness, he is an embryonic "con man." In an extreme form, he may become the kind of "model family man" who startles the community by committing grand larceny.

Another reason for presenting Mark is to counteract the stereotype of antisocial behavior as primarily a psychopathology of children with low socioeconomic status. On the contrary, white-collar crime is responsible for more stolen money than blue-collar crime. The $11 billion cost of violent crimes is nothing compared with the $200 billion taken by white-collar criminals annually. Moreover, the risk of white-collar crime is less and the punishment more benign (*U.S. News and World Report*, 1985). A thief does not have to be a punk from the slums holding up a convenience store; he may well be a man in a Brooks Brothers suit driving home to the suburbs. Why the developmental roots of white-collar crime are being ignored has more to do with the psychology and sociology of scientific enquiry than with the need to understand deviant behavior.

One final word concerning nomenclature. *Conduct disorder* is the psychological term for antisocial acting out. It should not be equated with *delinquency*, which is a legal term that includes offenses that are criminal if committed by an adult, such as robbery or homicide, and behaviors regarded as illegal in children but not in adults, such as truancy from school, drinking alcoholic beverages, and driving without a license. These latter are called *status*

offenses. While there is considerable overlap between conduct disorders and delinquency, they are distinct categories. Much of the antisocial behavior of the preschool period and early childhood may be contained within the family or school and is not regarded as delinquent; by the same token, there are illegal acts, such as drug use, which may represent expected unconventional behavior in certain adolescents rather than psychopathology. (See Chapter 11.)

UNDERSOCIALIZED, AGGRESSIVE CONDUCT DISORDER

Traditionally *undersocialized, aggressive conduct disorder* has been regarded as the most severe of the conduct disorders. This pattern is marked by active, antisocial behavior. Aggression may take such forms as temper tantrums, fighting, assault, or mugging. Disregard for social values is evidenced in behaviors such as stealing, lying, robbery, vandalism, drinking, and rape. Difficulty in accepting authority leads to conflict with parents, with the school, and with the law. The undersocialized, aggressive child is impulsive, fails to learn from experience, and is deficient in guilt feelings and anxiety. Relations with family and peers are shallow.

In discussing undersocialized, aggressive conduct disorder we shall draw on the rich literature on aggression. However, a conduct disorder is a syndrome or complex of behaviors; aggression does not define it any more than a depressed mood defines depression. As we have seen, aggression is part of normal development, and there is no reason for assuming that a "hothead" or a "scrapper" has a conduct disorder if the other crucial aspects of his or her personality are proceeding apace.

Characteristics

Referrals for conduct problems, aggressiveness, and antisocial behavior make up about one-third to one-half of all child and adolescent cases. *Prevalence* estimates depend on the strictness of criteria used and range from 4 to 10% of the population. In regard to *sex differences*, antisocial behavior is at least three times more common in boys than in girls. Sex even affects age of onset: antisocial behavior usually starts before age 10 with boys, while for girls it generally appears at age 14 to 16. Aggression and theft are the frequent bases for referring boys, while sexual misbehavior is more likely for girls. Self-report data, in contrast with records of arrests, do not support the view that male and female delinquency have been converging since the advent of the women's movement, and feminist attitudes are not linked with delinquent behavior. In addition, similar variables are associated with delinquency for both sexes. In spite of the lower rate for females, the juvenile justice system treats them more punitively than males (Henggeler, 1989).

While there is more conduct disorder and delinquency from lower *socioeconomic classes*, this may well be because this class has more of the variables known to be related to such disturbances, including large family size, overcrowding, and poor child supervision. (For a more detailed presentation of the research, see Kazdin, 1987.) While conduct-disordered youths are apt to have below-average scores on tests of *intelligence and academic achievement*, there is no strong evidence that such differences hold up when groups carefully matched for SES are used (Martin and Hoffman, 1990).

Conduct disorders can *co-occur* with other disturbances; the association with attention-deficit hyperactivity disorder is particularly high, as we have seen in Chapter 6. There is also a close relation between conduct disorders and oppositional-defiant disorder (Chapter 5). Lahey and colleagues (1992), in their review of objective studies, conclude that the two disturbances are developmentally related in that virtually all clinically referred youth with prepubertal onset of conduct disorder

have retained symptoms of an earlier-onset oppositional-defiant disorder. Moreover, the appearance of aggression seems to mark the transition from one disorder to the other. However, the authors note that the two should not be considered levels of severity of the same disorder since many youths with oppositional-defiant disorder never develop conduct disorders, while conduct disorders originating in adolescence appear independent of oppositional-defiant disorder. Finally, depression occurs in one-fifth to one-third of the conduct-disordered population (Baum, 1989).

NORMAL AND INADEQUATE SELF-CONTROL

Self-control is essential to socialization. A 4-year-old may not attack a 2-year-old sibling in a rage, masturbate in the supermarket, or try out a new toy hammer on the hi-fi set. Honesty, truthfulness, respect for the rights and property of others, obedience to the authority first of parents, then of teachers, and finally of the law are required. The requirements are essential because toddlers and preschoolers have a strong desire for immediate gratification of their aggressive, sexual, and exploratory urges, and they tend to be greedy, egocentric, selfish, and self-seeking. Our concern here is with the reasons why adequate self-control fails to develop or to function properly.

We shall call behaviors resulting from inadequate self-control *acting out*, which includes aggression, temper tantrums, lying, stealing, truancy, vandalism, fire setting, disobedience, and bullying. Note that some of the behaviors, such as aggression and temper tantrums, have a high-intensity, impulsive quality; others such as lying and stealing, may be of low intensity and premeditated. But they all involve a breach of socially accepted behavior.

For the first time in our discussions the *societal* context rivals the home and the school in importance: the 12-year-old who is caught cutting up all the clothes in her mother's closet or clogging the school toilets with sanitary napkins is in a different social situation from the one who is arrested for shoplifting. Getting into trouble with the law may involve the child in juvenile court and correctional institutions, both of which may have a special impact on the child's future.

The Development of Normal Control

At this point a review of the variables involved in the development of normal self-control is in order. First there are ones that give an *affective* charge to socializing directives—the bond of affection that makes the child educable, and later, sympathy and empathy, which counteract self-centeredness. Then there are a host of *intellectual* and *cognitive* variables. At the most basic level, the child must be able to remember the socializing message and recall it at appropriate times. Increased intellectual sophistication enables the child to progress from simple directives ("Don't touch that vase") to generalizations ("Everything in the living room is off limits") to conditional statements ("Don't take anything that belongs to somebody else unless you ask them first"). The development of *language* significantly facilitates the process of delaying and guiding action in accordance with socially accepted values. Concomitantly, the child becomes increasingly practiced in making decisions and taking responsibility for actions. A dependable, trustworthy *environment* also aids the child in postponing immediate gratification, as does the ability to find substitute gratifications or alternative means of achieving a goal.

The development of *conscience* and *ego ideals* plays a part in countering impulsivity and egocentrism. Cognitively, moral judgment progresses from a concern with immediate rewards and punishments for specific acts to the morality of shared standards, rights, and duties, while the ego ideal changes from superficial and exaggerated images of glamour and

success to realistic, socially oriented images. The affects involved in the conscience and ego ideal are self-satisfaction and self-esteem on the one hand, guilt, shame, and inferiority on the other.

In the interpersonal sphere both *parents* and *peers* play an important role in the development of self-control. In general, the optimal family setting includes affection and consistency, age-appropriate requirements for self-control and autonomy, help in understanding consequences of one's actions, and explicitness as to values. Peers counter egocentrism by forcing accommodations and by valuing proven worth over pedigree.

Clearly, an impressive array of factors contributes to self-control. Now let us see what blocks and undermines its development.

THE PRESCHOOL PERIOD

We will start with the hypothesis that many instances of acting out in the preschool period represent *fixations* or *developmental lags*. In the case of temper tantrums, we expect infants to react to frustrations with rage. During the terrible twos, willful toddlers are also apt to strike out in anger when they do not have their way, but now they can intentionally try to hurt. By 5 to 6 years of age the incidence of severe explosions should be rare (Macfarlane, Allen, and Honzik, 1954). Their persistence suggests both that the child is not making appropriate progress in achieving self-control and that he or she will be ill equipped to adjust to the demands of school successfully.

The hypothesis of a fixation or developmental lag also holds for stealing and lying. Let us examine the former. For the toddler every attractive object is fair game for exploration; it is the socializing adult who divides the world into things that are "OK" and things that are "no-no's." Prohibitions based on property rights are particularly difficult for the toddler to grasp. There is nothing in an object itself which proclaims its status as "mine" or "yours," so other cues must be utilized such as location ("mine" comes out of the big box by the bed I sleep in) or frequency of use (the fire engine big brother plays with all the time is a "not-mine"). Concurrently the toddler must learn that it is wrong to take objects that do not belong to him or her. While taking property peaks at 3 years of age (Macfarlane et al., 1954), this should not be regarded as stealing, since the idea of property rights has not registered. Only after the meaning of prohibitions has been grasped and intentional transgression has occurred does "taking" become "stealing."

And so it goes for lying. In early thinking, "lying" may represent a failure to differentiate the physical world from the psychological world of thoughts, feeling, and wishes. The 3-year-old boy who believes there is a wolf under his bed at night may also honestly believe that his big sister started a fight, when he himself was to blame. Only after objective and subjective social reality have been differentiated can the concept of lying become meaningful.

There is another cognitive problem arising from preschoolers' tendency to be quite literal in their understanding of terms. To lie is not telling the truth—period. Thus people who inadvertently communicate incorrect information are lying. For example, if a little girl was told by a mischievous older sister that a picture of a cat was a picture of a lion and the little girl subsequently told her younger brother that the pictured cat was a lion, the typical 4-year-old would say the little girl was lying! Many 4-year-olds and even some 6-year-olds reason in this way (Wimmer, Gruber, and Perner, 1984). The contingent nature of a lie, the fact that it is a deliberate deviation from a known truth, may be cognitively too difficult for the literal-minded preschooler to understand. By 6 years of age the child should have grasped the basic mean-

ing of stealing and lying, although the understanding of both will continue to develop.

Now suppose a mother came to you as a clinician and said, "My 4-year-old is always lying to me." Suppose further that you found out these were mainly face-saving lies. Would you reassure the mother that "most children her age tell such lies, and there is nothing to worry about?" Not at all. The chance that there is nothing to worry about does not negate the importance of exploring context variables. In regard to the little girl, you would at least want to know if this is the only sign of disturbance. The clinician should look not only for other symptoms but also for evidence of a generalized developmental lag. For example, does the girl habitually shun peers and play alone? Is her play repetitive? Is she withdrawn whenever she goes outside the protection of the home? Does she prefer to be only with her mother? The context of the mother's complaint is equally important. Does it arise from a lack of information concerning normal development, or does the mother talk about the child with the kind of controlled exasperation which suggests that lying just provides an excuse for expressing an underlying resentment? You might also ask about the father and the general pattern of family interaction before deciding that information coupled with reassurance is all that is needed. While the developmental approach helps put behavior in perspective, it does not supply categorical answers.

One final clinical example: A 19-year-old mother is complaining about her 3-year-old.

He don't do nothing but bad [things]. If he don't like what I make him [to eat], he throw it on the floor. I tell him I'm going to take a strap to him, and he just yells back at me, "Shut up, you old mother fucker," and I whip him with all I got and he still don't cry until he have to. . . . He pees in the closet every time he takes a mind to, and he takes his BMs and rubs them in his hair right while I'm looking at him. . . . Now he's taken to getting up in the middle of the night and turning on the bath water with the stopper in so there's water all over _the place. . . . If somebody don't straighten him out soon, I'm going to kill him!_

At first glance the boy's behavior would seem primitive and uncontrolled. However, note that he smears feces in front of his mother and gets up in the middle of the night to flood the bathroom, both of which suggest purposeful behavior. As it turns out, he knows quite well what he is doing. The mother is unmarried, childish, already worn down by poverty and lovelessness. Both emotionally and intellectually she was unprepared to be a mother at 16 years of age and felt burdened and resentful toward the baby. Fortunately for the boy, his grandmother was able to care for him, although only fitfully and grudgingly. The attention the boy received from his mother was primarily angry shouts and whippings. He was a resilient child, and in the toddler period he not only grasped the connection between doing "bad" things and exasperating his mother but also began to use it for all it was worth. The negative attention he gained from the mother was better than neglect, while her distress was his revenge.

Is Acting-Out Behavior "Outgrown"?

Data to answer this question come from Kohn's (1977) five-year longitudinal study of 1232 lower- and middle-class preschoolers. Kohn developed two scales, one entitled Interest-Participation versus Apathy-Withdrawal, the other entitled Cooperation-Compliance versus Anger-Defiance. It is the latter that interests us. Items at the Anger-Defiance extreme include "child expresses open defiance against teacher's rules and regulations" and "child is hostile or aggressive with other children (teases, taunts, bullies, etc.)." The children's behavior was evaluated by their teachers.

High anger and apathy scores in the preschool period were more predictive of overall evaluations of disturbance and need for psychological treatment in the fourth grade than were social class, race, ethnicity, and broken homes. In fact, gender was the only demographic variable of any predictive potency; boys became more disturbed than girls. Both sexes tended to become more disturbed and to achieve less as they progressed through school; boys showed the greatest change in the first and second grades, and girls became more apathetic during the first three grades but showed no consistent pattern of change in aggressiveness. Kohn notes that there is no evidence that the emphasis on "feminine" values of obedience and docility caused boys to become disturbed; rather, schooling accentuated the behavioral problems already present.

While aggressiveness was the most stable behavior over the five-year period, the significant correlation of .36 was sufficiently low to indicate that a good deal of change was also taking place. Analysis of the data revealed that 59 percent of the preschoolers scoring high in aggressiveness were no longer disturbed in the fourth grade; moreover, 14 percent of the highest-scoring aggressive children were subsequently among the healthiest fourth graders, while 13 percent and 16 percent, respectively, of the preschoolers scoring highest on Interest and Cooperation were now rated either extremely aggressive or extremely apathetic.

The findings are both significant and sobering in light of the emphasis on early detection and remediation of psychological disturbances. Kohn rightfully points out that his scales are a giant step forward in detecting high-risk preschoolers. But he also admits that predictability becomes increasingly inaccurate with the passage of time. As they stand, his data mean that an intervention program at the preschool level would be wasted on 59 percent of the aggressive children, who would "spontaneously outgrow" their problem, while missing the 29 percent of extremely well-adjusted preschoolers who subsequently would become disturbed.

Would a preventive program be worth the

time and money involved? The question has no easy answer. In part, it depends on how readily the early difficulties could be remedied and how serious the consequences if they were not. If a year of psychological help would save 40 percent of the children from severe academic underachievement and eventual delinquency, a preventive program would clearly be called for. As the time-and-money cost of change goes up and the severity of the ultimate disturbance declines, the need for early intervention becomes less clear. While no one would quarrel with the idea of preventive mental health, some of the problems involved in its implementation are concretely illustrated by Kohn's data.

Campbell (1991) enriches Kohn's research with her finding that aggression and noncompliance in kindergarten children, when accompanied by symptoms of hyperactivity and inattention, are likely to persist into the early school years and should not be considered normal turbulence that will be outgrown. Persistence was also related to increased stress in the family and a negative, conflicted mother-child relationship. Campbell infers a bidirectional interaction whereby the stressed mother becomes more restrictive and negative in trying to cope with her impulsive, noncompliant child; this in turn, makes the child more difficult to handle.

In a longitudinal study of preschoolers, Egeland and coworkers (1990) found that acting out was highly stable in at least the first three grades of school. More important, discontinuous development in the form of an increase or decrease in behavior problems was positively related to an increase or decrease in maternal depression. There was a negative relation to the degree of stimulation, predictability, and organization in the home, along with a positive relation to the number of stresses in the family such as loss of income or a severe illness.

We now have two clues as to how to make our hypothetical preventive program more ef-

ficient. Aggressive preschoolers who are also hyperactive and who have a conflicted relation with their mother are apt to continue to be aggressive. Maternal depressive symptoms should be monitored to detect cross-over children who are apt to grow out of or into aggressive behavior. Degree of stress in the family is important in both cases. (Reid, 1993, discusses early prevention in detail.)

MIDDLE CHILDHOOD AND ADOLESCENCE

Longitudinal studies of aggression and of disturbed children document the fixed nature of acting-out behavior. It will be worthwhile to examine these studies in detail. (For a summary of studies of adolescence, see Weiner, 1992.)

Aggression

Olweus's (1979) review of sixteen longitudinal studies of aggression in males sets the stage. While not concerned with psychopathology, these studies do trace the course of a behavior that lies at the heart of self-control. Olweus concludes that there is a substantial degree of stability of aggression over time; indeed, it seems to be as stable as intelligence. Since there is a tendency for the most aggressive boys to drop out of longitudinal studies, the available data may even underestimate the degree of stability.

Olweus was able to summarize the findings with a simple formula: the younger the subject and the longer the interval of time between evaluations, the less the stability. Thus, for example, over the same interval of time, a 2-year-old's aggressive behavior will vary more than that of a 10-year-old; and at any given age, predictability decreases with the passage of time, so aggression is less predictable over a six-year interval than over a three-year interval. By the time the boy is 8 or 9, there is a substantial correlation with aggressive patterns ten to fourteen years later; by 12 to 13 years of age, the stability is even higher for the next 10 years and, as we shall see, has considerable predictive capacity for later antisocial aggression.

The stability of aggressive behavior in the face of environmental variation and influences designed to change it leads Olweus to conclude that it is a relatively consistent reaction tendency or motivational system within the individual. Far from reacting to environmental provocation, highly aggressive children may actively seek out situations in which to express their need.

Psychopathological Development

In the 1950s, Robins (1966) compared 491 adults who had been seen at a child guidance center thirty years previously with a control group of 100 normal children matched for age, sex, IQ scores, race, and socioeconomic status. Children with IQs below 80 were eliminated. The population was predominantly male children of American-born Protestant parents of low socioeconomic status. Family disruption was high in the child guidance group, with only one-third of the children living with both parents. Approximately one-quarter to one-third of the fathers drank excessively and failed to provide financial support, while almost half of the mothers were extremely nervous, mentally ill, or feeble minded.

The continuity of antisocial behavior was striking: 45 percent of the clinic group had five or more antisocial symptoms as adults, compared with 4 percent of the control group. Conversely, the absence of antisocial behavior in childhood made the appearance of adult sociopathy extremely unlikely. Children referred for problems other than antisocial behavior—temper tantrums, irritability, fears, shyness, insomnia, tics—tended to be diagnosed as hysterics, alcoholics, or psychotics somewhat more frequently than the control group, but the differences were not as striking

as with antisocial behavior; in fact, antisocial children were equally liable to become psychotic adults as were children referred for other behavior.

Antisocial—or what Robins calls sociopathic—behavior occurred solely in males, beginning early in the boy's schooling. Theft, incorrigibility, running away, associating with bad companions, sexual activities, and staying out late were prominent reasons for referral. Most children were discipline problems in school—62 percent never graduated from grammar school—and were variously described as aggressive, reckless, impulsive, slovenly, enuretic, lacking guilt, and lying without cause. Almost four out of five appeared in juvenile court, and around half were sent to correctional institutions. Antisocial behavior was directed toward parents and teachers, businesses and strangers. Approximately half of the future sociopaths had fathers who were themselves sociopathic or alcoholic, while two-thirds came from broken homes.

As adults, almost every sociopath had marital problems and a poor work history and had been financially dependent on social agents or relatives. Three-fourths had multiple arrests and prison terms. They were impulsive, sexually promiscuous, vagrant, belligerent, and socially isolated.

Of greatest interest to us are Robins's findings concerning the predictive potential of childhood variables. The single best predictor was the *degree of antisocial behavior* as evidenced by the number of symptoms, the number of episodes, and the seriousness of the behaviors as measured by appearance in juvenile court and being sent to a correctional institution. Surprisingly, many variables frequently reported as childhood characteristics of adult sociopaths—parental deprivation and rejection, being a school dropout, poverty, foster home or orphanage placement, and antisocial behavior on the part of the mother—were not predictive when the level of the child's antisocial behavior was taken into account.

Sex, age, class, and ethnic values determined the *kind* of deviancy, not the deviancy itself: for example, antisocial acts among women were confined to sexual and maternal areas and the Irish children were more likely to develop alcoholism than other ethnic groups. Nor does "bad company" predict future sociopathy. Rather than the good child being led astray by the availability of delinquent gangs, the antisocial child seeks out other children on the basis of common interests—a point which Olweus made about normally aggressive children.

For boys who had fewer than six antisocial symptoms and therefore were not deeply enmeshed in antisocial behavior, it was the fathers who played the central role in determining their fate. More than two-thirds of such boys had fathers who were themselves sociopaths or alcoholics. These children were likely to live in lower-class neighborhoods, to receive little or inconsistent discipline, or to be sent to a correctional institution by a juvenile court wishing to remove them from the home environment. However, sociopathic behavior in middle-class fathers had the same detrimental effect upon predelinquent middle-class sons. For the boys with six or more antisocial symptoms, lack of discipline or inconsistent discipline was important in determining which ones would and would not become adult sociopaths.

One final point: in reviewing all the predictive variables, eleven involved characteristics of the child or the severity of his antisocial behavior; only two involved parental behavior, one involved family size, and two involved social institutions (juvenile court and correctional institutions). Thus, the child's current behavior predicts his future better than any context variable.

Subsequent research has corroborated and expanded Robins's findings (Loeber, 1991). In general, the four factors associated with the persistence of antisocial behavior are extremely high rates of such behavior; occur-

rence in more than one setting, such as home, school, and community; a variety of antisocial behaviors; and early onset. The evidence is conflicting in regard to whether socialized (group) or solitary aggression is more likely to lead to delinquency. (For specific studies, see Martin and Hoffman, 1990.) While most adult antisocial behavior is rooted in childhood, only half of the at-risk children grow up to be antisocial adults (Loeber and LeBlanc, 1990).

Relying on reconstructive data, Loeber and colleagues (1992) were able to arrive at a more differentiated picture. Children with early onset had both a higher level of disruptive behavior and progressed more rapidly to more serious problems. Regardless of age of onset, there was a developmental sequence going from hyperactivity and inattention, to oppositional behavior, to conduct problems, although there was considerable overlap among the steps in the sequence (Figure 9.1).

Finally, Kolvin and coworkers (1989) conducted a longitudinal study of the factors protecting high-risk children from becoming delinquent adults. They found that intelligence and temperament; parents, peers, and school; social factors such as SES and family size; and adverse physical events such as accidents; were important but played different roles in different developmental periods. For the first five years, good parental care, positive social circumstances, and few adverse physical experiences in the perinatal as well as in the current period were protective factors. Five factors emerged in the preadolescent period: good supervision, absence of developmental delays, relatively good intelligence and academic achievement, positive temperamental qualities, and a positive response to peers and social activities.

Criminal Careers

Criminal behavior is one form of antisocial acting out. The longitudinal sequencing of such behavior is called a criminal career. The study

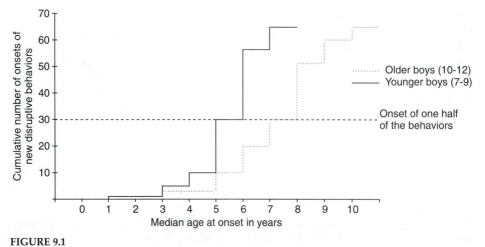

FIGURE 9.1
Cumulative onsets of new disruptive behavior in younger and older boys. (*Source:* Loeber et al., 1992.)

of these careers has revealed a number of developmental pathways. (Our presentation follows Loeber's 1988 integrative summary unless otherwise indicated. Also see Hinshaw, Lahey, and Hart, 1993.)

Age of Onset The age of onset is one of the most significant predictors of the subsequent seriousness of delinquent behavior. There is clear evidence that those who begin their antisocial activities before the teenage years will continue to commit a large number of offenses at a high rate over a long period of time. However, violent crimes, homicides, and armed robbery have a comparatively late onset in midadolescence (Loeber and LeBlanc, 1990). In spite of the importance of early onset, researchers have failed to find causes of antisocial behavior that are specific to this period (Farrington et al., 1990).

Seriousness of Offense As a rule there is a progression from less to more serious offenses (Loeber, 1991). Since more delinquent acts concern property offenses, we use these to illustrate the rule. Theft progresses from theft at

home to shoplifting to theft of school property and culminates in vehicle theft and breaking and entering between 10.1 and 12.7 years of age. As another illustration, LeBlanc (1990) found that criminal careers went from shoplifting and vandalism, which began between 11 and 14 years of age, to different types of theft—petty theft, burglary, personal larceny, and automobile theft—between ages 14 and 17, to personal attack, armed robbery, and drug trafficking between ages 16 and 19.

Developmental Progression Plotting antisocial behaviors against age of onset reveals a sequential progression, so that one form of problem behavior virtually always occurs before the emergence of another problem behavior. Loeber (1988) goes as far as to call it an *invariant sequence.* However, this does not mean that all individuals are fated to go through all the steps; on the contrary, most individuals progress to different stages of increasing seriousness of antisocial behavior, while few progress through all of them. Finally, as youngsters progress to new levels they tend to maintain their prior antisocial behaviors. Because behaviors are retained rather than replaced, the change is better described as accretion than succession

The Aggressive-Versatile Path Loeber (1988) derived two distinctive developmental paths from his examination of developmental studies. He called the first *aggressive-versatile*. These youngsters often experience an early onset of conduct problems, including aggression, some as early as the preschool years. In addition to aggression a high proportion are hyperactive and have poor impulse control and attention problems. Subsequently, they add nonaggressive antisocial acts such as stealing while still retaining their aggressiveness. The number of categories of antisocial behaviors is relatively high, and their desistence rate is low over time. Males outnumber females. These youngsters are at risk for having long criminal careers and for becoming chronic offenders and multiple drug users. Within this path there is also a subgroup of violent offenders. While their early aggressiveness makes them at risk for violent crime, they are also likely to have educational problems, poor social skills, and poor relationships with peers and adults.

Magnusson and Bergman's (1990) longitudinal research supplements Loeber's findings. While aggression may be stable, it predicts criminal behavior at 18 through 23 years of age only when it is accompanied by hyperactivity or is part of multiple problems. In fact they found that none of the variables they studied—aggressiveness, motor restlessness, lack of concentration, low motivation and achievement in school, and peer relations—predicted adult criminal behavior by themselves, pointing to the importance of multiple problem behavior for prediction.

The Nonaggressive Path The onset here is later than for the aggressive-versatile path, typically in late childhood or early to middle adolescence. There is also little hyperactivity.

Early problem behaviors are confined to nonaggressive ones such as chronic disobedience, lying, theft, and truancy. The rate at which children on this path add new categories of antisocial behaviors is slower than it is in the aggressive-versatile path, and the desistance rate is higher. While males still outnumber females, the proportion of females is higher here than in the aggressive-versatile path. Social skills of youngsters in this group are not impaired, and they form good relations with peers, although they are apt to associate with deviant groups.

Desistence Longitudinal studies indicate that the further an individual has progressed along a path of antisocial behavior, the less likely he or she is to desist. This is logical because the smaller the variety of antisocial behaviors, the fewer behaviors there are to change. For example, there is evidence that youngsters with fewer than three antisocial acts are less likely to become antisocial adults than those with six or more. This also means that youngsters at both extremes of the deviancy distribution have the highest degree of stability; neither those who are not deviant nor those who are very deviant are apt to change in regard to delinquency.

THE INTRAPERSONAL CONTEXT

Fritz Redl's writings will serve as our guide to understanding acting out (Redl and Wineman, 1951). Redl presents a detailed account of five 8- to 10-year-old boys who received milieu therapy in a residential home called Pioneer House for fifteen to nineteen months. Five other boys were also observed for one to three months. They all were healthy, had normal intelligence, and were of lower socioeconomic status. Their behaviors included destructiveness, hyperaggressiveness, stealing, running away from home, truancy from school, temper tantrums, lying, "sassing" adults, and profan-

Magnusson (1988) is conducting a landmark longitudinal study that may well have a major impact on our understanding of developmental psychopathology. By now we are familiar with his general thesis: psychopathology is the result of the interaction between intrapersonal, interpersonal, and organic contexts as well as the interaction between variables within each of these contexts. In fact, his project is an implementation of the interactive model introduced in Chapter 1. This in itself is noteworthy since only a few researchers have been bold enough to tackle the challenge of multivariable, interactive research head on.

Magnusson's design is impressive. His sample consisted of 3244 children drawn from a Swedish community of about 100,000 inhabitants. He conducted two longitudinal studies—one from 10 to 23 years of age, the other from 15 to 27 years of age. Follow-up data were available on 1393 subjects.

A distinguishing feature of Magnusson's approach is its emphasis on variables within individuals rather than on variables within populations. To illustrate, Magnusson obtained measures of six problem behaviors of 13-year-old males: aggression, motor restlessness, lack of concentration, poor peer relations, underachievement, and low motivation for school. A cluster analysis yielded groups of boys who had no problems, who had single problems (poor peer relations or underachievement), two problems (aggression and motor restlessness), three problems (motor restlessness, lack of concentration, and low school motivation—a pattern suggesting a learning disability), and four to five problems. There were three groups in this last category, which Magnusson called multiproblem boys.

We shall concentrate on data concerning criminality and alcohol abuse. Some of the findings were to be expected: boys with no problems at 13 years of age had few problems as adults, while aggression and hyperactivity predicted both criminality and alcohol abuse. Moreover, it was the multiple-problem boys who became disturbed adults, about half those with four to five problems becoming criminals, for example. The unexpected finding was that single variables alone were unrelated to adult criminality or alcohol abuse. This applied to peer relations and, more surprisingly, to aggression. It was only when aggression was accompanied by hyperactivity that it predicted criminality, and only as poor peer relations were accompanied by four other problem behaviors that it also became predictive.

Magnusson's point is that if one looks at only a single variable within a population and studies its relation to adult psychopathology, one might reach an erroneous conclusion concerning its importance. In reality, it is the limited number of multiple-problem children—only around a quarter of the population in this instance—who are responsible for the significant predictions. Not that Magnusson is against studying "pure" cases or single variables in a population. His concern is that researchers have been neglecting the group of multiple-problem children who, ironically, are the most liable to grow up to become criminals and alcoholics.

ity; however, they were not so disturbed that they could not function in the community, since they attended public school and used neighborhood recreational facilities.

The boys had no positive, sustained relation with any adult. Their parents were brutal, neglectful, or self-absorbed; their homes were broken by divorce and desertion; and they had been shuttled between foster homes and institutions. They were in special classes at school or had been expelled. They ran with a delinquent gang or were lone wolves, committing impulsive delinquent acts. Thus there was a total absence of positive experiences in the home, the school, and with peers.

Some of Redl's vivid descriptions of the boys' behavior are primarily illustrative of low self-control; others offer clues as to etiology.

Poor Control of Inner Impulses

The boys at Pioneer House had little ability to modulate or contain high states of arousal. Even mild frustrations would produce strong, disruptive affective reactions: a door that accidentally jammed was immediately kicked

A teen age shoplifter: normal problem behavior or conduct disorder?

and pounded and cursed with furious rage; a slight mishap during an enjoyable game would throw the group into wild outbursts of bickering, fighting, and griping. Neither anxiety nor guilt could be tolerated. The former would so quickly lead either to total flight or ferocious attack and diffuse destruction that the boys literally were only fleetingly aware of their fearfulness; for example, one boy reacted to his fear at bedtime by emitting high banshee wails, striking and cursing his pillow, and attacking other boys with a combination of vicious aggression and erotic teasing.

Objective studies provide evidence of a limited ability to delay impulses and tolerate frustration; aggressive boys respond more quickly

and impulsively on cognitive tasks, while their hasty reactions to social situations are associated with overattribution of hostility to others. (For specific studies, see Martin and Hoffman, 1990.)

Overreaction to External Stimuli

Weak control was also evidenced by low resistance to environmental lures. As might be expected, temptations to delinquent acts proved irresistible for the boys; a bit of loose change lying unnoticed on a desk was apt to be stolen, even if the boy had no prior intention of stealing. But the behavior did not have to be delinquent; it might just as well be mischievous or playful. One boy could not resist picking up and throwing a plastic knife on display in a store; the group could not resist wildly jumping up and down and breaking the springs on a mattress in a new bedroom where they were spending the night during Easter vacation. For these boys, it was as if to see was to act.

Of all environmental lures, excitement was the most irresistible. The mere sight of a boy throwing clothes or banging his fork ferociously against his plate or jumping back and forth on the furniture would trigger similar behavior in the onlooker. Redl calls this spread of excitement *contagion*. The exposure to even mildly excited group moods was apt to undermine control. Thus, when one boy escalated a game of sailing cards idly across the room to heaving several cards around, the other joined in until "the air was thick with checkers, cards, pieces of candy, all in motion." Redl aptly describes the behavior as group psychological intoxication.

Developmental Implications

Throughout his discussion, Redl points to the normal counterparts of acting-out behavior. His theme is that all these signs of weak self-control would be developmentally appropriate for younger children. His point is well taken. One can readily imagine toddlers and preschoolers going into a rage when frustrated or sulking after failure or dashing heedlessly into the street at the sound of the ice-cream truck; and the phenomenon of contagion is well known to any preschool teacher desperately trying to bring her little savages back under control after a game of tag has escalated to the point of intoxication. Thus the model of poor self-control as a *developmental delay* is appropriate.

Etiologic Factors

Memory   One of Redl's most provocative observations is that the boys at Pioneer House literally did not seem to remember past experiences; for example, the boys would insist on taking a favorite toy or gadget to school despite having such toys broken or destroyed time and time again in a playground battle. There was never a flicker of awareness of the relation between bringing the gadget to school and its certain destruction. Most puzzling of all was the boys' failure to remember pleasant experiences. When the staff tried to reexpose them to activities and games they had enjoyed, the boys would at first deny they had ever done anything like that before or, when they did remember, deny that it was fun.

When memory and recognition go, so does anticipation. There is nothing at the beginning of a sequence to signal, "This will lead to punishment" or "This will lead to pleasure." The result is the common observation that antisocial, impulsive children fail to learn from experience.

Perspective   The boys in Pioneer House were pathologically weak in assessing social reality. They did not stop to consider the feelings and motives of others or to predict how others might react toward them. This same insensitivity was also evidenced in relation to the

group code and social norms of proper behavior. One boy, for example, went around bragging that he was going to get a haircut, when he should have known that any evidence of special treatment would throw the group into a jealous rage—which it did; another boy took off his pants in a public park because he had gotten them wet and they itched.

This insensitivity to the thoughts, feelings, and actions of others was included in the discussion of *social perspective taking* (Chapter 2). One of the pivotal developments between the preschool period and middle childhood is decentering, that is, shifting from cognitive egocentrism—in which the world is viewed primarily from the child's own vantage point—to cognitive perspectivism—in which a situation can be seen from the diverse views of the individuals involved. Objective studies tend to confirm Redl's clinical impression that impulsive, antisocial children are deficient in social perspective taking. Chandler (1973) found chronically delinquent 11- to 13-year-old boys significantly lower in perspective taking compared with a control group matched for socioeconomic status and ethnic background. In this instance, perspective taking involved the realization that a latecomer viewing the final cartoon in a sequence (for example, a father observing his son's alarm at a knock on the door) would have no basis for interpreting it in the same way as a person who had viewed the entire sequence (in this instance, pictures showing the boy accidentally breaking a window with a baseball). (See Eisenberg and Miller, 1990, for a more detailed presentation of research on perspective taking.)

However, more is involved here than mere insensitivity. Egocentrism also may include a tendency to attribute one's own thoughts and feelings to others. Dodge and Frame (1982) investigated this tendency using *attribution theory*, which in this instance concerns inferences individuals make about causes of behavior. One would predict that aggressive children would tend to attribute aggressive intent to others. Such is the case when the situation is ambiguous. If the actions of others are clearly accidental or purposeful it is realistically evaluated. There is also evidence that the attribution of hostile intent is exaggerated under conditions of social anxiety and threat (Dodge and Somberg, 1987).

Let us return once more to Pioneer House using perspective taking as a concrete illustration of the "guiding and controlling function of thought" (Chapter 2). If the boys immediately translate feeling into action, thinking can serve neither function (see Camp, 1977). On the other hand, the question, "How will others perceive and react to what I do?" of necessity serves to check action. The answer to the question changes as the child is progressively capable of grasping the values, motives, and intentions of others and, ultimately, of simultaneously being aware of his own perspective and the perspective of others. As this guiding function advances, behavior becomes more socially adaptive. The unfortunate braggart who was to have his hair cut should have been able to think, "I want to lord it over the others, but this is just the thing that will drive them wild, because they can't stand the idea of someone getting anything special." Once having decentered, he now would be in a position to act in a socially appropriate manner. However, as Redl cautions, knowing what is right is not equivalent to doing what is right. The boys at Pioneer House often were not able to decenter; other types of acting-out-children—such as Mark, who was described earlier—know but cannot resist the force of their impulses.

In normal development parental discipline, empathy, and peer interaction play central roles in the development of perspective taking (Gibbs, 1987). *Inductive discipline* in particular fosters perspective taking. Here the parent explains and reasons with the child and directs the child's attention to the effects of his or her behavior on the other person by saying, for example, "How do you think that made the other child feel?" or "How would you feel if someone did that to you?" Successful *peer relations* require that, in order to accommodate to others, the individual child give up the egocentric need to do only what he wants to when he wants to do it. Through peer relations the child is also confronted with ideas, opinions, and values different from his own. Perspective taking is a purely cognitive achievement, however, which requires a strong motivational force to compete with the young child's egocentrism. According to Hoffman (1978) this affective charge is provided by *empathy*, which initially is an innate response but which is subsequently elaborated by conditioning and by cognitive development. Despite the plausibility of the rationale, research on the relation of perspective taking and empathy to prosocial behavior has produced mixed findings. However, the weight of evidence does support a relationship between the two (Eisenberg and Miller, 1990).

It would be difficult to imagine the parents of the Pioneer House boys sensitizing them to the feelings of others; in addition, the boys' own failure to develop stable peer relations might have been particularly detrimental to the ability to decenter. Since peers, like any other group, cannot tolerate impulsivity and egocentrism, the boys might have been caught in a vicious circle: their inability to cooperate prevented them from having access to the very experiences that could have helped them advance in their social awareness. (See Carlson, Lahey, and Neeper, 1984.)

The Pioneer House boys not only lacked perspective on others, they lacked perspective on themselves. Redl describes it as "the evaporation of self-contributed links in the causal chain" (Redl and Wineman, 1951, p. 128). Children literally would not remember, even after a short time, their own share in provoking a fight or a chaotic scene. They forgot not only their feeling, motivations, and intentions but also their surface behavior, such as being the first one to throw a stone, thus beginning a free-for-all, or mishandling a favorite toy so that it eventually broke.

We are now in an area different from social perspective (which involves understanding how others perceive the self); we are in the realm of self-observation. The psychoanalysts write of the "observing ego" when dealing with the ability to be a spectator in relation to one's own thoughts and actions. Piaget (1967) sketches the development of the ability of children to reflect on their own thinking. Egocentric preschoolers believe that something is true, immediately comprehended, and universally accepted because they say or think it. It is only as this belief is challenged by social encounters that they can, in middle childhood, begin to challenge themselves as to what they mean and why they believe it to be true. This "inner social discussion" is the beginning of reflection or the ability to examine one's own thoughts. Why reflection fails to develop in acting-out boys is not known, although Minuchin and colleagues (1967) speculate that "fast and externally geared resolution of cognitive-affective stress that becomes the dominant coping style" inhibits cultivation of reflection (p. 198).

Initiative   Instead of being expansive and seeking new challenges, the boys at Pioneer House were frightened of newness. Perhaps because their environment had been both unpredictable and punitive, newness had become equated with danger. In place of normal exploration, their examination of a new object was characterized by "panicky haste, nervous incompleteness and a flustered jumpiness" or a "frenzy of aggressive handling and poking around" (Redl and Wineman, 1951, p. 119). Goal-directed behavior was well-nigh impossible.

But initiative was lacking in an even more important way, namely, in the boys' inability to generate constructive activities or alterna-

tive coping devices. As Redl properly notes, normal school-age children, when left on their own, can call up memories of past interests or pleasures and proceed to pursue them. Normal children also have a variety of techniques to help them tolerate the tension of delayed gratification: they can take their minds off the unavailable goal by thinking of or actually doing other things, or they can use the "sour-grapes" technique of depreciating the desired goal, or they can reward themselves for having delayed so long or punish themselves for starting to yield to temptation, or they can transform the desired object into an abstract, less tempting image, or they can even go to sleep (Mischel, 1978). But all these devices must be generated, and it is just this generative ability which acting-out children lack. When they have nothing to do, they literally can think of nothing constructive to do; when faced with frustration, they literally have no alternative to acting out their anger.

Twenty-five years after Redl stressed the importance of generating alternatives to boredom and frustration, psychologists began exploring the phenomenon under the label of *interpersonal problem solving*. While interpersonal problem solving can be simply defined as the analysis and resolution of problems involving other people, there is a certain amount of disagreement as to the specific functions involved. Spivack, Platt, and Shure (1976) postulate the following components: an initial sensitivity to human problems, an ability to imagine alternative courses of action, an ability to conceptualize the means to solve the problem, sensitivity to consequences, and understanding cause and effects in human relations.

Of all the components, generating alternatives and means-end thinking proved the most important in their research. In the preschool period, *generating alternative solutions* to problems such as, What could you do if your sister were playing with a toy you wanted? was the single most significant predictor of interpersonal behavior in a classroom setting. Children who were deficient were rated by their teachers as being high on acting out or inhibition; for example, they were disruptive, disrespectful, and defiant, they could not wait to take turns, or they needed to be close to the teacher. In middle childhood, alternative thinking was still related to classroom adjustment, although not as strongly as it was previously, while *means-end thinking* emerged as an equally important correlate. For instance, when presented with the problem of a boy's feeling lonely after moving to a new neighborhood, the well-adjusted child could think not only of different solutions but also of ways to implement the solutions and overcome the obstacles involved, such as saying, "It would be easy if he found someone who liked to play soccer like he does, but he'd better not go to a kid's house at suppertime or his mother will be plenty mad!" Again, both impulsive and inhibited children were deficient in these two cognitive skills. It is interesting to note that the capacity to think in means-end terms was a developmental achievement, since it did not emerge until middle childhood. The data on adolescence were meager but suggested that means-end thinking and alternative thinking continued to be correlated with adjustment. The new component involved *thinking of consequences* or weighing the pros and cons of potential action: "If I do X, then someone else will do Y and that will be good (or bad)." Thus the developing child is able to utilize progressively advanced cognitive skills to solve interpersonal problems. Incidentally, such problem solving is not closely related to measured IQ.

Spivak and coworkers also have data on the kinds of parenting which facilitated interpersonal problem solving. An example of such parenting is the mother who focused on the child's own thinking ("Tell me what happened." "Why did it happen?" "What did you feel?" "How do you think the other child felt?" and so forth) and supported the child's attempts at solutions, though not always approving of the solution itself. In the process the parent served as a model of problem-evaluation, solution-attempting behavior. There was an interesting sex difference, however, the mother being effective only in relation to her daughter's problem-solving skills; wherever the son learned his, it was not at his mother's knee. Problem solving was discouraged by ignoring or disparaging the child ("Don't be a baby"), by absolutistic directives ("Stop crying and go outside and hit him back"), or by depreciating the child's alternatives ("That's the silliest thing I've ever heard of"). Under such conditions social problem-solving skills atrophied from sheer lack of use.

Other investigators have corroborated Spivak, Platt, and Shure's finding that aggressive children generate more aggressive and ineffectual solutions and fewer constructive ones than do nonaggressive children in their social problem solving. In addition, research has expanded to include situational variables that significantly affect the kind of solution an aggressive child will give. Lochman and Lampron (1986) found that 10-year-old aggressive boys were more likely to use aggressive solutions with peers than with parents and teachers. Also, aggressive solutions were more likely when there was hostile rather than ambiguous intent—for example, when a peer called the child an insulting name as contrasted with a peer who wanted to use the boy's baseball when the boy himself wanted to go home.

Returning once again to the Pioneer House boys, we can better appreciate how impoverished they were in terms of their repertoire of solutions to interpersonal problems. While Redl states that they were unable to use their past to provide alternative courses of action in the present, he might also agree that their past was barren soil for the cultivation of problem-solving skills.

Selman and his colleagues take a different approach to interpersonal problem solving, or what they call interpersonal negotiating strategies (INS), from that of Spivak, Platt, and Shure. Instead of using a social information-processing model and atomizing social behavior into specific skills, they are in the Piagetian tradition of postulating *stages* of cognitive development. (Our presentation follows Selman and Schultz, 1988.) These stages are ways of thinking about problems of social interaction—conceptual categories extracted from and embracing specific behaviors. They are analogous to Kohlberg's stages of moral development. In addition, stages represent qualitatively different ways of thinking and therefore do not fit the information-processing model, which favors quantitative changes. Finally, development goes from lower to higher levels in terms of increasing cognitive complexity and comprehensiveness.

Selman and Schultz's INS model has both a thinking (cognitive) and a doing (action) component. The first derives from responses children and adolescents give to problem situations, such as, "John's boss asks him to work late Friday night, and he does not want to. What does he do?" The situations involve parents, peers, and extrafamilial adults. The authors delineate four cognitive stages of INS:

*Stage 0: Impulsive.*The strategies are primitive—for example, based on fight or flight—and show no evidence of perspective taking. In the above situation both, "Tell him to screw off!" and "Just do what he says!" would be at this level.

Stage 1: Unilateral. Strategies here show an awareness of the other person's point of view and of the conflict that exists, but strategies are based on assertions of the child's needs or wants (e.g., "Tell him you are not going to show up") or simple accommodation (e.g., "He's the boss, so you've got to do what he says").

Stage 2: Self-reflective and reciprocal. Strategies are now based on reciprocal exchanges, with an awareness of the other party's point of view. However, negotiations are de-

signed to protect the interests of the child: for example, "He'll help the boss out this time, and then the boss will owe him one."

Stage 3: Collaborative. The child or adolescent is now able to view the situation objectively, taking his or her own and the other person's perspective into account and recognizing that negotiations are necessary for the continuity of the relationship: for example, "The boss and he have to work it out together, so they might as well talk out their differences."

An interesting finding is that the children's INS level varied with the social context; thus a child might be at the collaboration stage with peers but at the unilateral level with parents. A teenager, for example, might be able to see a problem from a peer's point of view and try to find some way of working it out collaboratively, while viewing a problem with parents primarily as a clash between what the parents and they themselves want.

The *action* stages of INS were derived from observing ongoing behavior, say, on the playground or in prearranged pairings of children. The stages parallel the cognitive ones, going from physically aggressive or withdrawing at Stage 0, to assertively ordering or submissively obedient at Stage 1, to persuasive and deferential at Stage 2, and, finally, to collaboration at Stage 3.

Conscience As could be predicted, the lack of love, of models, and of tutelage produced a defective conscience in the Pioneer House boys. While not completely absent, their conscience was fragmented and inefficient. There was a certain amount of acceptance of delinquent mores, along with pride in being tough, smart, and daring. There were fragments of middle-class values, which were isolated vestiges from the past; for example, one boy would suddenly berate another for swearing. Inefficiency was evidenced by the lack of anticipatory guilt; when it appeared, guilt typically followed a transgression. Guilt also seemed specific to the individual making the original demands for good behavior; for example, after stealing, a boy might feel ashamed in his mother's presence, but only in that one setting and only in relation to that one incident. Such situationalism nicely illustrates our point concerning the importance of generalizing rules for proper behavior in the development of self control.

The Pioneer House boys were more likely to think in terms of *preconventional morality* and less likely to think in terms of *conventional morality*. This means they were concerned primarily with avoiding punishment, with giving in order to get in return, and with deferring to the power of the maker of rules; they were less concerned with living up to family or group expectations regardless of the immediate consequences to themselves and with conforming to the "good-boy" image of being nice, obeying rules, doing one's best, maintaining order, and respecting authority.

In her comprehensive review of the research, Smetana (1990) found that twenty-two of twenty-eight studies supported the hypothesis that juvenile delinquents are more developmentally immature in their moral reasoning than are nondelinquents. This confirms Redl's observations.

The "Delinquent Ego" The behaviors examined so far could fit into a model of *developmental delays* of various types and to varying degrees. However, the delay is not pervasive, since many functions are intact or even highly developed. The problem is that they are used to maintain and justify impulsive behavior rather than to enhance self-control. Redl cites many examples of what he calls "the delinquent ego." The boys were past masters of the "He did it first" and "Everyone else does it" technique for justifying their impulsivity. Other techniques included: "He had it coming to him," "I did it to save face with the others," "He's a no-good so-and-so himself," "But I

made it up with him afterwards," and "Nobody likes me; they're always picking on me." Such defenses sound suspiciously like those that parents of healthy preadolescents have to contend with.

In a similar vein, Gibbs (1991) discusses and cites supportive research for two rationalizations of delinquent behavior: externalization of blame and mislabeling. In the first, the victim is blamed; for example, a woman who is "stupid enough" to walk in the park at night deserves to be robbed. Mislabeling also serves to avoid responsibility, but this time by minimizing the behavior. Thus vandalism becomes "mischief," rape becomes "wilding," or "having fun."

Initiative that was so lacking in many areas was fully developed in supporting delinquent gratifications. In contrast to their usual imperviousness to adults, the children knew the staff's whims and weaknesses, sensing the kind of argument which would appease or divert them and knowing when cajoling or affection seeking would throw them off guard. They knew how to act cute in public, to wheedle things out of a suspicious storekeeper, to convince a guard that they were "good kids." They remembered all too well that people could not be trusted and were constantly on guard against anticipated harm or against forming a positive attachment. To protect themselves from the latter, they provoked rejection (for example, by making impossible demands) or anger. Thus they avoided one more betrayal by "proving" that the staff was no different from all the other adults they had known.

This contrast between deviant and normal behavior has an interesting counterpart in the experimental literature. (For a more detailed presentation, see Achenbach, 1982). Initial evidence indicated that psychopaths might be different from normal individuals since they did not learn from noxious experiences; for example, they showed smaller galvanic skin responses (GSR) than control subjects to a buzzer which had repeatedly been paired with an uncomfortable shock and preferred frightening activities over onerous ones. Thus, they seemed to be deficient in normal anxiety. However, subsequent research revealed that their reaction depended on the kind of punishment involved: true, when learning a maze they were relatively unaffected by physical punishment or social censure such as being told they were wrong in a disapproving voice; but when deprived of money their maze performance was slightly better than that of normal subjects, while their GSR was the same! Instead of being incapable of experiencing anxiety, psychopaths have a different set of values. When these values are threatened, they, like the Pioneer House boys, react as normal boys do.

THE INTERPERSONAL CONTEXT: THE FAMILY

There are two approaches to studying the families of conduct-disordered children: one is concerned with general characteristics, and the other with specific parent-child interactions.

General Characteristics

Criminal and psychopathological behavior in the parent puts the child at risk, often for similar behavior (Kazdin, 1987). As we have seen, alcoholism and an antisocial personality on the part of the father are two of the strongest factors increasing the likelihood that his son will engage in similar behavior. Moreover, the risk is compounded by associative mating, or the tendency of two antisocial individuals to be attracted to one another and to have children (Robins, 1991). While psychiatric disturbances and maternal anxiety and depression have also been implicated, they are not specific to conduct disorder.

Family discord is fertile soil for producing antisocial acting out, especially in boys. In fact, it has replaced the rather vague concept of the "broken home" as an etiologic agent. It is not the literal breaking up of the family—say, by divorce or death—but the turmoil surrounding the disruption which increases the likelihood of antisocial acting out. If, for example, a divorce produces a decrease in parental conflict, the child's conduct disorder also decreases; on the other hand, if parental conflicts

---

Redl's *naturalistic* research is a prime example of the *clinical eye* nourishing a conceptualizing mind. Unlike the majority of clinicians, who are content with collecting vivid anecdotes, Redl was constantly asking, Why? In this, he differed from Kanner, who was primarily asking, What? That Redl was able to tease out so many variables involved in acting-out behavior and to place them in a developmental context is an achievement of the first order. His technique of observing children for prolonged periods in natural settings is also very much in keeping with the current emphasis on ecological validity, even though the research was conducted forty or so years ago.

Yet Redl's research also illustrates the limitations of naturalistic research. There is no concern for reliability, which could serve as a check for observer bias and increase the likelihood that the data are accessible to the scientific community. More important is the question of generalizability. Redl's observations were made on ten boys at most. What can one infer from such a small sample? Did Redl capture the essence of all such conduct disorders, or did he merely illuminate the psychological workings of a limited subpopulation? His ecological approach also prevented him from determining which of the many variables he delineated are essential and which are peripheral or even noncontributory to delinquency. More controlled studies, which could manipulate variables, would be required to answer such questions. Thus Redl's research is best regarded as hypothesis generating; while of great value, his findings need further testing either in the laboratory or through objective techniques in naturalistic settings.

persist, the likelihood of repeated antisocial behavior is increased (Rutter and Garmezy, 1983). Going one step beyond the divorce, there is evidence that boys are rarely juvenile delinquents in mother-alone families if the mother is competent (McCord, 1990). Again, it is not the broken home per se that matters but how well or how poorly the parents handle the rupture.

Parental discipline has been studied by many investigators over a considerable period of time. As we have seen, an inconsistent mix of harshness and laxness either within or between parents is related to antisocial acting out. Youths with conduct disorders are more likely than other disturbed children to be victims of child abuse or to come from homes where spouse abuse exists. Laxness may be evidenced in a number of ways: lack of supervision, parents being unconcerned with the children's whereabouts, absence of rules concerning where the children can go and whom they can be with.

There is also evidence of the *relative importance* of family factors. In a comprehensive analysis of longitudinal studies, Loeber and Stouthamer-Loeber (1986) found that the family characteristics that were the most potent predictors of later conduct disorders and delinquency were lack of parental supervision, lack of parent-child involvement, and parental rejection; next came marital conflict and parental criminality, while harsh discipline, parental health, and separation from home were among the weaker predictors.

While the role of *siblings* has been neglected, there is evidence that they initiate and sustain aggression more frequently than do siblings of nonaggressive children, especially in middle childhood and adolescence (Baum, 1989).

Finally, there is evidence that aggression is not only stable within a single generation but across generations as well. Huesmann and colleagues (1984), in their twenty-two-year follow-up study, compiled data on eighty-two subjects when they were 8 and 30 years of age

and also on their 8-year-old children. The correlation between the parents when they were 8 years old and their 8-year-old children was higher than the correlation between the parents' own behavior at age 8 and at age 30 (.65 versus .46). Similarly, truancy in the parents when they were children was related to truancy in their children, the risk increasing if both parents truanted. It is not clear what mechanisms are responsible for this continuity of behavior; neither genetic nor environmental explanations are totally satisfactory. (For a more detailed presentation of intergenerational transmission of aggression, see Eron and Huesmann, 1990.)

Specific Parent-Child Interactions

Coercion Theory Our presentation is based on Patterson's (1986) seminal research. Because of his learning-theory orientation, Patterson was particularly interested in patterns of reinforcement. He found that, especially with preschoolers, parents would positively reinforce aggressive behavior, for example, by regarding it as amusing. He also observed inconsistent outbursts of anger and punitiveness, or threats with no follow-through, both of which were ineffectual in curbing behavior. Finally, children's prosocial behavior was either ignored or reinforced noncontingently.

However, Patterson's most ingenious and important discovery was a pattern of interaction which he variously calls *coercion theory* or the *reinforcement trap*. This is how parents unwittingly systematically train their children to be aggressive and antisocial. The basic pattern is a series of escalating attacks and counterattacks which are negatively reinforced for both parties by the cessation of the noxious interaction while also increasing the likelihood that the interaction will be repeated in the future. Children discover by experience that if they are denied something, they can eventually get it if they just yell loud enough or have a tan-

Patterson's research technique serves as a nice counterpart to Redl's. Both began with naturalistic observation—Redl in Pioneer House, Patterson in the homes of children with conduct disorders—and both used their clinically trained eye to search out meaningful patterns of behavior. However, while Redl remained at the level of clinical observation, Patterson has translated his observations into objective measures. Since he suspected that the coercive interaction might be a critical one in the etiology of an antisocial behavior, he set about developing a training procedure whereby other investigators could recognize the pattern when it occurred in a natural setting. Such a training procedure is often essential for reliable data since descriptions alone do not suffice.

One of the many admirable features of Patterson's research program is the effort he put into developing robust measures of his major variables—antisocial behavior, academic failures, and peer rejection. Often investigators rely on only one or two measures in a given situation. This runs the risk of nonreplication of results when other measures of the same variable are used in different settings. Patterson, by contrast, had multiple methods, settings, and agents. Using antisocial behavior as an example, he had a telephone interview with both parents and had them fill out two questionnaires, interviewed the child over the telephone, had the teacher fill out a questionnaire, and obtained nominations concerning popularity from peers. He then did a factor analysis to determine how well the measures coalesced, rejecting the parental interview, for example, as being too divergent from the other data. He finally ended up with two agents in each setting: teacher and peers at school, parents and child at home, each contributing equally to the definition of antisocial behavior.

Finally, as a validity check, Patterson conducted two studies to see how well the measures correlated with a measure of delinquency obtained from official records and from self-report. The results were surprisingly good, accounting for 54 percent of the variance in the delinquency construct. (For a more detailed account of his methodology, see Patterson, 1986.)

For methodological soundness in translating ecologically valid data into objective measures, and for astuteness in generating fruitful hypotheses, Patterson's is a model of programmatic research.

---

trum. The termination of their behavior likewise reinforces the parents by providing relief from the children's obstreperousness (see Figure 9.2). However, the parents have paid a heavy price. Not only is their socializing effort negated, but they are also reinforcing the children's tendency to use aversive techniques to get what they want.

Patterson found that, for highly aggressive children, about one-third of their coercive behaviors, such as yelling and tantrums, was a reaction to aversive intrusions by other family members and that 70 percent of the time such behaviors were followed by the attacker's withdrawal. In distressed families, the coercive sequence may happen hundreds of times each day, being physically assaultive merely being the final step in the escalating process. While Patterson says that the coercion pattern becomes central in middle years, it has been related to conduct problems in the preschoolers as well (Gardner, 1989).

Other Interpersonal Factors

The Child's Contribution   Note that the research thus far can be interpreted as meaning that "bad parents produce bad children" and that causation goes only from parent to child. However, Lytton (1990a) reviews the evidence of the child's own contribution to conduct disorders. Much of it comes from the organic context, indicating that the child has a hereditary and constitutional bias to be aggressive, difficult to manage, and underresponsive to rewards and punishments. There is also evidence at the behavioral level; for example, when they were observed interacting with a

FIGURE 9.2
Coercion. (*Source:* Calvin and Hobbes copyright 1986 by Bill Watterson. Dist. by Universal Press
Syndicate. Reprinted by permission. All rights reserved.)

nonconduct-disordered child, mothers of con-duct-disordered children behaved like any other mother, while mothers of nonconduct-disordered children become more negative and controlling when they interacted with conduct-disordered children (Anderson, Lytton, and Romney, 1986). (For a lively series of objections to and defenses of Lytton's position, see Dodge, 1990a; Lytton, 1990b; and Wahler, 1990.)

Peer Interaction   While a potent force for healthy socialization, peer relations can also increase aggression, although the picture here is sketchy. (Our presentation follows Perry, Perry, and Boldizar's 1990 summary of research unless otherwise noted.) As early as the *preschool* period passive children can start initiating aggressive interactions if they begin defending themselves and discover that such counterattacks are successful. On the other hand, aggressive preschoolers may contribute to their own rejection through the following sequence of interactions: the aggressive child initiates aversive behavior which, even when not initially reciprocated, comes to produce counteraggression in peers. Ironically, even when the aggressive child wants to withdraw, peers will continue their active victimization (Olson, 1992).

In *middle childhood* the group may treat aggressive children with open hostility. Aggressive children are more apt to be accepted into groups which either tolerate or value aggressive behavior. For example, Dishion and colleagues (1991) found that peer rejection at age 10 (along with academic failure) predicted involvement with antisocial peers at age 12, more so than did parental discipline and monitoring practices. In general, association with delinquent peers still explains a substantial amount of variance in delinquent behavior, even after family factors have been controlled for (Farrington et al., 1990).

THE SUPERORDINATE CONTEXT

Schools

Since schools play a role in the etiology of conduct disorder, the question arises as to what aspects of this complex variable are responsible for the relationship. (Our presentation follows Rutter, 1983.)

Factors related to an absence of acting-out behavior in the school, such as classroom disruption, damage to school property, and graffiti, are the teacher's skill in classroom management and the model of behavior he or she provides, the amount of rewards and encouragement, the granting of responsibilities to the students, the degree of academic emphasis, and the general quality of the school's physical plant. Thus classes that are poorly organized, where expectations for achievement are low, where there is a good deal of punishment and little praise, and where students are given little or no responsibility in planning activities are apt to foster acting-out behavior. Moreover Kasen, Johnson, and Cohen (1990) found that a school environment characterized by a high degree of conflict (fighting, vandalism, teachers unable to maintain order, and defiant students) was significantly related to an increase in conduct disorder and alcohol use over a two-year period in students between 9 and 16 years of age.

While poor *school achievement* has been linked to conduct disorder, the causal direction is not clear. Tremblay and coworkers

(1992) analyzed longitudinal data in children between 7 and 14 years of age. They found that while there was a direct causal line between disruptive behavior in grade 1 and subsequent behavior for boys, poor school achievement was not a causal factor.

The Media

The effects of television violence on aggression is a hotly debated topic (Freedman, 1986). There is evidence that children with strong preferences for viewing violent television programs are more aggressive than their peers, while laboratory studies also show a relation between increased viewing of aggressive material and increased aggressive behavior. Longitudinal studies also show that children who prefer violent television programs during elementary school engage in more violent and

The lure of TV violence.

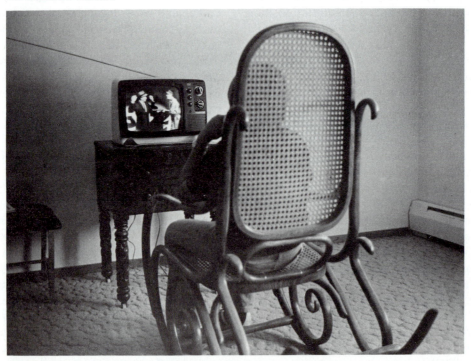

criminal activity as adults (Eron, 1982). (For a more detailed presentation, see Perry, Perry, and Boldizar, 1990.)

THE ORGANIC CONTEXT

Genetic factors are of only minor importance in the broad spectrum of conduct disorders (Robins, 1991). While an enlarged or YY chromosome was implicated in antisocial behavior for a time, this accounted for only a small proportion of antisocial individuals; the link was more likely to be with lower IQ than with aggression (Baum, 1989). (Plomin, Nitz, and Rowe, 1990, have a detailed discussion of genetics and aggressive behavior.) Obviously, criminality per se cannot be inherited, and it is not known just what aspects of personality functioning are affected and how these, in conjunction with environmental factors, produce severe antisocial conduct disorders (Rutter and Giller, 1983).

Among *psychophysiological* correlates, there is a well-established finding of lower resting heart rate in antisocial preadolescents and adolescents. Similar findings have been obtained for skin-conductance responses. Such results indicate lower autonomic responses in antisocial individuals, especially those who exhibit a greater number of and more severe behaviors and who are persistent offenders (Magnusson, 1992).

The bridge between the organic and the psychological domains is a matter of speculation. One explanation is that a low level of arousal is akin to a painful state of boredom and restlessness is an attempt to escape such boredom by increasing sensory stimulation. While this explanation might be tenable for those cases in which conduct disorders coexist with an attention-deficit hyperactive disorder, stimulus seeking per se is not the essence of antisocial behavior. Another explanation is that low autonomic responsiveness impairs learning by diminishing the reactivity both to

punishments and rewards. There is some evidence supporting this hypothesis but it is far from conclusive. (For a more detailed presentation of psychophysiological correlates, see Baum, 1989.)

A number of *biochemical* correlates have also been investigated. Plasma testosterone was a likely candidate because of its relation to aggression in animals. However, research on humans indicates that such hormonal differences are not sufficient to account for aggressive and antisocial behavior, although they may serve a mediating roles in individual responses to particular environmental circumstances. Serotonin and norepinephrine have also been studied because of their complementary roles of arousal-inhibition and excitation, respectively. However, no specific relation has been found to impulsive-aggressive behavior as serotonin and norepinephrine are also present in depressives and schizophrenics. The low reliabilities of biochemical measures, the wide range of values in the normal population, and their sensitivity to diet, stress, and exercise, are a few of the obstacles to obtaining stable findings, even though the search itself is worth pursuing. (Baum, 1989, has a more detailed presentation of research.)

As we have seen, the relation between conduct disorder and *temperament* is weak. However, *sexual maturation,* which is heritable, and early initiation of sexual intercourse, are powerful predictors of antisocial behavior. While some maintain that hormonal effects are directly causal, there is evidence that such effects depend upon nonorganic factors. Early-maturing girls' antisocial behavior is mediated by their preference for older friends as well as by the sex composition of the school they attend. Specifically, early-maturing girls in mixed-sex settings are at a greater risk for delinquency than are early-maturing girls in all-girls school or late-maturing girls in either school setting (Caspi et al., 1993; see also Farrington et al., 1990).

AN INTEGRATIVE MODEL

As we have said, we are particularly interested in attempts to integrate the multiple causes of a given psychopathology rather than to merely list them. Patterson provides such a model based partly on research, partly on his own observations and experience, and partly on his creative intellect. Devising the model involved both selecting the variables thought to be crucial to producing antisocial or delinquent behavior and hypothesizing the relationship among them. (Our presentation is based on Patterson, Reid, and Dishion, 1992.)

The key hypothesis is that the basic training for subsequent antisocial behavior takes place in the home, and family members are the primary trainers. Training itself begins with the breakdown of effectiveness in disciplinary confrontations; the initial coercive interaction escalates into increasingly intense exchanges. Other poor family management skills include little parental involvement and monitoring of the child, lack of contingent positive reinforcement on the part of the parents, and an absence of problem solving when difficult situations arise.

There are also a number of other risk variables—low SES, a difficult temperament in infancy, antisocial parents, divorce, stress, living in a high-crime neighborhood, and unskilled grandparents—but these do not directly lead to antisocial behavior. Rather, their effect has to be mediated by the family variables. The result of these untoward family interactions is an antisocial, socially incompetent child with low self-esteem. The entire sequence of events is called Stage 1.

Stage 2 occurs when the child enters school. His or her antisocial behavior and incompetence result in peer and parental rejection on the one hand, poor academic performance on the other, and depressed mood. In Stage 3 the adolescent is drawn to a deviant peer group that has a negative attitude toward school and

authority and becomes involved in delinquency and substance abuse. In Stage 4, the adult faces a chaotic employment career, a disrupted marriage, and institutionalization for crimes or mental disorder (see Figure 9.3). At each stage the number of individuals becomes smaller, but the risk of becoming an antisocial adult increases.

The Developmental Dimension Patterson's model is developmental since changes take place from early childhood to adolescence. He even writes of poor family management skills, antisocial behavior, and poor academic and peer relations as being "different stages of the same process" (Patterson, 1986, p. 432). However, he is not using "stage" as Piaget, Kohlberg, or Freud do because there is no qualitative change and no inevitable progression. Rather, he means that each development places the child at risk for the subsequent development: noncompliance with parents is apt to generalize to noncompliance with teachers; aggression at home is apt subsequently to block the formation of healthy peer relations; and so on. All such progressions can be accounted for in terms of well-established principles of learning, and there is no need to hypothesize a predetermined sequencing.

As befits a learning-theory orientation, the general model of psychopathology is one of *excess*, or extreme deviation from the norm. Neither parent nor child is a unique kind of person; rather they are more coercive or more aggressive than usual.

TREATMENT

The continuity of conduct disorders from childhood to adulthood means that individuals and society pay a high price, in terms of personal suffering and in dollars and cents for the violence and antisocial behavior that characterize this disturbance. Thus there is an ur-

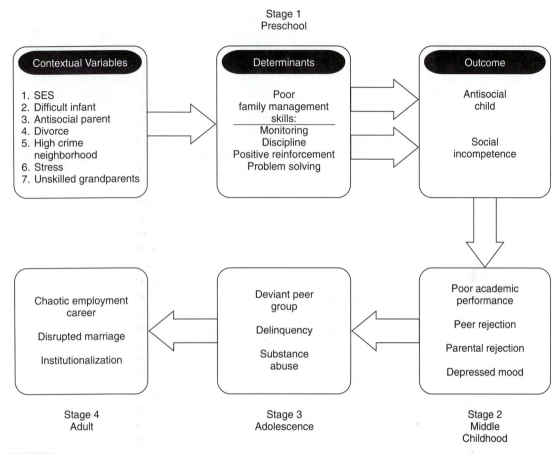

FIGURE 9.3
Patterson's model of conduct disorder. (*Source:* Patterson, Reid, and Dishion, 1992.)

gent need for prevention and treatment. Yet the multiple roots of conduct disorders—the cognitive and affective dysfunctions within the child, the psychopathology and discord within the family, the peer support by similarly disordered youths, the insensitivity and punitiveness in the schools and society at large—present major obstacles to success in both undertakings. While no program has clearly demonstrated its effectiveness in returning all conduct-disordered children to the path of normal development, there are a number of promising leads. (Our presentation follows Farrington et al.'s 1990 review, unless otherwise noted. Also see Kazdin, 1993.)

Improving Parenting

Since faulty child-rearing practices and discord are closely related to conduct disorders, it is logical to assume that altering the pattern of family interaction in a positive direction would have a therapeutic effect on the child. One of the most successful and best documented techniques is called Parent Management Training (PMT) and is based on altering the interaction patterns described in Patterson's coercion theory (Kazdin, 1987). As the name implies, it is the parents who are trained by the therapist and who implement the recommended procedures in the home.

Reinforcement for prosocial behavior ("Try to catch the child doing something good") counteracts the image of the family as an armed camp. Establishing firm rules and adhering to them helps circumvent the coercive interaction. Negotiating compromises introduces an element of reasonableness and mutuality into the parent-child interactions. Punishments are mild, such as temporary loss of privileges.The immediate goal is to develop specific parenting skills. Typically, the skills are first applied to relatively simple, easily observed behavioral sequences. As parents become more skilled, the focus shifts to more encompassing and problematic behaviors.

Parent Management Training has been extensively evaluated with behavior-problem children and has shown to bring problematic behaviors within the levels of adequately functioning peers. The gains are maintained from one to four years. In addition, sibling behaviors improve even though siblings are not the direct focus of treatment, while maternal depression tends to decrease. Thus PMT may alter many aspects of dysfunctional families.

Several factors contribute to treatment effectiveness. Families with multiple risk factors such as parental psychopathology and poverty show fewer gains than less pervasively disturbed families. Mothers who have social supports outside the home, such as friends or organizations, profit more from treatment than do socially isolated mothers. PMT also has limitations, the most obvious one being the need for parents who are willing and able to engage in the extensive training. A considerable number are too disturbed or too despairing to become involved or drop out during treatment. The high dropout rate during fol-

low-up also suggests that the data on long-term effectiveness may be on the optimistic side.

The effectiveness of PMT with adolescents is uncertain. There is some evidence that it is more effective with aggressive than with non-aggressive behavior disorders such as stealing and truanting. Finally, the failure of several studies to find treatment effects has led to the suggestion that parent training should be supplemented by other techniques focusing on social skills training and academic remediation (Patterson, DeBaryshe, and Ramsey, 1989).

Social Problem-Solving Skills

Kazdin and colleagues' (1989) study of social problem-solving skills has been singled out as a model of research into therapeutic effectiveness. They compared two variations of cognitive-behavioral therapy with relationship therapy, the criterion being enhancing antisocial children's ability to solve interpersonal problems in a constructive way. The subjects were ninety-seven boys between 7 and 13 years of age. The diagnosis was made both in terms of DSM-III criteria and a behavior checklist. The boys were evaluated before, immediately after, and one year after treatment either by standardized checklists with known reliability and validity or by standard interviews which could be reliably scored. The techniques covered a broad range of dysfunctions. Information was obtained from multiple sources in both the home and school setting.

Next, the boys were randomly assigned to one of three treatments. In the first, problem-solving skill training involved generating alternatives, thinking of consequences, and taking the perspective of others in various social situations. Role playing and modeling were used to make the situations more salient, and the boys were rewarded for versatile and constructive solutions. The second group received the same training, but it was supplemented by in vivo practice; for example, they were given "homework" involving applying what they learned in the treatment session to situations with parents, peers, and teachers. The third group received relationship or client-centered therapy that emphasized empathy, warmth, and unconditional positive regard on the therapists' part, along with helping the boys express their feelings and discuss their interpersonal problems.

The therapists had six months to a year's experience and were given six months' intensive training in the particular technique they were to implement. Moreover, their performance during the twenty-five treatment sessions was monitored by a series of ongoing reports they had to fill out and by constant supervision. All this was done to insure the integrity of the treatment.

The children in the cognitive-behavioral groups showed significantly greater reductions in antisocial behavior and overall behavior problems and greater increases in prosocial behavior than children in the relationship group. The effects were present in the one-year follow-up in the home and at school. In spite of their improvement, the children were still outside the range of normal behavior. The authors speculate that the multiple etiologies of antisocial behavior may require multiple treatment techniques.

Peer Influences

Some therapeutic techniques in this category emphasize training in *social skills* and *problem-solving skills.* Goals include increasing the frequency of children's positive social interactions and enabling them to generate constructive solutions to interpersonal problems with peers. A variety of methods are used— from coaching socially rejected youths in interaction skills to classroom instruction in handling interpersonal problems. While short-term follow-up studies of effectiveness have shown desirable changes in behavior, effectiveness has not been demonstrated over the long term.

Other treatments involve the peer group itself (Henggeler, 1989). *Guided group interaction* consists of daily group discussions aimed at directly confronting a child with his or her negative behavior and helping the child to assume responsibility for it, uncovering personal and interpersonal problems and discussing alternatives for handling them, and caring for others and helping them cope with difficulties. In spite of its popularity, there is scant empirical evidence of its effectiveness. More promising results have been obtained by involving antisocial and prosocial peers in community and educational events such as team sports. However, more studies need to be done. *Cooperative learning* in the classroom involves small, heterogeneous groups of students as learning partners. Students of diverse ability, ethnicity, and background work together to master curriculum material and receive recognition as a team. Controlled studies show positive effects on achievement, attitudes toward school and peers, and reduced rates of suspension and expulsion from school (Farrington et al., 1990).

School Achievement

A number of different treatment approaches have been tried in an effort to break the link between low academic achievement and delinquency. Early childhood education intervention, as epitomized by the Perry Preschool Program, combines a cognitively oriented preschool curriculum with weekly home visits to teach skills in child management and reinforcement of learning to mothers. Those who attended the program had lower arrest rates, fewer arrests, and lower rates of fighting than did a control group at the age of 19.

Other academically oriented interventions have had some success in improving academically related variables over short periods of time. Their long-term effectiveness and ability to prevent antisocial behaviors have yet to be proved.

Multisystemic Therapy

Multisystemic therapy specifically recognizes the multiple roots of antisocial behavior. It is individualized and flexible, offering a variety of treatments depending on the special needs of a particular adolescent. Thus, treatment may focus on family disharmony or school underachievement or lack of social skills or vocational guidance. A variety of remedial techniques may be used. Treatment is problem-focused, while setting, length, and frequency of sessions vary on a case-by-case basis. Preliminary results are encouraging (Henggeler, 1989).

Institutional Treatment

There is evidence that institutions do have a substantial effect on the delinquents during their stay. The characteristics of successful institutions include firmness combined with warmth, harmony, high expectations of appropriate behavior, nonpunitive discipline, and a practical approach to training. Interestingly, many of these qualities are found in families associated with protecting the children from delinquency. Reviews of effectiveness have produced mixed results but, in general, programs are more successful in improving behavior in the institutions than in reducing recidivism significantly (Henggeler, 1989).

Utah and Massachusetts have been leaders in devising effective institutional treatment. They closed their large training schools and replaced them with a network of small, secure units for violent and dangerous youths, who receive milieu and group therapy, are taught academic skills, and are given vocational training. Their progress is monitored when they return to the community. As a result, the number of new adult prisoners who are graduates of the juvenile system in Massachusetts has declined each year for the last eleven years (Schwartz and Levi, 1986).

Behavioral principles have been used to establish a *token economy*, in which delinquents earn tokens for acceptable behavior. These tokens can be exchanged for tangible rewards such as cigarettes or privileges. Despite the initial enthusiasm for the token economy, there is little evidence that it is superior to other programs in well-run institutions. There is also no evidence of long-term benefits in regard to reducing recidivism rates when the delinquent returns to the community (Rutter and Giller, 1983).

Community-Based Treatment

The basic tenet here is that remedial measures should be applied in the child's everyday environment such as local recreational or youth centers. The general goal is to foster competence and prosocial behavior, especially in regard to peer relations, thus providing an alternative to the child's antisocial pattern. Among other things, this approach is seen as a solution to the problem of gains made in one setting, such as in well-run institutions, being lost when the delinquent returns to the community.

Community-based treatment is difficult to implement and to evaluate. However, there is some evidence that youths can benefit from such programs if they are run by experienced rather than inexperienced leaders, if the groups contain a mixture of youths with and without conduct disorders rather than containing only those with conduct disorders, and if the program is behaviorally oriented in that it reinforces prosocial behavior rather than dealing with group processes and social organizations (Kazdin, 1987).

A variation on the community approach is court or police-referred *juvenile diversion projects*, which, as the name implies, try to divert children and youths who have not yet been involved in serious offenses from further legal involvement (Peterson and Roberts, 1986). While there is great diversity among the programs, they typically rely on establishing an important personal relationship with the delinquent and providing recreational opportunities as well as "curbside counseling." Features of specific programs might include teaching interpersonal and academic skills, improving physical fitness, and vocational, personal, and social counseling. Reviews of effectiveness have produced mixed results and there is even some evidence that diversion increases adolescents' involvement with the juvenile justice system and can have harmful effects (Henggeler, 1989).

Other Approaches

Deterrence theory suggests that the threat or imposition of sanctions, such as suspension from school or arrests, can decrease the rate of adolescent delinquent behavior. However, research shows that sanctions are associated with an increase in self-reported delinquent behavior and are not associated with changes in perceived certainty of punishment. There is also no evidence that institutionalization suppresses rates of subsequent delinquent behavior more than community treatment. Scared Straight and similar programs, while having some initially positive effects, have no effect on subsequent recidivism. There is preliminary evidence that restitution, in which an offender either pays a sum of money or performs a useful service for the victim, does lead to a lower recidivism rate in a two- to three-year period (Henggeler, 1989).

Behavioral therapies can alter specific aggressive and antisocial behavior, but durable changes among clinical populations have not been demonstrated. *Pharmacotherapy* has similarly been effective in altering aggressive behavior but not in changing everyday adjustment (Kazdin, 1987). *Individual psychotherapy* is generally ineffective except for those individuals who have a high level of anxiety, are introspective, and desire change (Rutter and Giller, 1983).

Final Comments on Treatment

The literature on remediation is frustrating because so many studies are poorly designed and describe populations, procedures, and outcomes in vague terms. Granted, well-designed and executed studies are difficult to do, but they remain the only means of evaluating the success or failure of a therapeutic procedure. Two conclusions seem justified from the literature. First, there is no "cure" for conduct disorders, no therapy of choice with demonstrated effectiveness on the entire range of disturbances. However, there are a number of important leads as to how to increase the success rates of future endeavors. Next, in light of the multiple roots of the disturbance, it is unlikely that a single treatment of choice will be forthcoming. As we have seen, even successful procedures in a given setting may fail to generalize to or may be nullified by other settings. The implication is that a combination of procedures may be necessary to bring about significant and sustained change. Yet as Kazdin (1987) notes, the procedures should not be merely a jumble of well-intentioned efforts, but should be tailored to remedying the specific deficiencies and dysfunctions responsible for the conduct disorder at hand. While a prodigious undertaking, remedying or, ideally, preventing conduct disorders is the most important challenge facing clinical child psychologists today.

CHAPTER 10

SCHIZOPHRENIA: A SEVERE DEVIATION OF MIDDLE CHILDHOOD AND ADOLESCENCE

Schizophrenia shares characteristics with both autism and depression. Like autism, it is a severe and pervasive psychopathology evidenced by cognitive, affective, and social deviations. In its extreme form it is incapacitating. Like depression, schizophrenia originates at two points in time, although these points are middle childhood and adolescence rather than infancy and middle childhood. The challenge is to understand the manifestations of the disturbance and its roots in prior developmental periods. The picture in regard to roots is a perplexing one because, while child-hood-onset schizophrenia continues through adolescence and into adulthood, adolescent-onset schizophrenia is not preceded by any of the defining symptoms of schizophrenia. The final challenge is to learn why schizophrenia has two periods of onset. We will not be able to meet this challenge as we did with depression, however, because research, especially in regard to childhood-onset schizophrenia, is scant and conceptualizations often skirt the developmental issue.

In our presentation, we will begin with childhood schizophrenia and then turn to the adolescent form. Finally, we will juxtapose the two sets of findings to see whether any developmental patterns can be detected.

CHILDHOOD SCHIZOPHRENIA

Characteristics

The *prevalence* of childhood schizophrenia is uncertain because of the lack of high-quality epidemiological studies. It is thought to have a lower prevalence than autism. Childhood schizophrenia is extremely rare before 6 years of age, after which it increases somewhat in frequency and is stable from 7 to 12 years of age. Males outnumber females, except in puberty, where the sexes are equal.

The primary *symptoms* here, as in adulthood, are hallucinations or perceptions with no external stimuli, delusions or irrational beliefs, thought disorders, and blunted or inappropriate affect. Such symptoms are rare before 8 years of age but are present and stable in middle childhood since there is no evidence of a developmental trend between 8 and 13 years of age. (Our presentation of research follows Russell, Bott, and Sammons, 1989, unless otherwise noted.)

Hallucinations Around 80 percent of schizophrenic children experience auditory hallucinations. Commands, such as hearing a man's voice saying "Murder your stepfather," are common. Visual hallucinations are less frequent, occurring in 30 to 46 percent of the population. For example, one child reported seeing a ghost with a burned and scarred face. The structure of hallucinations increases in complexity with age, while the content reflects age-appropriate concerns; for example, younger children may have hallucinations about monsters and pets, while older children's hallucinations may involve sex.

Delusions About 58 percent of schizophrenic children experience delusions. As with hallucinations, they become more com-

plex with age and reflect age-appropriate concerns. A young child may believe that his parents want to kill him, while an older one would have an elaborate delusion about the children at school plotting to turn her into a drug dealer. Persecutory delusions, such as the two just mentioned, and somatic delusions, such as a boy believing that a girl's brain lives inside his head, are common.

Thought Disorders There are a number of thought disorders, the most florid involving loose associations in which the child's language may be fragmented, dissociated, and bizarre. For example, "It's open in front but closed behind. I'm open in front but closed behind. Did you see me today? I think I was here, but Mommy wasn't. They don't take it away from Mommy. My dolly won't mind. I won't mind. (Enumerates all the members of the family who won't mind.) I was there yesterday. Was I here today?" There is little agreement among studies as to the prevalence of thought disorders in childhood schizophrenia; estimates range from 40 to 100 percent.

Controlled studies of thought disorders have been facilitated by the development of a storytelling technique which permits the measurement of loose and illogical thinking (Caplan and Sherman, 1990). The former is defined as an unpredictable change of topics; for example, answering the question, "Why don't you like Tim" with "I call my mother Sweetie." The latter involves contradictions and inappropriate causal relations; for example, "I left my hat in the office because her name is Mary" (Caplan et al., 1989). These thinking disorders, which are not found in children diagnosed with ADHD, conduct disorder, and oppositional disorder, may be specific to schizophrenia (Caplan et al., 1990).

Research suggests that the two kinds of disturbed thinking are not correlated. Loose thinking is related to distractibility, as manifested by low scores on certain of the WISC-R subtests. Illogical thinking is related to a short attention span, as measured by the ability to see the letter T or F when it is embedded in four to nine other letters, all of which are presented for a brief interval (Caplan et al., 1990). Children with schizophrenia use the same strategies as do normal ones, but for some reason, they use them less efficiently (Asarnow et al., 1991). This attentional deficit may underlie the children's digressive speech, since they lack the short-term attentional processes required for coherent conversation.

Finally, Thompson and colleagues (1990) showed that children with schizophrenia exhibit more attentional drift and thought disorders in conversations with their parents than did depressed children. Parents of schizophrenic children also showed communication deviance in that their style was confusing and unclear, although this quality was revealed in response to projective techniques and not during observed interaction with the children. Thus, it may be that the children's difficulty in processing information is compounded by the lack of clarity of messages sent by parents (Asarnow et al., 1991). (For a further study of thought disorder, see Caplan, Guthrie, and Foy, 1992.)

Other Deviations   Here we find emotional disturbances such as showing little or flat affect; situationally inappropriate affect such as laughing in situations that would ordinarily elicit fear or sadness; and moodiness, anxiety, or depression. Social difficulties have been reported, such as isolation, ineptness, and anxiety. Finally, there is frequent reference to motor deficiencies, such as awkwardness, delayed development, poor coordination, and peculiar posture (See Watkins, Asarnow, and Tanguay, 1988).

Developmental Pathway

The Early Years   Information concerning infancy through preschool is derived from three studies. (Incidentally, these studies illustrate three of the techniques for obtaining developmental data described in Chapter 3.) Cantor (1988) obtained retrospective data from a standard series of interview questions administered to twenty-nine mothers of schizophrenic children who were 10 years of age or younger. Watkins, Asarnow, and Tanguay (1988) did a follow-back study of eighteen children who became schizophrenic at 10 years of age or younger, obtaining data on prior behavior from records of pediatricians, clinics, hospitals, schools, and mental health and other public agencies. Fish (1971, 1976) conducted a follow-up study of infants of schizophrenic mothers, some of whom became schizophrenic.

In Cantor's study, twenty-five of the twenty-nine children were symptom-free in infancy, an increasing percent of them coming to professional attention during the preschool period for problems such as speech delay, social withdrawal, being a slow learner, and hyperactivity. In the Watkins study, seven of the eighty-one children had symptoms meeting the criteria of autism in the newborn to 30-month period. For the rest of the group there was a gradual worsening of symptoms from infancy to middle childhood. Fish was more impressed with the disjointed nature of change characterized by precocities and lags among the various facets of development, such as motor activity, perception, and cognition.

All three investigations reported deviant motor and speech development. The latter included little babbling and slowness in imitating sounds in infancy and no or seriously delayed speech along with making up words in the toddler and preschool period. There were social deviations which included preference for being alone, perseverative play, being "hyper" with peers, and lack of or bizarre responses to the social environment. Cantor and Watkins agree that the social deviations were particularly ominous in terms of presaging future disturbance. Other unusual behaviors were also observed: aimless wandering, smelling or perseverative touching of objects, and labile mood.

While findings are preliminary because of the small number of children studied, they indicate that schizophrenia does not have a sudden onset in middle childhood. On the contrary, it is preceded by serious disturbances in a number of psychological functions and a poor level of premorbid adjustment. Watkins, Asarnow, and Tanguay (1988) reconstruct the following developmental sequence: language abnormalities and delays, motor delays, and hypotonic, bizarre responses along with lack of social responsiveness during infancy; extreme mood lability, inappropriate clinging, unexplained rage reactions, and hyperactivity during early childhood; thought disorder, flat or inappropriate affect at 6 years of age or older; and, finally, hallucinations and delusions after 9 years of age.

Adult Adjustment   Data on adult adjustment are limited. Results suggest that about half of the children with schizophrenia will show improvement, 20 percent to the point of recovery. On the other hand, one-third will continue to be severely disturbed. Age of onset is an important predictor; the later the onset, the better the prognosis. A good premorbid personality, acute onset, easily identifiable symptoms and precipitating events are all related to better outcome (Prior and Werry, 1986).

The Organic Context

Bender's work (1947) is a comprehensive account of the etiology and manifestations of childhood schizophrenia in terms of organic dysfunction. Her basic premise is that schizophrenia is an organic pathology of the central nervous system involving the total organism. While a single entity, its expression differs as a function of the child's developmental level.

Moreover, the timing of developmental events is out of joint. Not only are daily rhythms of sleeping, eating, and elimination erratic but so are long-term growth patterns. Consequently, the nice developmental synchrony guaranteed by normal maturation is missing. In fact, Bender's term for this erratic growth pattern is *dysmaturation*. It corresponds to our concept of asynchrony. Finally, Bender's clinical observations led her to place particular emphasis on motor behavior and postural responses. She observed that toddlers and preschoolers were awkward and insecure in mastering the many motor skills of the period, from walking and climbing stairs to using swings and tricycles. However, primitive behavior can alternate with precocious grace and coordination.

Empirical support for Bender's position comes from Fish's (1984) ten-year follow-up study of infants of schizophrenic mothers. Five of the eight infants who showed clear evidence of dysmaturation were severely disturbed in middle childhood; only four of the thirteen infants showing no evidence of dysmaturation were moderately disturbed, the others having mild or no disturbance.

Turning to other variables in the organic context, family, twin, and adoption studies provide evidence of a hereditary factor in childhood schizophrenia. In addition, there is also a high incidence of abnormal EEG activity, brain scans and biochemical analyses. Finally, there may be an increased incidence of prenatal and birth complications, although these are not inevitable (Cantor, 1988).

Developmental Models

While acknowledging the importance of developmental factors, investigators have paid little attention to developmental models. There is evidence that the performance of schizophrenic children on span-of-attention tasks is like that of younger children (Asarnow et al., 1991). Loose thinking is related to low scores on certain intelligence test items. Caplan and coworkers (1990) speculate that formal thought disorders result from a lag in the development of perspective taking. Thus all of the models conform to that of a developmental lag—in information processing, in certain aspects of intelligence, and in perspective taking. However, too little is known about childhood schizophrenia to assume that a single model will suffice.

The Invulnerables

Bleuler (1974) followed 184 children of 206 schizophrenic parents and found that approximately 72 percent were functioning normally. The percentage is higher than is usually reported (which ranges between 35 and 50 percent), perhaps owing to the uncertainty of the definition of normality, perhaps because, as a family psychiatrist, Bleuler came to know his patients more thoroughly than most researchers know their subjects. But the mystery of normal functioning has deepened with the discovery of high-risk children who are making exceptionally good adjustments. Some have schizophrenic parents; some come from poverty backgrounds, and their home environment would seem inimical to normal development. For example, one 8-year-old girl's father was in jail, her mother was severely depressed and unable to see even to her children's basic needs for food, while her four siblings were either retarded or predelinquent school dropouts.

While the study of these invulnerable children has only recently begun, certain of their characteristics have been delineated. (Unless otherwise noted, our presentation follows Cohler, 1987.) Rather than being engulfed by their parents' psychopathology, the invulnerable children have the ability to distance themselves psychologically, showing a detached curiosity and understanding of what is troubling their parents while also being compassionate toward them. They have a high level of *initiative*. In the interpersonal realm this is

evidenced by their taking advantage of the well parent's support or lacking that, seeking out adults outside the family. Their capacity to make friends further enlarges their circle of growth-promoting social relationships. In the intrapersonal realm, the children's initiative is evidenced by their engaging in diverse activities outside of the home, holding down jobs, and having hobbies, all of which serve as buffers against the noxious influences of the home environment. While the invulnerable children are intelligent, more important is their ability to try to understand the events in their lives and figure out ways of coping with them. They also tend to be physically and personally attractive. A final finding is that the ability to cope effectively is increased if the disturbed parent is hospitalized later in the children's lives rather than early, and if the parent has some ability to relate positively to the children.

Subsequently, however, invulnerable children pay a price for their remarkable ability to cope effectively with adversity. As adults they have a diminished capacity to form a sustained intimate relationship. They are concerned with their own needs and interests but reluctant to explore their feelings. They gravitate toward impersonal pursuits and vocations such as science and technology and are most comfortable in tasks requiring group cooperation rather than close relations. They gain support from participation in religious and social groups. Such a life pattern results from their defenses of distancing, suppression of affect, and intellectualizing. When they seek psychotherapy, it is because they have vague feelings of being unsatisfied despite being successful (Anthony, 1987).

Finally, the intensive study of these children and their lives suggests that "invulnerable" might not be the most appropriate adjective for describing them because it suggests they somehow have developed an immunity to all of life's stresses and distresses. On the contrary, they, like most other people, have their periods of setback marked by discouragement, uncertainty, and fear. However, they also have a basic strength that enables them to overcome such periods and to resume the positive course of their lives. Thus it is not their immunity that marks them but their resilience.

Schizophrenia versus Autism

Since schizophrenia and autism are both severe disturbances, the question arises as to whether they are two manifestations of the same basic process. While the issue has been hotly debated in the past, there now is evidence that autism differs from childhood schizophrenia. The clinical picture of the two psychopathologies is different from middle childhood on. Autism lacks the delusions and hallucinations, the loose associations, and the mood disturbances which characterize schizophrenia. The autistic child is a highly ritualized, very odd outsider; the schizophrenic child's behavior is florid, excessive, and bizarre. A greater percent of autistic children are intellectually retarded. In their developmental courses, schizophrenia is marked by progressions and regressions, while autism is highly stable.

There are important differences in context factors. Parents of autistic children tend to have average or above average intelligence and do not come from any one socioeconomic group, while parents of schizophrenic children tend to have below average intelligence and come from a low socioeconomic stratum. Schizophrenia in parents of autistic children is no higher than in the normal population, while it is elevated in parents of schizophrenic children. (For a detailed presentation, see Kolvin, Ounsted, Humphrey, and McNay, 1971; Kolvin, Ounsted, Richardson, and Garside, 1971.)

So far we have painted the differences between schizophrenia and autism in broad strokes. What remains to be done are the more refined comparative studies. As we saw in Chapter 4, we now know a good deal about the variables that differentiate autism from other disturbances. What is needed is a point-by-point comparison between autistic and schizophrenic children. For example, do schizophrenic children show the same deviations in imitation, higher-order thinking, and language as autistic children?

ADOLESCENT SCHIZOPHRENIA

Description

The *prevalence* rate of adolescent schizophrenia is 0.33 percent. Of adolescents hospitalized for psychiatric care, 15 to 30 percent are schizophrenic. There is no sex difference in prevalence (Weiner, 1992).

Symptomatology   As was the case with childhood schizophrenia, the defining symptoms in adolescence are essentially the same as those found in adult schizophrenia.

Disorders of Thought   Certain disturbances involve the process of thinking itself rather than the content of thought: "It's like someone poured molasses into my thinking machinery. I've got to work and work to get from one idea to another, and sometimes the whole thing just stops running." "My mind keeps going in all directions at once. I don't know what's going to pop up next. That's why I'm so scared. My mind's going haywire."

These two adolescents are describing the collapse of directed attention, which is essential to orderly thinking. One result is *blocking*, which may be clinically manifested by long pauses before the adolescent can answer a question. Such sluggishness is different from the defiant silence or purposeful negativism of the sociopath or the frozen fearfulness of the adolescent with an anxiety disorder. At the other extreme is *fragmentation*, in which tangentially related or even unrelated ideas constantly intrude and disrupt the adolescent's train of thought.

The content of thinking is disturbed in a

number of ways. We shall describe only two. *Delusions* and *hallucinations* represent an extreme loss of contact with reality. The former include delusions of grandeur (for example, an adolescent boy picked up a book he had never read, briefly flipped through the pages from beginning to end, and announced, "I know everything that's in this book.") and delusions of persecution (for example, a young girl was certain a neighborhood gang was planning to capture, rape, and torture her "like Patty Hearst"). Hallucinations are often auditory (for example, hearing voices); visual hallucinations are infrequent. Perception of bodily sensations and functions can also be radically distorted (for example, the body is emitting a foul odor, there are roaches eating at the brain, or feces will come out of the mouth if the adolescent speaks).

Social Isolation The social withdrawal of schizophrenics can be evidenced in a variety of ways. They may be oblivious to others, puzzled or confused by things happening around them, excessively preoccupied with their own thoughts. Their affect might be blunted, or they might be touchy and hypersensitive, subject to inappropriate outbursts of anger or to silly laughter. Finally, ineptness and a lack of social skills can contribute to social isolation, particularly in regard to peers.

Disorders of Motor Behavior Here one finds facial grimaces, odd postures and movements such as persistent rocking while standing or sitting, long periods of immobility, bizarre repetitive actions such as incessantly rubbing the forehead or angrily slapping the wrist or scratching the skin to the point of producing open, bleeding sores. (For a detailed account of adolescent schizophrenia, see Weiner, 1992.)

Further Characteristics The symptoms of schizophrenia have also been subsumed under two broad categories. *Positive* symptoms include thought disorders, delusions, and hallucinations. *Negative* symptoms are characterized by an absence of sociability, pleasure, energy, and affect.

A number of factors contribute to *chronicity* of schizophrenia. (Our presentation follows Weiner, 1992.) A predominance of negative symptoms is one, especially if the symptoms are severe. Next are brain abnormalities, which are present in 20 to 35 percent of diagnosed schizophrenics. A past history of interpersonal and school- or work-related adjustment difficulties is a third factor. Slow deterioration over a period of months with no clear precipitating events, along with a lack of concern for or insight into problems and impairment, are final contributing factors. By contrast, an acutely disturbed schizophrenic typically has an unremarkable history, is reacting to a clearly identifiable precipitating event, is worried about the unusual nature of the symptoms, which are primarily positive and mild, and has no neuropathological involvement.

Developmental Studies

Two comments are in order before reviewing the data: (1) One would think that so dramatic a disturbance as schizophrenia would have equally dramatic precursors. Such is not the case. In fact, research findings are often inconsistent and inconclusive. (2) The majority of the findings differentiate schizophrenic from normal populations but do not differentiate schizophrenic from other severely disturbed populations. This does not mean such findings are trivial, but it does mean that many of the striking clinical features that define schizophrenia are yet to be explained.

Methodological Issues Since our presentation of research will rely heavily on longitudinal data, we will first discuss some of the problems with this approach to studying the precursors of adolescent schizophrenia.

A major problem involves *locating a population* (Garmezy and Streitman, 1974). Because schizophrenia occurs in less than 1 percent of the population, one would have to follow 1000 randomly selected infants in the hope of obtaining only 10 schizophrenic adolescents. It would facilitate research considerably if one could locate a group of infants or children at risk for developing schizophrenia. The most popular solution is to study children of schizophrenic parents: regardless of whether one holds a genetic or environmental position, the chances of such children becoming schizophrenic are significantly increased.

Other problems arise from the *nature of schizophrenia* itself. Rather than being a single entity, it may well be a family of disturbances, possibly with a number of etiologies (Watt, 1984). Consequently, an investigator may account for only a subgroup of the entire population, or differentiating etiologic patterns may be lost when data are combined and represented only in terms of mean scores. Next, the etiologic variables involved may not be stable, traitlike ones that persist over time, but may *wax and wane*. We know, for example, that IQ, usually a highly stable measure from middle childhood on, is highly unstable in children of schizophrenics, the correlation over time being around .59 rather than in the .80s as it is with other groups, including children of psychotically depressed mothers (Lewine, 1984). Instability undermines long-range predictability, requiring instead periodic monitoring of variables to chart their changing course. Added to this picture of instability is the fact that the definition of schizophrenia itself changed with DSM-III, requiring reclassification of original samples and reanalysis of data (Watt, 1984).

Next is the problem of *sample bias*. As we have seen, the design of choice has been to study children of schizophrenic mothers because there is an increased probability that the children will also become schizophrenic. However, since only 10 percent of adult schizophrenics have schizophrenic parents, the population followed longitudinally cannot be considered representative of schizophrenics in

general. Schizophrenic women are also more apt to marry disturbed men, such as criminals, who in turn may bias the children's behavior by their own psychopathology (Rutter and Garmezy, 1983). Moreover, older, unmarried, anxious, socially incompetent, lower-class schizophrenic mothers who have had difficult pregnancies and deliveries are apt to give up their babies for adoption or foster-parent placement (Watt, 1984). Far from being a random sample of infants, these would be at risk for a number of psychopathologies, even if their mothers were not schizophrenic. In short, investigators cannot control the situation to make sure that only variables intrinsic to schizophrenia are coming into play; instead, they confront a variety of potentially pathogenic variables that function as confounds in the developmental picture.

Finally, there is the problem of *attrition*, common to many longitudinal studies. The most severely disturbed subjects often are the most likely to drop out of the research with time, either because of uncooperativeness or because they have drifted on to other locations leaving no word behind.

Two further characteristics of the studies we shall examine should be mentioned. In some studies, the subjects have not been followed into adolescence and adulthood, so they are best regarded as "at risk" rather than having developed schizophrenia. This gives a tentative cast to the findings. Other studies failed to yield a sufficient number of schizophrenic adolescents, so related disturbances such as schizoid, paranoid, and borderline personality disorder were added. This cluster of related disturbances is called *schizophrenia spectrum disorder*.

Although there are problems, one methodological advance which the current crop of longitudinal studies shares is the inclusion of a severely disturbed but nonschizophrenic comparison group, typically psychotically depressed mothers and their offspring. This allows the investigators to make statements as to which variables are specific to schizophrenia and which are common to severe disturbances in general. It also avoids the pitfall of designs that compare schizophrenic populations only with normal ones and then interpret findings as if they were specific to schizophrenia.

Developmental Pathway

Pregnancy and Birth Schizophrenic women experience more stress during pregnancy and engage in more risk-increasing behaviors such as heavy smoking and drinking. However, since such behaviors are also characteristic of women with other psychiatric disorders, they should be regarded as nonspecific factors associated with the severity and chronicity of maternal disturbance (Asarnow, 1988). There is an elevated incidence of prenatal complications, a long and difficult delivery, and low birth weight for the neonate. Once again, the picture does not differ significantly from that found in other psychotically disturbed but nonschizophrenic mothers. Some studies find a relation between prenatal events and socioeconomic status; others do not. (For a more detailed account of findings, see Watt et al., 1984.)

Infancy through Preschool Some, but not all, infants of schizophrenic mothers evidence *neurological damage,* although no particular abnormality (such as reflexes, muscle tone, activity level) has been consistently implicated. During the first year of life there is evidence of a lag in motor and sensory development which exceeds that in infants of normal and psychologically disturbed mothers. Although not consistent, there are data suggesting that at least a subgroup of infants are underaroused and unresponsive to external stimuli as evidenced by low activity level, poor alertness and orientation, and poor muscle tonus. Since all the above findings are based on only half a dozen studies, they should be con-

sidered preliminary. (See Hans and Marcus, 1991, for a comprehensive review of the research.)

In the *interpersonal* domain, only two studies concern attachment, and their findings are inconclusive. A special subgroup of neonates were found to be less cuddly and consolable, but this does not characterize the group as a whole. Toddlers of schizophrenic mothers are less communicatively competent, more active, anxious, angry, and hostile with others, while affectively flat, withdrawn, and isolated from their mothers. However, beyond 2 years of age, these qualities are more related to severity and chronicity of psychopathology in disturbed mothers rather than being specific to schizophrenia. The four studies of temperament yielded divergent findings.

In the *preschool* period there is suggestive evidence of a lag in social behavior; as observed in a testing situation, the children act in a less mature manner than do their counterparts in the normal and depressed-mother groups. In regard to adaptive behavior, such as cooperation with the family and others, fearfulness, whining or bizarre behavior, children of schizophrenic mothers are as well adapted as children of other-disordered or (in a single instance) well parents. Severity and chronicity of disturbance are more important than kind of disturbance.

Finally, there is evidence from a single study that children in the schizophrenic group show more psychological disturbance by the end of the preschool period than children in comparison or control groups. The meager data on parenting suggests that schizophrenic mothers are less affectionately involved, more hostile, and less stimulating than nonschizophrenic mothers. (For a detailed account of objective studies, see Goodman, 1991.)

Overall, the findings make sense in terms of maternal and child disturbances in general but tell us little about what is unique to schizophrenia. We would expect disturbed mothers as a group to provide less adequate care for their offspring, who, in turn, would display more deviant behavior, but this fails to capture the distinguishing features of schizophrenia. Perhaps such features do not emerge this early in development, or perhaps researchers have not hit upon the crucial differentiating variables.

Middle Childhood and Adolescence *Motor development.* Neuromotor impairment characterizes at-risk populations. This may be evidenced by problems in both fine and gross motor coordination and by motor delays.

Personality Variables As for personality variables, in no instance is the socially withdrawn, bizarre adolescent schizophrenic an odd, socially isolated child. Rather, the picture more often is of a "stormy" middle childhood in which there is a mixture of internalizing and externalizing behaviors. The children tend to be rated as aggressive and disruptive by teachers and as unhappy, withdrawn and not liked by peers. While prospective studies of such children reveal that they develop schizophrenic-like symptomatology, the same pattern can be found in children who become delinquent or substance abusers (Ledingham, 1990).

Cognitive Variables While overall IQ is slightly lower in at-risk children, the difference is not clinically significant. Verbal scores are more adversely affected than performance scores, suggesting that impairment of verbal intellectual functions is the more sensitive measure of psychopathology (Asarnow, 1988). IQ scores are more variable over time in the at-risk group and in adolescence, the decline in IQ scores is greater for the schizophrenic than for the children of depressed mothers (Watts, 1984).

A number of investigations concern various aspects of *attention*. (Our presentation follows Harvey's 1991 review unless otherwise indicated.) Distractibility or deficit in selective at-

tention may be a marker of vulnerability for schizophrenia. It also seems to emerge in the adolescent period rather than being present in middle childhood. Difficulties in sustained attention have also been found but, unlike distractability, are present in preadolescent children. Although a frequently used measure of sustained attention—the continual performance test—is the same one used for children with an attention-deficit hyperactive disorder, the kind of deficit is different. Specifically, children of schizophrenic mothers have lower perceptual sensitivity scores; for example, they do particularly poorly when the continuous series of numbers projected onto a screen are slightly out of focus, making them appear fuzzy rather than clearly defined (Nuechterlein, 1983).

While studies of *language and communication* are sparse, there is some evidence that the speech of high-risk subjects is vaguer than that of normal subjects and has a lower overall information content. The result is speech that is confusing, unclear, and poorly elaborated, although not sufficiently deviant to qualify as a formal thought disorder.

Summary Table 10.1 summarizes findings from studies of high-risk children. The clearest signs of vulnerability to schizophrenia are deviations in neuromotor integration and in attentional and information-processing abilities, along with variability in IQ (Watt and Saiz, 1991).

Adult Outcome Of all adolescents hospitalized for schizophrenia, one-quarter recover, one-quarter improve but suffer lingering symptoms and occasional relapses, while half require continual residential care. (Our presentation follows Weiner, 1992.) There are no reliable data on nonhospitalized schizophrenics, but their prospect for improvement and recovery is probably better. There are no sex differences in long-term outcome.

Positive prognostic signs for recovery are as follows:

TABLE 10.1
Etiological Factors in Adolescent Schizophrenia

Developmental period	Nonspecific factors		Specific child factors
	Mother	Child	
Prenatal	Increased stress; risk behavior		
Delivery	Increased complications	Low birth weight	
Infancy			Increased neurological signs;* lag in sensory, motor development; increased arousal problems;* deviant attachment*
Toddler		Increased problem behaviors; less communicative competence	
Preschool	Increased deviant mothering†	Increased adaptive behavior problems	Socially immature;† increased disturbance†
Middle childhood		Internalizing and externalizing behaviors; vague, unelaborated speech†	Increased neuromotor impairment, IQ variability; sustained attention difficulties
Adolescence			Distractibility; IQ decline

* Factors found in subgroups only.
† Data are meager.

Age: Appearance in late rather than early adolescence

Manifestation: A sudden breakdown in response to an identifiable event

Symptom picture: Confused and distressed rather than unperturbed and bland

History: Good social and school adjustment

Family: No severe parental psychopathology; understanding and supportive family involvement

Treatment: A positive response to treatment

The Family

First we will review the clinical and observational studies of families that have a schizophrenic member. (The presentation follows Mishler and Waxler, 1965.)

Gregory Bateson traces the origin of schizophrenia to a particularly vicious pattern of parental *communication* called the *double bind,* which traps the child between two negative injunctions. The often-cited example is of a mother who stiffened when her schizophrenic son impulsively put his arm around her shoulder but, when he withdrew, reproached him with, "Don't you love me anymore?" This "damned if you do and damned if you don't" dilemma is compounded by a prohibition against escaping from the family and a further prohibition against calling the parent's attention to his or her incongruous messages.

The only way out of the intolerable dilemma of repeated exposure to the double bind is to shatter the bond of communication itself. Rather than trying to convey meaning, schizophrenics purposefully attempt to avoid conveying meaning. Making it impossible for the ordinary listener to understand them and their ideas is the schizophrenics' intent, escape, and protection.

Lyman Wynne locates the psychopathology not in communication but in the *structure* of the family as a whole. The drifting or scattered thinking of the schizophrenic represents the internalization of a diffuse or fragmented family structure. Amorphous patterns of interaction are marked by vague ideas, by blurring of meaning, and by irrelevancies. Note the following responses of a mother being interviewed for her schizophrenic child's developmental history.

Psychologist: Was it a difficult delivery, or did everything go OK?

Mother: I know just what you mean. And I can say for certain that I'm not one of those women you read about where they are so brave and natural childbirth is just the greatest thing in their life. (Laughs) Believe me, when the time comes, I want the works when it comes to care.

Psychologist: But did everything go OK?

Mother: Well, there was this Dr. Wisekoff that I never liked, and he said all kinds of doom and gloom things, but I told my husband I was the one who had the baby and I was the one who ought to know, so my husband got into this big fight and didn't pay the bill for a whole year, and the doctor threatened to hire one of these collection agencies, and what that was all about don't ask me—just don't ask me.

Psychologist: I see, but I'm still not sure . . .

Mother: (interrupting) But that's just what I mean.

Later the psychologist, who was just beginning his clinical internship, told his supervisor that he wanted to shake the mother and yell at the top of his lungs: "But was the delivery difficult or easy!" One can only imagine how difficult it would be for a child to grow up surrounded by such diffuseness, accompanied by a total obliviousness to the diffuseness itself.

Like amorphous thinking, fragmented thinking can be traced to parental communication. In this case, parental communication is marked by digression from topic to topic, non sequitur reasoning, and extraneous, illogical, or contradictory comments. In fragmented thinking itself, attention can be focused for brief moments, but bits and pieces of memories become intermixed with current stimuli. The technical name for this abrupt shift from one topic to another is *overinclusive* thinking (Singer, Wynne, and Toohey, 1979).

Wynne delineates other faults in the family structure. The family members cannot maintain an appropriate psychological distance, detached impersonality unpredictably alternating with highly personal remarks and confrontations. However, there is a concerted effort to act as if there were a strong sense of unity, which results in what Wynne calls *pseudo-mutuality.* There are great pressures to maintain a facade of harmony, the child being allowed neither to deviate from nor to question a prescribed role. Beneath this facade lie pervasive feelings of futility and meaninglessness.

Our final theorist, Theodore Lidz, deals less in terms of total family structure than Wynne and more in terms of *roles and functions.* In the healthy family, maternal and paternal roles are clearly delineated as are generational or parent-child roles, while parents transmit to their children useful ways of adapting to the demands of society. There is also role reciprocity which requires the acceptance of each member's role, values, and goals.

In the family with a schizophrenic child, roles are blurred and parents use children to serve their own egocentric needs. Lidz delineated two kinds of distorted patterns. In the *skewed family,* more commonly found with schizophrenic boys than girls, the mother is overprotective, intrusive, dominating, and seductive, while the father is passive and weak. Because of her tenuous emotional equilibrium, the mother perceives events according to her own needs and insists that her son do likewise. The adolescent boy becomes increasingly fearful of being engulfed by his mother but moves toward autonomy produce unbearable guilt. In the *schismatic family*, more characteristic of schizophrenic girls than boys, there is continuing overt conflict between the parents, each depreciating the other to their children and often competing for the children's loyalty. The mother has little self-esteem or security and is constantly being undermined by her husband's contempt; the father is insecure in his masculinity, is in constant need of admiration, and uses domination as a substitute for strength of character. Disappointed in his wife, the father turns to his daughter to fill his emotional needs. His behavior may be highly inconsistent, alternating between tyrannical tempers and seductiveness or even maternal tenderness. The daughter is caught in a bind, since pleasing one parent alienates the other. The mother, who disparages herself, is a poor model of mature femininity, while the father, who disparages women, is an equally poor model of adult masculinity.

Research   A fifteen-year follow-up study was done on sixty-four families with mild to moderately disturbed adolescents. The families were evaluated in terms of Lyman Wynne's concept of *communication deviance* (CD) and *affective style* (AS), or *expressed emotion* (EE), both of which include personal criticism, guilt induction, and excessive intrusiveness without strong positive support. The incidence of schizophrenia or schizophrenic spectrum disorders was highest in families classified as CD fifteen years earlier. In fact, there were no cases of schizophrenia in low-CD families. Adding a measure of affective climate (AS or EE) increased the ability to correctly identify cases

likely to manifest schizophrenia or schizophrenia spectrum disorders (see Goldstein, 1990).

The research results make sense in terms of what we know about the basic symptoms of schizophrenia. Communication deviance may be an important factor undermining the adolescent's ability to think coherently and realistically; the expression of negative emotions may contribute to social isolation by making social interactions noxious (see Weiner, 1992).

Other objective studies confirm the general importance of the family, although not the specific patterns described by clinical observations. (Our presentation follows Goldstein, 1990.) The clearest evidence for the family's *etiological* role comes from a Finnish study (Tienari et al., 1983) in which ninety-two children of schizophrenic and nondisturbed mothers were adopted into healthy and disturbed family environments. All the children who subsequently became schizophrenic were in the schizophrenic-mother, disturbed-family group. However, schizophrenia was not totally determined by the family environment, since it did not develop in the disturbed families that adopted children of nondisturbed mothers. Thus, schizophrenia may result when a genetically vulnerable child is reared in an uncongenial family environment. There is also evidence that the family plays a role in *relapse* after treatment, particularly negative maternal overinvolvement and an oppositional response on the adolescent's part to parental criticism. Finally, intervention aimed at moderating negative family interactions reduces relapse more than individually oriented intervention.

The Organic Context

There is no doubt that *genetic* factors play an etiologic role in schizophrenia. However, the modest concordance rate of 25 to 30 percent between monozygotic twins means that other, nonhereditary factors are also relevant; for example, as many as 75 percent of monozygotic pairs include only one schizophrenic member. (See Walker et al., 1991, for a critical examination of the research.) The most prevalent conceptualization of the relation between heredity and environment is the *diathesis-stress hypothesis*, which states that only a predisposition to schizophrenia is inherited, not the disturbance itself; its actual appearance is contingent upon the kind and amount of environmental stress the individual encounters.

In regard to other organic variables, autonomic studies, typically involving electrodermal hyperresponsiveness, have generally failed to differentiate children at risk for schizophrenia. Low levels of platelet monoamine oxidase (MAO) have also been investigated. MAO is a major agent in the breakdown of biologic amines, including the neurotransmitter dopamine, and high levels of dopamine have been implicated in the etiology of schizophrenia. However, low MAO is related to a number of disturbances; it does not seem to be specific to schizophrenia. (For details concerning these findings, see Ledingham, 1990.)

In regard to *brain structure,* there is evidence of ventricular enlargement, cortical atrophy, and hippocampal cell disarray from autopsy studies of brains of schizophrenic patients, but such abnormalities are associated with a variety of disturbances. Thus there is no strong evidence supporting the role of any particular brain structure or neurotransmitter abnormality that is specific to adolescent schizophrenia (Walker et al., 1991).

Evaluation

Prospective studies of populations at risk for schizophrenia may well be the most admirable in child psychopathology in terms of implementing sophisticated research designs over considerable periods of time. However, while much has been learned about severe disturbances in general, comparatively little has been learned about specific etiological agents. (See Ledingham, 1990, for different possible models relating general to specific etiological agents.) Even the few differentiating variables are difficult to relate to the defining characteristics of schizophrenia itself. For example, clumsiness suggests neurodevelopmental immaturity, attention deficit suggests difficulties in processing information, and both the variability of IQ scores over time and the "stormy" personality characteristics suggest general instability, but it is not at all clear how these produce the cognitive and affective behaviors unique to schizophrenia.

Moreover, it is impossible to place the findings in a meaningful *developmental* context. Rather, the conceptualizations of various investigators present a picture that is fragmented—to borrow a term from the description of schizophrenia itself. Using Piaget's stages of egocentric thinking, Lidz proposes a regression model to account for certain thought disorders. On the other hand, data showing preschizophrenics to be emotionally immature in middle childhood suggest fixation rather than regression. Aspects of family theory, along with learning theory, suggest that bizarre patterns of thinking are modeled on parental behavior and need not represent fixations or regressions. Finally, conceptualizing schizophrenia as a solution to an intolerable situation suggests that it might be a new development unrelated to the past; for example, the decision to shatter communication and obscure one's self-definition may have no counterpart in normal or preschizophrenic development.

Integrative Models

To maintain that many kinds of deviations are involved in a disturbance as severe as schizophrenia is probably correct, but too general. The challenge is to come to grips with specifics and to narrow down possible etiologies to necessary and sufficient ones. While the challenge is far from being met, there are a few models from diverse sources—longitudinal data, statistical analyses, and conceptualization of research findings.

The Danish Study   Mednick, who pioneered at-risk prospective research with his so-called Danish study, has integrated the various factors in the organic, intrapersonal and interpersonal contexts that increase the chances of developing schizophrenia spectrum disorders. (Our presentation follows Cannon, Barr, and Mednick, 1991.) First, the *genetic predisposition* to schizophrenia disrupts fetal brain development. CT scans of high-risk subjects have revealed two separate conditions: multisite neural developmental deficits and periventricular damage reflected in enlargement of the third and lateral ventricles. Prenatal and perinatal *environmental events,* such as contracting influenza in the second trimester of gestation, can similarly disrupt fetal neurological development. Delivery complications can also produce ventricular damage and increase the risk for schizophrenia spectrum disorders in infants with an especially high genetic risk (both parents are schizophrenic). Thus, there is a genetic-perinatal determination of ventricular damage. Among *postnatal environmental variables,* separation from parents and institutionalization increase the likelihood of schizophrenia in high-risk, but not low-risk, groups. Furthermore, while negative affective style and communication deviance in families predict schizophrenia spectrum disorders in general, the more severe forms of family instability represented by separation and institutionalization are unique to producing schizophrenia.

The authors have further analyzed their data in terms of schizophrenics with positive and negative symptoms. Enlarged third ventricles damage the diencephalic and limbic structures involved in excitatory autonomic functioning. The resulting reduction in autonomic responsiveness contributes to schizo-

phrenia characterized by negative symptoms. High-risk subjects who have normal births but unstable early families and who also have genetically determined high levels of autonomic reactivity in adolescence tend to develop schizophrenia with positive symptoms.

Mednick's synthesis is not without its problems. His study includes only seven active and eight passive subjects, and as we have seen, other studies have failed to find a relation between autonomic nervous system arousal and schizophrenia. However, the study does serve as a model for integrating variables in terms of their predictive power and for differentiating crucial from peripheral ones.

Statistical Techniques   Statistical techniques can also integrate variables, although such analyses are few and have been done only for psychosocial variables. In descending order of predictive importance the variables are: lack of goal directedness and poor identity; anxiety; interpersonal difficulties evidenced by undependability and social isolation; self-directed anger or inexplicable outbursts; low competence evidenced by developmental delays, poor school work and a lack of self-confidence; and, finally, distractibility, daydreaming and tangential thinking (Watt and Saiz, 1991).

One reason for the failure to find differences between schizophrenic and other severely disturbed populations may be that only single variables have typically been studied. When constellations of variables are used, such as poor motor development, high intraindividual variability on cognitive tasks, social withdrawal, emotional flatness, irritability, and emotional instability, children of schizophrenics can more readily be distinguished from both normal and other disturbed populations (see Ledingham, 1990, for examples). Thus, high risk may be a matter of the *patterning* of risk variables.

Conceptual Integration   Note how many variables in the statistical analyses concern lacks or deficiencies. In a similar vein but at a conceptual level, Watt and Saiz (1991) epitomize the findings concerning schizophrenic thinking in terms of *"passivising,"* which is evidenced in may ways. There is the weakness of sustained effort and attention, as if the schizophrenic cannot summon the mental energy necessary for organized thought; there is helplessness and a sense of being the passive recipient of environmental events; there is the failure to sustain the more demanding kinds of cognition, such as abstract thinking and complex learning. Ironically, there is evidence that flatness of affect, which seems congruent with the notion of passivity, is more potent in differentiating schizophrenia from other severe disturbances and more stable and predictive of schizophrenia than thinking disorders (Knight and Roff, 1985). Yet flat affect is rarely studied, perhaps because of assessment difficulties, perhaps because of the strong cognitive bias in current research. If Watt and Saiz are correct, then the basic defect in schizophrenia is a motivational one. In terms of our variables, passivizing represents an extreme deficiency in initiative.

On the Other Hand . . .

The overarching assumption in all the research so far is that adolescent schizophrenia has its roots in earlier developmental periods. Certain investigators have challenged this assumption on empirical and conceptual grounds.

After reviewing the results of follow-up, follow-back, and high-risk studies, Hanson, Gottesman, and Heston (1990) conclude that none of them establish a causal relation between the resulting variables and schizophrenia. They also maintain that the variables are related to disturbance in general, while genetic data are schizophrenia-specific.

Conceptually, according to Hanson and colleagues, researchers make the mistake of thinking linearly ("puppies become dogs") in-

stead of nonlinearly ("caterpillars become moths, but one will search in vain for embryonic wings on them"). Specifically, genetic events happen in adolescence that have little or no relation to prior development. Here the authors use a term we have not encountered since our discussion of autism: they state that schizophrenia is a *qualitatively* different disorder. However, they use the term to denote developmental discontinuity rather than behavior that has little or no counterpart in normal development (Chapter 4). Whether the latter is true of schizophrenia remains to be seen.

In a similar vein, Pogue-Geile (1991), drawing upon developmental behavior genetics, postulates that a defect in genes controlling postpubertal brain development plays the crucial role in causing schizophrenia. Thus, abnormalities in genetically controlled brain development during adolescence are the key etiological agent. The early obstetrical complications and insults to the organism that experts like Mednick regard as causal, do nothing more than increase the probability that the genetic abnormalities will produce clinical symptoms. They are basically ancillary and nonspecific. In sum, the relation between early and late specific and nonspecific causes is reversed. However, it is not clear how researchers who emphasize genetically defective programs in adolescence would account for childhood schizophrenia.

As for our own quest for models, we are left with two plausible but irreconcilable ones—the continuous and the discontinuous—with no data that could help us decide between them.

Summary of Findings

We will now summarize the major findings concerning child and adolescent schizophrenia. First, we learned that the clinical picture for adults, adolescents, and children is basically the same—hallucinations, delusions, and thinking disorders in the cognitive realm, along with flat and inappropriate affect. However, as we shall see when we discuss treatment, the middle-childhood schizophrenic does not respond as well to neuroleptics as do adolescents and adults, suggesting differences at the organic level which may have some yet to be discovered reverberations at the behavioral level. We also learned that many of the predictors at both levels are not unique to schizophrenia but are found in other severe deviations as well. This may mean that there are large areas of overlap among the disturbances, and teasing out the differentiating variables has eluded researchers so far; or it may mean that the variables are the same but the patterning is different and has different developmental trajectories.

In order to juxtapose specific findings we will collapse comparable variables into two periods—0 to 5 years and 6 to 15 years. If one interprets the data in general rather than specific terms, one is struck by the similarity of childhood-onset schizophrenia (COS) and adolescent-onset schizophrenia (AOS). (See Table 10.2.) In the 0-to-5-year period both have lags in motor development. Speech is difficult to compare because of lack of comparable data. The deviant and delayed speech of COS, which includes making up words, is juxtaposed to the more general deficiency in communicative competence of AOS. In the personality and social realm, the constellation of autistic and "hyper" with peers of COS corresponds to the constellation of isolated from mother and active/anxious with others of AOS. The labile mood of COS may have its counterpart in increased psychological disturbance in AOS. Mothers in the AOS group are uninvolved and hostile in their caregiving, but comparable data on the COS group are lacking.

Turning to the middle-childhood and adolescent period, motor delays and deviations are present in both groups. Both groups also have attention defects. Those with AOS exhibit poor sustained attention owing to low perceptual sensitivity and distractibility which emerges in adolescence; the group with COS has short span of attention, distractibility, and attentional drift. There is no evidence as to whether the increased variability in IQ over time evident in AOS also characterizes the COS group. In the personality and social area the moodiness and extreme lability found in COS is similar to the "stormy" picture of withdrawal coupled with aggression and disruptive behavior in AOS. The family interaction in both groups is characterized by communication deviance, to which the AOS group adds a negative affective style and a negatively involved child.

It may be that this summary strives too hard for consistency. If we could examine the actual data, it might turn out that "delayed and deviant speech" is different from "deficient communication." The comparisons are also limited to variables shared by both groups. The provisional nature of many of the findings themselves adds a final note of caution concerning the similarity of the two groups.

Ironically, the very consistency of our summary makes it impossible to answer our developmental question: Why are there two different points of origin? The hope is that future research will provide more comprehensive and more directly comparable data, which, in turn, will reveal differentiating deviations and protective factors that fit a developmental pattern.

Developmental Models

We have already encountered most of the developmental models used to account for research findings on schizophrenia. Developmental *lag* is the primary model of deviation mentioned in or implied by the research data. Others include the *deficiency* model, which un-

TABLE 10.2
Childhood and Adolescent Onset Schizophrenia Compared

	Childhood onset (COS)		Adolescent onset (AOS)
Age 0–5			
Motor development	Deviant; delayed	=	Lag
Speech	Delayed; deviant (makes up words)	=?	Deficient communication
Personal/Social	"Autistic"; unresponsive	=?	Affectively flat; isolated from mother
	"Hyper" with peers	=?	Active, anxious, angry with others
	Labile mood	=?	More disturbed
Age 6–15			
Motor development	Delayed, deficient	=	Delayed, impaired
Personality	Moody, extreme lability	=?	"Stormy" internalizing, externalizing behaviors
Cognitive	Distractible; short attention span	=	Distractible; sustained attention difficulties
Family	Communication deviance	=	Communication deviance

=   same behaviors in both groups.
=?   behaviors possibly the same in both groups.

derlies passivizing, and the disjointed or *asynchronous* development of infancy.

However, the data also present us with two new phenomena. Deviant motor development such as awkwardness and lack of coordination is found from infancy to adolescence. This means that we have come across a *nondevelopmental* variable. It also means that the developmental approach does not require that all variables change over time; rather, both changing and unchanging variables must be discovered and considered. Motor deviancy, for example, may result from a central nervous system dysfunction, which, since it is not directly subject to social pressures, remains relatively unchanged.

The next new model of psychopathology is *developmental discontinuity*, in which the pres-

ent clinical picture bears little or no relation to the past. In adolescent-onset schizophrenia, a genetic malfunctioning deflects the developmental trajectory and sends it off in a completely new direction. Whether the resulting behavior is qualitatively different, in that it has little or no counterpart in normal adolescent behavior, is a separate issue to be studied in its own right.

Treatment

The treatment of choice with adults is antipsychotic *medication*, the effectiveness of neuroleptics having been well established. Neuroleptics are a family of drugs that block postsynaptic receptor cells for dopamine, noradrenaline, and acetylcholine, so less is available to the brain. The drugs are effective both with withdrawn, retarded, uncommunicative adult schizophrenics and with agitated, excited, overactive ones. Therefore they are not tranquilizers, as was originally thought, but may affect an underlying defect common to both types of patients. Despite the success of neuroleptics with adults, well-controlled studies of children are rare. The evidence indicates that adolescents respond like adults but, for some unknown reason, neuroleptics are less effective with childhood schizophrenics. Many other medications have been tried, among them antidepressants, hallucinogens, lithium, megavitamin therapy, and stimulants, but their efficacy has not been established (Campbell and Spencer, 1988).

Weiner (1992) describes a program of *individual psychotherapy* aimed at counteracting the social isolation and impaired reality contact of the schizophrenic through relationship building and reality testing. The first involves a combination of warmth and nurturance for those who have been deprived of love and firmness without anger or punitiveness for those who cannot control their aggressive acting out. The therapist indicates that delusions and hallucinations, while real to the patient, are not real to the therapist. The next step involves identifying the needs giving rise to the cognitive distortions and dealing constructively with them. At a more practical level, the therapist helps the patient develop more effective social skills so as to counter social isolation.

Weiner also says that it is essential to involve the family in the treatment process in order to help them correct any of the communication and affective patterns which, as we have seen, can be preludes to a relapse. Finally, support from individuals outside the family, such as teachers or coaches, is enlisted.

Behavior therapy involves reinforcing adaptive responses, such as realistic thinking, and weakening maladaptive ones, such as delusions, by not reinforcing them. Behavior therapists use social skills training to help the schizophrenic overcome social isolation. Finally, *educational* and *milieu* therapy have been used either alone or in combination with other therapeutic approaches.

Well-designed studies of effectiveness are rare, so it is impossible to evaluate different therapeutic approaches or to decide whether there is a treatment of choice.

As we have noted, investigators have paid little attention to the developmental dimension in schizophrenia so our questions, Why childhood? and Why adolescence? have gone unanswered. By contrast, the psychopathologies we will next discuss—substance abuse and eating disorders—are closely tied in to the developments characterizing the adolescent period. In addition we will discuss homosexual identity which, while not a psychopathology, increases the risk that the adolescent will experience greater distress and have more problems than his or her heterosexual counterpart. The theme of risk itself will recur later on when we take up the risks of deviations from organic intactness, of maltreatment, and of divorce.

CHAPTER 11

PSYCHOPATHOLOGIES AND RISKS OF THE ADOLESCENT TRANSITION

Adolescence marks the transition from childhood to adulthood. The body itself sets the stage with physical changes more rapid than those of any other developmental period except infancy, with hormonal changes during puberty, and with the advent of adult sexuality. (See Rutter, 1979a.) Society follows suit by requiring the adolescent to relinquish dependence on the family and assume responsibility for making decisions regarding those dual foci of adulthood, love and work. The transition is facilitated by the increasingly important role peer relations play and by the newfound cognitive sophistication that enables the adolescent both to envision future possibilities and to expand the situation-specific self-examination of middle childhood into the overarching question, Who am I?

Traditionally, the adolescent transition has been viewed as one of turmoil, the inherent instability of the period being epitomized by G. Stanley Hall's phrase "storm and stress," coined in his classic turn-of-the-century study. Psychoanalysts, in a similar vein, characterize the period as marking the return of primitive impulses and unresolved conflicts from the early stages of psychosexual development while, according to Erikson, a weakened ego struggles to master an identity crisis and role diffusion. As if this were not enough, the more recent literature emphasizes the distress brought about by the generation gap and by alienation.

However, it is becoming increasingly clear that the image of adolescent turmoil is applicable primarily to the more visible and the more disturbed minority of adolescents. Most adolescents make the transition without significant emotional problems. While peer relations deepen and bickering with parents over everyday issues such as clothing and hair-style increases, the parent-adolescent relationship is generally harmonious, lines of communication remain open, and adolescents continue to share parental values and to turn to parents for guidance on matters of major concern. In a like manner, the search for identity goes on unaccompanied by crises, although there may be an increased anxiety about the future.

The revised picture should not be taken to mean that adolescence is uniformly serene. Moodiness, depression, and self-depreciation reach a peak in adolescence, even though such feelings characterize only a minority of this age group. Certain psychopathologies also show a sharp rise in adolescence: suicide and suicide attempts, alcoholism, drug abuse, schizophrenia, anorexia nervosa, and depression. Although the overall rate of psychopathology increases only slightly since other disturbances are on the decline, the new disturbances are far more serious than the ones they replace, making the overall picture an ominous one.

Erikson's concept of *identity* integrates many of the diverse strands of adolescent transition as well as providing specific leads as to assets and liabilities. (For a summary of research on identity, see Marcia, 1980, 1991.) Identity involves both inner continuity and interpersonal mutuality. It is a coming to terms with oneself and finding one's place in society. Adolescence is marked by an identity crisis because it is a "necessary turning point, a crucial moment" (Erikson, 1968, p. 16), in which the adolescent mind must master the tripartite challenge of finding a fulfilling vocation, sexual role, and ideology, or risk stagnation and regression.

The adolescent faces the task of achieving an identity with the accumulated resources and vulnerabilities from the past—trust, autonomy, initiative, and industry on the positive side; mistrust, shame, doubt, guilt, and inferiority on the negative side. Cognitively the adolescent is capable of a more sophisticated level of self-exploration and a more realistic grasp of the options that society offers, so choices and decisions now have an air of commitment, of "playing for keeps," which was absent from middle childhood.

Adolescence engages and gives special meaning to many of the personality variables we have been using. Initiative propels the forward thrust toward adulthood, and control allows for experimenting with new experiences while avoiding the extremes of inhibition and impulsivity. The intimacy of attachment merges with the sexual drive, and social relations with peers take on a new importance. In the realm of work, vocational choice becomes a realistic concern. Because of physiological changes, the psychological representation of the body, or the body image, is more salient than it has been since the early years. Finally, increased cognitive sophistication allows the adolescent both to entertain hypothetical possibilities and to ask abstract questions concerning the self and its future: Who am I? Where am I going?

The two psychopathologies we will discuss represent different ways in which the variables can go awry. In the anorectic or bulimic adolescent's relentless pursuit of thinness, the body image becomes a destructive tyrant, while the self-defeating need for autonomy is reminiscent of the oppositional behavior of the toddler period. In substance abuse, initiative propels the adolescent into assuming adult responsibilities in the areas of intimacy and work for which he or she is ill prepared. We will also discuss homosexual identity, which, while not a psychopathology, can be a source of distress for adolescents whose sexual identity deviates from society's standards of what is natural, acceptable, and moral.

ANOREXIA NERVOSA

Anorexia is a voluntary pursuit of thinness to the point of extreme emaciation or even death. It occurs primarily, but not exclusively, in adolescent females. However, anorectics use two different means of achieving thinness. The first group relies solely on strict dieting and are called *restricting type* or *restricters*. The second group, which alternates between dieting and binge eating followed by self-induced vomiting or purging, are called *bulimic type* or *bulimics*. To further complicate matters, there is also a group of adolescents who have a pattern of frequent binge eating followed by vomiting or purging, but who have normal weight or may even be overweight. This kind of eating disorder, which is separate from anorexia nervosa, is called *bulimia nervosa*. Thus there are restricters and bulimics within the population

of anorectics, and there is a separate category for bulimia (Schlundt and Johnson, 1990).

While the DSM-IV Draft Criteria (APA, 1993) recommends anorexia nervosa be divided into the restricting type and the binge eating/purging type, we prefer the designations in the above paragraph.

Description

Anorexia nervosa is a voluntary restriction of food and an active pursuit of thinness, usually with pride in control over eating. As a result, there is at least a 15 percent loss of body weight without organic cause. Anorectics have a normal awareness of hunger but are terrified of giving in to the impulse to eat. There is also evidence that their perception of satiety may be distorted because they report feeling bloated or nauseated after eating small amounts of food (Garfinkel and Garner, 1986). The startling feature is that, unlike in ordinary dieting, the individual wastes away to a dangerous state of emaciation in pursuit of some ideal image of thinness. As the condition advances, diets become increasingly restrictive; one girl would eat only two chicken livers a day, another ate only celery sticks and chewing gum for a year before her death (Bruch, 1973). In fact, anorexia nervosa is one of the few psychopathologies that can lead to death; studies have reported a fatality rate varying between 3 and 21 percent (Leon and Dinklage, 1989).

Among the secondary symptoms of anorexia nervosa, excessive activity is one of the most common. At times the intensity of the activity is masked by its socially acceptable form, such as doing homework or participating in sports; but an activity such as running up and down the driveway until exhausted or literally walking around in circles has a deviant quality. (Yates, 1989, reviews studies relating hunger and activity.) Amenorrhea is another common secondary symptom, menstruation often ceasing prior to weight loss.

Peak periods of onset are ages 14 and 18. While predominantly a disorder of females, 5 to 15 percent of anorectics are male (Leon and Dinklage, 1989). Among females the *prevalence* is estimated to be 1 in 100. It is most common among high-achieving high school students (Yates, 1989). There is evidence that anorexia nervosa is increasing, especially in industrialized societies. While it is most prevalent in white middle- and upper-class adolescents, it is found in all social classes and also among African Americans and Latinos (Pate et al., 1992).

Outcome is varied. For some, anorexia nervosa is a single, relatively mild disturbance, while for others, it is the beginning of a lifelong disorder. Follow-up studies show that 40 percent of anorectics totally recover, and 30 percent are considerably improved. However, 20 percent are unimproved or seriously impaired by depression, social phobias, or recurrent symptoms. Early onset (i.e., before 16 years of age) is associated with a favorable prognosis, while chronicity, pronounced family difficulties, and poor vocational adjustment are associated with a poor outcome (Leon and Phelan, 1985). While it was originally thought that bulimics had a poorer prognosis than restricters, it now seems there is no significant difference in the prognosis except that bulimics have more substance disorders (drug use and abuse) than restricters (Toner, Garfinkel, and Garner, 1986).

One final point: Research on anorectics is complicated by the fact that starvation per se significantly affects behavior, producing depression, irritability, social isolation, decreased sexual interest, and amenorrhea. Starvation can also significantly alter family interactions as members are helpless to alter eating patterns that produce striking emaciation and might eventuate in death. Thus the problem of distinguishing causes from consequences is a knotty one here, as it is in all severe disturbances.

Comorbidity Depression is present in both the anorectic adolescent and the family. One study of anorexia nervosa subjects found a comorbidity of 73 percent (Herzog et al., 1992). Such high comorbidity led to the speculation that the eating disorder and depression share a common etiology. However, subsequent research indicated that, while they occur together, they are independent disturbances: e.g., improvement in an eating disorder does not necessarily relieve the depression. Also, it is important to distinguish depression as a psychopathology from the depressed mood that accompanies any form of starvation.

While there have been reports of a high incidence of prior sexual abuse, many of the studies are methodologically flawed. The correlation may in fact exist because childhood sexual abuse and eating disorders have a high base rate in female clinical populations (Lask and Bryant-Waugh, 1992).

Etiology: A Multidimensional Model

Recognizing that anorexia nervosa is not due to a single cause but is the result of multiple factors, Garfinkel and Garner (1982) devised a multidimensional model of predisposing, precipitating, and sustaining factors. Intrapersonal predisposing factors include being female, lack of a sense of mastery and autonomy, maturational fears, conscientiousness and conformity, early feeding difficulties, rigid thinking, and physiological dysfunctions. Interpersonal factors include parents who emphasize achievement and fitness or who are conflicted, depressed, and impulsive. Superordinate factors include society's emphasis on thinness and the middle- and upper-class pressure for achievement. Precipitating factors include perceived loss of self-esteem and self-control (for example, through social or academic failure), new and unfamiliar situations, especially sexual intimacy, separation, or loss. We will now examine these factors in detail.

The Organic Context   There is evidence of a *genetic* component in anorexia nervosa; one study, for example, found that the concordance for dizygotic twins was 5 percent, while it was 56 percent for monozygotic twins. The exact mechanism of transmission is not known, nor has the relative contribution of environment been clarified. Numerous *biological correlates* of anorexia nervosa have also been studied but most appear to be secondary to weight loss and are reversible with weight gain. The search for a primary hypothalamic disorder has not been successful to date. (For a more detailed presentation of the organic context, see Lask and Bryant-Waugh, 1992.)

The Intrapersonal Context: The Body Image   Along with menarche and breast development in female puberty there is a "fat spurt," or an accumulation of large quantities of fat in subcutaneous tissue which adds an average of 24 pounds of weight. However, as we pointed out in Chapter 1, there is a distinction between the physiological body and the psychological representation of the body or the body image. It is the psychological reaction to the physiological change that interests us. (Our presentation follows Attie, Brooks-Gunn, and Petersen, 1990.)

To begin with, in normal female populations, there is evidence that dieting is associated with the above-mentioned pubertal changes independent of age. More important, such changes force the adolescent to make a fundamental reorganization of her body image, which—coupled with her increased capacity for self-reflection—may result in a preoccupation with her body self and with the responses of others to it. Adolescents who perceive themselves as underweight are most satisfied with their body image, followed by those who think they are simply average. Interestingly, body image is more predictive of dieting than maturational status and weight—a nice illustration of the importance of distinguishing the physical body from its psychological representation.

Psychological factors are also important in regulating eating behavior. Adherence to a diet is cognitively controlled, often in terms of quotas on food intake. Moreover, chronic dieters are vulnerable to "counterregulatory" eating, or binging on high-calorie food; for example, the mere belief that one has transgressed one's diet can break the dieter's resolve and trigger increased food consumption. Anxiety and depression can have a similar disinhibiting influence. Such findings on normal populations are relevant to the binge eating of the bulimic.

There are similarities and differences between weight-preoccupied chronic dieters and anorectics. Faust (1987) found that 11- to 14-year-old girls with a strong drive for thinness were like anorectic adolescents in their body dissatisfaction, relative insensitivity to hunger cues and depression, but they did not have the anorectic's feelings of ineffectiveness, perfectionism, and dependence nor did they perceive the family as conflicted or enmeshed.

Finally Bruch (1973), on the basis of clinical observations, claims that girls with anorexia nervosa literally do not *perceive* how thin their bodies have become. One patient had difficulty discriminating between two photographs of herself even though there was a 70-pound difference in her weight. Another said she could see how emaciated her body was when looking in a mirror, but when she looked away she reverted to her belief that she was larger. Thus the image of the body, which is a reasonably accurate psychological construction in normal development, borders on a somatic delusion in the anorectic. Perception is determined not by reality but by deeply felt needs. According to Bruch, the anorectic's vain pursuit of self-respect through food refusal is expressed in the vain pursuit of a body which literally is never perceived as sufficiently thin.

Bruch's hypothesis concerning a perceptual disturbance in body size has had a checkered history. On the positive side, Brown, Cash, and Lewis (1989), who compared 114 anorectic and normal adolescents matched for age, height, and weight, found that the former group distorted body size as heavier than did the control group regardless of weight. There is also evidence that persistent body image distortion predicts a poor response to treatment. However, on the nonconfirmatory side, studies show that overestimation of body size in normal women is related to lower self-esteem and, again in non–eating-disordered women, overestimation increases as weight deviates from normal. (See Yates, 1989, for a more comprehensive review of objective studies.) We can conclude that there is no evidence that perceptual distortion of the body image plays the crucial role Bruch assigns it. However, it cannot be dismissed as irrelevant since it does seem to be one of the ingredients in the total mix of characteristics.

The Interpersonal Context: Other Variables   There is evidence that young children who have digestive problems and are picky eaters may become anorectics in adolescence, suggesting a tendency for eating to become involved in psychological problems (Marchi and Cohen, 1990). Obsessive traits are often found, both restricters and bulimics being chronically preoccupied with counting calories and images of food.

Anorectics are reluctant to form close relationships outside the family, thereby isolating themselves from the important growth-promoting functions of peer relations in the adolescent period. Sexual relations, in particular, are avoided; Leon et al. (1985) found that both restricters and bulimics had a markedly negative evaluation of sex and lacked interest in sexual relations. While a decline in sexual interest is found in normal individuals who are starving, the negative evaluation is not typical. Even in treated anorectics, sexual aversions and fears remain in 20 percent of the population. Social problems also tend to persist in a number of recovered anorectics.

While both groups of anorectics are united by their pursuit of thinness, restricters tend to be conforming, reliable, socially insecure, obsessional, and both inflexible and nonpsychological in their thinking. Bulimics, who comprise about half the population of anorectics, are more extroverted and sociable but are more unstable and feel hunger more intensely. They tend to have problems with impulse control, such as stealing and substance abuse. While socially more skillful than restricters, their relations tend to be brief, superficial, and troubled. Their families also tend to be more unstable than those of restricters; there is more discord, maternal depression, paternal depression and impulsivity, and substance abuse.

In their study of fifty hospitalized women with anorexia nervosa, for example, Casper, Hedeker, and McClough (1992) found that restricters had an increase in self-control, self-discipline, inhibition of emotionality, and conscientiousness. By contrast, bulimic patients were more impulsive (although still in the normal range), and while they shared the restricters' belief in moral family values, were emotionally more adventurous and had more characterological problems.

There may also be a prior history of obesity in the adolescent and the family. In fact, there is speculation that the bulimic's constitutional bias toward obesity makes weight loss difficult, the constant vulnerability to breakthroughs of uncontrolled binge eating subjecting them to greater psychological distress than that experienced by the excessively controlled restricters. (For a detailed presentation of personality factors, see Yates, 1989.)

The Superordinate Context: The Family   In the family approach, each member is seen as affecting and being affected by the behavior of every other member in a dynamic interplay of influences. Thus the basic task is that of understanding patterns of interaction and the ways in which such patterns enhance or impede growth. Minuchin and his coworkers (1975) describe four characteristic patterns of interaction in families of anorectic children.

1. *Enmeshment.* Members of the pathologically enmeshed family are highly involved and responsive to one another but in an intrusive way. They have no strong sense of individuality, so changes in one member or in the interaction of two members quickly reverberate throughout the entire family system. There is a lack of privacy, an exaggerated "togetherness." Minuchin and his group cite the example of a 15-year-old who complained that his mother always moved the furniture around when he was not at home—as if this were as much his business as hers. Enmeshed families have poorly differentiated perceptions of each other, and parents often speak of their children as a group. Roles and lines of authority are diffuse; children assume parental roles, or one parent enlists a child's support in struggles with the other parent.

2. *Overprotectiveness.* Family members of psychosomatically ill children are overly concerned for each other's welfare. A sneeze can set off "a flurry of handkerchief offers," criticism must be cushioned by pacifying behavior. The family's exaggerated concern for the ill child retards the development of autonomy, and the child, in turn, feels responsible for protecting the family from distress.

3. *Rigidity.* Pathological families resist change. Particularly in periods of normal growth, such as adolescence, they intensify their efforts to retain their customary patterns. One consequence is that the child's illness is used as an excuse for avoiding problems accompanying change. Since attending to the child's illness diverts the family from facing conflicts, the illness is constantly reinforced.

4. *Lack of conflict resolution.* This final characteristic is the result of the first three, although its manifest forms differ. Some families deny conflict; others bicker in a diffuse, scattered, ineffectual way; some have a parent who is an avoider, such as a father who leaves the house every time a confrontation threatens. An honest facing up to conflicts is often bypassed by adherence to a strong religious or ethical code that provides a prefabricated answer to all interpersonal problems.

Minuchin enlarges our understanding of how the child's illness supports the entire network of family relationships. He also expands our understanding of the various roles the child may play within the family pattern. *Triangulation* puts the child in the distressing position of siding with one parent against the other in a parental disagreement. In a parent-child *coalition,* the child does side with one parent; for example, a girl might staunchly defend her mother's being incapacitated by "sick headaches" while the father taunts her for pampering herself and "putting on an act." In *detouring,* the parents escape their conflicts by regarding the sick child as their only problem. Some require the child to reassure them that they are indeed concerned only with her welfare; others alternate between concern and exasperation over the child who is such a "burden" and "does not try to help herself."

The family of the future anorectic is overly concerned with diet, food fads, and table manners. Their intrusiveness undermines the child's autonomy, and both her psychological and bodily functions are continually subject to scrutiny. Adolescence is a particularly stressful time for the family. The child, sensing the stress, responds with a behavior such as dieting, which is subsequently used as a detouring mechanism and is subtly reinforced by the family. As the symptom becomes enmeshed in the family pathology, it gradually escalates into a full-blown anorexia.

Humphrey's (1989) observational study of seventy-four families with anorexia, bulimic-anorexia, bulimia nervosa, and normal female adolescents, supports Minuchin. Parents of anorectic daughters communicated a double message of nurturant affection combined with neglect of the daughter's need to express herself and her feelings. The daughters, in turn, vacillated between discussing their feelings and submitting to their parents. The author speculates that too much nurturance in concert with ignoring and negating self-expression, undermines the daughter's effort to individuate and keeps her in a dependent state. Families of bulimics, by contrast, did not show much affection in their interactions but were hostilely enmeshed, with both parents and daughters blaming or controlling each other. Both mothers and daughters were also sulky and resentful of their interactions; the daughters' efforts to assert their individuality were undermined by their hostile submission.

On the other hand, there is evidence that the family pathology in anorexia is not unique, being found in families of children with other physical conditions such as asthma and diabetes (Minuchin, Rosman, and Baker, 1978). In addition, Yager (1982) warns against prematurely stereotyping families because of the diversity of family patterns and personality characteristics in anorectic adolescents. For example, some initially disorganized families become integrated and resourceful as the adolescent recovers, while others begin to show serious signs of maladjustment.

The Superordinate Context: Society　In our society the ideal of beauty has changed from the curvaceous, voluptuous figure popular a few decades ago to the lean, lithe, and svelte look of today. (Our presentation follows Striegel-Moore, Silberstein, and Rodin, 1986.) In addition, cultural norms dictate that fat is ugly and what is ugly is bad, while thin is beautiful and what is beautiful is good. Moreover, the message is more powerful in certain groups and settings: women of higher socioeconomic status who are concerned with current trends in beauty and fashion, colleges and boarding schools where beauty and dating are emphasized, professions such as dancing and modeling which dictate certain body weights—all are fertile breeding grounds for anorexia nervosa. In addition, there is evidence that beauty is central in the female sex-role stereotype, while being peripheral to the masculine sex role stereotype. There is even some evidence that eating small meals is associated with being feminine, while hearty eating is regarded as masculine.

The adolescent period is merely the culmination of lifelong acculturation since the family, the school, children's books, and the mass media all send the message that girls should be physically attractive. As early as the fourth grade, girls are more concerned than boys about becoming overweight, want to be thinner, and are generally dissatisfied with their perceived body image (Thelen et al., 1992).

Two other sex-linked forces are at work. By middle childhood, a girl's self-concept is related more to what others think of her than a boy's and thus is more interpersonal. Next, a girl's body image of being thin is related to her self-concept of feeling attractive, popular, and academically successful. In adolescence, the pubertal increase in fat, coupled with the social sensitivity and the intertwining of body image and self-esteem, is especially distressing and may well underlie adolescent girls' preoccupation with weight and dieting.

The above account of the adolescent's concern with thinness and dieting leaves unanswered the question why a selected few become anorectic or bulimic. The most obvious answer is that they have adopted the cultural stereotype of femininity to a greater degree than have other adolescent girls, but the evidence concerning this hypothesis is mixed. Consequently, Striegel-Moore, Silberstein, and Rodin (1986) state that there is not a single cause but a variety of risk factors. The girls may be genetically programmed to be heavier than the svelte ideal and, in the case of bulimic anorectics, also may feel hunger more intensely. These girls may begin puberty earlier, making them particularly unhappy with their weight. Personality characteristics may include an unusually strong need for social approval and immediate need gratification, poor impulse control, a tendency toward depression, and a fragile sense of self. (Gordon, 1990, discusses societal factors in detail.)

Speculative Integration

Attempts to integrate the findings within a developmental framework come primarily from the clinical literature and are therefore speculative. They are also addressed to restricters and ignore the superordinate context (Bruch, 1973; Sours, 1969).

The initial caretaking of the infant is marred by insensitivity, usually taking the form of intrusive overprotectiveness or excessive control. The result is a hostile-dependent relationship in which the exploited child cannot express her rage because of the fear that the mother will leave her alone and helpless. The damage during this early period is perpetuated by ingrained patterns of interaction which prevent the school-age child from correcting or compensating for it. The characteristic picture, surprisingly, is of attentive, concerned parents of a model child who is obedient, dependable, and considerate at home and a popular high-achiever at school. When one examines the picture more closely, however, one sees that the child is living out a

parental image of proper behavior which permeates every facet of her life—her physical appearance (thinness being especially valued), the food she eats, the clothes she wears, her friends, her activities. Any sign of resistance or self-assertion would result in painful self-recrimination. How could she go against the wishes of parents who are so obviously concerned about her welfare? Her own misery is either banished from consciousness or borne in silence.

Eventually, the child comes to think that her life and her self are not her own, and even her body is not her own. Gaining or losing weight, sickness or health are viewed not in terms of bodily pleasures and pains but in terms of pleasing or displeasing parents. Eating, in particular, has nothing to do with personal enjoyment but everything to do with parental preferences and values.

Adolescence, with its heightened sexual drive and its mandate to establish an independent identity, is shattering to the anorectic. She becomes increasingly preoccupied with restricting food intake and pursuing the unattainable goal of thinness. In part this is a desperate attempt to gain self-respect by achieving an idealized self-image. In part it is a caricature of autonomy in the form of controlling food intake. Note that the girl tries to resolve her problem by involving her body rather than directly confronting the people responsible for producing the problem. Yet as she continues to fast, she may well produce a belated control over her parents through their worried concern, their catering to her culinary eccentricities, their helplessness to change her. While the victory in the battle for control may finally be hers, it is won at the price of impoverishing her life and endangering her health.

Finally, anorexia nervosa illustrates self-destructive opposition, in contrast to healthy self-assertiveness (see Chapter 5). The anorectic's rejection of parental attempts to help are understandable. But therapists often encounter the same stubborn refusal both to eat and to cooperate. The resistance may be passive, such as taking two hours to eat a bowl of corn flakes and trying the therapist's patience to the limit, but it is, nonetheless, a powerful impediment to treatment.

BULIMIA NERVOSA

Bulimia nervosa was classified as a separate eating disorder in 1980, and so the clinical and research literature is limited. It is characterized by recurrent episodes of binge eating, or the rapid consumption of large quantities of food in a brief period of time, and repeated attempts to lose weight by severe dieting, self-induced vomiting, or the use of cathartics or diuretics. The typical picture is of a white female who begins overeating at about 18 years of age and begins purging by vomiting a year later. Although she may be either under- or overweight, her weight is often within the normal range. Her family history usually includes obesity or alcoholism. It is estimated that 4 percent of college females have bulimia nervosa (Yates, 1989). (For a review of the literature on bulimia, see Rodin, Striegel-Moore, and Silberstein, 1990.)

The adolescent with bulimia nervosa is preoccupied with thoughts of food, eating, and vomiting to the point that concentration on everyday matters is impaired. Johnson and Larson (1982), using an ingenious time-sampling method, found that bulimics spent less time socializing and more time alone than normal controls. As one of them remarked, "Food has become my closest companion." Binges include foods not allowed at other times—frequently ice cream, bread, candy, doughnuts, and soft drinks (Gandour, 1984). Ironically, adolescents with bulimia nervosa are terrified of losing control over eating. In their "all or none" way of thinking, even eating a small amount of a favorite food would result in a binge. In a less extreme form, they also share the anorectic's fear of becoming obese and perceive themselves as fat even when their body weight is normal. Thus the uncontrolled desire

Binge eating.

to gorge herself traps her between anxiety over anticipated loss of control and becoming obese, on the one hand, and guilt, shame, and self-contempt following a binge, on the other.

Personality Adolescents with bulimia nervosa present a different personality picture from that of the anorectic adolescent. (Except when noted, we follow Yates, 1989.) Their behavior is more extroverted, and they are more likely to abuse alcohol, to steal, to attempt suicide, and to be affectively unstable rather than depressed. Thus their behavior, like their eating pattern, suggests a basic difficulty in self-regulation. A history of pica (eating inedible substances such as sand, paint chips, and paper) in early childhood has also been interpreted as early evidence of indiscriminate eating (Marchi and Cohen, 1990).

Adolescents with bulimia nervosa are sensitive to rejection and are high achievers, the latter being channeled into their dogged pursuit of thinness. While guilt about sex is high in restricting anorectics, it is low in adolescents with bulimia nervosa who, in turn, are more sexually active than adolescents with noneating disorders. There is also suggestive evidence that, in spite of their greater frequency of sexual activity, these adolescents are less interested in sex and enjoy it less. (Coovert, Kinder, and Thompson, 1989, review the research on sexual behavior in eating disorders.) Finally, individuals with bulimia nervosa are likely to have a history of childhood maladjustment and to be alienated from their family. The family, in turn, is characterized by an increase in psychological disturbances and in maternal obesity.

A COMPARISON OF EATING DISORDERS

At a purely descriptive level, one is struck by the overlap among eating disorders. There is "pure" restricter anorexia, bulimia anorexia,

and "pure" bulimia nervosa. Is there some meaningful continuum here in terms of failures to regulate eating, and can this continuum be conceptualized in developmental terms? Neither question can be answered at present, although there are some relevant empirical data.

What little evidence there is suggests that the two groups of bulimics have more in common than the restricter and bulimic anorectic. Garner, Garfinkel, and O'Shaughnessy (1985) found that normal-weight bulimia nervosa adolescents and anorectic bulimics resemble each other in frequency, duration, and quality of food eaten during a binge episode, in the increase in impulse-related behavior and perceived family pathology, and in a predisposition to obesity. However, the normal-weight bulimia nervosa adolescents were more trusting than both types of anorectics. Finally, the three groups had a good deal in common. They all shared eating and weight-related disturbances such as a drive for thinness and an ideal body size lower than their actual one; they all had accompanying psychological problems, particularly depression, anxiety, and obsessiveness; and they all were equally perfectionistic and fearful of maturity while viewing themselves as ineffectual. While such data tentatively suggests that it might be more meaningful psychologically to regard anorectic bulimics as a special subgroup of bulimia nervosa rather than as a special subgroup of anorexia nervosa, more comparative studies must be done before the issue of classification can be solved (Schlundt and Johnson, 1990).

Table 11.1 summarizes the empirical findings concerning anorexia and bulimia nervosa.

TREATMENT

Anorectic adolescents are difficult to treat successfully. Half of them continue having eating difficulties and psychological impairment, and even recovered patients continue to have distorted attitudes toward eating and weight

TABLE 11.1
Summary of Eating Disorders

Anorexia nervosa		Bulimia nervosa
Voluntary food restrictions (PS)		Binging and efforts to lose weight (PS)
Active pursuit of thinness (PS)		Fears lack of control of eating (PS)
Weight loss of 15 percent (PS)		Normal weight
Excessive activity (SS)		
Amenorrhea (SS)		
Faulty perception of satiety		
Self image unduly influenced by body image	=	Self image unduly influenced by body image
Perceptual distortion of body	=?	Perceives self as too fat
Obsessive about food	=	Preoccupied with food
Problem eater as child		Pica as child Maladjusted, alienated as child
Depression		
Isolated from peers		
Negative view of or disinterest in sex		Sexually active but little enjoyment
Family: enmeshed; overprotective, rigid, no conflict resolution; nurturant but negates self-expression	=?	Family: enmeshed; hostile, increased psychological disturbance
Genetic component		Mother obese

Restricting	Bulimic		
	Binges	=	Binges
Conforming, overcontrolled	Unstable; poor impulse control	=	Unstable
Socially insecure	Socially skillful but superficial	=?	Extroverted; rejection-sensitive
Obsessive, inflexible thinking	Feels intense hunger History of obesity Predisposed to obesity	=	Predisposed to obesity

PS, primary symptom; SS, secondary symptom; =, equivalent characteristics; =?, possibly equivalent characteristics.
Note: All groups may share the same characteristics of perfectionism, increased psychological problems, and an ineffectual self-perception.

along with depression and unsatisfactory social relations. Thus there is a tendency toward chronicity even with long and intensive treatment. However, outcome varies considerably, good prognostic indicators being less immaturity and denial of illness, admission of hunger, overactivity, and positive self-esteem. Even those who do not improve can do well at school and in their job. The outlook for bulimia nervosa is more positive. While the disturbance may wax and wane, there is an overall trend toward improvement (Yates, 1990).

The multiple etiological theories of anorexia have spawned complementary treatment approaches. The only eating disorder for which *medication* has been effective is bulimia nervosa. Placebo-controlled studies show that various antidepressants can reduce the frequency of binging and vomiting. Although research was conducted on adults, adolescents were often included in the study samples (Gadow, 1992).

The goals of *individual psychotherapy* are to help the adolescent adopt a more realistic approach to eating, to focus upon and correct her feelings of inadequacy and need for perfection, and to achieve a feeling of self-esteem and autonomy. Because of the many ways in which the adolescent tries to undermine these treatment goals, therapists are usually advised to be sympathetic but firm in their approach. By the same token, nondirective approaches and classical psychoanalytic procedures for exploring unconscious motivations meet with little success.

Family therapies aim at restructuring family interactions in order to break the pattern of enmeshment and rigidity and enhance autonomy and flexibility. *Group therapy* may help the adolescent share her problems with others like herself while avoiding her fear that the therapist will be just another controlling adult like her parents. *Eclectic therapists* recommend a flexible use of many techniques depending on the needs of the individual.

While clinical reports of success abound, objective studies within and between different treatments are rare. A survey of ten studies of interventions for bulimia nervosa showed that the percentage of patients abstaining from binge eating and purging ranged from 15 to 90 percent; the wide range of outcomes suggests that unknown differences between treatments have an important influence. Therapeutic gains were relatively stable, lasting as long as four years (Craighead and Agras, 1991).

The hospitalized anorectic adolescent presents a special problem because of the urgent need to restore body weight and save her life. *Behavior therapy* is based on operant principles of rewarding eating by individualized reinforcers such as watching TV or having friends visit and withholding rewards when there is noncompliance. While there is no evidence that the behavioral approach is more effective than milieu or individual psychotherapy, this may be because, regardless of the kind of treatment, they all employ the operant techniques of praising and offering various rewards for weight gains. (See Linscheid, Tarnowski, and Richmond, 1988, for a detailed presentation of behavioral approaches to anorexia and bulimia nervosa.)

There is evidence that the operant behavioral approach, while effective in achieving the goal of weight gain, does not affect faulty notions concerning eating or personality and interpersonal problems. These may be addressed by *cognitive-behavior therapy*. The therapy aims at changing specific faulty beliefs both about eating and about the self, such as "I must be thin in order to be happy." "Anorexia is a sign of self-control." "I must be successful in everything I do." (See Garner and Rosen, 1990.) One of the problems with evaluating relative effectiveness is that cognitive-behavior therapy admittedly has much in common with individual psychotherapy. However, in a study designed to eliminate this overlap, subjects in cognitive-behavioral treatment, an exclusively behavioral approach, and individual psychotherapy, improved equally in terms of frequency of overeating and general psychological well-being, but the cognitive-behavioral approach was more effective in changing attitudes about shape and weight and attempts to diet (Fairburn, et al., 1991).

In sum, while there is suggestive evidence that cognitive-behavior therapy may have some advantages over other approaches, objective studies of comparative effectiveness do not clearly point to a treatment of choice. (For a comprehensive coverage of treatment, see Schlundt and Johnson, 1990.)

SUBSTANCE ABUSE

You are a clinical child psychologist. The time is 11:42 on a Saturday night. You get out of bed to answer the phone. It is Mitzi, the younger sister of your client Ada. She says Ada is high (on drugs) and has just hit her mother, knocking her down on the kitchen floor and bloodying her nose. You say you will be right over and hurriedly dress. Your husband grumbles about having "one hell of a family life, to say nothing of a sex life," adding, "I hope you charge them double for overtime." The last remark is ironic. Ada's mother has not paid you in two years. A widow, whose husband's jewelry business was going bankrupt at his death, she is a borderline psychotic barely able to keep herself together, much less manage her four children. As you are about to leave, your husband says, "How about me coming with you?" but you refuse. The family lives in a deteriorating middle-class neighborhood, which is relatively safe.

When you arrive, the household is surprisingly quiet. Mitzi meets you at the door. She is a miracle—a mature, sensible, assured 14-year old. She says her mother is upstairs resting. You will talk with her later. Ada is lying on the living room sofa. She is a strikingly beautiful 17-year-old, her voluptuous figure spilling over her tight, low-cut dress. "I'll sleep with anything," she had once told you, "man, woman, horse, dog, or pig." Then she had added with mock suffering, "But I'm really not bad; I'm just terribly, terribly lonely."

Ada has a brilliant, facile mind, and listening to her, you often cannot tell fact from fantasy, true feeling from mock sincerity. You are sure she frequently rode on a motorcycle with various gangs of delinquents, committed minor thefts, and then delighted in avoiding arrest either by crying or by being seductive with the police. "Pigs" is her favorite expression of contempt, which she applies to everyone—family, peers, teachers, the world in general. In spite of her obvious provocativeness, she constantly sees herself as unfairly victimized. Her one genuine desire is to graduate from high school (her father had been awed by education and "learning"), yet her uncontrollable restlessness in class has caused her to fail continually. Right now she is asleep on the sofa, snoring slightly—or perhaps she is pretending to sleep to avoid talking to you.

You try to decide what to do. Ada has a 22-year-old brother. (A second brother stays in his room much of the time, immobilized by fears and depression.) A high school dropout, he has already amassed a good deal of money by charming elderly people into buying expensive, un-

necessary, defective hearing aids. Although Ada violently dislikes him, he is quite fond of her. Tomorrow you will phone to see if he will pay for a boarding school so that Ada can realize her ambition of completing high school while receiving psychotherapy. If he agrees, you will have to talk Ada into accepting the idea. Mitzi will help, and Ada's mother would be glad to get her out of the house. If that fails, you will have to try to find some other resource, as you have been doing for over two years. While some would call this supportive psychotherapy, you think of it more in terms of "rolling with the punches."

Clearly Ada is not a well-adjusted adolescent. But in many cases the clinical child psychologist must decide whether to regard drug use as part of normal development or as a symptom of maladjustment. Making this determination requires knowledge of all the contexts we have encountered and the historical context as well. This last is important since history offers scant support for equating drug use with deviant behavior. (While DSM-IV Draft Criteria uses substance related disorders as the diagnostic label [APA, 1993], drug abuse is also frequently found in the literature. We will use drug and substance abuse interchangeably.)

The Historical Context

Most cultures have used alcohol: mead was possibly used around 8000 B.C. in the Paleolithic era, the biblical Noah became drunk, and the Indians who met Columbus had their own "home brew." Drugs have been used in religious ceremonies, to medicate, to counteract fatigue, to increase fierceness in battle, as well as for recreation. Cultures have applied different sanctions to drugs; one drug may have multiple uses, while another is strongly prohibited.

In modern times, there were more opiate addicts in the United States at the turn of the century than there are now, many being women using opiate-based patent medicines to treat various physical complaints. Some physicians considered opium as a cure for alcoholism, while heroin was regarded as less harmful still, medical journals stressing its nonaddictive properties. It was after the Harrison Narcotics Act of 1914, banning opiates, that the number of women addicts decreased, while male addicts turned increasingly to crime in order to obtain the now illegal drugs. The current drug scene is as much a patchwork as its historical context. By far the most lethal forms of drug abuse are alcoholism and smoking, almost 1000 Americans a day dying prematurely of medical problems associated with smoking (Davison and Neale, 1990). Yet only in recent years have local governments passed ordinances regulating smoking in public places, while legal sanctions against alcohol consumption are relatively benign.

The Current Picture

In the late 1960s and 1970s use of illicit drugs burgeoned into what some described as a drug epidemic, as marijuana along with other stimulants, sedatives, and analgesics joined the traditional drugs of nicotine, alcohol, and caffeine (Johnston, 1985). Since the early 1970s the majority of adolescents have experimented with one or more of these illicit drugs by the end of high school. The fact that the so-called epidemic spreads primarily among adolescents and young adults suggests that the teens and early twenties are particularly important developmental stages for the establishment of drug behavior.

Since the 1970s, *age of onset* has changed as an increasing number of young people in grades 6 to 9 became involved in drugs. In fact, there is even some drug use among children in grades 4 to 6 (Oetting and Beauvais, 1990). The period of highest risk for initiation of legal and illegal drugs peaks at 18 and declines sharply after that. Stabilization of use of both kinds of drugs appears within one year after high school graduation and declines around

22 years of age, perhaps as a result of psychosocial maturity and the assumption of an adult role (Kandel and Yamaguchi, 1985).

Overall use of most drugs increased from the mid-1970s to 1982, after which there has been a gradual reduction (Oetting and Beauvais, 1990). However, the decline does not mean that the problem has disappeared. The absolute level of drug use is still the highest of any industrialized nation. Next, the overall decline masks differential effects in terms of specific drugs and specific subgroups. The decline in marijuana—the third most commonly used drug—has been dramatic, going from 10.7 to 2.7 percent for daily users since 1980 (Oetting and Beauvais, 1990). Yet alcohol, the most widely used drug, is used at progressively higher levels for children in higher grades, going from 10 percent of sixth-graders to over 90 percent of twelfth-graders. Daily cigarette smoking declined rapidly after 1975, leveling off in 1980, while crack increased sharply from 1975 to 1985 (Johnston, O'Malley, and Jerald, 1987). Multiple use has also increased, so regular use of a variety of psychoactive substances is the norm among users of any drug.

The highest rate of drug involvement is in places where economically disadvantaged minorities live in separate enclaves—such as the black ghetto, the Hispanic barrio, the Indian reservations. Here social isolation compounds the problems of poverty, prejudice, unemployment, deviant role models, and gang influence to produce heavy drug involvement (Oetting and Beauvais, 1990. Moncher, Holden, and Trimble, 1990, discuss substance abuse among Native American youths.)

Finally, AIDS has cast its spectral shadow over injection drug use, one study finding a rate of HIV infection of 0.35 per 1000 males and 0.32 per 1000 females. Moreover, many babies born to HIV-positive mothers are themselves HIV-positive. The management of HIV-infected mothers and children has placed a heavy burden on social and medical services (Farrell and Strang, 1991).

What forces determined this long-range waxing and waning of drug use is a matter of speculation. Certainly the original epidemic was part of the massive rebellion of youth against the political, social, and moral values of the adult world which swept the country during the decade between 1960 and 1970. However, its very prevalence gradually may have eroded the shock value of drug use as a symbol of rebellion, while youth, along with the entire country, turned to a generally more conservative set of values and toward an emphasis on health and fitness inconsistent with drug use.

Description of Drugs

A number of terms are used in connection with drug use. *Dependence* involves excessive use with serious psychological or physical impairment. *Abuse* is a less severe condition but still significantly in excess of use. *Addiction* involves both a tolerance for a drug and withdrawal reactions when it is not available. In our own presentation we will only refer to use or abuse, since the literature often does not make finer distinctions. Finally, sedatives and stimulants are called *hard* drugs and are both illegal and addicting.

Our coverage of drugs will be selective. Caffeine (coffee, Coca-Cola, NoDoz), nicotine (cigarettes and cigars), tranquilizers (Valium, Miltown), antidepressants (Elavil), and miscellaneous drugs such as nonprescription sedatives, antihistamines, and glue will be omitted. Selectivity within categories will also be maintained, the concern being with the physiological and psychological effects of the drug under scrutiny. (For a comprehensive drug chart, see Calhoun, Acocella, and Goodstein, 1977.) All the drugs are *psychoactive* in that they affect the central nervous system in such a way as to produce alterations in subjective feeling states.

Cannabis This classification includes marijuana ("grass," "pot") and hashish ("hash"), small doses of which produce relaxation and euphoria. With intermediate doses there is the illusion of thinking more clearly, although judgment and memory become impaired, while heavy doses induce hallucinations, delusions, and thought disorders. Cannabis is used to get high, to escape, to relax.

Hallucinogens This category includes PCP—phencyclidine ("angel dust"), lysergic acid diethylamide—LSD ("acid"), and mescaline (peyote), which produce visual imagery and increased sensory awareness, as well as anxiety and nausea. They may also cause panic in unprepared individuals and sometimes precipitate or intensify an already existing psychosis. Curiosity, consciousness expansion, and seeking for meaning are typical reasons for use. LSD and mescaline are sometimes called psychedelic drugs.

Sedatives Sedatives are central nervous system depressants inducing relaxation and sleep, producing relief from pain, impairing intellectual functioning and motor coordination, and weakening emotional control. They can also produce euphoria. There are two main classes. *Narcotics* include opium and its derivatives, heroin ("horse," "H"), codeine, morphine, and even cough syrup. *Barbiturates* include Nembutal ("yellow jackets"), Seconal ("red devils"), Quaalude ("'ludes") and Doriden ("goofers"). Sedatives are usually taken to relax and escape.

Stimulants There are two principle stimulants: amphetamines ("speed," "uppers," "pep pills"), which include Benzedrine ("bennies") and Dexedrine ("dexies"), and cocaine ("coke," "crack," "snow"). Both are central nervous system stimulants that increase alertness and produce euphoria, along with insomnia and loss of appetite. They are taken for stimulation, to get high, and to relieve fatigue.

Alcohol Whiskey, gin, beer, and wine ("booze," "hooch") are all central nervous system depressants inducing relaxation and drowsiness, while interfering with reaction time, coordination, judgment, and emotional control. Alcohol is drunk to relax, to escape tensions and inhibitions, and to get high.

Risk Factors

Drugs vary in psychological and physical dependence potential, narcotics, barbiturates, and alcohol being high on both, cannibis and hallucinogens being moderate to low on psychological dependence while entailing no physical dependence. In addition, physical tolerance affects the course of drug taking; the body seems to become sensitized to marijuana so that the individual requires less of the drug to achieve a high with time, while opiates produce high tolerance resulting in an ever-increasing need for larger quantities. Note that tolerance and dependence (or addiction) may vary independently; tolerance develops rapidly for most hallucinogens, although they are not physically addictive. Both factors affect the lengths to which the adolescent must go to maintain a habit, as well as the degree of difficulty in breaking it.

In addition to the differential legal risks involved in maintaining various drug habits, there are differential risks in regard to physical consequences. Marijuana used to be regarded as a harmless recreational drug. However, its effects on intellectual functioning and motor coordination can impair classroom learning and driving skills; long-term use may seriously impair lung functioning. The long-term effects of LSD are in doubt. By contrast, chronic heroin use may be devastating. Loss of appetite leads to malnutrition and susceptibility to disease; carelessness concerning in-

jection techniques and the sterility of needles may result in tetanus, blood poisoning, and hepatitis; too large a dose may result in a coma and death. Overdoses of barbiturates cause accidental deaths as well as suicides, while withdrawal from both barbiturates and alcohol is harrowing, dangerous, and potentially fatal. In most instances, adverse effects come about by habitual use of high dosages, both of which indicate drug abuse rather than casual or recreational use.

As we have already noted, many individuals are multiple drug users. At times drugs are combined to heighten their effect, such as the "speedball," which is a vicious combination of cocaine and heroin. Sometimes one drug will be used to offset the negative features of another; for example, a depressant such as a barbiturate can be used to counteract the "crash" that comes when the effect of amphetamines wears off.

Overview

By the age of 18 almost all adolescents have had some exposure to substance use; over 90 percent have had an alcoholic drink, two-thirds have smoked tobacco, and more than half have tried marijuana (Robins and McEvoy, 1990). Since substance use is normative, our first questions are, What sets the process in motion? and, Why does it occur in adolescence? Next we will ask why use turns into abuse. In seeking an answer we will reintroduce conduct disorder, which can occur with substance use and can play a determining role in escalation. We will then round out our developmental picture by describing the effect of drug abuse in adolescence on adjustment in early adulthood.

While we will touch on organic factors, we will primarily be dealing with the intrapersonal and interpersonal contexts. In the former, we will pay particular attention to the characteristic of unconventionality. In the latter, peer relations will loom large, as we would expect in adolescence. Parents also play their part both as role models and sources of support. Our developmental orientation will allow us to see how the nature and impact of these variables change as the adolescent goes from legal to illegal substances and from use to abuse. Finally, we will see how one conceptualization of substance abuse introduces a new model of how normal development can go awry.

The Organic Context

Although environmental factors play a dominant role in substance abuse, *genetics* contributes a modest but significant component in some individuals. (Our presentation follows Farrell and Strang, 1991.) The most substantial work has been in the field of alcohol problems. While both twin and adoption studies have yielded conflicting findings, the consensus supports a genetic component for alcoholism, at least for males.

In regard to *prenatal factors,* the evidence is clear concerning the destructive effects on children born of drug-taking mothers. A pregnant mother who has six or more drinks per day over a period of time is placing her child at risk for developing fetal alcohol syndrome (FAS), characterized by central nervous system dysfunction, mild to moderate retardation, motor skill deficits, growth deficiency, and dysmorphic facial characteristics. Perinatal mortality is also increased after fetal exposure to both alcohol and cocaine. Marijuana, opiates, and cocaine may lead to impaired fetal growth. Following birth, the opiate-dependent neonate will show signs of withdrawal such as CNS hyperirritability, gastrointestinal dysfunction, respiratory distress, sneezing, sweating, crying, and fever.

Precursors in Early Childhood

With drug use beginning in junior high school, its precursors are being sought during the grammar school period. (Our presentation follows Hawkins, Lishner, and Catalano, 1985, unless otherwise noted.) Among *intraindividual variables,* aggressiveness and rebelliousness are related to subsequent drug use. One study, for example, showed that aggression in first-grade boys predicted drug use ten years later. Conversely, a strong investment in prosocial behavior prevents both antisocial behavior and drug use. Other intraindividual variables, including self-esteem, locus of control, sensation seeking, and psychopathology, are only weak predictors of drug use.

Among *family* variables, parental modeling of drug use and a direct involvement in parental drug use are particularly important in the grammar school years. Thus the more family members use alcohol or marijuana, the more likely it is that the children will use them. Children serving alcohol or buying cigarettes for their parents is also related to future drug use. By contrast, parental beliefs have little effect (Bush and Iannotti, 1985). This finding that modeling is more potent in determining children's behavior than are expressed beliefs is a common one in normal development. Generally positive family relations discourage initiation into drug use, even if parents themselves are users, while disharmonious family interactions increase the likelihood of both imitating drug-using parents and of becoming a user. While parental variables are important, their relative strength as an etiologic variable is disputed.

The data concerning *school* are mixed. Low performance in grammar school is related to subsequent drug use, but it is not clear whether the relation is a direct one or whether it is due to antisocial acting out in school, which results in low performance as well as being a precursor of drug use in its own right.

Early *peer relations* have not been sufficiently investigated to cast any light on how they influence future drug users who are still in grammar school. Research on this most important variable is clearly needed. Among *su-*

perordinate variables, socioeconomic status, race, and ethnicity have not been conclusively shown to be related to drug use. (For a largely speculative reconstruction of the developmental pathway from infancy through childhood, see Glantz, 1992.)

Substance Use and Adolescence

Risk Factors Before proceeding with our developmental enquiry, it will be helpful to present Clayton's (1992) list of risk factors derived from various studies (see Table 11.2). The details of the list need not concern us here since they will figure in our subsequent presentations. What is of interest is the variety of risks drawn from all the contexts except the organic, which was not included in any of the studies. Thus drug use is not due to any single cause but to the interaction of a number of variables. Multiple risk factors also suggest that there is no single path leading to drug use; rather, there are numerous possible patterns of etiological agents (Glantz and Pickens, 1992). While our subsequent reconstruction of the transition from nonuse to use will apply to a certain portion of the population, other children will travel other roads.

Why Adolescence? In answering our first question concerning why substance use acceleratse in adolescence we will present Jessor and Jessor's (1977) classical study in detail since it both has a developmental conceptual framework and places substance use in the context of related variables rather than viewing it in isolation.

Variables Studied Jessor and Jessor regard behavior as a result of interactions between the individual's personality and the perceived environment. All variables were studied by means of an annual questionnaire submitted to 432 high school and 205 college students every year for a four-year period. This longitudinal design enabled the authors to investi-

gate the factors related to beginning drug use at different ages. The population was drawn from a small, university-dominated city known for its attractive natural setting and comfortable standard of living.

Problem Behavior The Jessors found a high correlation among alcohol use, cigarette smoking, marijuana use, and the use of other illicit substances. They also found that substance use was correlated with precocious sexual intercourse and delinquent behavior. They labeled this constellation *problem behavior*, defined as behavior which is regarded as undesirable by the norms of conventional society, is a source of concern and elicits some kind of social-control response. A subsequent study showed that problem behavior generalized across sex, educational level, socioeconomic status, and ethnic background and was not an artifact of the "counterculture" of the late 1960s and early 1970s (Donovan and Jessor, 1985).

Conventionality-Unconventionality In the personality realm, drug use in both high school and college was positively correlated with tolerance of deviance and with a perception of drug use as being more positive than negative. It was also negatively correlated with religiousness. Among high school students, academic achievement and the need for peer affection (both of which were negatively related to drug use) and the valuing of independence over achievement were second in importance, while a critical attitude toward society was third.

Jessor and Jessor epitomize the personality dimension underlying their findings in terms of *conventionality-unconventionality*. The adolescent who does not use drugs is likely to value academic achievement, to be unconcerned with independence from the family, to be accepting of the social status quo and involved in a religion, and to regard transgressions as having more negative than positive consequences. The individual with high proneness to problem behavior in general and

TABLE 11.2

Typologies of Risk Factors for Adolescent Drug Use

Bry et al. (1982)	Newcomb et al. (1986)	Labouvie et al. (1986)	Hawkins & Catalano (1989)
Low grade point average	Low grade point average	Low academic performance, educational aspirations, and achievement orientation	Low commitment to school; cognitive impairment; intelligence
Lack of religious involvement	Lack of religious involvement		Low religious involvement
Early alcohol use	Early alcohol use		Early persistent problem behaviors; early onset high-risk behavior
Low self-esteem	Low self-esteem	Low self-esteem; self-derogation	
Psychopathology	Psychopathology	Emotional outbursts	
Poor relationship with parents	Poor relationship with parents	Low parental warmth; parental hostile control	Poor, inconsistent family management practices; family conflict; low bonding to family; alienation/and rebelliousness
	Lack of conformity		Attitudes favorable to drug use
	Sensation seeking	Impulsivity	Sensation seeking; attention deficit and hyperactivity; low autonomic and central nervous system arousal; hormonal factors
	Perceived peer drug use	Friends' deviance; negative activities with friends	Peer rejection in elementary school; association with drug using peers
	Perceived adult drug use		
			Laws/norms; availability; extreme economic deprivation; neighborhood disorganization; school organization factors; intergenerational transmission

Source: Clayton, 1992.

drug use in particular has the opposite characteristics.

Among environmental variables, friends' approval and modeling of problem behavior, along with parental approval (or lack of disapproval), were all significant correlates for both high school and college students. For high school students, parental support and control were negatively related to drug use, while these variables were no longer important for college students.

The Jessors also analyzed their data in terms of the relative contribution of each variable to problem behavior and drug use. In general, both personality and environmental variables always appeared as major contributors, underscoring the authors' thesis that behavior is a product of both intrapersonal and context variables. The specific variables contributing most to marijuana use were having friends who serve as models for problem behavior, a critical attitude toward society, and a tolerance of deviant behavior. The social-criticism variable distinguished marijuana use from the other problem behaviors studied.

In sum, the use of various substances is only one component of a constellation of problem behaviors which includes sexual intercourse and delinquent behaviors. There is a developmental pattern in which the valuing of independence progressively increases while the valuing of academic achievement declines; tolerance of unconventional behavior increases while acceptance of conventional ideology in regard to society and religion declines; the influence of the family declines while peer orientation and a utilization of peers as models increases. Thus problem behavior in general and substance use in particular are expressions of an underlying characteristic of unconventionality.

Conceptual Framework According to the Jessors, highly prized roles and rewards vary with age in our society. The adolescent, especially the early adolescent, has limited access to the valued goals of adulthood, such as autonomy, prestige, sex, and mobility. In addition, age norms ignore individual differences in the desire and readiness to pursue adult goals. Consequently, certain adolescents who are ready to make the transition are constantly frustrated and tantalized by the perceived attractiveness of mature status.

Furthermore, the Jessors state, the transition from a less mature to a more mature adult status is marked by problem behavior, which they define as behavior that is undesirable by the norms of conventional society. It should in no way be regarded as deviant or psychopathological. Many problem behaviors, such as drinking and sexual intercourse, will be regarded as acceptable and will be encouraged when the adolescent is old enough to be considered an adult. In essence, the Jessors regard adolescence as a period in which departure from accepted norms is not only to be expected but also may be a sign of healthy development. Their particular term for an adolescent's readiness to engage in problem behavior is *transition proneness*. According to the Jessors, then, "Problem behavior may be viewed, at least in part, as an aspect of growing up" (p. 238). We are reminded of the terrible twos—which have humorously been described as the first adolescence—when difficult to manage and socially disruptive behavior is also a part of normal development.

The Organic Component Magnusson's (1988) study of early and late maturing girls (defined in terms of age of menarche) complements Jessor and Jessor's study. He found that early maturers engaged in more norm-violating behavior—or what the Jessors would call problem behavior—such as staying out late without parental permission, cheating on exams, truanting, smoking hashish, and getting drunk. Peer relations proved to be the link between physiological maturation and norm violation, early maturers seeking out older peers. These older peers actually engaged in or were perceived as engaging in norm-violating behaviors. Late maturers evidenced similar problem behaviors after they had biologically "caught up" with their early maturing peers. In sum, Magnusson's data indicate that, with girls, the organic variable of age of menarche is an important determinant of what the Jessors call transition proneness.

Abstainers, Experimenters, and Frequent Users Shedler and Block (1990) present a more differentiated view of drug use by dividing their population into three groups rather than the bipartite division of the Jessors. Their subjects were 101 eighteen-year-olds who had been extensively evaluated since they were preschoolers. Abstainers had never tried marijuana or any other drug; experimenters had used marijuana a few times and no more than one drug other than marijuana; frequent users used marijuana once a week or more and had tried at least one drug other than marijuana. Thus both groups were still in the early stages of substance use in that they had not graduated to frequent use of hard drugs.

The personality picture of the *frequent user* was one of a troubled, manifestly unhappy adolescent who was interpersonally alienated and emotionally withdrawn and who expressed his or her disturbance through overly antisocial behavior. In terms of our personality variables, these adolescents were deficient in social relations, being mistrustful, hostile, and withdrawn; in the realm of work, they were neither invested in school nor in channeling their energies toward meaningful vocational goals; finally, their self-control was weak, resulting in antisocial acting out.

The picture of *abstainers* was a surprising one. Far from being well-adjusted, they were relatively tense, emotionally constricted individuals who were prone to delay gratification unnecessarily, unable to enjoy sensuous experiences. They avoided close interpersonal relationships and were not liked and accepted by others. While not as disturbed as the frequent users, they shared the quality of social alienation, while being overcontrolled rather than impulsive.

It was the *experimenters* who were the healthiest, in that they were sociable and warm, had the least amount of distress, and had stable self-control. They also had the freedom to experiment with values, beliefs, and roles as part of the process of forging a new identity. Thus, the authors would agree with the Jessors that, in adolescence, a certain amount of behavior which society judges as being a problem may be part of the normal growth process. They also show that, again in this period, abstainers should not be regarded as the normal control group, either statistically or psychologically.

Shedler and Block's (1990) analysis of their longitudinal data showed that the personality characteristics of the three groups were present in early childhood. Thus, as early as 7 years of age, frequent users were maladjusted; they were unable to form good relationships, insecure, and emotionally distressed. Abstainers were relatively overcontrolled, timid, fearful, and morose. The mothers of both groups of children were relatively cold and unresponsive, giving their children little encouragement while pressuring them to perform.

The authors conclude that abstinence, experimentation, and frequent use represent three relatively distinct personality constellations which were established early in life. In facing the drug scene, adolescents react in character rather than having their character shaped by abstinence and use. Their research also suggests that the Jessor's division of users into conventional and unconventional youths may have missed the more disturbed members of both groups.

From Marijuana to Hard Drugs

Research data allow us to trace the line of development from the use of marijuana, which is a relatively benign drug, to the use of more potent and dangerous ones. But before tracing the path, it is important to note that escalation is not inevitable. Adolescents may stop at any step along the way or may desist altogether. The fact that drug use peaks around 22 years of age and then declines to a relatively low level afterward argues against a simple escalation model of increasingly serious involvement.

When escalation does take place, it follows a predictable pattern: for males, the progression is from alcohol to marijuana to illicit drugs; females follow the same pattern except that cigarettes are part of the initial step along with alcohol. Thus legal drugs are a necessary intermediate between nonuse and marijuana, and there is a low probability that those who never use marijuana will progress to other illegal drugs (Kandel and Yamaguchi, 1985). Although subsequent research does not substantiate a fixed sequence for all populations, the basic progression has been verified as a common developmental pattern (Glantz, 1992).

There is also evidence that different *determinants* may be involved at each stage of escalation (Kandel, Kessler, and Margulies, 1978). Adolescents who begin to drink have engaged in a number of minor delinquent activities, enjoy high levels of sociability with peers, and are exposed to peers and parents who drink. The transition to marijuana use is preceded by involvement with peers who use marijuana, by a belief and value system that favors or condones marijuana use, and by participation in the same minor forms of deviant behaviors which precede involvement with hard liquor. While parental and peer models of illicit drug use precede the transition to the use of hard drugs, depression and lack of closeness to parents are equally important.

Thus the influence of peers, while the most important determiner of drug use, changes in nature: in the early stages a general sociability or group membership makes the adolescent susceptible to using drugs, while in the final

stage a single best friend plays an important role. Parental behavior is also influential in leading the adolescent to experiment with hard liquor, the model they present being more important then their beliefs and values. In the final stage, it is the quality of the parent-child relationship that matters, warmth and closeness shielding the adolescent from involvement in more serious drugs. The intrapersonal variables change from values and beliefs condoning drug use to feelings of despair as the adolescent moves into involvement with hard drugs. This changing pattern of risk variables means that escalation is not merely a matter of "more of the same"—a quantitative increase. Rather, the variables responsible for the transition from nonuse to use and from use to abuse are different (Glantz and Pickens, 1992).

The developmental progression is of more than academic interest. Locating individuals within the sequence furnishes important leads as to the focus of psychotherapy, since peers are particularly influential in the early stages, while the transition to hard drugs adds the element of negative self-esteem and alienation from the family.

From Use to Abuse

Conceptual Guide   Recall that, in discussing negativism (Chapter 5) we saw that the exaggeration of normal problem behavior which threatens to jeopardize future growth could be regarded as psychopathological. The same principle can be applied here. When rebellion, defiance, and antisocial behaviors become ends in themselves rather than means for promoting autonomy, adolescents may be in a state not of transition but of stagnation. Or again, if problem behaviors seem primarily directed against the parents—if adolescents seem to be going out of their way to defy and upset parents, if unconsciously they are behaving like "bad children" in order to prolong their status as children—then we begin to suspect that fixation rather than transition is calling the tune.

Erikson's writings on identity are useful at this point. In keeping with the Jessors he states that youths often go to extremes in order to test the "rock bottom of some truth" before committing themselves to a particular way of life (1968, p. 236). These extremes may include not only rebelliousness but also deviant, delinquent, and self-destructive behaviors. It is only when such tendencies defeat the purpose of experimentation by fixating the adolescent or necessitating a permanent retreat to primitive behavior that they become psychopathological. Take for example a *negative identity*, which in many ways is the adolescent counterpart of the toddler's negativism. Here the adolescent perversely identifies with all the roles that have been presented as undesirable or dangerous in the past; in despair of realizing the unattainable positive roles, the adolescents become "the last thing in the world" the parent would want them to be. If, in addition, authorities such as judges or mental health workers also label them as "delinquents" or "addicts" or "psychopaths" or "alcoholics," adolescents will make sure they become what the community has called them, thus abandoning the freedom of choice essential to a constructive outcome. (For a conceptualization of adolescent delinquency in terms of negative identity, see Gold and Petronio, 1980.) In a like manner, the depression and moodiness of the normal adolescent is different from the *despair* evidenced in the abandonment of the desire to grow, expand, and find new meanings in life. The devaluing of academic achievement also differs from a *work paralysis,* which suffocates even recreational and avocational activities in a pall of futility, just as an antireligious stance differs from an immobilizing *confusion of values.* Thus the difference between normality and deviance is a quantitative one, psychopathology not only being more extreme but (and this is the essence) representing a retreat from the struggle to establish an identity rather than a progression—no matter how painful to the adolescent and to society—along the way to reaching that goal.

Specific Criteria DSM-IV Draft Criteria lists eleven specific criteria for a diagnosis of Substance-Related Disorder (see Table 11.3). Among them are tolerance for the substance, unsuccessful efforts to control use in spite of knowledge of its physical, psychological, and interpersonal dangers, wthdrawal symptoms and an inability to fulfill major obligations at work, school, or home. Symptoms must occur almost daily for a month or repeatedly over a longer period of time.

Empirical Findings Two of the most important determinants of the transition from substance use to abuse are *timing,* or the age when use began, and the presence of a *conduct disorder.* Robins and McEvoy's (1990) research using retrospective accounts of drug users and abusers depicts the interplay of these two variables.

To begin with, the earlier substance use began (i.e., before the age of 15), the more likely the progression to subsequent abuse. In regard to conduct problems, it was the sheer quantity of such problems—five or more—that predicted subsequent abuse rather than any specific problem or groups of problems. In fact, number of problems was a better predictor of substance abuse than age of onset; of those beginning substance use before age 15 with seven or more problems, more than half developed serious substance abuse. While there was an interaction between the two variables, the number of problems remained a powerful predictor of substance abuse even when age and exposure were controlled.

Gender had little direct predictive value in regard to use or abuse. It had an indirect effect

TABLE 11.3
DSM-IV Draft Criteria for Substance Dependence

A maladaptive pattern of substance use, leading to clinically significant impairment or distress, as manifested by three or more of the following occurring at any time in the same twelve month period:

1. Tolerance, as defined by either of the following:
   a. Need for markedly increased amounts of the substance to achieve intoxication or desired effect
   b. Markedly diminished effect with continued use of the same amount of the substance

2. Withdrawal, as manifested by either of the following:
   a. The characteristic Withdrawal syndrome for the substance
   b. The same (or closely related) substance is taken to relieve or avoid withdrawal symptoms

3. The substance is often taken in larger amounts or over a longer period than was intended

4. A persistent desire or unsuccessful efforts to cut down or control substance use

5. A great deal of time is spent in activities necessary to obtain the substance (e.g., visiting multiple doctors or driving long distances), use the substance (e.g., chain-smoking), or recover from its effects

6. Important social, occupational, or recreational activities given up or reduced because of substance use

7. Continued substance use despite knowledge of having had a persistent or recurrent physical or psychological problem that was likely to have been caused or exacerbated by the substance (e.g., current cocaine use despite recognition of cocaine-induced depression, or continued drinking despite recognition that an ulcer was made worse by alcohol consumption)

Source: American Psychiatric Association, 1993.

because girls have fewer conduct problems than boys and begin substance use later. But those who did have conduct problems and started substance use early were at as great a risk for later substance abuse as were boys with a similar history.

Loeber's (1988) review of longitudinal studies looks at whether substance use and abuse lead to antisocial behaviors or vice versa. The answer is not simple. In the early stages of drug use, conduct problems or delinquency precede substance use for males. The picture for females is not so clear, studies finding that marijuana use predicted interpersonal aggression and use of other illicit drugs predicted theft. Once substance addiction has taken place, it is not uncommon for the frequency of delinquent activity and general deviant behavior to increase as well. Finally, Loeber notes that, as with conduct disorder, earlier substances tend to be retained as later ones are added, resulting in multiple drug use or abuse.

Elliott, Huizinga, and Menard's (1989) analysis of prospective data on 1725 youths between 11 and 17 years of age complements Loeber's review. In general, serious drug use has more influence on maintaining serious delinquency than the reverse. However, the pull to *desistence* is stronger than the pull to escalation, since the probability for regression to less serious behaviors is greater than the probability of progression to more serious behaviors. This would be expected in light of the fact that both substance use and delinquency decline with age, the former leveling off in young adulthood, the latter declining after mid-adolescence.

Multiple-problem youth represent a countercurrent in this general trend toward health. Such youths, who are multiple-drug users and engage in a variety of delinquent behaviors have longer criminal and drug careers, are less likely to "outgrow" their deviant behaviors, and are less responsive to treatment or intervention.

From Adolescence to Early Adulthood

Newcomb and Bentler's (1988)'s nine-year prospective study of 654 adolescents provides information on multiple aspects of their adult life. Following the authors, we will summarize the results in terms of developmental tasks which the adolescent faces in the transition to adulthood.

1. *Social integration.* (This corresponds to our variable of social relations.) Hard-drug use interferes with this development by reducing social support and increasing loneliness. In general, hard-drug users feel more disconnected and unsupported. On the other hand, early alcohol use seems to help social integration, perhaps by decreasing social inhibitions and permitting the learning of appropriate social competencies.
2. *Occupation* (which corresponds to our variable of work). Teenage drug use facilitates early involvement in the job market, which both augments the young adult's income and reduces chances of success by increasing the probability of being fired. In the process, traditional educational pursuits are abandoned, thereby limiting the range of career opportunities. However, job satisfaction, amount of work, and use of public assistance are not affected; the young adult is by no means a "lazy bum living off the government."
3. *Family and heterosexual relations* (which corresponds to our variables of attachment and sex). Drug use has both an accelerating and detrimental impact, leading to early involvement in getting married and bearing children, on the one hand, and divorce, on the other. Drug use changes very few aspects of sexual behavior and satisfaction beyond those experienced as a teenager.
4. *Criminal behavior.* Youthful drug use is differentially related to criminal behavior. Multiple substance use is predictive of increased stealing and drug law violation, such as driving while intoxicated or selling drugs, but decreases violent crimes.
5. *Mental health.* Multiple drug use is related to a small but significant increase in psychosis and a decreased ability to plan, organize, and direct behavior. Hard-drug use increases suicidal ideation in young adulthood, while alcohol decreases depression.

In sum, teenage drug use disrupts the timing of and the competencies required for meeting the critical developmental tasks involved in making the transition to adulthood. Timing is affected by generating a premature involvement in work and family prior to acquiring adequate competence to handle such challenges. The use of hard drugs also directly interferes with social integration and acceptance of adult civic and societal responsibilities while increasing feelings of social isolation from peers. Finally, drug use can affect cognition by making thinking more disorganized and bizarre, as well as resulting in increased suicidal ideation when hard drugs are involved.

Conceptualization Newcomb and Bentler (1988) conceptualize their findings in terms of *precocious development*. This involves a significant discrepancy between developmental level and competence. Teenage drug users push themselves toward a maturity that they are incapable of assuming effectively because they have not given themselves time to accumulate the needed skills and experience. The result is failure. This pattern is seen most clearly in regard to family and work.

The concept of precocious development resembles that of transition proneness. However, the latter terms applies to the early phases of substance use and is still within the realm of normal problem behavior. Precocious development, perhaps because it involves a later developmental period and the use of hard drugs, has consequences that are more clearly deviant.

The Developmental Model

This is our first encounter with *precocity* as normal development gone awry, the other timing models involving various kinds of delays in normal progression or regression. While the model plays only a minor role in the literature, it has been discussed. A. Freud (1965) states that precocity is part of normal development. We expect children to have musical talents or athletic abilities or social skills or intellectual capabilities which are beyond their general developmental level. Pathogenic precocity is a quantitative deviation which jeopardizes normal development. For example, clinicians will see children who are old before their time, who have been burdened by adult responsibilities and have paid the price both in terms of being robbed of their childhood and in

terms of psychopathologies. Adolescent drug abusers run a similar risk by taking on adult functions for which they are poorly prepared. The outcome is often failure or, in certain extreme cases, social isolation, despair, and loss of contact with reality.

Prevention

One general rationale for prevention is that it is less costly than treatment. Our review of the research on substance use and abuse provides a more specific reason. If timing plays such a prominent role and if there is a stepwise progression from less to more serious involvement, then a significant delay in age of onset should pay off handsomely in terms of less serious involvement and increased chances of desistance. (Unless otherwise noted, our presentation follows Schinke, Botvin, and Orlandi's 1991 summary of the research literature. The authors also discuss issues involved in evaluating programs.)

A number of traditional approaches have proven to be ineffective. *Information dissemination* focuses on increasing knowledge of drugs and the consequences of use and on fostering antidrug use attitudes. *Affective education* bypasses drugs and aims at increasing self-esteem, responsible decision making, and personal growth. *Alternative programs* have similar goals but offer alternatives to substance use such as recreational and youth center activities. While such programs sound plausible, studies of effectiveness have shown that increases in drug knowledge, self-esteem, decision making and changes in attitudes do not significantly affect substance use itself.

Recent psychosocial approaches are more promising because they are based on a better understanding of the causes of substance use and on accepted theories of human behavior, while using well-tested intervention techniques. They also have been evaluated more rigorously and modified when warranted.

Resistance skill training teaches students how to recognize, handle, and avoid situations in which they experience peer pressure to smoke, drink, or use drugs. (Recall that peers are one of the most powerful influences on initiating substance use.) Students role-play and practice ways of delivering specific refusal messages effectively. Many programs use peer leaders who often have higher credibility with adolescents than adults. Programs also combat the perception that substance use is widespread, thus countering the tendency to conform to "what everybody else is doing." Evaluation studies show that resistance-skills training is effective in reducing smoking, alcohol, and marijuana use by 35 to 45 percent.

Personal and social-skills training teaches a broad range of general skills for coping with life situations and thus differs from the problem-specific focus of resistance-skills training. Among the components are general problem-solving and decision-making skills, general cognitive skills for resisting interpersonal or media influences, skills for increasing self-control and self-esteem and relieving anxiety, general interpersonal skills, and assertiveness skills. These skills are taught by a combination of instruction, demonstration, feedback, reinforcement, behavioral rehearsal, and extended practice through behavioral homework assignments. Studies of effectiveness range from 42 to 87 percent reduction in initial smoking as well as a reduction in later use.

As the name implies, comprehensive *community-based prevention* involves school, parents, media, community organizations, and health-policy interventions. A prime example is Kansas City's Students Taught Awareness and Resistance (STAR) program. The three levels of intervention, based on the principles of social-learning theory, are direct training of youth to acquire drug-resistance skills; train-

ing of teachers, parents, and other program implementers; and ongoing booster sessions for both youth and program implementers. Eight representative Kansas City communities were assigned randomly to program and control conditions. Youths received the program in the sixth or seventh grade and were followed for three years.

The primary findings were a significant reduction in tobacco and marijuana use for both high-risk and low-risk youths. This finding is particularly important because preventive programs tend to have mainly low-risk youths, who are more readily available but who need the programs less. Finally, STAR was not effective in reducing alcohol use. (For details, see Johnson et al., 1990.) A subsequent analysis showed that, of the many components in the program, changing the perception of friends' reactions to drug use was the most important in regard to decreasing cigarette and alcohol use—a finding which again attests to the importance of peers. Decreased intentions to use both drugs and reduced beliefs in their positive consequences were also important components (MacKinnon et al., 1991).

Finally, the *media* is more noted for promoting than preventing substance use. Television, magazines, records, movies, and radio shows promote beer, wine, and cigarettes. Compared with this onslaught, efforts to counteract substance use seem puny indeed. While it is claimed that public service announcements were the most important factor in persuading the tobacco industry to eliminate cigarette ads on television, the overwhelming majority of mass media prevention programs have failed to achieve their goal of changing behavior. However, this may be because the media's potential has not been properly tapped. Many PSA announcements, for example, do not occur during prime time and therefore do not reach their intended audience; nor have they employed the principle of

Treatment

redundancy, which is so important in advertisement. (Schilling and McAlister, 1990, have a detailed discussion of media interventions.)

No specific treatment or combination of treatments has been successful in eliminating drug abuse, much less proving itself to be the treatment of choice. Moreover, the majority of programs have been developed for adults rather than being tailored to the special needs of adolescents.(SeeSchinke,Botvin,andOrlandi,1991. A more comprehensive presentation of treatment can be found in Davison and Neale, 1990.)

Drugs that produce a physical dependency, such as alcohol and heroin, require a *detoxification* program under medical management. The physiological and psychological withdrawal reactions may be treated with tranquilizers, while vitamins and a high-carbohydrate diet combat the effects of poor nourishment. In the case of heroin addiction, methadone—a synthetic opiatelike drug—can be substituted. It blocks the craving for heroin, can be taken orally rather than intravenously, and has a longer-lasting effect. Moreover, since it is legally available, it eliminates the necessity of engaging in criminal activities to support the habit. However, methadone maintenance involves substituting one drug for another and does not alter a life-style that may include criminal activities and the use of other drugs such as alcohol and barbiturates.

Individual treatment of drug abuse has been unsuccessful, whether it is psychotherapeutically or behaviorally oriented. The former often requires a willingness to change and the formation of a positive relationship between client and therapist, both of which may be lacking in the drug abuser. The latter often involves pairing of a noxious stimulus, such as a nausea-inducing chemical or a painful electric shock, with the drug, or manipulating

cue exposure. Efficacy remains in doubt, however (Farrell and Strang, 1991).

Outpatient counseling programs represent another approach to treatment and are useful when the drug abuser is unwilling to become involved in residential treatment. Here the individual is provided support in developing a drug-free lifestyle, is given opportunities for acquiring vocational skills, and is offered help in dealing with personal problems through individual or group therapy Unfortunately, evaluations have found that many outpatient programs have only limited effectiveness, perhaps because they do not remove adolescents from the powerful lures of their everyday environment (Schinke, Botvin, and Orlandi, 1991).

Group approaches to treatment have met with some success, although satisfactory evaluative data are often lacking. Alcoholics Anonymous capitalizes on group support. Each new member may choose a fellow member to be a "sponsor," someone who is available at any time to give advice and to help the member resist the temptation to drink. During regularly held meetings, members recount past experiences and express thoughts about their recovery, and recovered alcoholics give inspirational speeches. There is a strong religious element, members being encouraged to rely on the healing power of a "higher power."

The difficulty in judging treatment *effectiveness* is that many of the programs have not been adequately evaluated, and well-controlled studies with objective data are extremely rare. One of the more ambitious studies was conducted by Sells and Simpson (1980), who evaluated 3131 individuals in fifty-two treatment units representing four kinds of treatment. The definition of success was drug abstinence along with absence of criminal and other severely deviant behaviors. A four-year follow-up study revealed that success rates ranged from 20 to 37 percent, which might suggest modest effectiveness were it not for the fact that individuals seen for drug-related intake evaluations but not treated showed a 21 percent success rate. Two of the most effective programs involved methadone maintenance plus a therapeutic community approach for heroin and other opiate addicts, and an outpatient drug-free program for polydrug (excluding marijuana) and nonaddicted opiate users. Outpatient detoxification programs were not successful. Other than this unsuccessful program, the programs had a lower rate of highly unfavorable outcomes than the untreated controls, ranging from 14 to 16 percent compared with 24.5 percent. Thus, while certain forms of treatment may be better than no treatment at all, the success rate is low.

RISKS OF A HOMOSEXUAL IDENTITY

Homosexuality does not appear as a diagnostic category in DSM-IV Draft Criteria (APA, 1993). Gender Identity Disorders is the only sexual psychopathology listed for children. It consists of an intense and persistent distress over one's own sexual identity and an intense desire to have the identity of the opposite sex, (See Zucker and Green, 1992, for a review of the literature.)

If homosexuality is not a psychopathology, why discuss homosexual identity in adolescence? There are a number of reasons. First, developmental psychopathology, contrary to its obvious meaning, has broadened to include conditions that are not psychopathological, child maltreatment and physical illness being the most common examples (see Chapter 1). Such conditions do not necessarily place children at risk for developing a psychopathology. However, they do place such children at risk for developing serious problems that are in excess of those that are part of normal development.

Adolescents with a homosexual identity belongs in this category of at-risk children; for example they are more likely to make suicide attempts and to contract AIDS than are heterosexual adolescents. Quite literally, their lives are in danger. Most risks arise not from the inherent nature of homosexuality but from society. In Judeo-Christian cultures, the taboo against homosexuality is deeply rooted, the term *homophobia* being used to denote an irrational fear or distorted perception of homosexuality. Homophobia can be internalized by the adolescent and may result in bewilderment and despair (Remafedi, 1991).

The next reason for discussing homosexual identity is a practical one. Troubled homosexual youths and their families may seek professional help from clinical child psychologists. This help should be offered on the basis of understanding and of knowledge of relevant research. Ironically, information concerning homosexuality is difficult for the student of clinical child psychology to come by. It is rarely found in texts on child psychopathology and is not included in texts on normal sexual development. Lacking a reliable source of information, there is a danger that the interested student will either remain ignorant of the facts concerning homosexual identity or even share in society's distorted perceptions. Thus, conveying accurate information is another reason for discussing homosexual identity, as it is for all of our discussions.

Definition

The simplest definition of homosexuality is sexual behavior between people of the same sex. More differentiated definitions add the elements of frequency of sexual behavior and number of partners in a given time span. At a more covert level, homosexuality has been defined as a desire for same-sex contact and/or conscious sexual arousal from thinking about or seeing persons of the same sex. In such instances, the individuals may not engage in homosexual behavior because fear or moral scruples prevent them. Some definitions locate homosexuality in the self-image and require that individuals consider themselves homosexual regardless of their actual behavior. Finally, there are latent homosexuals, whose desires are either unconscious or who will turn to homosexual behavior only when heterosexual outlets are unavailable, such as in prison. When diverse behaviors are subsumed under a common label, one can expect a contradictory and confused literature.

In spite of varying definitions, there is general agreement concerning certain characteristics of homosexuality. The landmark research of Kinsey, Pomeroy, and Martin (1948) showed that, rather than being dichotomous, there is a continuum of behavior from heterosexual to homosexual. The Kinsey study found, for example, that 37 percent of adult males had one homosexual experience to orgasm since adolescence, 18 percent had as much homosexual as heterosexual experience, and 13 percent had homosexual impulses, which they did not act on. The incidence of homosexuality in women was lower, being only 13 percent. In spite of the sexual permissiveness of the 1960s and 1970s, there seems to have been little change since Kinsey's study (Sarason and Sarason, 1987). The estimate of individuals who are exclusively homosexual in terms of persistent and exclusive behavior ranges between 2 and 6 percent (Zucker and Green, 1992). Homosexuals vary as widely as heterosexuals in behavior and personality, the effeminate male and the tough female representing only a small minority. Nor can homosexuals be classified in terms of their assuming an "active" or a "passive" role in their sexual relations; both males and females alternate between the roles.

Homosexuality is distinct from *transvestism,* which involves obtaining sexual gratification through dressing in the clothes of the opposite sex. While some transvestites may be homosexuals they typically are not. Homosexuality should also be distinguished from *transsexualism,* which is a gender identification with the opposite sex; for example, from early childhood a boy may be convinced that he really is a girl and has been assigned the wrong body. It is the transsexual who typically seeks sex reassignment through surgery and sex hormones. Most transvestites and transsexuals are male. (For further discussion, see Bootzin and Acocella, 1988.)

Multiple Dimensions of Sexuality   A number of dimensions of sexuality will be relevant to our discussion. There is variability within and there are complex relations among these dimensions.

First, there is *anatomic sex differentiation.* Variability ranges from distinct differentiation into male or female at one extreme to hermaphroditism (in which a single individual has both male and female reproductive organs) at the other extreme. It also includes instances in which the external genitalia appear to be at variance with the internal reproductive system owing to a physiological anomaly; for example, a malformation of the infant's penis may result in his being called a girl (Money and Ehrhardt, 1972). Then there is *gender identity* or the self-classification as male or female which develops in the toddler and preschool period. It is not unusual for children during this period to believe they can change their gender identity merely by changing their appearance. And while cultures may prescribe distinct *sex roles,* individuals combine all degrees of masculinity and femininity in their behavior, as we shall soon see. Then there is *erotic preference,* which involves the ideal choice of a sexual object. Finally, there is the capacity to enjoy and sustain a *love relationship* over time. Erotic preferences are numerous—they can involve not only the same or the opposite sex but also children, animals, and inanimate objects such as clothes—while a love relationship can last from a brief period to a lifetime.

Just to give a sample of the complex inter-relations that exist among these varying dimensions, an infant who is physiologically a girl can be raised as a boy because of an anomaly of external genitals, while a preschool boy with no anomalies can become convinced that he is really a girl—a conviction that might last into his adult years and eventuate in his seeking a sex change. A woman may submit to intercourse with her husband as required by her sex role while ideally preferring a homosexual partner, and prisoners or sailors might engage in homosexual behavior not from preference but because only males are available.

Conceptualizations   In Chapter 2 we learned that there were two different conceptions of sexual development. The first is in terms of sex role and involves the learning of behaviors and feelings society regards as appropriate for the male and the female. This conceptualization is favored by social-learning theorists, who account for sexual development in terms of reinforcement by and imitation of socializing agents. The psychoanalytic theory views sexual development in terms of eroticized intimacy, which begins in infancy and goes through the special transformations that comprise the psychosexual stages. Psychoanalysts are concerned with understanding the love relations that exist between and among individuals. Their term for this relation is *object choice.*

Sex role and object choice are not only conceptually distinct but behaviorally distinct as well. Certain heterosexual men, for example, are aroused by the sight and touch of female clothing, especially underwear, which they put on in order to increase the pleasure of their heterosexual foreplay and intercourse. Thus, feminine sex-role behavior can serve a masculine sexual preference.

In reviewing the literature on homosexuality, consequently, the distinction between sex role and object choice must be kept in mind, so we do not assume that findings concerning one automatically apply to the other. Incidentally, the literature often implies that the difference is a theoretical one involving the psychoanalytic and social-learning theories, rather than an actual distinction between two aspects of sexuality.

We are now ready to examine homosexuality in adolescence. In our presentation it is important to keep in mind that there are only a handful of objective studies of youths. Most of the literature consists of clinical observations or retrospective reconstructions of homosexual adults, the former being biased in terms of degree of disturbances, the latter being subject to distorted memory (see Savin-Williams, 1991). The lack of longitudinal studies as well as ones directly comparing homosexuals and heterosexuals is particularly regrettable.

The Organic Context

Until recently, the case for an organic etiology of homosexuality was weak. Certain studies suggested a *genetic* component in that they found a higher concordance rate for homosexuality among identical twins than among fraternal twins and a higher rate of homosexuality among brothers than among males in general. However, some findings failed to replicate, while others could not satisfactorily eliminate a determining role for the environment (see Zucker and Green, 1992). Studies of *circulating sex hormones* have also failed to find convincing evidence of differences between adult homosexuals and heterosexuals. However, a number of experimental studies of animals and a smaller group of studies of humans suggest that the key to understanding both homosexuality and heterosexuality lies in the *prenatal brain differentiation.* (Our presentation follows Ellis and Ames, 1987.)

Sexual orientation is determined primarily by the degree to which the nervous system is exposed to testosterone and certain other sex hormones while neuro-organization is taking place in the fetus. According to Ellis and Ames's hypothesis, there are two stages to this brain organization, the first of which determines sexual orientation, or what we call erotic preference. If the level of the sex hormones is in the typical female range, the individual will prefer males on sexual maturity; if the level in the brain is in the typical male range, the postpubertal preference will be for female sexual partners. Sexually typical behavior, or what we have called sex role behavior, is determined in the second stage, again due to the biochemical processes determining masculinization and feminization of the brain. The crucial timing seems to be between the middle of the second month and the middle of the fifth month of gestation. Sexual inversions, such as homosexuality, occur either because of unusual features in the genetic programs that control these biochemical processes or because of external agents that interfere with such processes.

Ellis and Ames (1987) cite a number of studies in which such inversion has taken place in humans. Certain *drugs* taken by the pregnant mother can be one cause of sexual inversion. Mothers who took various types of progestins during pregnancy had genetic females with ambiguous external genitals which were surgically feminized. The infants were reared as females, but their sex-type behavior was highly masculine although, at puberty, they did not become homosexual. Thus the drug affected sexually typical behavior, which is determined in the second stage of fetal development, but not sexual orientation, which is determined in the first.

Ellis and Ames assign only a minor role to environmental factors. Stress on the mother during pregnancy is one such factor. For example, the significant increase in the proportion of homosexuals born in Germany during and immediately after World War II has been attributed to the unusual stress on German citizens (Dorner et al., 1980). While subsequent research suggested there might possibly be a relation between general maternal stress and homosexuality in the child, the evidence is far from conclusive (Zucker and Green, 1992).

Ellis and Ames's findings have subsequently been challenged and their position hotly debated by those who question whether variations in the prenatal hormonal milieu have any effect at all and, if so, whether such effects are of practical significance. In addition, the clear-cut results of animal research in this area are not typical of the findings with humans. (For details, see Zucker and Green, 1992.)

While concluding that Ellis and Ames's (1987) case might not be proven, we also must recognize that an extreme environmental position is also not tenable. Granted that it is best to think in terms of an interaction, little is known of the relative weight to assign to organic and environmental influences.

Homosexual Identity Development

Achieving a homosexual identity, like achieving an identity in general, is the result of a process which takes place over a number of years. Bell, Weinberg, and Hammersmith (1981) in their retrospective study of 979 adult homosexual and 447 adult heterosexual men and women found that early homosexual feelings played a determining role in ultimate sexual preference. These erotic feelings were a constant feature of the homosexual experience from childhood to adulthood. Homosexual arousal occurred around 11.6 years of age, which is somewhat earlier than heterosexual arousal, which was around 12.9 years. It antedated homosexual activities by three years or so. It also did not preclude heterosexual experiences during adolescence; however, homosexuals did not find such experiences fulfilling, just as their heterosexual counterparts did not find homosexual ones fulfilling.

From early childhood through early adolescence, adults are likely to recall nonspecific feelings of being different rather than identifying themselves as homosexuals; for example, they felt they were unusually sensitive or lacked interest in heterosexual activities. Between 10 and 18 years of age, an increasing number of youths began to equate being different with being homosexual. Although the realization could be a positive experience, it was usually accompanied by a period of duress marked by conflict, guilt, and fear of disclosure, this last often leading to an attempt to pass as a heterosexual. The final stage of acceptance, preference, and unwillingness to change, along with coming out and revealing their homosexuality to others, did not occur until late adolescence or early adulthood (Remafedi, 1987b, 1991).

There can be a number of discrepancies between sexual behavior and sexual identification within the above developmental pattern. Many future adult homosexuals engage in adolescent homosexual activities before defining themselves as gay or lesbian, while some gay and lesbian youths are sexual virgins. By the same token heterosexual youths experience more cross-sex contacts than they later will as adults. Thus, adolescents distinguish "doing" from "being." (See Savin-Williams, 1990 and Savin-Williams and Rodriguez, 1992, for a review of conceptualizations and research findings concerning homosexual identity.)

Risk Factors

The psychological and health problems accompanying adolescent homosexuality have been reasonably well documented. Most suicide attempts among homosexuals occur during adolescence and involve roughly a third of the populations studied—a much higher incidence than in the heterosexual population. Other problems include deteriorating school performance, truancy, drug abuse, running away from home, and prostitution (Remafedi,

1991). In Remafedi's (1987c) study of a non-clinical population of twenty-nine gay and bisexual men, approximately one-third to one-half reported strong negative attitudes toward their sexuality from parents and friends, discrimination, verbal abuse from peers, and physical assaults. They viewed the future with trepidation or experienced loss of self-esteem, masculinity, or spiritual worth. On the positive side, 52 percent were satisfied with their sexual orientation, 38 percent saw no difference in homosexual and heterosexual lifestyles aside from sexual orientation, while 28 percent attributed positive qualities to gays such as self-awareness, strength, and understanding.

In regard to health risks, a variety of sexually transmitted diseases are prevalent among the male homosexual population, although they are uncommon among exclusively lesbian women. The AIDS epidemic has added its staggering toll of fatalities. While the AIDS virus itself is indifferent to sexual orientation, 30 percent of cases in adolescents are attributable to homosexual intercourse—considerably higher than any other cause except hemophilia. (Henggeler, Melton, and Rodrigue, 1992. This reference contains a comprehensive review of the literature on pediatric and adolescent AIDS, including prevention and intervention.) (See Figure 11.1.) While there was a leveling off of incidence after a dramatic rise, recent data indicate that HIV infection is on the rise again, adolescents being one of the at-risk populations (Mann, Tarantola, and Netter (1992).

Other Intrapersonal Variables

Self-Esteem and Coming Out Savin-William's (1990) study of 214 gays and 103 lesbians between 14 and 23 years of age stands out in an otherwise bleak research landscape.

In regard to *self-esteem*, there were few group differences. There were also no differences between gays and lesbians in regard to

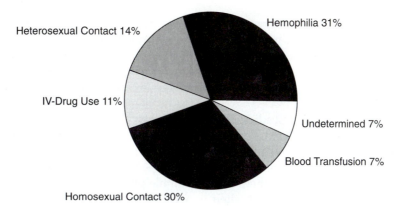

FIGURE 11.1
Percentage of adolescent AIDS cases by patient risk group, through 1990.
(*Source:* Henggeler, Melton, and Rodrigue, 1992.)

the following variables which, in turn, were related to self-esteem: demographics such as SES and education; attitudes and interests, such as religiosity, political liberalism, feminism, and sports; commitment to and satisfaction with homosexuality, and participation in gay and lesbian rights and social activities. In certain respects, however, the two groups diverged. For males, self-esteem was correlated with having a large number of gay affairs and with career and academic success. For females, self-esteem was correlated with having a large number of bisexual friends and, at a marginal level of significance, being accepted and supported by the family.

Savin-Williams defines *coming out* as the extent to which one believes that others know that he or she is gay or lesbian. For both males and females the most potent predictor of coming out was involvement in gay and lesbian social and political activities. The second most important variable for both groups was support from family and friends, although family was more important for lesbians, friends for gays. Age was important for males, the older ones being more likely to come out, while it was not important for females. Also, coming out was positively related to the self-esteem of males but not of females. These last results

speak to the controversy over whether coming out subjects youth to increased stress which lowers self-esteem or whether it is a liberating experience which enhances self-esteem. Being correlational, the data cannot answer the question of direction of effect in the male population, however (Savin-Williams, 1990).

The Same or Different? Savin-Williams (1990) also raises the question of whether sex-role behavior is the same or different for heterosexuals and homosexuals. Lacking a heterosexual control group, his answer had to involve results from other studies. The finding that lesbians had more sustained love affairs than gays is similar to findings with heterosexual women and men. The fact that gays' self-esteem depended on sexual prowess and achievement while lesbians' was dependent upon interpersonal relationships also fit in with the traditional view of sex roles. Yet, not all the data conform to the "no difference" model; for example, the high prevalence of cross-sex friends among both lesbian and gay youths is not typical of heterosexual friendships. Savin-Williams concludes that homosexuals may both be the same as or different from heterosexuals depending on the variable being studied. To take a stand in favor of one position or another would be premature in light of how little is known about homosexual youths.

Parental Relations

In seeming agreement with other studies, Bell, Weinberg, and Hammersmith (1981) found that gays, more than heterosexual men, felt close to their mothers, whom they also viewed as strong and dominant. However, there was no evidence that they identified with their mothers. Gays more than heterosexual men had a negative relation with their father marked by anger, dislike, and lack of closeness, admiration, and respect. This negative relationship went along with a weak identification with the father, who was perceived as ineffectual. The unexpected finding and the unique contribution of Bell, Weinberg, and Hammersmith's path analysis is that these early parental relations had either no effect on adult gender preference or a very weak one at best. What influence they had was primarily an indirect one in that, taken together, they played a role, although not a major role, in determining the child's gender conformity.

There is one more finding relevant to the issue of the role of parents. The special subgroup of adults who sought psychotherapy were different from the population as a whole in that having a cold, distant, hostile father did play an important role in the etiology of their sexual preference. This means, for one thing, that therapists wrongly generalized from their clients to the population of gays as a whole, a common pitfall in clinical research. But it also suggests that the quality of the father-son relation may be important not to the development of homosexuality but to the degree of distress that accompanies that sexual preference in adulthood.

Cross Gender Behavior   Capitalizing on the general finding that cross-gender behavior (or

what Bell, Weinberg, and Hammersmith call gender nonconformity) is one of the best predictors of adult homosexuality, Green (1987) studied sixty-six boys between 4 and 12 years of age (average age 7.1 years), whose parents had contacted a clinic because of their concern over their sons' effeminate behavior. Specifically, the boys preferred girls' clothes, toys, and companionship, evaded such traditional sex-typed activities as sports and rough-and-tumble play, and more than once expressed a wish to be a girl. The comparison group consisted of fifty-six nonclinic families matched for demographic variables including age, sibling position, parents' marital status, educational level, and ethnic background. Of the forty-four boys available for a follow-up evaluation at adolescence and young manhood, three-fourths were homosexuals or bisexuals, while only one of the boys in the control group had become homosexual.

Green's (in Roberts, Green, Williams, and Goodman, 1987) data permitted him to raise the question: Are the factors responsible for cross-gender behavior in a group of feminine boys the same as or different from those responsible for cross-gender behavior in boys considered masculine (since even masculine boys display some feminine behaviors)? In the feminine group, the mother's low level of premarital sexual experience, the father's desire for a daughter when the mother was pregnant, and the mother's approval of her son's early cross-gender behavior were significantly related to the boy's feminine behavior. In the comparison group, the father's masculinity was negatively related while parental dislike for household nudity, masturbation, and sex play (a general measure of conservative sexual standards) was positively related to the boy's femininity.

The authors rightly conclude that the findings do not readily fit into any model of sexual identity formation. One might say that, in the feminine group, the father's desire for a girl and the mother's approval of feminine behavior might fit a social learning or reinforcement model. However, the overall results are more impressive for the variables that did not turn out to be significant than for those that did. Among the former category were the mother's desire for a girl, her domination and masculinity, the unavailability of the father in intact homes, and his initial approval of feminine behavior. According to a social learning or reinforcement model, these should have contributed to feminine behavior as well. While Zucker and Green (1992) conclude that parental tolerance or encouragement of feminine behavior are two of the conditions for such behavior to emerge, note that only the latter—encouragement—conforms to a social-learning paradigm, while the former—tolerance—suggests behavior determined by some undiscovered intrapersonal variable.

Where do these studies leave us? First, Bell, Weinberg, and Hammersmith (1981) and Roberts, Green, Williams, and Goodman (1987) agree that biological factors play an important role in the etiology of homosexuality. The question now is, How much of a role? Moreover, both studies conclude that there is no simple relation between parental behavior and eventual sexual preference. Rather, the adult outcome is probably due to a complex sequencing of events functioning as metaphorical "choice points" which can be decided in a number of ways, each resolution inclining the child toward a homosexual or a bisexual or a heterosexual adult orientation. In the psychoanalytic camp the same image of sexual development was expressed by Anna Freud (1965), who wrote, "the balance between heterosexuality and homosexuality during the whole period of childhood is . . . precarious, and the scales are . . . readily tipped in one direction or the other by a multitude of influences" (p. 197).

This image of sexual identity being the result of a series of contingencies, with organic, intrapersonal, and interpersonal factors playing an uncertain role, highlights how incomplete our understanding of homosexuality is. However, this awareness of incompleteness protects us from accepting absolute statements claiming otherwise—for example, that homosexuality is determined by factors in the organic context or by parental behavior or by choice.

Adult Outcomes

Freud helps us frame the proper question to ask of adult outcomes. He clearly recognized that homosexuality was not a psychopathology; however, he maintained that it was a fixation which prevented the development of a mature relationship in adulthood (Bootzin and Acocella, 1988). Thus, the proper question is not, Is the homosexual disturbed? but, Is he or she capable of mature love? The question is particularly appropriate for us since love has been one of our primary personality dimensions.

The most relevant data for answering our question come from Bell and Weinberg's (1978) study of 979 homosexual adults and 425 matched heterosexuals in the San Francisco Bay area. Unlike other studies, which treat homosexuals as a group, these investigators divided their population into five empirically derived subgroups.

1. The *Close-Coupled homosexuals* would correspond to the "happily married" heterosexuals. They were living with a same-sex partner, had few sexual problems, engaged in relatively little cruising (that is, seeking contacts for the sole purpose of a temporary sexual outlet) but were not worried when they did, had few difficulties in finding and maintaining affection from their partners, were sexually active, and had few regrets about being homosexual.

2. The *Open-Coupled homosexuals,* while also living with a special sexual partner, were

not happy in the arrangement. They tended to seek sexual satisfactions outside the relationship through cruising but were worried about this activity. While they were quite active sexually they were concerned about their partner's or their own responsiveness to sexual requests. They also tended to regret their homosexuality.

3. The *Functionals* come closest to the image of the "swinging single": they scored high on the number of sexual partners and level of sexual activity, low on concern over their homosexuality.

4. Like the Functionals, the *Dysfunctionals* also had a high level of sexual activity and many partners but had a number of sexual problems in regard to their adequacy and regretted being homosexual. They most closely conform to the stereotype of the tormented homosexual, being poorly adjusted not only sexually but socially and psychologically as well.

5. Finally, the *Asexuals* were not "coupled" and rated low on sexual activity, number of partners, and amount of cruising. They had more sexual problems than the group as a whole, more regrets over their homosexuality, and were less exclusively homosexual than the group as a whole. They led lonely, solitary, withdrawn lives.

Since Bell and Weinberg did not similarly classify their heterosexual group, no comparison of categories is possible. However, as they stand, the categories clearly refute any stereotype of "the homosexual" as well as the idea that homosexuals somehow have different kinds of relationships with their sexual partners. Certainly, heterosexuals also are happily or unhappily married, happy or unhappy swinging singles, or isolates.

While the categories were applicable to men and women, interesting differences were found. The lesbian was more apt to be involved in a quasi-marriage requiring a high degree of fidelity (that is, there were many Close-Couples); lacking this, they tended to find their homosexuality problematical, since they did not enjoy brief, varied sexual relations (that is, there were few Functionals). Gays were less satisfied with quasi-marriages (there were more Open- than Close-Couples) but could enjoy the pleasures of being "swinging singles" (or Functionals).

The homosexual's psychological adjustment was related to sex and category. Generally speaking, lesbians were as well adjusted as their heterosexual counterparts while gays were less well adjusted. On the positive side, gays and, to a lesser extent, lesbians experienced more happiness and exuberance than did heterosexuals. Among categories, the Dysfunctionals, Asexuals, and to a lesser extent, the Open-Coupled gays accounted largely for the greater degree of maladjustment in homosexuals. Signs of lowered adjustment included psychosomatic symptoms, lowered self-acceptance, loneliness, increased worry, depression, tension, paranoia, and suicidal feelings. The Close-Couple and Functional males were generally as well adjusted as their heterosexual counterparts except, interestingly, for heightened loneliness and tension in the latter.

About half the males and two-thirds of the females had no regret concerning being homosexual. Those who were unhappy listed as reasons social rejection, restrictive opportunities for social participation, not being able to have children, and loneliness.

In sum, Bell and Weinberg's data show that adult homosexuality per se should not be equated with psychopathology, although it increases the likelihood that specific categories of males will be less well-adjusted than heterosexual males in general. The study also suggests that Freud was wrong in assuming a necessary limitation in the ability to love maturely. The impression of the Close-Couples is that they have a sustained, mutually gratifying relationship.

Another sign of psychosexual maturity is

the ability to love and care for offspring. A review of the literature on lesbian and gay parents (Patterson, 1992) concludes that there is no evidence that the psychosocial development of children of such parents is compromised in any respect relative to that of offspring of heterosexual parents. On the contrary, the home environment provided by gay and lesbian parents is as likely as that of heterosexual parents to support and enhance the children's psychosocial growth.

Juxtaposing the findings on adolescents and adults, there seems to be a *developmental trend* in general adjustment. The early adolescent has the most serious problems, which decline toward late adolescence (Ramafedi, 1991) and decline even further in adulthood.

Helping the Troubled Adolescent Homosexual

Savin-Williams (1991) paints a gloomy picture in regard to troubled adolescents receiving the help they need. To begin with, there are few resources, even gay and lesbian organizations being reluctant or unable to offer them support, advice, or counseling. Professionals, particularly pediatricians, use the fact that homosexuality declines from adolescence to adulthood as evidence that it is just a passing phase on the road to heterosexuality and is therefore nothing to worry about.

Remafedi (1991) is more hopeful. Special programs that foster peer and family support, offer positive adult role models, and educate professionals are being designed and implemented. Some programs provide academic and vocational training for those who have left traditional school settings, others are aimed at counteracting chemical dependency or prosti-

tution, while still others emphasize safe sex as a means of curtailing the spread of AIDS.

Gonsiorek (1988) summarizes the needed services for gay and lesbian adolescents. He regards support groups as the most valuable resource for developing social skills, discussing the meaning of sexual identity, sharing information, and interacting with understanding peers. In addition, family support organizations reduce the isolation and discomfort of families of homosexual youths. Finally, such youths need health care and social services, role models, advocates, and AIDS education.

While there is a tendency in the literature to downplay the role of traditional therapeutic techniques in dealing with problems of social and internalized homophobia, they should be used in cases where psychopathological conditions occur with homosexuality. Behavior therapy and psychotherapy have also been used for those cases in which a change from a homosexual to a heterosexual orientation has been deemed advisable (Zucker and Green, 1992).

Thus far, these discussions have implicitly assumed that the developing child is not significantly deviant either intellectually or physiologically. The assumption has not always proved correct; in the instance of autism, for example, both mental retardation and organic brain pathology have been shown to be present. However, the etiologic import of intellectual and organic deviations has had to be demonstrated. The procedure will now be reversed, and mental retardation or a lack of organic intactness will be assumed, so that we may ask, What developmental deviations—if any—ensue?

CHAPTER 12

THE DEVELOPMENTAL CONSEQUENCES OF MENTAL RETARDATION

CHANGING DEFINITIONS

"Mental retardation is not something you have, like blue eyes or a bad heart. Nor is it something you are, like being short or thin. It is not a medical disorder. . . . Nor is it a mental disorder" (American Association of Mental Retardation, AAMR, 1992, p. 9). "Mental retardation is present when specific intellectual limitations affect the person's ability to cope with the ordinary challenges of everyday living in the community. If the intellectual limi-

tations have no real effect on functioning, then the person does not have mental retardation" (AAMR, 1992, p. 13).

These are startling statements for those who believe that mental retardation (MR) is defined in terms of a low IQ and that "once retarded, always retarded." They represent the latest in a series of definitions and conceptualizations by the American Association on Mental Retardation.

The original definition was in terms of subnormal intelligence but, in 1959, the AAMR added adaptive behavior as a criterion. If a person were adapting adequately to the environment, why regard him or her as psychopathologically disturbed or deviant or abnormal just because the IQ score was below a given cut-off point? For example, there is a group called "six-hour retardates" who do poorly in school but function well, say in a rural or inner city environment. Thus the key to MR is not an IQ score but the way an individual *functions*.

The current revision (1992) goes one step further. Adaptation itself is not some kind of trait or absolute quality individuals possess. Rather, adaptation is always in relation to an environment. Therefore the environment must be scrutinized before one calls an individual mentally retarded.

The new conceptualization of MR is represented in Figure 12.1. Note that *Functioning* is at the base of the triangle, signifying that it is the basic, or fundament, term. Capabilities and Environments, the other two variables, contribute equally to functioning.

Capabilities (or competence) is an intrapersonal variable. There are two kinds:

1. Inner capabilities are aspects of conceptual intelligence, which encompasses cognition and learning.
2. Social competencies include practical and social intelligence, which, in turn, form the basis for adaptive behavior.

Adaptive difficulties derive from limitations in practical and social intelligence. The former limits the ability to maintain oneself as an independent person in managing the ordinary activities of daily living. The latter limits the ability to comprehend social behavior (e.g., via perspective taking), to develop social skills, and to show good ethical judgment in interpersonal situations. (We will deal more directly with adaptive behavior later.)

Environments are conceptualized as the specific settings in which the person lives, learns, plays, works, socializes, and interacts. The environment must be typical of the child's same-age peers and appropriate to the child's socioeconomic background. MR disappears when

FIGURE 12.1
General structure of the definition of mental retardation. (*Source:* American Association on Mental Retardation, 1992.)

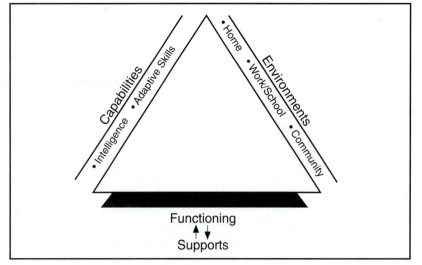

the individual is able to function well in the community without special support services. However, if the individual requires special supports or services, such as a sheltered workshop or institutional care, that person is considered to be mentally retarded.

According to this definition, *duration* need not be lifelong. If the environment becomes less demanding, such as the child leaving school, and the child adapts to it, then MR is "outgrown." It is important to note that intellectual functioning as measured by an IQ score is fairly stable from childhood on; however, it is the impact of intellectual limitations on functioning that may change.

Finally, this conceptualization explicitly states that MR is not a psychopathology. In addition, the definition in no way implies that MR places the child at risk for behavior problems. The essence of the definition is the child's adapting or failing to adapt to the environment. It therefore represents a new way of regarding deviance, since it differs from those we have already considered.

Definition *Mental retardation* refers to substantial limitations in present functioning. It is characterized by significantly subaverage intellectual functioning, existing concurrently with related limitations in two or more of the following applicable adaptive skills areas: communication, self-care, home living, social skills, community use, self-direction, health, and safety (AAMR, 1992, p. 5). Age of onset is under 18 years.

We will now examine two key terms in the definition: subaverage intellectual functioning and adaptive skills.

THE INTELLECTUAL DEFICIT

The first criterion for mental retardation (MR) involves "significantly subaverage general intellectual functioning," typically as measured by a standardized intelligence test, such as the Stanford-Binet or the Wechsler Intelligence Scale for Children. Numerically, an IQ score that is more than two standard deviations below the mean is regarded as a significant deviation from average intelligence. Depending on the test, such a score is between 67 and 69. IQ scores are also used to make finer classifications within the retarded range, although the nomenclature varies. For purposes of this discussion, IQ scores in the range of 52 to 69 would classify a child as mildly retarded, 36 to 51 as moderately retarded, 20 to 35 as severely retarded, and below 20 as profoundly retarded. For educational purposes, children with IQs between 55 and 80 are classified as educable, those with IQs between 25 and 55 are classified as trainable, while those with IQs below 25 are classified as custodial. (Morgenstern and Klass, 1991, discuss intelligence tests and the controversies surrounding them.)

Prevalence Using the statistical criterion of an IQ score two standard deviations or more below the mean, 2.3 percent of the population is mentally retarded. However, this statistical estimate cannot be regarded as absolute because there is a larger number of children at the lower end of the curve than would be predicted because of the addition of organically damaged children to those whose IQ is genetically determined. (For a detailed discussion of prevalence, see Deitz and Repp, 1989.)

ADAPTIVE BEHAVIOR

Intellectual level and adaptation are undoubtedly related; however, the correlation is not so high that the latter can accurately be inferred from the former. In certain instances the correlation may be low.

We will present the AAMD Adaptive Behavior Scale (Nihira et al., 1974) as an example of an instrument which assesses adaptive behavior (see Table 12.1). Statistical analyses showed that the ten behavior domains contain three factors—personal self-sufficiency, community self-sufficiency, and personal-social re-

TABLE 12.1
AAMD Adaptive Behavior Scale Domains

Part I (10 behavior domains)

I. Independent Functioning
   A. Eating
   B. Toilet use
   C. Cleanliness
   D. Appearance
   E. Care of clothing
   F. Dressing and undressing
   G. Travel
   H. General independent functioning
II. Physical development
   A. Sensory development
   B. Motor development
III. Economic activity
   A. Money handling and budgeting
   B. Shopping skills
IV. Language development
   A. Expression
   B. Comprehension
   C. Social language development
V. Numbers and time
VI. Domestic activity
   A. Cleaning
   B. Kitchen duties
   C. Other domestic activities
VII. Vocational activity
VIII. Self-direction
   A. Initiative
   B. Perseverance
   C. Leisure time
IX. Responsibility
X. Socialization

Part II (14 domains related to personality and behavior disorders)

I. Violent and destructive behavior
II. Antisocial behavior
III. Rebellious behavior
IV. Untrustworthy behavior
V. Withdrawal
VI. Stereotyped behavior and odd mannerisms
VII. Inappropriate interpersonal manners
VIII. Unacceptable vocal habits
IX. Unacceptable or eccentric habits
X. Self-abusive behavior
XI. Hyperactive tendencies
XII. Sexually aberrant behavior
XIII. Psychological disturbances
XIV. Use of medications

Source: Fogelman, 1974. Reprinted by permission.

sponsibility. Nihira's study of 3354 institutionalized subjects between 4 and 69 years of age adds a developmental perspective to these factors (Nihira, 1976).

Personal self-sufficiency is found at all ages and involves the ability to satisfy immediate personal needs such as eating, toileting, and dressing. Community self-sufficiency involves independence beyond immediate needs, along with self-sufficiency in relation to others; for example, using money, traveling, shopping, and communicating adequately. Personal-social responsibility involves initiative and perseverance, the ability to undertake a task on one's own and see it through to completion. These last two factors emerge around 10 years of age and are either weak or nonexistent in younger children. They also represent higher-level behavior than the mere satisfaction of immediate needs.

Developmental trends differ according to the degree of retardation. In general, the greater the retardation, the less rapid the development during childhood and the lower the final level of adaptation. For personal self-sufficiency, for example, 90 percent of total growth is achieved by 10 to 12 years of age in the mildly retarded groups, while the severely retarded groups achieve the same percent of growth between 16 and 18 years of age. Only the profoundly retarded continue to grow throughout the life cycle, although their rate is the slowest and their level the lowest of all the groups.

For the mildly, or what Nihira calls borderline, retarded children there is a rapid increase in personal self-sufficiency during childhood, which gradually tapers off during adolescence at the same time that community self-sufficiency is growing at an accelerated rate and surpassing it. This pattern seems congruent with development in non-retarded children. In moderately retarded children, community self-sufficiency grows more slowly, equaling personal self-sufficiency by adolescence but never rising above it subsequently. In the severely retarded, community self-sufficiency is consistently lower than personal self-sufficiency throughout the life span, indicating that in an institutionalized population competence in caring for immediate physical needs is the area of highest achievement (see Figure 12.2). (For other measures of adaptive behavior, see Deitz and Repp, 1989.)

ETIOLOGY

The Organic Context

A number of *genetic anomalies* can be accompanied by MR, the best known being Down syndrome (mongolism). Children with this anomaly have three number 21 chromosomes instead of the normal two. Hence, the condition is also called "trisomy 21." However, Down syndrome can also be caused by a num-

ber of other chromosome abnormalities. These children have distinctive physical features: almond-shaped eyes that slant upward; a flat nasal bridge; a relatively small mouth with a furrowed tongue that tends to protrude intermittently in infancy; small abnormally shaped and positioned teeth; small, square hands with a short first finger and a single crease running across the palm. Their IQs vary widely from profound to mild retardation, although the modal mental age of school-age children is approximately that of a 3½- to 5-year-old.

Phenylketonuria (PKU) is caused by a specific recessive gene. The affected infant lacks certain liver enzymes necessary for metabolizing the amino acid phenylalanine. Instead, phenylalanine accumulates and is converted to phenylpyruvic acid, a toxic substance that damages the brain. Although not totally satisfactory, screening methods based on the newborn's blood plasma can detect PKU, and a special phenylalanine-restricted diet can prevent retardation. The successfully treated child's intelligence is within the average range but somewhat lower than the intellectual level of the family.

A host of *prenatal and postnatal factors* can damage the central nervous system and result in MR. Rubella (German measles) contracted by the mother during the first trimester of pregnancy can cause a number of impairments, MR being one. Syphilis is another cause of MR as well as of fetal death. Exposure to massive doses of radiation in the first few months of pregnancy, chronic alcoholism, age (35 years or older), and severe emotional stress throughout pregnancy are among the numerous maternal factors that increase the risk of MR in the infant. Prematurity and prenatal asphyxia (oxygen deprivation during or immediately after delivery) are hazards of birth. Postnatal sources of mental subnormality are head injuries (most commonly resulting from automobile accidents and child abuse), encephalitis, and meningitis (inflammations of the brain resulting from infections by bacteria,

FIGURE 12.2
Developmental trends in personal and community self-sufficiency for borderline, moderately, and severely retarded individuals. (*Source:* Nihira, 1976.)

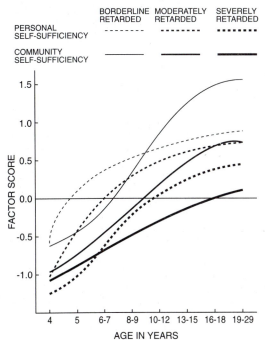

viruses, or tuberculosis organisms), particularly if they occur during infancy.

Clinical disorders associated with MR include cerebral palsy, seizure disorders (epilepsy), and lead and mercury poisoning from chemical pollutants ingested by the child (for example, by eating lead-based paint or shellfish that have absorbed methyl mercury from industrial waste.)

The foregoing list is intended solely to provide an overview of genetic and physical etiologies. In each instance the relation to MR, the degree of retardation, and the percent of affected children vary widely; it would be erroneous to conclude, for example, that all children with cerebral palsy or with seizures are also retarded, since a considerable portion are not. (A more detailed list of organic factors can be found in Deitz and Repp, 1989. Bregman and Hodapp, 1991, present current developments in biological research.)

The Intrapersonal Context

Both *cognitive* and *motivational* factors may be responsible for MR, although, understandably, the former have received the lion's share of attention from researchers. Since much of the cognitive research can be organized within an *information-processing model*, we will first describe the features of this model that will be relevant to our presentation.

Information processing analyzes thinking into a series of processes that bridge the gap between incoming information and an individual's response. A simplified version of this model will be presented here. First, there is the *sensory register*, which receives information from the environment. While its capacity is relatively large, it can hold impressions only briefly. Consequently, some information is lost while the remainder is passed on to *short-term memory, attention* playing a role in determining what information is transmitted. Short-term memory can hold information only 30 seconds

or so and is therefore a temporary working memory. Information is passed on to *long-term memory*, again with a certain loss. Long-term memory has a large capacity and can hold information more or less permanently.

What we have described are the *structural* features of the model which operate automatically. Other processes involve techniques that facilitate memory and are under the volitional control of the individual. These processes or *strategies*, such as *rehearsal, mediation*, and *clustering*, are particularly important because they increase the chances that information will be held longer in short-term memory and will fit with information already stored in long-term memory. They will be discussed in detail later. In order to be useful, information has to be not only stored in memory but *retrieved* as well, although relatively little research has been done on retrieval in mentally retarded children. The challenge for investigators using the information processing model, therefore, is to atomize the learning process into its basic components to determine which are and which are not functioning as they do in children with normal intelligence. (For a more elaborate model, see Hale and Borkowski, 1991.)

Attention to Relevant Cues   In the basic research paradigm, which is called *discrimination learning*, the child is presented with a succession of stimuli, two or three at a time—say, objects differing in color, shape, and size—and on the basis of being told that a choice is either right or wrong, the child must learn to choose the correct stimulus—say, the red object. To illustrate: A girl is presented with a red circle and a blue square; guessing that "circle" is the correct response, she chooses the first figure and is told she made a correct choice. Next time a green circle and a blue triangle are presented and she is told her choice of the circle is incorrect. She must now change her hypothesis. If she remembers the original circle was also red, she strongly suspects "red" to be the solution, which she verifies when another red object is shown. If she does not remember, she must adopt another hypothesis such as "triangle" or "green."

The learning curve for children of normal intelligence rises quickly at first and then levels off. For retarded children, choices are no better than chance for a number of trials, followed by rapid improvement.

Further investigation reveals that MR children often do not attend to relevant aspects of the situation; they are not asking themselves, Is it color? or shape? or size? On the contrary, they have a strong initial preference for position which they persist in using despite being told that their choice is frequently incorrect. Once they can break this irrelevant set, they learn rapidly. By the same token, if given a task in which position is the relevant cue—for example, the correct object is the first one—they learn as fast as or faster than normal children. In a special sense they are not slow learners but slow to catch on.

The retarded child's preference for position responses has its counterpart in normal development, since position habits have been observed to interfere with discrimination learning in l-year-olds. Such habits no longer seem to affect discrimination learning in the toddler and preschooler, although the evidence is not conclusive on this point. If the retarded child's preference does in fact represent a fixation, it is one that goes back to earliest childhood and may significantly interfere with subsequent learning. (For a review of the studies see Reese and Lipsitt, 1970.)

However, investigators have not been satisfied with the general explanation of failure to attend to relevant cues and, using the information processing model, have set out to pinpoint the source or sources of malfunctioning. Most of the studies have been done on mild to moderately retarded children who are organically intact. (Unless otherwise specified, our presentation follows Borkowski, Peck, and Damberg, 1983, and the more detailed and complex presentation of Hale and Borkowski, 1991.)

Attention Mentally retarded children may have a basic attentional deficit. For example, they have slower reaction times in simple reaction time experiments involving a preparatory signal, such as a buzzer, followed by a stimulus, such as a light, to which the subject must respond as quickly as possible, by pressing a button, for example. Another kind of evidence of a decreased ability to maintain adequate attentional levels is the increase in off-task glancing both in simple and complex tasks.

Memory There is no evidence that retarded children have a deficit in *short-term memory*. The situation in regard to *long-term memory* is more complicated because long-term memory depends on the use of a number of strategies designed to aid retention and organize the incoming information. Such strategies include rehearsal, mediation, and clustering, and, as has already been stated, are under volitional control.

Rehearsal, which is clearly evident by the third grade in nonretarded children, typically consists of repeating each new item along with all the prior ones; for example, in remembering a series of numbers a child may think, "six, six-three, six-three-eight," and so forth. Research indicates that MR children are deficient in rehearsal. If they are trained, their performance improves, but frequently they will not spontaneously use such aids. As with discrimination learning, they fail to do what they are capable of doing. And again, as with learning, this failure has its counterpart in normal development, since first-graders also make no use of their ability to rehearse (Flavell, 1977).

Remembering improves if incoming information is organized in a meaningful manner, a strategy called *clustering*. Present the average child with, say, a list comprised of three categories of words arranged in random order, and the child will tend to recall them by categories; for example, the words following "dog" will tend to be other animal words in the list, those following "apple" will be the other food words. Both retarded and young children of normal intelligence show little evidence of using the strategy of clustering. While retarded children can be taught to do so, once again they fail to use this aid spontaneously.

Memory is also facilitated by *mediation strategies*. The research paradigm here is paired-associate learning. Initially two stimuli are presented and subsequently, only the first is shown, with the child being asked to recall the second. Paired-associate learning can be facilitated if the child ties the two stimuli together in a meaningful manner; for example, *sun* and *bird* are more readily associated if related by, "the sun shines on the bird." While 5- to 6-year-olds can produce and use mediational strategies, younger and retarded children do not use them. If retarded children are provided with mediators or even instructed to generate them, their learning is significantly improved. However, if the experimenter no longer instructs the children, they may fail to continue using mediators on their own. Training them to "get into the habit" has met with only limited success, being effective primarily with the mildly retarded. Thus it is not that MR children are deficient in and cannot use higher-level strategies; for some unknown reason, they fail spontaneously to use the abilities they possess.

The findings concerning a possible deficit in long-term memory are contradictory and inconclusive because it is exceedingly difficult to control all the prior processes in order to obtain an unconfounded evaluation of this one alone.

There is evidence that the same deficiency in categorization which hampers memory also adversely affects *retrieval*. It makes sense to assume that items stored singly in memory would be more difficult to retrieve than ones stored by categories that represent superordinate organizations of such individual items. As was the case in short-term memory, the deficit seems to be one of lack of use of category knowledge rather than lack of category knowledge itself.

More recently, two higher-order processes that affect memory strategies have been added to the information processing model. The first is called *metacognition*, which is an understanding or awareness of when, where, and how to employ a strategy. In short, it is information about one's own cognitive processing. Metamemory refers specifically to information about memory, such as knowing it takes more time and effort to memorize a long list of words than a short one. While metamemory improves dramatically with age in normal children, the rate of improvement is variable in populations with MR; for example, mentally retarded children's understanding of the relation between amount of study time or the delay of recall on performance is commensurate with MA-matched peers, but even children with higher levels of intellectual functioning lack awareness of the advantage of relearning versus learning new material.

Executive function refers to the child's ability to select, monitor, evaluate, and revise strategies depending on the situation. Preliminary evidence indicates large individual differences among retarded children, some being capable of sizing up task demands and inventing strategies that lead to good performance, others being deficient. The reasons for this variability remain to be discovered. However, executive functioning may be one of the most important keys to understanding mental deficiency. Much of the evidence so far suggests that retarded children do not uniformly suffer from a cognitive deficit but that they may fail to use the abilities they possess.

Problem Solving While problem solving was not in our simplified model of information processing, it has been a topic of interest among investigators. Problem solving typically requires attention, abstraction, planning, and logical thinking. The same failure to generate relevant hypotheses that mars discrimination learning in MR children also affects the more complex task of solving problems. The classic twenty-questions task has been modified so that, in the simplest case, only one question is sufficient to supply the information necessary to make a correct choice. Even here, retarded children ask noncritical questions as frequently as critical ones. Once the information is supplied, they can use it effectively, however.

Generalization While MR children can be trained to do a specific problem successfully, they characteristically do not generalize to similar problems. It is as if each task is a new one that must be mastered in its own right. The impediment to learning is obvious.

Motivational Factors There is evidence that motivational factors play an important role in the performance and adjustment of mentally retarded children. (Our summary follows Merighi, Edison, and Zigler's, 1990, more detailed presentation of research.) Most studies are of mildly retarded school-aged children and adolescents.

Probably as a consequence of social deprivation, mentally retarded children tend to go to the extremes of *dependency* in relating to adults. Social deprivation can produce a heightened motivation to interact with warm, supportive adults; this, in turn, can interfere with concentrating on problem solving when such an individual is present as well as hampering the development of self-reliance. A characteristic related to overdependency is *outer-directedness* or seeking guidance from adults after failure. Such outer-directedness

can be growth-promoting especially for young children who lack the cognitive abilities to solve a number of problems. However, mentally retarded children carry this tendency to an extreme since repeated failure has led to a distrust of their problem-solving abilities. In terms of our variables, self-reliance suffers. At the other extreme, social deprivation can also lead to a reluctance to interact socially. This can result in an avoidance of tasks presented by adults and can hamper peer relations and friendships. (For the relation between MR and other psychopathologies, see Bregman, 1991.)

We now see that the MR child has a dual handicap, one intellectual, the other motivational. The problem may further be compounded in institutional settings where docility and conformity to a drab routine are rewarded, while assertiveness and initiative are punished. The challenge to researchers is to disentangle basic intellectual handicaps from those that result from motivational and environment influences. The therapeutic challenge is to find ways our society can accommodate the realistic limitations while maximizing the assets of the retarded child, which in turn will result in a more balanced mixture of successes and failures than presently exists. It is helpful to remind ourselves that in certain societies MR is not stigmatized or even viewed as a problem that needs correcting. Our achievement-oriented society might profit from such examples of acceptance.

The Interpersonal Context: Family Variables

Sameroff (1990) conducted the landmark studies showing that, aside from cases of extreme biological dysfunction, children's intelligence will be determined by environmental factors rather than by perinatal complications. For example, in 1975 he found that infants in advantaged families who suffered perinatal complications showed no or small residual effects, while infants from lower-class homes with identical medical histories showed significant retardation subsequently.

In the particular study we will describe, Sameroff further explored the environmental variable, hypothesizing that it was not the kind but the number of risks which determined intellectual functioning in children of comparable biological status. He extracted ten such risk factors from previous research: maternal mental illness, rigid values in regard to child development, large family, minimal education, etc. Using longitudinal data, Sameroff found that when the subjects were 4 years old, children with no risks scored more than 30 IQ points higher than children with eight or nine risks. In general, IQ declined as risk factors increased; for example, in multiple-risk families, 24 percent of the children had IQ scores below 85, while none of the children in the low-risk families did. Further analysis of the data revealed that no single risk variable reduced intellectual performance; rather, different families had different constellations of risk factors.

While the low-SES group had more high-risk families, high-risk middle- and upper-class families were equally damaging to their children's intellectual growth. Finally, Sameroff found that the correlations between environmental factors when children were 4 and 13 years of age were as high as the correlations between IQ scores at these two ages. In other words, the same lack of environmental support which undermined the children's competence at an early age would continue to do so through early adolescence.

The picture was not totally pessimistic, however, since 20 percent of the high-risk children escaped the fate of the group at large. The variables responsible for a more favorable outcome were parental restrictiveness, little democracy, clarity of rules, and emotional warmth. This pattern of "tough love" was sufficiently potent to counteract environmental risks.

The Interpersonal Context: Peer Relations

Guralnick (1986), in a short-term longitudinal study of fifty-two mildly delayed 4½-year-olds, found that social interaction lagged substantially behind the children's cognitive development. More ominous was the finding that progress during the year was so fragile that, at the beginning of the next school year, the children reverted to the level of social behavior that was characteristic of them at the beginning of the previous year.

One possible factor contributing to the developmental lag in social interaction is that retarded children are often grouped together in an educational setting and therefore cannot learn from or model themselves on children progressing at a normal rate. Since social interaction is facilitated when normal children of different chronological age are grouped together, one might expect a similar facilitation when MR children are *mainstreamed,* or placed in educational settings with normally developing children. However, the limited data available suggest that involvement with normal children produces only modest improvement in social and play interactions among preschoolers, perhaps because the tendency to form socially separate subgroups is a powerful one during this period (Guralnick, 1986). Thus while mildly retarded and normal children interact frequently and in similar ways, moderately and severely retarded children receive only infrequent attention from normal classmates. Interestingly, the interactions that do occur are not aversive, nor is there a failure in communication; on the contrary, the speech of normal children is simpler and more repetitive when they address cognitively less advanced children, and they are extremely persistent, creative, and successful in achieving their interpersonal goals. Even with mildly retarded children, the pattern of communication shows subtle differences, the normal children assuming an instructional mode, thereby being more "adultlike" than "peerlike" in their communication style.

The Superordinate Context

Approximately 75 percent of retarded individuals have no specific organic or genetic anomalies or unusual physical characteristics. (Our presentation is based on the more detailed review of Weisz, 1990, unless otherwise noted.) Their level of retardation is usually mild, with IQs rarely lower than 45 to 50, and they have at least one other immediate family member who is also retarded. Such retardation is most prevalent in lower-socioeconomic groups where there is an increased frequency of conditions inimical to intellectual growth: prenatal and postnatal risk, inadequate health care, large families, disorganized home environments lacking in personal attention and

growth-promoting objects such as books and "readiness" games.

This group of retarded individuals is called *cultural-familial.* Both environmental and genetic factors are involved, the contribution of the two being about equal (Plomin, 1989). Cultural-familial individuals represent the lower end of the normal distribution of intelligence.

The Difference-versus-Development Issue

At the most general level there are two distinct answers to the why of mental retardation. The first is that mentally retarded individuals are cognitively defective and their thinking is *qualitatively different* from that of individuals with normal intelligence. The second answer is that mentally retarded individuals' thinking is like that of nonretarded individuals, but they progress at a slower rate and cease growing intellectually at a lower level. However, the same principles of cognitive *development* apply to them (see Figure 12.3).

The developmentalists have derived two

FIGURE 12.3
Developmental model of cognitive growth. The single vertical arrow represents the passage of time. The horizontal arrows represent environmental events impinging on the individual, who is represented as a pair of vertical lines. The individual's cognitive development appears as an internal ascending spiral, in which the numbered loops represent successive stages of cognitive growth. (*Source:* Hodapp and Zigler, 1990.)

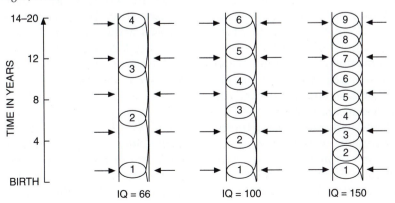

specific hypotheses from their general claim. The *similar-sequence* hypothesis states that mentally retarded individuals proceed through the various stages of cognitive development in much the same manner as nonretarded individuals. This hypothesis has been most extensively tested using Piaget's stages. The *similar-structure* hypothesis states that when retarded individuals are matched with nonretarded ones in regard to overall cognitive level, their functioning on specific cognitive tasks such as memory should be comparable. Matching is typically done in terms of MA. (For details of the difference vs. developmental issue, see Hodapp, Burack, and Zigler, 1990.)

How have the two hypotheses fared when put to the test of objective studies? Both can claim victories, but the record of the developmentalists is more impressive. With the possible exception of children with seizure disorders, both organically and familial retarded children proceed through the same Piagetian stages as do nonretarded children. This finding applies to a large number of Piagetian variables such as object permanence, causality, and moral reasoning. However, earlier developments, such as those in the sensorimotor stage show a greater degree of invariance than do later, more culturally determined ones such as moral development (Hodapp, 1990).

The similar-structure hypothesis has not been so uniformly favorable to the developmentalists. Retarded children perform significantly worse on information-processing tasks; for example, the familial group scores significantly lower on memory, distractibility, attention, and discrimination tasks than the MA-matched group. Because both groups are at the same general level of cognitive development, the deficits are interpreted as a qualitative difference from normality. It is not clear at this point whether the two models can be reconciled or whether one will be needed for Piagetian tasks and the other for information-processing tasks (Mundy and Kasari, 1990).

DOWN SYNDROME CHILDREN

The Organic Context

As we have seen, Down syndrome (DS) is due to various chromosome anomalies, the most frequent being a trisomy 21. There is also evidence of abnormalities in the postnatal growth and elaboration of neuronal networks, as measured by the growth and structure of dendrites and extensions of neurons. This decreased maturation may account for the persistence of primitive reflexes beyond the early months of life, poor muscle tone and motor control, and, more speculatively, the difficulty in synthesizing information quickly and efficiently. It may also underlie an inherent decrease in reactivity to stimulation (Ganiban, Wagner, and Cicchetti, 1990).

Among constitutional variables, the higher arousal thresholds and dampened affective intensity are of special interest since they impact upon the variables of attachment and anxiety. Infants with Down syndrome show a decreased positive and negative affect even when their delayed cognitive development is taken into account (Cicchetti and Beeghly, 1990). For example, their smiling is delayed, less frequent, and less intense than it is in normally developing infants, while there is decreased fear in the "visual cliff" situation and in response to looming objects (Berger, 1990; Cicchetti and Beeghly, 1990). However, decreased affective intensity does not imply decreased general responsiveness, since the infants are highly attentive to the environment and their activity level is normal (Ganiban, Wagner, and Cicchetti, 1990).

The Intrapersonal Context: Cognition

The decline in intelligence in Down syndrome children begins in infancy and proceeds at a decelerated rate thereafter; the Development Quotient is 71 to 75 between 16 and 40 weeks, 69 at 1 year, and 58 at 18 months. While some children have average intelligence, the mean IQ of the group as a whole is around 50. The reason for this decelerated pattern is unknown (Hodapp and Zigler, 1990).

Sensorimotor progress conforms to the developmental model described above; the sequencing is the same as in intellectually normal children, but there is a progressive slowing down in acquisition of competencies and a lower level of maximal growth (Dunst, 1990).

The limited number of studies of *information processing* indicate that infants with Down syndrome are less efficient in processing visual information such as visual patterns than are normally developing infants. Consequently, both infants and toddlers are more persistent and attentive, while lagging behind in shifting to different patterns and preference for novelty. This need for longer time to process information may, in turn, be related to a delay in maturation of their visual cortex (Ganiban, Wagner, and Cicchetti, 1990.)

The *structure* of intelligence in children with Down syndrome does not resemble that of normally developing children. In normal development various cognitive skills are at more or less comparable levels, while in Down syndrome development is disjointed. Thus, social skills are in advance of general intelligence, so that a 15-year-old might have an MA of 4 years and the social intelligence of a 7-year-old; or again, the purely cognitive aspects of language such as syntax may lag behind the social aspects of pragmatics, as we shall soon see. The reasons for such disjointed development are not understood (Hodapp and Zigler, 1990).

The *conceptual development* of children with Down syndrome parallels that of developmentally nondisabled children, always keeping in mind the difference in absolute level. For example, the initial vocabulary of both groups of children consists of the same level of categorizing objects, and even within levels, the choice of particular words is often identical, so

that "shoe" and "sockie" come before "shirt" and "pants." These findings suggest that basic categories are universal, both ordering the potential chaos of individual experiences and making communication possible (Mervis, 1990).

Generally speaking, *language* conforms to the developmental model of delay without deviance, although all aspects cannot be reduced to that simple formula (Fowler, 1990). Infants, like their nondisabled counterparts, prefer the human voice over other auditory stimuli and prefer the mother's "baby talk" to her "adult talk," but there is less vocal imitation and understanding of speech (Wagner, Ganiban, and Cicchetti, 1990). Turning to subsequent periods, a large body of studies documents a significant delay in speech relative to intellectual, social, and motor development; for example, while a few children will read at the level of a 5-year-old and have limited writing skills, the majority will not progress beyond the level of the simple phrase structure grammar found in nondisabled 2- to 3-year olds. On the other hand, lexical knowledge (vocabulary) is relatively unaffected (Fowler, 1990). The social aspects of language or pragmatics are also relatively spared; conversational relevance, topic maintenance, and turn-taking skills are comparable to MA-matched controls. While there has been speculation concerning the reasons for this disjointed development, the causes remain to be discovered. (See, Beeghly, Weiss-Perry, and Cicchetti, 1990.)

Developmental Pathway

Infancy Carr (1975) found that, in regard to *feeding*, Down syndrome infants were less alert and eager for food, had weaker sucking reflexes, and were sleepier than the normal controls. The mothers did not feed on demand simply because the infants were so undemanding—rarely crying and having to be awakened in certain instances—and fewer infants were breast-fed because of the difficulty involved in getting them to suck. Understandably, the mothers were more anxious over feeding than were mothers of normal infants.

Not only was bottle-feeding the rule, but DS children also remained dependent on the bottle owing to their lag in motor development. At 12 months they were like 8-month-olds, lacking the control of grasping necessary for self-feeding. More mothers of DS than normal children reacted with concern over feeding, forcing or encouraging the toddler or saving the food until later. While the 4-year-old DS preschoolers lagged behind the controls in self-feeding, two-thirds were capable of eating ordinary family meals, and feeding was no longer a problem to most of the mothers. Here, we see the infant "outgrowing" a problem and maternal concern diminishing.

Attachment conforms to the developmental model in that progression is broadly the same in infants with Down syndrome as in nondisabled infants, although one does not exactly mirror the other. In the preattachment months eye contact is delayed, the social smile is less frequent and intense, and, while the infant vocalizes more than nondisabled ones after the first two to three months of life, there is less coordinated vocal turn-taking and more vocal clashes between mother and infant. Yet mothers are able to accommodate to these deviations and mother and infant are able to enter into reciprocal interactions which are the prelude to attachment (Berger, 1990). The complex behaviors comprising attachment itself (following, separation protest, wariness of strangers) are organized in the same manner as they are in nondisabled infants, and in the majority of cases a secure attachment is formed. However, there are differences in the quality of certain component behaviors—affect is dampened, the latency of crying at separation is increased, and soothability is decreased (Cicchetti and Beeghly, 1990).

The period following attachment (9 to 36 months) has its own special problems. In normal development, the mother and child begin to do things together, and their interaction increasingly incorporates objects such as toys and pictures. The child with Down syndrome both has less interest in exploring objects and greater difficulty in maintaining joint attention to objects and caretaker, tending to withdraw from playing. Unfortunately, perhaps out of their own concern or because of literature stressing the importance of stimulation to cognitive growth, mothers may begin to make too great demands on their child's ability to understand and perform. Consequently, the interaction becomes frustrating to both partners (Berger, 1990).

The Toddler Period   Carr (1975) found that *toilet training* showed the opposite development from feeding, in that the DS children "grew into" deviant behavior. At 15 months there was no difference between groups in terms of the age at which training was started and in terms of maternal attitudes; by 4 years of age the DS children were significantly retarded in all aspects of toileting—they wet their beds and wet or dirtied their pants more and were less adept at self-care. Unlike early feeding, differences in toilet training did not differentially affect the mother's attitudes even though the DS children had many more accidents.

As to *initiative*, toddlers with Down syndrome are reactive to the environment but have neither the intensity of investment nor the attraction to novelty that characterizes their nondisabled peers. Thus, they are described as high in approach, low in intensity of response, positive in mood, and perseverative (Ganiban, Wagner, and Cicchetti, 1990). Toddlers also initiate fewer behaviors with caregivers (Beeghly, Weiss-Perry, and Cicchetti, 1990). The adjective "passive" crops up in the descriptive literature. The children are not withdrawn; rather they are deficient in the expansive, enterprising aspects of initiative.

Kopp (1990) studied *self-control* in fifteen children with Down syndrome between 2 years and 3 years 4 months of age and a group of developmentally matched nonretarded children between 18 months and 2½ years of age. Mothers and children were observed in a room where a number of toys were available. The children were instructed not to touch an attractive red plastic telephone in the 150 seconds during which the experimenter was out of the room and the mothers were ostensibly reading a magazine. Children with Down syndrome were significantly less able to control the impulse to touch the toy even when taking their developmental level into account. This might have been due to the fact that, unlike the control group, they did not divert their attention from the toy, for example, by looking around the room.

The Preschool Period   Carr's (1975) longitudinal data present a fluctuating picture in the first four years of life, children growing into and out of *behavior problems.* However, by 4 years of age, there was no difference between children with Down syndrome and the control group in terms of temper tantrums, aggressiveness, distress and upset, although the Down syndrome children got into mischief more frequently, for example, fiddling with light switches, putting things in the toilet. There was also no difference in either the amount or the kind of behavior problems such as rudeness, attention seeking, and oppositional behavior.

Overall Trends   The stereotype of children with Down syndrome is that they are friendly, sociable, and open. However, research has only partially supported this picture. Hodapp

and Zigler (1990) show that the children score higher than their MA on tests of social maturity and, as we have seen, they are most adept at the "social" aspects of language or pragmatics (Hodapp and Zigler, 1990). Other studies are at variance with the stereotype, while there are both age and sex differences. The placid, minimally responsive infant becomes outgoing, amiable, and extroverted in middle childhood and, subsequently, sullen and stubborn in adolescence. In addition, girls are more sociable than boys. (For a detailed presentation of sociability, see Serafica, 1990.)

The Interpersonal Context: The Family

Carr's (1975) research found that the DS child did not seriously disrupt family life, at least in the early years. Contacts with friends, relatives, and casual acquaintances continued as before. Only 21 percent of the mothers described themselves as lonely, especially if they did not receive psychological support from relatives and friends, although there is no way to tell how much their own behavior contributed to their isolation.

A good deal of consistency was found in parental life: the same mothers were working, the same fathers were participating in child care, parents were going out or staying at home as frequently and expressing the same degrees of contentment with their lot. The overall picture, then, is of parents continuing to behave "in character," of family styles being preserved, and of children being influenced in the same manner by early experiences. However, mothers of preschoolers were markedly worried over the future, anticipating—probably realistically—that the most difficult problems were yet to come. Crnic's (1990) review of the literature arrived at a similar conclusion. In spite of added stress, most families were coping adequately. (See Sloper et al., 1991, for factors related to stress and satisfaction.)

A child with Down syndrome can be an enjoyable playmate.

DEVELOPMENTAL MODELS

Our exploration of the intellectual functioning and personality of mentally retarded children has revealed a variety of models of deviant development. In certain instances retarded children are hampered by a slow rate of growth or a *developmental lag;* for example, the progress of community self-sufficiency in moderately retarded children or the DS child's mischievousness at 4 years of age when normal counterparts have passed through this stage. There may be growth failures or *fixations,* such as the utilization of position in discrimination learning or the failure to rehearse as an aid to remembering. There is the *exaggeration* of normal behavior as evidenced in the retarded child's outer-directedness and reliance on external cues. There is disjointed development, or what we call *asynchrony,* such as social intelligence being in advance of general intelligence, or syntax lagging behind

pragmatics in language. Finally, there is the possibility of *qualitatively different thinking* in retarded children whose performance is inferior even when their general intellectual level is taken into account. However, this is a different meaning of the term than that used in connection with autism (typical behavior that has little or no counterpart in normal development) and schizophrenia (behavior that is not rooted in prior development). How or whether these usages are related is impossible to say.

REMEDIAL AND PREVENTIVE PROGRAMS

The Overall Need

Because severe and profound levels of retardation tend to persist into adulthood rather than being "outgrown," it is clear that special preventive and remedial measures need to be taken. However, the situation is somewhat deceptive in regard to children at less retarded levels who comprise the vast majority of the MR population. Most of them live in the homes of parents or other relatives or with foster parents. And most of them function well, going to school during middle childhood, moving reasonably freely about the community, and participating in family life. Many of them subsequently hold jobs. Thus one may have the impression that these mildly to moderately retarded adults are absorbed into society and that their difficulties are solely in connection with having to attend school. However, the impression is misleading, because they turn up in a disproportionate number both on the welfare rolls and on police blotters (Haywood, Meyers, and Switzky, 1982). While they do not need the kind of extensive care that severely retarded children do, they are clearly at risk in regard to making an adequate adjustment to society.

Government Involvement

One aspect of programs for the mentally retarded that is of special interest is the involvement of the federal government. Legislative activity was climaxed by Public Law 94-142, known as the Education for All Handicapped Children Act of 1975. Its purpose was to assure that all handicapped children have a free public education tailored to their unique needs, to assure the rights of handicapped children and their parents or guardians, to assist states in providing education, and to assess and assure the effectiveness of efforts toward education. Two specific requirements have had far-reaching effects. The first is that an individualized education program (IEP) be devised for each child. Implementing an IEP involves assessment of the child's present level of functioning, setting goals, and providing educational services and procedures for evaluating educational progress. Parents as well as various

professionals participate in the decision-making process. The second requirement is that handicapped children be educated in the least restrictive environment. This requirement reversed the seventy-five-year-old trend of placing disabled children in self-contained special settings, such as special classrooms for the educably mentally retarded (EMR). The contention was that such classes were ineffective in helping many EMR children learn basic academic and occupational skills, that minorities were overrepresented and that advances in education have made individualized instruction in regular classes feasible (Beyer, 1991).

Special Education

Children with IQ scores between 55 and 80 are classified by most school systems as educable mentally retarded and are expected to perform at least at a third-grade level and occasionally as high as a sixth-grade level by the time they finish school. The trainable mentally retarded (TMR) with IQ scores between 25 and 55 are taught to function in a restricted environment because they are not expected to master traditional academic skills.

In special education classes, EMR pupils are taught academic subjects as tools to enhance social competence and occupational skills. Small classes with individualized attention are recommended. Between 6 and 10 years of age the EMR child, whose MA is between 3 and 6 years, is given the kind of readiness programs usually found in kindergarten; the emphasis is on language enrichment and self-confidence, along with good health, work, and play habits. EMR children between 9 and 13 years of age, whose MA is about 6 to 9 years, can master the basic academic skills involved in the three R's. At the junior and senior high school levels the applied emphasis continues; for example, the children are trained to read the newspaper and job application forms and to make correct change. Occupational education stresses appropriate work habits such as punctuality and following directions, since most vocational failures are due to poor adjustment rather than low mental ability. After formal schooling, sheltered workshops and vocational rehabilitation centers help the mildly retarded adjust to our complex society.

The curriculum for TMRs emphasizes self-care and communication skills, work habits, following directions, and rudimentary social participation. Reading instruction, for example, is likely to include recognizing signs such as "Stop," "Men," and "Women," while arithmetic is limited to making change. The majority of these children do not achieve social or economic independence as adults, although they can engage in useful work and adjust well in the protective setting of the family.

Educating MR children in regular classrooms is called *mainstreaming*. In keeping with the social fervor of the times, special classes have been labeled another form of discrimination and segregation. The claim has been buttressed by poorly designed studies showing that MR children in special classes fare worse than those in regular classes. Such studies ignored the fact that children were often placed in special classes because they were doing poorly or were so disruptive that it was impossible for the teacher to handle them in the regular classroom.

Research indicates that mainstreaming does not affect the academic achievement of EMR children. Observational studies show that there are few differences in the kind of education EMR children receive in either setting. In addition, mainstreaming does not increase social acceptance, nor does it uniformly result in a more positive self-concept (Gottleib, Alter, and Gottleib, 1991).

Treatment

Psychopharmacotherapy has been used not for mental retardation itself but for some of its accompanying disturbances. In their review, Aman and Singh (1991) conclude that, after 35 years of research, most studies are so poorly designed that findings cannot be accepted with any degree of confidence. While recognizing the methodological shortcomings of the research, Gadow (1992) is more sanguine in his review, citing instances in which drugs have been effective in reducing depression, self-injuries, and stereotypic behaviors. Since he had to include studies of adults as well as children, the case for psychopharmacotherapy remains a weak one.

Until recently, MR children were deemed unsuited for *psychotherapy* because of their limited comprehension and verbal ability, poor impulse control, and passivity in problem-solving situations (LaVietes, 1978). Typically, "environmental manipulation" was recommended in terms of consulting with parents and teachers and exploring resources in the community. While such counseling still plays a prominent role in remediation, a number of therapeutic techniques have been adapted to the special needs of the MR child. Nonverbal techniques such as play and art therapy can serve the dual function of tension release and self-expression. Verbal techniques can be used for reassurance, support, discussion, and advice, as well as for clarifying and interpreting feelings. Group therapies have become the most popular variant of psychotherapy; some take the form of discussions, others revolve around activities such as play, handicrafts, movies, or trips, while still others focus on the reflection and interpretation of feelings. Parent groups offer the opportunity for discussion in a setting of shared problems and mutual concern.

By far the most successful and widely used therapeutic technique is *behavior modification*, employing the operant principles of changing undesirable behaviors by altering the specific consequences which reinforce them and by reinforcing new, more socially acceptable responses (Huguenin, Weidenman, and Mulick,

1991). This technique has been used to increase a wide array of behaviors: self-help behaviors (toileting, feeding, dressing), work-oriented behaviors (productivity, task completion), social behaviors (cooperation, group activities), nonacademic classroom behaviors (attending, taking turns, talking at appropriate times), academic learning (arithmetic, sight vocabulary), as well as decreasing undesirable behaviors such as attention getting and aggressive or self-injurious behaviors. An important benefit is that parents can actively participate in the therapeutic program in the home setting.

While a number of parental training programs have been devised and successfully implemented, lower-SES parents—the very group that needs such programs most—often terminate or, when they stay, acquire lower proficiency in implementation (Harris, Alessandri, and Gill, 1991).

Most important of all, behavior modification, more than any other single therapeutic technique, has been responsible for changing the prevailing attitude of hopelessness among professional and nonprofessional caretakers. While data on relative effectiveness of various psychotherapies are meager, behavior modification has provided the clearest evidence that the behavior of MR children can be changed. (For a more detailed presentation of treatment, see Erickson, 1992).

Prevention

The diversity of preventive programs reflects the diverse etiologies of MR itself. A number are medically oriented—such as genetic counseling, therapeutic abortions, elimination of defect-producing illnesses, and compulsory tests for phenylketonuria (See Pueschel and Goldstein, 1991, for a discussion of genetic counseling.) More relevant are the compensatory educational programs, especially those involving preschool children. Head Start is probably the best known (see Chapter 17).

While there have been literally hundreds of compensatory education programs designed to prevent the decline of IQ often found in lower-class children, only a handful meet the minimal criteria for adequate evaluation of effectiveness. *Infant stimulation* programs have been particularly popular. Typically they are based on the "sensitive period" hypothesis that early experiences play a particularly important role in determining subsequent development, and on the observation that a number of lower-class mothers, perhaps from ignorance or immaturity or realistic burdens or different value systems, were not providing infants with the kind of stimulation that enhances cognitive development. While such programs played an important role in finding ways to involve mothers who were disinterested or suspicious or uncooperative, they were often so poorly designed and unsatisfactorily evaluated that it is impossible to judge their effectiveness.

One of the few programs that meets the criteria for evaluation of effectiveness and is closely linked with developmental data and theory was conducted by Slaughter (1983). She studied eighty-three black mother–child dyads randomly recruited from low-income housing projects. The two-year short-term longitudinal design began when the infants were 18 months of age and ended when they were 44 months. The choice of age was based on developmental studies showing that the difference in average IQ performance between children of higher status and children of lower status backgrounds emerges between 18 and 42 months of age. The purpose of the study was to prevent the decline.

On the basis of the findings from previous studies, Slaughter (1983) devised two kinds of interventions. Because of the importance of play as a facilitator of cognitive development, her first intervention was a demonstration program stressing the role of the adult in stimulating play through the use of toys. A primary goal of the program was to encourage verbal interaction between mother and child using play as a vehicle. The toys were selected for their cognitive stimulus value and were demonstrated by a specially trained "toy demonstrator" who modeled the play with a new item while the mother observed. The demonstrator then invited the mother to imitate this approach and encouraged her to use it in subsequent play. The second intervention was called the "mothers discussion group program" and consisted of weekly 1½-hour meetings of ten to fifteen mothers, initially to share concerns about child rearing and, later, to discuss more general problems. Under the guidance of a trained group leader, the mothers were expected to learn from each other as well as receiving psychological support. The goal was to provide educational experiences that would promote independent thinking and decision making in regard to child rearing and family life in general. Finally, there was a control group that did not receive any intervention.

In the final evaluation, children in the intervention groups were intellectually superior to those in the control group. While the intervention did not significantly raise IQ scores, it prevented the 13-point decline found in the control group. Mothers in the discussion group were significantly higher than the control group in a measure of ego development involving the perception of the self and relations to significant people in the social environment. These mothers also interacted more with their child and were more likely to expand on the child's ongoing play. The children of mothers in the discussion group also verbalized more during play. Finally, mothers in the discussion group were more open to outsiders (i.e., persons other than relatives and friends) in that they were willing to use social institutions as resources and perceived them as beneficial.

Thus, while both interventions were effective in regard to maintaining the children's level of IQ, the discussion group had more wide ranging effects, involving the mother's personality, her interaction with her child, and her attitude toward community resources. The finding was unexpected since it was thought that the toy demonstration program, being more specific, would be the greater facilitator of constructive maternal behavior and of children's verbalization. In accounting for the change, Slaughter speculated that the discussion group developed an interaction akin to that of an extended family in that the mothers felt close and comfortable enough to share problems and to give and receive help. Equally important, the problems and solutions were congruent with their own experiences rather than having the aura of being imposed upon them by well-meaning professionals.

While Slaughter did not do a follow-up study, a number of such studies have been conducted. We will discuss these studies in Chapter 17.

From this point on, we will be concerned with children at risk for developing behavior problems. Some have to cope with stress arising from chronic illness and brain damage, some with stress arising from parents or caretaking adults, some with stress from a prejudicial society. While they may become psychopathologically disturbed, typically they do not. In fact, many adjust remakably well as we shall see.

RISKS OF PHYSICAL ILLNESS AND BRAIN DAMAGE

Throughout life, but particularly during childhood, the body is the stage on which some of the most significant developmental dramas are enacted. We have already explored the importance of eating and elimination in the normal and psychopathological development of children who are physically healthy. If children are chronically ill or brain-damaged, we might rightly suspect that they must contend with special stresses and problems. They may be able to take such stresses in stride and even be stronger because of them. But they may also be taxed beyond their ability to cope successfully.

PEDIATRIC PSYCHOLOGY

It is natural initially to view the unknown in terms of the known. At times the strategy is successful. At times it misses the mark. A case in point is *pediatric psychology*. Clinical child psychologists who became interested in understanding and helping pediatric patients tended to ask the clinician's questions: How is physical illness related to traditional disturbances such as anxiety disorder, depression, and conduct disorders? and What traditional treatments would benefit such children? While these are legitimate questions they are too narrow to capture essential features of physical illness in children. Our own preference is to ask the developmental psychopathologist's questions: What is the child's experience and understanding of illness at various developmental levels? and How do these affect the intrapersonal and interpersonal variables (particularly the family) that have concerned us all along? In short, what we are searching for is a *developmental psychology of illness*. Here, as in our other inquiries, we are concerned with stresses and functional impairments on the one hand, coping mechanisms and resources on the other. Before pursuing this theme, we need to define the field itself.

Pediatric psychology is also known as behavioral medicine and health psychology. Its basic assumption is that both sickness and health result from the interplay between organic factors on the one hand and psychological, social, and cultural factors on the other, thus conforming to our now familiar interactional model. In regard to disease in particular, this interplay is present at every stage, from etiology to course and treatment, although at different points one or another factor may be predominant. In addition, the field includes the psychological and social variables involved in prevention and health maintenance. Finally, the primary concern is with chronically ill children, as life-threatening illnesses are increasingly being controlled. (See Barbarin, 1990; for a general reference, see Gross and Drabman, 1990).

Children's Understanding of Chronic Illness

We will begin with the understanding of pain and chronic illnesses at different developmental phases. (Unless otherwise indicated, our presentation follows Garrison and Mc-Quiston's 1989 review of objective studies.) In the past, researchers and professionals believed that *neonates* did not feel pain, so analgesics or pain-reducing medication was not necessary. Recent studies have proven the belief to be erroneous, although the practice of withholding analgesics is only slowly dying out. (See Craig and Grunau, 1991; Bush and Harkins, 1991, present the general topic of pain from a developmental perspective.) By 3 to 10 months pain is localized to a specific part of the body, while memory of a painful experience emerges after 6 months. *Toddlers* understand illness egocentrically in terms of how it affects them and how it interferes with activities and choice. Thus, illness hurts, sometimes requires painful medical treatments, separates them from important adults, and interferes with play. Extrapolating from Piaget's theory of early cognitive development, one would also expect magical thinking in terms of assuming responsibility for sickness: If something bad happens to me, then I must have done something bad.

In the *preschool* period thinking becomes more differentiated in that the child realizes that certain familiar painful experiences such as getting a cold and skinning a knee are not due to badness; however, magical thinking in terms of personal responsibility can still appear in regard to less familiar discomforts and illnesses.

Middle childhood thinking is accurate but concrete. The child now knows that illnesses involve some interaction of events occurring outside the body ("People get colds from going out in the winter") or that they are internalized from the outside to the inside ("People get colds from breathing in germs"). Prevention is particularly difficult to grasp perhaps because of the concreteness of the children's thinking: How can you do something about an illness that does not even exist yet?

Adolescents are now cognitively capable of abstract adultlike definitions of illness, but their concepts are still predominantly concrete. As often happens, cognitive advances do not guarantee the disappearance of more primitive ideas, particularly in the face of stressors. Again we have an illustration of regression. As a 12-year-old leukemic patient remarked, "I know that my doctor told me that my illness was caused by too many white cells, but I still wonder if it was caused by something I did."

Tracing the changes in the meaning of illness is of more than academic interest. There is a general belief that the more information children have about an illness, the better they will be able to cope with its stresses and the more compliant they will be with therapeutic recommendations. This approach is particularly important from middle childhood on when children are given increasing responsibilities for implementing therapeutic regimens. Yet research suggests that such a generalization is incorrect; as we have already seen, information concerning prevention is wasted on children too cognitively immature to grasp the basic concept. We will soon see other examples. Rather, the effectiveness of information depends on the kind of chronic illness, the kind of child, and the kind of parent.

The Effects of Chronic Illness on Development

Chronically ill and healthy children face the same developmental tasks and challenges, but illness adds special stresses: the disease itself, medication and other forms of treatment, fre-

quent hospitalizations, disruption of school and other daily activities, alterations in family relationships. These stresses differ at different developmental phases (Garrison and Mc-Quiston, 1989).

The hospitalized, chronically ill *infant* experiences highly intrusive, often painful medical procedures, intense and often noncontingent stimulation such as the continuous noise of monitors, ventilators, and staff conversations in the intensive care unit, plus repeated change of caregivers. All this interferes with the integration of autonomic and motor systems, such as digestion, respiration, posture, and movement, as well as with the formation of an attachment.

The *toddler* faces similar stresses from a painful illness and medical procedures along with separation due to hospitalization and increased parental anxiety. Physical restraint or restriction of movement, and parental worry or possible overprotectiveness frustrate the desire to explore and master the environment. The realistic increased dependence on parents for health care, particularly when compounded by parental overconcern in regard to the toddler's vulnerability, makes the struggle for autonomy more difficult and tempts the toddler to regress to the infantile stage.

Middle childhood has been relatively neglected in regard to clinical and objective studies, which have concentrated primarily on *adolescence*. Just at the time when peer relations take on an increased importance, chronic illness may diminish such contacts by limiting participation in social events and school. Delayed physical development or physical disfigurement, such as the small stature, chronic cough, barrel chest, and low exercise tolerance that may accompany cystic fibrosis, can be particularly distressing for the body-conscious adolescent. For its part, the medical community tends to perceive the adolescent as a chronic noncomplier; therapeutic procedures, even those essential to health, may be caught up in the adolescent's general need to defy authority and assert independence.

Departing briefly from Garrison and McQuiston, we can see how the same event—hospitalization—might have different meanings depending on when it occurs in development. Infants under 6 months who have not formed an attachment are relatively unfazed by separation anxiety, while those who have attached may suffer from it. The toddler and certain preschoolers may worry about what they have done wrong, while in middle childhood the concern may center on the pain that might be inflicted. For adolescents, isolation from peers and missing out on social and school activities may be a primary concern. This is one reason why it is important to have a developmental psychology of illness. (See Table 13.1 for a summary of findings concerning a developmental psychology of illness.)

This survey of what is known about the developmental psychology of illness highlights how far we have to go to achieve a comprehensive account. The understanding of illness is only one of many cognitive factors that may have to be investigated and integrated into a developmental framework. For example, nondevelopmentally oriented research indicates that children with an internal locus of control concerning illness (i.e., those who believe their health is in their own hands rather than being controlled by powerful others or chance) have a more sophisticated understanding of diseases and are more knowledgeable about illness (Tinsley, 1992). Still in the intrapersonal context, the relation between cognition and behavior at different phases of development needs to be understood, since it is the latter that is the ultimate concern of clinical child psychologists.

In the interpersonal context we need to

TABLE 13.1
Developmental Psychology of Illness

Age	Understanding	Hospitalization	General
Infancy	Pain localized and remembered	Heightened pain and stress delay autonomic and motor integration; separation anxiety after attachment	
Toddler	Egocentric: effects on self; magical beliefs: badness as cause	Heightened pain and stress; separation anxiety; badness as cause	Frustrated if physically restrained; dependency hampers autonomy
Preschooler	Realistic and magical ideas of cause	Badness as cause	
Midchildhood	Accurate but concrete grasp of cause; prevention hard to grasp	Worry about pain	
Adolescence	Accurate conceptual understanding but concreteness predominates	Worry about social isolation and school	Worry about social isolation, school, physical deviations; resists compliance with medical regimens

know more about parents as models of coping with sickness, what mix of sympathy and expectation of age-appropriate behavior is best, and how this mix changes with age. Peer and sibling relations, along with interactions with health care professionals, are largely unexplored from a developmental standpoint. In the superordinate context we need to know how schools deal with the extra demands and increased absence of chronically ill children. Finally, the impact of different cultural beliefs concerning sickness on children of different ages needs investigating; for example, the belief that sickness is caused by germs or by evil agents. (See Tinsley, 1992, for an integrative review of the related topic of children's health attitudes and behavior.)

While the developmental literature is of most interest to us, much of the research has not been specifically concerned with developmental issues. It is this literature that we will turn to now.

Chronic Illness and Psychopathological Disturbance

The blanket assumption that the stresses of chronic illness lead to psychopathology is erroneous. Many chronically ill children are adjusting well (Barbarin, 1990). However, risk of developing some kind of problem behavior is twice that of healthy children (Garrison and McQuiston, 1989). While the adjustment of the population as a whole is poorer than that of the general population of well children, it is still better than that of clinically referred children (Wallander et al., 1988).

The type of chronic illness is not linked to psychological disturbance, but the presence of cerebral involvement is. While severity of illness is positively related, there are a number of specific exceptions. In regard to demographic factors, the risk of problems increases with age, while socioeconomic status is not an important risk factor. Interestingly, children

with visible evidence of illness are better adjusted than those whose appearance is normal. (See Pless and Nolan, 1991, for objective studies.)

Research shows that chronic illnesses are not globally damaging but affect some functions and not others. Contrary to what one might predict, children with chronic illnesses do not have a less favorable self-concept than their healthy peers. However, serious illness does interfere with participation in social activities, resulting in increased isolation, shyness, loneliness, and withdrawal. Chronically ill children may be more distant or dependent or oppositional in the family. There is also some evidence that there is increased concern over adequacy in regard to sexual functioning and work.

Academic adjustment again presents a mixed picture. There is no increase in behavior problems or decline in motivation to attend school. However, chronically ill children are more inhibited and less willing to venture into novel activities, while both school attendance and academic achievement decline. (For specific studies, see Barbarin, 1990).

Interaction of Contexts: Asthma

We have chosen asthma to illustrate the complex interaction between organic and psychological factors, although all illnesses conform to this interactive model. (For a comprehensive review, see Creer and Kotses, 1989.)

Asthma is the most common chronic childhood disease, occurring in 38 per 1000 children. In addition to the distress it causes, it accounts for approximately 25 percent of school days lost due to all chronic diseases combined. Its course is unpredictable, attacks occurring on an irregular basis both for individual children and the group as a whole. With appropriate treatment, asthma tends to get better with age; approximately 70 percent are improved or free of attacks after a twenty-year period. While it can be fatal, the fatality rate is low.

Organic Factors Asthma is a disorder of the respiratory system. Hyperresponsiveness of the trachea, bronchi, and bronchioles result in the narrowing of air passages. The result may be intermittent episodes of wheezing and shortness of breath called *dyspnea*. Severe attacks, known as *status asthmaticus*, can be life-threatening and require emergency medical treatment.

What causes the hypersensitivity of the air passages is a matter of debate. The hypersensitivity, in turn, makes children sensitive to a number of irritants which are regarded as *trigger mechanisms* rather than etiological agents. At the organic level, viral infections can set off or worsen the severity of an attack. Allergies may also be related to the development and occurrence of attacks. The child may be allergic to inhaled substances such as dust, the dander of pets, or pollen or to ingested substances such as milk, wheat, or chocolate. Finally, physical factors such as cold temperature, tobacco smoke, pungent odors, exercise, and rapid breathing may trigger an attack.

Psychological Factors Psychological factors can also serve as trigger mechanisms. Anxiety may occur in anticipation of or during attacks, and this can subsequently increase probability of occurrence or the intensity of such attacks. The interpersonal context may be the source of another set of psychological factors if the natural concern of parents becomes exaggerated anxiety and overprotection. This may lead to age-inappropriate dependency on the parents, isolation from peers, and an increase in behavior problems. The causal loop is completed when the child's emotional upset becomes yet another trigger mechanism for an asthmatic attack. (For a discussion of prevention and management techniques, see Creer and Kotses, 1989.) (See Figure 13.1.)

The Role of the Family: Juvenile Rheumatoid Arthritis

Chronic illness confronts families with a host of challenges and problems. Parents, particularly the mother, are responsible for relating to medical personnel, understanding information concerning the nature and treatment of the illness, and implementing the medical regimens. Family routines must accommodate changes ranging from special diets to having the child at home rather than in school to lengthy hospital stays. Parents must strike the proper balance between sympathy with the child's distress and encouraging healthy coping mechanisms and age-appropriate behavior. They must also find ways of dealing with added financial burdens as well as with their own anxieties, frustrations, and heartbreaks.

Most families, like most children, do meet such challenges successfully. Some even find the experience brings a new sense of closeness. Yet, again as with children, the added stresses increase the risk of dysfunction; marital distress, although not divorce, is more prevalent among parents of chronically ill than among parents of healthy children (Barbarin, 1990). Such distress may not be due solely to the illness, which may be an unwelcome addition to other sources of tension (Kalnins, Churchill, and Terry, 1980).

We have arbitrarily chosen juvenile rheumatoid arthritis to illustrate interaction of family functioning and chronic illness, although we will broaden our scope to include other illnesses as well.

Juvenile rheumatoid arthritis is a connective-tissue disease affecting body joints with characteristic symptoms of swelling, pain, heat, and redness. Different types of the disease are characterized by differences in kind (abrupt or insidious), age of onset, number of joints affected, and etiology. Estimated prevalence is about 250,000 children; girls are affected twice as frequently as boys. Treatment

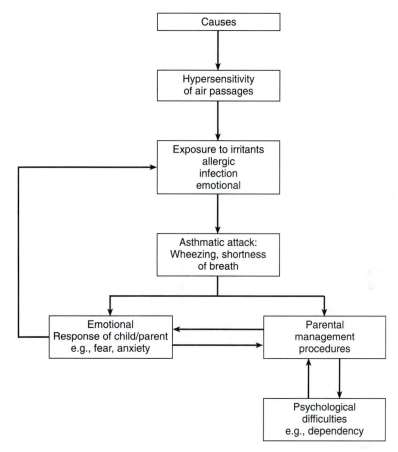

FIGURE 13.1
Schematic diagram of a general model for the development of asthma and its
concomitant psychosocial effects. (*Source:* Wicks-Nelson, and Israel, 1991.)

includes pharmacology, with aspirin being the
preferred drug; physical and occupational
therapy; and orthopedic surgery. Most children are responsive to minimal intervention,
although 10 to 20 percent have severe manifestations and considerable functional impairment (Garrison and McQuiston, 1989).

The study by Daniels and colleagues (1987)
of ninety-three juvenile rheumatic disease
(RD) children with a mean age of 10.8 years is
notable for its inclusion of siblings and for
evaluating family resources as well as family

risk factors. They found that background factors, such as parental education, ethnicity,
child's gender, and age were unrelated to adaptation in the RD children. While severity
and length of illness was related to adjustment, it accounted for only a small portion of
the variance. Finally, compared with healthy
controls, both patients and their siblings had
significantly more adjustment problems.

For RD children in the Daniels study, maternal and paternal functioning and family
stressors had the greatest impact on adjust-

ment. Unexpectedly, family resources were not significantly related. Thus, the adjustment of the RD child was adversely affected by parental and familial problems but was not helped by the positive features of family life. Since these were correlational findings, there is no way of disentangling the interactions among the various contexts; for example, does maternal depression further burden the RD child, or is RD responsible for maternal depression?

Turning now to more general findings concerning chronically ill children and the family, there is evidence that emotional support, open communication, and sharing information about diagnosis and treatment enhance the children's ability to cope with the stresses of illness (Barbarin, 1990). There is an increase in *maternal mental health* problems, possibly because mothers assume the major responsibility for the care of the children. Kovacs and colleagues (1990), for example, in a six-year longitudinal study of ninety-five subjects, found an initial reaction of mild depression and overall emotional distress which subsided in about six to nine months but which increased slightly over subsequent years. Other research has found that maternal mental health is related to perceived severity of illness rather than to objective criteria of the burdens the child's medical condition places upon her (Garrison and McQuiston, 1989). Other factors that determine maternal adjustment are her own physical health, the impact of the illness on the family, the presence of other stressors, and whether the mother has someone to talk to about her problem.

While most *siblings* of chronically ill children are functioning well, there is some increased risk for aggression and delinquency, withdrawal and internalizing disorders, along with medical problems. There is also some evidence that siblings are sensitive to parental worries and that they resent the increased responsibilities and decreased attention result-

ing from the illness. In general, research has focused on the negative aspects of sibling relationships while ignoring the growth-promoting aspects in regard to socialization, education, altruism, and empathy (Eiser, 1990).

Comment In discussing normal development we saw that there are periods of upset marked by an increase in problem behaviors. A developmental psychology of illness, in a like manner, should furnish us with guides as to an expected degree of upset, especially in the face of severe illnesses. We already have one such guide: the children should have more problems than healthy children do but should not be as disturbed as a clinical population. In like manner mothers may feel depressed but should not be psychopathologically disturbed (Kovacs et al., 1990). However, more information and more differentiated information are needed in order to help the clinical child psychologist decide what degree of disturbance is to be expected in response to the stresses of severe illnesses.

NEW CHALLENGES IN INTERVENTION

The concern with illness per se has been expanded to include a host of health-related issues. One involves the psychological aspects of *treatment* of physical disorders. This would include various facets of the hospitalization experience, some of which are social, such as separation from parents and relating to other hospitalized children, some of which involve medical treatments that may be painful or frightening, some of which involve academic and recreational activities. In regard to *health maintenance*, noncompliance with medication and treatment regimens is surprisingly frequent, even when the child's health or life is at stake. Obviously, there are significant personal and interpersonal problems involved with the *dying child*. Finally, a recent phenomenon in the area of *prevention* involves psychologists being consultants to well-baby clinics or to pediatricians in the community (See Gross and Drabman, 1990). We will present two of these health-related issues—adherence to medical regimens and pain management—in detail.

Adherence to Medical Regimens: Diabetes Mellitus

It has been estimated that the overall adherence rate to prescribed medical procedures is only 50 percent for the pediatric population in general. (Unless otherwise noted, our presentation follows La Greca's 1988 detailed summary of issues and research. A succinct presentation can be found in La Greca, 1990.) At a commonsense level, one would think that compliance would be greatest if there were acute, painful symptoms that would be relieved by some simple measure, such as taking a pill. And one would be correct. It would also follow that the treatment for diabetes mellitus, which meets none of those basic conditions, would present major problems in regard to adherence. Again, that is the case.

Diabetes is a chronic, lifelong disorder which results when the pancreas does not produce sufficient insulin. (Our presentation follows Johnson, 1989.) It is characterized by free fatty acids (ketones) in the blood as well as increased sugar in the blood (hyperglycemia) and urine (glycosuria). The overt symptoms are fatigue, weight loss, increased urination, and excessive thirst. If not controlled, diabetes can lead to coma and death. The long-term consequences of uncontrolled diabetes are equally ominous and include blindness, end-stage renal (kidney) disease, limb amputation, and fatal heart disease. The risk for developing diabetes is higher than for most other chronic diseases, and while there are no sex differences, whites are 1.5 times more likely to get the disease than African Americans.

The treatment regimen is complex. Blood glucose must be monitored daily to prevent hypoglycemia or hyperglycemia, and insulin dosages must be adjusted accordingly. Monitoring is accomplished by obtaining a small sample of blood from a finger stick, placing it on a strip that changes color, and comparing the color with those of a chart showing the glucose levels. Blood glucose variability is to be expected since diet, exercise, illness, and emotional state all affect it. Moreover, a special diet is necessary to prevent excessively high or low blood sugar, and frequent small meals throughout the day are recommended (Johnson, 1989).

The first problem in regard to adherence is *complexity*. Generally speaking, prescriptions of more than one medication have lower adherence rates than single prescriptions, while activity limitations or changes in personal habits and lifestyles are more difficult to adhere to than medication. Diabetes involves both a complex monitoring procedure and a lifestyle change, especially in regard to eating. Furthermore, the complexity of treating diabetes requires greater knowledge and skill on the part of the parent and child than does simple medication; the skill of glucose testing, for example, is not mastered until the child is 12 years of age. Ironically, adolescents, who now have the requisite knowledge and skill, are less apt to adhere to the regimen because of the many social obstacles. These include feeling different from peers because of disease-associated delayed sexual maturation, the unusual behaviors of injections and glucose testing, and dietary restrictions which forbid them to eat the very sweets and junk food that their peers favor.

The next problem in regard to adherence is *chronicity*, which is associated with poorer compliance regardless of the particular illness. Once symptoms have abated, there is also a tendency to discontinue some or all medication. Finally, there is the problem that, since diabetes is an asymptomatic disease, adherence does not involve *relief from pain,* so there is no immediate positive result. As we have seen, prevention is a difficult idea to grasp, even in middle childhood, and while adolescents are cognitively capable of understanding it, they must weigh it against the present unhappiness of dietary and activity restrictions and being different from their peers.

General Factors   In addition to factors inherent in diabetes, there are more general ones that play a role in nonadherence. Developmental status is important. Concrete thinking in middle childhood leads to a belief that recovery results from strict adherence to rigid health rules, which, in turn, promotes compliance. Although they are more cognitively sophisticated, adolescents tend to deny or neglect medical care in order to avoid appearing different from peers. At an even more general level, treatment adherence declines among children with serious emotional difficulties. Finally, the family, and the mother in particular, play a crucial role; dysfunctional families increase problems with treatment adherence, while family support decreases them.

Increasing Adherence   Providing verbal and written instructions, visual cues or reminders (such as a clock with times for medication in red pasted on the prescription label), and increased medical supervision (such as phone calls from nurses) have had some success in the cases of acute illnesses with short-term regimens. For chronic illnesses, multicomponent intervention programs combining intensive education, self-monitoring, and reinforcement procedures seem to be the most effective, although the evidence is preliminary. In spite of some encouraging initial attempts, the challenge of significantly improving treatment adherence is yet to be successfully met (see La Greca, 1988).

One final point: Professionals have different amounts of information about and interest in the developmental approach. Nor are they equally motivated to individualize their approach to a particular patient. Consequently, there are those who view their patients as undifferentiated "children" and prescribe standardized measures of treatment. In such cases it is left to the more sensitive parent to monitor the effects of regimens and to modify them as they fail to help or even do more harm than good. Thus, noncompliance should not be viewed uniformly as a failure by parents to do what is best for their children.

Pain Management: Cancer

In our presentation of pain management we will concentrate on bone marrow aspirations (BMAs), which pediatric cancer patients are required to undergo frequently.

Childhood cancer itself, while comparatively rare, accounts for the largest number of disease-related deaths in persons under 16 years of age. However, there has been a heartening increase in survival rate. Forty years ago it was three to six months; now 50 to 60 percent of patients achieve a five-year disease-free survival and probable cure. Moreover, this upward trend is expected to continue. Cancer in children, rather than being a single entity, includes a heterogeneous group of conditions, the common characteristic being a proliferation of malignant cells. Hematological malignancies involving the blood-forming tissues (i.e., leukemia and lymphoma) account for approximately half of the cancer diagnoses; tumors of the brain and central nervous system comprise the second-largest group, followed by tumors affecting specific tissues and organ systems, such as bone or kidney. (For a detailed discussion of childhood cancer, see Dolgin and Jay, 1989.)

BMAs involve inserting a needle into the child's hip bone and suctioning marrow out with a syringe. The marrow is then examined for cancer cells. It is a painful and anxiety-provoking procedure. (We follow Jay's 1988 summary of research.) Anticipatory anxiety can produce nausea, vomiting, insomnia, and crying days before the procedures are scheduled, while young children in particular often kick, scream, and physically resist to the point of having to be carried into the treatment room. Because of the traumatic nature of the procedure, it may take as long as two to three years for some children to learn to cope with it.

A number of *intraindividual* variables are relevant to the issue of controlling the anxiety and pain of BMAs. First, there are developmental factors, since the distress levels of patients under 7 years of age are 5 to 10 times higher than those of older children. Clinical observations suggest that children in the terminal stages of cancer have less tolerance than those who can view BMAs as a promise of cure. Finally, there are individual differences in coping styles (Jay, 1988). Some individuals are sensitizers ("approachers"), who cope by actively seeking information as a means of preparing to experience pain. Others are repressors ("avoiders"), who avoid information and deal with threat by not thinking about it, rationalizing or denying its potential stressfulness. Information helps the sensitizers master stress; the repressors, however, become more distressed, as in the case of the girl who wanted to shut her eyes and scream, "Just do it!" Preliminary evidence suggests that sensitizers have less difficulty coping with stressful medical situations, although the variable of coping style has not received the attention it deserves.

In the *interpersonal* context, there is a strong positive relationship between parental anxiety and children's distress during BMAs. There is also clinical evidence that the children who handle stress are those whose parents emphasize coping rather than being oversolicitous and anxiously concerned about the children's suffering. There is no clear answer to the question of whether parents should be present during BMAs. With less painful procedures the evidence indicates that children show more overt signs of distress, such as crying, with the mother present. However, there is also evidence that most children feel that having their parents present is the thing that helped them most during a painful experience. This finding suggests that overt behavior cannot be taken as the sole criterion in deciding the issue of parental presence, since the child's feeling of security must also be taken into account.

Still in the interpersonal context, the expectations and reactions of medical staff also affect the children's ability to cope. Children's anxiety level often varies as a function of the trust they have in the persons conducting the procedures. However, the question of the optimal blend of empathic concern and confidence in coping ability has not been settled.

Helping Children Cope A number of procures have been devised to help children cope with the pain and anxiety of BMAs. The most common preparation involves providing *information* concerning the details of the upcoming medical procedure. The underlying rationale is that unexpected stress is more anxiety-provoking and more difficult to cope with than predictable stress. While numerous ways have been devised to convey information—hospital tours, puppet shows, storybooks, modeling films, coloring books—well designed studies of effectiveness are lacking.

Hypnosis is the most frequently reported intervention for acute pain and distress. Patients are given suggestions for progressive muscle relaxation, slow rhythmic breathing, and an increasing sense of well-being. After having achieved deep relaxation, posthypnotic suggestions for reduced discomfort and greater mastery during the procedure are given. While there are documented reports of success, the technique cannot be used with children under 6 years of age—the very group most in need of intervention.

Instead of discussing *behavioral* and *cognitive-behavioral* techniques separately, we will present Jay's multicomponent "package," which combines a number of them (Jay et al., 1987). Children are first shown a film of another child receiving a BMA, in which the model describes her thoughts and feelings at each step of the procedure and models positive coping behaviors and positive self-statements, such as "I can do it." Thus the film recognizes the reality of the pain children will experience but provides them with ways of dealing with it. This is called the *coping model* as distinct from the mastery model, which aims to reduce or eliminate the pain and anxiety themselves. The film also provides information concerning the procedures and why they are being done.

Following the film, children are taught a simple breathing exercise which serves as an attention distraction and gives them something active to do. Ever since Freud's day, clinicians have recognized that being an active agent reduces anxiety, while having passively to endure pain increases anxiety. Next, the child is shown a small trophy which serves as positive reinforcement for courage and "doing their very best." The purpose is to change the meaning of pain from an aversive, punitive event to a challenge to be mastered.

Emotive imagery, the next component, involves weaving the child's image of a superhero into the present medical situation, such as Wonderwoman testing her superpowers by withstanding the pain of BMAs. The purpose is again to transform the meaning of pain while providing another distraction. The final component is behavior rehearsal in which the child plays doctor and gives a doll the BMA. The psychologist next has the child practice undergoing the procedure by lying still, doing the breathing exercises, and so forth. The intervention package is administered in the hour before the BMA and initial studies of effectiveness are encouraging.

BRAIN DAMAGE

Because of its importance, it is understandable that attempts to build a bridge between organic and intra-individual contexts initially concentrated on the brain.

The Problems

The Problem Of Definition   "Brain damage" can be defined in a number of different ways. A strictly neurological definition concerns itself with the nature, site, and size of damage to the brain. A behavioral definition is concerned with the functions impaired by the damage: motor and communication disorders, sensory and perceptual deficits, intellectual impairment, convulsive disorders, and so on. Brain damage can also be conceptualized in terms of a wide array of etiologic factors, such as traumatic injury, anoxia, encephalitis, epilepsy, cerebral palsy, and lead poisoning, to name a few. Each approach is valid, but the complex interrelations among them have yet to be worked out. Therefore, it is important for us to realize at the outset that "the brain-damaged child" is an abstraction that glosses over crucial distinctions among children. The diagnosis "brain damage" is meaningless without reference to etiology and, more important, to the specific psychological functions that have been impaired and the nature of the impairment itself.

Moreover, there is a *quantitative versus qualitative* controversy among experts. Those championing the former claim that behavioral deviations are a function of the sheer amount of brain damage. At one extreme of the quantitative continuum lies massive damage which can result in death; at the other extreme lies minimal brain dysfunction and its presumed psychological correlates, including hyperactivity. The qualitative viewpoint, by contrast, argues that in light of the well-known localization of brain functions, the effects of damage depend on the site and size of the damage as well as the age at which it occurs. The controversy is far from settled. (For a more detailed account of the points presented in this and subsequent sections, see Werry, 1986a.)

The Problem with Assessment Because of the delicacy, inaccessibility, and complexity of the brain, most assessments are indirect and inferential. For example, there are "silent" sections of the brain which have no externally measurable functions; consequently, diagnostic techniques may fail to detect substantial brain damage. Conversely, positive diagnostic signs can occur in the absence of brain damage. (Our presentation follows Schwartz and Johnson, 1985.)

While *autopsy* is the surest technique for establishing brain damage, it is, of course, no help in diagnosing a living child. Diagnosis of brain damage frequently relies on the child's *history*, covering factors such as pregnancy and delivery complications, developmental milestones such as sitting up, walking, and speaking, and illnesses. Not only is there evidence that such information is often unreliable, but there is also no direct relation between the information and brain damage. Paradoxically, developmental histories are the least useful yet most frequently used of all diagnostic procedures. The *neurological examination* covers such classic signs as failure of the patellar (knee-jerk) reflex and presence of a Babinski reflex, restriction of the visual field, and loss of sensation and function in any part of the body. The examination is most accurate when there are lesions in nonsilent areas of the brain. In other kinds of brain damage the findings may be ambiguous, or they may even be normal in children with head injuries and encephalitis. While *psychological tests* are invaluable in assessing specific cognitive deficiencies in the

brain-damaged child, in and of themselves they are insufficient for making a diagnosis of brain damage.

Remarkable progress has recently been made in techniques for visualizing brain structure and functioning. The traditional *electroencephalogram* (EEG), which measures electrical activity of the brain, can detect gross damage, but most of the records fall in a no-man's-land between normality and pathology (Werry, 1986a). In fact, 10 to 20 percent of normal children also display abnormal records. However, there have been two advances in electroencephalographic techniques which hold promise of increased sensitivity to brain damage. The first is the *event-related potential,* or ERP. When a stimulus such as a light or sound is presented, the brain produces a characteristic response or ERP. Knowing the ERP in the intact brain allows diagnosticians to detect malfunctions such as visual disorders and deafness in very young or mentally retarded children who cannot be tested by the usual techniques. Next, developments in computer analysis and computer graphics have made it possible to use many recording leads simultaneously rather than the few recording leads of traditional EEGs. Consequently, a computer-drawn, detailed picture of the brain is now available.

There have also been advances in *imaging techniques* for visualizing brain structure. The traditional *x-ray* could detect only gross abnormalities. However, *computerized axial tomography,* or CAT scans (also called computer-assisted tomography and abbreviated CT scans), using computer-driven x-ray machines, produces exceptionally detailed images both of the brain's surface and of the levels below, making it possible to localize lesions at any level of the brain. A newer imaging method called *nuclear magnetic resonance* (NMR) produces even clearer images. *Positron emission tomography* (PET scans), unlike imaging techniques which produce static pictures of the brain and reveal only structural or anatomical deficits, can detect abnormal functioning in brains that might look structurally intact. Because brain cells metabolize glucose, radioactive glucose is introduced into the cerebral artery and the rate at which it is metabolized in various parts of the brain is recorded. The resulting PET images are compared with those of a normally functioning brain.

The Problem with Timing The Kennard principle states that it is better to have your brain lesion early—if you can arrange it. Indeed, there is evidence of greater "sparing" of psychological functions if the damage occurs early in development rather than late. Recently, however, the principle has been challenged as being overly simple (Fletcher and Levin, 1988). An unusually thorough study of children who had localized head injuries found no relation between age and the presence or absence of psychopathology. The age range was from the preschool period through adolescence (Rutter and Garmezy, 1983).

Whether early lesions are more or less disruptive of subsequent behavior than similar lesions sustained at maturity depends on a number of factors. (Our discussion follows Teuber, 1975.) Most obviously, the effects on behavior depend on the site and size of the lesion, some parts of the brain showing resilience after early lesion, other parts showing less or none at all. Next, the effects of lesions depend on the nature of the particular psychological function being studied. Finally, time itself is the most important variable, since some deficits take time to recede after early lesions, whereas others take time to appear. Thus no conclusions can be drawn from assessments made at only one point in time.

The Problem of Recovery The search for mechanisms responsible for recovery of function after brain damage has yielded a number

of leads, some physiological, others psychological. We will sample only a few.

Sprouting is an example of a neural mechanism aiding recovery. Here an undamaged neuron makes synaptic contact with neurons beyond the lesion. At a more global level, the *vicarious-functioning* hypothesis states that another area of the brain takes over the functions subserved by the damaged area, such as the transfer of speech from the left to the right hemisphere. In the psychological realm, *substitution* is a mechanism by which one function is replaced by another, such as learning new strategies for solving cognitive tasks. In spite of a wealth of plausible explanations, the relationship between neural reorganization and the acquisition of new skills is virtually unexplored in human studies. (A more comprehensive review of concepts and research data can be found in Fletcher and Levin, 1988.)

The Problem of Causality Correlation does not prove causation, as we all know. Yet, when a study shows a correlation between psychopathological behavior and brain damage, we tend to assume that the latter is the cause. The assumption is naive and may be misleading. Brain damage occurs within the same intrapersonal and interpersonal contexts as all the psychopathologies discussed so far. Such context factors may significantly affect the child's reaction to brain damage or in certain instances be more potent in determining future behavior than brain damage itself.

Let us take an example. Suppose we find a correlation between brain damage and the now familiar pattern of acting out in school, evidenced by inattention, disobedience, truanting, and underachievement. In all probability a sizable number of the children will also come from homes characterized by parental disharmony, emotionally disturbed or irresponsible parents, and a large number of siblings—conditions that increase the likelihood of acting-out behavior in organically intact children. Thus, the onus would be on the organicist to show that the presence of brain damage significantly affected our understanding of etiology, our prognosis, and our therapeutic interventions.

Brain Damage and Deviant Behavior

As we have just seen, "brain damage" or "the brain-damaged child" covers such a variety of pathological conditions that they are more a convenient fiction than a specific, clearly delineated entity. We have also seen that the constant interweaving of physiological and psychological variables makes it difficult to establish what is cause and what is effect. However, the age-old challenge of relating the functioning and malfunctioning of the brain to normal and deviant behavior has yielded a number of reasonably established relationships. (Unless otherwise noted, our summary follows Rutter and Garmezy, 1983, and Werry, 1986a.)

There is evidence that brain damage increases the risk for psychological disturbances. Rutter (1977) compared 99 children between 5 and 14 years of age with cerebral palsy, epilepsy, or other clearly established brain disorders with 189 children from the general population of 10- and 11-year-olds and 139 10- to 12-year-olds with physical disorders not involving the brain, such as asthma, diabetes, and heart disease. The rate of psychological disturbance in the brain-damaged group was 34.3 percent of the population, while the rate of psychological disturbance in the group with other physical handicaps was 11.5 percent (which still was almost twice that of the normal population). A subsequent study (Rutter, 1981) showed the risk of psychopathology in brain-damaged children was increased threefold over that in children suffering orthopedic injuries. This does not mean that all brain-damaged children are at risk, however; on the contrary, only when biological factors result in *major brain disorders* is the risk of psychopathology significantly increased, although, even here, it is not inevitable. Aside from this special group, the risk of psychopathology is minimal and difficult to detect. Finally, the functions most powerfully affected by brain damage are cognition, sensory and motor functions, and seizure thresholds. It is when these are impaired that psychopathology is most likely to appear.

In light of the importance of the brain, the above findings may seem unexpectedly benign. However, it is important to remember the remarkable recuperative powers of the brain—for example, from injuries, strokes, or infections. It has reserve capacity, duplication of functions, and the impetus of growth itself to aid its recovery. Also, as we have seen, the ameliorating potential of the social environment has been underestimated until relatively recently.

Generally speaking, there is no evidence that brain damage leads to a characteristic clinical picture that can be labeled "the brain-damaged child." Effects tend to be nonspecific, with behavior the same as that found in other disturbed populations.

The situation in regard to *prenatal and postnatal* factors mirrors that of brain damage itself. In certain extreme instances the risk is high; for example, fetal immaturity or true prematurity increases the risk of anoxia and deep brain damage, which, in turn, can result in death or in mental retardation, cerebral palsy, or epilepsy. But in the majority of cases, so-called high-risk babies fail to show subsequent abnormalities of behavior. To be more precise, the immediate effects of the insult to the brain become less important with time, while the effects of the social environment become increasingly important.

Werry (1986a) neatly sums up the empirical

findings. "The child's behavior is a complex, ever-changing distillate of past and present forces—biological, psychological, and social. In this melange of influences, unless accompanied by gross distortions such as physical or mental handicap or active epilepsy, most brain insults or disorders appear as only an 'inefficient predictor' of later behavior" (p. 316).

Head Injury

Traumatic *head injury* is the leading cause of death in children (Fletcher and Levin, 1988). Mortality rates are 10 per 100,000 as compared with 2 per 100,000 for leukemia. Mortality is more frequent in boys and in children under 4 years of age. However, fatalities represent only 10 percent of all head injuries.

Head injury is associated with a variety of cognitive and personality changes. Injury severity, particularly duration of coma, is the most important determinant of recovery. There is a significant decline in *intelligence test scores* following head injury, recovery again being a function of severity of injury along with type of task. Severely damaged children continue to do poorly on tasks requiring speed, while moderately damaged ones gradually improve regardless of task, although it is not clear whether they return to the level of premorbid functioning. In regard to *language*, mutism and expressive aphasia are common symptoms in the acute phase of recovery but not in the long run. However, some subtle deficiencies may be present, for example in the areas of writing to dictation, object descriptions, and verbal fluency. Skills that are being acquired are more vulnerable to injury than fully developed ones.

There is a high frequency of *memory and attentional deficits* in head-injured children. Perhaps related to this is the fact that *scholastic achievement* is often significantly lower in these children. Finally, severe but not mild head in-

jury is associated with a significant increase in *behavior disorders*. Such disturbances reflect preinjury behavior problems that are exaggerated after injury rather than a unitary syndrome of the "brain-damaged child."

As we can see, the developmental dimension has not been given the attention it deserves. In general, children show the same pattern of recovery as adults, while there is suggestive evidence that younger children are more vulnerable to the effects of head injury than adults. However, the real work of studying differentiated cognitive and personality variables, rather than IQ and psychopathologies, and of relating these variables to age-appropriate intrapersonal and interpersonal tasks, has hardly begun. (For a detailed account of developmental neuropsychology and rehabilitation, see Tupper and Cicerone, 1991.)

An Illustrative Developmental Study

A longitudinal study evaluated anoxic infants when they were 3 and 7 years of age (Corah et al., 1965; Graham et al., 1962). In the first phase, 116 anoxic and 159 normal 3-year-olds were assessed in terms of their cognitive and personality development. Anoxic children did significantly poorer than the controls on all tests of cognitive functioning, including the Stanford-Binet, a vocabulary test, and a concept test. In general, the differences in personality were not as striking as those in cognitive development.

By 7 years of age, when 134 normal and 101 anoxic infants were located, the pattern was reversed. The overall difference in intelligence was no longer significant, while the most striking differences between groups were in the area of social competence. However, such differences between groups, even when significant, were minimal. In some of the discriminating measures, the differences were smaller than sex or socioeconomic status.

We learn two lessons from this study. The

first is a variation on a theme we have encountered before: behavioral correlates of brain damage are a function of when one evaluates the children, since they are apt to "grow out of" certain deficits (such as a lower IQ score) and "grow into" others (such as a deficit in social competence). The second lesson is that, while anoxia increases the risk for subsequent deviant behavior, most such infants will be developing normally when they enter school.

MINIMAL BRAIN DYSFUNCTION

Definition

Minimal brain damage or minimal brain dysfunction (MBD) syndrome refers to children of near average or higher intelligence in whom deviations of central nervous system functioning are manifested by various symptoms, the most characteristic being hyperactivity, perceptual-motor impairment, emotional lability, coordination deficits, disorders of attention, memory, thinking, and speech, impulsivity, and specific learning disabilities (H. E. Rie, 1980). Since the child may have average or above-average intelligence and since the signs of disturbed functioning are subtle, he or she may be regarded as merely "lazy" or "nervous." Etiologic factors implicated in MBD include genetic influences, temperament, brain damage, perinatal stress, lead poisoning, food additives, and early sensory deprivation, among others, but none of the evidence is definitive.

The definition has an appealing plausibility. It makes sense to postulate that (1) there are degrees of brain dysfunction; (2) minimal CNS dysfunction is difficult to detect; and (3) such dysfunctions selectively affect specific psychological functions. Furthermore, it seems reasonable to assume that organically caused psychological dysfunctions should be responsive to medication. Undoubtedly there are children

in whom this constellation of factors occurs. However, whether it occurs frequently is open to serious question and there is concern that it might not occur in the majority of children diagnosed as MBD and treated with drugs. As we shall now see, the evidence supporting the definition of an MBD syndrome is often flimsy or controversial.

The Assessment of MBD

If clear-cut instances of brain damage are difficult to detect, how much more problematic are instances of presumed MBD, which elude the traditional neurological assessment techniques. Since the majority of MBD children have no evidence of gross, demonstrable neurological impairment, the diagnosis must depend on the so-called soft signs of CNS dysfunction (see Table 13.2). Rutter (1977) lists three groups of such signs. The first group involves developmental delays in functions, such as speech, motor coordination, or perception. Being developmental in nature, lack of skill in the various functions is normal in young children, and their clinical significance depends on the degree of impairment in relation to the child's mental and chronological age. Unfortunately, there is no way to determine whether such signs are indicative of brain damage rather than a maturational delay or intellectual retardation not related to CNS damage. The second group of soft signs involve nystagmus or strabismus, which also may be due to either neurological or nonneurological causes. The third group consists of slight abnormalities that are often minor examples of classical neurological signs, such as slight asymmetries of tone or reflex. The difficulty in detecting these abnormalities adversely affects the reliability of the assessment.

Minor congenital physical anomalies have also been used as evidence of MBD. Such anomalies include malformed or asymmetrical ears, a curved fifth finger, a furrowed tongue, and

Shaffer and coworkers' research nicely solves many of the problems of using naturally occurring behavior in a longitudinal design while introducing the kind of rigorous analysis of data typically associated with the controlled laboratory study.

Subjects were children of every fifth woman registered in one year at a large pediatric clinic. Children with obvious neurological damage and mental retardation were eliminated. The decision to use a *nonclinical sample* was an important one. We have seen the danger of generalizing to all children on the basis of data from a clinical population, such as generalizing to all obese children on the basis of ones who were sufficiently distressed to seek out special weight reduction clinics. This all too frequent error in clinical research results in exaggerating the degree of disturbance in the population as a whole. In addition, an unselected population provides a base rate for the occurrence of a given behavior (such as soft signs) and furnishes a guide to how frequently the behavior must appear in order to place the child at risk for developing a psychopathology (this frequency is two or more in the case of soft signs). The selection of every fifth woman eliminated *sample bias,* which might result in spurious generalization to populations significantly different from the one studied, say in education or socioeconomic status. The *control* group was drawn from the same population and matched with the experimental group in terms of age, income, anomalous family situations, welfare dependency, and maternal education. This strategy solved the difficult problem of locating children comparable to the experimental ones in all important respects except the variable being studied which, in this case, was soft signs. Finally, the *attrition rate* was around 10 percent, which is remarkably low for a longitudinal study.

The investigators used either standardized instruments or ones that achieved satisfactory reliability with this particular research group. *Instrumentation* is particularly important in doing research with soft signs, which are often unreliable because of the high degree of subjectivity involved in the criteria, such as "awkward" or "lack of rhythmical alternation".

Data on behavior variables were gathered from the adolescents, parents, and teachers, insuring that assessment of disturbances was based on information from a *variety of sources.* The behavioral ratings and the soft sign evaluation were made by different investigators and were therefore done *blind.* This means that the ones making the behavioral evaluations would not be biased by knowing whether

a third toe longer than the second. While the detection of these anomalies is reliable and stable over time, and while they may well represent some type of atypical physical development, their relation to organic brain dysfunction is obscure (Rutter and Garmezy, 1983).

Neeper and Greenwood (1987) sum up the status of soft signs as follows. Their origin is uncertain, but they most likely have multiple origins. There may well be a genetic component and a relation to brain damage, especially in children with clear postnatal insult. The uniform assumption of brain damage, however, is unwarranted. While soft signs are not a useful diagnostic tool at present, there is sufficient evidence of their relation to important psychological variables to warrant continued research. There is reasonably convincing data indicating that they increase as IQ declines and decrease with age and that they are more frequent in boys than in girls. There is some evidence that soft signs differentiate children with attention-deficit disorders, learning disabilities, anxiety, depression, conduct disorders, risk for schizophrenia, enuresis, encopresis, and neurological impairment from normal children, although they do not differentiate one disturbance from another.

One constant criticism of the research on soft signs has been its poor quality. Therefore, Shaffer and coworkers' (1985) exemplary the adolescents had soft signs. Such independence of evaluation is not routinely done in clinical research; for example, it is not unusual for therapist to evaluate the results of therapy. The danger of this procedure is obvious.

The researchers evaluated a broad range of psychological disturbances rather than focusing on attention-deficit hyperactivity disorders and conduct disorders, the two most frequently linked with soft signs. The choice of a broad-gauged approach was particularly apt in light of the uncertain relation between soft signs and specific psychopathologies. Next, variables other than soft signs were studied for their possible relation to psychological disturbances. Specifically, the variables of being a single parent, of having four or more children, of having psychiatric treatment or a police record, of low income and education, and of marital dissatisfaction were combined into a category called social disadvantage. By means of a statistical technique called regression analysis, the investigators were able to ascertain that social disadvantage made no significant contribution to their findings. In sum, the investigators' *broad-gauged approach* to both the dependent and independent variables allowed them to capture significant relations and eliminate nonsignificant but plausible ones.

Finally, the investigators analyzed the data for possible *confounding* of variables. Because soft signs at 7 years were correlated both with low IQ and anxiety-withdrawal in adolescence, it was possible that low intelligence, rather than soft signs, might have led to anxious-withdrawn behavior. However, statistical analysis indicated that the relation between soft signs and anxiety-withdrawal was independent of IQ. Next, anxiety might have confounded the results in that high anxiety in the initial testing situation might have caused the kind of motor incoordination judged to be indicative of soft signs. However, this possibility was eliminated by the finding that the 7-year-olds who were high in anxiety but did not have at least two soft signs did not become anxious-withdrawn adolescents.

Like all skilled researchers, the investigators not only made a good case for their interpretation of the data but systematically eliminated other plausible interpretations as well. In general, this process of entertaining and testing alternate hypotheses either results in a strengthening of the hypothesis under investigation or points to the need for further research. In either case it is the mark of a sophisticated investigation.

---

study is particularly impressive. In this study the investigators reevaluated sixty-three male and twenty-seven female adolescents who had soft signs when they were 7 years old. The sample was drawn from a normal rather than a disturbed population. The most frequent soft signs involved motor coordination, such as awkwardness in finger-nose touching and the inability to perform alternating movements of hands and feet in a smooth, rhythmical fashion. The investigators found that adolescent males with two or more soft signs had significantly lower IQ scores and significantly more psychological disturbances than males with zero to one soft signs. These findings did not hold for females, however. For both male and

female adolescents two or more soft signs were related to a significant increase in anxiety-withdrawal and, for males only, a significant increase in affective disorders. For both groups, soft signs were more potent predictors of subsequent anxious-withdrawn behavior than a host of other variables such as socioeconomic status, family disharmony, and anxiety-dependency at 7 years of age. However, the combination of soft signs and anxiety-dependency in early childhood was the most potent predictor of subsequent anxiety-withdrawal. Of equal interest was the failure to find any relation between soft signs and the subsequent appearance of attention-deficit hyperactivity disorder or conduct disorder, both

TABLE 13.2
Examples of "Soft" Neurological Signs of Defects

Sign	Tests or symptoms
Poor coordination	*Tests:* Finger-to-nose, heel-to-knee (eyes open and closed), finger pursuit, rapid individual finger movements, rapid alternating movements, tying shoes, using buttons and zippers, writing, picking up small objects. *Symptoms:* dysmetria (abnormal difficulty in positioning a limb), ataxia (poor muscle control resulting from cerebellar difficulty in positioning a limb), dysdiadochokinesia (difficulty in executing rapid alternating movements)
Abnormal gait	*Tests:* Walking, running, walking on toes, walking on heels, hopping
Impaired position sense	*Tests:* Passive movement of great toe (child is asked to give direction of movement in at least five trials), location of finger in space (examiner places one of child's index fingers in space, and child is asked with eyes closed, to touch it with the other index finger)
Astereognosis	*Tests:* Identify by touch, with eyes closed, a bottle cap, nickel, button, key, marble, 3/4-inch block (the symptom is reflected by an inability to recognize the objects)
Nystagmus	*Symptoms:* Jerky eye movements when looking ahead, on directed horizontal or vertical gaze, or in one eye when the other is covered
Strabismus	*Symptoms:* Unilateral or bilateral esotropia (deviation of visual axis toward that of the other eye) or exotropia (deviation of visual axis away from that of the other eye), alternating internal strabismus (a convergent deviation of the eye that affects each eye alternately), alternating external strabismus (a divergent deviation of the eye that affects each eye alternately), other impaired extraocular movements
Abnormal reflexes	*Symptoms:* Hypoactive, hyperactive, or asymmetrical biceps, triceps, ankle, or knee jerk, with sustained ankle clonus (at least six rapid contractions of the triceps surae muscle); abnormal plantar response
Mirror movements	*Tests:* Examinee performs rapid thumb-forefinger apposition on one hand—examiner checks whether movements occurred on the other hand
Other abnormal movements	*Symptoms:* Fasciculation (quick involuntary contraction of muscle), myoclonus (quick nonrhythmic repetitive contractions of muscle, usually associated with limb movement), spontaneous tremor (including tremor present at rest), intention tremor (tremor elicited by attempted voluntary activity), athetosis (slow, worm-like writhing, spasmodic and repetitive movements affecting peripheral muscle of limbs and face), chorea (rapid involuntary jerks of trunk, head, face, or extremities), dystonia (involuntary fluctuations of tone and muscle spasms of the neck, trunk, and proximal musculature of the limbs), ballismus (large-scale, violent flinging movements involving major portions of a limb), tic (repeated stereotyped movement resembling voluntary movements), other unclassified abnormal or unwanted movements
Abnormal tactile finger recognition	*Tests:* Identify finger lightly touched, with fingers out of sight (each of the 10 fingers)

Source: Adapted from Nichols and Chen (1981).

of which have been regarded as being due to minimal brain damage. Finally, unlike other studies, this one did not find a decline in the number of soft signs with age, perhaps because it was longitudinal rather than cross-sectional, or because it evaluated a nonclinical population. However, the quality of the study is sufficiently high for this single result to raise questions about previous findings.

Returning now to MBD, there is no evidence that the behaviors that define the syndrome are in fact related (Weiss, 1980). Typically, there is a low degree of interrelatedness among organic measures (such as neurological and EEG findings) and behavioral ones (such as cognitive deficits and emotional lability).

Note that, unlike the situation with autism, subsequent research is disconfirming rather than confirming the existence of a clinical entity of MBD. Yet the children so diagnosed are undoubtedly disturbed and require a comprehensive assessment, including a careful history, an evaluation of intrapersonal factors (such as specific cognitive functions and personality variables) and of context variables (such as family and school), along with a neurological examination (Weiss, 1980; Wohl, 1980). Instead of the global diagnosis of MBD, however, specific areas of dysfunction should be delineated, such as "poor visual-motor coordination and short attention span when dealing with numerical problems"; and, instead of assuming an organic substratum, the entire gamut of etiologic possibilities from neurological to intrapersonal to interpersonal should be explored.

CHAPTER 14

RISKS IN THE INTERPERSONAL CONTEXT: CHILD MALTREATMENT AND DIVORCE

Chapter Outline

Privation
  The Effects of Privation
  Reversibility

Physical Abuse and Neglect
  Definition and Prevalence
  The Abused Child
  Developmental Pathway
  The Abusing Parent
  Conceptual Integration
  Direction of Effect
  The Superordinate Context
  Prevention and Remediation

Emotional Maltreatment
  Definition
  Research
  Evaluation

Sexual Abuse
  Description
  Risk Factors
  Short-Term and Long-Term Effects
  Conceptual Integration
  The Abuser
  Assessment
  Legal Aspects
  The Child as Witness
  Prevention and Treatment

The Risk of Divorce
  The Predivorce Period
  Immediate Reactions
  Chronic Problems
  Period of Recovery
  Good Divorce versus Bad Marriage
  Developmental Considerations
  Effects of Remarriage

One of the most interesting chapters in the history of clinical child psychology concerns child maltreatment. The very existence of physical and sexual abuse of children was hushed up until early in the 1960s. The gradual recognition of their prevalence sent shock waves throughout the country at large and galvanized professionals into seeking ways of protecting the child from further abuse as well as searching for causes that could serve as the basis for remedial and preventive measures. The search has proved difficult. The initial assumption that abusing parents must be psychopathologically disturbed was fallacious and simplistic. Child abuse came to be viewed as multidetermined, involving the interaction among variables from all contexts. Understanding this complex interaction will be our primary concern.

There has also been a shift in categorization so that child maltreatment has become a general category embracing physical, sexual, and emotional abuse and neglect. Along with this new categorization goes a growing recognition of the importance of interpersonal and superordinate variables rather than of physical acts and their physical consequences; for example, physical injuries are common among children, but it is injury at the hands of caretakers charged with loving, protecting, and comforting that makes abuse traumatic. The change is also congruent with our view of maltreatment as an extreme deviation from normal parenting and our interest in placing such deviation within a developmental context.

PRIVATION

Neglect is currently considered a form of child maltreatment. However, the literature is meager compared with that concerned with infants reared in bleak or substandard institutions. Studies of institutionally reared infants are also developmentally oriented, and so are more suited to our goal of viewing psychopathology as normal development gone awry. While the literature is typically conceptualized in terms of maternal deprivation, our preferred designation is *privation* because, rather than being deprived of adequate maternal care, these infants simply never have received it. In DSM-IV Draft Criteria, privation is subsumed under Reactive Attachment Disorders of Infancy or Early Childhood.

The pioneering investigation on privation was done by Spitz (1945), who opened the door to numerous subsequent studies. As is well known, Spitz was a consultant to a foundling home whose infants were wasting away and dying, a condition called *marasmus*. He found that while the institution was hygienic and the infants were given a nourishing diet, they received only minimal stimulation from the social and physical environment, as well as from the gross motor activities of their own bodies. There was one caretaker for every eight infants, and feeding and toileting were done in a routine, impersonal manner. There were no toys, while sheets hanging over the railing screened out the environment. Finally, a hollow worn in their mattresses prevented the infants from turning in any direction. A more isolated, sterile environment would be difficult to imagine. Spitz's famous prescription was "tender loving care in a one-to-one relation." Once the infants received adequate mothering, marasmus disappeared.

Spitz showed that, far from being a sentimental luxury, mothering is essential to healthy psychological development and, in certain instances, to life itself. However, neither Spitz nor subsequent research proved that institutions per se hamper normal development. It is privation—the absence of nurturance and appropriate stimulation—which is inimical to psychological growth, whether in institutions or in the home. Indeed, Russia and Israel have shown that institutions can embody the best of care, and infants seem to thrive in these settings. Nor did Spitz show that caretaking must be done by the mother or a mother substitute. The effects of a single caretaker compared with multiple caretakers are being vigorously investigated, and while the findings are not conclusive, it is clear that the number of caretakers does not tip the balance in favor of normality or severe psychopathology.

The Effects of Privation

Privation, or the lack of growth-promoting nurturance and stimulation from the social and physical environment, differs from deprivation, which is concerned with the loss of a loved one once the bond of love has been established. Loss was our concern in Chapter 7, while lack is our concern here.

One of the most detailed accounts of the effects of privation is presented by Provence and Lipton (1962), who studied seventy-five infants intensively during the first year of life. While the institution was orderly and clean, as was the one Spitz studied, it was not as psychologically sterile. The cribs were not shielded, there were age-appropriate toys, a radio played music softly. Yet it was clearly impoverished. The caretaker-to-infant ratio was 1:8 for eight hours of the day, 1:25 for the remaining sixteen. While most of the caretakers liked the infants and some even had favorites, the institutional policies and schedules limited caretaking to the bare essentials of feeding, bathing, and diapering. Motor activity was also limited, since the infants spent only four hours at most outside the crib, while visual and auditory stimulation was monotonously the same day after day.

In regard to the effects on development, there was a two- to five-month period of grace in which development proceeded normally. Then it began to deviate, primarily in the direction of retardation or failure of age-appropriate behavior to appear, although there were also some behaviors not typical of normal infants. As could be predicted, *language* and *social ties*, the functions most dependent on interpersonal interaction, were most adversely affected; *motor development*, with its strong maturational thrust, was least affected. But the effects were significant in all areas.

In the second half of the first year, the infants' behavior was characterized by an affective *blandness* and a *lack of initiative*. In relating to adults they were generally amiable and responded with mild pleasure. But there was no attachment to a single adult, no intense pleasure when one approached or distress at separation. Nor did the infants turn to adults for play and pleasure or for relief from distress.

We can readily understand the institutionalized infant's blandness in light of what we know about normal attachment. Why should the infant look to anyone to maximize pleasure and minimize pain when no one has provided the appropriate sensory stimulation and prompt relief from distress? Infrequent experience with caretakers hampers both discrimination and the pleasure of recognition. "People" are just that—an undifferentiated mass in which anyone can be substituted for anyone else. Similarly, the pervasive language delay—seen from the second month as a diminution in vocalization and, by the end of the first year, as a failure to use language to communicate and to develop simple words such as "mama"—is understandable in terms of the lack of verbal stimulation.

Reaction to toys had the same quality as reaction to people—blandness. Spontaneous play was meager, and there was little of the enterprising, experimental behavior seen in normal children. There was no toy preference, no distress at the loss of a toy or effort to regain it. The development of the object concept in Piaget's sense was markedly delayed. The infants were best in activities requiring imitation of adults and poorest in those requiring them to figure out a solution on their own.

As has been noted, motor development was less affected than other functions by lack of stimulation, although sitting, pulling to stand, and walking were all delayed. There were also unusual motor behaviors in the second six months—prolonged, affectless rocking on all fours, hand waving, or posturing. In addition, movement lacked the smoothness of performance seen in the normal infant; instead, it went by fits and starts, inactivity followed by sudden, jerky, poorly controlled activity.

Provence and Lipton frequently observed that the infants did not function in keeping with their *capabilities*. Motorically, they were able to approach, grasp, and manipulate objects, but from 6 months on they reached for toys less frequently than did normal infants. Their repertoire of sounds at 6 months was average for their age, but they did not communicate vocally or vocalize for their own entertainment. Maturationally, they were capable of stimulating and exploring their body and thereby defining their body image, but grasping their feet, sucking their thumb, poking their belly button, and all other normal body-oriented activities were strikingly absent. The decline in initiative in relation to people has already been described. In sum, neither the social environment nor the physical environment nor their own body was used as a source of stimulation and play or as comfort from distress.

What a striking contrast between the pervasive blandness of these infants and the imperviousness, repetitiousness, and resistance of the autistic child, or the disjointed, erratic behavior of the schizophrenic child—and incidentally, what a contrast to the mentally retarded child, who makes maximum use of his or her limited potential! These institutionalized infants seem to be basically normal individuals in whom the vitality of growth has been sapped. True, some of their behavior is strange—the mannerisms with the hands, the fitful outbursts of motor activity—but it generally does not puzzle the viewer. The lack of the vitalizing influence of sensitive caretaking seems to hold the key to understanding the infants' failure to attach, their lack of initiative, their superficial, indiscriminate social responsiveness, and the retarded development of specific psychological functions.

The total impact of privation depends on its duration and the kind of environment the child subsequently lives in; the child who goes from a bleak institution to a series of cold, rejecting foster homes will be more damaged than one who experiences consistent love and care in a single foster home.

Institutionally reared preschoolers tend to be lacking in deep attachments, clinging, overly friendly with strangers, and attention-seeking. Such behaviors continue into middle childhood. Institutional children also tend to be more attention-seeking, restless, disobedient, and unpopular in school than normal controls. They approach the teacher and other children more but tend to relate in socially unacceptable ways, such as calling out in class and disregarding the teacher's directions. In addition, they have greater difficulty in concentrating on the task at hand (Rutter, 1979b). In terms of our developmental model, their *work* orientation has been undermined.

Reversibility

That institutionalized children are not fated to deviant development is shown by the pioneering research of Skeels (1966). Again, there were two groups of infants being reared in an impoverished institutional environment, in this instance an orphanage. However, at 19 months of age, a group of thirteen toddlers was sent to an institution for the retarded, where each one was cared for by an adult who became particularly fond of him or her. In addition, this one-to-one relation was supplemented by frequent interactions with other adults in the environment.

Initially, the toddlers' average IQ score was 64, while the control group of twelve toddlers who remained in the orphanage had an average IQ score of 86. However, about eighteen months after the transfer, the "mentally retarded" experimental group now had an average IQ score of 92, while the control group's IQ score had declined to 61—a dramatic reversal of positions. Subsequently eleven of the toddlers were adopted and maintained their gains, while the two who were institutionalized suffered a decline. Most impressive of all were the results of a follow-up study when the experimental children were between 25 and 35 years of age. In general, their adult status was equivalent to that of children reared by natural parents in terms of education, occupation, and income. By contrast, the control group continued to function at a retarded level.

While the Skeels study proved that the adverse effects of a bleak environment are reversible, it also suggests that such dramatic results are not easily achieved. No less than a totally rehabilitative environment was required. Thus the cost of reversing initial damage is high, although the cost of doing nothing is even higher, not only in terms of wasted human potential but in monetary terms as well: the control group cost the state five times as much as the experimental group. (See also Dennis, 1973, and Kagan et al., 1979.)

Children adopted after infancy can also escape some of the damaging effects of privation. Although those adopted after 4 years of age can develop a deep relationship with their adoptive parents, they still tend to show attentional problems in the classroom and to have poor peer relations in middle childhood (Rutter, 1979b). Even without adoption, the picture is not totally gloomy. Rutter and Quinton (1984) studied the adult adjustment of eighty-one women whose institutional rearing was punctuated by episodes of living with their disharmonious families. The women clearly had been damaged: twenty-five had personality disorders and criminal records compared with none in a control group, and only one-fifth of them were making a good adjustment compared with three-fifths of the control group.

The unique feature of the study is its exploration of the factors that protected one-fifth of the group from the fate of the majority. The first was a *positive school experience*. This experience was not necessarily academic—the women did not have a higher IQ than the rest of the group—but it might have involved peer relations or sports or participation in the arts. Incidentally, such experiences had little effect on the women in the control group who were making a good adjustment and who presumably had other sources of feelings of self-worth. The next protective factor was a *good marriage*. While others in the group tended impulsively to marry inadequate, disturbed, or criminal men, the women who were doing well planned their marriage and had spouses who were making a good psychosocial adjustment. In fact, the characteristics of the spouse were by far the most powerful ameliorating factor. The results are interesting in themselves and also offer us a rare glimpse into the conditions under which children "outgrow" their deviant behavior (see Rutter, 1990b).

PHYSICAL ABUSE AND NEGLECT

While each form of maltreatment is sufficiently distinct to be presented in its own right, it is difficult to do so since, until recently, physical abuse and neglect were studied together. Thus, we are forced to present them under the general rubric of child abuse, differentiating them whenever possible.

Definition and Prevalence

Physical abuse involves the presence of nonaccidental injuries resulting from acts on the part of adults responsible for the child's care. Major injuries include brain damage, internal injuries, burns, severe cuts, bruises, and lacerations. Such injuries may result from acts of commission or acts of omission in which the child's life, health, or safety are endangered by extreme neglect. The definition of *neglect* has been broadened to include deprivation of necessities by caregivers such as nourishment, shelter, health care, supervision, and education. Finally, child abuse has also been broadened to include psychological as well as physical consequences.

Researchers are concerned that the definition does not take into account the kind, frequency, and intensity of the abuse or the developmental status of the child; for example, repeatedly burning an infant with cigarettes is not differentiated from a single beating causing severe lacerations on the back of an adolescent. (See Giovannoni's 1989 discussion of the definitional problem.) Researchers are also still wrestling with the problem of devising reliable and valid assessment instruments (Wolfe, 1988).

The Abused Child

The popular image of the abused child is one with traumatic injuries such as burns, lacerations, or broken bones. In reality, two-thirds of maltreated children experience neglect, while 88 percent of those physically abused suffer only minor injuries (Wolfe, 1987). This by no means trivializes physical abuse since 2000 to 5000 abuse-related deaths occur in the United States each year (Zigler and Hall, 1989). In regard to *prevalence*, 60,000 cases of child abuse were reported in 1974 which increased to 1.1 million in 1980 and more than doubled during the 1980s. About half of all reported cases are substantiated (U.S. Advisory Board on Child Abuse and Neglect, 1990).

While neglect is more prevalent in the infant and toddler period, physical abuse tends to occur at two age periods: the infant and toddler period and adolescence. There is no difference in incidence between black and white children, but the type of abuse is different: black children suffer more neglect, while white children suffer more physical abuse or combined physical abuse and neglect (Wolfe and St. Pierre, 1989).

Developmental Pathway

Physical abuse and neglect have different impacts on development at different ages. Unless otherwise noted, our presentation will follow Youngblade and Belsky's (1990) developmental reconstruction of the data on abused children.

Infancy   *Attachment.* There is general consensus that abuse is associated with the three types of *insecure attachment* (see Chapter 2). Furthermore, different types of insecure infants are associated with different types of abusing mothers. In general, research findings support the following predictions: rejecting, hostile mothers tend to have infants who try to avoid the noxious consequences of close contact (type A); neglecting mothers tend to have infants who exhibit an ambivalent mixture of longing for contact and anger that such longings are frustrated (type C); mothers who are both rejecting and neglecting tend to have infants who exhibit a similar mixture of consequences (type D). Finally, longitudinal studies reveal an instability of attachment classification in abused infants who, a year later, tend to shift from secure to insecure rather than the reverse. (See Cicchetti and Olsen, 1990; for a more detailed discussion of attachment and abuse, see Crittenden and Ainsworth, 1989, and Carlson et al., 1989.)

The Toddler and Preschool Period *Interpersonal relations.* The insecurity which marked attachment to the mother distorts the toddler's widening social world of caretakers and peers. Especially if they have been physically abused, toddlers are likely to avoid contacts with familiar persons who have not mistreated them and respond with aggression to prosocial encounters with adults and peers. Instead of being open to social contacts, they tend to display a mixture of approach and avoidance, walking toward another child and suddenly veering away or approaching a caregiver with their head or eyes turned away, for example. They respond to the distress of peers with aggression, diffuse anger, or distress instead of with sympathy or concern, as do nonabused toddlers.

In regard to play, Alessandri (1991) found that abused children engaged in less parallel and group play than nonabused peers and that they were more aggressive and conversed less. The play itself was less mature, and fantasy themes were concerned with nurturance and punishment rather than superheroes and monsters. Finally, there is some evidence that, while physically abused children are aggressive, neglected children interact less with peers but interact with teachers in the same prosocial manner as do nonabused toddlers (Cicchetti and Olsen, 1990). (For objective studies of peer relations, see Mueller and Silverman, 1989.)

The self One of the tests of the early development of the self as an independent entity assesses toddlers' ability to recognize their reflection in a mirror. Such visual self-recognition is delayed in insecurely attached toddlers. Moreover, they react with neutral or negative affect when they do inspect their faces in the mirror, rather than with positive affect as do nonabused children. In the early preschool period, the development of the self and the recognition of the selves of others is manifested verbally by labels for internal states. Abused children have fewer words for describing their internal states and for attributing internal states to others than do nonabused children. The inference is that they are lagging in the process of individuation (Cicchetti and Olsen, 1990).

Middle Childhood Middle childhood is marked by an increase in *adjustment problems,* especially externalizing ones of disobedience, tantrums, and aggression with family members and peers. This decreased self-control is due in part to cognitive and affective deficiencies. Cognitively, abused children have difficulty decentering and understanding the viewpoint of others, while affectively they are less empathetic and sensitive to the feelings of others. They have fewer social skills and fewer friends, while their communication skills continue to be inferior to those of nonabused peers. There is also an increase in internalizing problems evidenced by their being more withdrawn and depressed (Toth, Manly, and Cicchetti, 1992).

Initiative also suffers, since abused children are more dependent and less curious than nonabused children and less ambitious in regard to occupational goals. Finally, there is some evidence of lowered self-esteem, although the research has also produced contradictory findings.

Adolescence Although a large portion of abuse victims are adolescents, very little research has been done on this population (Garbarino, 1989). Families that are at risk for abuse tend to be low in adaptability, cohesion, support, and effective discipline, while being high in interparental conflict; e.g., they tend to score high on measures in the "chaotic" or "enmeshed" categories. For their part, adolescents are less socially competent and exhibit more problems such as isolation, temper, low self-esteem, and depression than do their peers. Finally, adolescent abuse is less likely to be transmitted intergenerationally than is child abuse.

The Developmental Model Recasting the findings concerning abuse in terms of our own personality variables, we have found that attachment, initiative, self-control, aggression, cognition, and sociability are all adversely affected. Since most investigators have not conceptualized their findings in developmental terms, we cannot be sure what model best fits their data. In addition, the paucity of longitudinal studies means that there is no way of knowing whether the reconstructed pathway is a typical line of development or a composite of diverse lines. Only the studies of insecure attachment chart the beginnings of a developmental trajectory. Keeping all these limitations in mind, our best guess is that the research findings can be regarded as *developmental lags.* (Table 14.1 summarizes the findings concerning child abuse.)

TABLE 14.1
Summary of Findings Concerning Child Abuse

	Infancy	Toddler and pre-school period	Middle childhood	Adolescence
		Interpersonal		
Social	Insecure attachment: Mother / Child Rejecting; hostile / Avoidant (Type A) Neglecting / Ambivalent (Type C) Rejecting & neglecting / Avoidant & ambivalent (Type D)	Avoids familiar people;* aggressive response to positive overtures;* ambivalent approach;* aggressive or distressed response to distress*	Fewer social and communicative skills; fewer friends; difficulty decentering; less empathy	Less competent; dysfunctional family
Play		Less mature, less group and parallel play; aggressive;* withdrawn;[†] interacts with teachers[†]		
		Intrapersonal		
Adjustment			Increased internalizing and externalizing of problems; less initiative	Increased internalizing and externalizing of problems
Self		Visual recognition delayed and affectless; fewer words for own and others' inner states		

* Physically Abused
[†] Neglected

The Abusing Parent

As much as the research will allow we will differentiate physical abuse from neglect, but when studies do not make this distinction, we will use the term *abusing parent*. (Unless otherwise indicated, our presentation follows Wolfe and St. Pierre, 1989.)

The proportion of female to male abusers is roughly 3:2. Females are associated more with neglect, while males are associated more with physical injury. Almost nothing is known about male abusers, however, since almost all studies are done with females. Abusing parents tend to marry younger than the norm and are teenagers at the birth of their first child.

When it was discovered that abusing parents were not severely disturbed psychologically, an effort was made to uncover distinguishing personality traits. Parents were described as less intelligent and more hostile, impulsive, self-centered, rigid, domineering, dependent, narcissistic, childlike, and passive—the very length of the list making the idea of an "abusive personality" sink under its own weight. However, abusing parents do share certain characteristics and, more important, certain parenting styles.

Characteristics   Abusing parents have more physical and emotional symptoms such as dissatisfaction, mood changes, and physical health problems, than do nonabusing parents from similar socioeconomic backgrounds. While they may not be more stressed in terms of objective measures, they perceive themselves as such. Neglecting parents tend to have a greater degree of global psychological impairment, as indicated by various psychiatric symptoms, than do physically abusing ones. Physical abusers tend to have low impulse control and frustration tolerance; for example, they respond to films of a screaming infant and a noncompliant child with heightened psychophysiological arousal as indexed by heart rate and galvanic skin response. Neglecters, on the other hand, respond to heightened stress by avoidance and passivity.

There are other differences between abusers and neglecters (LaRose and Wolfe, 1987). Neglect results from chronic adult inadequacies and failures, more stresses and unmet needs, more loneliness and discontent. Physical abuse is more likely to be influenced by contemporaneous events such as opposition, accidents, or sexual behavior on the child's part. The imbalance between positive and negative interactions is also not as great as in neglect.

Much has been made of the statement that abusing parents were themselves abused as children. Subsequent research has shown such an absolute statement to be an exaggeration (Kaufman and Zigler, 1989). An estimate of children repeating the cycle of all forms of maltreatment into adulthood (physical, sexual, and neglect) is around 30 percent. Parents who do not become abusers are likely to have had a supportive relation with the nonabusing parent while growing up. They also are apt to have a supportive adult relationship currently, to be experiencing fewer stressful events, and to be more openly angry and more explicit in recounting their past and their determination not to repeat it. (See Egeland, Jacobvitz, and Papatola, 1987; Rutter, 1989, reviews the general topic of intergenerational transmission of psychopathology.)

Abusing parents have also been described as *socially isolated*. The label is misleading. For example, Crittenden (1985) found that there was not a quantitative diminution in social contacts, nor was there a difference in the kinds of people contacted. However, there were qualitative differences. The support system of matched control mothers was characterized by long-term friendships; help from friends, relatives, and professionals; and mutuality in interactions. Neglecting mothers, by contrast, had only short-term friendships, relying unduly on relatives but generally being dissatisfied with the dependability of such support.

Parenting Style There is less communication with and stimulation of their infants among neglecting mothers, while abusive mothers are inappropriately interfering and occasionally hostile. Subsequently, abusive mothers are less positive, more intrusive and inconsistent, and less flexible in their child-rearing techniques than are nonabusing mothers. Even abusing parents who know about child development have unrealistic expectations and disregard the child's needs and abilities. Their discipline tends to be both inappropriate and ineffectual, while they react negatively even to the child's prosocial behaviors. (For a conceptual integration of the research on parenting, see Belsky and Vondra, 1989.)

Knowing what we now do about parenting, we might well question whether children of such parents might not be disturbed regardless of whether abuse occurs or not. Given the complex matrix of noxious influences that characterizes the environment of abused children, it is difficult to disentangle the role of abuse itself. For example, is it just one more stress to be added quantitatively to the others, or does it have a more specific effect on the child's behavior? As we shall see, we have a few initial clues to the answer but more needs to be learned.

Egeland conducted one of the few prospective, longitudinal studies of child maltreatment. We will see how his ingenious design throws light on many of the issues we have raised concerning maltreatment.

Egeland's research began with low-SES, high-risk mothers in the third trimester of pregnancy and followed the subjects until the children were 5 to 6 years old. Four types of abusive mothers were identified: physically abusive mothers; hostile and verbally abusive mothers (i.e., mothers who constantly berated and harassed their children); psychologically unavailable mothers (i.e., mothers who were detached, uninvolved, and affectless); and neglectful mothers (i.e., mothers who were fitfully interested but irresponsible or incompetent in their child care). The last three groups were further divided into those who did or did not physically abuse their child.

First, Egeland's research throws light on the issue of *risk*. While poverty is a risk factor and stressful life events increase that risk, most poor, stressed mothers do not abuse their children. What makes the difference? Egeland, Breitenbucher, and Rosenberg (1980) found that the kind of stress did not matter in the infancy period, but certain personality characteristics and competencies did. The abusing mothers were highly anxious, angry, and defensive, while the nonabusing ones were better able to take stress in stride. Abusing mothers were less sensitive and competent in caring for their infants who, in turn, were more difficult to care for than infants of nonabusing mothers. In a like manner, the mothers' emotional instability was the most important factor contributing to maltreatment in the early preschool period, while stress and social support were of secondary importance (Pianta, Egeland, and Erickson, 1989).

Because Egeland's research was longitudinal, it provided data on the issue of *continuity of effect* (Egeland, Sroufe, and Erickson, 1983). He found that the negative effects of maltreatment during the first two years of life were cumulative, particularly for children of psychologically unavailable mothers. There was also continuity in mothering: 71 percent of those classified as abusing when the children were 1 year of age retained that classification when the children were 6 years of age (Pianta, Egeland,

and Erickson, 1989).

The research design provided some tentative data on the question of whether the *addition of physical abuse* to an already deviant pattern of parenting would have a negative impact on the child. A comprehensive answer could not be given because small group sizes prevented statistical analyses. However, for neglectful mothers, the elimination of physical abuse did not significantly affect the findings on a variety of measures.

Finally, the research showed that, while all children suffered from maltreatment and there were overlaps among the groups, there were also *specific effects* of specific kinds of maltreatment. We can only sample some of the findings. Between 3 years, 6 months and 6 years of age, physically abused children were the most aggressive and noncompliant and least persistent when faced with a frustrating task. Children of verbally abusive mothers expressed the most anger and were most avoidant of their mother. Children of psychologically unavailable mothers, while dramatically disturbed in the infant and toddler period were, for some unknown reason, less disturbed by the preschool period, even though they had more problems than did the normal controls. However, it was the neglected group (even without physical abuse) that presented the least positive and most negative effects of all; they were distractable and inflexible in dealing with tasks, had the lowest self-esteem and the least initiative, and were the most dependent and least skillful in coping with various situations in preschool. They received little cognitive or social stimulation at home, their dirty and shabby clothes and unkempt appearance reflecting their mothers' lack of involvement (Erickson, Egeland, and Pianta, 1989).

The finding that neglect is more damaging than physical abuse is congruent with studies of the normal development of attachment in which hostile mothering does not take as great a toll on the infant as infrequent, capricious, inept mothering. While the pyrotechnics of violence have captured the public's imagination, the corrosive effects of fitful, unpredictable, inept mothering may be more insidious.(Paget, Philip, and Abramczy [1993] review the conceptual and empirical literature on neglect.)

Conceptual Integration

Wolfe (1987) has conceptualized the research findings on physically abusing parents in terms of deviations from the normal pattern of authoritarian child-rearing. Physical abuse itself is not viewed as an inexplicable outburst but as the result of forces that tip the omnipresent tension between anger and control. We will elaborate on both these themes. (For other conceptual integrations, see Belsky, 1980, and Cicchetti and Rizley, 1981.)

Discipline Physical abuse frequently (although not exclusively) occurs in the context of discipline. Among the types we have described (see Chapter 2) the one most akin to physical abuse is *authoritarian* discipline. Here parents control children's behavior according to an absolute set of standards, discourage ver-

bal give-and-take, and value obedience and respect for authority, work, and tradition. Such an "old-fashioned" approach to discipline ("children should be seen and not heard") can be used with respect for children and concern for their welfare. As with all discipline, as much depends on how the practices are implemented as on the nature of the practices themselves.

With physically abusive parents, however, there is an overemphasis on physical punitiveness and an insensitivity to the children's needs (LaRose and Wolfe, 1987). Ironically, such an authoritarian approach, while extreme, tends also to be ineffective. Because parents are locked into one kind of discipline, they cannot deal with different situations in a versatile, appropriate manner; neither can they serve as models for or help their children develop a flexible repertoire of ways to deal

Neglect can be more devastating than physical abuse.

with interpersonal problems. If, for any number of reasons, escalation occurs, punitiveness may become brutality.

What factors tip the scale in favor of brutality? (Our presentation, unless otherwise noted, will follow Wolfe, 1987.) Note that the question is phrased in terms of factors, meaning that we will be dealing with a number of variables rather than with a single cause. Also note that the question uses the image of tipping a scale. The implication is that a number of parents with different personalities may be living in a "zone of vulnerability," but will not physically abuse their children unless there are changes that undermine restraint and provoke a violent outburst. Thus physically abusive parents are not a breed set apart from all other parents.

Patterns of Interaction   Research on parent-child interactions allows us to view the family at closer range than does the description of disciplinary techniques. The data indicate that members of abusive families interact less frequently than do those of nonabusive controls, but, when they do, there is proportionately more negative than positive behavior. The latter finding is particularly important. Members of physically abusive families often engage in antagonistic behaviors such as criticism, threats, and shouting. However, such behaviors can be found in carefully matched control families as well. What sets the physically abusive family apart is the lack of positive exchanges that would offer relief from the atmosphere of imminent and overt hostility while allowing the family to develop constructive ways of relating to and supporting one another. In sum, the overall picture is of family members trapped between avoidance and anger.

The Role of Stress   Stress is the catalyst turning a difficult family situation into an abusive one. There is no one type of stress that leads to physical abuse, just as there is no one type of abusive parent. Rather, stress arises from multiple sources such as poverty, marital disharmony, or lack of preparation for parenting. Moreover, the impact of stress is not absolute but relative to the characteristics of the individual who must cope with it; for example, a child's school failure may infuriate one parent while being a matter of indifference to another. Finally, here as elsewhere, there are certain buffers, such as an experienced, stable grandparent in the home or a convivial work setting, that may serve as moderating factors. Thus one cannot expect a one-to-one relation between the amount of stress and the degree of violence.

Transitional Stages   It is possible to conceptualize physical abuse as developing in a series of stages if one keeps in mind that the transitions are not inevitable and that parents can move back and forth among them. (We continue to follow Wolfe, 1987.)

The *first stage* is marked by a reduced tolerance for stress and a disinhibition of aggression. There are three destabilizing or *risk factors* contributing to this state of affairs. The first is *poor preparation for parenting*. This may be due to the mother's own family, which relied upon punitive authoritarian discipline and was deficient in empathy, reasoning, and the cultivation of problem-solving and social skills. Thus the mother has learned that the principal way to cope with frustration is attack. The next component is *low control*, which may be viewed as another untoward consequence of punitive, authoritarian rearing. An impoverished repertoire of coping mechanisms is accompanied by a feeling of vulnerability to losing control: If attack does not work, what can I do then? The final component is *stressful life events*, which tend to be common, everyday problems of parenting, marriage, and work, rather than major crises such as severe illness.

Counterbalancing the three destabilizing factors are compensatory, or *protective factors:* a supportive spouse, friends or organizations, socioeconomic stability, success at work or school, or people who can serve as models of effective coping.

The *second stage* is characterized by poor management of acute crises and provocations. The punitive, authoritarian parent uses short-term and possibly self-defeating solutions to problems, such as excessive alcohol or drug use, relocation to escape from debtors, or, in the case of children, harsh punishment.

There are three destabilizing factors that turn punishment into abuse. The first is *conditioned emotional arousal.* The potentially abusive parent has had many experiences of being angry with the child. By a process of classical conditioning, specific aspects of the child's behavior or appearance, such as a facial expression or whining, can come to be associated with irritation or rage. In the future, similar behaviors or appearances on the child's part will serve as stimuli to arouse similar affects in the parent. Thus parents are increasingly likely to be in a mood that would result in aggression toward the child. The second destabilizing factor involves *attribution.* In this case a person who is unaware of the source of anger misattributes it to a current event, which provokes him to aggression. A common example is a man who feels irritable when he comes home from work and spanks his son for leaving the tricycle in the driveway. This has been called transfer of arousal and is akin to the defense mechanism of displacement. In any case, the child becomes the victim of the parent's anger. The third destabilizing factor is an intensification of aggression by the attribution of *intentionality.* Research has shown that aggression is more likely when an act is viewed as deliberate rather than accidental. In the second stage, the parent views the child's acts as purposely defiant or provocative, thereby justifying excessive punishment.

Compensatory factors in the second stage include improvements in the child's behavior, say, through maturation or a positive experience in school or with peers. They may be community resources that can offer relief from the home situation, such as day care facilities. Finally, parental coping resources can be increased through the intervention of concerned individuals or professionals, so that stress is perceived as less overwhelming.

The *third stage* is characterized by habitual patterns of arousal and aggression. Here the preceding pattern of increased stress, arousal, and overgeneralized response to the child becomes habitual. In part the change comes about because some children easily *habituate* to existing levels of intensity of punishment so that harsher measures are required to maintain a given level of compliance. In part, parents are immediately *reinforced* by venting their anger and making the child comply. However, in the long run they are paving the way for further escalation of punishment while concomitantly failing to help the child find alternative modes of behaving that would decrease or eliminate the necessity of punishment. Thus the parents' complaint, "No matter what I do he won't listen" and "He only listens if I get really mad" are justified to a certain extent. What the parents have failed to grasp is their own role in this impasse. Finally, as we have seen in Chapter 9, the combination of punitiveness and neglect is the breeding ground for *behavior problems* which, in turn, exasperate the parents.

Compensatory factors in this final stage, unfortunately, are minimal. Parents, either on their own or through help from others, may come to realize the self-defeating nature of their behavior. The child in turn may respond positively to noncoercive measures. Finally, community services such as crisis intervention centers may become involved and help change the pattern of parental behavior (see Figure 14.1).

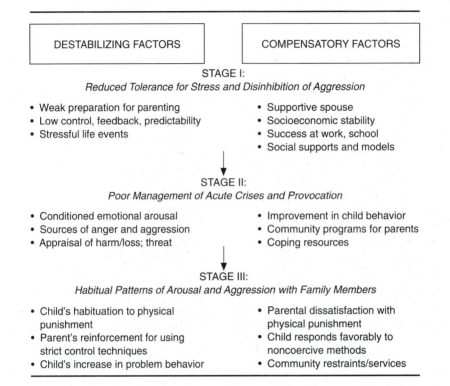

FIGURE 14.1
Destabilizing (risk) and compensatory (protective) factors and the stages of physical abuse. (*Source:* Wolfe, 1987.)

Direction of Effect

Most of the research on abusing adults and abused children is correlational. Our interactional approach requires that we consider the possibility that the direction of causation is from child to adult rather than the other way around. There is evidence suggesting that this might be the case. Abused infants are constitutionally more vulnerable than nonabused ones, are less socially responsive, and more difficult to care for (Egeland, Breitenbucher, and Rosenberg, 1980). Prematurity, mental retardation, physical handicaps, and congenital malformations are overrepresented among abused children.

However, after reviewing the research, Am-

merman (1990) concluded that it does not provide strong support for the causative role of the child. In cases where it could possibly be causative, its explanatory power is weak compared with other variables. More typically children's characteristics exist in a constellation of factors leading to parental abuse. On the other hand, there is evidence that once abuse has occurred, noncompliant and oppositional behavior plays an important role in sustaining it. For example, Oldershaw, Walters, and Hall (1986) describe the process by which the controlling but inept parent and the noncompliant child engage in an interaction that might well set the stage for escalation of conflict and eventual violence.

The Superordinate Context

This country has the highest level of violence of any Western society as evidenced by statistics on crime and murder. The right of schools to use corporal punishment on disobedient children has been upheld by the Supreme Court in *Ingraham v. Wright*. There are those who claim that child abuse is tacitly encouraged by an American society that is complacent about aggression in general and condones punitiveness toward children in particular (Belsky, 1980). Moreover, the rate of violence is higher among family members than among any other social group. As shocking as physical abuse of children is, it is even more disturbing to realize that it is just one manifestation of family violence in a society marked by violence.

While found at all socioeconomic levels, neglectful families are considerably below the national average on several socioeconomic indicators such as being employed. Physically abusing parents are closer to although still below the national average (Wolfe and St. Pierre, 1989).

In the past there was a tendency to regard low socioeconomic status as a cause of physical abuse. This mistake resulted from the failure of researchers to include a control group of subjects from the same class who did not abuse their children. When this was done, a different picture emerged. For example, in Starr's (1982) study of eighty-six abusive families matched for social class, only 10 of 190 variables significantly differentiated the two groups. Smith and Adler's (1991) study found that a number of variables regarded as related to abuse, such as financial and housing problems, drug use, physical arguments, and social isolation, did not differentiate abusing from matched nonabusing families. Thus, many of the so-called correlates of physical abuse turned out to be general characteristics of the lower-class population and had little or nothing to do with abuse.

Finally, to be maximally meaningful to us, findings concerning SES must be translated into relevant interpersonal variables. For example, the acceptance of physical punishment in discipline and the idea that children are the private property of parents are more frequently found in the lower classes and may well be two of the characteristics setting the stage for child abuse (Vondra, 1990).

Prevention and Remediation

Prevention The ideal goal of prevention is to keep abuse from occurring. At present, however, risk factors are neither sufficiently specific nor sensitive enough to achieve this goal; for example, targeting poor, stressed families is inefficient since the majority of them do not abuse (Ammerman and Hersen, 1990). Thus, many programs are aimed at the community at large or adopt a more limited goal of dealing with the early stages of abuse in order to prevent future abuse from occurring.

Community programs may use the media to disseminate information concerning the problem and sources of professional help or social support. There are also telephone hotlines and crisis centers for parents who feel they are in danger of abusing their children. Hospitals, which are in a good position to detect abuse in its early stages, have set up programs to help such families. Some community-based programs, recognizing the multidetermined nature of abuse, offer a wide variety of programs from prenatal to postnatal care to parenting skills to home management and nutrition to job finding. The goal of Project 12 Ways, for example, is to provide in-home services that will keep the family intact, increase parenting and living skills, decrease dysfunctional child behaviors, and decrease abuse and neglect. (For a more detailed presentation of prevention, see Newman and Lutzker, 1990).

The *effectiveness* of most preventive programs has not been satisfactorily evaluated, although the short-term efficacy of Project 12-Ways has been documented, and long-term efficacy seems promising. Dubowitz (1990) found that home health visitors, lay group counseling (rather than professional intervention), and family and group therapy were high on the list of cost-effective programs, although much more research needs to be done.

Remediation The primary form of intervention is *medical* and *legal*, since many children first come to the attention of medical professionals because of injuries. The medical profession then provides emergency services and refers families to social agencies. Child protective services carry out preliminary legal interventions and determine the child's disposition based on safety concerns. (Otto and Melton, 1990, discuss the legal aspects of maltreatment.) However, both medical and legal actions are primarily reactive and crisis-oriented rather than concerned with long-term functioning (Ammerman and Hersen, 1990).

Most remedial efforts involve abusing parents rather than the abused child. The most frequent goal is that of altering parents' reliance on ineffective control strategies and corporal punishment, both of which escalate the intensity and frequency of aversive parent-child interactions. Other programs target personality variables and involve rage reduction, stress management, and relaxation training. There is some evidence that such programs are as effective in reducing abuse as those involving parenting.

While there are some reports of successful family therapy, most remediation involves *behavioral techniques* used with individuals or groups. (Our summary follows Kelly, 1990.) These techniques are aimed at improving parenting skills and include explaining behavioral principles (such as positive reinforcement, time out, shaping, and appropriate punishment), problem solving of child management difficulties, therapist modeling of appropriate skills, role playing of problem situations, and feedback to parents following behavior rehearsal. While there is evidence that such behavioral techniques are successful in reducing abuse over a period of time, most treatment involves single-subject or small-sample demonstrations.

Remedial efforts with abused children have lagged, perhaps because the major treatment goal has been that of eliminating further abuse, perhaps because of the naive belief that change in parental behavior would automatically eliminate their children's problems. (Our presentation follows Mannarino and Cohen, 1990.) Such views overlook the child's role in perpetuating abuse and the self-perpetuating nature of some of their problems. Many of the approaches tried have a catch-as-catch-can quality and have not been adequately evaluated. However, improvement in a number of areas of functioning has been reported from placing preschoolers in a day treatment program as well as from counseling school-aged children and enhancing their problem-solving skills and self-esteem.

EMOTIONAL MALTREATMENT

At the beginning of our discussion we stated that attention had shifted from the abusive acts and their physical consequences to interpersonal and superordinate context variables. Emotional maltreatment takes up this theme and explores the full range of forces thwarting children's healthy development. This, in turn, raises the issues of conceptualizing, specifying, and operationalizing such forces so they can be used by researchers, clinicians, and social and legal agencies. (A full-dressed treatment of emotional maltreatment can be found in Brassard, Germain, and Hart, 1987.)

Definition

An entire issue of *Development and Psychopathology* (1991, No. 1) is devoted to the problem of defining emotional maltreatment. Diverse and often incompatible points of view were presented and defended, but no consensus emerged. All we can say for a certainty is that emotional maltreatment exists—that is, excluding physical and sexual abuse, adults behave in ways that are psychologically harmful to children and thwart their healthy development. Once we leave this obvious fact we find ourselves in the dismal swamp of uncertainty.

A good deal of attention has been paid to devising *categories* of emotional maltreatment in order to make the concept more specific and to facilitate operationalization. Categories include rejecting, terrorizing, isolating, degrading, corrupting, exploiting, and denying emotional responsiveness. They may also be expanded to include acts or situations not directly aimed at the child or under parental control such as modeling prejudiced behavior, divorce, and living in crime-ridden neighborhoods or in war zones.

Many objections have been raised to categories. First, they omit behaviors proven to be detrimental such as inconsistency (McGee and Wolfe, 1991) and psychological unavailability and emotional unresponsiveness (Egeland, 1991). They are nondevelopmental, as if it did not matter whether the child is 12 months or 12 years of age. Another objection is that the categories are presented as absolutes, whereas their effects are context-dependent; to require a child to do chores on a farm gives exploitation a different meaning than forcing a girl into prostitution to make money. Finally, Belsky (1991) makes the point that deviations from the norm are not necessarily dysfunctional and harmful. Preparing a child to survive in a crime-ridden inner-city neighborhood is different from preparing a child for Stanford, since the former may well involve an increase in punitiveness and a decrease in affection. It may even be that "beating the devil" out of children in colonial times prepared them for the harsh struggle for survival facing them (see Chapter 1).

Legal Implications The issue of definition takes on added seriousness in light of the fact that the legal system is involved in child maltreatment. Thompson and Jacobs (1991) argue persuasively that while broad, all encompassing definitions may be appropriate for research, they may have dangerous consequences should they be incorporated into the legal system. Labeling an overstressed, single mother as "psychologically unavailable" to her infant is socially denigrating and serves no useful purpose. At a practical level, broad definitions will strain already limited remedial resources while concomitantly expanding intrusions into family life with measures that have unproven effectiveness. For example, since removing the child from the home in the case of sexual or physical abuse may possibly do more harm than good, there is little justification for extending the range of cases treated in this manner. Thompson and Jacobs recommend that definitions of emotional maltreatment be narrow and explicit and that they reflect society's values concerning the necessity for care and treatment; for example, the need for intervention when parental behavior results in severe depression might be more readily accepted than when such behavior results in an insecure attachment or lower self-esteem.

Research

Perhaps because it is a relative newcomer on the clinical scene, emotional maltreatment of children has not yet generated a substantial body of research. (A more comprehensive coverage can be found in Hart, Germain, and Brassard, 1987.) In comparing 175 maltreated children with 176 normative children, Claussen and Crittenden (1991) found that while emotional maltreatment could exist alone, it almost always accompanied physical abuse. Moreover, the severity of physical injury was not related to detrimental outcome, whereas psychological maltreatment was.

Egeland, Sroufe, and Erickson (1983) found that emotional maltreatment, defined as hostile verbal behavior, had a different effect from physical abuse and neglect in the toddler and preschool period. While both groups were noncompliant, had low self-control, and lacked persistence and enthusiasm for tasks, the maltreated children had high levels of both anger at the mother and avoidance of her. There is also a high correlation between psychological maltreatment and developmental delay in young children (Hart and Brassard, 1991).

Evaluation

It is clear from our previous discussions that childhood psychopathology is, to a significant degree, related to noxious interpersonal and superordinate variables. To relabel such variables as emotional maltreatment would serve no useful purpose. But we are dealing with something different here. In the past we have, for the most part, started with the disturbed child and explored the variables that might be responsible for producing the disturbance. Emotional maltreatment reverses this process, beginning with interpersonal and superordinate variables assumed to be noxious and asking how they distort normal behavior. The ensuing child variables, such as aggression or mistrust or low self-esteem, may cut across traditional diagnostic categories.

What is to be gained by this reversal? One test is research productivity on the one hand, effective prevention and remediation on the other. As has already been mentioned, emotional maltreatment has not yet produced a body of well-controlled studies specifically growing out of the concept itself. And while it has added a persuasive voice to the clamor for preventive and remedial measures, to date it has not pioneered innovations in either.

There is much to be admired in the literature on emotional maltreatment—the humane values, the genuine concern for the plight of victimized children, the sense of urgency in regard to remediation which can spill over into social activism. Even our reservations about it are tempered by the fact that it is just coming into its own as a distinct concept. Its worth in terms of adding to our understanding of deviant behavior, serving as a basis for prevention and remediation, as well as providing well-documented guidelines to the legal profession, can only be judged at some later date.

SEXUAL ABUSE

Description

In a national survey by Finkelhor et al. (1990) of 2626 American men and women, they found that 27 percent of the women and 16 percent of the men reported at least one of four kinds of sexual abuse—sexual intercourse, touching or kissing or rubbing up against their body, taking nude photographs or exhibitionism, and oral sex or sodomy. While the sex difference was expected, the results reveal a considerable amount of abuse of boys. (Watkins and Bentovim, 1992, review the research on males.) Interestingly, there was no evidence of a significant increase in sexual abuse in the recent past, particularly during the "sexual revolution" of the 1960s. Race and parents' education were not related to victimization.

The median age of abuse was 9.9 for boys, 9.6 for girls. Boys were more likely than girls to be abused by strangers (40 percent vs. 21 percent), whereas girls were more likely to be abused by family members (29 percent vs. 11 percent), 6 percent of these being fathers or stepfathers. Most of the abusers were men. Most of the offenders were 10 or more years older than their victims, although boys were more likely to be abused by older adolescents.

Sixty-two percent of male victims and 49 percent of female victims experienced actual or attempted intercourse. While children experienced all four kinds of abuse, the majority of encounters were one-time events for both sexes; however a significant minority of both sexes had experiences lasting more than a year (42 percent of boys, 33 percent of girls). The incidence of use of force was low compared with findings from other studies (15 percent for boys, 19 percent for girls), perhaps because the survey questions stressed physical force and threats rather than bullying, intimidation, and being coerced into acting against their wishes.

Risk Factors

Finkelhor and colleagues (1990) found that growing up in an unhappy family was the most powerful risk factor. Furthermore, statistical analysis of the data indicated that such unhappiness was not merely the consequence of sexual abuse. Living without natural parents for a major portion of one's childhood was the next risk factor in this and other studies. For girls, all family circumstances other than living with two natural parents placed them at risk, particularly living alone with father or with two nonbiological parents. Boys, however, were at risk under only two conditions—living alone with their mothers or with nonbiological parents. The limitation of these descriptive findings is that they are so general they might apply to many kinds of childhood disturbances and fail to tell us why sexual abuse takes place, although the authors speculate as to reasons.

Short-Term and Long-Term Effects

Sexually abused children have more symptoms than nonabused ones, but are less symptomatic than a group of clinically referred children in treatment. (Our presentation follows Kendall-Tackett, Williams, and Finkelhor's 1993 research review.) The most frequent symptoms are fears, posttraumatic stress dis-

order (PTSD), behavior problems, sexualized behavior, and low self-esteem. No one symptom characterizes the entire population and there is no pattern of symptoms that can define a sexually abused child syndrome.

Depression is found across age groups from the preschool period to adolescence, while school and learning problems are also fairly consistent. Other symptoms evidence a possible developmental trend. Anxiety, nightmares, general PTSD, and internalizing and externalizing behaviors are prominent in the preschool period, while withdrawal, suicidal or self-injurious behavior, somatic complaints, illegal acts, running way, and substance abuse are prominent in adolescence. Sexual behavior is frequent in the preschool period but declines sharply in middle childhood to reemerge as promiscuity in adolescence. Between 20 and 52 percent of the children have various kinds of mental illnesses (mostly neuroses). In spite of the belief that boys are externalizers and girls internalizers, no sex differences are found in symptoms (see Table 14.2).

The factors that lead to the greatest number of symptoms are a perpetrator who is close to the victim, a high frequency and long duration of sexual contacts, the use of force, and sexual acts involving oral, anal, or vaginal penetration. However, approximately one-third of the victims have no symptoms.

Longitudinal studies indicate that symptoms tend to abate with time. About two-thirds of the children show recovery during the first 12 to 18 months after abuse. Signs of anxiety are most likely to disappear, while aggression persists or increases. On the other hand, 10 to 24 percent of children get worse with time; for example, sexual preoccupations may increase in children under 12. Neither age, gender, race, nor SES is related to recovery. However, there is some evidence that maternal support aids it.

The number of asymptomatic children and children who recover may seem surprisingly

TABLE 14.2

Percentage of Children with Symptoms by Age Group

Symptom	% of subjects (No. studies/No. subjects)		
	Preschool	School	Adolescent
Anxiety	61 (3/149)	23 (2/66)	8 (1/3)
Fear	13 (1/30)	45 (1/58)	—
Posttraumatic stress disorder			
Nightmares	55 (3/183)	47 (1/17)	0 (1/3)
General	77 (1/71)	—	—
Depression			
Depressed	33 (3/149)	31 (2/66)	46 (3/129)
Withdrawn	10 (1/30)	36 (1/58)	45 (2/126)
Suicidal	0 (1/37)	—	41 (3/172)
Poor self-esteem	0 (1/25)	6 (1/17)	33 (1/3)
Somatic complaints	13 (2/54)	—	34 (1/44)
Mental illness			
Neurotic	20 (1/30)	38 (1/58)	24 (1/25)
Other	0 (1/37)	19 (1/58)	16 (2/69)
Aggression			
Aggressive/antisocial	27 (3/154)	45 (1/58)	—
Delinquent	—	—	8 (1/25)

high in light of the inferred traumatic nature of the experience. It may be that those not affected had fewer of the high-risk factors; for example, they may have experienced only a single episode not involving violence or penetration, with the perpetrator being a stranger. The full story about long-term effects is yet to be told. In normal development there is a phenomenon called the "sleeper effect" in which the impact of an event occurs sometime later rather than immediately after. We would need to know how sexually abused preschoolers and school-aged children manage the sexual maturation of adolescence and the sexual adjustment of young adulthood before we can fully assess the impact of their earlier experience.

Conceptual Integration

Finkelhor and Browne (1986) have conceptualized the effects of sexual abuse in terms of four trauma-causing or *traumagenic dynamics*.

TABLE 14.2 *(continued)*
Percentage of Children with Symptoms by Age Group

Symptom	% of subjects (No. studies/No. subjects)		
	Preschool	School	Adolescent
Sexualized behavior			
Inappropriate sexual behavior	35 (6/334)	6 (1/17)	0 (1/3)
Promiscuity	—	—	38 (2/128)
School/learning problems	19 (2/107)	31 (1/58)	23 (2/69)
Behavior problems			
Hyperactivity	9 (2/55)	23 (2/75)	0 (1/3)
Regression/immaturity	36 (4/159)	39 (2/75)	0 (1/3)
Illegal acts	—	—	27 (1/101)
Running away	—	—	45 (3/172)
General	62 (1/17)	—	—
Self-destructive behavior			
Substance abuse	—	—	53 (2/128)
Self-injurious behavior	—	—	71 (2/128)
Composite symptoms			
Internalizing	48 (1/69)	—	—
Externalizing	38 (1/69)	—	—

Source: Kendall-Tackett, Williams, and Finkelhor, 1993.

Traumatic Sexualization Sexual abuse may result in shaping the child's sexuality in a developmentally inappropriate and interpersonally dysfunctional manner. This can come about in a variety of ways. The child may be repeatedly rewarded by affection, privileges, and gifts for developmentally inappropriate behavior and may also learn sexual behavior is a means of manipulating others into meeting developmentally inappropriate needs. Traumatic sexualization may occur when certain parts of the child's body are given distorted importance or become a fetish and when the offender transmits misconceptions and confusions about sexual behavior and sexual morality to the child.

The psychological impact of traumatic sexualization is an increased salience of sexual issues, a confusion of sex with caregiving or caregetting, and negative associations or aversion to sex or intimacy. The behavioral consequences of this impact might be sexual preoccupations, precocious or aggressive sexual behavior, promiscuity, or prostitution on the one hand, and sexual dysfunctions and avoidance of or phobic reactions to sexual intimacy on the other.

Betrayal   Betrayal is the children's discovery that a trusted person on whom they depend has done them harm. During or after abuse, for example, children can come to realize that they have been manipulated through lies or misrepresentations about proper standards of behavior, or they can realize that a loved adult treated them with callous disregard. Children can also feel betrayed by family members not involved in the abuse but who are unwilling to protect or believe them or who change their attitude after disclosure.

Betrayal can lead to a number of affective reactions: depression and grief on the one hand, anger and hostility on the other. Young children in particular can become clinging because of an intense need to regain a sense of trust and security. Betrayal can produce a mistrust of others and subsequently can impair the adult's ability to judge the trustworthiness of others.

Powerlessness   When a child's will, desires, and initiative are constantly opposed, disregarded, or undermined, the result is a feeling of powerlessness. In sexual abuse, this can result when a child's body is repeatedly invaded against the child's will and when the process of abuse involves coercion and manipulation on the part of the offender. Powerlessness is strongly reinforced when the child's attempts to halt the abuse are frustrated and when efforts to make adults understand what is happening are ignored. Finally, a child's inevitable dependence on the very adults who abuse and ignore them produces a feeling of being trapped.

Powerlessness can have two opposite effects. The children may feel anxious or helpless and perceive themselves as victims. As a protection against such terrifying feelings they may go to the opposite extreme of identifying with the aggressive abuser or, less dramatically, have an exaggerated need to dominate and be in control of every situation. The behavioral manifestations of powerlessness may be a number of neurotic symptoms such as nightmares, phobias, eating disorders, along with running away from home and truancy. There may also be learning and employment difficulties as victims feel unable to cope with the usual demands of life. At the other extreme, the children may become aggressive and antisocial or subsequently engage in child abuse themselves.

Stigmatization   Stigmatization refers to the negative connotations such as badness, shame, and guilt that are communicated to the child and then become incorporated into the child's self-image. Such negative meanings can come directly from the abuser, who may blame or denigrate the victim, or they may be implicit in the pressure for secrecy with its implication of having done something shameful. Stigmatization may result from the child's prior knowledge that the sexual activity is deviant and taboo, and it may result from the reaction of others who blame the child or regard her as "damaged goods" because of the molestation.

The psychological impact on the child consists of guilt, shame, and lowered self-esteem. Behaviorally, it may be manifested by isolation, and, in extreme cases, suicide. The child may gravitate to various stigmatized levels of society and become involved in drug abuse, criminal activity, or prostitution. Stigmatization may result in a sense of being different from everyone else and a constant concern over being rejected if the truth were discovered.

The Abuser

As was true of physical abuse, there is no type of person who sexually abuses children, nor is there a simple cause. To begin with, child sexual abuse is just one manifestation of a more general state of being sexually aroused by children, or *pedophilia*. Pedophilia can be manifested in manifold ways: masturbating to advertisements of children in their underwear, a lifelong pattern of being sexually aroused by fondling children, or a sudden incestuous impulse toward a daughter in a man who had heretofore engaged only in adult heterosexual relations. Since the diversity of the behavior has its counterpart in the diversity of theories and since the research data tend to be somewhat scattered, it will be helpful to present Araji and Finkelhor's (1986) summary of empirical findings. (See also Conte, 1991.)

Limiting this summary only to better established findings, the child sexual abuser can be characterized as follows. He is sexually aroused by children, is immature and socially inadequate, has difficulty relating to adult females, commits abuse while under the influence of alcohol, and was sexually abused himself. The picture, while sketchy, is at least a coherent one of early childhood vulnerability, a general social ineptness, blocking of adult heterosexual gratification along with being sexually aroused by children and disinhibition of prohibitions through drinking.

The picture is different from the one characterizing the physical abuser. There the punitiveness that may play a predominant role in authoritarian discipline is exaggerated by a number of factors—stress, impoverished parenting skills, and social isolation, among others—so that it becomes violence. The transition from normality to psychopathology can be traced with reasonable ease. Not so with sexual abuse. Normal parental love involves many sensual pleasures for the child—snuggling, kissing, bathing, and "riding horsey," to name only a few. While these may be erotically arousing to the child on occasion, such arousal is not their intent since both tenderness and playfulness are part of nonerotic pa-

rental love. What then goes wrong with the normal process? There has been a plethora of speculation but a paucity of empirical evidence. Only as more definitive data accumulate will we be able to decide which normal processes have gone awry and in what ways.

Assessment

Sexual abuse is by far the most difficult deviation to detect. Especially in the preschool period there are *cognitive* impediments since preschoolers' thinking tends to be concrete, their attention span short, and they can mouth ideas they do not really understand. Moreover, they do not have a firmly established understanding of chronological time, causality, or logical sequencing. Consequently, responses to questions might be rambling, full of irrelevances, inaccuracies, and idiosyncratic meanings. Equally important, preschoolers are mindful of pleasing or displeasing adults and might agree or disagree with statements on that basis alone rather than trying to decide whether a statement were true or not. (For details, see Waterman, 1986.)

Yet at any age obtaining accurate information is difficult. The subject matter itself is taboo so that the child does not have a readily available *vocabulary* to describe events that happened. Abuse often takes place with a familiar adult or family member in the context of seductive promises and flattery along with intimidations and threats. Thus the event is embedded in a highly charged *affective context* which can lead to various defensive maneuvers on the child's part such as denial or avoidance.

There is yet another complication in that the accusation of being a sexual abuser is part of a more general pattern of *parental relations*. In divorce proceedings, for example, the accusation may be motivated by vindictiveness rather than reality or by a misperception of reality born of vindictiveness. (For a detailed examination of this issue, see MacFarlane, 1986.) While it is important to protect the child from further sexual abuse, it is equally important to protect adults falsely accused. A different kind of complication arises when the sexual abusers are stepfathers or, to a lesser degree, natural fathers. Here, the mother may be forced to choose between believing either her child or her mate, who denies any wrongdoing. She may well side with her mate, dismissing the child's report as foolish, imaginary, or naughty. The child, in turn, feels betrayed, powerless, and entrapped, as we have seen.

It follows that interviewing a child concerning sexual abuse requires a number of skills. Foremost is the ability to establish and maintain the kind of relationship that will make the child feel sufficiently secure to talk about affectively charged experiences. With younger children, puppets and toys may lessen anxiety by transferring frightening events into the world of pretend. However, the child must understand that the purpose of such props is to make it easier to talk about an event that really happened. In this sense, the situation is basically different from pretend play, which allows the child unlimited freedom to fantasy.

There are a number of more specific interviewing skills. The interviewer must learn the child's names for body parts, sexual activities, and people. Especially with toddlers and preschoolers genitals are almost never known by their correct anatomic labels but are given a variety of nicknames such as "pee-pee" or "Suzie" or "pottie" (Schetky, 1991). Again at this age different people can be called by the same name such as "Uncle," or a person may be given a fabricated name such as "Mr. Tickle." Another source of confusion is that a general word like "hurt" may be the only one the child has to describe a sexual encounter, although it equally well might refer to a physical injury. Anatomically correct drawings and dolls and, whenever possible, photographs of implicated adults are helpful in decoding the child's terminology. However, the use of anatomically correct dolls as the sole diagnostic tool for determining whether sexual abuse occurred is of questionable validity (Cohn, 1991; Britton and O'Keefe, 1991). (See Figure 14.2.)

Answering the question of *how* the interview should be conducted presents something of a Hobson's choice. General questions elicit more accurate information. Specific questions yield a more complete account but also contain

FIGURE 14.2 (*Source:* Copyright 1993 by Bill Watterson. Dist. by Universal Press Syndicate. Reprinted with permission. All rights reserved.)

more errors (Dent, 1991). Unfortunately, there is evidence that general questions are not apt to elicit the kind of sensitive and embarrassing sexual information that is crucial. Leading questions also might be necessary to overcome the child's promise to keep abuse a secret (Goodman and Clarke-Stewart, 1991). While there is no resolution to the issue of preferred kind of questioning, interviewers at least should be aware of the trade-off in terms of accuracy as they move from general to specific enquiries.

Although much needs to be learned, enough is known to spell out some guidelines (see Ornstein, 1991; Heiman, 1992). These would include a supportive, skillful interviewer solely concerned with finding out what the child knows, conducting an interview as soon after the incident as possible, relying first on general questions and introducing specific ones only as necessary. While such guidelines should be elaborated as new findings come in, they would help counter the inept, biased, affect-laden interviewing that can characterize this affect-laden issue.

Finally, it is worth noting that medical findings, whether from a general physical examination, from genital and rectal examinations, or from the laboratory, are not sufficiently reliable to be considered diagnostic. Rather they should be considered, along with psychological findings, as another source of data relevant to answering the question of whether abuse occurred or not (Krugman, 1991).

Legal Aspects

Public concern over physical and sexual abuse has resulted in an increased involvement of the law which, in turn, has impacted on clinical child psychologists in their roles of assessing and treating such children. (Our presentation of maltreatment follows Otto and Melton, 1990, while the specific topic of sexual abuse follows Guyer, 1991, unless otherwise

specified.) At the most general level, legal action is justified under the state's *parens patriae* ("sovereign as parent") power to protect individuals unable to protect or care for themselves. Such power can override even fundamental rights such as the family's right to privacy. However, there is disagreement as to when the state should intervene, some advocating early intervention when there is only a suspicion of maltreatment, others favoring intervention only when there is proof.

Regardless of such disagreements, the general direction of the law since 1960 has been toward more expansive definitions, neglect and emotional abuse having been added to physical and sexual abuse; toward greater use of criminal sanctions especially in the area of sexual abuse; and toward a "get tough" strategy and easier prosecution of suspected abusers. The fact that a considerable number of alleged abuses have proven to be false indicates that the community in general shares this zeal to bring abusers to justice, even to the point of disregarding the right to privacy of the accused to say nothing of the potential psychological damage. (Yates, 1991, discusses false allegations of sexual abuse in detail.)

Certain modifications of judicial procedures have been made because of the concerns about the reliability of children as witnesses. An example of stretching the law is the use of hearsay evidence (Guyer, 1991). Traditionally, hearsay evidence is not allowed except in the case of physicians, the assumption being that patients would tell their doctor the truth in order to ensure proper diagnosis and treatment. However, the zeal to prosecute combined with the wariness of children as witnesses has lead to the inclusion of mental health workers as individuals who can give hearsay testimony about children they have interviewed. It has also led to a decision that a 3-year-old can understand that telling the truth about alleged sexual abuse will make him or her feel better through therapy! However, such liberalizations have not gone un-contested, and courts may differ in what they will and will not allow.

Traumatization of the Child   There is a basic conflict between the sixth Amendment guarantee that the accused has the right to confront his or her accuser and the desire to protect children from the assumed trauma of having to testify against their parents or caretakers. States have adopted various compromise solutions to this conflict. Some use closed-circuit television so the accused and accuser can confront one another on the television screen while the child is protected from actually being in the courtroom. Other states allow children to testify from behind a screen that blocks the defendant from their view but allows the defendant to see them, albeit dimly. The ultimate fate of such devices is yet to be decided.

Ironically, traumatization has been assumed, and only recently have investigators begun to collect data on the topic. Goodman and coworkers (1992) found that, in general, children who testified were more disturbed seven months after the testimony than those who did not. Once the trial ended, the negative effects tended to diminish but were still present. Continued behavior disturbances were related to having to take the stand multiple times, being deprived of maternal support, and lack of corroboration of the child's story. Finally, having to face the defendant was a source of great distress to the child. Thus, those concerned with making the trial less stressful for children need to focus on a number of its features in addition to facing the defendant.

Otto and Melton's (1990) summary of the overall legal situation is a sobering one. They state:

Because no consistent orientation exists among child advocates regarding the nature of child mal-

treatment, reforms have been based on emotional responses to the problem of abuse as much as empirical evidence or a theoretical basis. Many reforms have been instituted rather hastily, with little foresight and planning. According, we are left with procedures that are of questionable utility, some of which are also of questionable constitutionality. (p. 78)

Mandatory Reporting   In order to protect children and punish abusers, all states now mandate that professionals and laypersons report suspected abuse to agencies responsible for abuse investigation. While effective in increasing the reports of suspected abuse, these laws have created problems. One problem in implementation is that experts do not agree as to what constitutes physical and sexual abuse, while neglect and emotional abuse are even more vague. There is the further danger that the law would penalize what are stylistic differences among families, for example, in terms of physical punishment or nudity. Even more serious is the possibility that abuse and neglect would be used in a discriminatory manner to intrude into the lives of impoverished families (Kalichman, 1992).

Mandatory reporting creates a special problem for the therapist when abuse is revealed in the course of treating children or adults, or when adults seek treatment to help them change their behavior. If reporting would jeopardize treatment, which has greater claim on the therapist—the law or the good of the client? A survey of psychotherapists indicated that 25 percent would never break the confidentiality of the relationship in order to report suspected abuse while 32 percent sometimes would. While legal action can be taken against such psychotherapists, it may or may not be and the therapist may or may not be convicted, depending on individual circumstances (Guyer, 1991). (A general discussion of legal and ethical issues is found in Levine, Anderson, Ferretti, and Steinberg, 1993.)

The Child as Witness

Reliability of Testimony   Opinions concerning the reliability of children's testimony have varied all the way from claims that children never lie about having been sexually abused to claims that young children cannot tell fantasy from reality.

While the matter of reliability is beginning to receive the attention it deserves from researchers, the issue of ecological validity is crucial. How can one generalize from viewing and recalling a film of an auto accident in the classroom to being forced to submit to intercourse by a family member (Ceci, 1991)? At present there is no pat answer to this question. (For two different views, see Yuille and Wells, 1991, and Loftus and Ceci, 1991.) However, there is general agreement that laboratory findings should be complemented by naturalistic investigations. As an example of the latter, Raskin and Esplin (1991) analyzed children's accounts of sexual abuse in cases where the abuse was confirmed and not confirmed by other information. They found both structural and content difference. In regard to the former, coached children are apt to maintain the same story without modification, not to raise doubts about the believability of the story or to blame themselves for the event. In regard to content, there are certain details of sexual behavior that many children do not know unless they have actually experienced them.

Another study is worth singling out because, unlike the others, it most closely resembles the situation of sexual abuse (see Saywitz, et al., 1991). It concerns a medical checkup of seventy-two 5- to 7-year-old girls, half of whom had an external genital-anal examination and half of whom did not. Only three girls in the latter group responded positively to the question concerning genital-anal touching, two of whom could not provide details. However, the third falsely claimed the doctor placed a stick in her rectum. The authors conclude that the chances of obtaining a false report were extremely low. However, Steller (1991) counters that, even a paltry 6 percent of false reports becomes a sizable number when viewed in light of the total of 210,000 new cases of sexual abuse each year (Hartman and Burgess, 1989).

Suggestibility   Suggestibility is a possible variable in unreliable accounts of sexual abuse. Since it is not a personality trait, the search for suggestible versus nonsuggestible children is liable to prove fruitless (Davies, 1991). Rather, suggestibility takes place in the context of the adults' interviewing the child. Researchers are beginning to tease out the conditions that do and do not induce children to change their account. The typical procedure is for children to witness an event and, on subsequent questioning, for the experimenter to suggest that they witnessed something different; for example, suggesting that a man who said he was cleaning a doll when he lifted up her skirt was really playing with the doll.

Goodman and Clarke-Stewart (1991) summarize a number of important findings. As one would predict from studies of memory, children are apt to accept an interviewer's suggestions the longer the delay between event and interview (See Ornstein, Larus, and Clubb, 1991). Children between 3 and 5 years of age are more vulnerable to suggestion than are older ones. Suggestions tend to be accepted when children feel intimidated by the interviewer, when the interviewer's suggestions are strongly stated and frequently repeated, and when more than one interviewer makes the same strong suggestion. While the authors are careful not to claim that these findings can be extrapolated to false accusations of sexual abuse, they do seem relevant to the cases in which children are confronted with a variety of powerful adult questioners with vested interests in proving that abuse did occur. (For a review of research on suggestibility of the child as witness, see Ceci and Bruck, 1993)

Prevention and Treatment

Prevention Most preventive programs involve children and are aimed at teaching certain key concepts and skills. Among the most important are (1) children own their bodies and can control access to them; (2) there is a continuum from good to bad touching; (3) trusted adults should be informed after children are made to feel uncomfortable or strange. They are further informed that potential abusers are apt to be familiar individuals rather than strangers and taught ways of coping with sexual abuse such as saying no or running away (Daro, 1991).

There is evidence that programs are effective in informing children and that the information is retained for six weeks to six months. However, evidence that such knowledge is effective in preventing sexual abuse or increasing its reporting is still lacking. To assume that information alone can protect the child is to ignore the power differential between child and adult and the potency of the latter's seductions, threats, and rationalizations. On the positive side, there is evidence that sexual abuse offenders are deterred by children who indicate that they would tell a specific adult about an assault. Thus, teaching children, especially passive, lonely, or troubled ones, the simple task of telling an adult about sexual abuse may result in fewer abuses (See Daro, 1991; see also Reppucci and Herman, 1991, for a review of studies of child sexual abuse prevention programs in the school.)

Preventive programs with *parents* would be more palatable if sexual abuse were primarily committed by strangers and "perverts." That this is not true magnifies the already difficult task of explaining the various kinds of sexual overtures to children. Ironically, parents readily inform their children concerning the dangers of being kidnapped, but are reluctant to talk about someone touching their genitals, even though the latter is far more likely to happen than the former. There is some evidence that this abdication of responsibility to inform is uniform over all socioeconomic levels and over all ethnic backgrounds. In their defense, it can be said that parents are concerned about alarming their children unduly or making them mistrustful of closeness and affection.

Parents' avoidance of the admittedly difficult topic of sexual abuse is unfortunate because their close and continual contact puts them in a unique position to be effective educators. Their reluctance should be countered by information concerning the nature and extent of the problem, while their embarrassment over dealing with sexuality should be countered by guides concerning how to describe abuse in terms that children can understand and that are acceptable to the parents themselves. While promising preventive programs for achieving these goals have been devised, there are little data concerning how extensively they are used and how effective they are. (Conte, 1991, and Finkelhor, 1986a, have detailed presentations of prevention.)

Treatment The first challenge in treatment is deciding what is to be treated. (Our presentation follows Mannarino and Cohen, 1990. See also Dickstein, Hinz, and Eth's, 1991, more clinically detailed chapter.) As we have seen, there is no such thing as an abused child syndrome, and children do not necessarily have the usual clinical symptoms such as anxiety, depression, and low self-esteem. The family context can also vary widely, a single incident of abuse by a babysitter in an otherwise well-functioning family differing from chronic abuse by a father in a chaotic family. Thus, each child and family must be carefully and individually evaluated in order to establish treatment goals and decide appropriate techniques.

Most information about therapeutic techniques consists of clinical impressions rather than well-designed objective studies. (For an exception, see Gomes-Schwartz, Horowitz, and Cardarelli's 1990 study.) *Individual psychotherapy* can provide a safe setting for children to confront their sexual trauma, ventilate feelings about it, gain some perspective on it, and relearn trust. Play and art therapy are particularly useful with younger children who have difficulty verbalizing their feelings *Group therapy* is helpful in overcoming feelings of being different and therefore isolated from all other children. *Family therapy* addresses a variety of issues: poor supervision of the child, inappropriate sleeping arrangements, blurred role boundaries, feelings of guilt regarding the abuse, the loss when the perpetrator is removed from the family, and legal proceedings with regard to custody, visitation, and criminal charges.

THE RISK OF DIVORCE

When divorce was on the rise there seemed to be research showing that divorce is better for children than living in a family torn by conflict. The statement was premature, inaccurate, and simplistic. It was premature because rapid social changes outstripped researchers' ability to conduct well-designed studies. This problem is particularly acute with children, where it is essential to know long-term as well as immediate effects. The statement was inaccurate because it was simplistic. The effects of divorce are complex. Instead of a simple "If *X*, then *Y*" formula, the consequences are contingent on the interrelation of a number of variables. Thinking in terms of contingencies is more demanding than thinking in terms of a

simple formula, but it more faithfully reflects reality. It also helps the clinical child psychologist know where to probe in regard to both risk factors and resources.

Before tackling complexities, we will present an overview of the problem. The divorce rate rose rapidly between 1965 and 1979 and, despite a subsequent leveling off, it is estimated that between 40 and 50 percent of children born in the late 1970s and early 1980s will experience divorce and will spend an average of five years in a single-parent home. While 75 percent of divorced mothers and 80 percent of divorced fathers will remarry, the chances of a second divorce are even greater than for the initial one (Hetherington, 1989). Thus, the child must face a number of transitions: from dissolution of the original family to living with one parent, typically the mother, to adapting to a new family with a new parent and often new siblings.

The Predivorce Period

The period preceding divorce is one of parental conflict and acrimony. This raises the possibility that some of the children's problems which are regarded as the effects of divorce might have preceded it. There is evidence that this is indeed the case. Block, Block, and Gjerde (1986) analyzed longitudinal data from forty-one divorced or separated families and sixty intact families. The children were 14 to 15 years old at the time, but personality evaluations from teachers and researchers were available from when they were 3, 4, and 7 years old. The data showed that acting-out behaviors characteristic of boys after divorce were present at 3 or 4 years of age, which was as early as 11 years prior to separation or dissolution of the marriage. The constellation of early acting-out behaviors included being emotionally labile, stubborn, restless, aggressive, uncooperative, unresponsive to reason, and going to pieces under stress. There was no clearcut personality pattern for girls.

Immediate Reactions

It is to be expected that the period preceding and accompanying divorce is one of conflict and acrimony. (Our presentation follows Hetherington and Camara, 1984.) What is unexpected, especially to the partners who look on divorce as a solution to their problems, is that the period following separation and divorce is one of continued or even escalated conflict. Contact with the legal system intensifies problems over custody and visitation because of the adversarial nature of the legal process. In fact, clinical child psychologists' concern over the distress that legal battles cause children prompted them to advocate *mediating* child custody disputes (Saposnek, 1983). Mediation occurs independent of the legal proceedings. It is conducted by a skilled professional who helps the couples set aside their personal vindictiveness and concentrate on working out an arrangement that is best for the children. While mediation is typically voluntary, it has been sufficiently successful to be mandated by law in certain states. (For an evaluation, see Saposnek et al., 1984.)

To return now to immediate reactions to divorce, most children respond negatively to the loss of the parent and, while reactions vary with age, anger, anxiety, depression, dependency, yearning for the lost parent, and fantasized reconciliation are common to most. Children are apt to become more aggressive, noncompliant, whining, nagging, and unaffectionate with parents, teachers, and peers, such responses being more intense and enduring for boys than girls.

Chronic Problems

There are numerous sources of stress, conflict, and disruption during the *first year*. Some of the most pervasive changes are associated with finances. Women who usually have custody of the children suffer a decrease in income at the same time that they become head of the household. This may force them to seek employment for which they might not be well trained or to move to a poorer neighborhood with a loss of accustomed social networks and support. Both consequences seriously disrupt their lives.

Both parents are beset by problems ranging from management of household routines to lowered self-esteem. Divorced men find it difficult to shop, cook, and do the laundry, their lives being further complicated by the economic stress of maintaining two households. Divorced women are less likely to eat with their children than are mothers of intact families, bedtimes are more erratic, and the children are apt to be late for school. Both parents feel they have been failures. Divorced adults are overrepresented in admission rates to psychiatric facilities and have increased risk for automobile accidents, illness, physical disability, alcoholism, suicide, and death from homicide. Paradoxically, the relation between marital disruption and psychopathology is stronger for men than for women, even though women are exposed to greater stress over child rearing and finances.

Both parents communicate less well with their children, are more erratic in enforcing discipline, are less affectionate, and make fewer maturity demands of them, this list being an exact mirror image of growth-promoting parental behavior. The mothers, being unused to the authoritarian role, are both inconsistent and ineffectual, particularly in relation to their sons, who become increasingly aggressive and noncompliant. For their part, fathers become more indulgent and permissive and less available after divorce, although they still have more success in controlling their children than do mothers.

Because children handle stress best when

the environment is well structured and stable, predictable and secure, nurturing and supportive, it is not surprising that there is a significant increase in problem behavior after divorce, especially in boys. Finally, children of divorce are deprived of what has been called the *buffering effect* of intact families. This means that in an intact family a good relation with one parent can attenuate the effects of a conflictual relation with the other parent.

Period of Recovery

The *second year* usually marks a gradual recovery from the negative consequences of the divorce. The factors making for recovery are the expected ones. For parents, high self-esteem, low anxiety, feelings of being in control of the situation, tolerance for change, and freedom from economic concerns are associated with ease of adjustment to marital disruption. Within the family, low conflict, mutual support, and cohesiveness are related to coping with stress. Continued contact with a positively involved, non-custodial father is the most effective support in child rearing that a divorced mother can have. Friends also facilitate achieving a healthy adjustment while forming a new intimate relation plays a particularly important role for both men and women.

As the divorced parents can lead a more satisfying life, the children follow suit. An unexpected finding concerns the importance of grandparents, who frequently provide financial support to the mother and emotional support to both mother and child. Grandfathers help their grandsons by taking over skills training, educational, and recreational roles, while children in homes with both a mother and grandmother are better adjusted than those in which the mother is alone.

While schools and peers might be expected to play a positive role in helping children cope, they often do not. Even when boys' disruptive behavior begins to improve in the second year following divorce, teachers and peers continue to react negatively to them. Only if boys move to a new school where their reputation does not follow them are they treated well. In general, girls receive more support from teachers and peers than boys because they are more protected and because their internalizing behavior is more acceptable. In those rare instances in which schools do play a positive role, the teachers combine explicitly defined rules and regulations with consistent, warm discipline and expectations for mature behavior. In short, they behave as a good parent would.

Good Divorce versus Bad Marriage

Now let us examine the idea that a divorce is better for children than living in an intact but strife-torn family. The idea is too simplistic to be accurate because it fails to do justice to the dimension of *harmony-disharmony*. If this dimension is systematically added to the categories of intact-divorced, the following picture emerges. An intact, harmonious family is best for children. A harmonious divorce is better than being part of a disharmonious family. However, a disharmonious divorce has the most detrimental consequences for children. For example, in their meta-analysis of ninety-two studies of the effects of divorce, Amato and Keith (1991) found parental disharmony to be a prime variable responsible for children's lower scores on a measure of well-being, although economic disadvantage and absence of both parents also played an important role.

To view these findings in a slightly different way, "intactness" or "divorced" are not psychological variables. They may be considered descriptive or legal or sociological terms, but, in and of themselves, they define nothing psychological. Psychology enters when one begins to deal with the kinds of psychological variables that can be found in intact or divorced families. Either kind of family can have characteristics that promote or impede development, such as harmony and disharmony. It is these that affect children's lives. Thus divorce is detrimental to the extent that it contains features that incline children toward deviant development. By the same token, it can foster normal development to the extent that it contains growth-promoting features.

Developmental Considerations

One of the most interesting developmental studies is Wallerstein's (1984, 1985) ten-year follow-up of thirty children who were preschoolers and twenty-one children who were adolescents at the time of the divorce.

In the initial evaluation the preschoolers were significantly more disturbed than the adolescents. The general picture was one of severe distress: the children had extreme separation anxieties. They were clinging, demanding of attention, and needful. There were a number of regressive behaviors such as enuresis and soiling, thumb sucking, and masturbation. Eighteen months later half the children looked even more disturbed than initially, boys more so than girls.

The adolescents were also disturbed by the divorce, but less so. They experienced a painful sense of betrayal, feelings of loss and anger, along with conflicting loyalties. They were concerned about their own future marriages and about financial security. However, they were able to distance themselves from the family by increasing social activities and avoiding home. The protective maneuvers were successful because subsequently almost all of them were able to be supportive of and empathetic with their parents. Part of their healthy adjustment was the adoption of a realistic orientation toward the future.

The reactions of the two groups make sense in terms of their different developmental status. Preschoolers are significantly more dependent on caretakers than are adolescents, who are beginning to think of becoming independent of the family. Preschoolers' reactions are also more intense than those of adolescents, who have learned to keep their feelings under control. Preschoolers have access neither to the adolescents' defense of distancing nor to their diversity of interests outside the home, which offer both relief and substitute gratifications. Thus not only is their psychological world falling apart, but also they do not have the defenses and coping mechanisms to master their distress.

The picture ten years later was unexpected. The preschoolers, who were now 12 to 18 years of age, were less disturbed than the adolescents, who now were young adults. To begin with, the preschool group had no predivorce memories, although half of them were over 5 years of age at the time, and they remembered only fragments of the conflicts during and after the divorce.

Their relation with the custodial mother was close, open, and trusting. The father remained psychologically important even when the mother remarried, regardless of how often he was seen. In some instances the children knew of the father's failures and rejections, but still maintained a benign image, The importance of the father increased during adolescence, especially for girls. Significantly, the now-adolescents looked forward to the future with optimism.

The picture of the adolescent group, who now were young adults, was different. The effects of the divorce were long lasting and continued exerting a major influence on their lives. These young adults continued to be burdened by vivid memories of marital rupture. Lacking the preschoolers' protective forgetting or repression, they retained images of violent quarrels or their distraught, tearful mother or their brutal father. Feelings of sadness, continued resentment, and a sense of deprivation were strong. The women especially were apprehensive about repeating their parents' unhappy marriage in their own adulthood and eager to avoid divorce for the sake of future children. Yet both men and women continued to be strongly committed to the ideals of a lasting marriage and to a conservative morality.

Wallerstein's (1984, 1985) findings are noteworthy for a number of reasons. First, they contradict the critical period hypothesis, which states that events happening early in life are more potent than later events in determining subsequent development. Next, they show how spurious it can be to extrapolate future development from data taken at one point in time while also illustrating the frustration of having to wait ten years to obtain evidence that such an extrapolation was faulty! Finally, in regard to remediation, the data support the counterintuitive idea that it may be more important to help the seemingly well-adjusted adolescent than the obviously distressed preschooler if one had to make a choice.

On a more cautionary note, Wallerstein's was a clinical study relying heavily on intensive interview of the subjects. It is therefore open to the potential biases of such an approach to research; for example, the subjects may not be a representative sample and the data were not objective. (For a review of other long-term studies, see Wallerstein, 1991. Grych and Fincham, 1992, discuss the various interventions for children of divorce.)

Effects of Remarriage

Much of the information to be cited comes from Hetherington's (1989) study of divorce and remarriage. The study involved thirty sons and thirty daughters each in a nondivorced, a nonremarried, and a remarried group. The subjects were from a white middle-class population. One hundred and twenty-four of the children were part of a longitudinal investigation that began when they were 4 years of age and evaluated them when they were 6 and 10 years old. In order to equate the groups, subjects matching those who had been followed longitudinally were added during the second evaluation.

The Interpersonal Context: The Immediate Family As we have seen, divorce creates special problems for the boy who lives with the custodial mother. By contrast, remarriage creates special problems for the prepubescent girl. In the two years following remarriage, conflict between mothers and daughters was high, the daughters exhibiting more demandingness, hostility, and coercion and less warmth than girls in divorced or nondivorced families. While their behavior improved over time, they were still more antagonistic and disruptive with their parents than girls in the other two kinds of families. By contrast, the boys' behavior tended to improve in regard to aggressiveness and noncompliance. However, this improvement was not found in adolescent boys, although they still had fewer problems than did adolescent girls.

Paradoxically, closeness in the marital relationship and active involvement in parenting by the stepfather—the very factors that should be growth-promoting—were associated with problem behavior, especially with the girl. One reason may be that the remarriage was viewed as disrupting the positive mother-daughter relationship that was established after the stormy period of adjustment to the divorce. In this relationship the daughter was given more independence, authority, and decision-making responsibilities than she had before the divorce. The result was a more egalitarian, mutually supportive relationship, at least with prepubescent daughters, since puberty increased mother-daughter conflict. Thus, the prepubescent daughter might resent the mother's remarriage and be threatened by the stepfather, becoming sulky, resistant, and critical of both parents. Stepfathers fared best not by trying to be a good parent but by being like a polite stranger, spending time with the children but avoiding intense emotional involvement and making no concerted attempt to control the stepdaughter. Young and older children eventually accepted a warm, involved stepfather; but children between the age of 9 and 15 years continued to be resistant both because of their striving for independence and because of their strong sexual urges, which made closeness to a nonbiological father threatening.

The Interpersonal Context: Siblings, Grandparents and Peers

Hetherington's (1989) answer to the question of whether siblings play a supportive and buffering role during the stressful time of remarriage is a negative one. Ambivalent or hostile, alienated relationships were more common among siblings in remarried families than among siblings in nondivorced families. Moreover, sibling rivalry, aggression, and disengagement played an important role in increasing antisocial behavior. As might be expected, this pattern was more pronounced in boys than in girls. While sibling relations improved over time, they remained more disturbed than those in both nondivorced and divorced families.

Nor is there evidence that nonresidential grandparents played a major role in buffering the children or in the children's social, emotional, and cognitive development. However, they might have helped the children indirectly by supporting the mother during difficult times. In general, grandparents did not seem to play as positive a role in remarriages as in divorces.

Peers played an insignificant role in preschoolers' adjustment to family transitions. In middle childhood, active rejection or friendlessness increased problems in adjustment even though the support of a single friend could moderate the adverse effects of marital transitions and peer rejection. In adolescence, about one-third of the children became disengaged from the family following remarriage, becoming involved in school activities and peer groups. Whether this was a constructive or a detrimental development depended on the activities and associates the adolescent became involved with. Contact with an interested, supportive adult played a particularly important role in buffering the child against the development of behavior problems.

Developmental Considerations

Once again we see that the same event, remarriage, may have different meanings depending on the developmental stage of the child; however, we also see the importance of the child's sex as well. Prepubertal girls are at risk for developing behavior problems probably because remarriage intrudes upon the close mother-daughter relationship that has developed. For adolescent girls such closeness did not develop, so the problems of remarriage are more a continuation of those of the period following divorce. For prepubescent boys, remarriage produces a diminution of problem behaviors perhaps because the stepfather buffers the prior conflicted relation with the mother. For adolescent boys, no such improvement occurs, although they still are not as disturbed as girls.

Peer relations also play a different role at different developmental stages. In the preschool period they make little difference in regard to the children's adjustment. In middle childhood rejection increases problems in adjustment, while a single friend can moderate its effects. Adolescents become more involved in peer relations, but whether this fosters or hampers adjustment depends on the nature of the peer group itself.

Having explored some of the factors in the organic and interpersonal contexts that place children at risk for developing problem behavior, we now return to the superordinate context of society which was our focus in discussing the risk of a homosexual identity. This time our concern will be with minority children and the special stresses they face in trying to come to terms with two different sets of cultural values and expectations.

RISKS OF ETHNIC MINORITY CHILDREN

Ethnic minority children are of concern to the clinical child psychologist for a number of reasons. First, it is estimated that 20 percent of the population of the United States are members of ethnic minority groups and, by the turn of the century, it is projected that ethnic minority groups will constitute one-third of the population: 15 percent African American, 12 percent Latino, and 4.5 percent Asian American and Native American (Davis and Stiffman, 1990). Therefore there is a high probability that practicing clinicians will encounter these chil-

dren and their families. As with all clients, accurate assessment and effective treatment depend on the clinical child psychologist's ability to establish rapport and understand the client's point of view. This is not a problem for clinicians who work exclusively with children of their own ethnic or cultural background. Both literally and figuratively they can speak their clients' language. But this is not the case when client and clinician are from different ethnic backgrounds. It is therefore imperative that clinical child psychologists understand the impact of ethnic and cultural factors on their clients' lives.

Next the clinical child psychologist must decide whether a child is disturbed. This is difficult to do unless the clinician knows the child's culture. For example, many ethnic minority groups are family-oriented and authoritarian. The adolescent transition to independence, which plays such an important role in Anglo-American society, is not expected in cultures in which adolescents continue to be part of the family and subject to parental authority. Thus interpreting behavior as a "failure to resolve adolescent dependency needs" may be in error because such needs are not resolved in terms of independence. Similarly, the feminists' concern with equality that is increasingly valued in white American culture conflicts with the importance placed on parenting, particularly for women, which prevails in many cultures. Consequently, behavior that might be regarded as docile and subservient by Anglo-American standards might be fulfilling and adaptive in other cultures.

Ethnicity is bound up with mental health in a number of other ways (Gibbs and Huang, 1989a). First, it shapes the *belief systems* concerning what constitutes and causes mental illness. For example, Asian-American youth are more apt than white youth to believe that answering back to parents, becoming angry over minor insults, and talking openly with others about personal problems and secrets are signs of mental illness (Sue et al., 1976). Or again, there may be culture-specific psychopathologies, such as the Mexican-American syndrome called *susto,* consisting of restless sleep, listlessness, disinterest in dress and personal hygiene, loss of strength, depression, and introversion (Cuellar and Roberts, 1984). The Mexican American's belief in religious and folk spirits inclines them to attribute psychopathologies to the devil, punishment from God, witchcraft, or the evil eye (Cuellar and Roberts, 1984).

Culture influences children's *manifestations of symptoms;* some groups reinforce externalizing, while other groups internalize behaviors. For example, Weisz (1989) compared children from Thailand, where quietness, politeness, and inhibition are stressed, with American children, who are reared to be assertive and expressive. He found both similarities and differences in symptoms. Both groups had the same prevalence of problems, and in spite of dramatically different rearing, boys in both groups had more problems with lack of control than girls. However, Thai children as a whole had more problems with overcontrol, somatic symptoms being particularly prominent.

Next, ethnicity determines *help-seeking behavior.* Parents may consult a priest or minister, a spiritualist, or a tribal council of family elders rather than a mental health professional. Finally, as we shall see when we discuss African-American adolescents, ethnicity is a major factor in using and responding to *treatment,* for example, determining the initial level of trust and openness or the willingness to discuss certain topics.

But the clinical child psychologist must do more than learn to appreciate the perspectives of various minority groups. Many of these groups have to contend with the triple stressors of poverty, discrimination, and acculturation. The relation between poverty and psychopathology has long been known; adding the other two sources of stress may well increase the risk. At a practical level, the clinical child psychologist must tease out the role that all of these factors play in the problem at hand, since they may all impact upon assessment and remediation.

Aside from its importance to effective clinical practice, the study of ethnic minorities helps dispel the *ethnocentric belief* that "our way" is both the only way and the best. In reality, there are many ways of rearing children, many sets of values, each having its assets and liabilities. Clinical child psychologists have learned this lesson in regard to individuals. Children differ and, because of this, there are numerous fulfilling lifestyles. Both the sensitive scholar and the popular extravert can be developing normally although each has a different mix of the variables we regard as essential such as attachment, initiative, and self-control. The same is true of cultures. The Anglo-American culture is only one of many, and perspective on it can best be gained by a knowledge of diversity. In this way an ethnocentric view of what is good for children can be replaced by an understanding that our society, like all others, involves its special combination of factors that tend to promote and impede development. The United States has the highest rate of crime of any industrialized country, for example, while the crime rate in mainland China is low. Among the many variables contributing to the low crime rate is the closeness of the Chinese family, the constant surveillance of the child, and the deep sense of shame if the child commits an antisocial act. On the other hand, the Anglo-American emphasis on autonomy and independence opens up avenues of individual initiative that would not readily be available to the traditional Chinese adolescent.

One final point: Discussing characteristics of ethnic minorities is bound to run roughshod over variations within groups. A middle-class black family may have little in common with a black family from the slums, just as a third-generation Japanese family may have little in common with a first-generation one. In the category of Pacific Asian Americans there are an estimated twenty-nine distinct cultural groups ranging from preliterate to technologically advanced societies. Simplification is necessary in the initial stages of becoming acquainted with various cultural minorities, but the limitations of such simplification must be kept in mind.

Since it would be impossible to do justice to the richness of the field of ethnic minority children we have decided to concentrate on three themes, using a single minority group as an exemplar of each. While this strategy prevents comparisons among minority groups, the loss is unavoidable. (For a detailed presentation of the mental health of ethnic minorities, see Serafica et al., 1990; Gibbs and Huang, 1989b, deal specifically with minority youth.) The themes are *ethnic identity* in African-American adolescents, *cultural diversity* among Japanese-American children, and *clinical practice* with Mexican-American children. But first we will need some definitions and general observations to serve as a background for discussing these themes.

A note about *nomenclature:* There are no agreed-upon labels for various cultural groups. Some authors prefer the precision of Anglo-American or African American to more general terms such as black, white, or American. Certainly not all blacks or whites are Americans just as not all Americans are members of the white majority that defines the culture. At times terms are used to differentiate a minority from a majority status; for example, Mexican Americans are differentiated from Mexicans who still live in Mexico. However, in other instances, no such distinction is made since it is clear from the context; for example, one can read about the Japanese and know from what is written whether the reference is to the people in Japan or in the United States. Our presentation, like the literature in general, will not use a standard nomenclature throughout. Labels will be used interchangeably, and no differentiations are intended. The groups referred to should be clear from the context.

The decision to use labels interchangeably is a practical one. In no way does it deny the psychological and societal importance of such labeling. For example, the progression from negro-colored-darky to Black to African-American epitomizes the search for an accurate, nonpejorative group designation. Such designations impact on the way members of the group think of themselves as well as the way they are viewed by society. (See Ghee, 1990, for an elaboration of this theme.)

DEFINITIONS

Both "ethnic" and "minority" belong in the superordinate context and take us into the province of sociology and anthropology rather than psychology. In fact, this is the first time that the superordinate context serves as a point of departure. Because the realm is alien to psychology, we will not try to master its concepts and methodologies; rather, we will stay only long enough to become acquainted with some basic definitions and with some essential background data (Atkinson, Morten, and Sue, 1983). Then we shall return to the intra- and interpersonal contexts and concentrate our presentations there.

There is no general agreement on the definition of *ethnic groups*. We shall follow Gibbs and Huang (1989a) by defining *ethnicity* as membership in a group sharing a unique social and cultural heritage that is passed on from generation to generation. Such members believe themselves to be distinct from others in some significant way. While race often overlaps with ethnicity, it is not identical; Hispanics, for example, are defined by their common cultural heritage and language but may be white, black, or Indian or a mixture of all three.

For the purpose of federal surveys, the Office of Management and Budget has established five ethnic groups in the United States: American Indian or Native Alaskan, Asian or Pacific Islander, black, Hispanic, and white. In the literature, blacks may be referred to as African Americans and whites as Anglo-Americans. As of the 1990 census, there are 30 million African Americans, 22 million Hispanics, 7 million Asian/Pacific Islanders, and 2 million American Indians and Native Alaskans. All minorities are increasing at a more rapid rate than whites, Asian/Pacific Islanders in-

creasing by 108 percent over the past ten years, Hispanics by 53 percent, American Indian and Native Alaskans by 38 percent. By contrast African Americans have increased only 13 percent, whites by only 6 percent (U.S. Bureau of Census, 1991).

The simplest definition of a *minority group* is one having fewer members than the majority group. Obviously, not all ethnic groups are minorities, such as whites in the United States (although whites are a minority group worldwide), and not all minority groups are ethnic, such as the physically handicapped or the Quakers. M. E. Bernal (1989) adds two more characteristics which, while not generally agreed upon, are relevant to our concern with psychological adjustment. She regards an ethnic minority as being powerless or subordinate and the object of discrimination. Native Americans and blacks, for example, experience powerlessness and discrimination along with conflict with the dominant group; Polish or Irish Americans by contrast are not relegated to a subordinate role and are not in conflict with the dominant group.

Ethnic socialization refers to "the developmental processes by which children acquire the behaviors, perceptions, values, and attitudes of an ethnic group, and come to see themselves and others as members of such groups" (Rotheram and Phinney, 1987, p. 11). *Ethnic identity* is "one's sense of belonging to an ethnic group and the part of one's thinking, perceptions, feelings, and behavior that is due to ethnic group membership" (Rotheram and Phinney, 1987, p. 13). Ethnic identity is an important part of an individual's total identity but should not be equated with it.

GENERAL ISSUES

In this section we shall begin with the superordinate context and then proceed to the inter- and intrapersonal ones. As always, we shall be concerned with the context of time.

Changing Societies

As we saw in Chapter 1, societies, like individuals, change over time; being black or female or homosexual in 1950 was quite different from being black, female, or homosexual in 1980 because of the social revolution that took place in the interim. Other societies undergo their own changes; Mexico, for example, has seen increased industrialization while Japan has seen increased democratization. Thus it is important to know the cultural history of minority groups; one wave of immigrants, for example, may be predominantly illiterate farmers or factory workers, while another wave from the same country may represent a predominance of well-educated technicians and professionals. Even describing the "traditional" culture of a country involves an arbitrary stopping of the clock at one era in that country's continually evolving culture.

Ethnicity and Socioeconomic Status

Poverty, in and of itself, can have a number of risks and untoward consequences for children (see Figure 15.1). Therefore it is unfortunate that minority ethnicity and race have been confounded with poverty not only in popular thinking but in the research literature as well. This perpetuates negative stereotypes while making it impossible to know the relative contribution of each to disturbed behavior. We will cite findings from some of the few studies that have untangled race from SES. Patterson, Kupersmidt, and Vaden (1990) found that, overall, income level and gender rather than race were the strongest predictors of conduct problems, peer relations, and academic achievement in black and white elementary school children. In a similar vein, Stevenson, Chen, and Uttal (1990) found that children of poorly educated mothers, whether black,

FIGURE 15.1

Environmental relationships between poverty and educational failure. (*Source:* Birch and Gussow, 1970, p. 268. Reprinted by permission of publisher and authors.)

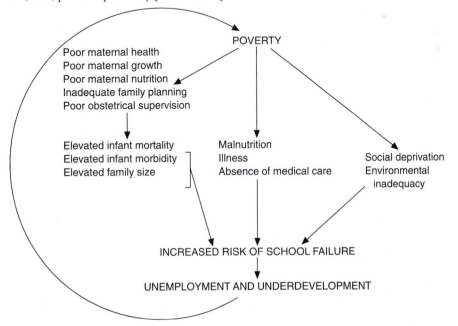

white, or Hispanic, did less well in grade school math than did children of better-educated mothers. Finally, in Achenbach and Edelbrock's (1981) standardization of their Child Behavior Checklist, neither SES nor race emerged as a significant contributor, although race was the weaker of the two. Thus, while not irrelevant, race contributes much less to children's school and general adjustment than does poverty. On the other hand, controlling for social class generally attenuates but does not eliminate racial differences in psychological distress among adults (McLoyd, 1990).

Ethnic Patterns

After reviewing the literature, Rotheram and Phinney (1987) were able to delineate four dimensions that are central to differentiating the social behavior of ethnic groups. These dimensions are:

(1) an orientation toward group affiliation and interdependence versus competition; (2) an active, achievement-oriented style versus a passive, accepting style; (3) authoritarianism and the acceptance of hierarchical relationships versus egalitarianism; and (4) an expressive, overt, personal style of communication versus a restrained, impersonal, and formal style. (p. 22)

The Anglo-American pattern values independence and competition, achievement, egalitarianism, and an expressive style of communication. This picture contrasts with many other patterns which emphasize the primacy of the family and the group, deference to and respect for the father and other authority figures, and valuing the good of the group over individual assertiveness and advancement.

Minority-Majority Relationships

Since many minority groups have ethnic patterns that are at variance with the Anglo-American pattern, what are the possible relationships that can result? One possibility is *assimilation,* in which the minority group loses its distinctiveness and becomes part of the majority group. This is the basis for the image of the United States as a "melting pot" in which diversity is homogenized into a uniform cultural pattern. At the other extreme is *pluralism,* in which the customs, values, and possibly even the language of different groups are maintained within a culture, resulting in a heterogeneous society made up of distinct groups. A middle position is *acculturation* or *accommodation,* in which elements of various groups are included in the culture. An analogy would be our government, which represents all the people but still accommodates to local interests of our geographic regions which are part of the country while retaining their distinctive local flavors (Rotheram and Phinney, 1987).

There is a difference of opinion concerning the result of the above relations between the minority and majority cultures. One view emphasizes the conflicts and dilemmas confronting children who must either identify with the dominant group and thereby alienate themselves from the family, or retain the minority group patterns and suffer various degrees of discrimination, ridicule, and rejection for being an outsider. Other authorities, while recognizing the stresses inherent in the situation, claim that the conflicts can be growth promoting. Just as bilingual children have advantages over children knowing only one language, so children who are knowledgeable about and can adapt to different cultures while maintaining their own identity have a richness of experience and a versatility in adapting which children knowing only one cultural pattern lack (Rosenthal, 1987). In all probability both outcomes are possible, but little is known about what determines whether children will go one way or the other.

Ethnic Identity

Ethnic identity, which will figure prominently in subsequent discussions, has a number of components. (Our presentation follows Rotheram and Phinney, 1987.) First there is ethnic *awareness,* or the understanding of one's own and other groups. This entails the acquisition of knowledge concerning the critical attributes of one's own ethnic group and how it differs from the ethnic groups of others. Next, there is *ethnic self-identification,* or adopting the labels used for one's group. This includes both formal and informal labels, the latter often having pejorative connotations, such as dago, spic, or coon. Then, there are ethnic *attitudes,* or the feelings about one's own and other groups. Such feelings may be the result of experience but may be based on stereotypes or prejudice. Finally, there are ethnic *behaviors,* or the behavior patterns specific to a given ethnic group. These may be specific, such as bowing versus shaking hands, or general, such as expressing feelings versus being self-contained.

Developmental Considerations

Ethnic self-identification may seem simple to adults but, in reality, it involves high-level cognitive processes. In many ways it is akin to gender identity. Preschoolers very early learn that certain labels are given them, such as "girl" or "Chinese," and they can parrot these labels. But then they are left on their own to figure out what the labels mean. This involves three basic processes. First, they must determine what are the essential elements in the label so that, if the elements were not present, the label would not be applicable. Next, they must discover what characteristics distinguish this particular label from labels given other groups, such as "boy" or "American." If there were no such differentiating features, then labels would not be necessary. Finally, they must learn that the label is consistent across situations and over time, that one is always a girl or Chinese wherever one is throughout one's lifetime (Aboud, 1987).

While children eventually master these three cognitive challenges, the process takes a number of years and may involve many errors

along the way. In our discussion of the development of the self (in Chapter 7) and of gender identity (in Chapter 11), we found that the preschooler thinks in concrete terms, such as, "A girl is a person who is small and wears dresses," or "The self is someone who plays ball"; only in middle childhood does thinking become abstract and accurate. A similar progression takes place with ethnic identification.

Some general trends in understanding ethnic identity can be summarized as follows. Simple *perceptual recognition* of different ethnic groups seems to be a function of the salience of perceptual cues, skin color and hair type being particularly important. Thus children can recognize blacks and whites by 3 to 4 years of age but not Chinese, Hispanics, or American Indians until around 8 years. Adults show a similar lack of differentiation within ethnic groups when they say that "all Asians look alike." In both instances, perception has not become sufficiently detailed to permit fine discriminations.

Self-identification is typically measured by presenting the child with dolls or pictures of children from different ethnic groups and asking, Which one looks most like you? Black and white children can perform the task by 5 years of age, although there is improvement in accuracy until 9 years of age. A similar technique can be used to determine which groups are different from the child, a task that children from various ethnic groups perform correctly more than 80 percent of the time by 4 or 5 years of age. Research also shows that children from different ethnic groups use different criteria for recognizing their own group and differentiating it from others. French Canadians use language, Chinese use eyes, food, and language, and American Indians use possessions and activities. Blacks rely on skin color and hair type as criteria (Aboud, 1987). This diversity of criteria shows the limitations of research techniques using appearance alone, such as dolls or drawings of different ethnic groups.

A more difficult challenge involves *conceptualizing* the essential features of ethnic groups and the self as a member of a group. One technique for measuring this conceptual ability involves presenting children with pictures of a number of people belonging to different ethnic groups and asking them to put all the members of the same group in separate piles. Next, the child is asked to place a stick figure representing himself or herself in one of the piles to determine the accuracy of self-identification with the group. The categorization task becomes accurate only around 7 years of age.

Ethnic constancy can be measured by asking children if they would be the same if dressed like another ethnic group—for example, asking a white child, "If you dressed like an Es-

kimo, would you be white or an Eskimo?" Temporal constancy can also be measured. For example, an American Indian child can be asked, "How long have you been an Indian?" and "Will you be an Indian ten years from now?" While achievement of constancy is not well documented, the evidence indicates that it happens around 8 years of age. (For more details concerning the research along with a critique of the limitations of the techniques used, see Aboud, 1987.) (Figure 15.2 summarizes ethnic identity.)

IDENTITY IN BLACK ADOLESCENTS

As we have seen, ethnic socialization refers to the developmental process by which children

FIGURE 15.2
Summary of ethnic identity.

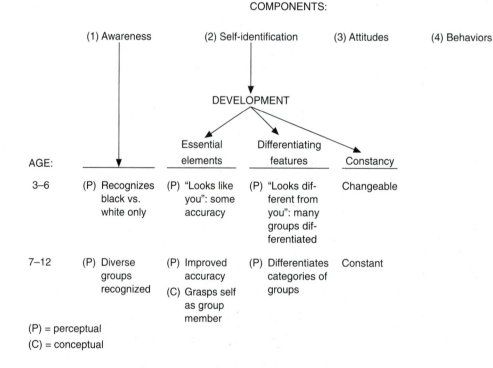

COMPONENTS:

(1) Awareness	(2) Self-identification	(3) Attitudes	(4) Behaviors

DEVELOPMENT

AGE:		Essential elements	Differentiating features	Constancy
3–6	(P) Recognizes black vs. white only	(P) "Looks like you": some accuracy	(P) "Looks different from you": many groups differentiated	Changeable
7–12	(P) Diverse groups recognized	(P) Improved accuracy (C) Grasps self as group member	(P) Differentiates categories of groups	Constant

(P) = perceptual
(C) = conceptual

acquire the behavior, perceptions, values, and attitudes of an ethnic group and come to see themselves and others as members of that group. Before discussing black adolescents, it will be helpful to have some general background information from the *superordinate context*.

Blacks, or African-Americans, as an ethnic group, have some special characteristics of their own. Primary among these is the fact that blacks were involuntarily incorporated into the existing society and permanently assigned an inferior status by legal, economic, and social forces (Spencer, 1991). During the 1960s civil rights movement blacks began to express increased pride in themselves as they had at other times of social change, beginning during the slave period and continuing throughout the twentieth century (Stuckey, 1987). This increased pride was epitomized by the change from being called Negro to being called black (Gibbs, 1990). For our purposes, the shift meant that black children could identify with a positive societal image of their ethnic group.

However, the process of change has been hampered by lingering prejudice and particularly by poverty. An already bleak picture became worse in the 1980s when the poverty rate for black children increased from 36 percent to 41 percent, compared to an increase from 12 percent to 13 percent for white children. Furthermore, 24 percent of black children live in poverty for ten out of fifteen years, compared with less than 1 percent of nonblack children (McLoyd, 1990).

A few more findings from the superordinate context will help flesh out the picture. The majority of black children are raised in families living in urban areas in predominantly black communities. The extended family is a common pattern serving many support functions. Black families of all income levels, for example, rely on relatives to care for children while they work and, in 1975, 40 percent of black children were living in households composed of the mother and other relatives (Norton, 1983).

Identity Formation

In conceptualizing identity formation in black adolescents, theorists tend to follow Erikson's formulation supplemented by an emphasis on the special problems engendered by ethnicity and color, poverty, prejudice, and social isolation. (See Phinney and Rosenthal, 1992, for a discussion of identity formation in a variety of minority adolescents.)

Coping Mechanisms Phinney (1990) describes four ways of coping with the above-mentioned special problems. One is to accept society's negative image and become an *alienated* member. This solution runs the risk of increasing personal problems and decreasing educational achievement. The next solution is to identify with the dominant white culture and *assimilate* into it. Anecdotal evidence attests to the strains of assimilation, such as not being totally accepted by whites while being rejected by blacks. Then there is *withdrawal*, which involves a retreat into the black culture and "being happy in the ghetto." There are advantages to this solution, research showing that self-esteem of blacks is higher in segregated than integrated schools. However, maintaining a lifelong pattern of withdrawal is difficult in the modern world, and such individuals are poorly equipped for confrontations with a white-dominated society. Finally, there is *biculturalism*, in which the adolescents retain their own culture but also adapt to the dominant one by learning the necessary skills. While there is research suggesting that this may be the best solution in terms of psychological adjustment, it also has its special stresses both in terms of parental opposition and social discrimination.

Process There are overlapping conceptualizations of the process by which a black identity is formed. We will follow Phinney's (1990) integrative summary. (See Helms, 1990, for an application of the model to other minorities.) The first stage is characterized by a *lack of exploration* of ethnicity. Here there are two possibilities. The first is identity *diffusion,* or a lack of interest in or concern with ethnicity. The second is identity *foreclosure,* or adopting the views of ethnicity based on the opinions of others. An example would be a doctor's son who is not allowed to think of any other vocation other than being a doctor or the adolescent who uncritically adopts the preferences and prejudices of the dominant culture.

The next stage is ethnic *identity search,* characterized by an involvement in exploring and seeking to understand the meaning of ethnicity for oneself. This stage may be initiated by a significant experience that forces awareness of one's ethnicity, which has variously been called "encounter" or "awakening." Recall that the adolescent is now cognitively capable of weighing and balancing divergent viewpoints before arriving at a decision. The final stage is one of *identity achievement,* or a clear, confident sense of one's own ethnicity. Individuals differ in how this achievement is expressed; some, for example, want to maintain

Identity achievement: being one's self while being part of the group.

ethnic language and customs, while others choose not to.

Adjustment Phinney, Lochner, and Murphy (1990) maintain that the development of ethnic identity described in the above section is an important factor mediating the relation between minority status and adjustment. There is beginning to be research support for this assumption. (Unless otherwise noted, we rely on Phinney, 1990, and Spencer and Markstrom-Adams, 1990.) The first two stages tend to be marked by anxiety and inferiority, while the final one is associated with a positive self-evaluation, a sense of mastery, and positive family and social relations. The final stage is also associated with endorsement of Afrocentric values (Table 15.1) (Helms, 1990).

The concept of stages also has implications for *treatment*. (Here we follow Helms, 1990. The chapter also describes the different kind of relationships that are established when counselor and client are at different stages of identity development.) Those in the early stage prefer white counselors, those in the middle stage prefer black, while those in the final stage have no preferences or prefer blacks. Clients in the initial stages will attend more sessions with white than black therapists, although those in the second and third stages will be more satisfied with the sessions. There is also tentative evidence that racial issues will play a more prominent role in counseling if the client is in the exploratory phase rather than in the final phase. The findings concerning stages help the clinician individualize the client at hand, rather than assuming that he or she is characterized by a single set of characteristics such as having low self-esteem and being hostile toward white therapists.

Other studies, while not conceptualized in terms of stages of identity formation, provide clues as to the variables distinguishing well-adjusted from poorly adjusted adolescents. In a study of 377 black youths between 14 and 24 years of age, Bowman and Howard (1985) found that those with a greater sense of personal efficacy had parents who emphasized self-development and individual achievement, while those who had better grades had parents who sensitized them to racial barriers to achievement and how to adapt to them. It was the 38 percent of youths whose parents taught them nothing about racial issues who lagged both in a sense of personal efficacy and achievement.

The next study concerns the 10 percent of black children who attend and are generally successful in private schools. (For a comprehensive account of concepts and research, see Slaughter and Johnson, 1988.) The mothers who sent their children to such schools were distinguished from nonblack mothers by feeling personally responsible for the quality of their children's education, along with protecting them from adverse in-school experiences, and by requiring teachers to demonstrate care and concern for the children as well as providing quality instruction in basic skills (Slaughter, Johnson, and Schneider, 1988). There is also some evidence that the successful children have a positive self-concept and a strong sense of personal control as well as a strong sense of racial identity (Epps, 1988). Finally, there is evidence that African-American adolescents with high self-esteem rely on the family as helpers with emotional problems, while those with low self-esteem do not (Coates, 1990).

Mental Health

While the relation between poverty, distress, and maladjustment has long been established, research findings in regard to race are inconclusive (Gibbs, 1990). Among *internalizing* disorders, the increase in depression among blacks disappears once SES, age, and sex are

TABLE 15.1
A Portrait of the African Perspective

1. *Spirituality.* Spirituality entails approaching life as though its primary essence were vitalistic rather than mechanistic. Permeating all sectors of one's life space is the conviction that greater powers than man are continuously at play. One strives to remain in touch with the greater spiritual essences.

2. *Harmony.* Rather than seeing oneself as distinct from one's environmental surroundings, one sees oneself as, and in turn acts as though one were, inextricably linked to one's surroundings. The conviction is that what will happen will happen, mainly because it is supposed to or because it is best that it does. Rather than attempting to maximize one's effort or attain excellence with regard to a single dimension or a relatively narrow range of expertise, one strives to be versatile.

3. *Movement.* Movement is actually a shorthand designation for the interwoven mosaic of movement, music, dance, percussiveness, and rhythm, personified by the musical beat. Also implied is a rhythmic orientation toward life: a complex and multidimensional recurrent pattern that typifies one's personal conduct and self-presentation.

4. *Verve.* This dimension is essentially extracted from the psychological residue of the movement dimension. It connotes a disdain for the routinized, the dull, and the bland, regardless of what ends are served. It implies a propensity for the energetic, the intense, the stimulating, and the lively.

5. *Affect.* Affect implies integration of feelings with thoughts and actions, such that it would be difficult to engage in an activity if one's feelings toward the activity ran counter to such engagement. Also implied is the importance of emotional expressiveness, the affective value of information, and a particular sensitivity to emotional cues given off by others.

6. *Communalism.* Communalism denotes awareness of the interdependence of people. One's orientation is social rather than being directed toward objects. Sharing is promoted because it signifies the affirmation of social interconnectedness; self-centeredness and individual greed are disdained.

7. *Expressive individualism.* Expressive individualism refers to the cultivation of a unique or distinctive personality or essence and putting one's own personal brand on an activity, a concern with style more than with being correct or efficient. It implies genuineness and sincerity of self-expression, an emphasis on spontaneity rather than on systematic planning. It implies approaching life as though it were an artistic endeavor.

8. *Orality.* Orality refers to the special importance attached to knowledge gained and passed on through word of mouth and the cultivation of oral virtuosity. It implies a special sensitivity to aural modes of communication and a reliance on oral expression to carry meanings and feelings. There is a reliance on the call-and-response mode of communication; to be quiet and wait one's turn to speak often implies a lack of interest in what the other is saying. Speaking is construed as a performance and not merely as a vehicle for interacting or communicating information.

9. *Social time perspective.* Commitment to time as a social phenomenon implies construing time primarily in terms of the significant events to be engaged in and not to be rigidly bound to clocks and calendars. It also connotes that behavior is bound to social traditions and customs of the past that serve as guideposts and beacons for future endeavors.

Source: Excerpted from Boykin, 1983. *Achievement and Achievement Motives* Copyright © 1983 W. H. Freeman and Company. Reprinted with permission.

controlled. The same applies to asthma, although race may play a role in the increase in hypertension. Eating disorders are also low among blacks. While the suicide rate is less than that of whites, it is increasing so that it is now the third leading cause of death.

In regard to *externalizing* disorders, there is less alcohol and marijuana use among blacks but more cocaine and heroin use; recently, this has also led to an increase in drug-related AIDS. The picture in regard to conduct disorders and juvenile delinquency is unclear. While more blacks than whites are arrested for serious felonies, this may be due, in part, to discrimination. Self-report surveys reveal no difference in delinquent behavior between blacks and whites, but such surveys were conducted on students attending high school, thus missing the dropouts. However, there is evidence that the psychological and neurological symptoms of the black delinquent are more likely to be handled by the juvenile justice sys-

tem, while whites exhibiting similar symptoms are referred for treatment in the mental health system. School dropouts have declined since 1970 until they approximate that of whites (17.3 percent versus 14.1 percent); however, in the inner city the rate is between 40 and 60 percent. Finally, homicide is the leading cause of death among black males, perhaps because of the drug trade and the availability of guns at home (see Figure 15.3). (Stiffman and Davis, 1990, have a detailed presentation of various externalizing disorders. For a discussion of assessment and treatment of black adolescents, see Gibbs, 1990, and Ho, 1992.)

CULTURAL DIVERSITY AND THE JAPANESE CHILD

Minority groups differ not only between themselves but within themselves as well, as acculturation brings about intergenerational shifts

FIGURE 15.3

Child and adolescent homicide rates by age, ethnicity, and gender. (*Source:* Halberstein, 1991, p. 43. Reprinted by permission.)

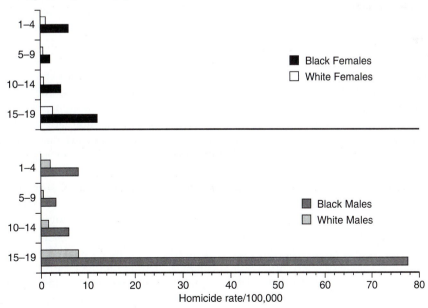

in values. Thus, for example, a minority adolescent trying to find his or her niche in society may be faced with disagreements between grandparents and parents as to acceptable and unacceptable choices. The clinical child psychologist trying to help such an adolescent must be mindful of these sources of stress as well as being skillful in dealing with them. While many minority groups change over time, we will discuss the Japanese Americans, whose history is particularly dramatic.

Traditional Japanese Culture

We begin with a reminder: while it is possible to describe general characteristics of the Japanese culture, the culture itself is undergoing change. After World War II both Western and democratic ideas began to play an increasingly important role in Japanese society, while national goals were changed from concerns with war to industrial productivity. While such changes are not our direct concern, they do affect the characteristics of immigrants to this country at different points in time.

At the most general level American and Japanese cultures can be contrasted in the following manner. In America the emphasis is on change, individuality, self-assertion, and equality. The Japanese culture emphasizes tradition, vertical relationships, interdependence, and self-denial. Both cultures value diligence, education, and postponement of immediate pleasures for future gratifications. (Our presentation will follow Yamamoto and Iga, 1983, unless otherwise noted.)

Vertical Organization The culture in the United States values equality and upward mobility; even rail splitters, peanut farmers, and actors can become president. The Japanese culture, by contrast, is highly stratified, making for keen status consciousness. Even language varies according to whether the person is of higher or lower rank, and a person of higher rank does not bow as deeply as one of lower

rank (Yamamoto and Kubota, 1983). While the lower strata are required to serve the people in the higher strata, the emphasis is on mutual obligation and loyalty. Thus the relation between classes is not like that of master and servant but one of interlocking responsibilities, individuals in the higher strata being as bound by prescribed duties and behaviors as those in the lower.

Interdependence Instead of Anglo-American individualism, the Japanese culture's pervasive emphasis is on interdependence. A person identifies himself or herself within a social group such as the family, the school, or the workplace. Group cooperation and participation are taken for granted in everyday activities. This cooperation in turn fosters a sense of togetherness and results in long-lasting relationships. Finally, not only subordinates but authority figures as well must conform to group objectives. Thus a corporation must be as totally committed to the employee as the employee is to the corporation. In fact, executives and production line workers may dress alike and eat in the same cafeteria, a custom that symbolizes interdependence and subordination of all individuals to group objectives.

Another aspect of interdependence is an emphasis on *empathy*, which is a highly valued virtue as well as being a far cry from "looking out for number one." The cultivation of the ability to feel what another person is feeling goes along with the motivation to help others achieve their wishes and goals. Part of this emphasis on empathy is an attempt to maintain consensus or positive feelings of agreement between people. Confrontations are avoided; accommodations are essential. Self-restraint is another means by which problems are avoided.

Finally, at the national level, the strong sense of group membership is related to an equally strong sense of being different from others. Traditionally, Japanese people have perceived themselves as separate and unique with their sense of interdependence referring exclusively to relationships among those of Japanese heritage.

Generational Changes

The Issei Generation   The Issei, or first-generation Japanese, arrived shortly after the turn of the century when Japan was only beginning to be industrialized and the tradition of caste and class was strong. (We continue to follow Yamamoto and Kubota, 1983.) The majority of immigrants were poorly educated, tended to be from rural areas, were disadvantaged educationally and culturally, and had been without employment in their native country. Most spoke only Japanese and were preoccupied with the problem of survival.

First regarded as a source of cheap labor in this country, they were subsequently subjected to blatant racism, violence, restrictive legislation, and antimiscegenational statutes. They coped with their strange and hostile environment by trying to be inconspicuous, adopting Western dress, and being polite, stoic, nonemotional, and self-effacing, as well as hardworking and conscientious. While adaptive, such mechanisms also perpetuated both a physical and psychological "ghettoization."

The Nisei   The Nisei are American-born children of the Issei immigrants and are considered second-generation Japanese Americans. They were raised before World War II and were bilingual, with Japanese as their primary language. They came to be called the model minority, although they did not view themselves in this manner. However, they were the most educated and successful ethnic group in the United States, even though the process by which they achieved this status was a painful one.

The hysteria following the bombing of Pearl Harbor was a turning point for Japanese Americans. The majority of their community leaders were arrested, separated from their families, and placed in a segregated facility in Crystal City, Texas, with the designation of dangerous aliens. West Coast families were uprooted and placed in concentration camps in the spring of 1942.

The people found they had to live in cramped quarters and use centralized eating, bathroom, and laundry facilities. The lack of privacy and the communal facilities disrupted traditional family life, depriving the Nisei of its stabilizing influence. But it emancipated them as well. The necessity of communicating in English with federal representatives escalated Nisei into roles of prominence overnight, while it simultaneously contributed to the erosion of established roles and functions within the family unit. Peer groups, organized around athletic competition between blocks, became primary socialization units. Older Nisei were selected as coaches and parent surrogates, while parental supervision itself gradually dissipated over time.

Because it was possible to leave the camps under special dispensation between 1942 and 1946, Nisei attended colleges and universities in unprecedented numbers, making them the most educated ethnic subgroup within the United States. They also formed an all-Nisei combat unit, which became the most decorated battle unit in World War II.

The post–World War II era had an air of starting over. Compared with the Issei, the Nisei were better educated and more worldly and were sufficiently flexible to abandon ghetto life and its attitude of coexistence in exchange for an assimilated form of living in mainstream America. Their diligence and education enhanced employment opportunities and facilitated acceptance by the majority culture.

The Sansei   The Sansei, or grandchildren of Issei immigrants, in many ways resemble middle-class white American children in attitudes, belief, and life-style. Most no longer speak Japanese. Sansei, like Nisei, tend to identify themselves not with Japan but with the camp in which the Nisei spent the four impressionable years between 1942 and 1946. They continue to show some of their parents' characteristics in that they are less aggressive socially than Anglo-Americans and overachieve in school. The majority do well and have the reputation of being model children.

Changing Family Patterns

The vertical organization of traditional Japanese culture was to be found in the family as well. (Our presentation follows Yamamoto and Kubota, 1983, unless otherwise noted.) Primogeniture and lineage were an integral part of Japanese culture. The eldest son became head of the household and was responsible for both his parents in their old age and for his brothers and sisters. Consequently, males were preferred above females, the first-born male being of special importance.

In the traditional family, rankings were related to seniority and gender, the father having the most authority, followed by the mother in an unofficial capacity, the eldest and then the next eldest sons. In fact, the Japanese language contains no words for brother and sister per se, but designates whether they are older or younger.

Interdependence was expressed in a high degree of family togetherness. Families did everything together, including eating, bathing, sleeping, and participating in recreational activities. Characteristically, hierarchical relationships were preserved, the members with the highest status being served or bathed first, for example. Family members were restrained rather than autonomous and spontaneous as in the American culture. Other-directedness and externality were further consequences of interdependence, children not only being concerned for the welfare of other family members but also feeling that their behavior was constantly monitored by them.

Future orientation was shown in two ways. First, parents were frugal in order to provide their children with the best educational advantages. Children, in turn, were expected to show filial piety and take care of their parents in old age. Consequently, there was no need for social security.

The Current Picture   Many but not all of the traditional Japanese values have been modified so that the current picture is a mixed one. (Our presentation is based on del Carmen's 1990 integrative summary of objective studies.) Both here and in Japan the extended family has been replaced by the nuclear family. Japanese families also have a lower rate of divorce, a lower proportion of households headed by a woman, and a lower rate of fertility than non-Asian families. Ironically, this "nuclearization" occurred at the same time that the nuclear family in the United States was undermined by an increase in divorce and single-parent households.

Marital roles are shifting away from the strong paternalism of traditional Japanese culture to a more egalitarian arrangement between husband and wife. However, Japanese-American women have more readily adopted this perspective than Japanese-American men, who are still more in the traditional mold. Decision making, which used to be unilateral, is being modified, with the more educated and Americanized women enjoying higher status within the family and a complementary relationship among more acculturated couples.

Yet the Americanization is not total. Japanese-American parents value having well-behaved children more highly than do white parents. They also still value sharing deep thoughts, rather than feelings, with their children. In their family communications, Japanese Americans are more cautious, indirect and restrained and show less warmth and affection. Thus, it is important for the clinical child psychologist not to interpret such behavior as evidence of coldness or hostility or inhibition. One final example of the persistence of tradition: while ethnic group identity usually declines in successive generations, there are no differences among third- and fourth-generation Japanese Americans in this regard (Wooden, Leon, and Toshima, 1988). (Del Carmen, 1990, discusses the assessment and treatment implications of the changes in Japanese-American family life. See also Ho, 1992.)

Parenting   The general trend in parenting is from indulgence in the early years to strict discipline in middle childhood and adolescence. (We follow Serafica's 1990 integration of objective studies.) *Infancy* and *early childhood* are apt to be the least stressful times. While parents are more indulgent in weaning, toileting, and bedtime than are Anglo-Americans, they can also adapt to demands for autonomy if necessary.

In *middle childhood* there is much emphasis on academic achievement, both to bring honor to the family and to prepare for a future occupation. While this goal coincides with that of the dominant society, there is no information on the possible personal price the child pays in achieving it. However, the assertive, questioning method that is often encouraged in the classroom is at variance with the family's values of filial piety and obedience. Parental desires to maintain close family ties may also hamper participation in peer group activities. There is evidence that Japanese-American children's physical self-concept is lower than that of their peers. They are particularly sensitive about their flat nose and general appearance because of the negative reactions of others to such characteristics. In this connection it is important to remember that physical appearance becomes increasingly central to self-esteem from middle childhood on.

In *adolescence* the clash of cultural values can become severe. Parents believe family members should prefer to be with each other rather than with outsiders and that decisions and deep thoughts should be shared. The adolescent feels equally strongly that each member has a right to keep certain thoughts private and to express feelings, especially angry ones, openly. Divergence from traditional values increases with age until by the twelfth grade the views of Japanese Americans are similar to those of their Anglo-American peers. While Japanese Americans may have higher career aspirations than their white peers, freedom of choice may be viewed by parents as a sign of disobedience or even betrayal. In a recent survey, for example, many students reported a conflict between their preferred career goals and parental aspirations for them, resulting in stress, anxiety and depression (Task Force on Asian-American Students, 1991). Dating may be stressful both because of racial prejudice among adolescents themselves and because of traditional values discouraging marrying non-Japanese. Sex-related guilt has decreased with successive generations but is still stronger than in Anglo-Americans (Nagata, 1989). (Serafica, 1990, discusses the implications of these findings for counseling parents.)

Mental Health

Information on specific psychopathologies is meager. The incidence of suicide is low, 9.4 per 100,000 as of 1980, compared with 13.5 per 100,000 for whites. However, suicide accounts for a larger proportion of deaths than it does for whites, 19.0 percent versus 11.9 percent (See Liu et al., 1990). The rate of juvenile delinquency and alcohol consumption is lower than it is with white Americans, although it is increasing with successive generations (Fugita, 1990).

Unfortunately, the true extent of psychopathology is unknown because of the lack of epidemiologic data and because of the underuse of mental health facilities. There are a number of reasons for the latter: the feeling that problems should be handled by family and friends, the concern with losing face, and the language barrier. However, there is evidence that utilization rates increase dramatically if resources are publicized, accessible, and culturally appropriate (Fugita, 1990). Even with more acculturated populations, such referrals tend to be for psychopathological conditions rather than for marital and family problems (Nagata, 1989). Mental illness in general tends to be viewed as inappropriate behavior or malingering. There is also a greater number of somatic complaints among Japanese-American college students than among their peers, perhaps because somatization is more acceptable than a direct expression of a psychological problem (Nagata, 1989).

The stereotype of the Japanese American as the ideal minority has a number of drawbacks, not the least of which is a trivializing of their problems. For example, among minorities, they have the lowest priorities for federal and state funding for physical and mental treatment and intervention, as well as for research and training (Liu et al., 1990). While it is true that Japanese Americans have the lowest poverty rate among minorities, it is also true that they are underemployed, earning several thousand dollars less than college-educated non-Asian peers (Nagata, 1989).

Finally, the mental health picture is far from positive for Sansei who stop with a high school education or earlier. The blue-collar class tends to discriminate against them more openly than the middle class, the options for work are more limited, and these Sansei become progressively alienated from their college-bound peers. Consequently, they are at risk for drug abuse and narcotic addiction as well as for conflicts with family, peers, and police (Santa, 1983).

Evaluation The American emphasis on equality and autonomy might give Japanese-Amer-

ican children opportunities for maximizing their potential which otherwise might not be available to Japanese children locked into specified roles and stratified classes. One thinks particularly of the traditional role for Japanese girls in this regard. Yet the very emphasis on individuality may not provide sufficient protection against isolation on the one hand and social irresponsibility on the other. Such vulnerabilities may not exist in traditional Japanese child rearing with its emphasis on interdependence, group identity, and group monitoring. In sum, we are dealing with a balancing of assets and vulnerabilities between cultural patterns just as we do among individual children.

HELPING MEXICAN-AMERICAN FAMILIES AND CHILDREN

While understanding ethnic socialization and diverse ethnic values is important, the pragmatic reason for learning about ethnic groups is to enable clinical child psychologists to evaluate and help families and children who are having problems. Our thesis is that these clinical goals of accurate evaluation and effective help can be achieved only by understanding ethnic backgrounds and modifying clinical procedures accordingly. We have arbitrarily chosen the Mexican-American culture to illustrate this thesis.

Before proceeding to clinical considerations, however, it will be necessary to describe the traditional Mexican values and how they have been modified over successive generations of immigrants.

Family Structure The *interdependence* of the Mexican Americans is nicely illustrated by the structure of the family, which is neither nuclear nor extended but a combination of the two. As in Mexico, the family unit is of prime importance to its members, with grandparents playing an important part in family life. Sex roles are clearly demarcated; males are

A multigenerational Mexican family.

granted independence at an earlier age than females and are expected to achieve in the outside world (Diaz-Guerrero and Szalay, 1991).

Family members also have ancillary relationships that serve as a support system as well as transmitting information and providing access to resources such as jobs. There is a fictive kin system called *compadrazgo,* or godparents, whose members are usually selected from close friends and relatives. They are responsible for the well-being of the child, thereby serving as a source of security for him or her and support for the parents. There are neighborhood helpers (*servidores*) who further extend the social network in terms of assisting with chores and providing companionship.

Friends and friendships are broader in scope, more enduring, and affectively deeper than they are in the dominant American culture (Diaz-Guerrero and Szalay, 1991).

Finally, belief in the supernatural can play an important role both as an explanation for distress and as a source of comfort. Mexican Americans may seek supernatural intervention not only from religious figures but from folk beliefs and healers (Argueta-Bernal, 1990). For example, natural healers bring relief from various health, mental health, and life crisis problems through a variety of healing modalities such as massage, herbs, and spiritual treatment. Religious counselors also play a role in helping Mexican-American families cope with problems (Vega, Hough, and Romero, 1983).

In short, Mexican Americans have an extensive support system which can help them cope with stress and which can also be used as a resource by mental health workers.

Family Values The prime values of Mexican-American families are religion, interdependence, honor, self-respect, and self-sufficiency. All members are expected to protect the family image, honor, and well-being. Respect within the family is hierarchically organized by age and sex, with older males being given the most respect. Family members are expected to do assigned chores and other family-related physical tasks and to contribute to the family's economic well-being (Mejia, 1983).

Family Roles The traditional male role is epitomized by *machismo*. However, the terms means more than masculine superiority and forcefulness. It encompasses a strong sense of personal honor, family loyalty, love of children and respect for the aged, as well as status in the community. There is evidence that the more extreme emphasis on masculine dominance has moderated in the modern Mexican-American family; there is more joint decision making with the wife and greater equality of roles in regard to vocational opportunities. While the father is still the authority and disciplinarian for his children, he is also friend and companion (Ramirez, 1989; Diaz-Guerrero and Szalay, 1991).

The more narrowly defined aspects of machismo are present in the *palomillos*, or social groups, in which young males display their prowess through drinking and feats of daring. In addition, the groups offer social support, giving help and advice to members who are having marital, familial, or work problems.

The traditional female role is a family-centered and subservient one. The mother is expected to be nurturant and self-sacrificing, while the daughter's socialization stresses caring for the children and the home. The daughter is allowed to spend less time away from the house than the son, and her social activities are more limited and carefully monitored. However, this situation is undergoing rapid change as women want more education and vocational opportunities and more freedom in their social and sexual life (Mejia, 1983).

Childrearing The parent-child relationship is the central focus of family life rather than the husband-wife relationship as it is in the dominant American culture (Diaz-Guerrero and Szalay, 1991). Parents express their family-centeredness not only with their children but also in their close relation with their own parents and the frequency of visiting relatives. Parents encourage their children to be more dependent on the family than do Anglo-Americans, for example, believing that their child's best friend should be a sibling. They allow fewer small decisions such as what to wear, encourage the children to play near home, worry when a child is not at home, and do not encourage children to bring their friends home as much as do Anglo-American parents. Obedience to authority and loyalty to the family are essential (Diaz-Guerrero, 1990).

The *model child* is not viewed as one who is achievement-oriented and successful in the academic and economic spheres. Rather, model children are skilled in human understanding and interpersonal relationships. They are polite, socially adept, courteous, respectful of elders, and deserving of respect, as well as being mindful of the dignity and individuality of others.

Such values, along with their noncompetitiveness, place Mexican-American children at a disadvantage in achievement-oriented *schools*. There is evidence, for example, that teachers praise, encourage, and direct questions to Anglo-American children more frequently than to Mexican-American children. Teachers also view Mexican-American children as lower in confidence and eagerness to learn (Mejia, 1983). Mexican-American children who start school close to Anglo-Americans in measured achievement will fall behind them at each grade level. They may be subjected to discrimination and cultural exclusion, being regarded stereotypically as lazy, dirty, satisfied with a subordinate role, or products of a rural folk culture. The children may react with confusion and may look to their peers for support. Such groups, in turn, may be viewed as a threat to the stability and safety of the school by administrators and school personnel (Trankina, 1983). On the positive side, successful students, as distinguished from unsuccessful ones, have confidence in their intellectual ability, a strong sense of responsibility for their academic future, and a supportive network of teachers and friends (Alva, 1991).

Generational Changes and Socioeconomic Influences

The Mexican immigrants who came after the Mexican Revolution of 1910 were laborers with little if any formal education. (Our presentation follows Vega, Hough, and Romero, 1983.) Today, immigrants come from midsized cities and reflect changes in Mexico itself in regard to urbanization and technological advances. They are in better health, have more education, may be acquainted with current production processes, and have more of a middle-class ideology.

As to *socioeconomic status*, a disproportionate number of Mexican Americans live in poverty. There is the *underclass*, consisting of poor, uneducated transients who migrate in search of employment and a stable support system to tide them over until they can cope using their own resources. The families are large, Spanish-speaking households living in chronically overcrowded conditions. The *low-income* families resemble the underclass except for employment and residential stability. They have limited education, work at semiskilled or service jobs, and have large, unacculturated families. The children are unlikely to be high achievers or to do well in school, thereby continuing the cycle of poverty.

The immigrant *working-class* family tends to be better educated than the previous two classes, some having completed high school. They have stable employment in skilled or semiskilled occupations, their homes are ample if overcrowded, and they have the resources to save money and take an occasional vacation. Their involvement in the community facilitates the social mobility of their children, who are aggressive, mobile, articulate, and independent, some eventually acquiring a good deal of wealth.

The *middle class* is similar to the Anglo-American middle class. The parents are rarely immigrants unless they were also from the middle class in Mexico, the household is English-speaking, and education is stressed. However adolescents, because they stand out as a distinct minority, may have a particularly difficult time with their ethnic identity, not knowing whether to renounce their cultural origins or to be proud of their Mexican-American heritage and participate in networks that provide ethnic support.

It would be a mistake to equate increased acculturation with increased adjustment. On the contrary, research suggests that the optimal mix is a *bicultural* one marked by adaptation to the dominant culture while maintaining an identification with the traditional Mexican-American culture. The evidence is clearest in the area of academic achievement. In elementary school, there is little evidence that failure is due to the discrepancy between the two cultures (Ocampo et al., 1991); in high school, earlier-generation students obtain higher grades than their later-generation, more-acculturated counterparts, while college-bound adolescents are more bicultural than non-college-bound ones. Finally, those who retain the traditional Mexican-American culture stay in college longer and receive higher grades than later-generation students (Chavez and Rodney, 1990).

Traditional Mexican-American values concerning the family can protect adolescents from delinquent behavior (Rodriguez and Zayas, 1990). In addition, bicultural Mexican-American mothers who retain values and beliefs from their own culture as well as adapting to those of the Anglo-American culture have the ability to view development from different perspectives and are more flexible even than Anglo-American mothers (Gutierrez and Sameroff, 1990).

Mental Health

Information concerning psychopathology is limited and often concerns Hispanics in general rather than Mexican-Americans in particular. (Our presentation follows Chavez and Rodney, 1990, unless otherwise noted.) Both drug and alcohol use are suspected to be higher among the Mexican-American population than the population in general, although the data are far from conclusive. There is evidence that Mexican Americans begin using drugs at an earlier age and prefer inhalants. Data on other drugs such as crack are lacking. Heavy drinking is more prevalent among men than women, probably because it is less culturally acceptable for the latter. However, cultural taboos can also prevent women with a drinking problem from seeking help (Delgado, 1989). Available data suggest that suicide is increasing and there is evidence that AIDS occurs more frequently among Hispanics than in the general population. (For a longitudinal study of inhalant use, see Simpson and Chatham, 1991, while Marín and Marín, 1990, present studies on AIDS among Hispanics.) Finally, Mexican Americans, perhaps those of the lower class in particular, have an elevated rate of somatizing symptoms (Fabrega, 1990).

Helping the Children and Their Families

Like all children, Mexican-American children may be seen by a clinical child psychologist because of one of the psychopathologies we have discussed. Like all impoverished children, their chances of becoming psychologically disturbed are significantly increased. In addition, the children may have problems unique to being a minority such as experiencing racial discrimination or cultural conflict. At this point there are few studies of the independent effects of poverty and ethnicity on the development of psychological disturbances (Farrington, 1986).

Regardless of the nature of the problem or the source of risk, Mexican-American children and their families must be treated in a manner congruent with their ethnic values and customs if psychological services are to be maximally effective or, indeed, if they are even to be accepted. We shall now examine a number of implications of this theme.

Mental Health Services Despite the increased risk for psychopathology, mental health services are underused by Mexican Americans and, incidentally, by other minorities as well (Trankina, 1983). A number of factors contribute to underuse. Mental health facilities located in middle-class neighborhoods are apt to be perceived as foreign, unfriendly, and not really there to serve Mexican Americans. Poor people in general are unaccustomed to forms and paperwork, while Mexican Americans may be especially suspicious if they have relatives or friends who are illegal aliens. The initial personal questioning may arouse feelings of vulnerability or being intruded upon. Moreover, many families view mental health care as similar to medical care, expecting expedient appointments and prescriptive courses of action. Finally, there is the communication problem: an English-speaking staff can do little for families who speak only Spanish or whose understanding of English is limited.

Ideally, then, facilities should be near the *barrio* and have bilingual staff members. Bilingualism is important not only for communication and rapport but for diagnosis as well; for example, interviewing in English may result in an underestimation of the degree of psychopathology in general and an overestimation of the degree of disturbance in schizophrenics (Fabrega, 1990). To solve the problem of lack of bilingual clinicians, innovative use has been made of paraprofessionals recruited from the community as interpreters. They also serve as cultural consultants to the English-speaking therapists as well as being a link between the community and the clinic (Rogler et al., 1987).

Forms should be in Spanish and reduced to a bare minimum. Long waiting periods should be avoided, crisis intervention should be available to the more pressing cases, along with casual contacts with the family during a waiting period. Clinic hours should be extended to accommodate working parents (Trankina, 1983). (For a detailed discussion of culturally sensitive mental health services, see Rogler et al., 1987.)

Although more controversial, it is also possible that forces within the culture itself serve as impediments to using mental health facilities. Family pride may lead to an attempt to conceal disturbances, and fatalism may produce a tendency to accept rather than remedy them. Natural healers may be consulted initially since they are familiar and their methods are congruent with cultural traditions. The extended social network as a resource may be preferred to professional advice.

Assessment   Since the diversity of the Mexican-American population makes generaliza-

tion difficult, we will deal primarily with the immigrant group, which has the greatest number of culture-specific stresses. Such stresses begin with emigration itself, which might involve the disruption of the family and social support systems. Crossing the border for undocumented individuals may be a harrowing experience marked by robbery, rape, and murder. Once in this country, the immigrant faces the stress of not finding employment or of an unsatisfactory job, of exploitation, discrimination and powerlessness, of adapting to an alien culture and language. In addition to assessing the nature and sources of stresses, sources of support should also be evaluated—the family, the social network, organizations, religion, and folk beliefs and practices. (For details, see Argueta-Bernal, 1990. For a general discussion, see Sattler, 1992.)

Assessment instruments such as psychological tests which have been standardized on Anglo-Americans cannot be used uncritically with minorities as was frequently done in the past, not only in clinical practice but in research as well. Typically minority groups were found to be inferior, not necessarily because of a basic inferiority but because of biases in the tests themselves.

E. M. Bernal (1990) lists a number of biases that might spuriously lower the scores of Mexican-American children on intelligence and achievement tests. Many of these tests require a degree of proficiency in English which Mexican-American children may not have. Clinicians may mistakenly assume that the ability to engage in a conversation is a sufficiently sensitive measure of mastery of English when it is not. Specifically designed tests of proficiency should be used instead. If proficiency is low, test results may reflect a limited ability to understand the task itself rather than an inability to do it well. To take just one example: a number of words in a vocabulary test may have no exact equivalent in Spanish; consequently, a child's vague definition may represent his lack of familiarity with the word or his attempt to define it in terms of its nearest Spanish equivalent.

Various extraneous interpersonal and intrapersonal variables may adversely affect test scores. While acculturated children score highest with English-speaking examiners, less acculturated ones score highest with Spanish-speaking ones. Some children lack test-taking skills, hurrying through as quickly as possible to escape an unpleasant situation. Merely having taken tests over the years does not necessarily remedy the situation. Personality factors, particularly high anxiety and self-deprecation, may lower scores. Both of these personality variables may increase with age rather than dissipating, while children in transition from a lower to a higher socioeconomic status are particularly prone to having them.

Knowing the sources of bias suggests remedies: devising special tests for Mexican-American children or using English proficiency measures in interpreting standard test results; having the test administered by a Spanish-speaking psychologist for certain groups of children; helping children develop useful test-taking attitudes and skills as well as reassuring them and relieving their anxiety.

Even standardized test results can be useful to the clinicians if properly interpreted, however. Achievement tests, for example, may be important measures of the level of a child's current functioning as compared with Anglo-American peers. However, saying "Juan is two years behind in reading and arithmetic" is different from saying "Juan is a slow learner." The first sentence leaves open the issues of etiology and ability; the second does not.

Treatment   Just as culturally sensitive assessment is attuned to the special values, stresses, and resources of Mexican Americans, so guidelines for treatment follow from what we have learned of their culture, particularly in regard to the family and to family roles. To begin with, the prime importance of the family unit means that treatment should be *family-oriented,* although individual or group therapy might be appropriate on occasion. There are also other cultural values that can serve as guides to establishing rapport and conducting the initial sessions.

The friendly impersonality and task orientation of the professional dealing with Anglo-Americans is not suited to Mexican Americans. Rather, the quality Mexican Americans value is *personalismo,* which is a combination of warmth, empathy, and equality between clinician and client. Since touching is more frequent than in Anglo-American society, a clinician might extend her hand upon meeting a new client, introduce herself by including her first name rather than a formal title, and engage in small talk in order to establish an atmosphere of friendly give-and-take. The clinician may talk about her own past as she inquires into the past of the parent. *Personalismo* also includes an attitude of respect and tactfulness. Thus sensitive clinical topics should be approached slowly and cautiously, and confrontations should be avoided (Ramirez, 1989; Trankina, 1983).

Because many low-SES clients view the clinician as they would a medical doctor, they tend to expect advice and direction. Thus they expect an active approach such as questions focused on the presenting problems followed by concrete solutions. The nondirective approach, a probing into details of childhood history, or requests for introspection should be used sparingly (Ruiz and Padilla, 1983).

Respect for family structure means that the father should be addressed first, then the mother, then the older children. Since Mexican-American families believe it is impolite to disagree, the therapist must watch for overt compliance which masks resistance to treatment. Respect for family values also means that the therapist might postpone advice that could be readily given to Anglo-American parents; for example, to suggest that the mother needs more time for herself might imply that she is not putting the family's needs ahead of her own as a good mother should (Ramirez, 1989; Trankina, 1983).

By knowing familial values, the clinician can interpret behavior differently than with Anglo-Americans. A mother walking her children to and from school, for example, may be a natural expression of family closeness rather than suggesting overprotection. A respectful, cooperative school-age child should not be suspected of having difficulty expressing aggression toward parents or competitiveness toward peers; in fact, anger toward parents is often indicative of a significant rupture in the parent-child relationship. While rebelliousness is considered part of normal development for Anglo-American teenagers, the same is not true for Mexican Americans. For a clinician to encourage rebellion on the assumption that it is essential to the development of adult autonomy might only create overwhelming guilt in the teenager. Mexican-American adolescents may also be more mature than Anglo-Americans since the older sons are encouraged to contribute to the family's finances while the older daughters care for the younger siblings. To treat them as typical teenagers, rather than as young adults, would be demeaning. Finally, values can be more rigid in certain areas than they are in Anglo-American families: pregnancy can result in the teenager being disowned, perhaps having to live with relatives or friends, while homosexuality is impossible for many parents to accept no matter how much effort is made to change their attitudes.

One risk of machismo is that the young boy will identify only with its aggressive aspects or even that he will be encouraged by his father to be too aggressive. If acting-out behavior brings such a boy to a clinical child psychologist, the relation with the father must be handled with the utmost tact. The clinician might accommodate the father in scheduling visits after hours or meeting the father at home, rather than assuming the stance of the expert who knows best what the father should do. It also might be a good strategy to appeal to paternal values incompatible with aggressiveness, such as pride in the family whose reputation is being threatened by the boy's antisocial acting out. Whatever is done, the father cannot feel that his authority is being threatened by the clinician, but rather that the clinician needs his help in making important decisions about the family.

The clinician should constantly be mindful of the reverberations of remedial measures throughout the network of familial relations. In one case intrusive grandparents were causing marital problems, and the therapist made the mistake of recommending that the grandparents stay out of the picture. This recommendation only intensified the problems. The therapist then changed tactics so as to increase the couple's self-confidence, only gradually focusing on the grandparents' involvement at a level the parents themselves determined. This tactful approach, in which change took place within the context of respect for traditional relationships, succeeded where the confrontational approach had failed.

One final point: the authoritarian male and the dependent female are no longer the accepted images of sex roles for Anglo-Americans. Rather, there is overlap and sharing of qualities between males and females. Because we are in a state of transition, feelings may run high concerning how faulty traditional sex roles were and how much better the current situation is. However, the clinical child psychologist cannot let such personal feelings interfere with the desire to do what is best for the child. In certain instances the clinician may decide that masculine dominance or feminine dependence should be supported because a change in roles would engender intense family conflict and individual guilt and because the child would be more fulfilled in the traditional rather than in the contemporary model. Respect for ethnic culture entails this kind of respect for ethnic diversity. To decide that minorities must conform to the culture of the majority is to devalue diversity and to make decisions that may be detrimental to the children and their families. Recall the research showing that individuals who are making the best adjustment are not the ones who are most thoroughly "Americanized" but those who can incorporate elements of Mexican and American culture.

Other therapeutic approaches   While the literature is primarily concerned with family therapy, other approaches are also mentioned. Group therapy may be recommended for adolescents who need the support of peers in their rejection of traditional values in the family. Individual play therapy may also be effective in helping younger children master special problems (Ramirez, 1989). Finally, traditional folktales can be used as a vehicle for confronting children with problems and challenging them to find optimal solutions. Although this technique was devised for Puerto Rican children it is not necessarily limited to them. (See Rogler et al., 1987.) (For a general discussion of treatment, see Vargas and Koss-Chioino, 1992, and McGoldrick, Pearce, and Giordano, 1982.)

A FINAL CHALLENGE

Before leaving the topic of minorities, it will be worthwhile to present Fabrega's (1990) warning concerning the danger of treating Mexican Americans, and, by implication, all minority groups, in terms of classifications and procedures derived from the Anglo-American population. He questions whether minor adjustments in clinical procedures can do justice to the differences between the two groups—differences that might require a rethinking of basic assumptions concerning psy-

chopathology and that challenge current research findings.

In terms of *diagnosis,* DSM-IV Draft Criteria now has an appendix listing culturally-related syndromes that could be used to enlarge the scope of deviant behaviors and test the universality of current explanations (Alarcon, 1983). In regard to the classifications themselves, there is evidence that symptoms of affective disorders and alcoholism do not apply to Mexican Americans but those for psychotic disorders, phobic disorders, and somatization do; for example, when a Mexican American blames his alcoholism on a neighbor who put a hex on him, the attribution may be part of a culturally accepted belief in evil spirits rather than a delusion. Or again, the symptoms of depression have a somewhat different factor structure for unacculturated Mexican Americans than for the general population (Garcia and Marks, 1989).

Cultural differences also impact on *etiology.* For example, parental problems and peer influences play a less important role in Mexican-American youths' use of inhalants than they do in drug use by non-Hispanic youths (Joe and Simpson, 1991), while parental influences play a less important role in predicting alcohol and drug use as well as criminality.

In short, as the cultural context changes, so do the manifestations and etiologies of psychopathologies. This is our developmental orientation applied to the superordinate variable of culture. Fabrega's (1990) concern is that the tendency to regard traditional modes of thinking about clinical issues as universal will act as a barrier to recognizing their limitations and enlarging their scope. What is implied is that American society's challenge to accommodate to minority groups and minority groups' challenge to acculturate to American society have their counterpart in clinical child psychology. While Mexican Americans and other minorities have much in common with Anglo-Americans, there are also differences which need to be articulated and recognized so they can be embraced in clinical theory, practice, and research. If the process of mutual accommodation works as it should, minority groups will lead a more fulfilling life, while society and the mental health field will be expanded and enriched. (Harkness and Super, 1990, discuss the implications of a multicultural approach to clinical child psychology at a more general level.)

In many of our discussions we have included assessment and remediation. Because these are the activities that concern practicing clinical psychologists the most, they deserve a full-dress presentation of their own.

PSYCHOLOGICAL ASSESSMENT

We have repeatedly seen that in order to be understood, behavior must be evaluated in context. The context of time is crucial and includes not only the child's current age but past history as well. Within this temporal framework both intra- and interpersonal factors must be considered. Our goal has been the scientific one of understanding all variables relevant to the production of psychopathological behavior.

Clinicians, however, vary in their need to evaluate psychopathological behavior in terms of all relevant contexts. In part, this variability is a function of different theoretical allegiances. Psychoanalytically oriented clinicians strive for a comprehensive understanding not only of present and past but also of conscious and unconscious determinants of behavior. Clinicians with a systems orientation concentrate on current patterns of interpersonal interactions, particularly in the family. Behaviorally oriented clinicians focus on specific patterns of behavior in specific settings, while nondirective clinicians reduce assessment to a bare minimum.

Another kind of constraint on comprehensive assessment arises from the clinician's primary role as a help giver. Characteristically, he or she wants to understand a problem in terms that are congruent with a particular school of therapy and to devise and implement remedial plans as quickly as possible (Gordon and Schroeder, 1990).

The present discussion will begin with the clinician who seeks a comprehensive understanding of the child's psychopathology, noting how those with different goals, particularly behavioral clinicians, would abbreviate and alter the procedure. This strategy allows the widest scope in presenting assessment techniques, as well as affording a glimpse into the assessment process at its most complex. Coverage of specific techniques will be selective and knowledge of the construction, reliability, and validity of major psychological tests, commensurate with that gained in an introductory course in psychology, is assumed. (For a detailed coverage of assessment, see Sattler, 1992.)

THE ASSESSMENT PROCESS

Clinicians never assume that within the space of a few hours they will be able to understand the nature and origin of the problems that bring a particular child to their attention. They realize they are viewing parents and child under special circumstances that both limit and bias the data they will obtain: the child who is frightened by a clinic waiting room may not be a generally fearful child, just as one who is hyperactive in school may be a model of cooperation when taking an intelligence test; parents may have their own misperceptions and blind spots in regard to their child's behavior, along with varying degrees of willingness to reveal information about themselves and their child. Thus, an initial session is only the first step toward understanding.

In attempting to assimilate and integrate the massive amount of data they collect, clinicians implicitly proceed like hypothesis-testing scientists (Johnson and Goldman, 1990). No single bit of behavior is definitive, but each is suggestive. As these bits accumulate, certain initial hunches tend to be confirmed and others discarded. By the end of the assessment process, the clinician can make some statements concerning the child's problem with a reasonable degree of assurance; other statements will be tentative and qualified; and a number of questions will remain unanswered.

You are a clinical child psychologist about to assess Tom, a 10-year-old boy referred for a learning problem; specifically, he is lazy, failing reading and arithmetic, and beginning to be disruptive in class. Upon being introduced to you in the waiting room, Tom is unusually friendly and communicative. Most children are cautious initially, and rightly so. You mentally note Tom's behavior and wonder what it might represent. Perhaps this is a basically healthy boy whose problems have been exaggerated; perhaps he has been too close to adults at the expense of becoming alienated from peers; perhaps he is a charming sociopath; perhaps his social skills are a defense against some unknown fear. During the interview the boy continues to impress you as a bright, alert, open youngster.

However, Tom's behavior begins to change on the intelligence tests: he tends to say "I don't know" too readily when items become difficult; he quickly destroys a puzzle he had put together incorrectly as if trying to cover up his mistake; and he uses his conversational skills to divert attention away from the test material. When encouraged to respond to difficult items, it is clear that he does not know the correct answer.

At this point he seems neither a sociopath nor fearful nor prematurely adult; both his enjoyment of people and his openness seem genuine. Yet, the test adds a significant bit of data: he has only average intelligence. You begin speculating, "If his sociability misled me into thinking he was intellectually bright, his parents and teachers might have also been misled into setting unrealistically high goals and pressuring him to achieve them." This hypothesis naturally would have to be checked by interviewing the parents and a telephone call to the teacher. It also raises further questions, such as the effects of being regarded as lazy on the boy's self-image, which could be explored by further assessment.

In regard to diagnosis, you are tentatively thinking in terms of a learning disability which undermined his confidence on a variety of intellectual tasks.

Hypotheses are never generated out of the blue. Rather, clinicians use a variety of sources: their preferred theoretical framework, the clinical and research literature relevant to the problem at hand, accumulated knowledge passed on from seasoned clinicians to novitiates, as well as their own experience. In this instance, the hypothesis generated by the discrepancy between Tom's social and intellectual development derived from a discussion of a similar case with the hypothetical clinician's supervisor during his student days; the question concerning Tom's self-image came from the clinician's interest in the self-concept. Equally valid questions could be raised concerning the effects of Tom's failure on the family dynamics or on his status with teachers and peers at school.

THE DEVELOPMENTAL DIMENSION

The developmental dimension is part and parcel of every aspect of assessment. At times the clinical child psychologist must rely on his or her skills, sensitivity, and experience rather than on formal procedures. The best example concerns establishing *rapport*. In order for any assessment technique to be of use, the child must at least be minimally cooperative and ideally should participate wholeheartedly. Cooperation is not guaranteed, and the clinical child psychologist must be prepared to deal with a variety of obstacles at different ages—a crying infant; a toddler fearful of leaving his mother; a provocative, defiant school-aged child; a sullen teenager who resents all questioning by adults. But aside from such dramatic challenges, there is always the basic issue of how one goes about establishing oneself as an interested, friendly adult to children of different ages. What does one say and do with

a 5-year-old girl that is different from what one says and does with a 9-year-old boy? While there are some general guides to establishing rapport with children of different ages, much depends on experience and training. (For a detailed discussion, see Boggs and Eyberg, 1990.)

Rather than relying on experience and training, *standardized tests* incorporate development into the assessment technique itself. Such tests define the age of the population for which they are appropriate, such as infant intelligence tests or high school achievement tests. Only age-appropriate items are included and the progression of items is based on representative samples of the population. Consequently, the clinician can compare the developmental status of a given child with that of a population of children his or her age.

Finally, there are assessment techniques that contain both subjective and objective features. Projective techniques are an example. Here there is a standard set of stimuli along with guides for scoring and a certain amount of normative information. However, after completing the objective scoring, clinicians have considerable leeway in drawing inferences from responses that impress them as being significant. As always, this judgment of significance carries the implicit proviso, "for a child this age or at this developmental level."

INITIAL SOURCES OF DATA

Referrals

The first data concerning the child come from the referral, which usually contains information about the problem as perceived by concerned adults, its duration and onset, its effects on the child and on others, and what measures, if any, have been taken to remedy it. Parents and teachers are the major sources of referrals.

The fact that children are not self-referred,

as are most adults, has an important psychological implication. There is a great deal of difference between seeking help and being told one needs help. Children may or may not feel the need, may or may not understand why they are being brought to the clinic. Parents may either fail to tell them why or give them reasons they do not understand or agree with. After establishing some rapport, the clinician should clarify why the child is there, what the assessment procedures are, and why they are being done.

Observation

The clinician's assessment begins on first seeing the parents and child. Their appearance and interactions provide clues as to family characteristics and the relationships among its members. First impressions furnish information concerning the family's social class and general level of harmony or disharmony, as well as its stylistic characteristics—reserved, demonstrative, authoritarian, intellectual, and so on.

Once with the child, the clinician systematically gathers certain kinds of information. The *overall impression* of the child's personality is always important: "an all-American boy"; "he already has the worried look of an old man, as if he does not know what it is like to be a child"; "a perfect little lady, a real showpiece for her mother"; "he has that sullen look, like he is constantly spoiling for a fight"; "a direct, honest, no-nonsense pre-adolescent girl, somewhat on the tomboy side." Such impressions help define the child's social-stimulus value, which may be a potent elicitor of positive or negative reactions from others.

The child's *body* and *body language* provide important clues to a physiological intactness as well as to personality variables. Significant departures from the norms of height and weight may indicate a medical problem or, more important, may cause the child to be teased and rejected by peers. The body can be read for more subtle signs of disturbance: bruises and scars suggest accident proneness or abuse; needle marks on the arm suggest drug abuse; squinting or putting the face close to the paper when drawing or writing suggests a visual defect.

Body language includes a wide array of expressive behaviors. Psychological tension is often embodied in physical tension: a strained facial expression, a forced laugh, a tense posture when sitting, pressured speech or stuttering, "nervous gestures" such as nail biting. A monotonous voice, slouched posture, masklike face, and slow movements suggest depression or withdrawal.

Finally, the child's *relationship* to the clinician furnishes information concerning his or her perception of adults. It is natural for children to be reserved initially, since in reality the clinician is a stranger. However, as they discover that the clinician is interested, friendly, and benign, they should become relaxed, cooperative, and communicative, although still reluctant to talk about sensitive topics. Certain children never warm up; they sit as far back in their chair as possible, speak in an almost inaudible monotone, rarely look at the examiner or else watch intently, as if he or she were a kind of monster who might strike out at any minute. Provocative children begin to "test the limits," mischievously peeking when told to close their eyes or destroying a puzzle when told to leave it intact.

But a relationship involves two people, the clinician as well as the child. Clinicians are not standard stimuli; they have their own styles of behaving as well as their own talents and vulnerabilities. It is essential, therefore, that clinicians understand their own individual characteristics and include this understanding in their evaluation of the child. They may naturally be effusive or confronting or self-contained or intellectual, and such characteristics may naturally turn some children off or appeal to others. Knowing their own vulnerabilities, clinicians can see that they are becoming impatient with a whining child or angry with a provocative one or frightened by a hyperactive one and can then make sure that such reactions do not further undermine the child's self-control. While professionals can be expected to be objective about themselves as well as knowledgeable and resourceful in relating to children, they cannot be expected to transcend their own personalities.

Generally speaking, observation as used by many clinicians may be nearer an art than a science because the procedures are unstandardized and the target behaviors so wide ranging. However, observation per se is not unscientific. Behavioral clinicians, for example, bring to assessment the structure and reliability that the more open-ended approach lacks.

While our presentation has not been developmentally oriented, this was done only for the purpose of delineating certain dimensions of observational data. As always, the clinical child psychologist evaluates behavior in terms of its age appropriateness or inappropriateness, the former providing clues as to assets and resources, the latter providing clues to possible disturbances.

The Interview

Parent Interviews Information concerning the child and the family comes primarily from interviewing the parents (Perry, 1990). Typically, the interview begins with an account of the present problem. Next, a detailed history, technically known as a *case history*, is obtained in order to explore the antecedent conditions that might have contributed to the present difficulties. Among the topics covered are the child's prenatal history, birth history, and early development. The subsequent adjustment of the child within the family and with peers is explored, along with social and academic adjustment. For teenagers, information is obtained concerning sexual development and work history, as well as possible drug and alcohol use and delinquent behavior. The clinician also inquires about major illnesses and injuries. To complete the picture, the parents may be asked about their own marital and occupational adjustment, their specific goals, satisfactions, and dissatisfactions, and their relation to their own parents.

What about the studies showing the unreliability of parental histories? While disqualifying parents as sources of accurate information concerning many aspects of development, the studies do not render their histories useless, because it is still important for the clinician to know the parents' perception of the facts. Whether the child was a "difficult" infant and a "bad" toddler may not be as important as the parents' perception or memory of the child as difficult and bad. However, the argument that it is the parents' perceptions that matter has its limitations. If a mother says, "My boy was doing all right in school until he had that bad accident on his bike," it would be important to know that the trouble actually started a year before the accident when she and her husband were on the verge of getting a divorce because of his extramarital affair. The mother's account suggests an organic etiology, while the actual sequence suggests a psychogenic one. Incidentally, the mother may not be trying to deceive the clinician and may firmly believe the accuracy of her account. The clinician must realize that in cases where accuracy matters, interview data should be verified, say, by medical or school records. In many instances, however, accuracy is impossible to establish.

There is one final aspect to the interview. In the process of interviewing, the clinician is beginning to know the parents, while the parents are also beginning to know the clinician. Since there is no hard and fast line between assessment and therapy, skilled interviewers can use this initial contact to lay the groundwork for the trust and respect that will be so crucial in future contacts with the parents.

Child Interviews The clinical child psychologist also needs to obtain the child's own perception of clinically relevant issues. Topics covered might include the child's view of the problem; the home, school and peers; interests, fears and somatic concerns; self-concept; and, for adolescents, career aspirations, sexual relations, and drug or alcohol use.

Since we have already discussed the importance of rapport in assessment, we will concentrate on the *cognitive* aspects of interviewing (Kovacs, 1986; Stone and Lemanek, 1990a). For the interview to be valid, it must be tailored to the children's level of understanding. This level will affect many aspects of the situation.

Before 7 or 8 years of age, children's self-understanding is limited to isolated pieces of information about observable characteristics and actions ("I have brown hair," "I play ball," "I have a dog"). Consequently, questions about the *nature of the problem* that brought them to see a psychologist are apt to elicit responses couched in terms of specific behaviors ("I hit my brother"). These, in turn, probably echo what parents or other adults have said to them about being "bad." Recall that young children are never self-referred and often do not see themselves as having problems. In a like manner children's view of the *cause of the problem* is apt to be specific and external ("I hit my brother because he takes my things").

Preschoolers' evaluations of *affects* and of *other people* are equally concrete and situational; for example, being happy is having a party. Consequently, interview questions must be similarly concrete and action-oriented ("Do you cry?" rather than "Do you feel sad?"). The interviewer should also expect people to be described in terms of what they do rather than what they think or how they feel.

It is only in middle childhood that the self-concept becomes "psychological" and more differentiated; for example, instead of being judged "smart" or "dumb," the child can be smart in some things and dumb in others. In this period children are able to provide accurate reports of their own emotions by using internal, psychological cues. They also begin to attribute psychological characteristics to others and realize other people have perspectives different from their own. Along with these cognitive advances goes the ability to recognize deviance. However, even in early adolescence there is still the tendency to attribute cause to external, typically social, events such as family quarrels and conflicts.

Cognition determines how the child will understand the concept of the psychologist as *helper* as well as the concept of *being helped.* The preschooler is apt to view the former in terms of general traits, such as being "kind" or "nice," along with the psychologist's specific behaviors, such as "playing games." In middle childhood references to competence begin to appear, such as "She knows what she is doing," while the early adolescent recognizes the role of inner qualities of empathy and a desire to help. Being helped itself changes from denoting some form of direct action in the preschool period to a recognition of the importance of advice giving and other kinds of indirect help in early adolescence. Thus, in preparing a preschooler for the first visit, it is better for the parent to say the psychologist is a "nice person" like someone the child knows than to say that the psychologist "wants to help." (Subsequently, if the child goes into treatment the psychologist will have to deal with the issue that helping does not involve the environmental changes and tangible rewards that the preschooler envisioned; for example, "Tell my brother to quit picking on me and bring me a new game to play.")

The interview can have different degrees of *structure.* The unstructured interview has implicit guides regarding achieving its goals but allows the interviewer considerable leeway for improvising and following up unexpected leads. The semistructured interview consists of a series of questions designed to obtain specific information such as the presence or absence of diagnostic symptoms. There are also contingent probes on the order of ''If X, go to Y. If not, go to Z.'' The structured interview also consists of a series of specific questions or statements, but now the child's response is predetermined as well, either in a yes-no or in the more differentiated strongly agree–agree–

disagree–strongly disagree configuration. (See Figure 16.1 for excerpts from an interview containing both structured and semistructured components.)

Interviewing disturbed children may present special problems. Kovacs (1986) notes that depressed, nonretarded older children may show the same mislabeling of emotions characteristic of preschoolers. For example, when the interviewer asked a child when was the last time he felt sad, he described an incident in which a sibling made him feel mad. In dis-

FIGURE 16.1
Structured and semistructured questions in a child interview. (*Source:* Center for Stress and Anxiety Disorders, 1991.)

SCHOOL REFUSAL BEHAVIOR

1. Do you get very nervous or scared about having to go to school?

_____ Yes _____ No _____ Other

2. Do you stay home from school because you are nervous or scared?

_____ Yes _____ No _____ Other

If "YES", ask: How many times has that happened this year?_____

If "YES", ask 2A, otherwise skip to question 3.

2A. Can you give me an example of a "typical" day when you wake up and don't go to school? [What happens? What do you do? What do your parents do?]

_____

_____

3. Do you get very nervous or scared when you are in school?

_____ Yes _____ No _____ Other

A. If child responds "YES", ask: Have you ever left school because of this?

_____ Yes _____ No _____ Other

If "YES", ask: How many times has that happened this year?

_____

Ask child to elaborate on "YES" response to 3 or 3A.

_____

turbances that significantly impair attention, such as ADHD, the touch-and-go quality of the responses may lower the reliability of their content. For some children merely being questioned by an adult is perceived as an accusation of wrongdoing, resulting in minimal responses or no replies at all. (For a comprehensive presentation of interviewing children, see Hughes and Baker, 1990. Flanery, 1990, addresses the psychometric issues in such interviewing.)

PSYCHOLOGICAL TESTS

Of all professionals dealing with psychopathologically disturbed children, psychologists have been most concerned with developing assessment techniques that can be objectively administered and scored, that have norms based on clearly defined populations, and that have established reliability and validity.

Intelligence Tests

The two most widely used intelligence tests for children are the Stanford-Binet and the Wechsler Intelligence Scale for Children, or WISC.

Until its most recent revision, the format of the Stanford-Binet had remained the same. It consisted of six items located at mental age levels 2 through 14, with subsequent items going from average adult to superior adult. The content of the items varied widely, from building a tower of blocks, to copying a circle, to defining words, to repeating digits, to explaining why certain statements are absurd. No effort was made to have comparable items at the various mental age levels. The scoring allowed for the computation of a child's mental age and intelligence quotient.

The fourth edition of the Stanford-Binet (1986) represents a major revision of the format. To begin with, the concept of mental age has been abandoned. Instead of different kinds of items located at different mental age levels, items of the same type are grouped into fifteen tests, each test requiring a somewhat different cognitive skill and fund of information. Moreover, these fifteen tests have been organized into four broad areas of cognitive abilities. In the *Verbal Reasoning* category are tests on Vocabulary and Comprehension (e.g., questions such as "What does envelop mean?" and "Why are there traffic signs?"). *Quantitative Reasoning* includes tests on Quantitative Ability (e.g., counting and knowledge of fractions) and on Number Series (e.g., figuring out the next two numbers in a series of numbers which increases by 4). *Abstract/Visual Reasoning* includes tests on Copying Figures (e.g., copying a diamond or two intersecting circles) and on Pattern Analysis (e.g., putting blocks together to make a pattern depicted on a card). *Short-Term Memory* tests include remembering a series of digits and remembering sentences. At a higher level of abstraction, Verbal Reasoning and Quantitative Reasoning are regarded as *crystallized abilities,* which are greatly influenced by schooling although they also develop by general experiences outside school. Abstract/Visual Reasoning is regarded as a *fluid-analytic ability.* It requires the invention of new cognitive strategies and is more dependent on general experiences than on schooling.

The items in each test are arranged according to difficulty; thus the more items children successfully complete, the higher their intelligence compared with children their own age. However, instead of an IQ, the results are expressed in terms of Standard Age Scores (SASs). For the total scale, the mean score is 100 and the standard deviation is 16. For example, a child with a total score of 116 will be one standard deviation above the mean or in approximately the 84th percentile. Since the same formula was used for IQs, the SAS and the IQ scores are comparable. The test can be used from 2 to 23 years of age.

The trend away from tests comprised of disparate items and toward items based on categories of cognitive abilities is illustrated by the Kaufman Assessment Battery for Children (K-ABC) (1983). Here intelligence is defined in terms of two styles of functioning called *sequential processing* and *simultaneous processing*. The former involves temporal ordering of stimuli when solving problems; for example, repeating numbers spoken by the examiner or reproducing a series of hand movements made by the examiner. The latter requires simultaneous integration of stimuli that are spatial or pictorial in nature; for example, assembling several identical triangles into an abstract pattern to match a model, or naming an object in a partially completed drawing. The K-ABC also includes an achievement scale that measures knowledge of facts or crystalized abilities; for example, vocabulary, arithmetic, and reading comprehension. The test is for children from 2½ to 12½ years of age.

The most recent revision of the WISC is the WISC-III (Wechsler, 1991), which consists of thirteen subtests, the items in each being arranged according to increasing difficulty (see Figure 16.2). The Verbal Scale, which requires facility in using verbal symbols, consists of five basic subtests (Information, Similarities, Arithmetic, Vocabulary, and Comprehension) and one supplementary test (Digit Span). The Performance Scale, which involves concrete material such as pictures, blocks, and jigsaw puzzles, also consists of five basic subtests (Picture Completion, Coding, Picture Arrangement, Block Design, and Object Assembly) and two supplementary subtests (Symbol Search and Mazes). Note that "verbal" and "performance" refer to the form in which the task is presented, not the level of thinking required; certain performance subtests require higher-level thinking than certain verbal subtests. Scoring yields a Verbal IQ and Performance IQ, as well as a Full-Scale IQ. (For a detailed discussion, see Kaufman, 1979.)

While the IQ score is important, it is only one of many pieces of information gained from an intelligence test. The discrepancy between the Verbal and Performance IQs on the WISC-III furnishes clues as to the child's differential ability to handle the two kinds of tasks: the child who has a Full-Scale IQ of 100, a Verbal IQ of 120 and a Performance IQ of 80 is quite different from a child with the same overall IQ but with a Verbal IQ of 80 and a Performance IQ of 120. The second child may be particularly penalized in school, where the manipulation of verbal symbols becomes increasingly important, while being quite talented on tasks that minimize verbal facilty.

Analysis of successes and failures on individual items may provide further clues to intellectual strengths and weaknesses. A child may do well on problems involving rote learning and the accumulation of facts, but poorly on ones requiring reasoning and judgment; an otherwise bright child may be weak in visual-motor coordination which, in turn, might make learning to write difficult.

An intelligence test furnishes important clues as to the child's *style of thinking*, regardless of IQ. Note the responses of two equally bright 8-year-olds to the question, "What should you do when you lose a ball that belongs to someone else?" One child answered, "I'd get him another one." The other said, "I'd pay money for it. I'd look for it. I'd give him another ball." (The examiner asks her to choose one of the possibilities.) "I'd try to find it. If I couldn't, I'd give him money for it because I might not have the kind of ball he wants." Both answers receive the same high score, but one is clear, simple, and to the point, while the other is needlessly cluttered with alternatives.

Styles of thinking are closely related to psychological health or disturbance. Intelligence is not some kind of disembodied skill existing apart from the rest of the child's personality. On the contrary, a psychologically sound child tends to think clearly, an impulse-ridden child

Information (30 questions)

How many legs do you have?
What must you do to make water freeze?
Who discovered the North Pole?
What is the capital of France?

Similarities (17 questions)

In what way are pencil and crayon alike?
In what way are coffee and tea alike?
In what way are inch and mile alike?
In what way are binoculars and microscope alike?

Arithmetic (18 questions)

If I have one piece of candy and get another one, how
  many pieces will I have?
At 12 cents each, how much will 4 bars of soap cost?
If a suit sells for 1/2 of the ticket price, what is the cost
  of a $120 suit?

Vocabulary (32 words)

ball	poem
summer	obstreperous

Comprehension (17 questions)

Why do we wear shoes?
What is the thing to do if you see someone dropping his
  packages?
In what ways is a lamp better than a candle?
Why are we tried by a jury of our peers?

Digit Span

Digits Forward contains seven series of digits, 3 to 9 digits
  in length (Example: 1-8-9).
Digits Backward contains seven series of digits, 2 to 8 digits
  in length (Example: 5-8-1-9).

Picture Completion (26 items)

The task is to identify the essential missing part of the picture.
A picture of a car without a wheel.
A picture of a dog without a leg.
A picture of a telephone without numbers on the dial.
An example of a Picture Completion task is shown below.

Courtesy of The Psychological Corporation.

Picture Arrangement (12 items)

The task is to arrange a series of pictures into a
meaningful sequence.

Block Design (11 items)

The task is to reproduce stimulus designs using four or nine
blocks. An example of a Block Design item is shown below.

Object Assembly (4 items)

The task is to arrange pieces into a meaningful object.
An example of a Object Assembly item is shown below.

Courtesy of The Psychological Corporation.

Coding

The task is to copy symbols from a key (see below).

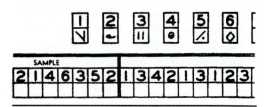

Courtesy of The Psychological Corporation.

Mazes

The task is to complete a series of mazes.

Note. The questions resemble those that appear on the
WISC-R but are not actually from the test.

tends to think impulsively, an obsessive child (like the one just quoted) tends to think in terms of a series of alternatives which, in turn, may hamstring the ability to act. And, surely, a schizophrenic child tends to think bizarrely, as is revealed in this rambling, fantasy-saturated answer to the simple question, "Why should a promise be kept?" "If you don't keep a promise you get into trouble; you go to court; like teenagers give up promises; they're usually armed, guys who run around the forest and woods, the woods near the house. We go there to catch frogs, and we always have to have older people go with us because of the teenagers with guns and knives. A child drowned there not long ago. If you don't keep a promise they start a gang and drown you."

For clinicians, an intelligence test has a rich yield of *observational data.* (See Figure 16.3 for an example of a checklist for observing behavior and attitudes.) To begin with, they can see how a given child copes with the challenge of solving intellectual problems. For some children, intellectual challenges are their "thing," and they work for the sheer pleasure of working. Others do what they are told in a joyless, dutiful manner; solving the problems is a burden, a chore. For still others, the tests are a chance to show off or just one more in a long series of humiliating failures.

The intelligence test also allows the clinician to evaluate the child's *work habits.* Some children are task-oriented and self-motivated; they need almost no encouragement or help from the examiner. Others are uncertain and insecure, giving up readily unless encouraged or prodded, constantly seeking reassurance that they are doing well, or asking to know whether their response was right or wrong. Finally, the tests yield information concerning

the child's capacity for self-monitoring, which is the ability to evaluate the quality of the responses. Some children seem to be implicitly asking, "Is that really correct?" or "Is that the best I can do?" while others seem to have little ability to judge when they are right or wrong, an incorrect response being given with the same air of uncritical assurance as a correct one.

In sum, it is for good reason that intelligence tests are so frequently administered as part of the assessment procedures. The IQ score itself is related to many aspects of the child's life—success in school, vocational choice, peer relations—and IQ is a better predictor of future adjustment than any score on a personality test. In addition, the test provides data concerning general areas of strength and weakness, the kind and degree of impairment of specific intellectual functions such as immediate recall or abstract reasoning, the child's coping techniques, work habits, and motivation, stylistic characteristics of thinking that may well be related to personality variables, and the presence of distorted thinking, that might indicate either organic brain pathology or psychosis (see Kaufman, 1979).

Yet care must be taken that an intelligence test is used appropriately and that results are properly understood. As *IQ* became a household term, so did the misconception that the score represents an unalterable intellectual potential existing independent of background and experience. In order to counteract this belief that IQ is destiny, many clinicians do not report the score to parents. Rather, they talk in terms of categories of intelligence, such as average, below average, superior. Then, taking into account the child's background and experience so as to correct for their possible biasing effects on the test score, they go on to describe strengths and weaknesses, which in turn may lead to a discussion of remedial plans.

FIGURE 16.2
WISC-R-like items. (*Source:* The Psychological Corporation, 1991.)

Behavior and Attitude Checklist

Child's name: _____ Examiner: _____

Age: _____ Date of report: _____

Test(s) administered: _____ Date of examination: _____

IQ: _____ Grade: _____

Instructions: Place an *X* on the appropriate line for each scale.

I. *Attitude toward examiner and test situation:*
    1. cooperative   ___ : ___ : ___ : ___ : ___ : ___ : ___   uncooperative
    2. passive   ___ : ___ : ___ : ___ : ___ : ___ : ___   aggressive
    3. tense   ___ : ___ : ___ : ___ : ___ : ___ : ___   relaxed
    4. gives up easily   ___ : ___ : ___ : ___ : ___ : ___ : ___   does not give up easily

II. *Attitude toward self:*
    5. confident   ___ : ___ : ___ : ___ : ___ : ___ : ___   not confident
    6. critical of own work   ___ : ___ : ___ : ___ : ___ : ___ : ___   accepting of own work

III. *Work habits:*
    7. fast   ___ : ___ : ___ : ___ : ___ : ___ : ___   slow
    8. deliberate   ___ : ___ : ___ : ___ : ___ : ___ : ___   impulsive
    9. thinks aloud   ___ : ___ : ___ : ___ : ___ : ___ : ___   thinks silently
    10. careless   ___ : ___ : ___ : ___ : ___ : ___ : ___   neat

IV. *Behavior:*
    11. calm   ___ : ___ : ___ : ___ : ___ : ___ : ___   hyperactive

V. *Reaction to failure:*
    12. aware of failure   ___ : ___ : ___ : ___ : ___ : ___ : ___   unaware of failure
    13. works harder after failure   ___ : ___ : ___ : ___ : ___ : ___ : ___   gives up easily after failure
    14. calm after failure   ___ : ___ : ___ : ___ : ___ : ___ : ___   agitated after failure
    15. apologetic after failure   ___ : ___ : ___ : ___ : ___ : ___ : ___   not apologetic after failure

VI. *Reaction to praise:*
    16. accepts praise gracefully   ___ : ___ : ___ : ___ : ___ : ___ : ___   accepts praise awkwardly
    17. works harder after praise   ___ : ___ : ___ : ___ : ___ : ___ : ___   retreats after praise

VII. *Speech and language:*
    18. speech poor   ___ : ___ : ___ : ___ : ___ : ___ : ___   speech good
    19. articulate language   ___ : ___ : ___ : ___ : ___ : ___ : ___   inarticulate language
    20. responses direct   ___ : ___ : ___ : ___ : ___ : ___ : ___   responses vague
    21. converses spontaneously   ___ : ___ : ___ : ___ : ___ : ___ : ___   only speaks when spoken to
    22. bizarre language   ___ : ___ : ___ : ___ : ___ : ___ : ___   reality-oriented language

VIII. *Visual-motor:*
    23. reaction time slow   ___ : ___ : ___ : ___ : ___ : ___ : ___   reaction time fast
    24. trial-and-error   ___ : ___ : ___ : ___ : ___ : ___ : ___   careful and systematic
    25. skillful movements   ___ : ___ : ___ : ___ : ___ : ___ : ___   awkward movements

IX. *Motor:*
    26. defective motor coordination   ___ : ___ : ___ : ___ : ___ : ___ : ___   good motor coordination

X. *Overall test results:*
    27. reliable   ___ : ___ : ___ : ___ : ___ : ___ : ___   unreliable
    28. valid   ___ : ___ : ___ : ___ : ___ : ___ : ___   invalid

FIGURE 16.3
Behavior and Attitude Checklist. (*Source:* Sattler, 1992.)

Infant intelligence testing requires special skill in accommodation so as to elicit an optimal performance. The examiner must know how to intrigue the infant with the test material, allow for distractions, temporarily become a comforting caretaker in response to fretting, postpone testing when distress becomes too great—in short, the good examiner must have the sensitivity, flexibility, and warmth of a good parent.

One of the best constructed standardized infant tests is the Bayley Scales of Infant Development, which evaluates development between 2 and 30 months of age (Bayley, 1969). The Mental Scale evaluates the infant's vocal and verbal behavior, memory, generalization, classification, and simple problem-solving ability, among other things; the Motor Scale evaluates gross-motor and fine-motor coordination and skills; and the Infant Behavior Record assesses the infant's social relations, responsiveness to objects, activity level, interests, emotions, and tendency to approach or withdraw from stimulation. (For other infant tests, see Culbertson and Gyurke, 1990, and Sattler, 1992.)

Brief intelligence tests, such as the Peabody Picture Vocabulary Test, or PPVT (Dunn, 1965), estimate intelligence in less time than it takes to administer the Stanford-Binet or the WISC, while *group tests,* such as the Otis-Lennon Mental Ability Test (Otis and Lennon, 1967) are especially suited for administration in school settings (see Sattler, 1992).

Personality Tests

Personality Inventories These consist of a series of statements to be judged as characteristic or not characteristic of an individual. The judgment is in terms of true-false or a more differentiated evaluation such as never, sometimes, often. One of the most widely used inventories is the Children's Behavior Check List (CBCL), which was described in Chapter 3.

There are special forms for parents, teachers, and the children themselves and norms for children from 4 to 16 years of age. Figure 16.4 presents a segment of the parent's form of the CBCL. (A detailed presentation of child behavior rating scales and checklists can be found in Barkley, 1988.)

Projective Techniques In all the assessment instruments discussed so far the stimulus material is as clear and unambiguous as possible. Projective techniques take the opposite tack by using ambiguous or unstructured material; either the stimulus has no meaning, such as an inkblot, or it has a number of different meanings, such as a picture that is to be used as the basis of a story. Theoretically, the particular meaning attributed to the unstructured material is a reflection of the individual's particular personality. The disguised nature of the responses allows the individual to express ideas that would be too threatening to talk about directly; for example, a girl who is too frightened to talk about her anger toward her mother may feel free to tell a story about a daughter being angry with and defying her mother.

The Rorschach test is a series of ten inkblots, which the child views one at a time after being instructed to tell the examiner everything the blots look like. The child's responses are recorded and subsequently scored and interpreted in terms of a number of personality variables. We shall briefly mention only two: intellectual characteristics and personality structure.

Rorschach responses reflect three kinds of thinking: abstract, global thinking—the need to "get it all together" and achieve a comprehensive overview or understanding; concrete, down-to-earth involvement with practical issues in the here-and-now; and concern with minutiae and a need for preciseness in the smallest detail. No one kind of thinking is ideal since healthy adaptation requires all

Below is a list of items that describe children. For each item that describes your child now or within the past 6 months, please circle the 2 if the item is very true or often true of your child. Circle the 1 if the item is somewhat or sometimes true of your child. If the item is not true of your child, circle the 0. Please answer all items as well as you can, even if some do not seem to apply to your child.

0 = Not True (as far as you know)   1 = Somewhat or Sometimes True   2 = Very True or Often True

0 1 2 1. Acts too young for his/her age	0 1 2 10. Can't sit still, restless, or hyperactive
0 1 2 2. Allergy (describe): _____	
_____	0 1 2 11. Clings to adults or too dependent
	0 1 2 12. Complains of loneliness
0 1 2 3. Argues a lot	
0 1 2 4. Asthma	0 1 2 13. Confused or seems to be in a fog
	0 1 2 14. Cries a lot
0 1 2 5. Behaves like opposite sex	
0 1 2 6. Bowel movements outside toilet	0 1 2 15. Cruel to animals
	0 1 2 16. Cruelty, bullying, or meanness to others
0 1 2 7. Bragging, boasting	
0 1 2 8. Can't concentrate, can't pay attention for long	0 1 2 17. Day-dreams or gets lost in his/her thought
	0 1 2 18. Deliberately harms self or attempts suicide
0 1 2 9. Can't get his/her mind off certain thoughts;	
obsessions (describe): _____	0 1 2 19. Demands a lot of attention
_____	0 1 2 20. Destroys his/her own things

FIGURE 16.4
Excerpt from parent's version of the Child Behavior Check List.

three; a successful Girl Scout camping trip entails an overall plan, a realistic grasp of what food and equipment will be needed, and maps that are accurate to the last detail. However, individuals differ in the kind of thinking most characteristic of them. Psychopathological conditions produce exaggerations of the three types of thinking: a psychotic adolescent boy in a manic phase may have grandiose ideas of his intellectual prowess, such as believing that he knows everything in the world there is to know; an anxious individual may cling desperately to the mundane requirements of a day-to-day existence, any slight deviation from a routine being viewed as a potential danger; while a compulsive girl may waste her energies on trivia such as making sure that her shoes are arranged in a perfectly straight line, that there is not a speck of dust on any of the

furniture, that her clothes are immaculately clean.

The Rorschach also reveals the kind and degree of emotional responsiveness (roughly translated as extraversion), inner resources and fantasy life (roughly translated as introversion), and rational self-control an individual has. As with the intellectual characteristics, all three elements are present in healthy individuals, but different ones predominate; some individuals have outgoing, expressive, convivial, and colorful personalities; others are reflective, intellectual, and "deep"; while still others are unemotional, self-controlled, and straight-laced. The Rorschach furnishes valuable information as to when such normal personality characteristics become extreme to a pathological degree: the reactive individual may become an impulse-ridden or violently acting-out one; inwardness may become pathological isolation and paranoid suspiciousness; while the self-contained individual may become so massively inhibited that any affect is perceived as a terrifying threat.

Exner (1974, 1978; Exner and Weiner, 1982) has made two important contributions to Rorschach analysis. First, he took the numerous scoring systems and integrated them into a single comprehensive one. Next, he provided norms for children between 5 and 16 years of age so that clinicians can now evaluate the deviancy of a given child's responses in terms of a normative population his or her age.

Exner's norms also made possible a *validation* study in which age changes in Rorschach scores were predicted on the basis of developmental theory and data. The majority of these predictions were verified. Rorschach scores reflected the predicted increase in the following variables: complexity, integration and precision of thinking, richness of ideas, conformity to acceptable ways of thinking, and affective control. They also reflected the predicted decrease in the following variables: unrealistic, egocentric ideas and uncontrolled affect. However, the scores failed to reflect the predicted decrease in anxiety and increase in depression (Wenar and Curtis, 1991).

Such positive findings are not typical of the body of Rorschach research, however. In fact the question of the Rorschach's validity continues to bedevil psychologists since it gained popularity some fifty years ago. Psychometricians have been dismayed by its poor performance, some recommending it be banished altogether, while some practicing clinicians regard it as indispensable in revealing information no other technique can match. A review of research (Klopfer and Taulbee, 1976) suggests that there have been a sufficient number of positive findings to reassure the clinicians and a sufficient number of negative ones to gladden the hearts of nihilistic psychometricians. The decision to use the Rorschach, therefore, becomes one of personal preference.

The Thematic Apperception Test (TAT) consists of thirty pictures, although only around ten are used for a given individual. The instructions are to tell a story identifying the people in the picture, explaining their thoughts and feelings, and describing their past, present, and future. The examiner records the story and asks questions concerning elements that may have been omitted. Some pictures are for males, others for females, and still others are for both sexes, but all are purposefully ambiguous; for example, a figure sitting on the floor leaning against a couch may be male or female, may be exhausted or depressed or suicidal or merely resting. Some cards contain single figures, others suggest interpersonal situations, such as the nuclear family, same- and opposite-sex parent-child interactions, and same- and opposite-sex adult relations.

Unlike the Rorschach, the TAT has no standard scoring procedure. However, most systems assume that the heroes of the stories represent various aspects of the individual's self-concept, although not necessarily the conscious view of the self. Thus special attention is paid to the hero's needs, interests, traits, and competences. In the interpersonal sphere, themes concerning parents and the family unit are of special interest, stories being analyzed for the way parents are viewed and the hero's interaction with parental figures. Stories also reveal the nature and strength of the affect accompanying the various themes, along with the effectiveness of coping devices in dealing with the problems generated in the stories.

Let us return to Tom, the hypothetical 10-year-old boy with the learning problem. The clinician was wondering whether the pressure to meet impossible academic goals had affected Tom's self-image and relations with his parents. Here one of Tom's TAT stories will be used to illustrate the process of analysis. However, a word of caution before starting: no one story—just like no one bit of behavior—is definitive in itself; it is merely suggestive. Only as themes occur repeatedly and can be fitted together into some cohesive entity does the clinician have confidence in the interpretation of the data.

The card depicts a boy looking at a violin that is on a table in front of him. His expression is ambiguous. The following is Tom's story.

Well, there is a little boy, and his mother told him to practice the violin, and he don't want to practice the violin, so he just sits there staring at it. After a while he fell asleep, and he has a dream and—now I have to think up a dream. He dreamed he was the greatest violinist in the world, and fame and success brought him riches and happiness. He bought his mother beautiful things, and his father—he bought him nice things and everything he wanted. He enjoyed living in such luxury. I don't want to end it yet. These are hard to figure out. He had a special violin, and no other violin could he play because this was the only one that ever worked for him, because there was only one that could play the right tunes. It seemed like magic that it played all right. He kept it by his bedside because if he lost the violin he would lose his wealth and everything. It was almost like magic. Finally, there came a time when his rival realized he could only play that one violin, and he sent some bandits to break up his violin and ruin his career. Just as the bandits were going to break the violin in half, he woke up.

This particular picture often elicits stories concerning responsibility and achievement; in terms of our conceptual scheme, the stories concern work. Tom's opening sentence contains the familiar theme of a child having to do something he does not want to do because his mother says he must. However, Tom's method of coping with this conflict is quite unusual—he escapes into a dream. It is as if telling a story about being pressured to work was not sufficiently safe, and Tom needs the twice-removed protection of a fantasy within a fantasy. The dream itself is richly imagina-

tive, suggesting a creative potential in Tom. And what a contrast between the initial picture of the boy who is incapable of resolving the conflict of imposed duty, and the grandiose, world-famous, supremely rich and happy achiever. The achievement is not solely egocentric, since it also enables the boy to give the parents everything they wanted. But, interestingly, Tom is not able to end on this theme of magical, compensatory fulfillment. Instead of bringing security, grandiose achievement is accompanied by a state of heightened vulnerability, since a competitive rival sets out to destroy him. Once again Tom cannot cope with the situation he creates, this time the anxiety over the competitive aspects of achievement. The boy in the story wakes up as one might from a nightmare in which anxiety has reached an intolerable level.

We can infer that Tom's situation of trying to meet unrealistic expectations has affected his view of himself in relation to his parents. Out of his impotence he has generated a compensatory image of grandiose success, which both allows him to fulfill parental expectations and to be on the giving end in regard to his parents. In its own right, this exaggerated image and reversal of parent-child roles could not be considered a healthy resolution. In addition, the wishful image cannot be sustained because of the destructive competitiveness Tom perceives to be an integral part of achievement. Thus there is an impasse at both the reality and the fantasy levels. In sum, the pressures of unattainable goals has engendered a feeling of helplessness and a concern over loveworthiness on the one hand and a fear of competitiveness and achievement on the other. However, Tom has the great assets of a lively imagination and an openness in expressing ideas in a disguised form when they are too painful to face directly. One would expect that he would be a good risk for psychotherapy and that he would make significant progress.

In general, the TAT has fared reasonably well in reliability and validity studies. Not only does it differentiate various psychopathological groups, such as psychotics and delinquents, but it has also stimulated interest in studying a number of the needs which it taps, the achievement need being the outstanding example. (For further information concerning validity studies, see Klopfer and Taulbee, 1976.)

Other Projective Techniques The Children's Apperception Test (CAT) was designed on the premise that children will more readily identify with and therefore tell more meaningful stories about animal than about human figures (Bellak, 1954) The fact that the original premise has not been confirmed has relegated the CAT to the status of an ancillary technique.

The Roberts Apperception Test for Children (RATC) (McArthur and Roberts, 1984) represents a more successful effort to adapt the thematic approach to children. There are twenty-seven stimulus cards (of which only sixteen are administered to a given child) depicting common situations, conflicts, and stresses in children's lives—for example, parental support and conflict, sibling rivalry, and peer interaction. The RATC provides criteria and examples for scoring the stories in terms of adaptive and maladaptive functioning; for example, a constructive resolution to a problem is healthier than an unrealistic, wishful, or magical solution. Interrater agreement on scores is high. Finally, there are norms on well-adjusted children ages 6 to 15 which aid the clinician in evaluating an individual child's disturbance.

Of the many *drawing techniques*, the Draw-A-Person Test (DAP) is one of the most widely used. According to Machover's (1949) procedure, the child is first asked to draw a person, then to draw a person of the opposite sex. Next, a series of questions follows, such as "What is the person doing?" "How old is he(she)?" "What does the person like and dislike?"—although such questions have not become part of a standard procedure. Theoretically, the child's drawing is a projection of both the self-image and the body image. Various characteristics of the drawing are interpreted in terms of psychological variables—a small figure indicating inferiority, faint lines suggesting anxiety or an amorphous identity, an overly large head indicating excessive intellectualization—while the answers to the questions are interpreted thematically; for example, a figure who is "just standing there" suggests passivity, while one who is a cheerleader suggests activity and exhibitionism. The figure may represent either the self or the idealized self; Tom, for example, may have drawn either a very small or a very large male figure. While its popularity attests to its clinical utility, the DAP only rarely has met the test of validation (see Klopfer and Taulbee, 1976).

Other Psychological Tests

Achievement Tests An assessment of academic achievement is important in deciding whether a child has a learning disability and in evaluating the effectiveness of a remedial program. Low academic achievement may also contribute to the development of a behavior problem. As with intelligence tests, there are individual, group, and short forms of achievement tests. Again, as with intelligence tests, individually administered achievement tests allow the clinician to make behavioral observations of the child and to analyze the nature of the child's failures, both of which may provide helpful clues as to motivational and academic problems; for example, a boy who gives up without trying is different from one who fails after trying his best, just as a girl who fails multiplication problems because of careless mistakes is different from another who fails because she has not grasped the basic process of multiplying. Typically, achievement tests are of the pencil-and-paper variety and cover reading, spelling, arithmetic, social studies, and science.

In many instances, a global measure of achievement in the principal school subjects suffices to answer the clinician's questions and the Wide-Range Achievement Test-Revised (WRAT-R) may be used (Jastak and Wilkinson, 1984). The WRAT-R provides tests for reading, spelling, and arithmetic, covers an age range from 5 years to adulthood, and can be administered in twenty to thirty minutes. Its reliability is high, as are correlations between WRAT-R scores and those on other tests measuring achievement in the same school subjects. Another achievement test which evaluates reading, math, written language (including grammar, punctuation, and spelling) and knowledge of social studies, science, and the humanities is the Woodcock-Johnson Tests of Achievement (1989). The Gray Oral Reading Tests (1986) and the Woodcock Reading Mastery Tests (1987) may be used when the clinician is particularly interested in evaluating a child's reading.

Among group-administered achievement tests, both the Iowa Test of Basic Skills (Lindquist and Hieronymus, 1955-1956), designed to assess vocabulary, reading comprehension, work-study skills, and arithmetic in children in grades three through nine, and the Stanford Achievement Test (Kelley et al., 1964), which has five batteries of tests for children from first through ninth grades covering word and paragraph meaning, science and social studies concepts, spelling, language, and arithmetic concepts, have satisfactory reliability and validity and are widely used (see Sattler, 1992).

Abilities Tests   A different approach to assessing learning disabilities is that of evaluating the abilities directly related to academic achievement rather than achievement per se. An example of such an approach is the Illinois Test of Psycholinguistic Ability (ITPA) (Kirk,

McCarthy, and Kirk, 1968). The scale is made up of twelve subtests sampling variables theoretically involved in language communication. Certain subtests, for example, evaluate simple abilities, such as auditory and visual reception, while vocal association uses analogy statements, such as "A dog has hair; a fish has _____," to tap the ability to relate concepts presented orally.

Tests for Organic Brain Damage   A neuropsychological assessment usually begins with an intelligence and an achievement test. These tests not only provide information as to the children's intellectual level and academic progress but, more important, they also provide clues as to what psychological functions might be affected by organic brain damage. As we have seen, the manifestations of brain damage may range from a slight deficit in sensorimotor abilities to a pervasive disruption of every aspect of a child's intellectual and personality functioning. It follows that there can be no single diagnostic test for organicity.

If brain damage potentially affects a variety of functions, then a battery of tests casting a wide psychological net would seem to provide a reasonable strategy for capturing the elusive diagnosis. Two of the most widely used are the Reitan-Indiana Neuropsychological Test Battery (1969) for children 5 to 8 years of age and the Halstead Neuropsychological Test Battery for Children (1969), which is applicable to children 9 through 14 years of age (see Table 16.1). The diversity of the tests may be seen in the following sampling. In the Tactual Performance Test, the blindfolded child is required to fit variously shaped blocks into a form board with the preferred, nonpreferred, and both hands and then, with blindfold, blocks, and form board removed, to draw a diagram of the board. This test evaluates memory and spatial location, both of which may be adversely affected by organicity. In Trailmaking B, the child is given a piece of paper on

TABLE 16.1

Selected Items From the Halstead-Reitan Neuropsychological Test Battery for Older Children and the Reitan-Indiana Neuropsychological Test Battery for Children

Test	Description
Category Test*	Measures concept formation; requires child to find a reason (or rule) for comparing or sorting objects.
Tactual Performance Test*	Measures somatosensory and sensorimotor ability; requires child, while blindfolded, to place blocks in appropriate recess using dominant hand alone, nondominant hand alone, and both hands.
Finger Tapping Test*	Measures fine motor speed; requires child to press and release a lever like a telegraph key as fast as possible.
Aphasia Screening Test*	Measures expressive and receptive language functions and laterality; requires child to name common objects, spell, identify numbers and letters, read, write, calculate, understand spoken language, identify body parts, and differentiate between right and left.
Matching Pictures Test[†]	Measures perceptual recognition; requires child to match figures at the top of a page with figures at the bottom of the page.
Marching Test[†]	Measures gross motor control; requires child to (a) connect a series of circles with a crayon in a given order with right hand alone and with left hand alone and (b) reproduce examiner's finger and arm movements.
Target Test[†]	Measures memory for figures; requires child to reproduce a visually presented pattern after a three-second delay.
Rhythm Test[‡]	Measures alertness, sustained attention, and auditory perception; requires child to indicate whether two rhythms are the same or different.
Trail Making Test (Parts A and B)[‡]	Measures appreciation of symbolic significance of numbers and letters, scanning ability, flexibility, and speed; requires child to connect circles that are numbered.
Tactile Form Recognition[‡]	Measures sensory-perceptual ability; requires child to identify various coins through touch alone with each hand separately.
Strength of Grip[‡]	Measures motor strength of upper extremities; requires child to use Smedley Hand Dynamometer with preferred hand and nonpreferred hand.

* This test appears both on the Halstead-Reitan Neuropsychological Test Battery for Older Children and on the Reitan-Indiana Neuropsychological Test Battery for Children.
[†] This test appears only on the Reitan-Indiana Neuropsychological Test Battery for Children.
[‡] This test appears only on the Halstead-Reitan Neuropsychological Test Battery for Older Children.
Note: The WISC-R (or WAIS-R) is often administered as part of the complete battery.

which twenty-five circles are scattered about; the circles are randomly numbered from 1 to 13 and randomly lettered from A through L. The child's task is to connect alternate numbers and letters, that is, to go from A to 1 to B to 2 and so on. The score is the time taken and the child is penalized for errors. Among other things, Trailmaking B is a test of flexibility of thinking, a facility that may be impaired in certain kinds of organic brain damage. (For a general discussion of neuropsychological assessment, see Hynd, Snow, and Becker, 1986).

Tests of individual functions are more widely used than time-consuming batteries, but their popularity is rarely buttressed by solid evidence of diagnostic accuracy. A frequently used means of evaluating *perceptual motor coordination* is the Bender Gestalt Test for Young Children (Koppitz, 1973). It consists of nine figures which are presented one at a time for the child to copy; for example, a row of dots, a juxtaposed circle and diamond, two wavy lines intersecting. As a test of *memory* the Benton Visual Retention Test (1974) may be used for visual material, and the Wechsler Memory Scale (1987) may be used for verbal memory in adolescents.

Currently, specialized techniques are being developed on the basis of research concerning the effects of various kinds of brain damage on children of different ages. These techniques have two advantages. First, they are tailored to children of different ages rather than representing downward extensions of adult techniques. Next, they are specific to the various kinds of brain damage such as seizures or head injuries. (For information concerning assessment of special populations such as learning disabled and sensorily impaired children, see Sattler, 1992. Family assessment is discussed by Jacob and Tennenbaum, 1988.)

BEHAVIORAL ASSESSMENT

As we have noted, the scientist's quest for comprehensive understanding of psychopathology differs from the clinician's pragmatic goal of obtaining information relevant to implementing a particular kind of remediation. A prime example of tailoring inquiry to a therapeutic procedure is behavioral assessment. Since behavior therapy concerns the current situation, assessment aims at obtaining a specific account of a child's problem behaviors along with their immediate antecedents and consequences.

Behavioral assessment utilizes many traditional diagnostic procedures but the emphasis differs. In obtaining *referral information* the clinician focuses on the question of who has seen what behaviors in which situations. Similarly, the *behavioral interview* aims primarily at obtaining behavior-specific accounts of the problem and the environmental factors that may be eliciting and maintaining it. The behavioral clinician also inquires into attempts to change the troublesome behavior and the results obtained. Adults directly involved with the child's problem, such as parents, teachers, and relatives, are interviewed. Generally speaking, obtaining historical information is minimized, since the clinician is only incidentally interested in reconstructing etiology. However, such information is sought to the extent to which it may throw light on the current situation.

Some of the main features of the behavioral interview deserve to be presented in detail. To begin with, general descriptions of the child, such as "nervous," "bad," or "lazy," must be translated into specific behaviors. Next, the interviewer inquires concerning *antecedents* or a description of the situations in which the problem behavior occurs. Again, specificity is of the essence: "Sue-Anne starts yelling when we're eating" is not as helpful as, "Sue-Anne starts yelling when her dad and me are at supper, and he tells her 'Eat all your corn' or 'Help clear the table' or 'Do the dishes' or some other (dinner) chore." Next, the clinician inquires as to events that occur immediately following the problem behavior, namely, its *consequences*.

Here, as in every aspect of the interview, behavioral specificity is sought in terms of exactly who is present and what is done: "After Sue-Anne starts yelling, her dad smacks her, and she just keeps on until sometime he can't stand the noise and leaves the house and I don't see him the rest of the evening" (see Table 16.2).

Certain ancillary information is helpful. The clinician may obtain an initial inventory of potential reinforcers to be used in therapy by asking what the child enjoys, such as favorite foods, recreational activities, or pastimes. The parents may be asked what behavior they would wish to have as a replacement for the present objectionable ones. The clinician may

TABLE 16.2

Illustration of Interview Format Suggested for ADHD Children

Examiner: How does your child generally behave when there are visitors at your home?

Mother: Terrible! He embarrasses me tremendously.

E: Can you give me some idea of what he does specifically that is bothersome in this situation?

M: Well, he won't let me talk with the visitors without interrupting our conversation, tugging on me for attention, or annoying the guests by running back and forth in front of us as we talk.

E: Yes? And what else is he likely to do?

M: Many times, he will fight with his sister or get into something he shouldn't in the kitchen.

E: How will you usually respond to him when these things happen?

M: At first I usually try to ignore him. When this doesn't work, I try to reason with him, promise I'll spend time with him after the visitors leave, or try to distract him with something he usually likes to do just to calm him down so I can talk to my guests.

E: How successfully does that work for you?

M: Not very well. He may slow down for a few moments, but then he's right back pestering us or his sister, or getting into mischief in the kitchen. I get so frustrated with him by this time. I know what my visitors must be thinking of me not being able to handle my own child.

E: Yes, I can imagine it's quite distressing. What will you do at this point to handle the situation?

M: I usually find myself telling him over and over again to stop what he is doing, until I get very angry with him and threaten him with punishment. By now, my visitors are making excuses to leave and I'm trying to talk with them while yelling at my son.

E: And then what happens?

M: Well, I know I shouldn't, but I'll usually grab him and hold him just to slow him down. More often, though, I may threaten to spank him or send him to his room. He usually doesn't listen to me though until I make a move to grab him.

E: How often does this usually happen when visitors are at your home?

M: Practically every time; it's frustrating.

E: I see. How do you feel about your child creating such problems in front of visitors?

M: I find myself really hating him at times *(cries)*; I know I'm his mother and I shouldn't feel that way, but I'm so angry with him, and nothing seems to work for me. Many of our friends have stopped coming to visit us, and we can't find a babysitter who will stay with him so we can go out. I resent having to sacrifice what little social life we have. I'm likely to be angry with him the rest of the day.

Source: Barkley, 1981. Copyright by Guilford Press. Reprinted with permission.

assess the amount of time the parent has to participate in a therapeutic program if one were deemed desirable and evaluate the parent's ability and willingness to do so. Finally, the child may be interviewed to obtain his or her perception of the problems as well as a list of likes and dislikes.

The interviewer's emphasis on specific behavior in no way eliminates the problems inherent in conducting any clinical interview. Parents are personally involved rather than objective reporters; for example, in the preceding illustration, the mother may have cited only the father's behavior as an antecedent and omitted her own out of defensiveness or vindictiveness toward her husband or dislike of the clinician—or out of honest obliviousness. Thus the behavioral clinician must be as skilled as any other in establishing rapport, constructively handling negative feelings, judging the accuracy of the information and when it is suspect, finding ways of eliciting a more realistic account without antagonizing or alienating the parent.

Psychological tests are used sparingly; personality tests which reveal underlying attitudes, motivations, and perceptions of self and others are regarded as useless. Preference is for *behavior checklists,* which are typically composed of a listing of behavior problems, such as disobedience, attention seeking, social withdrawal, or truancy from school. The adult who knows the child best checks the characteristic items. Some checklists also include positive items, while others are environmentally oriented, requiring the parent to designate the setting and social consequences for each of the problem behaviors.

Behavioral Observation

The behavioral approach has made a unique contribution by adapting the technique of naturalistic observation—previously used primarily for research purposes—to assessment goals and placing it at the heart of the process. It is easy to understand this emphasis on direct observation, since abnormal behavior is assumed to develop and to be maintained by environmental stimuli, while behavior modification corrects problem behaviors by altering the environmental conditions maintaining them.

On the basis of information obtained from the referral, checklist, and interview, the clinician identifies the target behaviors to be observed. These behaviors are, in effect, the operational definition of the child's problem, "bad" becoming translated into "yelling at her father during supper" in our example. While behavioral clinicians are always sensitive to the individuality of the child, they have found sufficient commonality among certain problems to have developed standard *behavior codes* for particular settings. Disruptive behaviors in the classroom, for instance, frequently fall within categories, such as the child being out of his or her chair without permission; touching, grabbing, or destroying another child's property; vocalizing, speaking, or noisemaking without permission; aggressiveness; and failure to do the assignment.

The behavioral clinician's next task is to determine the frequency of the target behavior in order to establish a *baseline* for its natural occurrence against which to evaluate the effectiveness of the therapeutic intervention. Observations are scheduled for the specific periods in which the problem behavior is most likely to happen. Depending on the natural occurrence of the target behavior, the period may last half an hour to an entire day, while observations may be made daily or only on particular days. Our obstreperous little girl, for example, needs to be observed for only about thirty minutes every day at suppertime, provided both parents are present.

There are a number of different methods for quantifying behavioral observations. *Frequency* involves counting the number of times the target behavior occurs within a specific period. Frequency divided by time yields a measure called *response rate;* for example, a disruptive boy may leave his seat without permission five times in a fifty-minute class period so his response rate would be 5/50 or .10. In *interval recording* an observer has a data sheet divided into small time units, such as twenty seconds; aided by a timing device such as a stopwatch attached to a clipboard, the observer indicates whether the target behavior occurred in a given unit. Frequently, a *time-sampling* method is used in which the observer observes the child's behavior for ten seconds, for example, and spends the next five seconds recording the target behaviors which occurred in that fifteen-second interval (see Figure 16.5). This sequence is repeated for the duration of the observational period. Typically, only the presence or absence of target behavior is recorded. Some data are lost if a behavior occurs more than once during an interval, but such losses are often unimportant. Interval recording is usually more practicable than the frequency method when the observer wishes to record a number of behaviors. Finally, *duration* consists of measuring the interval of time between the onset and termination of the target behavior. This method is appropriate when decreasing the time spent in a particular behavior, such as head-banging, is a therapeutic goal.

In addition to being used to determine the frequency or duration of target behavior, observation provides information concerning antecedent and consequent events. However, this aspect of data gathering has not been formalized into specific procedures. Often the data are in descriptive or narrative form rather than being quantified. As always, the observer is aware of the setting-specific nature of the relationships observed and is alert to the possibility that the setting may significantly alter the functional meaning of behavior; for example, a mother's reprimand may tend to de-

FIGURE 16.5
Example of a three-minute partial-interval time sample recording. Abbreviations are as follows: R = referred child, C = comparison child, X = behavior observed, O = behavior not observed, Tot. = Total. Each number reflects a 10-second observation period followed by a 5-second pause for recording data. Three types of behavior were recorded: passive off-task behavior, disruptive off-task behavior, and on-task behavior. Bill engaged in off-task behavior in 6 of the 12 intervals; 5 of the off-task behaviors were passive. Thus in 50 percent of the intervals he showed some kind of off-task behavior. In contrast, Ted had only one interval with off-task behavior (passive). (*Source:* Sattler, 1992.)

Referred child: Bill
Comparison child: Ted
Date: March 2, 1986

Class: Mrs. Jones
Time: 11:00 to 11:03 A.M.

Behavior	Tot.		1	2	3	4	5	6	7	8	9	10	11	12
Passive off-task	5	R	X	O	O	O	O	O	X	X	X	O	O	X
	1	C	O	O	O	O	O	O	X	O	O	O	O	O
Disruptive off-task	1	R	O	O	O	X	O	O	O	O	O	O	O	O
	0	C	O	O	O	O	O	O	O	O	O	O	O	O
On-task	6	R	O	X	X	O	X	X	O	O	O	X	X	O
	11	C	X	X	X	X	X	X	O	X	X	X	X	X

crease provocative behavior when mother and child are alone, but it may increase such behavior when the father comes home, especially if he sides with the child.

Theoretically the baseline phase should continue until the target behavior has become stable. Because of the variability of human behavior, such an ideal is often difficult to achieve. The general consensus is that there should be a minimal baseline period of one week of data collection. (For a more extended presentation, see Hartmann and Wood, 1990, and Mash and Terdal, 1988.)

Reliability

Everyone would agree that Sue-Anne's "badness" is nearer the behavioral level than is Tom's concept of himself as helpless. As personality characteristics become increasingly inferential, they become increasingly difficult to evaluate in terms of reliability and validity. How would you go about determining whether Tom "really" felt helpless, for example? Note, however, that we are dealing with *levels* of inferences from behavior, not with inferential versus noninferential personality characteristics. Certainly Sue-Anne's yelling is "out there" for anyone to see—and hear! In this particular instance the issue of reliability may be irrelevant. But for most problems the target behavior is not so clear; on the contrary, naturally occurring behavior may well be equivocal, while its variability makes interpretation and inference inevitable.

In order to insure reliability, researchers using naturalistic observation have found it necessary to train observers. Typically, two or more trainees observe, record, and score the behavior of the same child. Disagreements are discussed and reconciled. Additional observations are made and scored until agreement between observers is at least 80 to 85 percent. Even after training is completed, it is highly desirable to "recalibrate" the observers periodically by repeating the training procedures. Such intensive training further attests to the fact that problem behavior is not "out there"; the emperor's new clothes notwithstanding, the untrained eye is an inaccurate observational instrument.

Behavioral clinicians rarely have the time or the personnel to train for accurate observation. Consequently, they must rely on untrained adults, such as parents and teachers. The expected decline in reliability has been documented (Achenbach and Edelbrock, 1978). In general, a given individual is consistent with himself over a period of one week to one month; even after six months, consistency is marginal but adequate. Reliability between similar observers such as parents or teachers is satisfactory but not so high as to prevent disagreements between mother and father or between teachers. Reliability plunges precipitously between adults who view the same child in different situations, such as parents and teachers, teachers and mental health workers, or even teachers who see the child in different settings. This last finding suggests that many problem behaviors may be situation-specific. Thus reliability is affected both by the implicit definitions and biases of the observers, and by the different information input they have in terms of the situations in which they have observed the child.

The Developmental Dimension

Development has no formal status in behavior assessment. As late as 1991, Ollendick and King, after detailing the conceptual problems involved in combining a behavioral with a developmental approach, cautiously concluded that "The emergence of 'developmental-behavioral assessment' is on the horizon" (p. 70). They also listed the ways in which developmental considerations enter into the assessment process. The behavior therapist cannot naively accept every parent's or teacher's word that a child's behavior is deviant. Like all clinical child psychologists, they must know when behavior that others might regard as a problem is to be expected at a given age. Lacking such a developmental perspective, they could not decide whether to treat the child or change the adults' misperceptions. In addition, establishing rapport with children is a universal feature of assessment which, in turn, requires developmentally relevant knowledge and skills. Note that Ollendick and King are not trying to inject a developmental dimension into behavior assessment; rather they are making explicit the developmental aspects that have been implicit, ignored, or denied.

CLINICAL ASSESSMENT: ART AND SCIENCE

While differences in assessment procedures can best be understood in terms of clinicians' different theoretical and therapeutic allegiances, there is another, related source of disagreement. As scientists, psychologists strive for objectivity and precision, which require, among other things, clearly delineated procedures that are available to the scientific community. It is no accident that psychologists in the past championed intelligence tests in particular and the mental measurement movement in general over impressionistic evaluations. Nor is it by chance that behavioral assessment, with its explicit procedures for observation, its relative disinterest in historical antecedents, and its dismissal of inferred personality characteristics and motivations, is exercising a similar appeal. Concomitantly, there is a mistrust of the hypothesis-testing clinician initially described in this discussion. While utilizing theoretical and experiential guides, the process by which this clinician generates, tests, accepts, and discards ideas is nearer to an art than a science. He or she may indeed come up with impressive insights but also may

be seriously in error; more important—and this is what concerns the critical psychologist—there is no clearly established procedure for deciding in favor of one outcome over the other.

Certain clinicians might answer that scores are only one kind of information to be gained from a test, as we have seen in discussing intelligence tests. To limit assessment to such scores would be to eliminate the added behavioral data so vital to understanding an individual child. If such data have yet to be standardized and are of unknown reliability, their clinical utility justifies their use for the present.

These clinicians rightly claim that there are a number of important areas for which no standardized, clinically useful instruments exists. Thus they can do no more than put the pieces of assessment data together as best they can. Moreover, it is just such efforts to understand complex, heretofore unsystematized data that can ultimately serve as the basis for objective assessment techniques.

While techniques and goals may vary, all clinical assessment requires a high degree of *professional competence.* Clinicians must be skillful and sensitive in handling the many interpersonal problems inherent in dealing with troubled parents and children; they must be knowledgeable concerning the procedures they use and the problems they are called upon to evaluate; they must be well acquainted with and abide by the ethical principles of their profession; and they must have received adequate academic and professional preparation, which for a clinical child psychologist typically involves a Ph.D. or Psy.D. from an accredited university and at least two years of supervised experience (American Psychological Association, 1979).

The dovetailing of assessment and psychotherapy which has been emphasized will become clearer after we learn more about the major schools of psychotherapies themselves. This topic is covered in our final discussion.

REMEDIATION AND PREVENTION

Our discussion will now turn to some of the ways in which psychopathological behavior can be changed and ways to prevent it. In the realm of remediation, three of the major psychotherapies—psychoanalytic, client-centered, and behavioral—will be presented, with emphasis on the conceptualization of development that provides the basic rationale for the therapeutic techniques each employs. Next, the effectiveness of individual therapy with children will be discussed, followed by a brief survey of group and family psychotherapy. Prevention will take us into the realm of the community mental health movement. The origins and nature of this movement and some of the many efforts at prevention and remediation it has generated will be described and evaluated. Finally, we will present two preventive programs specifically based on research in developmental psychopathology. (For a summary of psychotherapy with children and adolescents, see Kazdin, 1993.)

THE PSYCHOANALYTIC APPROACH

Classical psychoanalysis is a highly specialized technique appropriate for only a limited range of psychopathologies. Here, as in the remainder of this section, the presentation will be based on the writings of Anna Freud (1965; see also Scharfman, 1978). Another influential figure in this field is Melanie Klein, who disagreed with Anna Freud on many points concerning child psychoanalysis (see Segal, 1973).

The Developmental Model

Psychoanalytic theory is inherently developmental, the psychosexual stages defining the pivotal conflicts to be mastered on the way to maturity. Consequently, the focus of therapy is on the particular psychosexual stage or stages presumed to be responsible for the psychopathology (see Chapter 1). Moreover, psychoanalysts have devised special therapeutic techniques suited to children at different developmental levels. In our presentation we will only be able to touch on this literature.

Classical psychoanalysis grows directly out of the psychoanalytic theory of neurosis. According to this theory, psychopathology originates in the psychosexual stages, where the possessiveness, rivalry, death wish, and castration anxiety of the Oedipus complex act as particularly fertile breeding grounds. Preschoolers who are unable to master psychosexual anxieties defend themselves against it, using repression and other defenses such as displacement and projection. In certain instances

the defenses work in the sense of providing developmental pathways that will be serviceable throughout life. But there is always the vulnerability attendant upon an unmastered phase of development and subsequent experiences may exacerbate the underlying disturbance, the special combination of fixation point and defenses producing the specific neurotic symptoms of hysteria, phobias, obsessions, or compulsions (see Chapter 1).

The essence of psychoanalysis consists of reversing the defensive process, reconfronting the individual with the original trauma so that it can be mastered belatedly. Successful psychoanalysis is epitomized by Freud's aphorism, "Where id was, there shall ego be." The once-overwhelming hates, jealousies, and fears can now be revived and viewed from a more mature perspective. The ensuing insight into the root of the problem exorcises it. The result is a "widening of consciousness" in two senses: the individual can face previously unacceptable aspects of his or her personality, and the energy used for defensive maneuvers can now be employed in growth-promoting activities.

The Therapeutic Process

Psychoanalysis depends on the establishment of a *therapeutic alliance* between therapist and patient—a bond sufficiently strong to sustain the patient through the many stormy sessions that lie ahead. The sessions themselves are held four to five times a week for a period of three years or more. Another general feature of psychoanalysis is the maximizing of free expression during the psychoanalytic hour. Adult patients are initially instructed to lie down on the couch, facing away from the analyst, and say anything that comes into their mind—a technique called *free association*. It is from the basic data of free association that the analyst tries to understand the patient's life as the patient perceives it. Suggestions, advice, directions as to how to handle problems, and medication are minimized and ideally avoided altogether.

There are two major techniques for undoing the work of defenses. The first is called analyzing the *resistance*. Since defenses protect the patient from anxiety, he or she will find numerous ways to retain them. This accounts for the paradox that despite great suffering the adult neurotic will resist attempts at cure. The maneuvers used to resist bringing painful ideas and feelings into consciousness are numerous. A patient may lie on the couch and say that nothing comes to mind, for example, or he may bring up a personal feeling and quickly change the subject by talking about the current state of society, or he may steep himself in psychoanalytic theory so that he "knows the answer" to his problem before the analyst, or he may even engage in a "flight into health," claiming that all his problems have been solved and that he never felt better in his life! The analyst's task is constantly to call attention to such evasive maneuvers and help the patient to focus on the threatening material which prompted them, the therapeutic alliance giving the client courage to explore such material.

Next, classical psychoanalysis involves analysis of the *transference*. The intense, prolonged one-to-one relationship stimulates the revival of previous intense relationships to the parents. Thus, feelings once directed toward parents are transferred to the therapist. Again it is the analyst's function to call attention to transferences, so that in exploring them, patients can begin to gain access to the distressing relationships that played a decisive role in their neurosis.

The patient's verbal productions form the leading edge of psychoanalysis. After a period of time, the analyst begins to make *interpretations* as to the meaning of these productions once the meaning seems reasonably clear.

Such interpretations are often very simple: "You must have been angry at your older brother for always being so much better than you were." "Wasn't it frustrating to have such a 'perfect' mother?" "You seem always to run away from this idea that you are as sexy as any other girl." Correctly timed, such interpretations produce *insights*; prematurely timed they are rejected and fuel the patient's resistance. Nor does a therapeutic cure come in one blinding flash of insight. Instead, the same material has to be approached again and again from many different directions and through many different experiences in order for the insight to be firmly established—a process called *working through*.

Child Psychoanalysis

Applying classical psychoanalysis to children has required certain major changes in procedures and techniques but not in the basic goal. For a number of reasons the therapeutic alliance is different with children than with adults. Children do not voluntarily seek therapy, nor do they necessarily suffer intensely from their neurotic problems. They live more in the present than do adults, so they cannot be expected to endure the pain of psychoanalysis for the sake of some future good. In attributing causes for their behavior, they tend to externalize and place the responsibility on others rather than examining their own actions. By the same token, they look to the therapist as someone who will change the environment, so that they will not have to go to school or obey their father, for example. Children often lack the capacity for self-observation or self-monitoring that enables adults to participate in an intense emotional experience while at the same time observing themselves reacting. One can readily understand how such an ability facilitates the gaining of insight. Finally, during times of developmental stress such as adolescence, children are reluctant to add to their emotional burdens by confronting their anxieties.

Children's personalities are also not as firmly structured as those of adults, who can maintain an intrapsychic conflict relatively independent of environmental events. A child is always more responsive to environmental influences even when neurotic; for example, the resolution of a phobia may come about by some growth-promoting forces within the environment and not represent a "flight into health." Thus the child analyst must keep track of reality to a much greater extent than is necessary with adults. Children's transferences, unlike those of adults, do not involve feelings toward parental ghosts dating back to the distant past. Because children are still living with and dependent upon parents, their transference tends to be more dilute and obscure; for example, the irrational anger a girl brings to a therapy session may be due to the fact that her parents have entered a stormy phase in their relationship or that a parent, envious of the therapist's influence, has begun catering to the child in order to win her over.

A radical change in technique is necessitated by the fact that the children cannot free-associate, and *play* has to be substituted. However, play is not the equivalent of free association. Through associations, adults provide the key to the idiosyncratic meaning of events or dreams; since children provide no such key, the analyst must actively try to decode the meaning of their fantasies. In addition, adults are encouraged to say anything that comes into their mind, while children cannot be similarly encouraged to do anything they like; such a lure too often leads to aggressive acting out, such as damaging property, endangering their safety, or attacking the analyst, all of which overwhelms their already weakened ability to reflect upon their own behavior.

The play material itself is the kind which taps fantasies rather than skills—a doll family, crayons, clay, etc. The analyst watches for signs that a theme is of special importance: repetition, excessive affect, an abrupt termination (which suggests anxiety), regression in the form of more infantile play or speech, loss of control, such as scattering the toys around, or a "they lived happily ever after" dismissal of a conflict situation (Peller, 1964). Interpretations are simple and closely attuned to the play: "I bet that family was really scared when the hurricane started coming toward their house." "I wonder why the little girl always wanted to look at the monkeys in the zoo." "Being locked in a closet for two years after being bad does seem a long time." After obtaining clues as to the meaning of the child's fantasy, both from play material and conversations, the analyst can begin building a bridge from the safe disguise of make-believe to the child's own feelings; for example, "That hurricane sounds like what you told me about your mother and father having all those fights." (See Figure 17.1.) Through such interpretations the child, like the adult, is led back to the original traumatic situation and helped to recognize, reevaluate, and master it. And as with adults, the roadblocks of resistance must be overcome, while the transference is used for clues concerning feelings toward parents.

The analyst recognizes that age itself significantly affects the manner in which a psychoanalysis can be conducted; the play material that delights the preschooler becomes increasingly inappropriate toward the end of middle childhood and would be considered demeaning to the adolescent. In fact, adolescents are particularly difficult to help since they eschew fantasy play, while their tenuous self-control makes them reluctant to explore their feelings via free association.

Recently, psychoanalytic theory has supplemented its traditional concern with the intrapsychic variables (id, ego, and superego) with an emphasis on interpersonal relations, epitomized by Bowlby's attachment theory. This

FIGURE 17.1
Fantasy as a clue to reality. (*Source:* Copyright 1988 by Bill Watterson. Dist. by Universal Press Syndicate. Reprinted with permission.)

emphasis has resulted in psychoanalysis being more interactive. The psychoanalyst is viewed as a person with very human reactions to the child rather than as a detached observer and interpreter. Parents are also regarded as participants in the therapeutic process rather than primarily as providers of information (see Shapiro and Esman, 1992).

Kohut's treatment, for example, aims to undo the damage of faulty parental mirroring and idealizing (see Chapter 1). The classical model of the psychoanalyst as a shadowy figure onto whom the patient transfers earlier unmastered aspects of psychosexual development is inappropriate for individuals with *narcissistic* disorders. Such individuals cannot

project emotions consistently because they are too personally preoccupied even when they appear to be relating to others. According to psychoanalytic theory, they have been unable to form a true object relation and their libido has remained concentrated on themselves to a large extent. Hence the term narcissistic.

Narcissistically disturbed individuals need the therapist to fill the voids in their experience. This may involve mirroring, or being appreciated, respected, and valued. Kohut's therapy in this regard resembles Roger's technique of unconditional positive regard, which we will discuss next. Therapy may also involve permitting the patient to idealize the therapist. Thus, the therapist must make himself or herself known as a person with whom the patient can identify (see Ornstein, 1981).

Psychoanalytically Oriented Psychotherapies

Since the conditions necessary for a classical psychoanalysis are difficult to meet in childhood, numerous adaptations have been made in order to help a wider variety of disturbed children. At times these variations serve the basic goal of enabling the child to deal with and master traumatic, unconscious material; more often the goal itself is changed to a general one of helping the child adapt, even though the core problem may go unresolved.

A number of the modifications involve the use of techniques which, in classical psychoanalysis, play only a minor role or are regarded as obstacles to achieving the basic goal. One of the most important modifications is that of providing a *corrective emotional experience*. This involves encouraging inhibited children to express forbidden feelings so they can discover that they are neither rejected nor punished for doing so. A too proper girl, for example, may find that there are no disastrous consequences to getting angry first with the therapist and then with significant people in her environment. Closely related to the corrective emotional experience is *reassurance,* in which the omnipotence the child invests in the therapist is used to counteract disabling fears and to bolster crippled self-confidence and self-esteem. The implicit message often is: "There is nothing to be afraid of; you can do it if you really try; you are worthy of love and respect."

The therapist can perform an *educational* function that has nothing to do with academic instruction despite its label, but which is more akin to good parenting. Educational measures may involve providing ways of dealing more effectively with id impulses, such as discussing sexual techniques with a shy adolescent. At times the measures are directed toward the ego, the therapist supplying adaptive techniques to substitute for maladaptive ones; for example, telling a socially isolated child that if she shared her toys rather than acting superior and keeping them to herself, she would have more friends. Finally, the measures may be directed to the superego, such as telling a child that stealing is wrong for a number of reasons and that he should not give in to his impulses.

The common denominator in this diversity of techniques is the therapist's allegiance to the genetic theory of psychosexual development and to the structural theory of id-ego-superego. In addition the psychoanalytic approach champions certain other concepts. The approach is comprehensive or *holistic* in that it assumes that psychopathology can be understood only in terms of intrapersonal factors (the balance between id, ego, and superego), interpersonal factors (the relation between the child and significant figures, particularly parents), and time, or the historical dimension. It offers a variety of therapeutic techniques aimed at *meeting the child's needs* as these are revealed by the comprehensive evaluation. Next there is an emphasis on the *affect* generated by intense interpersonal relationships. Freud's belief that the passions of love, hate, fear, and guilt hold the key to pathology clearly implies that such feelings and their interpersonal contexts should be central in correcting psychopathology—hence the emphasis not only on children's *relationship* to parents and sibs but also on their relationship to the therapist and the therapist's feelings toward them. There is the belief that broadly based *motivational systems* underlie specific behaviors and that, as much as possible, those systems should be changed. Castration anxiety, for example, has manifold expressions in terms of fear of authority and competition, as well as being expressed in maneuvers to circumvent such fears; as the anxiety is allayed, many maladaptive behaviors will lose their reason for being.

Psychoanalytically oriented psychotherapy with adults has not fared well in objective studies of *relative effectiveness*. In a review of nineteen comparative outcome studies, Svartberg and Stiles (1991), found that, while it was superior to no treatment, this superiority decreased as the quality of the study increased. In addition, it was inferior to other therapies, particularly in treating depression. Its relative effectiveness with children remains to be evaluated.

Cognitive Development and Child Psychotherapy

Recently, a diverse group of researchers who generally ascribe to a *stage model* rather than an information-processing model of cognitive development has begun exploring the cognitive components in psychodynamically oriented psychotherapy or in therapy centering on the exchange of ideas between therapist and child. While preliminary, their findings are worth sampling. (For a comprehensive account, see Shirk, 1988a).

Communication The rationale for the research should be clear by now. Children's communications to the therapist reflect their particular level of cognitive development, and therapists must be aware of this level in order to avoid misunderstanding and misinterpretation. Let us take the now familiar characteristic of preschoolers' and school-aged children's thinking as being simple, concrete, and situation-specific and look at some implications for psychotherapy.

In a divorce, for example, a 5-year-old might be concerned about where his gerbils will sleep, while a 14-year-old is worried about how to handle her feelings of divided loyalty. Each is expressing dismay at the ruptured family in terms congruent with his or her cognitive development. Thus, it would be a mistake to trivialize the concern of the preschooler

or to regard him as lacking in depth of attachment to the parents (Nannis, 1988).

In like manner, therapists' communications must be congruent with the child's cognitive level if they are to be correctly understood. Interpretations referring to distal causes, such as past interpersonal conflicts in the family, may exceed the school-age child's level of causal reasoning, just as references to psychological content may fail to engage the interest of the concrete, action-oriented preschooler or school-aged child (Shirk, 1988b). Thus, a therapist should not regard the child's behavior as resistance when it only reflects the level of cognitive development.

The Self-concept In addition to exploring the implications of cognitive development on communication, certain investigators are extrapolating from research in particular substantive areas to psychotherapy. We have arbitrarily chosen to present Harter's (1988) studies of the development of the self.

In her research Harter found that while school-aged children were capable of giving self-evaluative judgments—say, on their competencies in various areas—they showed little interest in examining these evaluations. Nor did they see them as a source of concern or in need of alteration. Recall that psychoanalysts also noted the tendency to externalize problems. Only in adolescence does analyzing the inner self come into its own, at times to an excessive degree. How then can a psychotherapist achieve self-related goals such as enhancing self-esteem?

Again Harter (1988) relies on her research showing that children with low self-worth highly value areas of low competence. Thus the therapist can concentrate on increasing the skills in areas the child values or help the child decrease the importance of areas of low competence. Next, since self-esteem is partially dependent on the way the child is evaluated by significant others, the therapist can work on changing the feedback from such individuals, particularly parents who apply negative labels to the child.

Development versus Training The cognitive model of development as a series of qualitatively different stages has never been acceptable to behaviorists, who prefer more atomistic, mechanistic models such as information processing and who view development in terms of quantitative changes. This difference also affects their preferences for treatment. We will use conduct-disordered children as an example.

Behaviorists prefer skills training in which socially appropriate behavior is analyzed into its components; these components are then used as targets for training procedures. By contrast, Selman and Schultz (1988) are interested in charting the stages of what they call interpersonal negotiating strategies (INS) (see Chapter 9). Data come from ways in which children go about resolving interpersonal conflicts presented in story form; for example, "John's boss asks him to work late Friday night and he does not want to. What does he do?" Simplifying the findings, the developmental levels of INS go from impulsive at one extreme (e.g., John says "I quit" in the above example) to collaboration at the other (e.g., John says, "Let's sit down and talk about this.") It follows that the goal of therapy is to help the child advance to a new, qualitatively different level of cognitive development—to change the way he or she thinks about handling interpersonal problems in general. This is a different image of treatment from that of training the child to use specific skills.

Finally, the choice of treatment strategies depends on the child's cognitive level, although Selman and Schultz (1988) offer only general guidelines as to how therapy should proceed. Children who are low in both cognition and self-control are usually so impulsive that cognitive therapy is impossible and

milieu therapy is necessary. As higher cognitive levels are achieved, psychotherapy can be introduced since problems are now amenable to discussion, reasoning, confrontation, and interpretation by the therapist.

At this point it is too early to tell which approach—developmental, or skills training—will prove to be the more effective, although skills training is currently enjoying a wider popularity.

THE CLIENT-CENTERED APPROACH

15-year-old girl: When Dad starts that same old lecture (in a singsong voice) "No nice girl *I* ever knew went around in dirty jeans, and no nice girl *I* ever knew let a boy touch her body on the first date," I could just explode on the inside.

Therapist: You feel all angry on the inside then.

Girl: Yeah. But then (glumly) sometimes I look at him and he looks so worn out and there's this cancer thing he's got . . .

Therapist: It sounds like you feel sad about your father's condition—getting old and sick, I mean.

Girl: Or just mixed up so I don't know where I'm going at times, except maybe crazy (with a little laugh).

Therapist: So it's as if the mad feeling and the sad feeling make you feel all mixed up?

The therapist is doing two things that epitomize the client-centered approach—*reflecting* and *accepting* the client's feelings. The therapist's manner is sincere, interested, warm. This type of therapist will never interpret, unlike the analyst, or tell clients how to solve their problems, unlike the behavior therapist. Primarily the therapist will accept and reflect feelings.

On the face of it, the client-centered approach makes little sense, and its practice seems too simple to be regarded as a skill. In reality, the therapy is based on an explicit developmental model of psychopathology, is one of the most demanding of its practitioners, and has exerted a powerful influence on the professional community.

The Developmental Model

Our discussion will be based on the ideas of Carl Rogers (1959), founder of client-centered therapy. Rogers stresses the primacy of the individual's experience and of the individual's self. Maturity is the ability to *experience a feeling fully* so that there is congruence between experiencing the feeling, awareness of the feeling, and expressing the feeling. If the three elements are not present, the individual is apt to be disturbed; a repressed individual cannot allow certain feelings into consciousness, an overintellectualized individual talks about feelings in an impersonal manner, while an inhibited individual is afraid to act upon feelings. The *self* is the concept of who one is and of one's relations with others. While it may not be totally conscious, it is available to consciousness.

Rogers is explicit about the conditions that facilitate or block the attainment of maturity. First he postulates an *actualizing tendency,* which is an inherent tendency in each organism to develop all of its capacities in ways that serve to maintain or enhance it. This is the growth principle—an innate push toward expansion, differentiation, and maximization. It includes the tendency to be creative, to learn new things painfully rather than to settle for the complacency of acquired learning, to develop toward autonomy rather than to be controlled by external forces. Moreover, each organism has an *organismic valuing process,* which leads it to value positively those experiences that maintain and enhance it, while valuing negatively those that have the opposite effect. Thus each individual has a built-in guide to what is best for personal growth, innately seeking enhancing experiences and avoiding

those that are detrimental. As awareness of the self emerges in the toddler period, the individual develops the *need for positive regard,* which is a universal need for warmth, respect, sympathy, and acceptance. With time, the need can become more potent than the organismic valuing process.

An essential requirement for healthy growth is that the need for positive regard continues to serve the organismic valuing process; in other words, it is essential that the people the child loves and values continue to foster the child's need to experience and decide for himself. In our terminology, affection must enhance initiative. This can be done only if the child receives *unconditional positive regard.* Here, no experience of the child is perceived by others as more or less worthy of positive regard. Children are intrinsically valued, and their experiences are not viewed judgmentally as being "good" or "bad" by adult standards.

But Rogers does not advocate total permissiveness. He recognizes that children cannot be allowed to do everything they like. However, discipline should take place in the context of an explicit and sympathetic recognition of the children's feelings: "I know you are mad at your baby brother, and I understand why, but I just can't let you hurt him because he has his feelings too." When this is done children never have to view themselves as "bad" and never have to disown their feelings. Consequently, their openness to experience and feelings is preserved.

Normal development goes awry because of what Rogers calls *conditions of worth.* Instead of unconditional positive regard, significant adults, particularly parents, say, in essence, "I will love you on the condition that you behave as I want you to." Because of the strong need for positive regard, children eventually make parental values into self values. At this point children are no longer in touch with their organismic valuing process, no longer open to experience and capable of deciding for themselves whether an experience is growth-promoting. By incorporating alien values they become alienated from themselves. Because of alienation, children begin to distort experiences in order to fit the imposed model of a "good boy" or a "good girl": the aesthetic boy believes he has to be a competitive go-getter because this is his father's ideal, the bright girl is hounded by feelings of inadequacy because her mother disparages intellectual achievement. Self-alienation is also a state of vulnerability to anxiety as the organismic values continue to press for their rightful place in the self. When distress becomes too intense, anxiety runs rampant and therapy is required.

How different the Rogerian model is from the Freudian. Freud sees humanity as endowed with primitive drives that must be socialized or else society itself could no longer exist. Rogers follows Rousseau's idea that the child, like the primitive "noble savage," is innately good, and it is socialization that has the potential for destroying the natural tendencies to growth and self-actualization. Understandably, Rogers has had a strong appeal for those who turn their backs on convention in order to "find themselves" and search for a way of life that would express "the real me." He is also in harmony with the existential emphasis on the primacy of the individual's experience and the importance of individual choice. One hears echoes of Shakespeare's "To thine own self be true" along with the "me" generation's "If it feels right, it is right."

The Therapeutic Process

In light of what we have learned, we can understand how the client-centered therapist, by offering the child unconditional positive regard, will help undo the damage of conditional love. The focus is continually on feelings because these hold the key to maturity. Because of the growth principle, the therapist has

complete confidence in the client's ability to solve his or her own problems with the minimum of direction—hence the general name *nondirective therapy.*

While a number of therapists have adapted Rogers's principles for children, Axeline's (1964, 1969) approach is presented here. The major change in procedure is the introduction of play material for children below the preadolescent age range. The material is simple and conducive to self-expression—dolls, animals, clay, sand, building materials. Construction toys and games of skill are avoided as being too structured to produce varied and individualized behavior. While the formal arrangement resembles that of psychoanalysis, the purpose is quite different. Rather than using play as the basis for interpretation, therapists limit their activity to reflecting the themes and affects the child introduces.

Some of the basic features of nondirective therapy deserve to be elaborated. Therapists are, quite literally, nondirective. After discussing the ground rules for the therapeutic hour and describing the procedure in general terms they leave the direction of the sessions up to the child. As we have seen, therapists do not interpret the meaning of the child's behavior, nor do they introduce any material from the child's past, from the reality of the child's present situation, or from previous sessions. If, for example, they learn that the child has started setting fires, they wait until the child is ready to make such behavior part of the therapeutic session. Thus responsibility is always on the child's shoulders. What therapists communicate implicitly is a faith in the child's ability to decide what is best for his or her own growth.

We can now understand both why the past has little intrinsic value and why diagnosis plays only a minor role in nondirective therapy. Therapists have no need to "know the answer" ahead of time; in fact, such a need might well interfere with the therapeutic process. Not only do they want to learn about the child only through the child, but as much as possible they also want to experience life as the child experiences it. Their reflection of feeling is not a mechanical technique; with it goes a genuine effort to feel their way into the child's experience. Therapists are not onlookers; they are empathetic participants.

We can also understand why it is so demanding to be a nondirective therapist. First it means relinquishing the role of authoritative adult. Moreover, the therapist's acceptance of and respect for the child must be genuine. As we have already learned from Anna Freud, when children are given freedom to do what they like, many of them begin to gravitate toward destructive acting out. Not only that, but they also have a genius for finding ways of teasing, testing, and provoking adults. For the therapist to maintain an attitude of acceptance and understanding rather than self-defense and retaliation requires a forebearing disposition and self-discipline.

However, not everything children do is accepted; certain limits are essential. There is the limit of time, since the children must leave at the end of the session whether they want to or not. Children are not permitted to do things that deviate significantly from the world of reality; specifically, they are not allowed to attack the therapist or themselves physically or to destroy the playroom and its contents. However, the therapist, like the good parent, is understanding of the motive, even while preventing the behavior, thus avoiding judging the children as "bad."

One final word about the technique of reflecting feelings. Its *structuring* properties are obvious, since the therapist is implicitly sending the message, "While we are together, feelings are what we will be dealing with." But there is more than that. In the permissive atmosphere of the therapeutic session, the child begins to explore feelings that formerly had to be banished from conscious awareness. In fact, some of these feelings may never have been clearly recognized for what they were. Thus, reflection also serves a *defining* function rather than being a mere echo of what the child already knows. What is more, as feelings are explicitly defined, they come under conscious control. As the boy realizes his resentment for being pushed into the alien role of a go-getter, as the girl can face her fear of being rejected by a nonintellectual mother, such feelings become part of the self. The once-divided self is whole again.

THE BEHAVIOR THERAPIES

The behavior therapies are the most vigorous cluster of treatments on the current scene. The past thirty years have witnessed an exuberant expansion of therapeutic techniques that has been somewhat disconcerting to those concerned with conceptual clarity. And if behavior therapy represents the marriage of the clinic and the laboratory, there are signs that the honeymoon is drawing to a close; little irritations are surfacing, and the two partners are searching for a more sober and mature basis for their relationship.

First, a conceptual framework sufficiently broad to embrace all the behavior therapies will be presented. Then the therapies themselves will be sampled in terms of their underlying rationales. Finally, we shall turn to some of the practical and theoretical problems that have accompanied the field's rapid growth.

A note on nomenclature: Conceptually the behavior therapies can fall under the rubric of psychotherapy. However, because of their distinctive features it is also possible to put them in a separate category and contrast them with psychoanalytic, nondirective, and other therapies that are more open-ended and involve more give and take between therapist and client. Thus, one can distinguish behavior therapy on the one hand from psychotherapy on the other.

Conceptual Framework

Behavior therapies are characterized by attention to specific, currently *observable behaviors* of the client, by a concern with *objective measures* of the outcomes of their interventions, and by a reliance on the *research laboratory* to provide general principles of behavior change that can be used as the basis of therapeutic intervention and as a place to put clinical findings to rigorous experimental tests. Rather than being a special set of techniques, behavior therapies are "an *approach* to abnormal behavior . . . characterized by (an) empirical methodology" (A.O. Ross and Nelson, 1979, p. 303). (Our presentation follows Ross and Nelson. For a more detailed presentation, see Ross, 1981.)

To elaborate: pragmatic considerations have dictated the emphasis on specific behaviors, since these are most amenable to change. Behavior therapists would not deny that such behaviors may be rooted in the past, but the past cannot be altered, the present and the future can. Among ongoing behaviors, the therapists deal with three response systems—overt-motor, physiological-emotional, and cognitive-verbal. All must be considered in a comprehensive treatment program, since they are not necessarily correlated; a boy who is constantly fighting in school may tell the therapist that "everything is OK" and he only fights "a little every now and then."

In the constant interplay between the clinic and the laboratory, principles of learning have been extensively used to generate therapeutic procedures, while both social and developmental psychology have provided conceptual underpinnings for therapeutic techniques, although to a lesser degree. Perhaps even more significant than the application of laboratory findings is the incorporation of experimental procedures into psychotherapeutic practice. Behavioral assessment (as described in Chapter 16) sets the stage for the objective, reliable measurement of target behavior, as well as providing leads to the specific antecedents and consequent events that elicit and maintain these behaviors. The behavior therapist then proceeds to reason very much like his or her experimental counterpart: if behavior X is due to antecedent Y and consequent Z, then as Y and Z are changed, so should X. The therapeutic intervention, like an experiment, consists of testing out the hypothesis, the crucial measure being a change in the base rate of the target behavior X in the desired direction.

The simplest design in evaluating therapeutic effectiveness is the *A-B* design, in which the dependent measure is evaluated both before intervention (baseline or *A*) and during intervention (*B*). If, for example, a therapist hypothesized that temper tantrums in a 3-year-old were being sustained by maternal attention, he might advise the mother to ignore them. If the base rate went down, the therapist would have evidence that the hypothesis was correct. Such a design is adequate for clinical work because it demonstrates whether change occurs. However, for a more stringent test of the hypothesis that change was caused by the intervention rather than by other variables, the reversal or *A-B-A-B* design is used, in which the therapeutic procedure is repeatedly applied and withdrawn. If change in the target behavior occurs only in the presence of the intervention, then a causal relationship can be more readily assumed (see Figure 17.2).

While the behavior therapist's procedure is akin to the experimentalist's, therapy cannot be equated with experimentation. Uncontrolled variables (such as a boy improving because his father obtained a better job), ethical considerations, and the inevitable complexity of dealing with ongoing problems of living prevent therapy from having the required purity. However, questions raised by therapeutic efficacy can be referred back to the laboratory to be examined under properly controlled conditions. If, for example, a child with a snake phobia begins to handle snakes after watching

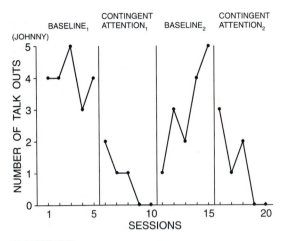

FIGURE 17.2

A record of talking out behavior of an educable mentally retarded student. Baseline₁—before experimental conditions. Contingent Teacher Attention₁—systematic ignoring of talking out and increased teacher attention to appropriate behavior. Baseline₂—reinstatement of teacher attention to talking out behavior. (*Source:* Hall et al., 1971, p. 143, Figure 2. Reproduced by permission.)

movies of other children doing so, is it because the anxiety has diminished or because the incentives and techniques for handling snakes are now enhanced, even though the anxiety level itself remains unchanged? The question whether it is better to diminish anxiety or enhance coping skills, along with a number of other questions raised in the context of behavior therapies, has provided grist for the experimental mill. In sum, the interaction between the clinic and the laboratory and the objective documentation of the efficacy of various intervention techniques are the hallmarks that clearly distinguish behavior therapies from other approaches to remediation.

Behavior Therapies Derived from Learning Theory

In the prototypical instances of behavior therapy, principles of learning—specifically, classical conditioning, operant learning, and imitation—have formed the bases of intervention procedures. Exemplars of the application of each principle will be examined. (For an account of how behavior therapies are applied to various psychopathologies, see Kratochwill and Morris, 1991.)

Classical Conditioning *Systematic desensitization,* as developed by Wolpe (1973), is a procedure for eliminating anxiety-mediated problems. In such problems, initially neutral stimuli come to elicit powerful anxiety responses as a result of classical conditioning. The bond between the conditioned stimulus and the anxiety response can be broken, however, by *reciprocal inhibition,* in which the stronger of two incompatible responses tends to inhibit the weaker. The therapist's task, therefore, becomes one of pairing anxiety-eliciting stimuli with a more powerful, incompatible response. The response Wolpe uses is deep muscle relaxation, since obviously an individual cannot be simultaneously anxious and relaxed.

Two preliminary steps are needed to implement the therapy. First, the child must be instructed in the technique of relaxing various muscle groups throughout the body. The child is also required to make up a graduated sequence of anxiety-eliciting stimuli, going from the least to the most intense. A girl with a school phobia, for example, may feel no anxiety when she awakens and dresses, mild anxiety at breakfast, increasingly strong anxiety while waiting for the bus and approaching school, while the most intense anxiety comes in the free period before classes start.

In the therapy proper, the children imagine each of the steps, pairing them with the relaxation response. If the anxiety is too strong at any particular step and they cannot relax, they return to the preceding step. Over a series of sessions the children gradually are able to relax in response to even the most intense anxiety-producing stimuli. For adults, around six-teen to twenty-three treatment sessions are required to reach this goal. It is interesting that the therapeutic gains, which relate solely to imagined representations of reality, transfer to reality itself. While Wolpe's rationale has been questioned and the specific variables respon-sible for improvement have not been satisfac-torily isolated, the therapy itself has been suc-cessful in treating a host of problems, including school and hospital phobias, exam-ination anxiety, fear of authority, maternal separation anxiety, and asthma.

Operant Learning   Behavior therapists have made extensive use of the operant principle that behavior is controlled by specific anteced-ent and consequent stimulus events. *Contin-gent management,* or the manipulation of re-wards and punishments that follow or are contingent upon the response, has been partic-ularly potent in decreasing the strength of un-desirable behaviors or increasing the strength of adaptive ones. There are two kinds of pos-itive consequences: reward or positive rein-forcement, and removal of an aversive stimu-lus or negative reinforcement. There are also two kinds of negative consequences: positive punishment or administering an aversive stimulus, and negative punishment or the re-moval of a pleasant stimulus. Two procedures are used if the behavior one wishes to strengthen is not present in the child's reper-toire or is infrequently emitted: *chaining* or *shaping,* in which components or successive approximations of the desired behavior are differentially reinforced, and *prompting,* in which instruction, modeling, or physical guid-ance is used to elicit the desired response. Be-havior therapists frequently combine these various ingredients to increase the effective-ness of their therapeutic program. To teach a very retarded child how to feed herself, for example, the therapist might use shaping by first reinforcing her hand movements toward a spoon, then her grasping the spoon, then her

lifting it up, and finally her bringing it to her mouth. The therapist might use prompting by demonstrating feeding himself or by actually guiding the girl's hand through feeding move-ments.

Examples of the application of operant prin-ciples are legion, some involving a therapist, others involving parents who not only can be taught how to implement a therapeutic pro-gram with relative ease but who also are in a position to control a wider range of behaviors than can be elicited in a therapeutic setting. (The examples are from Ross and Nelson, 1979.) We shall begin with instances of simple reward or punishment and proceed to pro-grams combining both. The language skills of 2- and 3-year-old children were enhanced when their mothers reinforced naming of ob-jects with praise or bits of food, while the tan-trums of a 21-month-old were extinguished when the mother ignored them, thereby with-drawing the attention that had been sustaining them. In programs combining extinction with reinforcement, aggressive dependent behavior was ignored while cooperative independent behavior received parental attention; the mother of an effeminate boy ignored his fem-inine behavior while praising his masculine behavior; self-stimulation and self-injurious behavior in severely disturbed children were punished by a brief electric shock or a slap, while adaptive behavior was rewarded.

Instead of direct reinforcement, a child can be a given a *token,* which subsequently can be redeemed for rewards such as prizes or priv-ileges. In one therapeutic program children were given tokens for cooperative behavior and doing chores while losing them for un-desirable social behavior. In *time out,* the child is isolated for a brief period, thereby being punished by the withdrawal of reinforcers. In one complex program an acting-out boy was isolated for two minutes when he was aggres-sive and disobedient, while less severe mis-behavior was ignored and cooperative behav-ior was rewarded by special attention and treats. In another complex program, the tantrums of a 3½-year-old autistic boy were treated by time out. A shaping technique was used to teach him to wear glasses, since he was in danger of losing his vision. First he was rewarded for holding the empty frames, then for bringing the frames to his eyes, and finally for wearing the prescriptive lenses. To treat his echolalic speech, he was first rewarded for saying the label for a picture the therapist held and then rewarded for saying the label without the therapist's prompting. His eating problems were decreased by temporarily removing his plate when he ate with his fingers and by temporarily removing him from the dining room when he threw food or took it from someone else's plate.

Training parents to be behavior therapists is not without its problems. The parent must be motivated to learn the techniques and sufficiently conscientious to use them over long periods of time. While parents typically want their children to change, they are not uniformly agreeable to the idea that they must also change. The problem of parental involvement may be compounded when the complaint originates in the school or in the court, as it often does. Thus parents themselves may need special reinforcement from the therapist.

Observational Learning Observational learning or modeling has not been extensively employed as a primary (rather than an auxiliary) therapeutic technique. However, observing fearless children interacting with a phobic stimulus, such as a snake or a dog, has successfully eliminated phobias. The model may be presented either in real life or on film. Modeling is often combined with reinforcement of the desired behavior; for example, in teaching verbal behavior to autistic children, the child is immediately rewarded with food upon each successful imitation of the therapist's vocalization.

Cognitive Behavior Therapies

Cognitive behavior therapies are one of the newer and more controversial additions to the family of behavioral techniques. Not that there is a strict dichotomy between traditional and cognitive behavior therapy. Traditional procedures employ cognitive elements as a means of achieving behavioral change; in desensitization, for example, children imagine various situations and instruct themselves to relax, both of which are cognitive activities. For their part, cognitive therapies are concerned with changing specific overt behaviors, are ahistoric, systematically monitor the relation between intervention and behavioral change, and retain allegiance to the clinic-laboratory symbiosis. However, cognition now becomes the primary object of the therapeutic thrust, since the basic goal is to change the way the child thinks. When this has been accomplished, behavior will also change. Of the varieties of cognitive therapies, only those concerned with self-control, cognitive restructuring, and social skills training will be discussed. (For a comprehensive discussion, see Kendall, 1991.)

Self-Control There is an Achilles heel to traditional behavioral techniques: the very design that proves their effectiveness—the *A-B-A-B* paradigm—leaves the child forever dependent on external agents for maintenance of the new, more adaptive behavior. Such a situation presents practical problems, since therapists cannot see children indefinitely, while the enthusiasm of parents and teachers may wane. The situation is also ethically unacceptable to a society that values self-determination so highly. Therefore behavior therapists have set about finding ways by which external control can become internalized. One technique, within the traditional model, is called *fading* and involves the gradual removal of contingencies. Delinquents, for example, were first given tokens for every acceptable specific behavior but, after reaching a level of consistently high performance, were placed on a merit system, where privileges were freely available as long as the delinquents continued to behave appropriately.

Other behavior therapists have attacked the problem of self-control directly (Kazdin, 1980). Rather than equating self-control with some vaguely defined trait, such as will power, these therapists conceptualize it as a deliberate undertaking by the individual to achieve a self-selected outcome. This involves, among other things, forgoing immediate rewards for future ones (for example, doing homework instead of looking at television), selecting cues congruent with eliciting the desired behavior (leaving the recreation room and finding a quiet place to study), monitoring one's behavior, and rewarding or punishing oneself as the goal is or is not realized. Each component can be subjected to study in a laboratory setting and, individually or in combination, can serve as the basis for intervention techniques.

One cognitive technique involves increasing self-control in impulsive or hyperactive children by means of *self-instruction* (Meichenbaum and Goodman, 1971). The rationale is the familiar one that verbal symbols (words) serve both to delay and to guide behavior. Impulsive children, who are presumably deficient in "self-talk," should perform better on specific tasks if they learn how to instruct themselves properly. The procedure relies on modeling, reinforcement, and a graduated performance task. For the purpose of illustration, the task of copying a rectangle has been chosen. First the adult performs the task, talking aloud in order to delineate each step in the procedure: defining the task ("Let's see, what do I have to do? I have to copy this picture"), focusing attention ("I'm going real slow and careful"), self-monitoring and self-reinforcement ("I did that corner really well"), and self-evaluation ("That's pretty good, except next time I could get that line straighter if I went

slower"). Next the children perform the same task with the therapist giving explicit instructions. Then the children perform the task, first instructing themselves aloud, then whispering the instructions, and finally guiding their performance via private speech. In short, the children's haphazard, impulsive self-instructions are replaced by planful and critical ones.

Understandably, self-control procedures are not without shortcomings. While designed partly to alleviate the problem of maintaining gains in traditional behavior therapies, the procedures themselves can begin to deteriorate over time in the absence of external reinforcement. For example, schoolchildren who have been taught to reward themselves for acceptable behavior in the classroom might gradually begin rewarding themselves for disruptive behavior. Once again we see how tenuous self-control is in middle childhood and the concomitant dependence on adult guidance.

Cognitive Restructuring Long a therapy in its own right, Ellis's (1970) rational emotive therapy (RET) has been included under the behavior-therapies umbrella. Ellis assumes that psychopathology results from misperceptions and mistaken cognitions. He lists twelve such irrational ideas, such as "Everyone must love me for everything I do," "I need someone stronger than myself to rely on," "It is easier to avoid than to face life's difficulties." The therapist, through a kind of Socratic dialogue and logical examination of the clients' ideas, helps them achieve emotional insight into erroneous beliefs while assigning specific tasks that enable them to put their newfound understanding into practice.

Like all behavior therapies, cognitive restructuring emphasizes specific behavioral change. With self-instruction, it shares an emphasis on the importance of private monologues and provides reinforcement for systematic observation and alteration of dysfunctional thought. While its technique of rational self-examination makes it poorly suited for young children.

Effectiveness Durlak, Fuhrman, and Lampman (1991) analyzed sixty-four studies of the effectiveness of various kinds of cognitive behavior therapies. Most of the studies involved 9-year-old boys with externalizing problems. Treatment was brief, averaging twelve sessions. The results showed that treated children had changed significantly as compared with untreated controls, although their behavior was still not within normal limits. Improvement was maintained over a four-month follow-up period. Effectiveness was a function of the children's cognitive level, those functioning at the formal operational level (ages 11 to 13) showing twice as much change as those at less advanced stages (ages 5 to 11). However, contrary to what the rationale of cognitive behavior therapy would predict, improvement was not related to changes in cognition. Thus, the underlying mechanism responsible for change remains to be discovered.

Theoretical and Practical Problems

The principle *theoretical* issue is whether cognitive behavior therapy should be regarded as behavior therapy at all. (See Ledwidge, 1978. For a lively exchange of ideas, see Mahoney and Kazdin, 1979, and Ledwidge, 1979.) Conservative behaviorists are reluctant to deal with "mental" events because the major thrust of behaviorism historically involved a rebellion against mentalism and a defining of psychology as the study of objective behavior. In their defense, cognitive behaviorists maintain that inner events such as thoughts or feelings are perfectly admissible as long as they can be operationally defined in behavioral terms and their inclusion increases the predictability and control of behavior.

The principle *practical* problem with tradi-tional behavior therapies is not with producing but with maintaining change (Ross and Nelson, 1979). In learning-theory terms, the problem is one of generalization over situations and over time. Generalization over situations, or stimulus generalization, cannot be assumed; behaviors changed in the home, for example, may remain at their pretreatment level in the school situation. This is congruent with the behaviorist's view that behavior is situation-specific rather than the result of underlying traits. Generalization over time is another problem. In our discussion of various psychopathologies we have seen many instances in which initial gains fail to be maintained, while even self-control techniques may deteriorate.

In regard to cognitive behavior therapy, there is no convincing evidence that therapeutic results are due to changes in cognitions, which in turn produce behavioral changes. Since most therapies include behavioral as well as cognitive components, the two variables are confounded and it is impossible to say which is the effective agent. In fact, in techniques aimed at eliminating phobias there is evidence that only after children are helped to practice new, nonfearful behaviors in connection with the phobic object do they begin to change their cognitions about themselves and their ability to master the situation. Thus one can make a case that cognitive changes are contingent on behavioral ones rather than vice versa.

Finally, there is evidence that, while cognitive behavior therapy is superior to no therapy at all, it is not superior to the more traditional behavioral techniques such as progressive desensitization (Beidel and Turner, 1986).

Further Proliferation

While behavior therapists were expanding into various cognitive realms, they were also finding that concentrating on a single target area was too confining. Consequently, they began including various contexts in their treatment plan—the family, the school, peers. (Our presentation follows Mash, 1989.) And for good reason. It makes little sense to change a deviant behavior while leaving a child in a disharmonious or dysfunctional setting. Research on effectiveness also shows that conduct-disordered children whose parents were trained to reduce marital conflict improved more than those whose parents had no such training.

Currently, behavioral therapists are primarily concerned with finding effective treatment procedures. They have been versatile and ingenious in their search. Howevei, the original concern that procedures be based on well-established principles of behavior change and the much-touted marriage of the clinic and laboratory have both fallen by the wayside. The emphasis on objective, observable behavior remains along with a commitment to evaluating outcome. Although a far cry from their original manifesto, behavior therapies are still sufficiently distinct to set them apart from other approaches to treatment. By the same token, they now have more in common with psychotherapies than they did in the past, and there are more opportunities for meaningful dialogues to replace the confrontational, "My therapy is better than your therapy."

Training Programs for Children and Parents

Training programs combine reinforcement and modeling from classical behavior modification with cognitive components. As with behavioral techniques in general, they have proliferated, becoming more complex and more difficult to place in a single category.

Social Skills Training   Social skills training derives from studies showing a positive correlation between social relations and adjustment.

Unfortunately, little is known concerning the specific behaviors that predict children's level of peer acceptance or ratings of social competence by parents, teachers, and other experts. Nor do we know how these behaviors are affected by age, as they surely are, or by sex, race, or setting. Lacking such information, social skills trainers are "flying blind," either using idiosyncratic definitions or regarding almost any behavior as a social skill (see Gresham, 1986). Such conceptual, definitional and empirical difficulties have not prevented social skills trainers from developing a rich repertoire of techniques, a few of which will be briefly described. (For a more comprehensive account, see Michelson and Mannarino, 1986.)

Some techniques involve *modeling* in which the child observes live or film exemplars performing the desired prosocial behaviors. Modeling in and of itself is not sufficiently potent to bring about significant change, but modeling followed by immediate rehearsal of the observed behavior is. Multiple models who are similar to the child and who display a wide range of behaviors are more effective than single, dissimilar ones displaying a narrow range of behavior. *Reinforcement* such as attention and approval has also been used to increase desirable and decrease undesirable social behavior.

In *coaching and practice* the trainer specifically instructs the child how to behave, such as how to speak to parents or teachers, and provides feedback concerning how well the child performed. *Interpersonal problem solving,* in which children are taught to identify interpersonal problems, generate alternative solutions, and evaluate consequences of behavior, has already been discussed in relation to conduct disorders (see Chapter 9).

Social skills *training packages* assume that multifaceted treatments will have greater impact, durability and generality than single treatments. A package might cover a number of specific social skills such as complimenting others, standing up for one's rights, initiating, maintaining, and terminating conversations, and dealing with authority figures and with mixed-sex interactions. The program itself might be implemented by lectures from the trainer, by modeling, by rehearsal with feedback from the trainer and peers, and by homework assignments.

Parent Training Programs Parent training programs are design to teach parents positive, effective ways of dealing with their children's disturbed behaviors. We have already encountered two of the most successful and extensively researched parent training programs, both based on careful analyses of parental behavior (see Chapters 5 and 9). Forehand and McMahon (1981) deal with parents of noncompliant children first by helping them identify and reward their children's prosocial behaviors and then by teaching them to give effective commands and to use time-out for noncompliance. The program is conducted in a clinic setting with individual parents. There is a one-way mirror for observation, and intervention involves role playing and a ''bug in the ear'' device through which the therapist can directly coach or prompt the parents while they are playing with the child.

Patterson's (Patterson, 1982; Patterson et al., 1975) training aims to counteract the coercive interaction that plays such an important role in producing conduct disorders. Five family management practices form the core of the program. Parents are taught to record problem behaviors at home along with being taught how to use reinforcement techniques for desirable behavior and time-out procedures for undesirable behavior. Next they are taught how to monitor and supervise their children's behavior and, finally, how to negotiate and solve problems.

Both programs have been successful in changing parents' and children's behaviors over a one- to four-year period. Results have generalized to untreated child behaviors, although, in the case of Forehand and Mc-

Mahon's technique, results have not generalized from home to school. Comparative studies have shown both techniques to be superior to other treatments such as family-based psychotherapy and a family systems therapy. However, the techniques have limitations. Some children, while improving, are still not within the normal range of behavior, and certain families either do not cooperate or fail to show significant gains, particularly those in which there is marital distress, spouse abuse, maternal depression, poor problem-solving skills, high life stress, and low socioeconomic status.

As with behavioral techniques in general, parent training has proliferated to include a wide variety of disorders, while therapeutic goals have expanded to include the family context beyond the child's specific problem. (See Webster-Stratton, 1991, for a summary of parent training programs. Schaefer and Briesmeister, 1989, have a comprehensive coverage of the technique.)

Developmental Considerations

Behavior therapies, like behavioral assessment, have long ignored developmental considerations in part because their early reliance on universal principles of learning rendered developmental considerations irrelevant. However, behavior therapists are now exploring the interface between their therapies and development. Since many of the points they make are familiar to us, we will only touch upon them briefly. (For a more detailed presentation, see Holmbeck and Kendall, 1991, and Masten and Braswell, 1991.)

Developmental studies help answer the question, ''To treat or not to treat?'' by providing guidelines as to which are normal problem behaviors, which problems are apt to persist, and which, while being outgrown, leave others in their wake. Development affects the choice of optimal treatment strategies. The clearest cases involve cognitive-behavioral therapies whose effectiveness is contingent upon the cognitive level of the children. For example, if one uses self-instruction to increase self-control, it is important to know that younger, preoperational children, as well as those with low IQs, are not apt to generalize beyond the specific task, thereby limiting the technique's efficacy. However, development also affects treatments based on learning principles as well. Reinforcers change with age, and age affects the amount of information that can be extracted from modeling. Again, there is evidence that desensitization is not as effective with children as with adults because, although they can imagine vividly, they cannot use imagery to change behavior for some unknown reason. (For more details, see Masten and Braswell, 1991.)

RESEARCH ON THE EFFECTIVENESS OF THERAPY

Methodological Problems

Evaluating the effectiveness of therapy in general and the relative effectiveness of particular therapies is a difficult undertaking. One problem in studying relative effectiveness concerns *matching* groups. Since psychopathologies differ in amenability to change, the groups should at least be equated in terms of the nature and severity of disturbance. Other variables might also affect outcome—not only demographic ones such as age, intelligence, and socioeconomic status, but also therapy-specific ones such as motivation for treatment and expectation of being helped.

The therapy or therapies being investigated must be competently conducted, and therapeutic *competence* is difficult to measure, although the number of years of experience has served as a practical guide. *Criteria of outcome* differ radically among psychotherapies; the specific changes a behavior therapist would accept as defining successful completion might well be rejected by a Freudian or Ro-

gerian. *Follow-up* evaluations are important to insure that initial differences in effectiveness do not wash out in time or even reverse themselves.

Finally, research on psychotherapy, like all psychological research, is hampered by lack of adequate *measuring instruments*. It is chancy to accept either the therapist's or the client's judgment concerning outcome because both are subject to bias; for example, parents report their children have continued to improve after therapy when objective measures indicate that they have not or that their behavior has actually worsened. To avoid bias, individuals not involved in the therapy should evaluate the client by means of objective instruments before and after treatment. Standardized tests may be used, but they may not be sensitive to crucial therapeutic variables, while specialized assessment techniques run the risk of being inadequately standardized. (A comprehensive discussion of methodological issues can be found in Kazdin, 1988, 1991.)

Findings

In child therapy everything works and nothing works. The literature on each technique is replete with evidence of successful implementation even though the evidence admittedly is not definitive. But taken all together, these techniques have yet to prove their effectiveness. The original study was done by Levitt who, in 1957, failed to find that treated children in general were better off than untreated ones. Over thirty-five years later, Levitt's challenge to therapists to prove their claim has not been successfully met.

In the late 1980s it seemed that Levitt's negative findings had been countered and the effectiveness of child therapy had been established. The evidence was largely based on a new statistical technique called meta-analysis, which was capable of dealing with aggregated data from a number of studies.

The basic research was conducted by Casey

and Berman (1985) on 75 studies of therapy outcome, and by Weisz, Weiss, Alicke, and Klotz (1987) on 108 studies. Both sets of investigators found that around 80 percent of the treated children were functioning at a higher level than untreated children, an impressive showing indeed. Weisz and coworkers (1987) also found that children between 4 and 12 years of age improved significantly more than adolescents between 13 and 18 years of age. In addition, gains were sustained in follow-up studies conducted five to six months later. Both studies agreed that whether children received individual, group, or play therapy or whether parents were also in therapy did not affect outcome significantly. Somewhat later Kazdin and coworkers (1990) found similar results in their survey of 223 treatment studies of children 4 to 18 years of age.

It has been argued that, since a number of studies were not conducted as rigorously as is desirable, the positive findings may be spuriously inflated. However Weiss and Weisz (1990) found just the opposite: the more rigorous the design, the greater the difference between the groups receiving therapy and the control groups.

While the overall findings are positive, the studies have limitations. Neither the full range of childhood disturbances nor the full range of psychotherapies has been studied. The internalizing disorders such as phobias and withdrawn behavior along with the externalizing disorders such as conduct disorder, aggression, and hyperactivity are adequately sampled, but not the severe disturbances such as autism and schizophrenia, somatic disturbances such as anorexia nervosa, or learning disabilities. The behavior therapies are well represented as is client-centered therapy but not the psychodynamic therapies since these typically do not employ the kind of research design and methodology that would lend itself to statistical analysis (Kovacs and Paulauskas, 1986). A perplexing result is that therapeutic efficacy depends on who is evaluating

it. Casey and Berman (1985), for example, found that while therapists, observers involved in the research, and parents reported improvement, the children themselves and their teachers and peers did not. There is no easy resolution to this problem of disagreement among evaluators. One might argue that therapists, observers, and parents are more skilled and knowledgeable judges, or that therapy is situation-specific, affecting home but not school and peer relations. But if significant change has taken place, why are the children themselves unaware of it?

One final result is important. Therapeutic effectiveness is enhanced when outcome is measured in terms of activities similar to those occurring during treatment. For example, if modeling has been used to help a child overcome a dog phobia, the effectiveness of treatment would be measured in terms of the child's subsequent reaction to dogs. The implication is that effectiveness is facilitated when children have specific problems that can be specifically targeted in treatment. The obverse of this implication is that children with diffuse or multiple problems may be more difficult to treat successfully.

In sum, instead of concluding that treatment of children works, it would be more accurate to say that there is evidence that many types of behavior therapy are effective, particularly with children who have a specific behavior that can be targeted for change. However, it may not be as effective with children who have diffuse and multiple problems. Moreover, effectiveness in treating a number of disturbances has not been evaluated. Finally, there is little evidence concerning psychodynamic therapies, even though these, along with client-centered therapies, are commonly used methods of treating children. In fact, child psychotherapists have lagged behind those working with adults in translating their psychodynamic techniques into specifically described procedures and then designing studies in which there are objective measures of the population and outcome along with appropriate control or comparison groups (Kovacs and Paulauskas, 1986). Until there is a willingness to undertake such studies, the effectiveness of psychodynamic therapies will remain unknown. (Heinicke, 1989, presents a model for doing research on psychodynamic psychotherapy with children.)

While meta-analysis seemed to have saved the day, Weisz, Weiss, and Donenberg (1992) pointed out another, more critical limitation: the majority of studies were conducted under conditions that differed from those of a clinical setting. A number of differences were cited. The children were not clinically referred but were recruited for research purposes; for example, they were children who were afraid of snakes rather than ones who were in treatment for a phobia. This raises a question as to whether the research populations were as disturbed as clinically referred children. In addition, the children had a single problem that became the focus of treatment. Therapists were trained to treat this problem, while treatment was guided by a structured manual and was monitored regularly by senior personnel. Weisz, Weiss, and Donenberg coined the term *research treatment* to epitomize such studies that were designed to meet the conditions of standardization and control that mark well-designed research.

Clinical treatment is different. The youngsters are more disturbed, often having multiple problems that require diverse therapies. Often therapists lack recent, intensive training on such techniques, while neither manuals nor external monitoring is common. Instead of having the luxury of concentrating solely on treatment, therapists must often deal with parents and teachers, to say nothing of paperwork. In short, the authors raise the issue of the *ecological validity* of the meta-analytic analyses.

While it is difficult to meet the requirements of well-controlled research in a clinical setting, such as equating the initial level of distur-

bance, random assignment of clients to treatment and control groups, and uniform criteria of improvement, such criteria have at least been approximated. The results of two of the more recent clinical studies failed to reveal significant improvement in the treatment group. For example, Weisz and Weiss (1989) compared ninety-three completers with sixty dropouts who had been judged in need of treatment but had not showed up after intake. At six and twelve months after treatment, the two groups were compared on the Child Behavior Check List; they were also rated by parents on the severity of the children's three major problems, and by teachers on the Teachers Report Form, which provided information on a variety of problems as observed by a person outside the family. While the treatment group showed some advantage in terms of improvement, in no case was the difference between groups significant from zero (see Figure 17.3).

Neither of these studies is definitive, of course, since the clinic rarely meets all the requirements of well-controlled research. On the other hand, the results cannot be dismissed on purely methodological grounds. Instead of being laid to rest, Levitt's ghost still haunts clinicians, challenging them to prove that therapy as practiced in clinical settings is more effective in helping children than no therapy at all.

Process Studies

Instead of studying outcome, some researchers are asking the process question: "What combinations of therapist, client, and technique produce what kinds of change?" In the summary that follows, the findings are derived primarily from research with adults unless otherwise specified, since studies of children are so sparse. (For comprehensive coverage, see Garfield and Bergin, 1978.) We will first discuss *nonbehavioral psychotherapies*.

For adults and children alike, the general rule is that the more disturbed the client, the

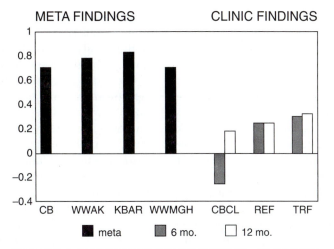

The four bars on the left show results of the meta-analyses: CB = Casey & Berman (1985); WWAK = Weisz, Weiss, Alicke, & Klotz (1987); KBAR = Kazdin, Bass, Ayers, & Rodgers (1990), bar represents our estimate of the pooled effect size, based on Kazdin et al.'s report; WWMGH = Weisz, Weiss, Morton, Granger, & Han (1992), bar represents preliminary findings. The three bars on the right show findings of the Weisz and Weiss (1989) study: CBCL = Child Behavior Checklist findings; REF = findings on severity of primary referral problems, TRF = Teacher Report Form findings.

FIGURE 17.3

Effect sizes found in four meta-analyses of child and adolescent psychotherapy outcome studies and in the clinic-based outcome study by Weisz and Weiss (1989) (*Source:* Weisz, Weiss, and Donenberg, 1992.)

less likely is improvement, and that children with conduct disorders and psychotics are less amenable to psychotherapy than are those with anxiety disorders. Younger children improve more than older ones, while sex is not systematically related to improvement. The long-standing belief that individuals of lower socioeconomic status do not respond to psychotherapy has been successfully challenged; evidence suggests that a good deal depends on how competent and comfortable the therapist is in dealing with racial and class differences between the client and himself or herself. The client's motivation to change is positively related to outcome. The role of expectations is more ambiguous, but the evidence suggests that if these are realistic and if the client is willing to work to fulfill them, they are facilitative. The client's willingness to collaborate actively in the therapy and to assume respon-

sibility for change are also facilitative, while readiness to reveal intimate information and feelings is not clearly related to outcome.

In regard to the therapist, a good personal adjustment facilitates positive change, perhaps because the client identifies with the healthy aspects of the therapist's personality. On the other hand, the importance of warmth, empathy, and genuineness has been recently challenged, while there is no evidence that the therapist's value systems or biases per se have a direct impact on therapeutic outcome. In the realm of the therapeutic alliance, it is important that therapist and client like one another, that there is relaxed rapport and open communication, that the therapist conveys a capacity to understand, and the client feels understood. Anger, boredom, or detachment on the part of the therapist hamper therapy or lead to termination. Therapy can be enhanced if both parties either share similar values or have complementary ones, such as a submissive client matched with an authoritative therapist.

Client variables such as *motivation to change* carry the most weight in determining outcome, with *therapists' personal characteristics* coming next and *techniques* running a weak third (Bergin and Lambert, 1978). Thus research findings contradict the widely held and strongly defended position that the choice of therapy is the most important determinant of outcome. The evidence suggests that in training therapists, the cultivation of interpersonal skills may be more advantageous to future clients than the teaching of a particular technique.

Behavioral therapists have also become interested in nonspecific variables that might influence therapeutic outcome, such as the client's expectancies and the therapist-client relationship. There is evidence, for example, that the relationship variable together with behavioral techniques can affect the outcome, either enhancing or hindering goal attainment. This should not be surprising because clients have been shown to improve under the so-called attention placebo condition in which they receive attention from a therapist, such as playing games or reading stories, but receive no formal kind of psychotherapy (Sweet, 1984). (For a discussion of the therapeutic relationship, see Shirk and Saiz, 1992.)

THE FAMILY APPROACH

While various schools of psychotherapy have adapted their techniques to treating families rather than individuals, it would be more fruitful to examine those conceptualizations that have broken new ground by regarding family interaction as an entity to be studied and understood in its own right. (Our presentation follows Whiteside, 1979.) Through the discussions of anorexia nervosa and schizo-phrenia, we are already familiar with the basic premise and some of the concepts generated by the family approach. Now we need to examine both in greater detail.

The basic premise is that the family is a superordinate unit, an entity over and above the interaction of its individual members. In searching for a congenial theoretical framework, family therapists have gravitated toward viewing the family as an *open system*. It is a system because it is the product of the dynamic interaction among a set of mutually interdependent components. It is open because it interacts with other systems. Expressed concretely, family members are in continual interaction with one another and each family interacts with other families as well as with other social institutions. As an open system, the family has certain characteristics:

Wholeness: Families, like individuals, have their own defining characteristics, which cannot be derived from the personalities of its members. At times, families are characterized by psychological terms, such as *hostile, inhibited,* or *inadequate;* at other times, therapists use colloquial expressions, such as *tough* or *slippery.* Thus family therapists subscribe to the principle that the whole is greater than the sum of its parts.

Interdependence: The family is formed by highly complex interlocking relationships, so that a change in any one member will affect the remaining members. The nature of relatedness ranges from trivial to profound, from routine functions such as putting out the garbage to meeting the deepest needs for love or for respect.

Feedback: Family therapists reject linear causality, in which *A* causes change in *B,* for a circular conceptualization in which *A* both affects and is affected by *B.* Since the family is a system, this feedback may well involve multiple reverberating influences among family members.

Homeostasis: A family limits the variations in behavior which each member is allowed, thereby bringing stability to the system. When the limits are exceeded, feedback functions to bring the system back in balance. Some states of equilibrium are maintained at the cost of curtailing individuality; for example, all the family members may be required to behave as if there were never any disharmony. Other states of equilibrium can allow for both individuality and adaptation to changing circumstances.

Rules: These are the persistent and observable regularities in family relationships. Rules may govern trivial behavior such as, "Brush your teeth before bedtime," or they may define broad areas of relationships such as, "Female family members are inferior to male members." While some rules are conscious and explicit, others are implemented without awareness.

Communication: Communication, the warp and woof of the fabric of family interaction, is the means by which interactions are established and negotiated. Indeed, a family member cannot avoid communicating, since silence itself can send potent messages such as "I will not do what you want me to do" or "I do not consider myself part of this group." A communication has a given content, an expressive component, and an implied relationship. "Go upstairs to bed," spoken in an angry voice, conveys both the literal message, the anger of the speaker, and the fact that he or she is in command. The same content could be conveyed in a way that indicates meekness and uncertainty as to authority.

Change: In first-order change, variation occurs within the rules of the system. Therapists have noted that if the system requires a disturbed member in order to maintain homeostasis and if that member improves, another may become disturbed. In second-order change, the system itself is altered;

instead of using a disturbed child as an excuse for not facing its basic conflicts, the family is helped by a therapist to confront such problems. Naturally, both first- and second-order change can occur outside of therapy, and the latter can be in the direction of greater or less adaptability.

A well-functioning family system is characterized by explicit rules, clarity of communication, flexibility, openness to change, and respect for individuality. Such qualities enable the family to successfully perform its functions of socializing the child while enhancing autonomy. A malfunctioning system is characterized by covertness, manipulation, and rigid, ambiguous, or amorphous rules; individuation is sacrificed to a false image of togetherness. The child feels bewildered or imprisoned or betrayed but, in the most insidious cases, is prevented by family maneuvers from realizing what is happening. We have seen many exemplars of such faulty systems. In Minuchin's concept of *enmeshment* and *overprotection,* family members are highly involved with one another in an intrusive, overconcerned manner that robs each member of a sense of individuality (Minuchin et al., 1975). In Bateson's concept of the *double bind,* the individual is confronted with an insolvable dilemma of being condemned regardless of what he or she does, while being prevented from calling attention to the trap that has been laid. Wynne, Toohey, and Doane (1979) describe the *diffuse* and *fragmented* family structure, along with the inability of family members to maintain an appropriate *psychological distance.* Lidz (1973) delineates the *skewed* family with its dominating mother and passive father, and the *schismatic* family in which conflicted parents compete for the child's loyalties.

The systems approach redefines the nature of psychopathology. The disturbed child becomes merely the "identified patient," the symptom, as it were, that something has gone wrong. The pathology itself is in the system.

The child may be a *scapegoat*, protecting parents from facing their own unresolved problems; concern over antisocial acting out, for example, may divert parents from facing their own chronic conflicts in regard to who makes decisions in the family. Confronting parents with the fact that the entire network of familial relationships must be examined and changed may be the jolt that initiates the process of change.

Family Therapy

At the beginning of therapy families are trapped in defensive maneuvers that block growth and distort reality. Therapists initially try to cut through defenses, to facilitate openness, and to uncover sources of pain. They are especially skilled in sensitizing families to mixed, contradictory, obscure, and vague communications, often pointing to the expressive as well as to the manifest content. They help family members face conflicting needs and the self-defeating results of their defensive protection. At times they support the system in order to convey a message of understanding and trustworthiness; at times they upset the system's equilibrium so that the underlying issues may be brought to light. One such technique involves confronting parents with an alternative interpretation of the child's behavior, such as pointing out that an immature adolescent boy wants to spare the parents the pain of his growing up and becoming independent of them. While catharsis or release of pent-up emotions might well take place in the process of therapy, this is not the goal. The goal is restructuring the family system. Only then can experiences that have been avoided or denied be mastered.

While there are many kinds of family therapy, we have chosen to discuss Satir's, since she pays greater attention than most therapists to the role of the child. (See Satir, 1967. For a comprehensive presentation of family thera-

pies, see Goldenberg and Goldenberg, 1991). Satir regards self-esteem as the basic human drive and defines the mature individual as one who is in touch with his or her own feelings, can communicate clearly, and can accept the individuality of others. Separating from the family and becoming a clearly delineated self represent the key to maturity.

There are a number of ways in which self-differentiation can be blocked. If either or both of the parents have a poor self-image they will tend to view the child as a means of achieving self-esteem. Consequently the child is not viewed as an individual and is saddled with the burden of fulfilling parental needs. Any difference in the child's outlook is translated as a lack of love for the parents. Since the parents themselves may well be in conflict, the child who turns to one for help risks losing the other. (One catches glimpses of Rogers in Satir's theorizing.)

Satir, like many other family therapists, emphasizes the role of communication in enhancing or blocking development. The parent who has low self-esteem does not communicate clearly. The messages are vague or uncertain or contradictory, or there is a disjuncture between the content and the expressive component. Since the child's self is formed partially by interactions with the parent, such communications prevent the child from achieving a clearly defined self-image.

Finally, there is the matter of family rules. Ideally the rules should give children the freedom to disagree, to ask questions when they do not understand, and to acknowledge their own feelings. However, family rules may be rigid and unrealistic such as, "Only good feelings may be expressed," or "You must not feel angry or jealous of your sibling." Family rules can also be uncertain or contradictory, leaving children baffled as to where they stand and what they should do.

It follows that one goal of therapy is to help the family discover the rules regarding emo-

Therapy with a single-parent family.

tional interchange in order to ascertain which are still valid and which no longer apply. This emphasis on rules has the advantage of relieving the child of the role of "the sick one," while relieving parents of guilt over having done something "wrong." In the good sense of the word, the situation is depersonalized as all members of the family set out to understand the causes of the pain they are feeling. As the rules causing pain are exposed, the family has a chance to change them, which, in turn, enhances the family's feeling of being in control of its destiny. Families must also learn to communicate and to individuate so that each member can report completely and congruently what he or she feels and thinks, while uniqueness is valued and differentness is openly acknowledged and used for growth.

Being both an experienced professional and an outsider, the therapist is in a favored position to detect incongruent, covert, and confused messages and to articulate implicit rules.

More important, the therapist must model open communication by being warm, empathetic, and involved while sending messages that are clear, congruent, and reality-based. Thus, while the family is examining the faults in its system that produce pain, they have constantly before them a model of what communication and a mature relationship should be like.

Effectiveness

In regard to effectiveness, Hazelrigg, Cooper, and Borduin (1987) found that family therapy had positive effects when compared with no treatment and with alternative treatment controls. Follow-up studies showed that positive effects continued over time, but the effects were weaker and more variable than at the end of treatment. Recidivism as a follow-up measure showed family therapy to be more effective than alternative treatments, however.

The above findings have a number of important qualifications. To begin with, only twenty studies were found which were sufficiently sophisticated methodologically and sufficiently objective in assessment techniques to be included in the statistical analysis. Thus the sampling of family therapy in general and of specific family therapies was limited. The same is true of the kind of problem treated; most of the studies involved children with conduct disorders. Only eleven studies had alternative treatments such as group therapy or medication. Much needs to be learned about the effectiveness of family therapy relative to a variety of other treatment approaches (see Fauber and Long, 1991).

GROUP THERAPIES

Group therapies are difficult if not impossible to epitomize. They involve diverse ages (from preschoolers to adolescents), psychopathologies (the entire gamut has been treated on a group basis), special-interest groups (father-absent boys, teenage pregnant girls), techniques (structured tasks, games, discussions ranging from dreams to current happenings, fantasy play, role playing, dance, body movement, and art), goals (release of inhibitions, relief of anxiety and guilt, increased controls and coping skills, modification of the self-concept, insight), and conceptual models (psychoanalytic, nondirective, behavioral, gestalt, and transactional analysis). They are performed in a variety of settings (child guidance clinics, private practice, schools, hospitals, detention homes), with the therapist's role varying from passive observer to active director. Adequate coverage would take us far afield (see Kraft, 1979). Unlike family therapy, group therapies have a catch-as-catch-can quality resulting from the lack of an overall integrating framework. Therefore our discussion will be limited to a presentation of some of their general characteristics.

The rationale of group therapy derives from the inherently social nature of human beings that is clearly evident from infancy on. The general goal is to enable children, isolated from healthy peer contact by withdrawal or hostility, to establish growth-promoting social interactions. A number of curative factors are at work in a group setting (Yalom, 1975). One is *universality,* or the reassuring discovery that many others share the child's feelings and experiences. There are various sources of *interpersonal learning experiences,* some coming from direct interaction among the group members, others from imitation of peers and modeling of the therapist's behavior, and still others from group cohesiveness and the sense of "we-ness" that develops with time. The therapist is also a source of information concerning ways children can get along together constructively. The group experience may involve *catharsis,* or the release of pent-up feelings in an accepting and sympathetic setting, as well as providing a chance to relive and correct *distortions originating in the family;* for example, the manipulatively helpless child finds no support from the group or the therapist, the disconfirmation of expectations serving as the opening wedge to change. There is the opportunity for children to see themselves as others see them, thus gaining *perspective* and ultimately a sense of responsibility for their actions. There are positive feelings that accompany *altruistic* behavior on the child's part, as well as the *hopefulness* that comes from the knowledge that previously insoluble problems can be resolved. (For a detailed account of group therapy, see Slavson and Schiffer, 1975.)

THE COMMUNITY MENTAL HEALTH MOVEMENT

In the 1960s, community mental health was heralded as the third mental health revolution. If Pinel had unshackled the insane in 1792, thereby proclaiming their right to be treated as human beings, if Freud had shown that neurosis conformed to the same principles that accounted for normal behavior, then community mental health would prevent psychopathology through social interventions. (Our presentation follows Korchin, 1976.)

Mental health problems were viewed as intimately connected with social problems—primarily poverty, along with racism, crime, inadequate housing and education, job discrimination, and unemployment. Concern shifted from the individual to the social institution, from therapy to prevention, from clinic to community. The mental health worker's place should be in the community rather than in an office, both to make services readily accessible to populations most in need of them and to mobilize human resources within the community itself. Social action and advocacy were added to the mental health worker's functions. As if that were not enough, the movement aimed at maximizing human potential as well as ameliorating psychological suffering.

A number of factors were responsible for such a radical departure from traditional clinical thought and practice. The connection between poverty and psychopathology had been convincingly demonstrated prior to the 1960s but largely ignored. Moreover, the greater need of the poor was accompanied by an equally great inequity in the delivery of services to them. The largely middle-class clinician preferred to treat the middle-class client, while the poor tended to be shunted into custodial hospitals where they received grossly inadequate care. It was the social ferment of the 1960s—the riots, the protests, the demands of impoverished blacks for equality—which opened the eyes and seared the conscience of mental health workers. That there was both ideological and financial support at the national level assured the translation of community mental health goals into actual programs.

The second factor contributing to the momentum of the community mental health movement was a *dissatisfaction with psychotherapy,* which was viewed as both ineffectual and inefficient. Finally, the deplorable condition of *mental hospitals* at the end of World War II was the third factor underlying the shift in concern from changing individuals to changing institutions. Not only were many of these hospitals grossly understaffed, but the requirement that patients be submissive and accept a role of being inadequate and incompetent also fostered regression rather than recovery. Neither brutality nor inhumane treatment was unknown; children were beaten, deprived of clothing and toilet facilities, placed in solitary confinement, and sexually abused. Mental institutions were a major disgrace in the affluent American society, just as prisons continue to be to this day.

The shift to *prevention* took its cue from the history of medicine, which shows that no major disease has been eliminated by therapeutic measures alone, but only through preventive ones. In addition, prevention captured the spirit of the mental health movement in that it required professionals to reach out to the most needy populations and to show members of these populations how to assume responsibility for helping themselves. Along with its high-minded ideology, the outreach approach had the potentiality for solving the practical problem of understaffing. (Peterson and Roberts, 1986, contains a more detailed account of community prevention and intervention than will be given here.)

Programs to Enhance Adjustment

We will describe three preventive programs targeting three different developmental periods: preschool, middle childhood, and adolescence.

Early Intervention A number of measures have been undertaken to enhance cognitive and personality growth in the infancy-to-pre-school period. (For a comprehensive description of early intervention programs, see McGuire and Earls, 1991.) The so-called *infant stimulation programs*, primarily involving low-income mothers, have a number of goals: imparting information about normal development, instructing the mothers in ways to stimulate cognitive growth, encouraging mothers to express warmth and pride in their infants, and enhancing their feelings of competence.

At the national level, the Education for All Handicapped Children Act (PL 94-142) provides funds to assist states with the tasks of developing and implementing comprehensive, multidisciplinary interventions for all developmentally delayed infants and their families. (For a critical evaluation of this law, see Black, 1991.) Undoubtedly, the most familiar early intervention program is *Sesame Street*, which was designed to enhance a number of cognitive and social skills.

Head Start, another well-known program of early intervention, is national in scope and provides educational and social experiences for disadvantaged preschoolers. The rationale for Head Start is that positive early experiences will counter the tendency for such children subsequently to do poorly in school and to have a number of social and adjustment problems.

In regard to efficacy, there is clear evidence that Head Start produces immediate effects on intellectual performance and personal adjustment. (Our presentation is based on Haskins, 1989.) However, there is also evidence that the cognitive and personality advantages decline each year as the children proceed through public school. Thus, the program does not inoculate children against subsequent failure. The evidence concerning repeated grades and placement in special classes is contradictory, some studies finding that Head Start decreases both, others not. The meager evidence on long-term effects suggests that Head Start does not

protect children from delinquency, teen pregnancy, welfare, or unemployment, although more research is needed.

Head Start should be distinguished from a number of model or demonstration preschool programs that were well-funded and conducted by skilled researchers and capable, well-trained staff. Such programs have a more impressive record of benefits than Head Start. There is strong evidence that they reduce placement in special education classes and grade retention, and suggestive evidence that they reduce teen pregnancy, delinquency, welfare participation, and unemployment. Somewhat ironically, it was the long-term effects of a model program that convinced legislators to increase funding for Head Start.

Middle Childhood It is estimated that 10 million children attending school have conditions warranting intervention. This is about 8 to 12 percent of the child population. (Our presentation follows Knitzer, Steinberg, and Fleisch, 1991.) The dropout rate of children with behavioral and emotional disorders is almost twice that of nondisturbed children, and one study found that, by the second year, 44 percent of dropouts were involved with the courts.

While the Education for All Handicapped Children Act provides for special education and related services for seriously emotionally disturbed children, the promise of PL 94-142 has been greater than the reality of its implementation. Behavioral management is often used for the sole purpose of maintaining order in the classroom, the children receiving little help in coping with their feelings of anger or anxiety and little intellectual stimulation. Mental health personnel are rarely present to work with the children as well as the teachers. When children receive individual therapy, it is often outside of and unrelated to the school. In spite of the rhetoric concerning family involvement, strategies to ensure that families are seen as partners are limited. While there are exceptions to this generally negative picture, the potential for using the school as an agent of change for disturbed children is largely untapped (see Conoley and Conoley, 1991).

Teenage Pregnancies Of the estimated 1 million adolescent pregnancies, the majority are unintended. (Our presentation follows White and White, 1991.) Those adolescents who give birth are at high risk for mortality, toxemia, anemia, and premature labor, while the infants have a greater-than-average chance of being of low birth weight or stillborn. The vast majority of mothers choose to raise their children and face economic problems associated with terminated educational opportunities, limited employment skills, and welfare dependency. An important obstacle to articulating a national policy concerning teenage pregnancies is the fact that political and religious leaders disagree on whether the primary mission should be encouraging abstinence or promoting the use of contraceptives.

The educational goal of the Adolescent Family Life Act (AFLA) is to prevent or postpone adolescent sexuality by increasing parent-child communication and strengthening the teenager psychologically. While unsatisfactory in many respects, the data do suggest that the program increases self-esteem and confidence in dealing with peers, increases parent-child communication about sexuality, increases knowledge about sexuality, and decreases permissive attitudes. There may also be an overall decrease in sexual activity and pregnancies, but such results are by no means universal. How the programs will fare under more rigorous scrutiny is impossible to say at this point.

Social Approaches

Recall that the community mental health movement aims at changing the social context in which psychopathology is apt to develop.

This involves establishing new community resources and changing existing ones.

One community resource is the *crisis center* for individuals or families experiencing a sudden traumatic change such as the death of a parent, an eruption of violence by an alcoholic father, or a suicide attempt by an adolescent. Crisis intervention is immediately available, brief, and focused on a specific problem. It may take place in drop-in centers, on hot lines, in pastoral counseling, or with police officers trained in family intervention. Depending on how the crisis is resolved, the client may or may not be referred for more extended help. There are *halfway houses* to help adolescents who were previously institutionalized for various psychopathologies make the transition to independent community living. *Day-care centers* enabling mothers to work without depriving their children of stimulation and attention have become a permanent fixture on the social scene.

By far the most ambitious addition to community resources, however, has been the *community mental health center* (CMHC), established by the Community Mental Health Act of 1963. Mandated services include inpatient and outpatient care, partial hospitalization such as night hospitals for patients able to work during the day, twenty-four-hour emergency services, and consultation with community agencies and professional personnel. CMHCs frequently foster self-help groups consisting of individuals who are at risk for or are showing early signs of psychological difficulties, such as single parents, children of divorced parents, or parents of children with chronic illnesses.

Despite its initial lofty ideals in regard to prevention, this function of CMHCs has all but vanished with time. Federal support has declined and, in order to survive, CMHCs have had to rely increasingly on money from other sources such as insurance reimbursement, which pays only for treatment of existing disorders. (Preventive and remedial programs for child physical and sexual abuse have been discussed in Chapter 14.)

Among *institutions*, the community mental health movement has had the greatest impact on mental hospitals. In part, the decline in population there has been due to the discovery of more effective psychopharmacological agents; but it also has been due to professional and public concern over the detrimental effect many large state hospitals were having on their patients. There has been a vigorous movement protecting the rights of psychologically disturbed and mentally retarded children in regard to the decision to institutionalize them, as well as their right to humane treatment, appropriate therapy, and periodical evaluation once institutionalized. While programs to capitalize on the therapeutic potential of mental institutions have been inaugurated, they cannot be said to have had a major impact. The same is true of programs for improving the juvenile justice system. One program which has been successfully implemented has been federal and state mandated *deinstitutionalization* which returned a large number of patients to the community. Unfortunately, the community did not always have adequate facilities to absorb and care for them so that they joined the ranks of the homeless.

Another important feature of the community mental health movement is *legislation* that has countered society's tendency to insulate itself from the fate of the deviant. Notable are the Education for All Handicapped Children Act of 1975, Public Law 94-142, which prescribes free appropriate public education for children who are mentally retarded, deaf, orthopedically and visually impaired, seriously emotionally disturbed, and learning disabled; legislation in regard to the mentally retarded; and the Child Abuse and Treatment Act, Public Law 93-274, which serves as a legal deterrent to child abuse by encouraging the reporting of such abuse and requiring that the abused child receive appropriate treatment.

Recent Developments Federal support ended abruptly in 1981 when President Reagan eviscerated the community mental health legislation, forcing states to take over funding. (Our presentation follows Wylie, 1992.) By the mid-1980s, declining tax bases and increasing demands from other public agencies, such as schools and correctional departments, relegated community mental health to the back burner. In addition, substance abuse, homelessness, and mental illness confronted mental health workers with a new, more seriously disturbed population—isolated, rootless, disturbed men and women, unable to work, to establish relationships, to care for themselves and sustain even the rudiments of a normal life. In response, *community support services* (CSS) were created whose aim was to help such individuals become independent, self-sustaining members of the community. A model CSS would include residential and emergency care, halfway houses, outpatient therapy, vocation training and job placement, social and recreational programs, self-help organizations and family programs. CSS providers expect to be involved in their clients' lives for a number of years, doing everything from teaching homeless women how to cook and clean house to combatting depression over loss.

Children's Rights, Advocacy, and Political Action

The concern for *children's rights* arose from the recognition of children's helplessness when adults failed to discharge their responsibilities. In the case of child abuse, adjudication, and in some states, institutionalization, children's rights are enforced by laws. Whether more rights should have legal backing is a matter of debate. The rights of children must be weighed against those of parents and siblings, and the legal profession has traditionally been reluctant to intrude in family life except under the special conditions of divorce and custody litigation. The developmental dimension further complicates the picture, 13- to 18-year olds being able to make decisions, such as receiving therapy, which would be meaningless for a child under 6 years of age. It may be that children's rights are too complex and individualized to be codified and implemented by lawyers and judges whose training includes little or nothing of child development. (For a more extended discussion, see Hayes, 1979.)

Another response to the "child as victim" has been *advocacy*. An advocate is a person who tries to insure that programs and services based on sound developmental knowledge are available to all children. Advocates perform diverse functions. Case advocacy is concerned that the individual child is appropriately treated by an agency; for example, an advocate might hear individual grievances, investigate, and render a judgment in a state training school for delinquents. Class action litigation is undertaken on behalf of a class of children who have been deprived of their constitutional rights, such as the case of handicapped children being excluded from public school or students suspended without due process. Legislative advocacy attempts to insure that statutory provisions serve the needs of children as well as protecting their rights (Knitzer, 1976).

It is clear that the community mental health movement has placed the clinical child psychologist and other mental health professionals in the *political arena*. One cannot strive to alter public policies and institutions, change laws, and accept federal, state, and local funds while avoiding politics.

However, political activism has another root. Our actual record of achievements has for years belied our stance that we are a nation deeply concerned with the welfare of our children. In fact, the number of children living in poverty has risen steadily from 1970 to the present, with children who are members of ethnic minorities being disproportionately

represented (see Figure 17.4). (For details, see Culbertson, 1991.) Two-thirds of the 3 million children who are seriously disturbed do not receive appropriate mental health services, while poor funding, political manipulation, fragmentation, and restrictions on services, along with poor coordination, limit the scope and effectiveness of federal, state, and local programs (Roberts, Alexander, and Davis, 1991). Periodically, the nation engages in well-intentioned exercises in futility on behalf of children: experts are assembled, needs are documented, recommendations are made, and little or nothing is done. This was the fate of President Carter's Select Panel for the Promotion of Child Health in 1981 as well as the International Year of the Child in 1991 (Roberts, Alexander, and Davis, 1991; Tarnowski, and Rohrbeck [1993] review the literature on disadvantaged children).

It is argued that one reason for national apathy is that children have no political constituencies; consequently, professionals along with concerned members of the community must spearhead the adoption of political measures on their behalf. Traditionally, clinical child psychologists have not been political activists. However, since the advent of the community mental health movement they have increasingly been involved in shaping social policy and legislation on such issues as day care, family planning, child support, the special needs of the physically handicapped and mentally retarded child, as well as funding for research relevant to the mental health of children. There are also training programs for graduate students who want to specialize in social policy.

Evaluation

The community mental health movement has not fulfilled its promise of being a third revolution for a number of reasons. Funding is too closely tied to the country's political mood and

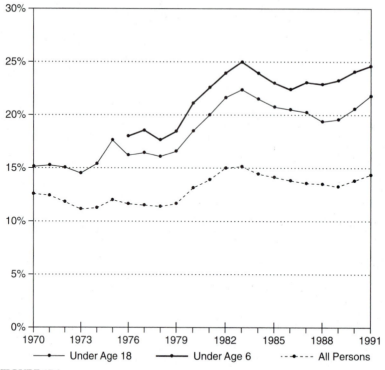

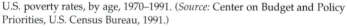

FIGURE 17.4

U.S. poverty rates, by age, 1970–1991. (*Source:* Center on Budget and Policy Priorities, U.S. Census Bureau, 1991.)

economic health; society has confronted the professional with a particularly intractable client—the drug-addicted, homeless, mentally disturbed individual—who was relatively rare when the movement began; and mental health workers too often fail to provide convincing evidence of effectiveness, partly because of the inherent difficulty in obtaining such data, partly because of lack of funds or lack of interest.

Yet, the movement has had a significant impact. Some of its institutions have become part of the social scene, such as Head Start, day care, crisis centers, hotlines, and *Sesame Street*. It forced psychologists to participate in the political scene through advocacy and involvement in legislation. Intellectually, its legacy is its emphasis on context. Psychopathology is not "in" the child but results from family in-

teractions as well as from large social forces such as poverty, joblessness, prejudice, and discrimination. The current concern with the mental health of minority children is very much in the spirit of the community mental health movement, as is any program involving reaching out to those in need of professional help. Finally, the community mental health movement shattered the myth that social ills and mental ills exist in isolation.

Psychologists' idealism and enthusiasm for involvement in social programs, which reached a fever pitch in the 1960s and 1970s, is only fitfully evident in the 1990s. Yet the lesson that psychologists can contribute to relieving the distress of social outcasts as well as learning from them, which lies at the heart of the community mental health movement, is too valuable a one to be lost.

Developmentally Based Prevention

Recall that when we first discussed developmental psychopathology (Chapter 1), we noted that the concepts of risk and developmental pathways could furnish guides for prevention. Developmentally oriented research has been sufficiently fruitful that some of those guides are now available. We will present two preventive programs, one based on the risk of an insecure attachment, the other on the developmental pathway of conduct disorder.

Insecure Attachment The STEEP program (Erickson, Korfmacher, and Egeland, 1992) was designed to offset the risk of an insecure attachment. The target population was first-time mothers at risk for parenting problems due to poverty, youth, lack of education, social isolation, and stressful life circumstances. Bimonthly home visits started when the mother was in the first trimester of pregnancy and continued until the child's first birthday.

The goal of the individual sessions was to help the mother see how her own early experiences of being inadequately cared for triggered her current feelings of sadness, loss, and anger and then to help her deal with these feelings. Thus, the sessions were a form of *insight therapy.* In addition, the facilitator (i.e., the person working with the mother) provided information about child care and helped the mother with issues regarding personal growth, education, work, and general life management. A therapeutic *relationship* was fostered by having the facilitator be consistent, predictable, and trustworthy, by identifying the strengths in the mother and her ability to help herself, and by encouraging open communication. There were also group sessions, which allowed the mothers to discuss defense mechanisms, air problems, and gain confidence from mutual support.

An evaluation when the children were 2 years old showed that the mothers provided a more appropriately stimulating and organized home environment for their child than did mothers in the control group, that they had fewer symptoms of depression and anxiety and better life management skills. Attachment security was not increased in the first year, but a trend in that direction was detected in the second year.

Conduct Disorder The Fast Track Program (Conduct Problems Prevention Research Group, 1992) is based on the developmental pathway that identifies the early signs of conduct disorder and the contribution of parents, school, and peers to its fruition (see Chapter 9). The target population was first-graders evidencing disruptive behaviors such as noncompliance, aggression, impulsivity, and immaturity. The techniques used were ones that had been tried already with some degree of success. However, the unique feature of the program was the integration of such techniques. In this way the separate components, such as dealing with parents and teachers, could be coordinated and could reinforce one another, and the chances of generalizing across settings could be maximized.

We are already familiar with two of the interventions: changing parents' ineffectual disciplinary practices and increasing the child's social skills so as to circumvent peer rejection (see Chapter 9). We will therefore concentrate on the more novel components of the program aimed at avoiding school failure. Sessions with the *family* focused on setting up a structured learning environment in the home and encouraged parental involvement in the child's learning as well as communication with the school. The importance of establishing a positive relation with the child's teacher was particularly emphasized. At *school,* teachers were trained by Fast Track staff in strategies for effective management of disruptive behaviors, such as establishing clear rules, rewarding appropriate behavior, and not rewarding, or punishing, inappropriate behavior. Teachers also implemented special classroom programs designed to strengthen the children's self-control, to build and maintain friendships, and to enhance problem-solving abilities. Finally, children who needed it were tutored, especially in reading.

Fast Track, along with recognizing the multidetermined nature of conduct disorder, is both integrated and solidly based on research. Thus it avoids the rather piecemeal, improvisational quality of many previous attempts at prevention. While studies of effectiveness are not available at present, it is a prime example of the practical application of developmental psychopathology.

GLOSSARY

Abilities tests. Tests designed to evaluate abilities directly related to academic achievement.

Achievement tests. Tests designed to assess academic achievement.

Actualizing tendency. In Carl Rogers's theory, the inherent tendency for an organism to develop all of its capacities in ways that serve to maintain and enhance it.

Adaptive behavior. The ability to cope with environmental demands, such as those for self-care, conventional social interactions, and independent functioning in the community, at an age-appropriate level.

Adjustment disorder. Deviant behavior that is a reaction to a specific event or events, such as parental death or divorce.

Advocacy. See *Child advocacy.*

Aggression. Behavior for which the goal is physical or psychological injury or destruction; anger or hatred may be the accompanying affect.

Anaclitic depression. The infant's reaction of despair following the loss of a loved and needed caretaker.

Anal stage. In Freud's psychosexual theory, the second stage of development, in which pleasure is derived from retaining and evacuating feces and the toddler confronts the issue of autonomy versus compliance.

Anorexia nervosa. An intense fear of gaining weight along with an undue influence of body weight on self-evaluation and a body weight of less than 85 percent of that expected. *Restricters* rely on dieting; *bulimics* alternate between binge eating and dieting and rely on vomiting and purging.

Anoxia. Deprivation of oxygen during or immediately following birth; may cause damage to or destroy brain cells.

Anxiety. As used here, anxiety refers to the anticipation of a painful experience.

Anxiety disorders. A group of disorders characterized by intense, chronic anxiety. Formerly called *psychoneurotic disorders.*

Asynchrony. Disjointed or markedly uneven rates of progression among developmental variables.

Attachment. The bond of love that develops between infant and caretaker.

Attention-deficit hyperactivity disorder. Developmentally inappropriate inattention accompanied by motor restlessness and impulsivity.

Attribution theory. A theory dealing with the inferences individuals make concerning the causes of behavior.

Authoritarian discipline. Discipline requiring strict, unquestioning obedience.

Authoritative discipline. Discipline requiring compliance with standards for mature behavior, accompanied by love, communication, and respect for the child.

Autism. A severe disorder of the infancy and toddler period marked by extreme aloneness, a pathological need for sameness, and mutism or noncommunicative speech.

Avoidance learning. A form of learning in which an organism, having experienced an aversive stimulus, behaves so as to prevent future encounters with that stimulus.

Baseline. In behavioral assessment, the frequency of the natural occurrence of behavior targeted for change by behavioral techniques.

Behavior therapies. A group of therapies characterized by attention to specific, current behaviors, objective measurement, and reliance on principles of behavior change derived from the laboratory.

Behavioral assessment. Procedures designed to locate specific behaviors—along with their antecedents and consequences—that subsequently can serve as targets for modification through behavioral techniques.

Behaviorism. A theory inaugurated by John B. Watson according to which the study of overt behavior is the sole basis for a scientific psychology.

Brain syndrome (or organic brain syndrome). A group of disorders caused by impairment of brain tissue, particularly the cerebral cortex. They may be characterized by impairment of cognitive functions, lability of affect, and personality disturbances.

Bulimia nervosa. Recurring episodes of binge eating accompanied by a fear of being unable to control such eating, followed by purging, dieting, exercise, or fasting.

Castration anxiety. In Freud's psychosexual theory, the universal fear among preschool boys in the oedipal stage that the rivalrous father will emasculate them for wanting to possess the mother.

Central nervous system (CNS). The part of the nervous system that includes the spinal cord and the brain.

Chaining. See *Shaping*.

Child abuse. See *Maltreatment*.

Child advocacy. The attempt to insure that programs and services based on sound developmental knowledge are available to all children.

Childhood schizophrenia. A psychosis appearing in middle childhood characterized by marked withdrawal, bizarre thinking and behavior, loss of reality contact, and inappropriate affect. Also called schizophreniform psychotic disorder.

Client-centered therapy. See *Nondirective therapy*.

Coalition. Salvador Minuchin's term for a family pattern in which a child sides with one parent against the other.

Coercion theory. A pattern of parent-child interaction in which a series of attacks and counterattacks are negatively reinforced by cessation, thus increasing the likelihood of their reoccurrence.

Cognitive behavior therapy. Behavior therapy aimed at changing cognitions so as to make behavior more adaptive.

Cognitive restructuring. A behavioral technique aimed at substituting adaptive for maladaptive cognitions through a logical analysis of the latter and the assignment of specific tasks putting the new understanding into practice.

Community mental health movement. The effort to eliminate the social conditions responsible for the production and perpetuation of mental health problems.

Comorbidity. The co-occurrence of two or more psychopathologies.

Compulsion. An irrational act that an individual is compelled to do.

Conditions of worth. Carl Rogers's term for conditions set by parents under which they will grant their love and respect for the child.

Conduct disorders. Behaviors in which children act out their feelings or impulses toward others in an antisocial or destructive fashion. Also called *undersocialized, aggressive type*.

Corrective emotional experience. In psychoanalytic therapy, the discovery that expression of anxiety-laden feelings does not lead to punishment or rejection.

Critical period. The assumption that early experiences have disproportionately potent influence on later development.

Defense mechanisms. Stratagems for reducing anxiety. (See also *Repression, Reaction formation, Projection,* and *Displacement*.)

Delinquency. A legal term for offenses that are criminal if committed by an adult.

Delusion. A firmly held, irrational belief that runs counter to reality and to the individual's culture or subculture.

Depression. In its psychopathological form, depression is marked by a depressed mood, loss of self-esteem, intense self-deprecation, and guilt. Eating and sleeping disturbances as well as agitation may also occur.

Deprivation. See *Privation.*

Detachment. The final phase of an infant's reaction to the loss of a loved caretaker when socially acceptable but superficial contact is established when the caretaker returns. Also called *restitution.*

Detouring. Salvador Minuchin's term for parents' avoidance of their own conflicts by regarding their child as their sole problem.

Developmental crises. Crises inherent in normal development.

Developmental pathway. Determining the risk and protective factors responsible for diverting development from its normal course, maintaining it, and returning it to its normal course.

Developmental psychopathology. Viewing each psychopathology within the context of antecedents and consequent events and relating it to normal development.

Diathesis-stress hypothesis. The hypothesis that abnormal behavior results from a genetic predisposition combined with environmental stress.

Displacement. A mechanism of defense in which an impulse is directed toward a target that is safer than the original one.

Double bind. A communication pattern that traps the recipient between two negative and inescapable injunctions. There is also a prohibition against drawing attention to the bind itself.

Down syndrome. A form of mental retardation caused by a chromosomal abnormality and accompanied by distinctive physical features. (Once called mongolism.)

Drug abuse. A pattern of pathological use of a chemical substance causing significant impairment of functioning or distress.

DSM. The *Diagnostic and Statistical Manual,* published by the American Psychiatric Association, providing diagnostic criteria for mental disorders. The latest edition is DSM-IV.

Ecology. The study of children in their natural environment.

Ego. In Freud's structural theory, the psychic component responsible for learning the nature of reality in order to gratify the id's demands for maximal pleasure, on the one hand, and avoid the painful censure of the superego, on the other hand.

Egocentrism. In Jean Piaget's theory, the tendency to view the physical and social world exclusively from one's own point of view.

Ego ideal. In Freudian theory, the individual's idealized self-image.

Electroencephalogram (EEG). An instrument used to record electrical activity in the brain by means of electrodes attached to the scalp.

Emotional maltreatment. Adult behavior that is psychologically harmful to the child to a significant degree and thwarts healthy psychological development.

Enmeshment. Salvador Minuchin's term for excessive involvement by individual members of a family with one another so that there is no strong sense of individuality.

Enuresis. Involuntary urination during the day or night in children 5 years of age or older.

Ethnic socialization. The process of acquiring the behaviors, perceptions, values, and attitudes of an ethnic group and seeing the self and others as members of such groups.

Externalization. See *Internalization-externalization.*

Extinction. The gradual disappearance of a learned behavior through the removal of reinforcements.

Fading. In behavior therapy, the gradual removal of reinforcements so that the desired behavior may become autonomous.

Family therapies. A group of specific techniques based on the assumption that it is necessary to treat the entire family to correct the faulty pattern responsible for producing a disturbance in single members.

Fixation. The persistence of normal behavior beyond the point where it is developmentally appropriate. This arrest of development may be psychopathological, depending on the degree or intensity.

Fragmentation. A thought disorder in which tangentially related or unrelated ideas disrupt the chain of thought.

Free association. The basic psychoanalytic technique for uncovering unconscious material by encouraging the patient to say whatever comes to mind.

Functional disorder. A designation given to disturbances that are primarily psychological rather than primarily organic in origin.

GAP report. A diagnostic classification system devised especially for children by the Group for the Advancement of Psychiatry.

Gender identity. Self-classification as male or female.

Generalized anxiety disorder. See *Overanxious disorder of childhood.*

Group therapies. Therapeutic techniques in which individuals work together to solve their problems through social interaction guided by a trained leader.

Guilt. The painful affect accompanying judgment of oneself as bad.

Hallucination. A sensory perception occurring in the absence of any appropriate external stimulus.

Homosexuality. A preferential erotic attraction to members of the same sex.

Hyperactivity (or **hyperkinetic syndrome**). See *Attention-deficit hyperactivity disorder.*

Id. In Freud's structural theory, the biologically based pleasure-seeking source of all psychic energy.

Identity. In Erik Erikson's theory, the search for inner continuity and interpersonal mutuality that begins in adolescence and is evidenced by a vocational choice.

Imitation (modeling). Learning by observing the behavior of others (models).

Induction discipline. Discipline based on reasoning and appeals to the child's pride and concern for others.

Information processing. The step-by-step conversion of sensory input into knowledge by means of operations such as attention, memory, organization, and retrieval.

Initiative. Self-reliant expansiveness.

Insecure attachment. There are three types: *resistant attachment* is marked by an ambivalent mixture of demands for and rejection of attention; in *avoidant attachment*, the child ignores the mother while *disorganized-disoriented attachment* is marked by contradictory responses to the mother

such as approaching her with depressed or flat affect.

Intelligence quotient (IQ). A measurement of intelligence derived from the relation between the child's mental age and chronological age.

Intelligence tests. Standardized techniques for measuring intellectual functioning.

Internalization. The process by which behavior that was once dependent on environmental factors for its maintenance comes to be maintained by intraindividual factors.

Internalization-externalization. A classification of psychopathologies based on whether the child suffers (internalization) or the environment suffers (externalization).

Interpretation. In psychoanalytic theory, interpretation consists of the therapist pointing out the meaning of material the patient is not aware of.

Lateralization hypothesis. The hypothesis that the cerebrum undergoes progressive left-hemisphere specialization as language develops.

Learned helplessness. Nonresponsiveness to a noxious stimulus that has occurred independently of the organism's efforts to avoid it.

Learning disabilities. Learning problems due to a disorder in one or more of the basic psychological processes involved in understanding or in using spoken or written language and not due to mental retardation, emotional disturbance, environmental disadvantage, or specific perceptual or motor handicaps.

Lesbianism. Female homosexuality.

Libido. Freud's term for the biologically based drive to obtain erotic bodily sensations; also equated with sexual drive.

Mainstreaming. The term given to placing retarded children in regular classes.

Maltreatment. A general category embracing neglect and physical, sexual, and emotional abuse.

Marasmus. René Spitz's term for infants who waste away and sometimes die due to a lack of adequate mothering.

Masked depression. Underlying depression in children in middle childhood which is masked by a wide variety of deviant but nondepressive behaviors.

Medical model. A model of psychopathology emphasizing the role of organic dysfunction in the etiology of psychopathologies as well as classification and interpretation of psychopathological behaviors in terms of diagnostic entities.

Mental retardation. Significantly subaverage general intelligence and deficits in adaptive behavior, manifested during the developmental period.

Milieu therapy. A mode of treatment in which the daily environment is ordered so as to be therapeutic.

Minimal brain damage (or minimal brain dysfunction). Term applied to children of average or above-average intelligence in whom deviations of function of the central nervous system are manifested by hyperactivity; perceptual-motor impairment; emotional lability; coordination deficits; disorders of attention, memory, thinking, and speech; and specific learning disabilities.

Modeling. See *Imitation*.

Multiaxial classification. A diagnostic system whereby individuals are assessed in terms of a number of dimensions rather than in terms of a single classification.

Multiculturalism. The comparative study of ethnic minority groups.

Multideterminism. A perspective that regards psychopathology as the result of the interaction among multiple factors rather than the result of a single cause.

Mutism. Refusal to speak despite an ability to do so.

Narcissistic disorders. Within psychoanalytic theory, disorders resulting from an inability to form true object relations owing to faulty early parenting.

Negative reinforcement. Increasing the probability that behavior will occur by removing unpleasant or aversive consequences.

Negativism. A heightened state of opposition to adults which flourishes in the toddler and early preschool period.

Neglect. Acts of omission on the part of caretakers which endanger the child's health or safety.

Nondirective therapy. Carl Rogers's therapeutic procedure that utilizes warmth, acceptance, and reflection of the client's ideas and feelings to remove the obstacles to self-actualization. Also called client-centered therapy.

Object concept. In Jean Piaget's cognitive theory, the infant's separation of the self from the physical world and the realization that objects have independent existence.

Object relation. In Freudian theory, the term used for an emotional attachment to another person.

Obsession. An irrational thought, the repeated occurrence of which is beyond the individual's conscious control.

Oedipus complex. In Freud's psychosexual theory, the universal desire of the preschool boy to take possession of the mother and eliminate the rivalrous father.

Omnipotent thinking. Belief that one can control events that, in reality, lie beyond one's power.

Operant conditioning (instrumental conditioning). A form of conditioning in which the persistence of a response depends on its effects on the environment.

Oppositional-defiant disorder. Purposeful defiance of adults' requests resulting in violation of minor rules. (See *Negativism*.)

Oral stage. In Freud's psychosexual theory, the first stage of development, in which pleasure is derived from sucking and biting and attachment to the caretaker is formed.

Organismic valuing process. In Carl Rogers's theory, the innate tendency for an organism to value experiences so as to optimize its development.

Overanxious disorder of childhood. Excessive anxiety or worry out of proportion to the likelihood or impact of the feared event.

Overinclusiveness. A thought disorder in which ideas flit from one tangential association to another.

Overprotection. Excessive and unrealistic concern over another's welfare.

Parent training programs. Behavioral techniques designed to teach parents positive, effective ways of dealing with their children's disturbed behavior.

Pediatric psychology. The study of the role of psychological factors in the origins, treatment, and prevention of physical disorders and the effects of such disorders on future development. Also called *behavioral medicine*, *behavioral pediatrics*, and *health psychology*.

Pedophilia. A state of being sexually aroused by children.

Permissive discipline. Indulgent or neglectful discipline.

Perseveration. A thought disorder in which the individual dwells on a single idea.

Personality disorders. Deeply ingrained, maladaptive behaviors that, while more pervasive than the anxiety disorders, still do not significantly diminish the individual's reality contact.

Personality inventories. Personality assessment techniques in which a series of statements is judged as characteristic or not characteristic of the individual.

Perspective taking. The cognitive ability to see the physical environment and social situations from the point of view of another person or persons.

Phallic stage. In Freud's psychosexual theory, the third stage of development, in which the preschooler is expansive and assertive and derives pleasure from stimulating the genitals.

Phobia. An intense, persistent, irrational fear of an animate or inanimate object or of a situation.

Physical abuse. Nonaccidental physical injury resulting from acts on the part of the child's caretakers.

Play therapy. Using play to encourage the child to express important ideas, conflicts, and feelings symbolically rather than through direct verbal communication. The procedure depends on the kind of psychotherapy being used, such as psychoanalytic or nondirective.

Positive reinforcement. Use of rewards to increase the probability that behavior will occur.

Posttraumatic stress disorder. A disorder resulting from experiencing an event involving actual or threatened death or injury to the self or others.

Precausal thinking. In Jean Piaget's theory, the tendency to view the physical world in animistic terms, as having life and purpose, for example.

Prevention. The emphasis in the community mental health movement on forestalling the development of mental health problems rather than on treating them after they have appeared.

Primary-process thinking. In Freudian theory, unrealistic thinking based on immediate need gratification rather than on reality.

Privation. A lack of growth-promoting stimulation from the social and physical environment. Privation refers to infants who never had such stimulation; *deprivation* implies that such stimulation was available but was withdrawn.

Projection. A mechanism of defense in which anxiety-provoking impulses are denied in oneself and attributed to others.

Projective techniques. Personality assessment methods using ambiguous or unstructured stimuli. The most popular are the Rorschach, consisting of a series of ink blots; the Thematic Apperception Test (TAT), consisting of a series of ambiguous pictures; and human figure drawing.

Prompting. In operant conditioning, the use of instructions, modeling, or guidance to elicit a desired response.

Protective factors. Factors that promote healthy development and counteract the negative effects of risks.

Pseudo-mutuality. L. C. Wynne's term for a facade of harmony used by families to cover pervasive feelings of futility.

Psychoactive drugs. Drugs that affect the central nervous system so as to alter subjective states of feeling.

Psychoanalysis. A psychotherapeutic technique relying upon free association, dream interpretation, play, and the analysis of resistance and transference to provide insights into the unconscious roots of disturbed behavior.

Psychodynamic theory. The Freudian and neo-Freudian theories that aim to understand the basic motivations of human behavior. Both emotions and unconscious motivations play a major role.

Psychoneurotic disorders. See *Anxiety disorders.*

Psychopathology. Abnormal behavior that may have psychological and/or biological causes.

Psychosexual theory. Freud's developmental theory in which each stage—the oral, anal, and phallic—is marked by a change in the source of erotic bodily sensations and a distinct personality development.

Psychosis. A disorder so severe and pervasive as to interfere with the individual's capacity to meet the ordinary demands of life.

Punishment. Presentation of an aversive stimulus which decreases the probability that the response leading to it will occur.

Rational emotive therapy. Albert Ellis's cognitive restructuring therapy in which the client is helped to identify and correct irrational ideas responsible for disturbed behavior.

Reaction formation. A mechanism of defense in which a child's thoughts and feelings are diametrically opposed to an anxiety-provoking impulse.

Reading disability. Failure to learn to read or to make appropriate progress despite normal intelligence and adequate instruction.

Reciprocal inhibition. The inhibition of the weaker of two incompatible responses by the stronger one. Utilized in systematic desensitization.

Regression. The return of behaviors that once were developmentally appropriate but no longer are. Whether or not the behaviors are psychopathological depends on the degree or intensity of regression.

Reinforcer. Any stimulus that increases the probability of a response.

Reliability. The consistency with which an assessment instrument performs.

Repression. The basic mechanism of defense in which anxiety-provoking impulses and ideas are banished from consciousness.

Resistance. In psychoanalytic therapy, devices used by patients to avoid bringing painful material to consciousness.

Restitution. See *Detachment.*

Rigidity. Excessive and unrealistic resistance to change.

Risks. Factors that increase the probability that development will be diverted from its normal path, resulting either in clinically significant problem behavior or psychopathology.

Rorschach. See *Projective techniques.*

Schismatic family. Theodore Lidz's term for families which are characterized by overt conflict between parents, mutual depreciation, and competition for the child's loyalty.

Schizophrenia. A severe, pervasive disorder consisting of delusions, hallucinations, disorganized speech, inappropriate affect, disorganized or bizarre behavior, and the negative symptoms of flat affect, avolition, alogia, and anhedonia.

School phobia. An irrational dread of school. Also called *school refusal.*

Self-actualization. See *Actualizing tendency.*

Self-control. The ability of the child to behave in a socially acceptable rather than a socially unacceptable manner when the two are in conflict.

Self-instruction. A behavioral therapy designed to increase self-control by teaching impulsive children how to guide their behavior by first talking out loud and then to themselves.

Self-psychology. Within psychoanalytic theory, the belief that the self has a more central role in development than that provided for by the classical theory.

Separation anxiety. The anxiety engendered by the caretaker's departure after an attachment has been formed in infancy.

Separation anxiety disorder. Excessive anxiety concerning separation from those to whom the child is attached.

Sex role. Culturally approved behaviors and attitudes for males and females.

Sexual abuse. Sexual activities between a child under 17 years of age and an individual at least 5 years his or her senior.

Shaping. An operant-conditioning technique in which responses that successively approximate the desired one are reinforced.

Situational crises. Crises that, while not inherent in normal development, are frequently encountered and are typically weathered.

Skewed family. Theodore Lidz's term for families in which the mother is dominating and overprotective and the father is weak and passive.

Social problem solving. The application of the information processing model specifically to coping with social situations.

Social skills training. A behavioral therapy applying techniques such as modeling, reinforcement, coaching, and interpersonal problem solving to the substitution of adaptive for maladaptive social behavior.

Soft neurological signs. A group of behavioral criteria from which, in the absence of demonstrable impairment, minimal CNS dysfunction is inferred.

Stage theories. Theories that assume that development proceeds by qualitatively distinct reorganizations of behavior and that the sequence of such reorganizations is invariant.

Status offense. Behavior regarded as illegal in children but not in adults, such as drinking alcoholic beverages.

Stimulus generalization. The tendency of an organism, conditioned to a particular stimulus, subsequently to respond to similar stimuli.

Substance abuse. See *Drug abuse.*

Superego. The moral component, or conscience,

in Freud's structural theory. Initially, it is perfectionistic, requiring absolute obedience and punishing transgressions with guilt feelings.

Symptom. A psychological, behavioral, or biological manifestation of a psychopathology.

Syndrome. A group of behaviors or symptoms which tend to occur together in a particular disorder.

Systematic desensitization. A behavior therapy for extinguishing anxiety by pairing a graded series of anxiety stimuli with the incompatible response of relaxation.

Thematic Apperception Test (TAT). See *Projective techniques*.

Theories of mind. A child's understanding of the content and function of mental life, such as perception, memory, and dreams.

Therapeutic alliance. In psychoanalytic therapy, the positive bond between patient and therapist.

Time out. In behavior therapy, isolating the child for brief periods in order to extinguish undesirable behaviors.

Token economy. A behavioral therapy in which socially desirable behavior is rewarded by tokens that can subsequently be exchanged for rewards of the client's choosing.

Transference. In psychoanalytic therapy, the projection onto the therapist of intense feelings once directed toward significant figures, typically the parents.

Transsexualism. Gender identity with the opposite sex.

Transvestism. Obtaining sexual gratification by dressing in the clothes of the opposite sex.

Triangulation. Salvador Minuchin's term for a family pattern in which the child is forced to side with one parent against the other.

Unconditional positive regard. In Carl Rogers's theory, the parents' intrinsic valuing and acceptance of the child.

Unconscious. In Freudian theory, the region of the mind that contains material that has been repressed or has never been conscious.

Validity. The degree to which an instrument evaluates what it intends to evaluate.

Vulnerability. Factors that intensify the effects of risks.

Work. The ability to do what is required to be done; task orientation.

Working through. In psychoanalytic theory, the process by which the patient gains insight into the many ways in which a single conflict is expressed.

REFERENCES

Abikoff, H. 1991. Cognitive training in ADHD children: Less than meets the eye. *Journal of Learning Disabilities* **24,** 205–219.

Aboud, F. E. 1987. The development of ethnic self-identification and attitudes. In J. S. Phinney and M. J. Rotheram (eds.), *Children's ethnic socialization: Pluralism and development,* pp. 32–55. Newbury Park, Calif.: Sage.

Abramowitz, R. 1976. Parenthood in America. *Journal of Clinical Child Psychology* **5,** 43–46.

Abramson, L. Y., and Sackeim, H. A. 1977. A paradox in depression: Uncontrollability and self-blame. *Psychological Bulletin* **84,** 838–851.

Abramson, L. Y., Seligman, M. E. P., and Teasdale, J. D. 1978. Learned helplessness in humans: Critique and reformulation. *Journal of Abnormal Psychology* **87,** 49–74.

Achenbach, T. M. 1966. The classification of children's psychiatric symptoms: A factor-analytic study. *Psychological Monographs* **80** (7, whole no. 609).

Achenbach, T. M. 1978. Psychopathology of childhood: Research problems and issues. *Journal of Consulting and Clinical Psychology* **46,** 759–776.

Achenbach, T. M. 1979. The child behavior profile: An empirically-based system for assessing children's behavior problems and competencies. *International Journal of Mental Health* **7,** 24–42.

Achenbach, T. M. 1980. DSM-III in light of empirical research in the classification of child psychopathology. *Journal of the American Academy of Child Psychiatry* **19,** 395–412.

Achenbach, T. M. 1982. *Developmental psychopathology,* 2d ed. New York: Ronald.

Achenbach, T. M. 1988. Integrating assessment and taxonomy. In M. Rutter, A. H. Tuman, and I. S. Lann (eds.), *Assessment and diagnosis in child psychopathology,* pp. 300–343. New York: Guilford.

Achenbach, T. M. 1991. The derivation of taxonomic constructs: A necessary stage in the development of developmental psychopathology. In D. Cicchetti and S. L. Toth (eds.), *Models and integrations. Rochester symposium on developmental psychopathology,* vol. 3, pp. 43–74. Rochester, N.Y.: University of Rochester Press.

Achenbach, T. M., Conners, C. K., Quay, H. C., Verhults, F. C., and Howell, C. T. 1989. Replication of empirically derived syndromes as a basis for a taxonomy of child/adolescent psychopathology. *Journal of Abnormal Child Psychology* **17,** 299–323.

Achenbach, T. M., and Edelbrock, C. S. 1978. The classification of child psychopathology: A review and analysis of empirical efforts. *Psychological Bulletin* **85,** 1275–1301.

Achenbach, T. M., and Edelbrock, C. S. 1981. Behavioral problems and competencies reported by parents of normal and disturbed children aged four through sixteen. *Monographs of the Society for Research in Child Development* **1** (46, series no. 188).

Achenbach, T. M., and McConaughy, S. H. 1987. *Empirically based assessment of child and adolescent psychopathology. Practical applications.* Newbury Park, Calif.: Sage.

Achenbach, T. M., McConaughy, S. H., and Howell, C. T. 1987. Child/adolescent behavioral and emotional problems: Implications of cross-informant correlations for situational specificity. *Psychological Bulletin* **101**, 213–232.

Adolinks. 1987. Risk factors for suicide attempts. **4**, No. 2.

Adrien, J. L., Faure, M., Perrot, A., Hameury, L., Garreau, B., Barthelemy, C., and Sauvage, D. 1991. Autism and family home movies: Preliminary findings. *Journal of Autism and Developmental Disorders* **21**, 43–50.

Ainsworth, M. D. S. 1969. Object relations, dependency and attachment. A theoretical review of the mother infant-relationship. *Child Development* **40**, 969–1025.

Ainsworth, M. D. S. 1973. The development of the infant-mother attachment. In B. M. Caldwell and H. N. Ricciuti (eds.), *Review of child development research,* vol. 3. Chicago: University of Chicago Press.

Ainsworth, M. D. S. 1991. Attachment and other affectional bonds across the life cycle. In C. M. Parkes, J. Stevenson-Hinde, and P. Marris (eds.), *Attachment across the life cycle,* pp. 33–51. London: Routledge.

Ainsworth, M. D. S., and Bell, S. M. 1969. Some contemporary patterns of mother-infant interaction in the feeding situation. In A. Ambrose (ed.), *Stimulation in early infancy,* pp. 133–162. New York: Academic Press.

Alarcon, R. D. 1983. A Latin American perspective on DSM-III. *American Journal of Psychiatry* **140**, 102–104.

Alessandri, S. M. 1991. Play and social behavior in maltreated preschoolers. *Development and Psychopathology* **3**, 191–205.

Alva, S. A. 1991. Academic invulnerability among Mexican-American students: The importance of protective resources and appraisals. *Hispanic Journal of Behavioral Sciences* **13**, 18–24.

Aman, M. G., and Singh, N. N. 1991. Pharmacolog-

ical intervention. In J. L. Matson and J. A. Mulick (eds.), *Handbook of mental retardation,* pp. 347–372. New York: Pergamon.

Amato, P. R., and Keith, B. 1991. Parental divorce and the well-being of children: A meta-analysis. *Psychological Bulletin* **110**, 26–46.

American Association of Mental Retardation (AAMR). 1992. *Mental retardation: Definition, classification, and systems of supports.* 9th ed. Washington, D.C.

American Psychiatric Association (APA). 1980. *Diagnostic and statistical manual of mental disorders.* 3d ed. Washington, D.C.

American Psychiatric Association (APA). 1987. *Diagnostic and statistical manual of mental disorders.* 3d ed., revised. Washington, D.C.

American Psychiatric Association (APA). 1991. *DSM-IV options book: Work in progress.* Washington, D.C.

American Psychiatric Association (APA). 1993. *DSM-IV Draft Criteria (3/1/1993).* Washington, D.C.

American Psychological Association. 1979. *Revised ethical standards of psychologists.* Washington, D.C.

Ammerman, R. T. 1990. Predisposing child factors. In R. T. Ammerman and M. Hersen (eds.), *Children at risk. An evaluation of factors contributing to child abuse and neglect,* pp. 119–224. New York: Plenum.

Ammerman, R. T., and Hersen, M. 1990. Research on child abuse and neglect: Current status and an agenda for the future. In R. T. Ammerman and M. Hersen (eds.), *Children at risk. An evaluation of factors contributing to child abuse and neglect,* pp. 3–21. New York: Plenum.

Anastopoulos, A., and Barkley, R. A. 1990. Counseling and training parents. In R. A. Barkley (ed.), *Attention-deficit hyperactive disorder: A handbook for diagnosis and treatment,* pp. 397–413. New York: Guilford.

Anastopoulos, A. D., DuPaul, C. J., and Barkley, R. A. 1991. Stimulant medication and parent training therapies of Attention Deficit-Hyperactive Disorder. *Journal of Learning Disabilities* **24**, 210–218.

Anderson, K. E., Lytton, H., and Romney, D. M. 1986. Mothers' interactions with normal and conduct-disordered boys. Who is affecting whom? *Developmental Psychology* **22**, 604–609.

Andrews, J. A., and Lewinsohn, P. M. 1992. Suicidal

attempts among older adolescents: Prevalence and co-occurrence with psychiatric disorders. *Journal of the American Academy of Child and Adolescent Psychiatry* **31,** 655–662.

Angold, A., and Rutter, M. 1992. Effects of age and pubertal status on depression in a large clinical sample. *Development and Psychopathology* **4,** 5–28.

Anthony, E. J. 1987. Children at risk for psychosis growing up successfully. In E. J. Anthony and B. J. Cohler (eds.), *The invulnerable child,* pp. 147–184. New York: Guilford.

Appleton, T., Clifton, R., and Goldberg, S. 1975. The development of behavioral competence in infancy. In F. D. Horowitz (ed.), *Review of child development research,* vol. 4. Chicago: University of Chicago Press.

Araji, S., and Finkelhor, D. 1986. Abusers: A review of the research. In D. Finkelhor (ed.), *A sourcebook of child sexual abuse,* pp. 89–118. Beverly Hills: Sage.

Argueta-Bernal, G. A. 1990. Stress and stress-related disorders in Hispanics: Biobehavioral approaches to treatment. In F. C. Serafica, A. I. Schwebel, R. K. Russell, P. D. Isaac, and L. B. Myers (eds.), *Mental health of ethnic minorities,* pp. 202–221. New York: Praeger.

Asarnow, J. R. 1988. Children at risk for schizophrenia: Converging lines of evidence. *Schizophrenia Bulletin* **14,** 613–628.

Asarnow, J. R., Asarnow, R. F., Hornstein, N., and Russell, A. 1991. Childhood-onset schizophrenia: Developmental perspectives on schizophrenic disorders. In E. F. Walker (ed.), *Schizophrenia: A life-course developmental perspective,* pp. 95–121. San Diego: Academic Press.

Asarnow, J. R., Goldstein, M. J., and Ben-Meir, S. 1988. Parental communication deviance in childhood onset schizophrenic spectrum and depressive disorders. *Journal of Child Psychology and Psychiatry* **29,** 825–838.

Asarnow, J. R., Lewis, J. M., Doane, J. A., Goldstein, M. J., and Rodnick, R. 1982. Family interaction and the course of adolescent psychopathology: An analysis of adolescent and parent effects. *Journal of Abnormal Child Psychology* **10,** 424–442.

Atkinson, D. R., Morten, G., and Sue, D. W. (eds.). 1983. *Counseling American minorities: A cross-cultural perspective,* 2d ed. Dubuque, Iowa: William C. Brown.

Attie, I., and Brooks-Gunn, J. 1989. Development of eating problems in adolescent girls. A longitudinal study. *Developmental Psychology* **25,** 70–79.

Attie, I., Brooks-Gunn, J., and Petersen, A. C. 1990. A developmental perspective on eating disorders and eating problems. In M. Lewis and S. M. Miller (eds.), *Handbook of developmental psychopathology,* pp. 409–420. New York: Plenum.

Attwood, A., Frith, U., and Hermelin, B. 1988. The understanding and use of interpersonal gestures by Down's syndrome children. *Journal of Autism and Developmental Disabilities* **18,** 241–257.

Axeline, V. 1964. *Dibbs in search of self.* New York: Ballantine.

Axeline, V. 1969. *Play therapy.* New York: Ballantine.

Bakwin, H. 1972. Depression: A mood disorder in children and adolescents. *Maryland State Medical Journal* **23,** 55–61.

Bakwin, H., and Bakwin, R. M. 1972. *Behavior disorders in children,* 4th ed. Philadelphia: Saunders.

Baltaxe, C. A. M., and Simmons, J. Q. III. 1985. Prosodic development in normal and autistic children. In E. Schopler and G. B. Mesibov (eds.), *Communication problems in autism,* pp. 95–125. New York: Plenum.

Bandura, A. 1968. A social learning interpretation of psychological dysfunctions. In P. London and D. Rosenhan (eds.), *Foundation of abnormal psychology.* New York: Holt, Rinehart & Winston.

Bandura, A. 1969. *Principles of behavior modification.* New York: Holt, Rinehart & Winston.

Bandura, A. 1977. *Social learning theory.* Englewood Cliffs, N.J.: Prentice-Hall.

Bandura, A. 1985. A model of causality in social learning theory. In M. Mahoney and A. Freedman (eds.), *Cognition and therapy.* New York: Plenum.

Bandura, A. 1986. *Social foundations of thought and action: A social cognitive theory.* Englewood Cliffs, N.J.: Prentice-Hall.

Bandura, A., and Walters, R. H. 1963. *Social learning and personality development.* New York: Holt, Rinehart & Winston.

Barbarin, O. A. 1990. Adjustment to serious childhood illness. In B. B. Lahey and A. E. Kazdin (eds.), *Advances in clinical child psychology,* vol. 13, pp. 377–401. New York: Plenum.

Barkley, R. A. (1981) Hyperactivity. In E. Mash and L. Terdal (eds.), *Behavioral Assessment of Childhood Disorders.* New York: Guilford.

Barkley, R. A. 1982. Guidelines for defining hyperactivity in children: Attention deficit disorder with hyperactivity. In B. B. Lahey and A. E. Kazdin (eds.), *Advances in clinical child psychology*, vol. 5, pp. 137–180. New York: Plenum.

Barkley, R. A. 1988. Child behavior scales and checklists. In M. Rutter, A. H. Tuma, and I. S. Lann (eds.), *Assessment and diagnosis in child psychopathology*, pp. 113–155. New York: Guilford.

Barkley, R. A. 1990. *Attention-deficit hyperactivity disorder: A handbook for diagnosis and treatment.* New York: Guilford.

Barkley, R. A. 1991. The ecological validity of laboratory and analogue assessment methods of ADHD. *Journal of Abnormal Child Psychology* **19**, 149–178.

Barkley, R. A., Anastopoulos, A. D., Guevremont, D. C., and Fletcher, K. E. 1992. Adolescents with Attention Deficit Hyperactivity Disorder: Mother-adolescent interactions, family beliefs and conflicts, and maternal psychopathology. *Journal of Abnormal Child Psychology* **20**, 263–286.

Barkley, R. A., Fischer, M., Edelbrock, C., and Smallish, L. 1991. The adolescent outcome of hyperactive children diagnosed by research criteria. Part 3: Mother-child interactions, family conflicts and maternal psychopathology. *Journal of Child Psychology and Psychiatry* **32**, 233–255.

Baron-Cohen, S. 1988. Social and pragmatic deficits in autism: Cognitive or affective? *Journal of Autism and Developmental Disorders* **18**, 379–401.

Baron-Cohen, S. 1989a. Are autistic children "behaviorists"? An examination of their mental-physical and appearance-reality distinctions. *Journal of Autism and Developmental Disorders* **19**, 579–600.

Baron-Cohen, S. 1989b. Joint-attention deficits in autism: Toward a cognitive analysis. *Development and Psychopathology* **1**, 185–189.

Baron-Cohen, S. 1991. Do people with autism understand what causes emotion? *Child Development* **62**, 385–395.

Barrios, B. A., and Hartmann, D. P. 1988. Fears and anxieties. In E. J. Mash and L. G. Terdal (eds.), *Behavior assessment of childhood disorders*, 2d ed., pp. 196–262. New York: Guilford.

Barrios, B. A., and O'Dell, S. L. 1989. Fears and anxieties. In E. J. Mash and R. A. Barkley (eds.), *Treatment of childhood disorders*, pp. 167–221. New York: Guilford.

Barth, R. P. 1991. An experimental evaluation of in-home child abuse prevention services. *Child Abuse and Neglect* **15**, 363–375.

Basta, S. M., and Peterson, R. F. 1990. Perpetrator status and the personality characteristics of molested children. *Child Abuse and Neglect* **14**, 555–566.

Battle, E. S., and Lacey, B. 1972. A context for hyperactivity in children over time. *Child Development* **43**, 757–773.

Bauermeister, J. J., Alegria, M., Bird, H. R., Rubio-Stipec, M., and Canino, G. 1992. Are attentional-hyperactivity deficits unidimensional or multidimensional syndromes? Empirical findings from a community survey. *Journal of the American Academy of Child and Adolescent Psychiatry* **31**, 423–431.

Baum, C. G. 1989. Conduct disorders. In T. H. Ollendick and M. Hersen (eds.), *Handbook of child psychopathology*, 2d ed., pp. 171–196. New York: Plenum.

Bayley, N. 1969. *Bayley Scales of Infant Development manual.* New York: Psychological Corporation.

Beeghly, M., Weiss-Perry, B., and Cicchetti, D. 1991. Beyond sensorimotor functioning: Early communicative and play development of children with Down syndrome. In D. Cicchetti and M. Beeghly (eds.), *Children with Down syndrome: A developmental perspective*, pp. 329–368. Cambridge: Cambridge University Press.

Beidel, D. C., and Turner, S. M. 1986. A critique of the theoretical bases of cognitive-behavioral theories and therapy. *Clinical Psychology Review* **6**, 177–197.

Bell, A. P., and Weinberg, M. S. 1978. *Homosexualities. A study of diversity among men and women.* New York: Simon & Schuster.

Bell, A. P., Weinberg, M. S., and Hammersmith, S. K. 1981. *Sexual preference: Its development in men and women.* Bloomington: Indiana University Press.

Bell, R. 1968. A reinterpretation of direction of effects in studies of socialization. *Psychological Review* **75**, 81–95.

Bell-Dolan, D. J., Last, C. G., and Strauss, C. C. 1990. Symptoms of anxiety disorders in normal children. *Journal of the Academy of Child and Adolescent Psychiatry* **29**, 759–765.

Bellak, L. 1954. *The Thematic Apperception Test and the Children's Apperception Test in clinical use.* New York: Grune & Stratton.

Belsky, J. 1978. A theoretical analysis of child abuse remediation strategies. *Journal of Clinical Child Psychology* **7,** 117–121.

Belsky, J. 1980. Child maltreatment: An ecological integration. *American Psychologist* **35,** 320–335.

Belsky, J. 1991. Psychological maltreatment: Definitional limitations and unstated assumptions. *Development and Psychopathology* **3,** 31–36.

Belsky, J., and Vondra, J. 1989. Lessons from child abuse: The determinants of parenting. In D. Cicchetti and V. Carlson (eds.), *Child maltreatment: Theory and research on the causes and consequences of child abuse and neglect,* pp. 153–202. Cambridge: Cambridge University Press.

Bem, S. L. 1989. Genital knowledge and gender constancy in preschool children. *Child Development* **60,** 649–662.

Bender, L. 1947. Childhood schizophrenia: Clinical studies of 100 schizophrenic children. *American Journal of Orthopsychiatry* **17,** 40–56.

Bender, L. 1957. Specific reading disability as a maturational lag. *Bulletin of the Orton Society* **7,** 9–18.

Bender, L. 1962. *The Bender Visual Motor Gestalt Test for Children.* Los Angeles: Western Psychological Services.

Bender, L., and Faretra, G. 1972. The relationship between childhood schizophrenia and adult schizophrenia. In A. Kaplan (ed.), *Genetic factors in schizophrenia.* Springfield, Ill.: Charles C. Thomas.

Benton Revised Visual Retention Test. 1974. San Antonio, Tex.: Psychological Corporation.

Berger, J. 1991. Interaction between parents and their infants with Down syndrome. In D. Cicchetti and M. Beeghly (eds.), *Children with Down syndrome: A developmental perspective,* pp. 101–146. Cambridge: Cambridge University Press.

Bergin, A. E., and Lambert, M. J. 1978. The evaluation of therapeutic outcomes. In S. L. Garfield and A. E. Bergin (eds.), *Handbook of psychotherapy and behavioral change: An empirical analysis,* 2d ed. New York: Wiley.

Berk, L. E. 1991. *Child development,* 2d ed. Boston: Allyn & Bacon.

Berkowitz, L. 1973. Control of aggression. In B. M. Caldwell and H. N. R. Ricciuti (eds.), *Review of child development research,* vol. 3. Chicago: University of Chicago Press.

Berman, A. L., and Jobes, D. A. 1991. *Adolescent suicide. Assessment and intervention.* Washington, D. C.: American Psychological Association.

Bernal, E. M. 1990. Increasing the interpretative validity and diagnostic utility of Hispanic children's scores on tests of achievement and intelligence. In F. C. Serafica, A. I. Schwebel, R. K. Russell, P. D. Isaac, and L. B. Myers (eds.), *Mental health of ethnic minorities.* New York: Praeger.

Bernal, M. E. 1989. Minority mental health curricula: Trends and issues. In F. C. Serafica, A. I. Schwebel, R. K. Russell, P. D. Isaac, and L. B. Myers (eds.), *Mental health of ethnic minorities.* New York: Praeger.

Bernstein, G. A., and Borchardt, C. M. 1991. Anxiety disorders in childhood and adolescence: A critical review. *Journal of the American Academy of Child and Adolescent Psychiatry* **30,** 519–533.

Beyer, H. A. 1991. Litigation involving people with mental retardation. In J. L. Matson and J. A. Mulick (eds.), *Handbook of mental retardation,* pp. 451–467. New York: Pergamon.

Bibring, E. 1953. The mechanism of depression. In P. Greenacre (ed.), *Affective disorders,* pp. 13–48. New York: Hallmark-Hubner.

Bifulco, A., Harris, T., and Brown, G. W. 1992. Mourning or early inadequate care? Reexamination of the relation of maternal loss in childhood with adult depression and anxiety. *Development and Psychopathology* **4,** 433–449.

Birch, H. G., and Gussow, J. D. 1970. *Disadvantaged children: Health, nutrition, and school failure.* New York: Grune & Stratton.

Birch, L. L. 1990. Development of food acceptance patterns. *Developmental Psychology* **26,** 515–519.

Birch, L. L., McPhee, L., Shoba, B. C., Steinberg, L., and Krehbiel, R. 1987. "Clean your plate": Effects of child feeding practices on the conditioning of meal size. *Learning and Motivation* **18,** 301–317.

Bird, H. R., Gould, M. S., and Staghezza, B. 1991. Aggregating data from multiple informants in child psychiatry epidemiology research. *Journal of the American Academy of Child and Adolescent Psychiatry* **31,** 78–85.

Black, B., and Robbins, D. R. 1990. Panic disorders in children and adolescents. *Journal of the American Academy of Child and Adolescent Psychiatry* **29,** 36–44.

Black, M. M. 1991. Early intervention services for

infants and toddlers: A focus on families. *Journal of Clinical Child Psychology* **20,** 51–57.

Blagg, N. R., and Yule, W. 1984. The behavioral treatment of school refusals. A comparative study. *Behaviour Research and Therapy* **22,** 119–127.

Blatt, S. J., and Homann, E. 1992. Parent-child interaction in the etiology of dependent and self-critical depression. *Clinical Psychology Review* **12,** 47–91.

Blatt, S. J., and Zuroff, D. C. 1992. Interpersonal relatedness and self-definition: Two prototypes for depression. *Clinical Psychology Review* **12,** 527–562.

Bleuler, M. 1974. The offspring of schizophrenics. *Schizophrenia Bulletin* **8,** 93–107.

Block, J. H. 1983. Differential premises arising from differential socialization of the sexes: Some conjectures. *Child Development* **54,** 1335–1354.

Block, J. H., Block, J., and Gjerde, P. F. 1986. The personality of children prior to divorce: A prospective study. *Child Development* **57,** 827–840.

Block, J., and Gjerde, P. F. 1990. Depressive symptoms in late adolescence: A longitudinal perspective on personality antecedents. In J. Rolf, A. S. Masten, D. Cicchetti, K. H. Nuechterlein, and S. Weintraub (eds.), *Risk and protective factors in the development of psychopathology*, pp. 334–360. Cambridge: Cambridge University Press.

Block, J., and Haan, N. 1971. *Lives through time.* Berkeley, Calif.: Bancroft.

Boggs, S. R., and Eyberg, S. 1990. Interview techniques and establishing rapport. In A. M. La Greca (ed.), *Through the eyes of the child: Obtaining self-reports from children and adolescents*, pp. 85–108. Boston: Allyn & Bacon.

Bootzin, R. R., and Acocella, J. R. 1988. *Abnormal psychology: Current perspectives*, 5th ed. New York: Random House.

Bootzin, R. R., Acocella, J. R., and Alloy, L. B. 1993. *Abnormal psychology: Current perspectives*, 6th ed. New York: McGraw-Hill.

Borkowski, J. G., Peck, V. A., and Damberg, P. R. 1983. Attention, memory, and cognition. In J. L. Matson and J. A. Mulick (eds.), *Handbook of mental retardation*, pp. 479–498. New York: Pergamon.

Botvin, G. J., Baker, E., Dusenbury, L., Tortu, S., and Botvin, E. M. 1990. Preventing adolescent drug abuse through a multimodal cognitive-behavioral approach: Results of a 3-year study. *Journal of Consulting and Clinical Psychology* **58,** 437–446.

Boucher, J., and Lewis, V. 1989. Memory impairments and communication in relatively able autistic children. *Journal of Child Psychology and Psychiatry* **30,** 99–122.

Bowlby, J. 1960. *The psychoanalytic study of the child.* Vol. 15: *Grief and mourning in infancy and early childhood.* New York: International Universities Press.

Bowlby, J. 1973. *Attachment and loss.* Vol. 2: *Separation: Anxiety and anger.* New York: Basic Books.

Bowlby, J. 1980. *Attachment and loss.* Vol. 3: *Loss, sadness and depression.* New York: Basic Books.

Bowman, P. J., and Howard, C. 1985. Race-related socialization, motivation, and academic achievement: Study of black youths in three-generation families. *Journal of the American Academy of Child Psychiatry* **24,** 134–141.

Boykin, A. W. 1983. The academic performance of Afro-American children. In J. T. Spence (ed.), *Achievement and achievement motives.* New York: Freeman.

Brady, E. U., and Kendall, P. C. 1992. Comorbidity of anxiety and depression in children and adolescents. *Psychological Bulletin* **111,** 244–255.

Brassard, M. R., Germain, R. B., and Hart, S. N. 1987. *Psychological maltreatment of youth.* New York: Plenum.

Bregman, J. D. 1991. Current developments in the understanding of mental retardation. Part 2: Psychopathology. *Journal of the American Academy of Child and Adolescent Psychiatry* **30,** 861–872.

Bregman, J. D., and Hodapp, R. 1991. Current developments in the understanding of mental retardation. Part 1: Biological and phenomenological perspectives. *Journal of the American Academy of Child and Adolescent Psychiatry* **30,** 707–719.

Breslau, N., and Marshall, I. A. 1985. Psychological disturbances in children with physical disabilities: Continuity and change in a 5-year follow up. *Journal of Abnormal Child Psychology* **13,** 199–216.

Bretherton, I. 1985. Attachment theory: Retrospect and prospect. In I. Bretherton and E. Waters (eds.), Growing points in attachment theory and research, pp. 3–38. *Monographs of the Society for Research in Child Development* **50** (1–2, series no. 209).

Bretherton, I. 1987. New perspectives in attachment relations: Security, communication, and internal working models. In J. D. Osofsky (ed.), *Handbook of infant development,* 2d ed., pp. 1061–1100. New York: Wiley.

Bretherton, I., and Waters, E. (eds.). 1985. Growing points in attachment theory and research. *Monographs of the Society for Research in Child Development* **50** (1–2, series no. 209).

Bridges, K. M. B. 1932. Emotional development in early infancy. *Child Development* **3,** 324–341.

Britton, H. L., and O'Keefe, M. A. 1991. Use of non-anatomical dolls in the sexual abuse interview. *Child Abuse and Neglect* **15,** 567–573.

Bronfenbrenner, U. 1977. Toward an experimental ecology of human development. *American Psychologist* **32,** 513–531.

Bronfenbrenner, U. (1989a). Ecological systems theory. *Annals of Child Development* **6,** 187–249.

Bronfenbrenner, U. 1989b. Ecological systems theory. In R. Vasta (ed.), *Annals of child development,* vol. 6, pp. 187–251. Greenwich, Conn.: JAI Press.

Brown, G. W. 1988. Causal paths, chains and strands. In M. Rutter (ed.), *Studies of psychosocial risk: The power of longitudinal data,* pp. 285–314. Cambridge: Cambridge University Press.

Brown, G. W., Harris, T. O., and Bifulco, A. 1986. Long-term effects of early loss of parent. In M. Rutter, C. E. Izard, and P. B. Read (eds.), *Depression in young people: Developmental and clinical perspectives,* pp. 251–296. New York: Guilford.

Brown, T. A., Cash, T. F., and Lewis, R. J. 1989. Body-image disturbances in adolescent female binge-purgers. A brief report of the results of a national survey in the U.S.A. *Journal of Child Psychology and Psychiatry and Allied Disciplines* **30,** 605–613.

Browne, A., and Finkelhor, D. 1986. Initial and long-term effects: A review of the research. In D. Finkelhor (ed.), *A sourcebook of child sexual abuse,* pp. 143–179. Beverly Hills: Sage.

Bruch, H. 1973. *Eating disorders: Obesity, anorexia nervosa, and the person within.* New York: Basic Books.

Bruck, M. 1987. Social and emotional adjustments of learning disabled children: A review of the issues. In S. J. Ceci (ed.), *Handbook of cognitive, social and neuropsychological aspects of learning disabilities,* vol. 1, pp. 361–380. Hillsdale, N.J.: Erlbaum.

Bryan, T., and Bryan, J. 1990. Social factors in learning disabilities: An overview. In H. L. Swanson and B. Keogh (eds.), *Learning disabilities: Theoret-*

ical and research issues, pp. 131–138. Hillsdale, N.J.: Erlbaum.

Bryan, T., and Pearl, R. 1979. Self-concepts and locus of control in children with learning disabilities. *Journal of Clinical Child Psychology* **8,** 223–226.

Buitelaar, J. K., van Engeland, H., de Kogel, K. H., de Vries, H., and van Hooff, J. A. R. A. M. 1991. Differences in the structure of social behaviour of autistic children and nonautistic retarded controls. *Journal of Child Psychology and Psychiatry* **32,** 995–1015.

Burack, J. A., and Volkmar, F. R. 1992. Development of low- and high-functioning autistic children. *Journal of Child Psychology and Psychiatry* **33,** 607–616.

Burke, P., and Puig-Antich, J. 1990. Psychobiology of childhood depression. In M. Lewis and S. M. Miller (eds.), *Handbook of developmental psychopathology,* pp. 327–339. New York: Plenum.

Bush, J. P., and Harkins, S. W. 1991. *Children in pain. Clinical and research issues from a developmental perspective.* New York: Springer-Verlag.

Bush, P. J., and Iannotti, R. J. 1985. The development of children's health orientations and behaviors: Lessons for substance use prevention. In C. L. Jones and R. J. Battjes (eds.), *Etiology of drug abuse: Implications for prevention,* pp. 45–74. NIDA Research Monograph 56. Rockville, Md.: National Institute on Drug Abuse.

Buss, D. M., Block, J. H., and Block, J. 1980. Preschool activity level: Personality correlates and developmental implications. *Child Development* **51,** 401–408.

Calhoun, J. F., Acocella, J. R., and Goodstein, L. D. 1977. *Abnormal psychology: Current perspectives.* New York: Random House.

Camp, B. W. 1977. Verbal mediation in young aggressive boys. *Journal of Abnormal Psychology* **86,** 145–153.

Campbell, M., and Spencer, E. K. 1988. Psychopharmacology in child and adolescent psychiatry: A review of the past few years. *Journal of the American Academy of Child and Adolescent Psychiatry* **27,** 269–279.

Campbell, S. B. 1986. Developmental issues in childhood anxiety. In R. Gittelman (ed.), *Anxiety disorders in childhood,* pp. 24–57. New York: Guilford.

Campbell, S. B. 1989. Developmental perspectives. In T. H. Ollendick and M. Hersen (eds.), *Handbook of child psychopathology,* 2d ed., pp. 5–25. New York: Plenum.

Campbell, S. B. 1990. The socialization and social development of hyperactive children. In M. Lewis and S. M. Miller (eds.), *Handbook of developmental psychopathology,* pp. 77–92. New York: Plenum.

Campbell, S. B. 1991. Longitudinal studies of active and aggressive preschoolers: Individual differences in early behavior and in outcome. In D. Cicchetti and S. L. Toth (eds.), *Internalizing and externalizing expressions of dysfunction. Rochester symposium on developmental psychopathology,* vol. 2, pp. 57–90. Hillsdale, N.J.: Erlbaum.

Campbell, S. B., Breaux, A. M., Ewing, L. J., and Szumowski, E. K. 1986. Correlates and predictors of hyperactivity and aggression: A longitudinal study of parent-referred problem preschoolers. *Journal of Abnormal Child Psychology* **14,** 217–234.

Campbell, S. B., Endman, M. W., and Bernfeld, G. 1977. A three-year follow-up of hyperactive preschoolers into elementary school. *Journal of Child Psychology and Psychiatry* **18,** 239–249.

Campbell, S. B., and Werry, J. S. 1986. Attention deficit disorder (hyperactivity). In H. C. Quay and J. S. Werry (eds.), *Psychological disorders of childhood,* 3d ed., pp. 111–155. New York: Wiley.

Cannon, T. D., Barr, C. E., and Mednick, S. A. 1991. Genetic and perinatal factors in the etiology of schizophrenia. In E. F. Walker (ed.), *Schizophrenia: A life-course developmental perspective,* pp. 9–31. San Diego: Academic Press.

Cantor, S. 1988. *Childhood schizophrenia.* New York: Guilford.

Cantor, S., and Kestenbaum, C. 1986. Psychotherapy with schizophrenic children. *Journal of the American Academy of Child Psychiatry* **25,** 623–630.

Cantwell, D. P. 1980. The diagnostic process and diagnostic classification in child psychiatry: DSM-III. *Journal of the American Academy of Child Psychiatry* **19,** 345–355.

Cantwell, D. P. 1988. DSM-III studies. In M. Rutter, A. H. Tuma, and I. S. Lann (eds.), *Assessment and diagnosis in child psychopathology,* pp. 3–36. New York: Guilford.

Capaldi, D. M. 1991. Co-occurrence of conduct problems and depressive symptoms in early adolescent boys. Part I: Familial factors and general adjustment at Grade 6. *Development and Psychopathology* **3,** 277–300.

Capaldi, D. M. 1992. Co-occurrence of conduct problems and depressive symptoms in early adolescent boys. Part II: A 2-year follow-up at Grade 8. *Development and Psychopathology* **4,** 125–144.

Caplan, R., Foy, J. G., Asarnow, R. F., and Sherman, T. 1990. Information processing deficits of schizophrenic children with formal thought disorder. *Psychiatric Research* **31,** 169–177.

Caplan, R., Guthrie, D., Fish, B., Tanguay, P. E., and David-Lando, G. 1989. The Kiddie Formal Thought Disorder Scale (K-FTDS). Clinical assessment, reliability, and validity. *Journal of the American Academy of Child and Adolescent Psychiatry* **28,** 408–416.

Caplan, R., Guthrie, D., and Foy, J. G. 1992. Communication deficits and formal thought disorder in schizophrenic children. *Journal of the American Academy of Child and Adolescent Psychiatry* **31,** 151–159.

Caplan, R., Perdue, S., Tanguay, P. E., and Fish, B. 1990. Formal thought disorder in childhood onset schizophrenia and schizotypal personality disorder. *Journal of Child Psychology and Psychiatry* **31,** 1103–1114.

Caplan, R., and Sherman, T. 1990. Thought disorder in the childhood psychoses. In B. B. Lahey and A. E. Kazdin (eds.), *Advances in clinical child psychology,* vol. 13, pp. 175–206. New York: Plenum.

Carlson, C. L., Figueroa, R. G., and Lahey, B. B. 1986. Behavior therapy for childhood anxiety disorders. In R. Gittelman (ed.), *Anxiety disorders of childhood,* pp. 204–232. New York: Guilford.

Carlson, C. L., Lahey, B. B., and Neeper, R. 1984. Peer assessment of the social behavior of accepted, rejected and neglected children. *Journal of Abnormal Child Psychology* **12,** 187–198.

Carlson, G. A., and Cantwell, D. P. 1980. A survey of depressive symptoms, syndrome, and disorder in a child psychiatric population. *Journal of Child Psychology and Psychiatry* **21,** 19–25.

Carlson, G. A., and Garber, J. 1986. Developmental issues in the classification of depression in children. In M. Rutter, C. E. Izard, and P. B. Read (eds.), *Depression in young people: Developmental and clinical perspectives,* pp. 339–434. New York: Guilford.

Carlson, V., Cicchetti, D., Barnett, D., and Braunwald, K. G. 1989. Disorganization/disoriented attachment relationships in maltreated infants. *Developmental Psychology* **25,** 525–531.

Caron, C., and Rutter, M. 1991. Comorbidity in child psychopathology: Concepts, issues and research strategies. *Journal of Child Psychology and Psychiatry* **32**, 1063–1080.

Carr, J. 1975. *Young children with Down's syndrome: Their development, upbringing and effect on their families.* London: Butterworth.

Carter, D. B., and Paterson, C. J. 1982. Sex roles as social conventions: The development of children's conception of sex-role stereotypes. *Developmental Psychology* **18**, 812–824.

Casey, R. J., and Berman, J. S. 1985. The outcome of psychotherapy with children. *Psychological Bulletin* **98**, 388–400.

Casper, R. C., Hedeker, D., and McClough, J. F. 1992. Personality dimensions in eating disorders and their relevance for subtyping. *Journal of the American Academy of Child and Adolescent Psychiatry* **31**, 830–840.

Caspi, A., Lynam, D., Mofitt, T. E., and Silva, P. A. 1993. Unraveling girls' delinquency: Biological, dispositional, and contextual contributions to adolescent misbehavior. *Developmental Psychology* **29**, 19–30.

Cass, L. K., and Thomas, C. B. 1979. *Childhood pathology and later adjustment: The question of prediction.* New York: Wiley.

Ceci, S. J. 1991. Some overarching issues in children's suggestibility debate. In J. Doris (ed.), *The suggestibility of children's recollections*, pp. 1–9. Washington, D.C.: American Psychological Association.

Ceci, S. J., and Baker, J. C. 1987. How shall we conceptualize the language problems of learning-disabled children? In S. J. Ceci (ed.), *Handbook of cognitive, social and neuropsychological aspects of learning disabilities*, vol. 2, pp. 103–114. Hillsdale, N.J.: Erlbaum.

Ceci, S. J., and Bruck, M. 1993. Suggestibility of the child witness: A historical review and synthesis. *Psychological Bulletin* **113**, 403–439.

Center for Stress and Anxiety Disorders. 1991. *Anxiety disorders interview schedule for children (child version).* Albany, N.Y.: Graywind Publications.

Center on Budget and Policy Priorities. 1991. *Poverty in the United States.* Washington, D. C.: U.S. Bureau of the Census.

Chambers, W. J., Puig-Antich, J., Hirsch, M., Paez, P., Ambrosini, P. J., Tabrizi, M. A., and Davies, M. 1985. The assessment of affective disorders in children and adolescents by semistructured interview: Test-retest reliability. *Archives of General Psychiatry* **43**, 696–702.

Chandler, M. J. 1973. Egocentrism and antisocial behavior: The assessment and training of social perspective-taking skills. *Developmental Psychology* **9**, 326–332.

Chavez, J. M., and Rodney, C. E. 1990. Psychocultural factors affecting the mental health status of Mexican American adolescents. In A. R. Stiffman and L. E. Davis (eds.), *Ethnic issues in adolescent mental health*, pp. 73–91. Newbury Park, Calif.: Sage.

Chess, S. 1971. Autism in children with congenital rubella. *Journal of Autism and Childhood Schizophrenia* **1**, 33–47.

Children and the law. 1978. *Journal of Clinical Child Psychology* **7**.

Cicchetti, D. 1989. Developmental psychopathology: Some thoughts on its evolution. *Development and Psychopathology*, **1**, 1–4.

Cicchetti, D., and Beeghly, M. 1991. An organizational approach to the study of Down syndrome: Contributions to an integrative theory of development. In D. Cicchetti and M. Beeghly (eds.), *Children with Down syndrome: A developmental perspective*, pp. 29–62. Cambridge: Cambridge University Press.

Cicchetti, D., and Olsen, K. 1990. The developmental psychopathology of child maltreatment. In M. Lewis and S. M. Miller (eds.), *Handbook of developmental psychopathology*, pp. 261–279. New York: Plenum.

Cicchetti, D., and Rizley, R. 1981. Developmental perspectives on the etiology, intergenerational transmission, and sequelae of child maltreatment. *New Directions for Child Development* **11**, 31–55.

Cicchetti, D., and Schneider-Rosen, K. 1986. An organizational approach to childhood depression. In M. Rutter, C. E. Izard, and P. B. Read (eds.), *Depression in young people: Developmental and clinical perspectives*, pp. 71–134. New York: Guilford.

Clarke, A. M., and Clarke, A. D. B. 1977. *Early experience: Myth and evidence.* New York: Free Press.

Claussen, A. H., and Crittenden, P. M. 1991. Physical and psychological maltreatment: Relations among types of maltreatment. *Child Abuse and Neglect* **15**, 5–18.

Clayton, R. R. 1992. Transition in drug use: Risk and protective factors. In M. Glantz and R. Pickens (eds.), *Vulnerability to drug abuse,* pp. 15–52. Washington, D.C.: American Psychological Association.

Coates, D. L. 1990. Social network analysis as mental health intervention with African-American adolescents. In F. C. Serafica, A. I. Schwebel, R. K. Russell, P. D. Isaac, and L. B. Myers (eds.), *Mental health of ethnic minorities,* pp. 5–37. New York: Praeger.

Cohler, B. J. 1987. Adversity, resilience, and the study of lives. In E. J. Anthony and B. J. Cohler (eds.), *The invulnerable child,* pp. 363–424. New York: Guilford.

Cohn, D. S. 1991. Anatomical doll play of preschoolers referred for sexual abuse and those not referred. *Child Abuse & Neglect* **15,** 455–466.

Coie, J. D., Dodge, K. A., and Coppotelli, H. 1982. Dimensions and types of social status. A cross-age perspective. *Developmental Psychology* **18,** 557–570.

Cole, M., and Cole, S. R. 1989. *The development of children.* New York: Freeman.

Coleman, J. C. 1980. Friendship and the peer group in adolescence. In J. Adelson (ed.), *Handbook of adolescent psychology.* New York: Wiley.

Conduct Problems Prevention Research Group. 1992. A developmental and clinical model for the prevention of conduct disorders: The FAST Track Program. *Development and Psychopathology* **4,** 509–528.

Conoley, J. C., and Conoley, C. W. 1991. Collaboration for child adjustment: Issues for school- and clinic-based child psychologists. *Journal of Consulting and Clinical Psychology* **59,** 821–829.

Conte, J. R. 1991. Overview of child sexual abuse. In A. Tasman and S. M. Goldfinger (eds.), *Review of psychiatry,* vol. 10, pp. 283–307. Washington, D.C.: American Psychiatric Press.

Coovert, D. L., Kinder, B. N., and Thompson, J. K. 1989. The psychosexual aspects of anorexia nervosa and bulimia nervosa: A review of the literature. *Clinical Psychology Review* **9,** 169–180.

Corah, N. L., Anthony, E. J., Painter, P., Stern, J. A., and Thurston, D. 1965. Effects of perinatal anoxia after seven years. *Psychological Monographs* **79** (3, whole no. 596).

Costanzo, P. R., and Woody, E. Z. 1985. Domain-specific parenting styles and their impact on the child's development of particular deviance. The

example of obesity proneness. *Journal of Social and Clinical Psychology* **3,** 425–445.

Costello, E. J., Loeber, R., and Stouthamer-Loeber, M. 1991. Pervasive and situational hyperactivity: Confounding effect of informant. A research note. *Journal of Child Psychology and Psychiatry* **32,** 367–376.

Craig, K. D., and Grunau, R. V. E. 1991. Developmental issues: Infants and toddlers. In J. P. Bush and S. W. Harkins, *Children in pain: Clinical and research issues from a developmental perspective,* pp. 171–193. New York: Springer-Verlag.

Craighead, L. W., and Agras, W. S. 1991. Mechanisms of action in cognitive-behavioral and pharmacological interventions for obesity and bulimia nervosa. *Journal of Consulting and Clinical Psychology* **59,** 115–125.

Cramer, P. 1991. *The development of defense mechanisms: Theory, research, and assessment.* New York: Springer-Verlag.

Creer, T. L., and Kotses, H. 1989. Asthma. In T. H. Ollendick and M. Hersen (eds.), *Handbook of child psychopathology,* 2d ed., pp. 341–358. New York: Plenum.

Crittenden, P. M. 1985. Social networks, quality of child rearing, and child development. *Child Development* **56,** 1299–1313.

Crittenden, P. M., and Ainsworth, M. D. S. 1989. Child maltreatment and attachment theory. In D. Cicchetti and V. Carlson (eds.), *Child maltreatment: Theories and research on the cause and consequences of child abuse and neglect,* pp. 432–463. Cambridge: Cambridge University Press.

Crnic, K. A. 1991. Families of children with Down syndrome: Ecological contexts and characteristics. In D. Cicchetti and M. Beeghly (eds.), *Children with Down syndrome: A developmental perspective,* pp. 399–423. Cambridge: Cambridge University Press.

Crockenberg, S., and Litman, C. 1990. Autonomy as competence in 2-year-olds: Maternal correlates of child defiance, compliance, and self-assertion. *Developmental Psychology* **26,** 961–971.

Crowell, J. A., and Waters, E. 1990. Separation anxiety. In M. Lewis and S. M. Miller (eds.), *Handbook of developmental psychopathology,* pp. 209–218. New York: Plenum.

Cuellar, I., and Roberts, R. E. 1984. Psychological disorders among Chicanos. In J. L. Martinez, Jr.

and R. H. Mendoza (eds.), *Chicano psychology*, 2d ed., pp. 133–162. Orlando, Fla.: Academic Press.

Culbertson, J. 1991. Child advocacy and clinical child psychology. *Journal of Clinical Child Psychology* **20,** 7–10.

Culbertson, J., and Gyurke, J. 1990. Assessment of cognitive and motor development in infancy and childhood. In J. H. Johnson and J. Goldman (eds.), *Developmental assessment in clinical child psychology*, pp. 100–131. New York: Pergamon.

Damon, W. 1977. *The social world of the child.* San Francisco: Jossey-Bass.

Daniels, D., Moos, R. H., Billings, A. G., and Miller III, J. J. 1987. Psychosocial risk and resistance factors among children with chronic illness, healthy siblings, and healthy controls. *Journal of Abnormal Child Psychology* **15,** 295–308.

Daro, D. 1991. Child sexual abuse prevention: Separating fact from fiction. *Child Abuse and Neglect* **15,** 1–4.

Davidson, L. M., and Baum, A. 1990. Posttraumatic stress in children following natural and human made trauma. In M. Lewis and S. M. Miller (eds.), *Handbook of developmental psychopathology*, pp. 252–260. New York: Plenum.

Davies, G. 1991. Concluding comments. In J. Doris (ed.), *Suggestibility in children's recollections*, pp. 177–186. Washington, D.C.: American Psychological Association.

Davis, C. M. 1929. Self selection of diet by newly weaned infants. *American Journal of Diseases of Children* **36,** 651–679.

Davis, C. M. 1935. Choice of formulas made by three infants throughout the nursing period. *American Journal of Diseases of Children* **50,** 385–394.

Davis, L. E., and Stiffman, A. R. 1990. Introduction. In A. R. Stiffman and L. E. Davis (eds.), *Ethnic issues in adolescent mental health*, pp. 13–18. Newbury Park, Calif.: Sage.

Davison, G. C., and Neale, J. M. 1990. *Abnormal psychology*, 5th ed. New York: Wiley.

Dawson, G. (ed.). 1989. *Autism. Nature, diagnosis and treatment.* New York: Guilford.

Dawson, G. 1991. A psychobiological perspective on the early socio-emotional development of children with autism. In D. Cicchetti and S. L. Toth (eds.), *Models and integrations. Rochester symposium on developmental psychopathology*, vol. 3, pp.

207–234. Rochester, N.Y.: University of Rochester Press.

Dawson, G., and Galpert, L. 1986. A developmental model for facilitating the social behavior in autistic children. In E. Schopler and G. B. Mesibov (eds.), *Social behavior in autism*, pp. 237–261. New York: Plenum.

Dawson, G., Hill, D., Spencer, A., Galpert, L., and Watson, L. 1990. Affect exchange between young autistic children and their mothers. *Journal of Abnormal Child Psychology* **18,** 335–345.

Dawson, G., and Levy, A. 1989. Arousal, attention, and the socioemotional impairment of individuals with autism. In G. Dawson (ed.), Autism. Nature and diagnosis, pp. 49–74. New York: Guilford.

de Hirsch, K., Jansky, J., and Langford, W. 1966. *Predicting reading failure: A preliminary study of reading, writing, and spelling disabilities in preschool children.* New York: Harper & Row.

Deitz, D. E. D., and Repp, A. C. 1989. Mental retardation. In T. H. Ollendick and M. Hersen (eds.), *Handbook of child psychopathology*, 2d ed., pp. 75–92. New York: Plenum.

del Carmen, R. 1990. Assessment of Asian-Americans for family therapy. In F. C. Serafica, A. I. Schwebel, R. K. Russell, P. D. Isaac, and L. B. Myers (eds.), *Mental health of ethnic minorities*, pp. 139–166. New York: Praeger.

Delgado, M. 1989. Treatment and prevention of Hispanic alcoholism. In T. D. Watts and R. Wright, Jr. (eds.), *Alcoholism in minority populations*, pp. 77–93. Springfield, Ill.: Charles C. Thomas.

Delprato, D. J. 1980. Hereditary determinants of fears and phobias: A critical review. *Behavior Therapy* **11,** 79–103.

Dennis, W. 1973. Children of the creche. New York: Appleton-Century-Crofts.

Dent, H. R. 1991. Experimental studies of interviewing child witnesses. In J. Doris (ed.), *The suggestibility of children's recollections*, pp. 138–146. Washington, D.C.: American Psychological Association.

Deshler, D. D., and Schumaker, J. B. 1986. Learning strategies: An instructional alternative for low-achieving adolescents. *Exceptional Children* **52,** 583–590.

Deutsch, C. K., and Kinsbourne, M. 1990. Genetics and biochemistry in Attention Deficit Disorder.

In M. Lewis and S. M. Miller (eds.), *Handbook of developmental psychopathology,* pp. 93–107. New York: Plenum.

Diaz-Guerrero, R. 1990. Commentary on "Limits to the use and generalizability of the views of life questionnaire." *Hispanic Journal of Behavioral Sciences* **12,** 322–327.

Diaz-Guerrero, R., and Szalay, L. B. 1991. *Understanding Mexicans and Americans. Cultural perspectives in conflict.* New York: Plenum.

Dickstein, L. J., Hinz, L. D., and Eth, S. 1991. Treatment of sexually abused children and adolescents. In A. Tasman and S. M. Goldfinger (eds.), *Review of psychiatry,* vol. 10, pp. 345–366. Washington, D.C.: American Psychiatric Press.

Digdon, N., and Gotlib, I. H. 1985. Developmental considerations in the study of childhood depression. *Developmental Review* **5,** 162–199.

Dishion, T. J., Patterson, G. R., Stoolmiller, M., and Skinner, M. L. 1991. Family, school, and behavioral antecedents to early adolescent involvement with antisocial peers. *Developmental Psychology* **27,** 172–180.

Dodge, K. A. 1983. Behavioral antecedents of peer social status. *Child Development* **54,** 1386–1399.

Dodge, K. A. 1986. A social information process model of social competence in children. In M. Perlmutter (ed.), *Eighteenth annual Minnesota symposium on child psychology,* pp. 77–125. Hillsdale, N.J.: Erlbaum.

Dodge, K. A. 1990a. Nature versus nurture in childhood conduct disorder: It is time to ask a different question. *Developmental Psychology* **26,** 698–701.

Dodge, K. A. 1990b. Developmental psychopathology in children of depressed mothers. *Developmental Psychology* **26,** 3–6.

Dodge, K. A., and Frame, C. L. 1982. Social cognitive biases and deficits in aggressive boys. *Child Development* **53,** 620–635.

Dodge, K. A., and Somberg, D. R. 1987. Hostile attributional biases among aggressive boys are exacerbated under conditions of threat to the self. *Child Development* **58,** 213–224.

Doehring, D. G., and Hoshko, I. M. 1977. Classification of reading problems by the Q-technique of factor analysis. *Cortex* **13**(3), 281–294.

Doleys, D. M. 1977. Behavioral treatments for nocturnal enuresis in children: A review of the recent literature. *Psychological Bulletin* **84,** 30–54.

Dolgin, M. J., and Jay, S. M. 1989. Childhood cancer. In T. H. Ollendick and M. Hersen (eds.), *Handbook of child psychopathology,* 2d ed., pp. 327–340. New York: Plenum.

Donovan, J. E., and Jessor, R. 1985. Structure of problem behavior in adolescence and young adulthood. *Journal of Consulting and Clinical Psychology* **53,** 890–904.

Dorner, G., Geier, T., Ahrens, L., Krell, L., Munx, G., Sieler, H., Kittner, E., and Muller, H. 1980. Prenatal stress and possible aetiogenetic factor homosexuality in human males. *Endokrinologie* **75,** 365–368.

Douglas, V. I. 1980. Treatment and training approaches to hyperactivity: Establishing internal or external control? In C. K. Whalen and B. Henker (eds.), *Hyperactive children: The social ecology of identification and treatment.* New York: Academic Press.

Douglas, V. I. 1983. Attention and cognitive problems. In M. Rutter (ed.), *Developmental neuropsychiatry,* pp. 280–329. New York: Guilford.

Douglas, V. I. 1989. Can Skinnerian theory explain attention deficit disorder? A reply to Barkley. In L. M. Bloomingdale and J. M. Swanson (eds.), *Attention deficit disorder, vol. IV: Current concepts and merging trends in attentional and behavioral disorders of childhood,* pp. 235–254. Oxford: Pergamon.

Douglas, V. I., and Peters, K. G. 1980. Toward a clearer definition of the attentional deficit of hyperactive children. In G. A. Hale and M. Lewis (eds.), *Attention and the development of cognitive skills.* New York: Plenum.

Downey, G., and Coyne, J. C. 1990. Children of depressed parents: An integrative review. *Psychological Bulletin* **108,** 50–76.

Dubowitz, H. 1990. Cost and effectiveness of interventions in child maltreatment. *Child Abuse and Neglect* **14,** 177–186.

Dunn, J. 1989. Normative life events as risk factors in childhood. In M. Rutter (ed.), *Studies of psychosocial risk: The power of longitudinal data,* pp. 227–243. Cambridge: Cambridge University Press.

Dunn, L. M. 1965. *Expanded manual for the Peabody Picture Vocabulary Test.* Minneapolis: American Guidance Service.

Dunst, C. J. 1991. Sensorimotor development in infants with Down syndrome. In D. Cicchetti and M. Beeghly (eds.), *Children with Down syndrome: A developmental perspective*, pp. 180–230. Cambridge: Cambridge University Press.

DuPaul, G. J., and Barkley, R. A. 1990. Medication therapy. In R. A. Barkley (ed.), *Attention-deficit hyperactivity disorder: A handbook for diagnosis and treatment*, pp. 573–612. New York: Guilford.

Durlak, J. A., Fuhrman, T., and Lampman, C. 1991. Effectiveness of cognitive-behavior therapy for maladapting children: A meta-analysis. *Psychological Bulletin* **110,** 204–214.

Dush, D. M., Hirt, M. L., and Schroeder, H. E. 1989. Self-statement modification in treatment of child behavior disorders: A meta-analysis. *Psychological Bulletin* **106,** 97–106.

Dweck, C. S., and Slaby, R. G. 1983. Achievement motivation. In P. H. Mussen (ed.), *Handbook of child psychology*, 4th ed., vol. 4, pp. 643–692. New York: Wiley.

Edelbrock, C., and Achenbach, T. M. 1980. A typology of child behavior profile patterns: Distribution and correlates for disturbed children aged 6–16. *Journal of Abnormal Child Psychology* **8,** 441–470.

Edelbrock, C., and Costello, A. J. 1988. Convergence between statistically derived behavior problem syndromes and child psychiatric diagnoses. *Journal of Abnormal Child Psychology* **16,** 219–231.

Egeland, B. 1991. From data to definition. *Development and Psychopathology* **3,** 37–44.

Egeland, B., Breitenbucher, M., and Rosenberg, D. 1980. Prospective study of the significance of life stress in the etiology of child abuse. *Journal of Consulting and Clinical Psychology* **48,** 195–205.

Egeland, B., Jacobvitz, D., and Papatola, K. 1987. Intergenerational continuity of abuse. In R. Gelles and J. Lancaster (eds.), *Child abuse and neglect: Biosocial dimensions*, pp. 255–276. New York: Aldine Gruyter.

Egeland, B., Kalkoske, M., Gottesman, N., and Erickson, M. E. 1990. Preschool behavior problems: Stability and factors accounting for change. *Journal of Child Psychology and Psychiatry* **31,** 891–909.

Egeland, B., Sroufe, L. A., and Erickson, M. 1984. The developmental consequences of different patterns of maltreatment. *International Journal of Child Abuse* **7,** 459–469.

Eisenberg, N., and Miller, P. A. 1987. The relation of empathy to prosocial and related behaviors. *Psychological Bulletin* **101,** 91–119.

Eisenberg, N., and Miller, P. A. 1990. The development of prosocial versus nonprosocial behavior in children. In M. Lewis and S. M. Miller (eds.), *Handbook of developmental psychopathology*, pp. 181–188. New York: Plenum.

Eiser, C. 1990. Psychological effects of chronic disease. *Journal of Child Psychology and Psychiatry* **31,** 85–98.

Elliott, D. S., Huizinga, D., and Menard, S. 1989. *Multiple problem youth. Delinquency, substance use, and mental health problems.* New York: Springer-Verlag.

Ellis, A. 1970. *The essence of rational psychotherapy: A comprehensive approach to treatment.* New York: Institute for Rational Living.

Ellis, L., and Ames, M. A. 1987. Neurohormonal functioning and sexual orientation: A theory of homosexuality-heterosexuality. *Psychological Bulletin* **101,** 233–258.

Elmer, E., Evans, S., and Reinhart, J. B. *Fragile families, troubled children.* Pittsburgh: University of Pittsburgh Press.

Epps, E. G. 1988. Summary and discussion. In D. T. Slaughter and D. J. Johnson (eds.), *Visible now: Blacks in private schools*, pp. 86–90. New York: Greenwood.

Erickson, M. F., Egeland, B., and Pianta, R. 1989. The effects of maltreatment on the development of young children. In D. Cicchetti and V. Carlson (eds.), *Child maltreatment: Theory and research on the causes and consequences of child abuse and neglect*, pp. 647–684. Cambridge: Cambridge University Press.

Erickson, M. F., Korfmacher, J., and Egeland, B. R. 1992. Attachment past and present: Implications for therapeutic intervention with mother-infant dyads. *Development and Psychopathology* **4,** 495–508.

Erickson, M. T. 1992. *Behavior disorders of children and adolescents*, 2d ed. Englewood Cliffs, N.J.: Prentice-Hall.

Erikson, E. 1950. *Childhood and society.* New York: Norton.

Erikson, E. 1968. *Identity: Youth and crisis.* New York: Norton.

Eron, L. D. 1982. Parent-child interaction, television,

and aggression of children. *American Psychologist* **37,** 197–211.

Eron, L. D., and Huesmann, L. R. 1990. The stability of aggressive behavior—even unto the third generation. In M. Lewis and S. M. Miller (eds.), *Handbook of developmental psychopathology*, pp. 147–156. New York: Plenum.

Escalona, S. 1948. Some considerations regarding psychotherapy for psychotic children. *Bulletin of the Menninger Clinic* **2,** 126–134.

Essen, J., and Peckham, C. 1976. Nocturnal enuresis in childhood. *Developmental Medicine and Child Neurology* **18,** 577–589.

Exner, J. E. 1974. *The Rorschach: A comprehensive system,* vol. 1. New York: Wiley.

Exner, J. E. 1978. *The Rorschach: A comprehensive approach,* vol. 2. *Current research and advanced interpretation.* New York: Wiley.

Exner, J. E., and Weiner, I. 1982. *The Rorschach: A comprehensive study,* vol. 3. *Assessment of children and adolescents.* New York: Wiley.

Eysenck, H. J. 1952. The effects of psychotherapy: An evaluation. *Journal of Consulting Psychology* **16,** 319–324.

Eysenck, H. J. 1960. *Handbook of abnormal psychology.* London: Pittman.

Fairburn, C. G., Jones, R., Peveler, R. C., Carr, S. J. (1991). Three Psychological Treatments for Bulimia Nervosa: A Comparative Trial. *Archives of General Psychiatry, 48,* 463–469.

Fabrega, Jr., H. 1990. Hispanic mental health research: A case for cultural psychiatry. *Hispanic Journal of Behavioral Sciences* **12,** 339–365.

Farrell, M., and Strang, J. 1991. Substance use and misuse in childhood and adolescence. *Journal of Child Psychology and Psychiatry* **32,** 109–128.

Farrington, D. P. 1986. The sociocultural context of childhood disorders. In H. C. Quay and J. S. Werry (eds.), *Psychopathological disorders of childhood,* 2d ed., pp. 391–422. New York: Wiley.

Farrington, D. P. 1991. Longitudinal research strategies: Advantages, problems, and prospects. *Journal of the American Academy of Child and Adolescent Psychiatry* **30,** 369–375.

Farrington, D. P., Loeber, R., Elliott, D. S., Hawkins, J. D., Kandel, D. B., Klein, M. W., McCord, J., Rowe, D. C., and Tremblay, R. E. 1990. Advancing knowledge about the onset of delinquency and crime. In B. B. Lahey and A. E. Kazdin (eds.), *Advances in clinical child psychology,* vol. 13, pp. 283–336. New York: Plenum.

Farrington, D. P., Loeber, R., and Van Kammen, W. B. 1990. Long-term criminal outcomes of hyperactivity-impulsivity-attention deficit and conduct problems in childhood. In L. N. Robins and M. Rutter (eds.), *Straight and devious pathways from childhood to adulthood,* pp. 62–81. Cambridge: Cambridge University Press.

Fauber, R. L., and Long, N. 1991. Children in context: The role of the family in child psychotherapy. *Journal of Consulting and Clinical Psychology* **59,** 813–820.

Faust, J. 1987. Correlates of the drive for thinness in young female adolescents. *Journal of Clinical Child Psychology* **16,** 313–319.

Fein, D., Humes, M., Kaplan, E., Lucci, D., and Waterhouse, L. 1984. The question of left hemisphere dysfunction in infantile autism. *Psychological Bulletin* **95,** 258–281.

Fergusson, D. M., Horwood, L. J., and Lloyd, M. 1991. Confirmatory factor models of attention deficit and conduct disorder. *Journal of Child Psychology and Psychiatry* **32,** 257–274.

Ferster, C. B., and DeMyer, M. K. 1962. A method for the experimental analysis of the behavior of autistic children. *American Journal of Orthopsychiatry* **32,** 89–98.

Field, T. 1992. Infants of depressed mothers. *Development and Psychopathology* **4,** 49–66.

Fielding, D. M., and Doleys, D. M. 1988. Elimination problems: Enuresis and encopresis. In E. J. Mash and L. G. Terdal (eds.), *Behavioral assessment of childhood disorders,* 2d ed., pp. 586–623. New York: Guilford.

Fincham, F. D., and Cain, K. M. 1986. Learned helplessness in humans: A developmental analysis. *Developmental Review* **6,** 301–333.

Finkelhor, D. (ed.). 1986a. *A sourcebook of child sexual abuse.* Beverly Hills: Sage.

Finkelhor, D. 1986b. Prevention: A review of programs and research. In D. Finkelhor (ed.), *A sourcebook of child sexual abuse,* pp. 224–254. Beverly Hills: Sage.

Finkelhor, D. 1990. Early and long-term effects of child sexual abuse: An update. *Professional Psychology: Research and Practice* **21,** 325–330.

Finkelhor, D., and Baron, L. 1986. High-risk children. In D. Finkelhor (ed.), *A sourcebook of child sexual abuse,* pp. 60–88. Beverly Hills: Sage.

Finkelhor, D., and Browne, A. 1986. Initial and long-term effects: A conceptual framework. In D. Finkelhor (ed.), *A sourcebook of child sexual abuse,* pp. 180–198. Beverly Hills: Sage.

Finkelhor, D., Hotaling, G., Lewis, I. A., and Smith, C. 1990. Sexual abuse in a national survey of adult men and women: Prevalence, characteristics, and risk factors. *Child Abuse & Neglect* **14,** 19–28.

Fischer, M., Barkley, R. A., Edelbrock, C. S., and Smallish, L. 1990. The adolescent outcome of hyperactive children diagnosed by research criteria: Academic, attentional, and neuropsychological status. *Journal of Consulting and Clinical Psychology* **58,** 580–588.

Fish, B. 1971. Contributions of developmental research to a theory of schizophrenia. In J. Hellmuth (ed.), *Exceptional infant: Studies in abnormalities.* New York: Brunner/Mazel.

Fish, B. 1976. Biological disorders in infants at risk for schizophrenia. In E. R. Ritvo, B. Freeman, E. M. Ornitz, and P. E. Tanquay (eds.), *Autism: Diagnosis, current research, and management.* New York: Spectrum.

Fish, B. 1984. Characteristics and sequelae of the neurointegrative disorder in infants at risk for schizophrenia: 1952–1982. In N. F. Watt, E. J. Anthony, L. C. Wynne, and J. E. Rolf (eds.), *Children at risk for schizophrenia: A longitudinal perspective,* pp. 423–439. Cambridge: Cambridge University Press.

Fisher, S., and Greenberg, R. P. 1977. *The scientific credibility of Freud's theories and therapy.* New York: Basic Books.

Flakierska, N., Lindstrom, M., and Gillberg, C. 1988. School refusals: A 15-20 year follow-up study of 35 Swedish urban children. *British Journal of Psychiatry* **152,** 834–837.

Flanery, R. C. 1990. Methodological and psychometric considerations in child reports. In A. M. La Greca (ed.), *Through the eyes of the child. Obtaining self-reports from children and adolescents,* pp. 57–82. Boston: Allyn & Bacon.

Flavell, J. H. 1977. *Cognitive development.* Englewood Cliffs, N.J.: Prentice-Hall.

Fletcher, J. M., and Levin, H. S. 1988. Neurobehavioral effects of brain injury in children. In D. K. Routh (ed.), *Handbook of pediatric psychology,* pp. 258–295. New York: Guilford.

Fogelman, C. J. (ed.). 1974. *AAMD Adaptive Behavior Scale Manual, 1974 revision.* Washington, D.C.: American Association on Mental Deficiency.

Folstein, S. E., and Rutter, M. 1988. Autism: Familial aggregation and genetic implications. *Journal of Autism and Developmental Disorders* **18,** 3–30.

Forehand, R. 1977. Child noncompliance to parental requests: Behavioral analysis and treatment. In M. Hersen, R. M. Eisler, and P. M. Miller (eds.), *Progress in behavior modification,* vol. 5, pp. 111–148. New York: Academic Press.

Forehand, R., and McMahon, R. 1981. *Helping the non-compliant child: A clinician's guide to parent training.* New York: Guilford.

Foreyt, J. P., and Goodrick, G. K. 1988. Childhood obesity. In E. J. Mash and L. G. Terdal (eds.), *Behavioral assessment of childhood disorders,* 2d ed., pp. 528–551. New York: Guilford.

Forness, S. R. 1990. Subtyping in learning disabilities: Introduction to the issues. In H. L. Swanson and B. Keogh (eds.), *Learning disabilities: Theoretical research issues,* pp. 195–200. Hillsdale, N.J.: Erlbaum.

Fowler, A. E. 1991. Language abilities in children with Down syndrome: Evidence for a specific syntactic delay. In D. Cicchetti and M. Beeghly (eds.), *Children with Down syndrome: A developmental perspective,* pp. 302–328. Cambridge: Cambridge University Press.

Fraiberg, S. 1977. *Insights from the blind: Comparative studies of blind and sighted infants.* New York: Basic Books.

Freedman, J. L. 1986. Television violence and aggression: A rejoinder. *Psychological Bulletin* **100,** 372–378.

Freud, A. 1946. *The ego and the mechanisms of defense.* New York: International Universities Press.

Freud, A. 1965. *Normality and pathology in childhood: Assessment of development.* New York: International Universities Press.

Freud, A., and Dann, S. 1951. An experiment in group upbringing. In R. S. Eisler, A. Freud, H. Hartmann, and E. Kris (eds.), *The psychoanalytic study of the child,* vol. 5. New York: International Universities Press.

Freud, S. 1938. The psychopathology of everyday life. In *The Basic Writings,* pp. 33–178. New York: Modern Library.

Frith, U., and Baron-Cohen, S. 1987. Perception in autistic children. In D. J. Cohen, A. M. Donnellan, and R. Paul (eds.), *Handbook of autism and developmental disabilities,* pp. 85–102. New York: Wiley.

Frostig, M. 1972. Visual perception, integrative functions and academic learning. *Journal of Learning Disabilities* **5,** 1–15.

Fuerst, D. R., Fisk, J. L., and Rourke, B. P. 1989. Psychosocial functioning of learning disabled children: Replicability of statistically derived subtypes. *Journal of Consulting and Clinical Psychology* **57,** 275–280.

Fugita, S. S. 1990. Asian/Pacific American mental health: Some needed research in epidemiology and service utilization. In F. C. Serafica, A. I. Schwebel, R. K. Russell, P. D. Isaac, and L. B. Myers (eds.), *Mental health of ethnic minorities,* pp. 66–86. New York: Praeger.

Gadow, K. D. 1985. Relative efficacy of pharmacological, behavioral, and combination treatment for enhancing academic performance. *Clinical Psychology Review* **5,** 513–533.

Gadow, K. D. 1992. Pediatric psychopharmacotherapy: A review of recent research. *Journal of Child Psychology and Psychiatry* **33,** 153–195.

Gandour, M. J. 1984. Bulimia: Clinical description, assessment, etiology and treatment. *International Journal of Eating Disorders* **3,** 3–38.

Ganiban, J., Wagner, S., and Cicchetti, D. 1991. Temperament and Down syndrome. In D. Cicchetti and M. Beeghly (eds.), *Children with Down syndrome: A developmental perspective,* pp. 63–100. Cambridge: Cambridge University Press.

Garbarino, J. 1989. Troubled youth, troubled families: The dynamics of adolescent maltreatment. In D. Cicchetti and V. Carlson (eds.), *Child maltreatment: Theory and research on the causes and consequences of child abuse and neglect,* pp. 685–706.

Garbarino, J., and Vondra, J. 1987. Psychological maltreatment: Issues and perspectives. In M. R. Brassard, R. B. Germain, and S. N. Hart (eds.), *Psychological maltreatment of youth,* pp. 25–44. New York: Pergamon.

Garcia, M., and Marks, G. 1989. Depressive symptomatology among Mexican-American adults: An examination with the CES-D Scale. *Psychiatric Research* **27,** 137–148.

Gard, G. C., and Berry, K. K. 1986. Oppositional children: Taming tyrants. *Journal of Clinical Child Psychology* **15,** 148–158.

Gardner, F. E. M. 1989. Inconsistent parenting: Is there evidence for a link with children's conduct problems? *Journal of Abnormal Child Psychology* **17,** 223–233.

Garfield, S. L., and Bergin, A. (eds.). 1978. *Handbook of psychotherapy and behavior change: An empirical analysis,* 2d ed. New York: Wiley.

Garfinkel, P. E., and Garner, D. M. 1982. *Anorexia nervosa: A multidimensional perspective.* New York: Brunner/Mazel.

Garfinkel, P. E., and Garner, D. M. 1986. Anorexia nervosa and adolescent mental health. In R. A. Feldman and A. R. Stiffman (eds.), *Advances in adolescent mental health,* vol. 1, part A, pp. 163–204. Greenwich, Conn.: JAI Press.

Garmezy, N. 1974. Children at risk: The search for antecedents of schizophrenia. Part II. Ongoing research programs, issues and intervention. *Schizophrenia Bulletin,* **9,** 55–125.

Garmezy, N. 1986. Developmental aspects of children's responses to the stress of separation and loss. In M. Rutter, C. E. Izard, and P. B. Read (eds.). *Depression in young people: Developmental and clinical perspectives,* pp. 297–324. New York: Guilford.

Garmezy, N., and Streitman, S. 1974. Children at risk: The search for antecedents of schizophrenia. Part I. Conceptual models and research methods. *Schizophrenia Bulletin* **8,** 14–90.

Garner, D. M., Garfinkel, P. E., and O'Shaughnessy, M. 1985. The validity of the distinction between bulimia with and without anorexia nervosa. *American Journal of Psychiatry* **142,** 581–587.

Garner, D. M., Olmsted, M. P., and Garfinkel, P. E. 1983. Does anorexia nervosa occur on a continuum? *International Journal of Eating Disorders* **2,** 11–20.

Garner, D. M., and Rosen, L. W. 1990. Anorexia nervosa and bulimia nervosa. In A. S. Bellack, M. Hersen, and A. E. Kazdin (eds.), *International handbook of behavior modification and therapy,* 2d ed., pp. 805–817. New York: Plenum.

Garrison, W. T., and McQuiston, S. 1989. *Chronic*

illness during childhood and adolescence. *Psychological aspects.* Newbury Park, Calif.: Sage.

Gelfand, D. M., Jenson, W. R., and Drew, C. J. 1988. *Understanding child behavior disorders,* 2d ed. New York: Holt, Rinehart and Winston.

Gelman, R., and Baillargeon, R. 1983. A review of some Piagetian concepts. In P. H. Mussen (ed.), *Handbook of child psychology,* vol. III. J. H. Flavell and E. M. Markman (eds.), pp. 167–230. New York: Wiley.

Gelman, R., and Schatz, M. 1977. Appropriate speech adjustment. The operation of conversational constraints on talk of two year olds. In M. Lewis and L. A. Rosenbaum (eds.), *Interaction, conversation and the development of language,* pp. 27–62. New York: Wiley.

Gesell, A., and Ilg, F. L. 1949. *Child development: An introduction to the study of human growth.* New York: Harper.

Gesell, A., Ilg, F. L., Ames, L. B., and Bullis, G. E. 1946. *The child from five to ten.* New York: Harper.

Ghee, K. L. 1990. The psychological importance of self-definition and labeling: Black versus African American. *Journal of Black Psychology* **17,** 75–93.

Gibbs, J. C. 1987. Social processes in delinquency: The need to facilitate empathy as well as sociomoral reasoning. In W. M. Kurtines and J. L. Gewirtz (eds.), *Moral development through social interaction,* pp. 296–316. New York: Wiley.

Gibbs, J. C. 1991. Sociomoral development delay and cognitive distortion: Implications for the treatment of antisocial youth. In W. M. Kurtines and J. L. Gewirtz (eds.), *Handbook of moral behavior and development,* vol. 3, pp. 95–110. Hillsdale, N.J.: Erlbaum.

Gibbs, J. T. 1990. Mental health issues of black adolescents: Implications for policy and practice. In A. R. Stiffman and L. E. Davis (eds.), *Ethnic issues in adolescent mental health,* pp. 21–52. Newbury Park, Calif.: Sage.

Gibbs, J. T., and Huang, L. N. 1989a. A conceptual framework for assessing and treating minority youth. In J. T. Gibbs and L. N. Huang (eds.), *Children of color: Psychological interventions with minority youths,* pp. 1–29. San Francisco: Jossey-Bass.

Gibbs, J. T., and Huang, L. N. 1989b. *Children of color. Psychological interventions with minority youth.* San Francisco: Jossey-Bass.

Gillberg, C. 1988. Annotation. The neurobiology of infantile autism. *Journal of Child Psychology and Psychiatry* **29,** 257–266.

Gillberg, C. 1990. Autism and pervasive developmental disorders. *Journal of Child Psychology and Psychiatry* **31,** 99–119.

Gillberg, C. 1991. Outcome in autism and autistic-like conditions. *Journal of the American Academy of Child and Adolescent Psychiatry* **30,** 375–382.

Giovannoni, J. 1989. Definitional issues in child maltreatment. In D. Cicchetti and V. Carlson (eds.), *Child maltreatment. Theory and research on the causes and consequences of child abuse and neglect,* pp. 3–37. Cambridge: Cambridge University Press.

Gittelman, R. 1983a. Hyperkinetic syndrome: Treatment issues and principles. In M. Rutter (ed.), *Developmental neuropsychiatry,* pp. 437–451. New York: Guilford.

Gittelman, R. 1983b. Treatment of reading disorders. In M. Rutter (ed.), *Developmental neuropsychiatry,* pp. 520–539. New York: Guilford.

Gittelman, R., and Kanner, A. 1986. Psychopharmacotherapy. In H. C. Quay and J. S. Werry (eds.), *Psychological disorders of childhood,* 3d ed., pp. 455–495. New York: Wiley.

Glantz, M. 1992. A developmental psychopathology model of drug abuse vulnerability. In M. Glantz and R. Pickens (eds.), *Vulnerability to drug abuse,* pp. 389–412. Washington, D.C.: American Psychological Association.

Glantz, M., and Pickens, R. (eds.) 1992. *Vulnerability to drug abuse.* Introduction and review. In M. Glantz and R. Pickens (eds.), *Vulnerability to drug abuse,* pp. 1–14. Washington, D.C.: American Psychological Association.

Gold, M., and Petronio, R. J. 1980. Delinquent behavior in adolescence. In J. Adelson (ed.), *Handbook of adolescent psychology.* New York: Wiley.

Goldenberg, I., and Goldenberg, H. 1991. *Family therapy: An overview,* 3d ed. Monterey, Calif.: Brooks/Cole.

Goldfarb, W. 1970. Childhood psychoses. In P. M. Mussen (ed.), *Carmichael's manual of child psychology,* vol. 2. New York: Wiley.

Goldstein, M. J. 1988. The family and psychopathology. *Annual review of psychology,* vol. 39, pp. 283–300. Palo Alto, Calif.: Annual Reviews.

Goldstein, M. J. 1990. Family relations as risk factors for the onset and course of schizophrenia. In J.

Rolf, A. S. Masten, D. Cicchetti, K. H. Nuechter-lein, and S. Weintraub (eds.), *Risk and protective factors in the development of psychopathology*, pp. 408–423. Cambridge: Cambridge University Press.

Gomes-Schwartz, B., Horowitz, J. M., and Carda-relli, A. P. 1990. *Child sexual abuse: The initial effects*. Newbury Park, Calif.: Sage.

Gonsiorek, J. C. 1988. Mental health issues of gay and lesbian adolescents. *Journal of Adolescent Health Care* **9,** 114–122.

Goodenough, F. L. 1931. *Anger in young children*. Minneapolis: University of Minnesota Press.

Goodman, G. S., and Clarke-Stewart, A. 1991. Suggestion of children's testimony: Implications for sexual abuse investigation. In J. Doris (ed.), *The suggestibility of children's recollections*, pp. 92–105. Washington, D.C.: American Psychological Association.

Goodman, G. S., Taub, E. P., Jones, D. P. H., En-gland, R., Port, L. K., Rudy, L., and Prado, L. 1992. Testifying in court. *Monographs of the Society for Research in Child Development* **57** (5, series no. 229).

Goodman, S. H. 1991. Early social and affective development in schizophrenic offsprings. In E. F. Walker (ed.), *Schizophrenia: A life-course developmental perspective*, pp. 59–91. San Diego: Academic Press.

Goodyear, P., and Hynd, G. W. 1992. Attention-Deficit Disorder with (ADD/H) and without (ADD/WO) hyperactivity: Behavioral and neuropsychological differentiation. *Journal of Clinical Child Psychology* **21,** 273–305.

Gordon, B. N., and Schroeder, C. S. 1990. Clinical practice: From assessment to intervention. In J. H. Johnson and J. Goldman (eds.), *Developmental assessment in clinical child psychology*, pp. 251–267. New York: Pergamon.

Gordon, R. A. 1990. *Anorexia and bulimia: Anatomy of a social epidemic*. Oxford, England: Basil Blackwell.

Gottesman, I. I. 1978. Schizophrenia and genetics: Where are we? Are you sure? In L. C. Wynne, R. L. Cromwell, and S. Matthyssse (eds.), *The nature of schizophrenia: New approaches to research and treatment*. New York: Wiley.

Gottlieb, J., Alter, M., and Gottlieb, B. W. 1991. Mainstreaming mentally retarded children. In J. L. Matson and J. A. Mulick (eds.), *Handbook of mental retardation*, pp. 63–73. New York: Perga-mon.

Graham, F. K., Ernhart, C. B., Thurston, D., and Craft, M. 1962. Development three years after perinatal anoxia and other potentially damaging newborn experiences. *Psychological Monographs* **76,** (3, whole no. 522).

Graham, S., Doubleday, C., and Guarino, P. A. 1984. The development of relations between perceived controllability and the emotions of pity, anger, and guilt. *Child Development* **55,** 561–565.

Gray Oral Reading Tests, Revised (GORT-R). 1986. Austin, Tex.: Pro-Ed.

Green, R. 1987. *The "sissy boy syndrome" and the development of homosexuality*. New Haven: Yale University Press.

Gresham, F. M. 1986. Conceptual and definitional issues in the assessment of children's social skills: Implications for classification and training. *Journal of Clinical Child Psychology* **15,** 3–15.

Gross, A. M., and Drabman, R. S. 1990. *Handbook of clinical behavioral pediatrics*. New York: Plenum.

Group for the Advancement of Psychiatry. 1966. *Psychopathological disorders in childhood: Theoretical considerations and a proposed classification*, vol. 6, no. 62.

Grych, J. H., and Fincham, F. D. 1992. Interventions for children of divorce: Toward greater integration of research and action. *Psychological Bulletin* **111,** 434–454.

Guevremont, D. 1990. Social skills and peer relationship training. In R. A. Barkley (ed.), *Attention-deficit hyperactivity disorder: A handbook for diagnosis and treatment*, pp. 540–572. New York: Guilford.

Guralnick, M. J. 1986. The peer relations of young handicapped and non-handicapped children. In P. S. Strain, M. J. Guralnick, and H. M. Walker (eds.), *Children's social behavior: Development, assessment and modification*, pp. 93–140. New York: Academic Press.

Gutierrez, J., and Sameroff, A. 1990. Determinants of complexity in Mexican-American and Anglo-American mothers' conceptions of child development. *Child Development* **16,** 384–394.

Guyer, M. J. 1991. Psychiatry, law, and child sexual abuse. In A. Tasman and S. M. Goldfinger (eds.), *Review of psychiatry*, vol. 10, pp. 367–390. Washington, D.C.: American Psychiatric Press.

Haaga, D. A. F., Dyck, M. J., and Ernst, D. 1991. Empirical studies of cognitive theory of depression. *Psychological Bulletin* **110,** 215–236.

Halberstein, D. 1991. *A data book of child and adolescent injury.* Washington, D.C.: National Center for Education in Maternal and Child Health.

Hale, C. A., and Borkowski, J. G. 1991. Attention, memory, and cognition. In J. L. Matson and J. A. Mulick (eds.), *Handbook of mental retardation,* pp. 505–528. New York: Pergamon.

Hall, R. V., Fox, R., Willard, D., Goldsmith, L., Emerson, M., Owen, M., Davis, T., and Porcia, E. 1971. The teacher as observer and experimenter in the modification of disputing and talking-out behaviors. *Journal of Applied Behavioral Analysis* **4,** 141–149.

Halperin, J. M., Matier, K., Bedi, G., Vanshdeep, S., and Newcorn, J. H. 1991. Specificity of inattention, impulsivity, and hyperactivity to the diagnosis of Attention-deficit Hyperactivity Disorder. *Journal of the American Academy of Child and Adolescent Psychiatry* **31,** 190–196.

Halstead Neuropsychological Test Battery for Children. 1969. Indianapolis: Reitan.

Hammen, C. 1990. Cognitive approaches to depression. In B. B. Lahey and A. E. Kazdin (eds.), *Advances in clinical child psychology,* vol. 13, pp. 139–173. New York: Plenum.

Hans, S. L., and Marcus, J. 1991. Neurobehavioral development of infants at risk for schizophrenia: A review. In E. F. Walker (ed.), *Schizophrenia. A life-course developmental perspective,* pp. 33–57. San Diego, Calif.: Academic Press.

Hanson, D. R., Gottesman, I. I., and Heston, L. L. 1990. Long-range schizophrenia forecasting: Many a slip twixt the cup and the lip. In J. Rolf, A. S. Masten, D. Cicchetti, K. H. Nuechterlein, and S. Weintraub (eds.), *Risk and protective factors in the development of psychopathology,* pp. 242–444. Cambridge: Cambridge University Press.

Hare, E. H. 1962. Masturbatory insanity: The history of an idea. *Journal of Mental Science* **108,** 1–25.

Harkness, S., and Super, C. M. 1990. Culture and psychopathology. In M. Lewis and S. M. Miller (eds.), *Handbook of developmental psychopathology,* pp. 41–52. New York: Plenum.

Harrington, R., Fudge, H., Rutter, M., Pickles, A., and Hill, J. 1991. Adult outcomes of childhood and adolescent depression. Part II: Links with antisocial disorders. *Journal of the American Academy of Child and Adolescent Psychiatry* **30,** 434–439.

Harris, P. 1989. The autistic child's impaired conception of mental states. *Development and Psychopathology* **1,** 191–196.

Harris, S. L., Alessandri, M., and Gill, M. J. 1991. Training parents of developmentally disabled children. In J. L. Matson and J. A. Mulick (eds.), *Handbook of mental retardation,* pp. 373–381. New York: Pergamon.

Harrison, A. O., Wilson, M. N., Pine, C. J., Chan, S. Q., and Buriel, R. 1990. Family ecologies of ethnic minority children. *Child Development* **61,** 347–362.

Hart, S. N., and Brassard, M. R. 1991. Psychological maltreatment: Progress achieved. *Development and Psychopathology* **3,** 71–78.

Hart, S. N., Germain, R. B., and Brassard, M. R. 1987. The challenge: To better understand and combat psychological maltreatment of children and youth. In M. R. Brassard, R. B. Germain, and S. N. Hart (eds.), *Psychological maltreatment of youth,* pp. 3–24. New York: Pergamon.

Harter, S. 1983. Developmental perspective on the self-system. In P. H. Mussen (ed.), *Handbook of child psychology.* New York: Wiley.

Harter, S. 1986. Processes underlying the construction, maintenance, and enhancement of the self-concept in children. In J. Suls and A. G. Greenwald (eds.), *Psychological perspectives on the self,* vol. 3, pp. 137–180. Hillsdale, N.J.: Erlbaum.

Harter, S. 1987. The determinants and mediational role of global self-worth in children. In N. Eisenberg (ed.), *Contemporary topics in developmental psychology,* pp. 242–291. New York: Wiley.

Harter, S. 1988. Developmental and dynamic changes in the nature of the self-concept: Implications for child psychotherapy. In S. R. Shirk (ed.), *Cognitive development and child psychotherapy,* pp. 119–160. New York: Plenum.

Harter, S. 1990a. Issues in the assessment of the self-concept of children and adolescents. In A. LaGreca (ed.), *Through the eyes of a child,* pp. 292–325. Boston: Allyn & Bacon.

Harter, S. 1990b. Causes, correlates, and the functional role of global self-worth: A life-span perspective. In R. J. Sternberg and J. Kolligian, Jr. (eds.), *Competence considered,* pp. 67–97. New Haven: Yale University Press.

Harter, S., Marold, D. B., and Whitesell, N. R. 1992. Model of psychosocial risk factors leading to suicidal ideation in young adolescents. *Development and Psychopathology* **4**, 167–188.

Hartman, C. R., and Burgess, A. W. 1989. Sexual abuse in children: Causes and consequences. In D. Cicchetti and V. Carlson (eds.), *Child maltreatment: Theory and research on the causes and consequences of child abuse and neglect*, pp. 95–128. Cambridge: Cambridge University Press.

Hartman, H. 1964. *Essays on ego psychology.* New York: International Universities Press.

Hartmann, D. P., and Wood, D. D. 1990. Observational methods. In A. S. Bellack, M. Hersen, and A. E. Kazdin (eds.), *International handbook of behavior modification and therapy*, 2d ed., pp. 107–128. New York: Plenum.

Hartup, W. W. 1983. Peer relations. In P. H. Mussen (ed.), *Handbook of child psychology*, vol. 4, 4th ed., pp. 103–196. New York: Wiley.

Hartup, W. W. 1974. Aggression in childhood: Developmental perspectives. *American Psychologist* **29**, 336–341.

Hartup, W. W. 1983. Peer relations. In E. M. Hetherington (ed.), *Handbook of child psychology*. Vol. 4: *Socialization, personality, and social development*, 4th ed., pp. 103–196. New York: Wiley.

Harvey, P. D. 1991. Cognitive and linguistic functions of adolescent children at risk for schizophrenia. In E. F. Walker (ed.), *Schizophrenia. A lifecourse developmental perspective*, pp. 139–156. San Diego, Calif.: Academic Press.

Haskett, M. E., and Kistner, J. A. 1991. Social interactions and peer perceptions of young physically abused children. *Child Development* **62**, 979–990.

Haskins, R. 1989. Beyond metaphor: The efficacy of early childhood education. *American Psychologist* **44**, 274–282.

Haswell, K. L., Hock, E., and Wenar, C. 1982. Techniques for dealing with oppositional behavior in preschool children. *Young Children*, March, pp. 13–18.

Haugaard, J. J., and Emery, R. E. 1989. Methodological issues in child sexual abuse research. *Child Abuse & Neglect* **13**, 89–100.

Hawkins, J. D., Lishner, D., and Catalano, R. F., Jr., 1985. Childhood predictors and the prevention of adolescent substance abuse. In C. L. Jones and R. J. Battjes (eds.), *Etiology of drug abuse: Implications for prevention*, pp. 75–126. NIDA Research Monograph 56. Rockville, Md.: National Institute on Drug Abuse.

Hawton, K. 1986. *Suicide and attempted suicide among children and adolescents.* Beverly Hills: Sage.

Hayes, M. 1979. Rights of the child. In J. D. Noshpitz (ed.), *Basic handbook of child psychiatry.* Vol. 4, *Prevention and current issues.* New York: Basic Books.

Haywood, H. C., Meyers, C. E., and Switzky, H. N. 1982. Mental retardation. In M. R. Rosenzweig and L. W. Porter (eds.), *Annual review of psychology*, vol. 33, pp. 309–342. Palo Alto, Calif.: Annual Reviews.

Hazelrigg, M. D., Cooper, H. M., and Borduin, C. M. 1987. Evaluating the effectiveness of family therapies: An integrative review and analysis. *Psychological Bulletin* **101**, 428–442.

Heiman, M. L. 1992. Annotation: Putting the puzzle together: Validating allegations of child sexual abuse. *Journal of Child Psychology and Psychiatry* **33**, 311–329.

Heinicke, C. M. 1956. Some effects of separating two-year-old children from their parents: A comparative study. *Human Relations* **9**, 105–176.

Heinicke, C. M. 1989. Psychodynamic psychotherapy with children: Current status and guidelines for future research. In B. B. Lahey and A. E. Kazdin (eds.), *Advances in clinical child psychology*, vol. 12, pp. 1–26. New York: Plenum.

Heinstein, M. I. 1963. Behavioral correlates of breast-bottle regimes under varying parent-infant relationships. *Monographs of the Society for Research in Child Development* **28** (4, serial no. 88).

Helms, J. E. 1990. Three perspectives on counseling and psychotherapy with visible racial/ethnic group clients. In F. C. Serafica, A. I. Schwebel, R. K. Russell, P. D. Isaac, and L. B. Myers (eds.), *Mental health of ethnic minorities*, pp. 171–201. New York: Praeger.

Henggeler, S. W. 1989. *Delinquency in adolescence.* Newbury Park, Calif.: Sage.

Henggeler, S. W., Borduin, C. M., and Mann, B. J. 1993. Advances in family therapy: Empirical foundations. In T. H. Ollendick and R. J. Prinz (eds.), *Advances in clinical child psychology*, vol. 15, pp. 207–242. New York: Plenum.

Henggeler, S. W., Melton, G. B., and Rodrigue, J. R. 1992. *Pediatric and adolescent AIDS. Research findings from the social sciences.* Newbury Park, Calif.: Sage.

Henggeler, S. W., Rodick, J. D., Borduin, C. M., Hanson, C. L., Watson, S. M., and Urey, J. R. 1986. Multisystemic treatment of juvenile offenders: Effects on adolescent behavior and family interaction. *Developmental Psychology* **22**, 132–141.

Herbert, M. 1974. *Emotional problems of development in children.* New York: Academic Press.

Hermelin, B. 1976. Coding and sense modalities. In L. Wing (ed.), *Early childhood autism: Clinical, educational and social aspects.* New York: Pergamon.

Hersov, L. 1960. Persistent non-attendance at school. *Journal of Child Psychology and Psychiatry* **1**, 130–136.

Hersov, L. 1977. Fecal soiling. In M. Rutter and L. Hersov (eds.), *Child psychiatry: Modern approaches.* Oxford: Blackwell Scientific Publications.

Herzog, D. B., Keller, M. B., Sacks, N. R., Yeh, C. J., and Lavori, P. W. 1992. Psychiatric comorbidity in treatment-seeking anorexics and bulimics. *Journal of the American Academy of Child and Adolescent Psychiatry* **31**, 810–818.

Herzog, E., and Sudia, C. E. 1973. Children in fatherless families. In B. E. Caldwell and H. N. Ricciuti (eds.), *Review of child development research,* vol. 3. Chicago: University of Chicago Press.

Hetherington, E. M. 1989. Coping with family transitions: Winners, losers, and survivors. *Child Psychology* **60**, 1–14.

Hetherington, E. M., and Camara, K. A. 1984. Families in transition: The process of dissolution and reconstitution. In R. E. Parke (ed.), *Review of child development research,* vol. 7, pp. 398–440. Chicago: University of Chicago Press.

Hetherington, E. M., and Martin, B. 1986. Family interaction. In H. C. Quay and J. S. Werry (eds.), *Psychopathological disorders of childhood,* 3d ed. New York: Wiley.

Hinshaw, S. P. 1987. On the distinction between attentional deficits/hyperactivity and conduct problems/aggression in child psychopathology. *Psychological Bulletin* **101**, 443–463.

Hinshaw, S. P., Lahey, B. B., and Hart, E. L. 1993. Issues of taxonomy and comorbidity in the development of conduct disorders. *Development and Psychopathology, 5,* 31–49.

Hirshfeld, D. R., Rosenbaum, J. F., Biederman, J., Bolduc, E. A., Faraone, S. V., Snidman, N., Reznick, J. S., and Kagan, J. 1992. Stable behavioral inhibition and its association with anxiety disorder. *Journal of the American Academy of Child and Adolescent Psychiatry* **31,** 103–111.

Ho, M. K. 1992. *Minority children and adolescents in therapy.* Newbury Park, Calif.: Sage.

Hobson, R. P. 1982. The question of childhood egocentrism: The coordination of perspectives in relation to operational thinking. *Journal of Child Psychology and Psychiatry* **23,** 43–60.

Hobson, R. P. 1984. Early childhood autism and the question of egocentrism. *Journal of Autism and Developmental Disorders* **14,** 85–104.

Hobson, R. P. 1986a. The autistic child's appraisal of expressions of emotion. *Journal of Child Psychology and Psychiatry* **27,** 321–342.

Hobson, R. P. 1986b. The autistic child's appraisal of expression of emotions: A further study. *Journal of Child Psychology and Psychiatry* **27,** 671–680.

Hobson, R. P. 1989. Beyond cognition: A theory of autism. In G. Dawson (ed.), *Autism. Nature, diagnosis and treatment,* pp. 22–48. New York: Guilford.

Hobson, R. P. 1991. Methodological issues for experiments on autistic individuals' perception and understanding of emotion. *Journal of Child Psychology and Psychiatry* **32,** 1135–1158.

Hobson, R. P., Ouston, J., and Lee, A. 1988. What's in a face? The case of autism. *British Journal of Psychology* **79,** 441–453.

Hodapp, R. M. 1990. One road or many? Issues in the similar-sequence hypothesis in relation to mentally retarded children. In R. M. Hodapp, J. A. Burack, and E. Zigler (eds.), *Issues in the developmental approach to mental retardation,* pp. 49–70. Cambridge: Cambridge University Press.

Hodapp, R. M., Burack, J. A., and Zigler, E. 1990. The developmental perspective in the field of mental retardation. In R. M. Hodapp, J. A. Burack, and E. Zigler (eds.), *Issues in the developmental approach to mental retardation,* pp. 3–20. Cambridge: Cambridge University Press.

Hodapp, R. M., and Zigler, E. 1991. Applying the developmental perspective to Down syndrome. In D. Cicchetti and M. Beeghly (eds.), *Children with Down syndrome: A developmental perspective,* pp. 1–28. Cambridge: Cambridge University Press.

Hodges, K., and Cools, J. N. 1990. Structured diagnostic interviews. In A. M. La Greca (ed.), *Through the eyes of the child: Obtaining self-reports from children and adolescents,* pp. 109–149. Boston: Allyn & Bacon.

Hoffman, M. L. 1978. Toward a theory of empathetic arousal and development. In M. Lewis and L. A. Rosenblum (eds.), *The development of affect,* vol. 1, pp. 227–256. New York: Plenum.

Holmbeck, G. N., and Kendall, P. C. 1991. Clinical-childhood-developmental interface: Implications for treatment. In P. R. Martin (ed.), *Handbook of behavior therapy and psychological science. An integrative approach,* pp. 73–99. New York: Pergamon.

Howlin, P. 1986. An overview of social behavior in autism. In E. Schopler and G. B. Mesibov (eds.), *Social behavior in autism,* pp. 103–131. New York: Plenum.

Huelsman, C. B. 1970. The WISC subtest syndrome for disabled readers. *Perceptual and Motor Skills* **30,** 535–550.

Huesmann, L. R., Eron, L. D., Lefkowitz, M. M., and Walder, L. O. 1984. Stability of aggression over time and generation. *Developmental Psychology* **20,** 1120–1134.

Hughes, J. N., and Baker, D. B. 1990. *The clinical child interview.* New York: Guilford.

Huguenin, N. H., Weidenman, L. E., and Mulick, J. A. 1991. Programmed instruction. In J. L. Matson and J. A. Mulick (eds.), *Handbook of mental retardation,* pp. 451–467. New York: Pergamon.

Humphrey, L. 1989. Observed family interactions among subtypes of eating disorders using structural analysis of social behavior. *Journal of Consulting and Clinical Psychology* **57,** 206–214.

Humphreys, L., Forehand, R., McMahon, R., and Roberts, M. 1978. Parent behavior training to modify child noncompliance: Effects on untreated siblings. *Journal of Behavior Therapy and Experimental Psychiatry* **9,** 235–238.

Hynd, G. W., and Semrud-Clikeman, M. 1989. Dyslexia and brain morphology. *Psychological Bulletin* **106,** 447–482.

Hynd, G. W., Snow, J., and Becker, M. G. 1986. Neuropsychological assessment. In B. B. Lahey and A. E. Kazdin (eds.), *Advances in clinical child psychology,* vol. 9, pp. 35–86. New York: Plenum.

Israel, A. C. 1990. Childhood obesity. In A. S. Bellack, M. Hersen, and A. E. Kazdin (eds.), *International handbook of behavior modification,* 2d ed., pp. 819–830. New York: Plenum.

Israel, A. C., & Shapiro, L. S., (1985) Behavior problems of obese children enrolling in weight reduc-

tion programs. *Journal of Pediatric Psychology, 10,* 449–460.

Israel, A. C., Stolmaker, L., and Andrian, C. A. G. 1985. The effects of training parents in general child management skills in a behavioral weight loss program for children. *Behavior Therapy* **16,** 169–180.

Israel, A. C., Weinstein, J. B., and Prince, R. 1985. Eating behavior, eating styles and children's weight status: Failure to find an obese eating style. *International Journal of Eating Disorders* **4,** 113–119.

Izard, C. E., and Schwartz, G. M. 1986. Patterns of emotion in depression. In M. Rutter, C. E. Izard, and P. B. Read (eds.), *Depression in young people: Developmental and clinical perspectives,* pp. 33–70. New York: Guilford.

Jacob, T., and Grounds, L. 1978. Confusions and conclusions: A response to Doane. *Family Process* **17,** 377–387.

Jacob, T., and Tennenbaum, D. L. 1988. Family assessment methods. In M. Rutter, A. H. Tuma, and I. S. Lann (eds.), *Assessment and diagnosis in child psychopathology,* pp. 196–231. New York: Guilford.

Jacobitz, D., and Sroufe, L. A. 1987. The early caregiver-child relationship and Attention-Deficit Disorder with Hyperactivity in kindergarten: A prospective study. *Child Development* **58,** 1496–1504.

Jacobs, J. 1971. *Adolescent suicide.* New York: Wiley-Interscience.

Jacobson, E. 1964. *The self and the object world.* New York: International Universities Press.

Janis, I. L. (ed.). 1969. *Personality: Dynamics, development, and assessment.* New York: Harcourt, Brace & World.

Jarvie, G. J., Lahey, B., Graziano, W., and Framer, E. 1983. Childhood obesity and social stigma: What we know and what we don't know. *Developmental Review* **3,** 237–273.

Jastak, S. R., and Wilkinson, G. S. 1984. *Wide-Range Achievement Test—Revised.* Wilmington, Del.: Jastak Associates.

Jay, S. M. 1988. Invasive medical procedures: Psychological intervention and assessment. In D. J. Routh (ed.), *Handbook of pediatric psychology,* pp. 401–425. New York: Guilford.

Jay, S. M., Elliot, C. H., Katz, E., and Siegel, S. E.

1987. Cognitive behavioral and pharmacologic intervention for children's distress during painful medical procedures. *Journal of Consulting and Clinical Psychology* **55,** 860–865.

Jenkins, J. H. 1988. Conceptions of schizophrenia as a problem of nerves: A cross-cultural comparison of Mexican-Americans and Anglo-Americans. *Social Science and Medicine* **26,** 1233–1243.

Jersild, A. T., and Holmes, F. B. 1935. *Children's fears.* Child Development, monograph no. 20. New York: Teachers College, Columbia University.

Jessor, R. 1979. Marijuana: A review of recent psychosocial research. In R. I. Dupont, A. Goldstein, and J. O'Donnell (eds.), *Handbook on drug abuse.* Washington, D.C.: National Institute on Drug Abuse.

Jessor, R. 1985. Bridging etiology and prevention in drug abuse research. In C. L. Jones and R. J. Battjes (eds.), *Etiology of drug abuse: Implications for prevention,* pp. 257–268. NIDA Research Monograph 56, Rockville, Md.: National Institute on Drug Abuse.

Jessor, R., and Jessor, S. L. 1977. *Problem behavior and psychosocial development: A longitudinal study of youth.* New York: Academic Press.

Joe, G. W., and Simpson, D. D. 1991. Reasons for inhalant use. *Hispanic Journal of Behavioral Sciences* **13,** 256–266.

Johnson, C., and Larson, R. 1982. Bulimia: An analysis of mood and behavior. *Psychosomatic Medicine* **44,** 341–351.

Johnson, C. A., Pentz, M. A., Weber, M. D., Dwyer, J. H., Baer, N., MacKinnon, D. P., Hamsem, W. B., and Flay, B. R. 1990. Relative effectiveness of comprehensive community programming for drug abuse prevention with high-risk and low-risk adolescents. *Journal of Consulting and Clinical Psychology* **58,** 447–456.

Johnson, C. N. 1988. Theory of mind and the structure of conscious experience. In J. W. Astington, P. L. Harris, and D. R. Olson (eds.), *Developing theories of mind,* pp. 47–63. Cambridge: Cambridge University Press.

Johnson, J. H., and Goldman, J. 1990. Developmental assessment: An introduction and overview. In J. H. Johnson and J. Goldman (eds.), *Developmental assessment in clinical child psychology,* pp. 1–14. New York: Pergamon.

Johnson, S. B. 1989. Juvenile diabetes. In T. H. Ol-lendick and M. Hersen (eds.), *Handbook of child psychopathology,* 2d ed., pp. 359–376. New York: Plenum.

Johnston, L. D. 1985. The etiology and prevention of substance use: What can we learn from recent historical changes? In C. L. Jones and R. J. Battjes (eds.), *Etiology of drug abuse: Implications for prevention,* pp. 155–177. NIDA Research Monograph 56. Rockville, Md.: National Institute on Drug Abuse.

Johnston, L. D., Bachman, J. G., and O'Malley, P. M. 1977. *Highlights from: Drug use among American high school students, 1975–1977.* Rockville, Md.: National Institute on Drug Abuse.

Johnston, L. D., O'Malley, P. M., and Bachman, J. G. 1988. Illicit drug use, smoking, and drinking by American high school students, college students, and young adults. *National Institute on Drug Abuse.* Rockville, Md.: U.S. Department of Health and Human Services.

Johnston, L. D., O'Malley, P. M., and Jerald, G. 1987. Psychotherapeutic, licit and illicit use of drugs among adolescents: An epidemiological perspective. *Journal of Adolescent Health Care* **8,** 36–51.

Kaffman, M., and Elizur, E. 1977. Infants who become enuretics: A longitudinal study of 161 kibbutz children. *Monographs of the Society for Research in Child Development,* vol. 42, no. 2.

Kagan, J., Klein, R. E., Finley, G. E., Rogoff, B., and Nolan, E. 1979. A cross-cultural study of cognitive development. *Monograph of the Society for Research in Child Development* **44** (5, series no. 180).

Kail, R. 1982. *The development of memory in children,* 2d ed. New York: Freeman.

Kalichman, S. C. (ed.). 1992. Impact of child maltreatment reporting (Special Issue). *The Child, Youth, and Family Service Quarterly* **15,** Winter.

Kalnins, I. V., Churchill, M. P., and Terry, G. E. 1980. Concurrent stresses in families with a leukemic child. *Journal of Pediatric Psychology* **5,** 81–92.

Kandel, D. B. 1978. Convergence in prospective longitudinal surveys of drug use in normal populations. In D. B. Kandel (ed.), *Longitudinal research in drug use: Empirical findings and methodological issues.* Washington, D. C.: Hemisphere.

Kandel, D. B., Kessler, R. C., and Margulies, R. Z. 1978. Antecedents of adolescent initiation into stages of drug use: A developmental analysis. In

D. B. Kandel (ed.), *Longitudinal research in drug use. Empirical findings and methodological issues.* Washington, D.C.: Hemisphere.

Kandel, D. B., and Yamaguchi, K. 1985. Developmental patterns of the use of legal, illegal, and medically prescribed psychotropic drugs from adolescence to young adulthood. In C. L. Jones and R. J. Battjes (eds.), *Etiology of drug abuse: Implications for prevention,* pp, 193–235. NIDA Research Monograph 56. Rockville, Md.: National Institute on Drug Abuse.

Kanner, L. 1943. Autistic disturbances of affective contact. *Nervous Child* **2,** 217–250.

Kanner, L. 1946–1947. Irrelevant and metaphorical language in early infantile autism. *American Journal of Psychiatry* **103,** 242–246.

Kanner, L. 1977. *Child Psychiatry,* 4th ed. Springfield, Ill.: Charles C. Thomas.

Kanner, L., Rodriguez, A., and Ashenden, B. 1972. How far can autistic children go in matters of social adaptation? *Journal of Autism and Childhood Schizophrenia* **2,** 9–33.

Kasari, C., Sigman, M., Mundy, P., and Yirmiya, N. 1990. Affective sharing in the context of joint attention interactions in normal, autistic, and mentally retarded children. *Journal of Autism and Developmental Disorders* **20,** 87–100.

Kasen, L., Johnson, J., and Cohen, P. 1990. The impact of school emotional climate on school psychopathology. *Journal of Abnormal Child Psychology* **18,** 165–177.

Kasik, M. M., Sabatino, D. A., and Spoentgen, P. 1987. Psychosocial aspects of learning disabilities. In S. J. Ceci (ed.), *Handbook of cognitive, social and neuropsychological aspects of learning disabilities,* vol. 2, pp. 251–272. Hillsdale, N.J.: Erlbaum.

Kaufman, A. S. 1979. *Intelligence Testing with WISC-R.* New York: Wiley.

Kaufman Assessment Battery for Children (K-ABC). 1983. Circle Pines, Minn.: American Guidance Service.

Kaufman, B. N., and Kaufman, R. K. 1976. *Son-rise.* New York: Warner Books.

Kaufman, J., and Zigler, E. 1989. The intergenerational transmission of child abuse. In D. Cicchetti and V. Carlson (eds.), *Child maltreatment: Theory and research on the causes and consequences of child abuse and neglect,* pp. 129–151. Cambridge: Cambridge University Press.

Kavale, K. A. 1990a. A critical appraisal of empirical subtyping research in learning disabilities. In H. L. Swanson and B. Keogh (eds.), *Learning disabilities: Theoretical and research issues,* pp. 215–230. Hillsdale, N.J.: Erlbaum.

Kavale, K. A. 1990b. Variance and verities in learning disability intervention. In T. E. Schruggs and B. Y. L. Wong (eds.), *Intervention research in learning disabilities,* pp. 3–33. New York: Springer-Verlag.

Kazdin, A. E. 1980. *Behavior modification in applied settings.* Homewood, Ill.: Dorsey.

Kazdin, A. E. 1987. *Conduct disorders in childhood and adolescence.* Newbury Park, Calif.: Sage.

Kazdin, A. E. 1988. *Child psychotherapy: Developing and identifying effective treatment.* New York: Pergamon.

Kazdin, A. E. 1989a. Developmental differences in depression. In B. B. Lahey and A. E. Kazdin (eds.), *Advances in clinical child psychology,* vol. 12, pp. 192–219. New York: Plenum.

Kazdin, A. E. 1989b. Identifying depression in children. A comparison of alternative selection criteria. *Journal of Abnormal Child Psychology* **17,** 437–454.

Kazdin, A. E. 1989c. Developmental psychopathology: Current research, issues and directions. *American Psychologist* **44,** 180–187.

Kazdin, A. E. 1990. Childhood depression. *Journal of Child Psychology and Psychiatry* **31,** 121–160.

Kazdin, A. E. 1991. Effectiveness of psychotherapy with children. *Journal of Consulting and Clinical Psychology* **59,** 785–798.

Kazdin, A. E. 1993a. Treatment of conduct disorders: Progress and directions in psychotherapy research. *Development and Psychopathology, 5,* 277–310.

Kazdin, A. E. 1993b. Psychotherapy for children and adolescents. Current progress and future research directions. *American Psychologist, 48,* 644–657.

Kazdin, A. E., Bass, D., Ayers, W. A., and Rodgers, A. 1990. Empirical and clinical focus of child and adolescent psychotherapy research. *Journal of Consulting and Clinical Psychology* **58,** 729–740.

Kazdin, A. E., Bass, D., Seigel, T., and Thomas, C. 1989. Cognitive-behavioral therapy and relationships therapy in the treatment of children referred for antisocial behavior. *Journal of Consulting and Clinical Psychology* **57,** 522–535.

Kazdin, A. E., French, N. H., Unis, A. S., Esveldt-

Dawson, K., and Sherick, R. B. 1983. Hopelessness, depression and suicidal intent among psychiatrically disturbed inpatient children. *Journal of Consulting and Clinical Psychology* **51,** 504–510.

Kearney, C. A., and Silverman, W. K. 1990. A preliminary analysis of a functional model of assessment and treatment of school refusal behavior. *Behavior Modification* **14,** 340–366.

Kearney, C. A., and Silverman, W. K. 1992. Let's not push the "panic" button: A critical analysis of panic and panic disorder in adolescents. *Clinical Psychology Review* **12,** 293–305.

Keller, M., and Wood, P. 1989. Development of friendship reasoning. A study of interindividual differences and intraindividual change. *Developmental Psychology* **25,** 820–826.

Kelley, T. L., Madden, R., Gardner, E. F., and Rudman, H. C. 1964. *The Stanford Achievement Test.* New York: Harcourt Brace Jovanovich.

Kelly, J. A. 1990. Treating the child abuser. In R. T. Ammerman and M. Hersen (eds.), *Children at risk: An evaluation of factors contributing to child abuse and neglect,* pp. 269–289. New York: Plenum.

Kelly, E. W., Jr. 1973. School phobia: A review of theory and treatment. *Psychology in the Schools* **10,** 33–42.

Kendall, P. C. 1991. *Child and adolescent therapy. Cognitive-behavioral procedures.* New York: Guilford.

Kendall, P. C., and Ronan, K. R. 1990. Assessment of children's anxieties, fears, and phobias: Cognitive-behavioral models and methods. In C. R. Reynolds and R. W. Kamphaus (eds.), *Handbook of psychological and educational assessment in children,* vol. 2, pp. 223–244. New York: Guilford.

Kendall, P. C., Stark, K. D., and Adam, T. 1990. Cognitive deficits or cognitive distortions in childhood depression. *Journal of Abnormal Child Psychology* **18,** 255–270.

Kendall-Tackett, K. A., Williams, L. M., and Finkelhor, D. 1993. Impact of sexual abuse on children: A review and synthesis of recent empirical studies. *Psychological Bulletin* **113,** 164–180.

Kenny, T. J. 1980. Hyperactivity. In H. E. Rie and E. D. Rie (eds.), *Handbook of minimal brain dysfunctions. A critical view.* New York: Wiley.

Kenny, T. J., and Burka, A. 1980. Coordinating multiple interventions. In H. E. Rie and E. D. Rie (eds.), *Handbook of minimal brain dysfunctions. A critical view.* New York: Wiley.

Keogh, B. K. 1990. Definitional assumptions and research issues. In H. L. Swanson and B. Keogh (eds.), *Learning disabilities: Theoretical and research issues,* pp. 15–22. Hillsdale, N.J.: Erlbaum.

Kephart, N. 1968. *Learning disability: An educational adventure.* West Lafayette, Ind.: Kappa Delta Pi.

Kessler, J. W. 1966. *Psychopathology of childhood.* Englewood Cliffs, N.J.: Prentice-Hall.

King, N. J. 1993. Simple and social phobias. In T. H. Ollendick and F. J. Prinz (eds.), *Advances in clinical child psychology,* vol. 15, pp. 305–341. New York: Plenum.

King, N. J., Hamilton, D. I., and Ollendick, T. H. 1988. *Children's phobias. A behavioural perspective.* New York: Wiley.

King, N. J., Ollier, K., Iacuone, R., Schuster, S., Bays, K., Gullone, E., and Ollendick, T. H. 1989. Fears of children and adolescents: A cross-sectional Australian study using the Revised-Fear Survey Schedule for Children. *Journal of Child Psychology and Psychiatry* **30,** 775–784.

Kinsbourne, M., and Caplan, P. J. 1979. *Children's learning and attention problems.* Boston: Little, Brown.

Kinsbourne, M., and Hiscock, M. 1978. Cerebral lateralization and cognitive development. In J. S. Chall and A. F. Mirsky (eds.), *Education and the brain: The seventy-seventh yearbook of the National Society for the Study of Education* (part 2). Chicago: University of Chicago Press.

Kinsey, A. C., Pomeroy, W. B., and Martin, C. E. 1948. *Sexual behavior in the human male.* Philadelphia: Saunders.

Kirk, S., McCarthy, J., and Kirk, W. 1968. *Illinois Test of Psycholinguistic Ability,* rev. ed. Urbana, Ill.: University of Illinois Press.

Klausmeier, H., and Allen, P. S. 1978. *Cognitive development of children and youth: A longitudinal study.* New York: Academic Press.

Klein, R. G., and Last, C. G. 1989. *Anxiety disorders in children.* Newbury Park, Calif.: Sage.

Klein, R. G., and Mannuzza, S. 1991. Long-term outcome of hyperactive children: A review. *Journal of the American Academy of Child and Adolescent Psychiatry* **30,** 383–387.

Klesges, R. C., Malott, J. M., Boschee, P. F., and Weber, J. M. 1986. The effects of parental influences on children's food intake, physical activity, and relative weight. *International Journal of Eating Disorders* **5,** 335–346.

Klopfer, W. G., and Taulbee, E. S. 1976. Projective

tests. In M. R. Rosenzweig and L. W. Porter (eds.), *Annual review of psychology*, vol. 27. Palo Alto, Calif.: Annual Reviews.

Knight, R. A., and Roff, J. D. 1985. Affectivity in schizophrenia. In M. Alpert (ed.), *Controversies in schizophrenia. Changes and constancies*, pp. 280–313. New York: Guilford.

Knitzer, J. E. 1976. Child advocacy: A perspective. *American Journal of Orthopsychiatry* **46**, 200–216.

Knitzer, J. E., Steinberg, Z., and Fleisch, B. 1991. Schools, children's mental health, and advocacy challenge. *Journal of Clinical Child Psychology* **20**, 102–111.

Kohlberg, L. 1976. Moral stages and moralization: The cognitive-developmental approach. In T. Lickona (ed.), *Moral development and behavior. Theory, research and social issues*. New York: Holt, Rinehart & Winston.

Kohlberg, L., LaCrosse, J., and Ricks, D. 1972. The predictability of adult mental health from childhood behavior. In B. J. Wolman (ed.), *Manual of child psychopathology*. New York: McGraw-Hill.

Kohn, M. 1977. *Social competence, symptoms and underachievement in childhood: A longitudinal perspective*. Silver Spring, Md.: V. H. Winston.

Kolvin, I., Miller, F. J. W., Fleeting, M., and Kolvin, P. A. 1989. Risk/protective factors for offending with particular reference to deprivation. In M. Rutter (ed.), *Studies in psychosocial risk: The power of longitudinal studies*, pp. 77–95. Cambridge: Cambridge University Press.

Kolvin, I., Ounsted, C., Humphrey, M., and McNay, A. 1971. Studies in childhood psychoses. Part 2. The phenomenology of childhood psychoses. *British Journal of Psychiatry* **118**, 385–395.

Kolvin, I., Ounsted, C., Richardson, L. M., and Garside, R. 1971. Studies in childhood psychoses. Part 3. The family and social background in childhood psychosis. *British Journal of Psychiatry* **118**, 396–402.

Kopp, C. B. 1982. Antecedents of self-regulation: A developmental perspective. *Developmental Psychology* **18**, 199–214.

Kopp, C. B. 1991. The growth of self-monitoring among young children with Down syndrome. In D. Cicchetti and M. Beeghly, (eds.), *Children with Down syndrome: A developmental perspective*, pp. 231–251. Cambridge: Cambridge University Press.

Koppitz, E. M. 1971. *Children with learning disabilities: A five-year follow-up study*. New York: Grune & Stratton.

Koppitz, E. M. 1973. *The Bender Gestalt Test for Young Children*. New York: Grune & Stratton.

Korchin, S. J. 1976. *Modern clinical psychology. Principles of intervention in the clinic and community*. New York: Basic Books.

Kovacs, M. 1981. Rating scale to assess depression in school aged children. *Acta Paedopsychiatrica* **46**, 305–315.

Kovacs, M. 1986. A developmental perspective on methods and measures in the assessment of depressive disorders: The clinical interview. In M. Rutter, C. E. Izard, and P. B. Read (eds.), *Depression in young people: Developmental and clinical perspectives*, pp. 435–466. New York: Guilford.

Kovacs, M., and Beck, A. T. 1977. An empirical-clinical approach toward a definition of childhood depression. In J. G. Schulterbrandt and A. Raskin (eds.), *Depression in childhood: Diagnosis, treatment and conceptual models*. New York: Raven.

Kovacs, M., Feinberg, T. L., Crouse-Novak, M., Paulauskas, S. L., Pollock, M., and Finkelstein, R. 1984. Depressive disorders in childhood. II. A longitudinal study of the risk for a subsequent major depression. *Archives of General Psychiatry* **41**, 643–649.

Kovacs, M., Feinberg, T. L., Paulauskas, S., Finkelstein, R., Pollack, M., and Crouse-Novak, M. 1985. Initial coping responses and psychosocial characteristics of children with insulin-dependent diabetes mellitus. *Journal of Pediatrics* **106**, 827–834.

Kovacs, M., Iyengar, S., Goldston, D., Obrosky, D. S., Stewart, J., and Marsh, J. 1990. Psychological functioning among mothers of children with insulin-dependent diabetes mellitus: A longitudinal study. *Journal of Consulting and Clinical Psychology* **58**, 189–195.

Kovacs, M., and Paulauskas, S. 1986. The traditional psychotherapies. In H. C. Quay and J. S. Werry (eds.), *Psychopathological disorders of childhood*, 3d ed., pp. 496–522. New York: Wiley.

Kraft, I. A. 1979. Group therapy. In J. D. Noshpitz (ed.), *Basic handbook of child psychiatry*. Vol. 3, *Therapeutic interventions*. New York: Basic Books.

Kratochwill, T. R., and Morris, R. J. 1991. *The practice of child therapy*, 2d ed. New York: Pergamon.

Krugman, R. D. 1991. Physical indicators of child

sexual abuse. In A. Tasman and S. M. Goldfinger (eds.), *Review of psychiatry*, vol. 10, pp. 336–344. Washington, D. C.: American Psychiatric Press.

Kuczynski, L., and Kochanska, G. 1990. Development of children's noncompliant strategies from toddlerhood to age 5. *Developmental Psychology* **26**, 398–408.

La Greca, A. M. 1988. Adherence to prescribed medical regimens. In D. J. Routh (ed.), *Handbook of pediatric psychology*, pp. 299–320. New York: Guilford.

La Greca, A. M. 1990. Issues in adherence with pediatric regimens. *Journal of Pediatric Psychology* **15**, 423–436.

La Greca, A. M., and Stone, W. L. 1990. Children with learning disabilities: The role of achievement in their social, personal, and behavioral functioning. In H. L. Swanson and B. Keogh (eds.), *Learning disabilities: Theoretical and research issues*, pp. 333–350. Hillsdale, N.J.: Erlbaum.

Lahey, B. B., Loeber, R., Quay, H. C., Frick, P. J., and Grimm, J. 1992. Oppositional defiant and conduct disorders: Issues to be resolved for DSM-IV. *Journal of the American Academy of Child and Adolescent Psychiatry* **31**, 539–546.

Lamborn, S. D., Mounts, N. S., Steinberg, L., and Dornbusch, S. M. 1991. Patterns of competence and adjustment among adolescents from authoritative, authoritarian, indulgent, and neglectful families. *Child Development* **62**, 1049–1065.

LaRose, L., and Wolfe, D. A. 1987. Psychological characteristics of parents who abuse or neglect their children. In B. B. Lahey and A. E. Kazdin (eds.), *Advances in clinical child psychology*, pp. 55–98. New York: Plenum.

Lask, B., and Bryant-Waugh, R. 1992. Early-onset anorexia nervosa and related eating disorders. *Journal of Child Psychology and Psychiatry* **33**, 281–300.

Last, C. G., and Francis, G. 1988. School phobia. In B. B. Lahey and A. E. Kazdin (eds.), *Advances in clinical child psychology*, vol. 11, pp. 193–222. New York: Plenum.

Last, C. G., and Strauss, C. C. 1990. School refusals in anxiety-disordered children and adolescents. *Journal of the American Academy of Child and Adolescent Psychiatry* **29**, 31–35.

LaVietes, R. 1978. Mental retardation: Psychological treatment. In B. J. Wolman (ed.), *Handbook of treatment of mental disorders in childhood and adolescence.* Englewood Cliffs, N.J.: Prentice-Hall.

LeBlanc, M. 1990. Two processes of the development of persistent offending: Activation and escalation. In L. N. Robins and M. Rutter (eds.), *Straight and devious pathways from childhood to adulthood*, pp. 82–100. Cambridge: Cambridge University Press.

Ledingham, J. E. 1981. Developmental patterns of aggressive and withdrawn behavior in childhood: A possible method for identifying preschizophrenics. *Journal of Abnormal Child Psychology* **9**, 1–22.

Ledingham, J. E. 1990. Recent developments in high-risk research. In B. B. Lahey and A. E. Kazdin (eds.), *Advances in clinical child psychology*, vol. 13, pp. 91–137. New York: Plenum.

Ledwidge, B. 1978. Cognitive behavior modification: A step in the wrong direction? *Psychological Bulletin* **85**, 353–375.

Ledwidge, B. 1979. Cognitive behavior modification or new ways to change minds: Reply to Mahoney and Kazdin. *Psychological Bulletin* **86**, 1050–1053.

Lefkowicz, M. M., and Tesiny, E. P. 1980. Assessment of childhood depression. *Journal of Consulting and Clinical Psychology* **48**, 43–50.

Leon, G. R. 1979. Cognitive-behavioral therapy for eating disturbances. In P. Kendall and S. Hollon (eds.), *Cognitive-behavioral interventions: Theory, research and procedures*, pp. 357–388. New York: Academic Press.

Leon, G. R., and Dinklage, D. 1983. Childhood obesity and anorexia nervosa. In T. H. Ollendick and M. Hersen (eds.), *Handbook of child psychopathology*, pp. 253–276. New York: Plenum.

Leon, G. R., and Dinklage, D. 1989. Obesity and anorexia nervosa. In T. H. Ollendick and M. Hersen (eds.), *Handbook of child psychopathology*, 2d ed., pp. 247–264. New York: Plenum.

Leon, G. R., Lucas, A. R., Colligan, R. C., Ferdinande, R. J., and Kamp, J. 1985. Sexuality, body-image, and personality attitudes in anorexia nervosa. *Journal of Abnormal Child Psychology* **13**, 245–258.

Leon, G. R., and Phelan, P. W. 1985. Anorexia nervosa. In B. B. Lahey and A. E. Kazdin (eds.), *Advances in clinical child psychology*, vol. 8, pp. 81–113. New York: Plenum.

Leonard, H. L., Goldberger, E. L., Rapoport, J. L.,

Cheslow, D. L., and Swedo, S. E. 1990. Childhood rituals: Normal development or obsessive-compulsive symptoms? *Journal of the American Academy of Child and Adolescent Psychiatry* **29,** 17–23.

Levine, M., Anderson, E., Ferretti, L., and Steinberg, K. 1993. Legal and ethical issues affecting clinical child psychology. In T. H. Ollendick and R. J. Prinz (eds.) *Advances in clinical child psychology,* vol. 5, 243–262. New York Plenum.

Levitt, E. E. 1957. The results of psychotherapy with children: An evaluation. *Journal of Consulting Psychology,* **21,** 189–196.

Levy, D. M. 1955. Oppositional syndrome and oppositional behavior. In P. H. Hoch and J. Zubin (eds.), *Psychopathology of childhood,* pp. 204–226. New York: Grune & Stratton.

Levy, F. 1980. The development of sustained attention (vigilance) and inhibition in children: Some normative data. *Journal of Child Psychology and Psychiatry* **21,** 77–84.

Levy, S., Zoltak, B., and Saelens, T. 1988. A comparison of obstetrical records of autistic and nonautistic referrals for psychoeducational evaluation. *Journal of Autism and Developmental Disorders* **18,** 573–581.

Lewine, R. R. J. 1984. Stalking the schizophrenia marker: Evidence for a general vulnerability model of psychopathology. In N. F. Watt, E. J. Anthony, L. C. Wynne, and J. E. Rolf (eds.), *Children at risk for schizophrenia: A longitudinal perspective,* pp. 545–550. Cambridge: Cambridge University Press.

Lewine, R. R. J., Watt, N. F., and Grubb, T. W. 1984. High-risk-for-schizophrenia research: Sampling bias and its implications. In N. F. Watt, E. J. Anthony, L. C. Wynne, and J. E. Rolf (eds.), *Children at risk for schizophrenia: A longitudinal perspective,* pp. 557–564. Cambridge: Cambridge University Press.

Lewis, M., and Miller, S. M. 1990. *Handbook of developmental psychology.* New York: Plenum.

Lidz, T. 1973. *The origin and treatment of schizophrenic disorders.* New York: Basic Books.

Lilienfeld, S. O., and Waldman, I. D. 1990. The relation between childhood attention-deficit hyperactivity disorder and adult antisocial behavior reexamined: The problem of heterogeneity. *Clinical Psychology Review* **10,** 699–725.

Lindquist, E. F., and Hieronymus, A. M. 1955–1956. *Iowa Tests of Basic Skills manuals.* Boston: Houghton-Mifflin.

Linscheid, T. R., Tarnowski, K. J., and Richmond, D. A. 1988. Behavioral approaches to anorexia nervosa, bulimia and obesity. In D. Routh (ed.), *Handbook of pediatric psychology.* New York: Guilford.

Liu, W. T., Yu, E. S. H., Chang, C., and Fernandez, M. 1990. The mental health of Asian-American teenagers: A research challenge. In A. R. Stiffman and L. E. Davis (eds.), *Ethnic issues in adolescent mental health,* pp. 92–112. Newbury Park, Calif.: Sage.

Lochman, J. E., and Lampron, L. B. 1986. Situational social problem-solving skills and self-esteem of aggressive and nonaggressive boys. *Journal of Abnormal Child Psychology* **14,** 605–617.

Loeber, R. 1988. Natural histories of conduct problems, delinquency, and associated substance use. Evidence for developmental progression. In B. B. Lahey and A. E. Kazdin (eds.), *Advances in clinical child psychology,* vol. 11, pp. 73–118. New York: Plenum.

Loeber, R. 1990. Antisocial behavior: More enduring than changeable? *Journal of the American Academy of Child and Adolescent Psychiatry* **30,** 393–397.

Loeber, R. 1991. Questions and advances in the study of developmental pathways. In D. Cicchetti and S. L. Toth (eds.), *Models and integrations. Rochester symposium on developmental psychopathology,* vol. 3, pp. 97–116. Rochester, N. Y.: University of Rochester Press.

Loeber, R., Green, S. M., Lahey, B. B., Christ, M. G., and Frick, P. J. 1992. Developmental sequences in age of onset of disruptive child behavior. *Journal of Child and Family Studies* **1,** 21–41.

Loeber, R., and LeBlanc, M. 1990. Toward a developmental criminology. In M. Tonry and N. Morris (eds.), *Crime and justice. A review of research,* vol. 12, pp. 375–473. Chicago: University of Chicago Press.

Loeber, R., and Stouthamer-Loeber, M. 1986. Family factors as correlates and predictors of juvenile conduct problems and delinquency. In M. Tonry and N. Morris (eds.), *Crime and justice: An annual review of research,* vol. 7, pp. 29–149. Chicago: University of Chicago Press.

Loftus, E. F., and Ceci, S. J. 1991. Commentary: Research findings: What do they mean? In J. Doris (ed.), *The suggestibility of children's recollections*, pp. 129–133. Washington, D.C.: American Psychological Association.

Lord, C. 1985. Autism and the comprehension of language. In E. Schopler and G. B. Mesibov (eds.), *Communication problems in autism*, pp. 257–282. New York: Plenum.

Losche, G. 1990. Sensorimotor and action development in autistic children from infancy to early childhood. *Journal of Child Psychology and Psychiatry* **31,** 749–761.

Lotter, V. 1978. Follow-up studies. In M. Rutter and E. Schopler (eds.), *Autism: A reappraisal of concepts and treatment*. New York: Plenum.

Lovaas, O. I. 1977. *The autistic child. Language development through behavior modification*. New York: Irvington.

Lovaas, O. I. 1987. Behavioral treatment and normal educational and intellectual functioning in young autistic children. *Journal of Consulting and Clinical Psychology* **55,** 3–9.

Lovaas, O. I., Koegel, R. L., and Schreibman, L. 1979. Stimulus overselectivity in autism: A review of research. *Psychological Bulletin* **86,** 1236–1254.

Lovaas, O. I., and Smith, T. 1988. Intensive behavioral treatment for young autistic children. In B. B. Lahey and A. E. Kazdin (eds.), *Advances in clinical child psychology*, vol. 11, pp. 285–324. New York: Plenum.

Lovaas, O. I., Smith, T., and McEachin, J. J. 1989. Clarifying comments on the Young Autism Study: Reply to Schopler, Short, and Mesibov. *Journal of Consulting and Clinical Psychology* **57,** 165–167.

Lovejoy, M. C. 1991. Maternal depression: Effects on social cognition and behavior in parent-child interactions. *Journal of Abnormal Psychology* **19,** 693–706.

Loveland, K. A., and Tunali, B. 1991. Social scripts for conversational interactions in autism and Down syndrome. *Journal of Autism and Developmental Disorders* **21,** 177–186.

Lovitt, T. C. 1978. Arithmetic. In N. G. Haring, T. C. Lovitt, M. D. Eaton, and C. L. Hansen (eds.), *The four r's: Research in the classroom*, pp. 127–166. Columbus, Ohio: Merrill.

Luthar, S. S., and Zigler, E. 1991. Vulnerability and competence: A review of research on resilience in childhood. *American Journal of Orthopsychiatry* **61,** 6–20.

Lyon, G. R., and Moats, L. C. 1988. Critical issues in the instruction of the learning disabled. *Journal of Consulting and Clinical Psychology* **56,** 830–835.

Lytton, H. 1990a. Child and parent effects in boys' conduct disorder: A reinterpretation. *Developmental Psychology* **26,** 683–688.

Lytton, H. 1990b. Child effects—Still unwelcome? Response to Dodge and Wahler. *Developmental Psychology* **26,** 705–709.

Maccoby, E. E., and Jacklin, C. N. 1980. Sex differences in aggression: A rejoinder and reprise. *Child Development* **51,** 964–980.

Maccoby, E. E., and Martin, J. A. 1983. Socialization in the context of the family: Parent child interaction. In P. H. Mussen (ed.), *Handbook of child psychology*. Vol. IV, E. M. Hetherington (ed.), pp. 1–102. New York: Wiley.

Macdonald, H., Rutter, M., Howlin, P., Rios, P., Le Conteur, A., Evered, C., and Folstein, F. 1989. Recognition and expression of emotional cues in autistic and normal adults. *Journal of Child Psychology and Psychiatry* **30,** 865–877.

Macfarlane, J. W. 1964. Perspectives on personal consistency and change: The guidance study. *Vita Humana,* **7,** 115–126.

Macfarlane, J. W., Allen, L., and Honzik, M. P. 1954. *A developmental study of the behavior problems of normal children between 21 months and 14 years of age*. Berkeley and Los Angeles: University of California Press.

MacFarlane, K. 1986. Child sexual abuse allegations in divorce proceedings. In K. McFarlane and J. Waterman (eds.), *Sexual abuse of young children: Evaluation and treatment*, pp. 121–150. New York: Guilford.

Machover, K. 1949. *Personality projection in the drawing of the human figure*. Springfield, Ill.: Charles C. Thomas.

MacKinnon, D. P., Johnson, C. A., Pentz, M. A., Dwyer, J. H., Hansen, W. B., Flay, B. R., and Wang, E. Y. 1991. Mediating mechanisms in a school-based drug prevention program: First-year effects of the Midwestern Prevention Project. *Health Psychology* **10,** 164–172.

Maddi, S. A. 1980. *Personality theories: A comparative analysis*, 4th ed. Homewood, Ill.: Dorsey Press.

Magnusson, D. 1988. *Individual development from an*

interactional perspective: A longitudinal study. Hillsdale, N.J.: Erlbaum.

Magnusson, D. 1992. Individual development: a longitudinal perspective. *European Journal of Personality, 6.* 119–138.

Magnusson, D., and Bergman, L. R. 1990. A pattern approach to the study of pathways from childhood to adulthood. In L. N. Robins and M. Rutter (eds.), *Straight and devious pathways from childhood to adulthood,* pp. 101–115. Cambridge: Cambridge University Press.

Magrab, P. R., and Lehr, E. 1982. Assessment techniques. In J. M. Tuma (ed.), *Handbook for the practice of pediatric psychology,* pp. 67–109. New York: Wiley.

Mahoney, M. J. 1977. Reflections on the cognitive-learning trend in psychotherapy. *American Psychologist 32,* 5–13.

Mahoney, M. J., and Kazdin, A. E. 1979. Cognitive behavior modification: Misconceptions and premature evacuation. *Psychological Bulletin* **86,** 1044–1049.

Mahoney, M. J., Kazdin, A. E., and Lesswing, N.J. 1974. Behavior modification: Delusion or deliverance? In C. M. Franks and G. T. Wilson (eds.), *Annual review of behavior therapy, theory and practice,* vol. 2. New York: Brunner/Mazel.

Main, M., Kaplan, N., and Cassidy, J. 1985. Security in infancy, childhood, and adulthood: A move to the level of representation. In I. Bretherton and E. Waters (eds.), Growing points of attachment theory and research. *Monographs of the Society for Research in Child Development* **50,** (1–2, Series no. 209), 66–104.

Malmquist, C. P. 1980. Depressive phenomena in children. In B. B. Wolman (ed.), *Manual of child psychopathology.* New York: McGraw-Hill.

Mann, J. M., Tarantola, D. J. M., and Netter, T. W. 1992. *AIDS in the world.* Cambridge: Harvard University Press.

Mann, V. A., and Brady, S. 1988. Reading disability: The role of language deficiencies. *Journal of Consulting and Clinical Psychology* **56,** 811–816.

Mann, V. A., and Liberman, I. Y. 1984. Phonological awareness and verbal short-term memory. *Journal of Learning Disabilities* **17,** 592–600.

Mannarino, A. P., and Cohen, J. A. 1990. Treating abused children. In R. T. Ammerman and M. Her-

sen (eds.), *Children at risk: An evaluation of factors contributing to child abuse and neglect,* pp. 249–268. New York: Plenum.

Marchi, M., and Cohen, P. 1990. Early childhood eating behavior and adolescent eating disorders. *Journal of the American Academy of Child and Adolescent Psychiatry* **29,** 112–117.

Marcia, J. E. 1980. Identity in adolescence. In J. Adelson (ed.), *Handbook of adolescent psychology.* New York: Wiley.

Marcia, J. E. 1991. Identity and self-development. In R. M. Lerner, A. C. Petersen, and J. Brooks-Gunn (eds.), *Encyclopedia of Adolescence,* vol. 1, pp. 529–533. New York: Garland.

Marcus, D. E., and Overton, W. F. 1978. The development of cognitive gender constancy and sex role preferences. *Child Development* **49,** 434–444.

Marín, B. V., and Marín, G. 1990. Special issue: Hispanics and AIDS. *Hispanic Journal of Behavioral Sciences* **12,** 107–227.

Martin, B., and Hoffman, J. A. 1990. Conduct disorders. In M. Lewis and S. M. Miller (eds.), *Handbook of developmental psychopathology,* pp. 109–118. New York: Plenum.

Mash, E. J. 1989. Treatment of child and family disturbance: A behavioral-systems perspective. In E. J. Mash and R. A. Barkley (eds.), *Treatment of childhood disorders,* pp. 3–35. New York: Guilford.

Mash, E. J., and Terdal, L. G. (eds.). 1988. *Behavioral assessment of childhood disorders,* 2d ed. New York: Guilford.

Massie, H. N. 1980. Pathological interactions in infancy. In T. M. Field (ed.), *High-risk infants and children. Adult and peer interaction.* New York: Academic Press.

Masten, A. S., Best, K. M., and Garmezy, N. 1990. Resilience and development: Contributions from the study of children who overcome adversity. *Development and Psychopathology* **2,** 425–444.

Masten, A. S., and Braswell, L. 1991. Developmental psychopathology: An integrative framework. In P. R. Martin (ed.), *Handbook of behavior therapy and psychological science: An integrative approach,* pp. 35–56. New York: Pergamon.

Masten, A. S., Morison, P., Pellegrini, D., and Tellegen, A. 1990. Competence under stress: Risk and protective factors. In J. Rolf, A. S. Masten, D. Cicchetti, K. H. Nuechterlein, and S. Weintraub (eds.), *Risk and protective factors in the development of psychopathology*, pp. 236–252. Cambridge: Cambridge University Press.

McAdoo, W. G., and DeMyer, M. K. 1978. Personality characteristics of parents. In M. Rutter and E. Schopler (eds.), *Autism: A reappraisal of concepts and treatment*, pp. 251–267. New York: Plenum.

McArthur, D. S., and Roberts, G. E. 1984. *Roberts apperception test for children*. Los Angeles: Western Psychological Services.

McBride, A. A., Joe, G. W., and Simpson, D. D. 1991. Prediction of long-term alcohol use, drug use, and criminality among inhalant users. *Hispanic Journal of Behavioral Sciences* **13,** 315–323.

McConaghy, M. J. 1979. Gender permanence and the genital basis of gender: Stages in the development of constancy of gender identity. *Child Development* **50,** 1223–1226.

McCord, J. 1978. A thirty-year follow-up of treatment effects. *American Psychologist* **33,** 284–289.

McCord, J. 1990. Long-term perspectives on parental absence. In L. N. Robins and M. Rutter (eds.), *Straight and devious pathways from childhood to adulthood*, pp. 116–134. Cambridge: Cambridge University Press.

McGee, R., and Share, D. L. 1988. Attention Deficit Disorder-Hyperactivity and academic failure: Which comes first and which should be treated? *Journal of the American Academy of Child and Adolescent Psychiatry* **27,** 318–325.

McGee, R., and Wolfe, D. A. 1991. Psychological maltreatment: Toward an operational definition. *Development and Psychopathology* **3,** 3–18.

McGoldrick, M.,. Pearce, J. K., and Giordano, J. (eds.). 1982. *Ethnicity and family therapy*. New York: Guilford.

McGuire, J., and Earls, F. 1991. Prevention of psychiatric disorders in early childhood. *Journal of Child Psychology and Psychiatry* **32,** 129–152.

McIntosh, R., Vaughn, S., and Zaragoza, N. 1991. A review of social interventions for students with learning disabilities. *Journal of Learning Disabilities* **24,** 451–458.

McLoyd, V. C. 1990. The impact of economic hardship on black families and children: Psychological distress, parenting, and socioemotional development. *Child Development* **61,** 311–346.

McMahon, R. J., and Wells, K. C. 1989. Conduct disorders. In E. J. Mash and R. A. Barkley (eds.), *Treatment of childhood disorders*, pp. 39–134. New York: Guilford.

Mednick, S. A., Schulsinger, H., and Schulsinger, F. 1975. Schizophrenia in children of schizophrenic mothers. In A. Davids (ed.), *Child personality and psychopathology: Current topics*, vol. 2. New York: Wiley.

Meehl, P. E. 1978. Theoretical risks and tabular asterisks: Sir Karl, Sir Ronald, and the slow progress of soft psychology. *Journal of Consulting and Clinical Psychology* **46,** 806–834.

Meichenbaum, D. H., and Goodman, J. 1971. Training impulsive children to talk to themselves: A means of developing self-control. *Journal of Abnormal Psychology* **77,** 115–126.

Mejia, D. 1983. The development of Mexican-American children. In G. J. Powell (ed.), *The psychosocial development of minority group children*, pp. 77–114. New York: Brunner/Mazel.

Menyuk, P. 1978. Language: What's wrong and why. In M. Rutter and E. Schopler (eds.), *Autism: A reappraisal of concepts and treatment*. New York: Plenum.

Menyuk, P., and Quill, K. 1985. Semantic problems in autistic children. In E. Schopler and G. B. Mesibov (eds.), *Communication problems in autism*, pp. 127–145. New York: Plenum.

Merighi, J., Edison, M., and Zigler, E. 1990. The role of motivational factors in the functioning of mentally retarded individuals. In R. M. Hodapp, J. A. Burack, and E. Zigler (eds.), *Issues in the developmental approach to mental retardation*, pp. 114–134. Cambridge: Cambridge University Press.

Mervis, C. B. 1991. Early conceptual development in children with Down syndrome. In D. Cicchetti and M. Beeghly (eds.), *Children with Down syndrome: A developmental perspective*, pp. 252–301. Cambridge: Cambridge University Press.

Michelson, L., and Mannarino, A. 1986. Social skills training with children: Research and clinical application. In P. S. Strain, M. J. Guralnick, and H. M. Walker (eds.), *Children's social behavior: Development, assessment, and modification*, pp. 373–406. Orlando: Academic Press.

Miller, L. C. 1983. Fears and anxieties in children. In C. F. Walker and M. C. Roberts (eds.),

Handbook of clinical child psychology. New York: Wiley.

Miller, L. C., Barrett, C. L., and Hampe, E. 1974. Phobias of childhood in a prescientific era. In A. Davids (ed.), *Child personality and psychopathology: Current topics,* vol. 1. New York: Wiley.

Miller, L. C., Barrett, C. L., Hampe, E., and Noble, H. 1972. Comparison of reciprocal inhibition, psychotherapy and waiting list control for phobic children. *Journal of Abnormal Psychology* **79,** 269–279.

Miller, N. E., and Dollard, J. 1941. *Social learning and imitation.* New Haven, Conn.: Yale University Press.

Miller, R. T. 1974. Childhood schizophrenia: A review of selected literature. *International Journal of Mental Health* **3,** 3–46.

Miller, S. B., Boyer, B. A., and Rodoletz, M. 1990. Anxiety in children: Nature and development. In M. Lewis and S. M. Miller (eds.), *Handbook of developmental psychopathology,* pp. 191–208. New York: Plenum.

Minuchin, P. P., and Shapiro, E. K. 1983. The school as a context for social development. In P. H. Mussen (ed.), *Handbook of child psychology,* vol. 4, 4th ed. New York: Wiley.

Minuchin, S., Baker, L. Rosman, B. L., Liebman, R., Milman, L., and Todd, T. C. 1975. A conceptual model of psychosomatic illness in children. *Archives of General Psychiatry* **32,** 1031–1038.

Minuchin, S., Montalvo, B., Guerney, B. G. Jr., Rosman, B. L., and Schumer, F. 1967. *Families of the slums.* New York: Basic Books.

Minuchin, S., Rosman, B. L., and Baker, L. 1978. *Psychosomatic families.* Cambridge: Cambridge University Press.

Mischel, W. 1974. Processes in delay of gratification. In L. Berkowitz (ed.), *Advances in experimental social psychology,* vol. 7. New York: Academic Press.

Mischel, W. 1978. How children postpone pleasure. *Human Nature* **1,** 50–55.

Mischel, W., and Baker, N. 1975. Cognitive appraisals and transformations in delay behavior. *Journal of Personality and Social Psychology* **31,** 254–261.

Mishler, E. G., and Waxler, N. E. 1965. Family interaction and schizophrenia: A review of current theories. *Merrill-Palmer Quarterly* **11,** 269–316.

Moncher, M. S., Holden, G. W., and Trimble, J. E.

1990. Substance abuse among Native-American youth. *Journal of Consulting and Clinical Psychology* **58,** 408–415.

Money, J. 1970. Sexual dimorphism and homosexual gender identity. *Psychological Bulletin* **74,** 425–440.

Money, J., and Ehrhardt, A. A. 1972. *Man and woman, boy and girl. The differentiation and dimorphism of gender identity from conception to maturity.* Baltimore: Johns Hopkins University Press.

Money, J., and Higham, E. 1976. Juvenile gender identity: Differentiation and transpositions. In A. Davids (ed.), *Child personality and psychopathology: Current topics,* vol. 3. New York: Wiley.

Montemayor, R., and Eisen, M. 1977. The development of self-concept from childhood to adolescence. *Developmental Psychology* **13,** 314–319.

Morgenstern, M., and Klass, E. 1991. Standard intelligence tests and related assessment techniques. In J. L. Matson and J. A. Mulick (eds.), *Handbook of mental retardation,* pp. 195–201. New York: Pergamon.

Morris, R. D. 1988. Classification of learning disabilities: Old problems and new approaches. *Journal of Consulting and Clinical Psychology* **56,** 789–794.

Morris, R. J., and Kratochwill, T. R. (eds.). 1983. *The practice of child therapy.* New York: Pergamon.

Mosher, L. R., and Keith, S. J. 1977. Research on the psychosocial treatment of schizophrenia: A summary report. *American Journal of Psychiatry* **136,** 623–631.

Mueller, E., and Silverman, N. 1989. Peer relations in maltreated children. In D. Cicchetti and V. Carlson (eds.), *Child maltreatment: Theory and research on the causes and consequences of child abuse and neglect,* pp. 529–578. Cambridge: Cambridge University Press.

Mundy, P., and Kasari, C. 1990. The similar-structure hypothesis and differential rate of development in mental retardation. In R. M. Hodapp, J. A. Burack, and E. Zigler (eds.), *Issues in the developmental approach to mental retardation,* pp. 71–92. Cambridge: Cambridge University Press.

Mundy, P., and Sigman, M. 1989a. The theoretical implications of joint-attention deficit in autism. *Development and Psychopathology* **1,** 173–183.

Mundy, P., and Sigman, M. 1989b. Specifying the

nature of the social impairment in autism. In G. Dawson (ed.), *Autism: Nature, diagnosis, and treatment*, pp. 3–21. New York: Guilford.

Mundy, P., Sigman, M., and Kasari, C. 1990. A longitudinal study of joint attention and language development in autistic children. *Journal of Autism and Developmental Disorders* **20**, 115–128.

Nagata, D. K. 1989. Japanese-American children and adolescents. In J. T. Gibbs and L. N. Huang (eds.), *Children of color: Psychological interventions with minority youth*, pp. 67–113. San Francisco: Jossey-Bass.

Nagera, H. 1966. Early childhood disturbances, the infantile neurosis, and the adult disturbances: Problems of a developmental psychoanalytic psychology. *The psychoanalytic study of the child*. Monograph no. 2. New York: International Universities Press.

Nannis, E. D. 1988. A cognitive-developmental view of emotional understanding and its implications for child psychotherapy. In S. R. Shirk (ed.), *Cognitive development and child psychotherapy*, pp. 91–115. New York: Plenum.

Naylor, H. 1980. Reading disability and lateral asymmetry: An information-processing analysis. *Psychological Bulletin* **87**, 531–545.

Neeper, R., and Greenwood, R. S. 1987. On the psychiatric importance of neurological soft signs. In B. B. Lahey and A. E. Kazdin (eds.), *Advances in clinical child psychology*, vol. 10, pp. 217–258. New York: Plenum.

Newcomb, A. F., Bukowski, W. M., and Pattee, L. 1993. Children's peer relations: A meta-analytic review of popular, rejected, neglected, controversial, and average sociometric status. *Psychological Bulletin* **113**, 99–128.

Newcomb, M. D., and Bentler, P. M. 1988. *Consequences of adolescent drug use. Impact on the lives of young adults*. Newbury Park, Calif.: Sage.

Newman, M. R., and Lutzker, J. R. 1990. Prevention programs. In R. T. Ammerman and M. Hersen, eds., *Children at risk. An evaluation of factors contributing to child abuse and neglect*, pp. 225–248. New York: Plenum.

Newsom, C., and Rincover, A. 1989. Autism. In E. J. Mash and R. A. Barkley (eds.), *Treatment of childhood disorders*, pp. 286–346. New York: Guilford.

Nihira, K. 1976. Dimensions of adaptive behavior in institutionalized mentally retarded children and adults: Developmental perspectives. *American Journal of Mental Deficiency* **81**, 215–226.

Nihira, K. 1978. Factorial descriptions of the AAMD Adaptive Behavior Scale. In W. A. Coulter and H. W. Morrow (eds.), *Adaptive behavior: Concepts and measurements*. New York: Grune & Stratton.

Nihira, K., Foster, R., Shellhaas, M., and Leland, H. 1974. *AAMD Adaptive Behavior Scale, 1974 revision*. Washington, D.C.: American Association on Mental Deficiency.

Norland, R. 1992, March 9. Deadly lessons. *Newsweek*.

Norton, D. G. 1983. Black family life patterns, the development of self and cognitive development of black children. In G. J. Powell (ed.), *The psychosocial development of minority group children*, pp. 181–193. New York: Brunner/Mazel.

Noshpitz, J. D. (ed.). 1979a. *Basic handbook of child psychiatry*. Vol. 3, *Therapeutic interventions*. New York: Basic Books.

Noshpitz, J. D. (ed.). 1979b. *Basic handbook of child psychiatry*. Vol. 4, *Prevention and current issues*. New York: Basic Books.

Nuechterlein, K. H. 1983. Signal detection in vigilance tasks and behavioral attributes among offspring of schizophrenic mothers and among hyperactive children. *Journal of Abnormal Psychology* **92**, 4–28.

Nuechterlein, K. H. 1984. Sustained attention among children vulnerable to adult schizophrenia and among hyperactive children. In N. F. Watt, E. J. Anthony, L. C. Wynne, and J. E. Rolf (eds.), *Children at risk for schizophrenia: A longitudinal perspective*, pp. 304–311. Cambridge: Cambridge University Press.

Nuechterlein, K. H. 1986. Childhood precursors of adult schizophrenia. *Journal of Child Psychology and Psychiatry* **27**, 133–144.

Nuechterlein, K. H., Edell, W. S., Norris, M., and Dawson, M. E. 1986. Attentional vulnerability indicators, thought disorders and negative symptoms. *Schizophrenia Bulletin* **12**, 408–426.

O'Brien, M., and Huston, A. C. 1985. Development of sex-typed play behavior in toddlers. *Developmental Psychology* **21**, 866–871.

Ocampo, K. A., Garza, C. A., Dabul, A. J., and Ruiz,

S. Y. 1991. Ethnic identity and school achievement in Mexican-American youths. *Hispanic Journal of Behavioral Sciences* **13**, 234–235.

O'Donohue, W. T., and Elliott, A. N. 1991. Treatment of sexually abused children: A review. *Journal of Clinical Child Psychology* **21**, 218–228.

Oetting, E. R., and Beauvais, F. 1990. Adolescent drug use: Findings of national and local surveys. *Journal of Consulting and Clinical Psychology* **58**, 385–394.

Ohta, M. 1987. Cognitive disorders in infantile autism: A study employing the WISC, spatial relationships, conceptualization, and gesture imitation. *Journal of Autism and Developmental Disorders* **17**, 45–62.

Oldershaw, L., Walters, G. C., and Hall, D. K. 1986. Control strategies and noncompliance in abusive mother-child dyads: An observational study. *Child Development* **57**, 722–732.

Ollendick, T. H., and Hersen, M. (eds.). 1989. *Handbook of child psychopathology*, 2d ed. New York: Plenum.

Ollendick, T. H., and King, N. J. 1991. Developmental factors in child behavioral assessment. In P. R. Martin (ed.), *Handbook of behavior therapy and psychological science: An integrative approach*, pp. 57–72. New York: Pergamon.

Ollendick, T. H., King, N. J., and Frary, R. B. 1989. Fears in children and adolescents: Reliability and generalizability across gender, age, and nationality. *Behaviour Research and Therapy* **27**, 19–26.

Ollendick, T. H., Yule, W., and Ollier, K. 1991. Fears in British children and their relationship to manifest anxiety and depression. *Journal of Child Psychology and Psychiatry* **32**, 321–331.

Olson, S. L. 1992. Development of conduct problems and peer rejection in preschool children: A social systems analysis. *Journal of Abnormal Child Psychology* **20**, 327–350.

Olweus, D. 1979. Stability of aggressive reaction patterns in males: A review. *Psychological Bulletin* **86**, 852–875.

Oppel, W. C., Harper, P. A., and Rider, R. V. 1968. The age of attaining bladder control. *Pediatrics* **42**(4), 614–626.

Ornitz, E. M. 1976. The modulation of sensory input and motor output in autistic children. In E. Schopler and R. J. Reichler (eds.), *Psychopathology and child development*. New York: Plenum.

Ornitz, E. M., and Ritvo, E. R. 1976. The syndrome of autism: A critical review. *American Journal of Psychiatry* **133**(6), 609–621.

Ornstein, A. 1981. Self-pathology in childhood: Developmental and clinical considerations. *Psychiatric Clinics of North America*, 4, 435–453.

Ornstein, P. A. 1991. Commentary: Putting interviewing in context. In J. Doris (ed.), *The suggestibility of children's recollections*, pp. 147–152. Washington, D.C.: American Psychological Association.

Ornstein, P. A., Larus, D. M., and Clubb, P. A. 1991. Understanding children's testimony: Implications of research on the development of memory. In R. Vasta (ed.), *Annals of child development*, vol. 8, pp. 145–176. London: Jessica Kingsley.

Otis, A. S., and Lennon, R. T. 1967. *Otis-Lennon Mental Abilities Test*. New York: Harcourt Brace.

Otto, R. K., and Melton, G. B. 1990. Trends in legislation and case law on child abuse and neglect. In R. T. Ammerman and M. Hersen (eds.), *Children at risk: An evaluation of factors contributing to child abuse and neglect*, pp. 55–84. New York: Plenum.

Ozonoff, S., Pennington, B. F., and Rogers, S. J. 1990. Are there emotion perception deficits in young autistic children? *Journal of Child Psychology and Psychiatry* **31**, 343–361.

Ozonoff, S., Pennington, B. F., and Rogers, S. J. 1991. Executive function deficits in high-functioning autistic individuals: Relationship to theory of mind. *Journal of Child Psychology and Psychiatry* **32**, 1081–1105.

Paget, K. D., Philp, J. D., and Abramczy, L. W. 1993. Recent developments in child neglect. In T. H. Ollendick and R. J. Prinz (eds.), *Advances in clinical child psychology*, vol. 15, pp. 121–174. New York: Plenum.

Panak, W. F., and Garber, J. 1992. Role of aggression, rejection, and attributions in the prediction of depression in children. *Development and Psychopathology* **4**, 145–166.

Parke, R. D., and Collmer, C. W. 1975. Child abuse: An interdisciplinary analysis. In E. M. Hetherington (ed.), *Review of child development research*, vol. 5. Chicago: University of Chicago Press.

Parke, R. D., and Slaby, R. G. 1983. The development of aggression. In E. M. Hetherington (ed.), *Handbook of child development*. Vol. 4: *Socialization*, *personality, and social development*, 4th ed., pp. 605–641. New York: Wiley.

Parker, J. G., and Asher, S. R. 1987. Peer relations and later personality adjustment: Are low-accepted children at risk? *Psychological Bulletin* **102,** 357–389.

Pate, J. E., Pumariega, A. J., Hester, C., and Garner, D. M. 1992. Cross-cultural patterns in eating disorders: A review. *Journal of the American Academy of Child and Adolescent Psychiatry* **31,** 802–808.

Patterson, C. J. 1992. Children of lesbian and gay parents. *Child Development* **63,** 1025–1042.

Patterson, C. J., Kupersmidt, J. B., and Vaden, N. A. 1990. Income level, gender, ethnicity, and household composition as predictors of children's school-based competence. *Child Development* **61,** 485–494.

Patterson, G. R. 1982. *Coercive family process.* Eugene, Ore.: Castalia.

Patterson, G. R. 1986. Performance models for antisocial boys. *American Psychologist* **41,** 432–444.

Patterson, G. R., and Capaldi, D. M. 1990. A mediational model for boys' depressed mood. In J. Rolf, A. S. Masten, D. Cicchetti, K. H. Nuechterlein, and S. Weintraub (eds.), *Risk and protective factors in the development of psychopathology,* pp. 141–163. Cambridge: Cambridge University Press.

Patterson, G. R., DeBaryshe, B. D., and Ramsey, E. 1989. A developmental perspective on antisocial behavior. *American Psychologist* **44,** 329–335.

Patterson, G. R., Littman, R. A., and Bricker, W. 1967. Assertive behavior in children: A step toward a theory of aggression. *Monographs of the Society for Research in Child Development* **32** (5, serial no. 113).

Patterson, G. R., Reid, J. B., and Dishion, T. J. 1992. *Antisocial boys.* Eugene, Ore.: Castalia.

Patterson, G. R., Reid, J. B., Jones, R. R., and Conger, R. W. 1975. *A social learning approach to family intervention,* vol. 1. Eugene, Ore.: Castalia.

Patterson, G. R., and Stoolmiller, M. 1991. Replications of a dual failure model for boys' depressed mood. *Journal of Consulting and Clinical Psychology* **59,** 491–498.

Paul, R. 1987. Natural history. In D. J. Cohen, A. M. Donnellan, and R. Paul (eds.), *Handbook of autism and pervasive developmental disorders,* pp. 121–130. New York: Wiley.

Pearl, R., and Bryan, T. 1990. Learning disabled ad-

olescents' vulnerability to victimization and delinquency. In H. L. Swanson and B. Keogh (eds.), *Learning disabilities: Theoretical and research issues,* pp. 139–154. Hillsdale, N.J.: Erlbaum.

Pellegrino, J. W., and Goldman, S. R. 1990. Cognitive science perspective on intelligence and learning disabilities. In H. L. Swanson and B. Keogh (eds.), *Learning disabilities: Theoretical and research issues,* pp. 41–58. Hillsdale, N.J.: Erlbaum.

Peller, L. E. 1964. Libidinal development as reflected in play. In M. R. Haworth (ed.), *Child psychotherapy.* New York: Basic Books.

Pennington, B. F. 1990. Annotation: The genetics of dyslexia. *Journal of Child Psychology and Psychiatry* **31,** 193–201.

Pennington, B. F., and Ozonoff, S. 1991. A neuroscientific perspective on continuity and discontinuity in developmental psychopathology. In D. Cicchetti and S. L. Toth (eds.), *Models and integrations. Rochester symposium on developmental psychopathology,* vol. 3, pp. 117–160. Rochester, N.Y.: University of Rochester Press.

Perner, J., Frith, U., Leslie, A. M., and Leekam, S. R. 1989. Exploration of the autistic child's theory of mind: Knowledge, belief and communication. *Child Development* **60,** 689–700.

Perry, D. G., Perry, L. C., and Boldizar, J. P. 1990. Learning of aggression. In M. Lewis and S. M. Miller (eds.), *Handbook of developmental psychopathology,* pp. 135–146. New York: Plenum.

Perry, M. A. 1990. The interview in development. In J. H. Johnson and J. Goldman (eds.), *Developmental assessment in clinical child psychology,* pp. 58–77. New York: Pergamon.

Peterson, L., and Roberts, M. C. 1986. Community intervention and prevention. In H. C. Quay and J. S. Werry (eds.), *Psychopathological disorders of childhood,* 3d ed., pp. 622–660. New York: Wiley.

Petti, T. A. 1989. Depression. In T. H. Ollendick and M. Hersen (eds.), *Handbook of child psychopathology,* pp. 229–246. New York: Plenum.

Pettit, G. S., and Bates, J. E. 1989. Family interaction patterns and children's behavior problems from infancy to 4 years. *Developmental Psychology* **25,** 413–420.

Pfiffner, L. J., and Barkley, R. A. 1990. Educational placement and classroom management. In R. A. Barkley (ed.), *Attention-deficit hyperactivity disor-*

der: A handbook for diagnosis and treatment, pp. 498–539. New York: Guilford.

Phares, E. J. 1976. *Locus of control in personality*. Morristown, N.J.: General Learning.

Phinney, J. S. 1990. Ethnic identity in adolescents and adults: Review of research. *Psychological Bulletin* **108,** 499–514.

Phinney, J. S., Lochner, B. T., and Murphy, R. 1990. Ethnic identity development and psychological adjustment in adolescence. In A. R. Stiffman and L. E. Davis (eds.), *Ethnic issues in mental health,* pp. 53–72. Newbury Park, Calif.: Sage.

Phinney, J. S., and Rosenthal, D. S. 1992. Ethnic identity in adolescence: Process, context, and outcome. In G. R. Adams, T. P. Gullotta, and R. Montemayor (eds.), *Adolescent identity formation,* pp. 145–172. Newbury Park, Calif.: Sage.

Piacentini, J. C., Cohen, P., and Cohen, J. 1992. Combining discrepant diagnostic information from multiple sources: Are complex algorithms better than simple ones? *Journal of Abnormal Child Psychology* **20,** 51–62.

Piaget, J. 1930. *The child's conception of physical causality*. London: Kegan Paul.

Piaget, J. 1932. *The moral judgment of the child*. London: Kegan Paul.

Piaget, J. 1954. *The construction of reality in the child*. New York: Basic Books.

Piaget, J. 1967. *Six psychological studies*. New York: Random House.

Pianta, R., Egeland, B., and Erickson, M. F. 1989. The antecedents of maltreatment: Results of the Mother-Child Interaction Project. In D. Cicchetti and V. Carlson (eds.), *Child maltreatment: Theory and research on the causes and consequences of child abuse and neglect,* pp. 203–253. Cambridge: Cambridge University Press.

Pless, I. B., and Nolan, T. 1991. Revision, replication and neglect: Research on maladjustment in chronic illness. *Journal of Child Psychology and Psychiatry* **32,** 347–365.

Plomin, R. 1989. Environment and genes: Determinants of behavior. *American Psychologist* **44,** 105–111.

Plomin, R., Nitz, K., and Rowe, D. C. 1990. Behavioral genetics and aggressive behavior in childhood. In M. Lewis and S. M. Miller (eds.), *Handbook of developmental psychopathology,* pp. 119–133. New York: Plenum.

Pogue-Geile, M. F. 1991. The development of liability to schizophrenia: Early and late developmental models. In E. F. Walker (ed.), *Schizophrenia. A life-course developmental perspective,* pp. 277–299. San Diego: Academic Press.

Politano, P. M., Stapleton, L. A., and Correll, J. A. 1992. Differences between children of depressed and nondepressed mothers: Locus of control, anxiety and self-esteem. A research note. *Journal of Child Psychology and Psychiatry* **33,** 451–455.

Premorbid adjustment and schizophrenic heterogeneity. 1977. *Schizophrenia Bulletin* **3**(2), 180–182.

Prior, M., Dahlstrom, B., and Tracie-Lee, S. 1990. Autistic children's knowledge of thinking and feeling states in other people. *Journal of Child Psychology and Psychiatry* **31,** 587–601.

Prior, M., and Sanson, A. 1986. Attention deficit disorder with hyperactivity: A critique. *Journal of Child Psychology and Psychiatry* **27,** 307–319.

Prior, M., and Werry, J. S. 1986. Autism, schizophrenia and allied disorders. In H. C. Quay and J. S. Werry (eds.), *Psychopathological disorders of childhood,* 3d ed., pp. 156–210. New York: Wiley.

Prior, M. R. 1979. Cognitive abilities and disabilities in infantile autism: A review. *Journal of Abnormal Child Psychology* **7,** 357–380.

Prior, M. R., and Chen, C. S. 1976. Short-term and serial memory in autistic, retarded, and normal children. *Journal of Autism and Childhood Schizophrenia* **6,** 121–131.

Provence, S., and Lipton, R. C. 1962. *Infants in institutions*. New York: International Universities Press.

Pueschel, S. M., and Goldstein, A. 1991. Genetic counseling. In J. L. Matson and J. A. Mulick (eds.), *Handbook of mental retardation,* pp. 279–307. New York: Pergamon.

Quay, H. C. 1986. Classification. In H. C. Quay and J. S. Werry (eds.), *Psychopathological disorders of childhood,* 3d ed., pp. 1–34. New York: Wiley.

Quiggle, N. L., Garber, N., Panak, W. F., and Dodge, K. A. 1992. Social information processing in aggressive and depressed children. *Child Development* **63,** 1305–1320.

Radke-Yarrow, M., Nottelmann, E., Martinez, P., Fox, M. B., and Belmont, B. 1992. Young children of affectively ill parents: A longitudinal study of psychosocial development. *Journal of the American Academy of Child and Adolescent Psychiatry* **31,** 68–77.

Ramirez, O. 1989. Mexican-American children and

adolescents. In J. T. Gibbs and L. N. Huang (eds.), *Children of color. Psychological interventions with minority youth,* pp. 224–250. San Francisco: Jossey-Bass.

Rapoport, J. L. 1986. Childhood obsessive compulsive disorders. *Journal of Child Psychology and Psychiatry* **27,** 289–295.

Raskin, D. C., and Esplin, P. W. 1991. Assessment of children's statements of sexual abuse. In J. Doris (ed.), *The suggestibility of children's recollections,* pp. 153–164. Washington, D.C.: American Psychological Association.

Redl, F., and Wineman, D. 1951. *Children who hate. The disorganization and breakdown of behavior controls.* New York: Free Press.

Reed, T., and Peterson, C. 1990. A comparative study of autistic subjects' performance at two levels of visual and cognitive perspective taking. *Journal of Autism and Developmental Disorders* **20,** 555–567.

Reese, H. W., and Lipsitt, L. P. 1970. *Experimental child psychology.* New York: Academic Press.

Reid, J. B. 1993. Prevention of conduct disorder before and after school entry: Relating interventions to developmental findings. *Development and Psychopathology, 5,* 243–262.

Reitan-Indiana Neuropsychological Test Battery. 1969. Indianapolis: Reitan.

Remafedi, G. 1987a. Adolescent homosexuality: Psychosocial and medical implications. *Pediatrics* **79,** 331–337.

Remafedi, G. 1987b. Homosexual youth. A challenge to contemporary society. *Journal of the American Medical Association* **258,** 222–225.

Remafedi, G. 1987c. Male homosexuality: The adolescent's perspective. *Pediatrics* **79,** 326–330.

Remafedi, G. 1991. Homosexuality, adolescent. In R. M. Lerner, A. Petersen, and J. Brooks-Gunn (eds.), *Encyclopedia of adolescence,* vol. 1, pp. 504–507. New York: Garland.

Reppucci, N. D., and Herman, J. 1991. Sexuality education and child sexual abuse preventive programs in the schools. In G. Grant (ed.), *Review of research in education,* vol. 17, pp. 127–166. Washington, D.C.: Education Research Association.

Rhodes, J. E., and Jason, L. A. 1990. A social stress model of substance abuse. *Journal of Consulting and Clinical Psychology* **58,** 395–401.

Rie, E. D. 1980. Effects of MBD on learning, intellectual functions and achievement. In H. E. Rie and E. D. Rie (eds.), *Handbook of minimal brain dysfunctions: A critical view.* New York: Wiley.

Rie, H. E. 1971. Historical perspective of concepts of child psychopathology. In H. E. Rie (ed.), *Perspectives in child psychopathology.* Chicago: Aldine-Atherton.

Rie, H. E. 1980. Definitional problems. In H. E. Rie and E. D. Rie (eds.), *Handbook of minimal brain dysfunctions: A critical view.* New York: Wiley.

Risk factors for suicide attempts. *Adolinks,* vol. 4, no. 2 (undated).

Ritvo, E. R., Freeman, B. J., Mason-Brother, A., Mo, A., and Ritvo, A. M. 1985. Concordance for the syndrome of autism in 40 pairs of afflicted twins. *American Journal of Psychiatry* **142,** 74–77.

Roberts, C. W., Green, R., Williams, K., and Goodman, M. 1987. Boyhood gender identity development: A statistical contrast of two family groups. *Developmental Psychology* **23,** 544–557.

Roberts, M. 1975. Persistent school refusal among children and adolescents. In R. D. Wirt, G. Winokur, and M. Roff (eds.), *Life history research in psychopathology,* vol. 4., pp. 79–108. Minneapolis: University of Minnesota Press.

Roberts, M. C., Alexander, K., and Davis, N. J. 1991. Children's rights to physical and mental health care: A case for advocacy. *Journal of Clinical Child Psychology* **20,** 18–27.

Robins, L. N. 1966. *Deviant children grown up: A sociological and psychiatric study of sociopathic personality.* Baltimore: Williams & Wilkins.

Robins, L. N. 1972. Follow-up studies of behavior disorders in children. In H. C. Quay and J. S. Werry (eds.), *Psychopathological disorders of childhood.* New York: Wiley.

Robins, L. N. 1979. Addict careers. In R. I. Dupont, A. Goldstein, and J. O'Donnell (eds.), *Handbook on drug abuse.* Washington, D.C.: National Institute on Drug Abuse.

Robins, L. N. 1980. The natural history of drug abuse. In D. J. Lettieri, M. Sayers, and H. W. Pearson (eds.), *Theories on drug abuse. Selected contemporary perspectives.* NIDA Research Monograph 30. Washington, D.C.: National Institute on Drug Abuse.

Robins, L. N. 1991. Conduct disorder. *Journal of Child Psychology and Psychiatry* **32,** 193–212.

Robins, L. N., Davis, D. H., and Nurco, D. N. 1974. How permanent was Vietnam drug addiction?

American Journal of Public Health **64** (suppl.), 38–43.

Robins, L. N., and McEvoy, L. 1990. Conduct problems as predictors of substance abuse. In L. E. Robins and M. Rutter (eds.), *Straight and devious pathways from childhood to adulthood,* pp. 182–204. Cambridge: Cambridge University Press.

Robins, L. N., and Przybeck, T. R. 1985. Age of onset of drug use as a factor in drug and other disorders. In C. L. Jones and R. J. Battjes (eds.), *Etiology of drug abuse: Implications for prevention,* pp. 178–192. NIDA Research Monograph 56. Rockville, Md.: National Institute on Drug Abuse.

Robinson, N. M., and Robinson, H. B. 1976. *The mentally retarded child: A psychological approach,* 2d ed. New York: McGraw-Hill.

Rodin, J., Striegel-Moore, R. H., and Silberstein, L. R. 1990. Vulnerability and resilience in the age of eating disorders: Risk and protective factors for bulimia nervosa. In J. Rolf, A. S. Masten, D. Cicchetti, K. H. Nuechterlein, and S. Weintraub (eds.), *Risk and protective factors in the development of psychopathology,* pp. 361–383. Cambridge: Cambridge University Press.

Rodnick, E. H., Goldstein, M. J., Lewis, J. M., and Doane, J. A. 1984. Parental communication style, affect and role as precursors of offspring schizophrenia-spectrum disorders. In N. F. Watt, E. J. Anthony, L. C. Wynne, and J. E. Rolf (eds.), *Children at risk for schizophrenia: A longitudinal perspective,* pp. 81–92. Cambridge: Cambridge University Press.

Rodriguez, O., and Zayas, L. H. 1990. Hispanic adolescents and antisocial behavior: Sociocultural factors and treatment implications. In A. R. Stiffman and L. E. Davis (eds.), *Ethnic issues in adolescent mental health,* pp. 147–174. Newbury Park, Calif.: Sage.

Roff, J. D. 1974. Adolescent schizophrenia: Variables related to differences in long-term adult outcome. *Journal of Consulting and Clinical Psychology* **42,** 180–183.

Rogers, C. R. 1959. A theory of therapy, personality, and interpersonal relationships as developed in the client-centered framework. In S. Koch (ed.), *Psychology: Study of a science.* Vol. 3: *Formulations of the person and the social context.* New York: McGraw-Hill.

Rogers, S., Ozonoff, S., and Maslin-Cole, C. 1991. A comparative study of attachment behavior in young children with autism and other psychiatric disorders. *Journal of the American Academy of Child and Adolescent Psychiatry* **30,** 483–489.

Rogers, S., and Pennington, B. F. 1991. A theoretical approach to the deficits in infantile autism. *Development and Psychopathology* **3,** 137–162.

Rogler, L. H., Malgady, R. G., Costantino, G., and Blumenthal, R. 1987. What do culturally sensitive mental health services mean? The case of Hispanics. *American Psychologist* **42,** 565–575.

Rolf, J., Masten, A., Cicchetti, D., Nuechterlein, K., and Weintraub, S. (eds.). 1990. *Risk and protective factors in the development of psychopathology.* Cambridge: Cambridge University Press.

Rosenblith, J. F., and Sims-Knight. 1985. *In the beginning: Development in the first two years of life.* Monterey, Calif.: Brooks/Cole.

Rosenblith, J. F., and Sims-Knight, J. 1992. *In the beginning: Development in the first two years of life,* 2d ed. Monterey, Calif.: Brooks/Cole.

Rosenthal, D., Wender, P. H., Kety, S. S., Schulsinger, F., Welner, J., and Rieder, R. O. 1975. Parent-child relationships and psychopathological disorder in the child. *Archives of General Psychiatry* **32,** 466–476.

Rosenthal, D. A. 1987. Ethnic identity development in adolescents. In J. S. Phinney and M. J. Rotheram (eds.), *Children's ethnic socialization: Pluralism and development,* pp. 153–155. Newbury Park, Calif.: Sage.

Rosenthal, P. A., and Rosenthal, S. 1984. Suicidal behavior by preschool children. *American Journal of Psychiatry* **141,** 520–525.

Ross, A. O. 1980. *Psychological disorders of children: A behavioral approach to theory, research, and therapy,* 2d ed. New York: McGraw-Hill.

Ross, A. O. 1981. *Child behavior therapy: Principles, procedures, and empirical basis.* New York: Wiley.

Ross, A. O., and Nelson, R. O. 1979. Behavior therapy. In H. C. Quay and J. S. Werry (eds.), *Psychopathological disorders of childhood,* 2d ed. New York: Wiley.

Ross, D. C. 1964. *A classification of child psychiatry.* 4951 McKean Ave., Philadelphia.

Ross, D. M., and Ross, S. A. 1976. *Hyperactivity: Research, theory, and action.* New York: Wiley.

Rotheram, M. J., and Phinney, J. S. 1987. Ethnic behavior patterns as an aspect of identity. In J. S.

Phinney and M. J. Rotheram (eds.), *Children's ethnic socialization: Pluralism and development*, pp. 180–200. Newbury Park, Calif.: Sage.

Rourke, B. P. 1988. Socioemotional disturbances of learning disabled children. *Journal of Consulting and Clinical Psychology* **56**, 801–810.

Rourke, B. P., Bakker, D. J., Fisk, J. L., and Strang, J. D. 1983. *Child neuropsychology. An introduction to theory, research, and clinical practice*. New York: Guilford.

Routh, D. K. 1979. Activity, attention and aggression in learning-disabled children. *Journal of Clinical Child Psychology* **8**, 183–187.

Routh, D. K. 1988. Introduction. In D. K. Routh (ed.), *Handbook of pediatric psychology*, pp. 1–5. New York: Guilford.

Routh, D. K. 1990. Taxonomy in developmental psychopathology. Consider the source. In M. Lewis and S. M. Miller (eds.), *Handbook of developmental psychopathology*, pp. 53–63. New York: Plenum.

Rubio-Stipec, M., Shrout, P. E., Bird, H., Canino, G., and Bravo, M. 1989. Symptom scales of the Diagnostic Interview Schedule: Factor results in Hispanic and Anglo samples. *Psychological Assessment: A Journal of Consulting and Clinical Psychology* **1**, 30–34.

Ruble, D. N. 1988. Sex-role development. In M. H. Bornstein and M. E. Lamb (eds.), *Developmental psychology: An advanced textbook*, 2d ed., pp. 411–460. Hillsdale, N.J.: Erlbaum.

Ruiz, R. A., and Padilla, A. M. 1983. Counseling Latinos. In D. R. Atkinson, G. Morten, and D. W. Sue (eds.), *Counseling American minorities: A cross-cultural perspective*, 2d ed., pp. 213–236. Dubuque, Iowa: William C. Brown.

Russell, A. T., Bott, L., and Sammons, C. 1989. The phenomenology of schizophrenia occurring in childhood. *Journal of the American Academy of Child and Adolescent Psychiatry* **28**, 399–407.

Ruttenberg, B. A. 1971. A psychoanalytic understanding of infantile autism and treatment. In D. W. Churchill, G. D. Alpern, and M. K. DeMyer (eds.), *Infantile autism*. Springfield, Ill.: Charles C. Thomas.

Ruttenberg, B. A., Kalish, B., Wenar, C., and Wolf, E. G. 1978. *Behavior rating instrument for autistic and other atypical children* (BRIACC). Chicago: Stolting.

Rutter, M. 1972. *Maternal deprivation reassessed*. New York: Penguin.

Rutter, M. 1977. Brain damage syndromes in childhood: Concepts and findings. *Journal of Child Psychology and Psychiatry* **18**, 1–21.

Rutter, M. 1978. Diagnoses and definition. In M. Rutter and E. Schopler (eds.), *Autism: A reappraisal of concepts and treatment*. New York: Plenum.

Rutter, M. 1979a. *Changing youth in a changing society: Patterns of adolescent development and disorder*. London: Nuffield Provincial Hospitals Trust.

Rutter, M. 1979b. Maternal deprivation, 1972–1978: New findings, new concepts, new approaches. *Child Development* **50**, 283–305.

Rutter, M. 1981. Psychological sequelae of brain-damaged children. *American Journal of Psychiatry* **138**, 1533–1544.

Rutter, M. 1983. School effects on pupil progress: Research findings and policy implications. *Child Development* **54**, 1–29.

Rutter, M. 1985. Infantile autism. In D. Shaffer, A. A. Ehrhardt, and L. L. Greenhill (eds.), *The clinical guide to child psychiatry*, pp. 49–78. New York: Free Press.

Rutter, M. 1986a. The developmental psychopathology of depression: Issues and perspectives. In M. Rutter, C. E. Izard, and P. B. Read (eds.), *Depression in young people: Developmental and clinical perspectives*, pp. 3–32. New York: Guilford.

Rutter, M. 1986b. Depressive feelings, cognitions, and disorders: A research postscript. In M. Rutter, C. E. Izard, and P. B. Read (eds.), *Depression in young people: Developmental and clinical perspectives*, pp. 491–520. New York: Guilford.

Rutter, M. 1988. DSM-III-R: A postscript. In M. Rutter, A. H. Tuma, and I. S. Lann (eds.), *Assessment and diagnosis in child psychopathology*, pp. 453–463. New York: Guilford.

Rutter, M. 1989. Intergenerational continuities and discontinuities in serious parenting difficulties. In D. Cicchetti and V. Carlson (eds.), *Child maltreatment: Theory and research on the causes and consequences of child abuse and neglect*, pp. 317–348. Cambridge: Cambridge University Press.

Rutter, M. 1990a. Commentary: Some focus and process considerations regarding effects of parental depression on children. *Developmental Psychology* **26**, 60–67.

Rutter, M. 1990b. Psychosocial resilience and protective mechanisms. In J. Rolf, A. S. Masten, D. Cicchetti, K. H. Nuechterlein, and S. Weintraub (eds.), *Risk and protective factors in the development of psychopathology*, pp. 181–214. Cambridge: Cambridge University Press.

Rutter, M. 1991. Nature, nurture, and psychopathology: A new look at an old topic. *Development and Psychopathology* **3**, 125–136.

Rutter, M., and Garmezy, N. 1983. Developmental psychopathology. In P. H. Mussen (ed.), *Handbook of child psychology*. Vol. 4: *Socialization, personality and social development*. E. M. Hetherington, ed., pp. 775–911. New York: Wiley.

Rutter, M., and Giller, H. 1983. *Juvenile delinquency: Trends and perspectives*. New York: Penguin.

Rutter, M., Macdonald, H., LeCouteur, A., Harrington, R., Bolton, P., and Bailey, A. 1990. Genetic factors in child psychiatric disorders. Part II: Empirical findings. *Journal of Child Psychology and Psychiatry* **31**, 39–83.

Rutter, M., and Quinton, D. 1984. Long-term follow-up of women institutionalized in childhood: Factors promoting good functioning in adult life. *British Journal of Developmental Psychology* **2**, 191–204.

Rutter, M., and Shaffer, D. 1980. DSM-III—A step forward or back in terms of the classification of child psychiatric disorders? *Journal of the American Academy of Child Psychiatry* **19**, 371–394.

Sameroff, A. J. 1990. Neo-environmental perspectives on developmental theory. In R. M. Hodapp, J. A. Burack, and E. Zigler (eds.), *Issues in the developmental approach to mental retardation*, pp. 93–113. Cambridge: Cambridge University Press.

Sameroff, A. J., and Chandler, M. J. 1975. Reproductive risk and the continuum of caretaking casualty. In F. D. Horowitz (ed.), *Review of child development research*, vol. 4. Chicago: University of Chicago Press.

Sander, L. W. 1964. Adaptive relationships in early mother–child interaction. *Journal of the American Academy of Child Psychiatry* **3**, 231–264.

Sanford, R. N., Adkins, M. M., Miller, R. B., and Cobb, E. A. 1943. Physique, personality, and scholarship: A cooperative study of school children. *Monograph of the Society for Research in Child Development* **8** (1, series no. 34).

Sanson, A., Oberklaid, F., Pedlow, R., and Prior, M. 1991. Risk indicators: Assessment of infancy predictors of preschool behavioural maladjustment. *Journal of Child Psychology and Psychiatry* **32**, 609–626.

Santa, L. S. 1983. Mental health issues of Japanese-American children. In G. J. Powell (ed.), *The psychosocial development of minority group children*, pp. 362–372. New York: Brunner/Mazel.

Santrock, J. W. 1990. *Adolescence: An introduction*, 3d ed. Madison, Wis.: Brown and Benchmark.

Saposnek, D. T. 1983. *Mediating child custody disputes*. San Francisco: Jossey-Bass.

Saposnek, D. T., Hamburg, J., Delano, C. D., and Michaelsen, H. 1984. How has mandatory mediation fared? Research findings of the first year's follow-up. *Conciliation Courts Review* **22**, 7–19.

Sarason, I. G., and Sarason, B. R. 1987. *Abnormal psychology. The problems of maladaptive behavior*, 5th ed. Englewood Cliffs, N.J.: Prentice-Hall.

Satir, V. 1967. *Conjoint family therapy: A guide to theory and technique*, 2d ed. Palo Alto, Calif.: Science and Behavior Books.

Sattler, J. M. 1982. *Assessment of children's intelligence and special abilities*. Philadelphia: Saunders.

Sattler, J. M. 1990. *Assessment of children*, 3d ed. San Diego, Calif.: Sattler.

Sattler, J. M. 1992. *Assessment of children*, 3d ed. rev. San Diego, Calif.: Sattler.

Savin-Williams, R. C. 1990. *Gay and lesbian youth. Expressions of identity*. New York: Hemisphere.

Savin-Williams, R. C. 1991. Gay and lesbian youth. In R. M. Lerner, A. C. Petersen, and J. Brooks-Gunn (eds.), *Encyclopedia of adolescence*, vol. 1, pp. 385–388. New York: Garland.

Savin-Williams, R. C., and Rodriguez, R. G. 1992. A developmental, clinical perspective on lesbian, gay male, and bisexual youths. In T. P. Gullotta, G. R. Adams, and R. Montemayor (eds.), *Adolescent sexuality*, pp. 77–102. Newbury Park, Calif.: Sage.

Saywitz, K. J., Goodman, G. S., Nicholas, E., and Moan, S. F. 1991. Children's memories of a physical examination involving genital touch: Implications for reports of child sexual abuse. *Journal of Consulting and Clinical Psychology* **59**, 682–691.

Scarr, S. 1992. Developmental theories for the 1990s:

Development and individual differences. *Child Development* **63,** 1–19.

Schachar, R. 1991. Childhood hyperactivity. *Journal of Child Psychology and Psychiatry* **32,** 155–191.

Schachar, R., and Logan, G. D. 1990. Impulsivity and inhibitory control in normal development and child psychopathology. *Developmental Psychology* **26,** 710–720.

Schachar, R., and Wachsmuth, R. 1991. Oppositional disorders in children: A validation study comparing conduct disorder, oppositional disorder and normal control children. *Journal of Child Psychology and Psychiatry* **31,** 1089–1102.

Schaefer, C. E., and Briesmeister, J. M. (eds.). 1989. *Handbook of parent training: Parents as co-therapists for children's behavior problems.* New York: Wiley.

Scharfman, M. A. 1978. Psychoanalytic treatment. In B. B. Wolman, J. Egan, and A. O. Ross (eds.), *Handbook of treatment of mental disorders in childhood and adolescence.* Englewood Cliffs, N.J.: Prentice-Hall.

Schetky, D. H. 1991. The sexual abuse of infants and toddlers. In A. Tasman and S. M. Goldfinger (eds.), *Review of psychiatry,* vol. 10, pp. 308–319. Washington, D.C.: American Psychiatric Press.

Schilling, R. F., and McAlister, A. L. 1990. Preventing drug use in adolescents through media interventions. *Journal of Consulting and Clinical Psychology* **58,** 416–424.

Schinke, S. P., Botvin, G. J., and Orlandi, M. A. 1991. *Substance abuse in children and adolescents. Evaluation and intervention.* Newbury Park, Calif.: Sage.

Schlundt, D. G., and Johnson, W. G. 1990. *Eating disorders: Assessment and treatment.* Boston: Allyn & Bacon.

Schneider, G. E. 1979. Is it really better to have your brain lesion early? A revision of the "Kennard principle." *Neuropsychologica* **17,** 557–583.

Schopler, E., and Mesibov, G. B. (eds.). 1985. *Communication problems in autism.* New York: Plenum.

Schopler, E., Short, A., and Mesibov, G. 1989. Relation of behavioral treatment to "normal functioning." Comment on Lovaas. *Journal of Consulting and Clinical Psychology* **57,** 162–164.

Schreibman, L., and Charlop, M. H. 1989. Infantile autism. In T. H. Ollendick and M. Hersen (eds.), *Handbook of child psychopathology,* pp. 105–130. New York: Plenum.

Schwartz, I. M., and Levi, L. B. 1986. The juvenile justice system: The lessons of "reform." *Division of Child, Youth and Family Services Newsletter,* vol. 4, Fall, pp. 1, 10.

Schwartz, S., and Johnson, J. H. 1985. *Psychopathology of childhood: A clinical experimental approach,* 2d ed. New York: Pergamon.

Segal, H. 1973. *Introduction to the work of Melanie Klein.* New York: Basic Books.

Seidel, W. T., and Joschko, M. 1990. Evidence of difficulties in sustaining attention in children with ADDH. *Journal of Abnormal Child Psychology* **18,** 271–229.

Seligman, M. E. P. 1975. *Helplessness: On depression, development and death.* San Francisco: Freeman.

Sells, S. B., and Simpson, D. D. 1980. The case for drug treatment effectiveness based on the DARP research program. *British Journal of Addications* **75,** 117–131.

Selman, R. L. 1980. *The growth of interpersonal understanding.* New York: Academic Press.

Selman, R. L., and Byrne, D. F. 1974. A structural-developmental analysis of levels of role taking in middle childhood. *Child Development* **45,** 803–806.

Selman, R. L., and Demorest, A. P. 1984. Observing the troubled children's interpersonal negotiational strategies: Implications of and for a developmental model. *Child Development* **55,** 288–304.

Selman, R. L., and Schultz, L. H. 1988. Interpersonal thought and action in the case of a troubled early adolescent: Toward a developmental model of the gap. In S. R. Shirk (ed.), *Cognitive development and child psychotherapy,* pp. 207–246. New York: Plenum.

Selman, R. L., Schultz, L. H., and Yeates, K. O. 1991. Interpersonal understanding and action: A development and psychopathology perspective on research and prevention. In D. Cicchetti and S. L. Toth, (eds.), *Models and integrations. Rochester symposium on developmental psychopathology,* vol. 3, pp. 289–326. Rochester, N.Y.: University of Rochester Press.

Selye, H. 1956. *The stress of life.* New York: McGraw-Hill.

Semrud-Clikeman, M., Biederman, J., Sprich-Buckminster, S., Lehman, B. K., Farone, S. V., and Norman, D. 1992. Comorbidity between ADDH and learning disability: A review and report of clinically referred sample. *Journal of the American Academy of Child and Adolescent Psychiatry* **31,** 439–448.

Serafica, F. C. 1990. Counseling Asian-American parents: A cultural-developmental approach. In F. C. Serafica, A. I. Schwebel, R. K. Russell, P. D. Isaac, and L. B. Myers (eds.), *Mental health of ethnic minorities,* pp. 222–244. New York: Praeger.

Serafica, F. C. 1991. Peer relations of children with Down syndrome. In D. Cicchetti and M. Beeghly (eds.), *Children with Down syndrome: A developmental perspective,* pp. 369–398. Cambridge: Cambridge University Press.

Serafica, F. C., and Cicchetti, D. 1976. Down's syndrome children in a strange situation: Attachment and exploration behaviors. *Merrill-Palmer Quarterly* **22,** 137–150.

Serafica, F. C., and Harway, N. I. 1979. Social relations and self-esteem of children with learning disabilities. *Journal of Clinical Child Psychology* **8,** 227–233.

Serafica, F. C., Schwebel, A. I., Russell, R. K., Isaac, P. D., and Myers, L. B. (eds.). 1990. *Mental health of ethnic minorities.* New York: Praeger.

Shaffer, D. 1977. Enuresis. In M. Rutter and L. Hersov (eds.), *Child psychiatry: Modern approaches.* Oxford: Blackwell Scientific Publications.

Shaffer, D. 1985. *Developmental psychology.* Monterey, Calif.: Brooks/Cole.

Shaffer, D., Chadwick, O., and Rutter, M. 1975. Psychiatric outcome of localized head injuries in children. Outcome of severe damage to the central nervous system. Ciba Foundation Symposium (new series) **34,** 191–209.

Shaffer, D., Schonfeld, I., O'Connor, P. A., Stokman, C., Trautman, P., Shafer, S., and Ng, S. 1985. Neurological soft signs: Their relation to psychiatric disorder and intelligence in childhood and adolescence. *Archives of General Psychiatry* **42,** 342–351.

Shakow, D. 1953. Experimental psychology. In R. R. Grinker (ed.), *Midcentury psychiatry.* Springfield, Ill.: Charles C. Thomas.

Shapiro, S. 1973. Disturbances in development and childhood neurosis. In S. L. Copel (ed.), *Behavior pathology of childhood and adolescence.* New York: Basic Books.

Shapiro, T., and Esman, A. 1992. Psychoanalysis

and child and adolescent psychiatry. *Journal of the American Academy of Child and Adolescent Psychiatry* **31,** 6–13.

Shedler, J., and Block, J. 1990. Adolescent drug use and psychological health. *American Psychologist* **45,** 612–630.

Shiffrin, R. M., and Atkinson, R. C. 1969. Storage and retrieval processes in long-term memory. *Psychological Review* **76,** 179–193.

Shirk, S. R. 1988a. *Cognitive development and child psychotherapy.* New York: Plenum.

Shirk, S. R. 1988b. Introduction: A cognitive-developmental perspective on child psychotherapy. In S. R. Shirk (ed.), *Cognitive development and child psychotherapy,* pp. 1–16. New York: Plenum.

Shirk, S. R. 1988c. Conclusion: Child development and child psychotherapy. In S. R. Shirk (ed.), *Cognitive development and child psychotherapy,* pp. 319–332. New York: Plenum.

Shirk, S. R., and Saiz, C. C. 1992. Clinical, empirical, and developmental perspectives on the therapeutic relationship in child psychotherapy. *Development and Psychopathology* **4,** 713–728.

Sigel, I. E., and Blechman, E. 1990. Reflections: A conceptual analysis and synthesis. In G. R. Patterson (ed.), *Depression and aggression in family interaction,* pp. 281–313. Hillsdale, N.J.: Erlbaum.

Sigman, M., Ungerer, J. A., Mundy, P., and Sherman, T. 1987. Cognition in autistic children. In D. J. Cohen, A. M. Donnellan, and R. Paul (eds.), *Handbook of autism and developmental disabilities,* pp. 103–120. New York: Wiley.

Simpson, D. D., and Chatham, L. R. 1991. Special issue: Inhalant use by Mexican American youth. Findings from a longitudinal study. *Hispanic Journal of Behavioral Sciences* **13,** 243–355.

Singer, M. T., Wynne, L. C., and Toohey, B. A. 1979. Communication disorders and the families of schizophrenics. In L. C. Wynne, R. L. Cromwell, and S. Matthysse (eds.), *The nature of schizophrenia: New approaches to research and treatment.* New York: Wiley.

Skeels, H. M. 1966. Adult status of children with contrasting early life experiences. *Monographs of the Society for Research in Child Development* **31** (3, serial no. 105).

Skinner, B. F. 1948. *Walden Two.* New York: Macmillan.

Skinner, B. F. 1953. *Science and human behavior.* New York: Macmillan.

Slaughter, D. T. 1983. Early intervention and its effects on maternal and child development. *Monographs of the Society for Research in Child Development* **48** (4, series no. 202).

Slaughter, D. T., and Johnson, D. J. (eds.). 1988. *Visible now. Blacks in private schools.* New York: Greenwood.

Slaughter, D. T., Johnson, D. J., and Schneider, B. L. 1988. The educational goals of black private school parents. In D. L. Slaughter and D. J. Johnson (eds.), *Visible now. Blacks in private schols,* pp. 225–250. New York: Greenwood.

Slavson, S. R., and Schiffer, M. 1975. *Group psychotherapies for children: A textbook.* New York: International Universities Press.

Sloane, R. B., Staples, F. R., Cristol, A. H., Yorkston, N. J., and Whipple, K. 1975. *Psychotherapy versus behavior therapy.* Cambridge, Mass.: Harvard University Press.

Sloper, P., Knussen, C., Turner, S., and Cunningham, C. 1991. Factors related to stress and satisfaction with life in families of children with Down's syndrome. *Journal of Child Psychology and Psychiatry* **32**, 655–676.

Smetana, J. G. 1990. Morality and conduct disorders. In M. Lewis and S. M. Miller (eds.), *Handbook of developmental psychopathology,* pp. 157–179. New York: Plenum.

Smith, J. A. S., and Adler, R. G. 1991. Children hospitalized with child abuse and neglect: A case-control study. *Child Abuse & Neglect* **15**, 437–445.

Snowling, M. J. 1991. Developmental reading disorders. *Journal of Child Psychology and Psychiatry* **32**, 49–77.

Sours, J. A. 1969. Anorexia nervosa: Nosology, diagnosis, developmental patterns, and power-control dynamics. In G. Caplan and S. Lebovici (eds.), *Adolescence: Psychosocial perspectives.* New York: Basic Books.

Spencer, M. B. 1991. Identity, minority development of. In R. M. Lerner, A. C. Petersen, and J. Brooks-Gunn (eds.), *Encyclopedia of adolescence,* vol. 1, pp. 525–528. New York: Garland.

Spencer, M. B., and Markstrom-Adams, C. 1990. Identity processes among racial and ethnic mi-nority children in America. *Child Development* **61,** 290–310.

Spirito, A., Brown, L., Overholser, J., and Fritz, G. 1989. Attempted suicide in adolescence: A review and critique of the literature. *Clinical Psychology Review* **9,** 335–363.

Spitz, R. A. 1945. Hospitalism: An inquiry into the genesis of psychiatric conditions in early childhood. *Psychoanalytic study of the child,* vol. 1. New York: International Universities Press.

Spitz, R. A. 1946. Anaclitic depression. *Psychoanalytic study of the child,* vol. 2. New York: International Universities Press.

Spitzer, R. L., and Cantwell, D. P. 1987. The DSM-III classification of the psychiatric disorders of infancy, childhood and adolescence. *Journal of the American Academy of Child Psychiatry* **19,** 356–370.

Spivack, G., Platt, J. J., and Shure, M. 1976. *The problem-solving approach to adjustment.* San Francisco: Jossey-Bass.

Spock, B. 1963. The striving for autonomy and regressive object relations. *Psychoanalytic study of the child,* vol. 18. New York: International Universities Press.

Spreen, O. 1988a. *Learning disabled children growing up. A follow-up into adulthood.* New York: Oxford University Press.

Spreen, O. 1988b. Prognosis of learning disability. *Journal of Consulting and Clinical Psychology* **56,** 836–842.

Sroufe, L. A. 1989. Pathways to adaptation and maladaption: Psychopathology as developmental deviation. In D. Cicchetti (ed.), *The emergence of a discipline. Rochester symposium on developmental psychopathology,* vol. 1, pp. 13–40. Hillsdale, N.J.: Erlbaum.

Sroufe, L. A. 1990. An organizational perspective on the self. In D. Cicchetti and M. Beeghly (eds.), *The self in transition: Infancy to childhood,* pp. 281–307. Chicago: University of Chicago Press.

Sroufe, L. A. 1990. Considering normal and abnormal together: The essence of developmental psychopathology. *Development and Psychopathology* **2,** 335–348.

Sroufe, L. A., Cooper, R. G., and DeHart, G. B. 1992. *Child development. Its nature and course,* 2d. ed. New York: McGraw-Hill.

Sroufe, L. A., and Rutter, M. 1984. The domain of

developmental psychopathology. *Child Development* **55,** 17–29.

Sroufe, L. A., and Ward, M. J. 1985. Seductive behavior of mother and toddlers. Occurrence, correlates and family origin. *Child Development* **51,** 1222–1229.

Sroufe, L. A., Waters, F., and Matas, L. 1974. Contextual determinants of infant affective response. In M. Lewis and L. Rosenblum (eds.), *The origins of fear,* pp. 49–72. New York: Wiley.

Stanford-Binet Intelligence Scale. 1986. 4th ed. Chicago: Riverside.

Stanovich, K. E. 1987. New beginnings, old problems. In S. J. Ceci (ed.), *Handbook of cognitive, social and neuropsychological aspects of learning disabilities,* vol. 1, pp. 229–238. Hillsdale, N.J.: Erlbaum.

Starr, R. 1982. *Child abuse and prediction.* Cambridge, Mass.: Gallinger.

Starr, R., Jr., Dubowitz, H., and Bush, B. A. 1990. The epidemiology of child maltreatment. In R. T. Ammerman and M. Hersen, (eds.), *Children at risk. An evaluation of factors contributing to child abuse and neglect,* pp. 23–54. New York: Plenum.

Steinhausen, H. C., and Glanville, K. 1983a. Retrospective and prospective follow-up studies in anorexia nervosa. *International Journal of Eating Disorders* **2,** 221–235.

Steketee, G., and Cleere, L. 1990. Obsessive-compulsive disorders. In A. S. Bellack, M. Hersen, and A. E. Kazdin (eds.), *International handbook of behavior modification and therapy,* 2d ed., pp. 307–332. New York: Plenum.

Steller, M. 1991. Commentary: Rehabilitation of the child witness. In J. Doris (ed.), *The suggestibility of children's recollections,* pp. 106–109. Washington, D.C.: American Psychological Association.

Stevenson, H. W., Chen, C., and Uttal, D. H. 1990. Beliefs and achievement: A study of black, white, and Hispanic children. *Child Development* **16,** 508–523.

Stiffman, A. R., and Davis, L. E. (eds.). 1990. *Ethnic issues in adolescent mental health.* Newbury Park, Calif.: Sage.

Stone, W. L., and Lemanek, K. L. 1990a. Developmental issues in children's self-report. In A. M. La Greca (ed.), *Through the eyes of the child. Obtaining self-reports from children and adolescents,* pp. 18–56. Boston: Allyn & Bacon.

Stone, W. L., and Lemanek, K. L. 1990b. Parental report of social behavior in autistic preschoolers. *Journal of Autism and Developmental Disorders* **20,** 513–522.

Streissguth, A. P., Martin, D. C., Barr, H. M., Sandman, B. M., Kirchner, G. L., and Darby, B. L. 1984. Intra-uterine alcohol and nicotine exposure: Attention and reaction time in 4-year-old children. *Developmental Psychology* **20,** 533–541.

Striegel-Moore, R. H., Silberstein, L. R., and Rodin, J. 1986. Toward an understanding of risk factors in bulimia. *American Psychologist* **41,** 245–263.

Stuckey, S. 1987. *Slave culture.* New York: Oxford University Press.

Sue, S., Wagner, N., Ja, D., Margullis, C., and Lew, L. 1976. Conceptions of mental illness among Asian and Caucasian-American students. *Psychological Reports* **38,** 703–708.

Sullivan, H. S. 1953. *The interpersonal theory of psychiatry.* New York: Norton.

Svartberg, M., and Stiles, T. C. 1991. Comparative effects of short-term psychodynamic psychotherapy: A meta-analysis. *Journal of Consulting and Clinical Psychology* **59,** 704–714.

Swedo, S. E., Rapoport, J. L., Leonard, H., Lenane, M., and Cheslow, D. 1989. Obsessive-compulsive disorder in children and adolescents: Clinical phenomenology of 70 consecutive cases. *Archives of General Psychiatry* **46,** 335–341.

Swedo, S. E., Schapiro, M. B., Grady, C. L., Cheslow, D. L., Leonard, H. L., Kumar, A., Friedland, R., Rapoport, S. I., and Rapoport, J. L. 1989. Cerebral glucose metabolism in childhood-onset obsessive-compulsive disorder. *Archives of General Psychiatry* **46,** 518–523.

Sweet, A. A. 1984. The therapeutic relationship in behavioral therapy. *Clinical Psychology Review* **4,** 253–272.

Swisher, L., and Demetras, M. J. 1985. The expressive language characteristics of autistic children compared with mentally retarded or specific language-impaired children. In E. Schopler and G. B. Mesibov (eds.), *Communication problems in autism,* pp. 147–162. New York: Plenum.

Szapocznik, J., Santisteban, D., Rio, A., Perez-Vidal, A., Santisteban, D., and Kurtines, W. K. 1989. Family effectiveness training: Drug abuse and problem behaviors in Hispanic adolescents. *Hispanic Journal of Behavioral Sciences* **11,** 4–27.

Szatmari, P., Bartolucci, G., Bremner, R., Bond, S., and Rich, S. 1989. A follow-up study of high functioning autistic children. *Journal of Autism and Developmental Disabilities* **19,** 213–224.

Tager-Flusberg, H. 1985. Psycholinguistic approaches to language and communication in autism. In E. Schopler and G. B. Mesibov (eds.), *Communication problems in autism*, pp. 89–92. New York: Plenum.

Tager-Flusberg, H. 1989. A psycholinguistic perspective on language development in the autistic child. In G. Dawson (ed.), *Autism: Nature, diagnosis and treatment*, pp. 92–115. New York: Guilford.

Tager-Flusberg, H. 1992. Autistic children's talk about psychological states: Deficits in the early acquisition of a theory of mind. *Child Development* **63,** 161–172.

Tager-Flusberg, H., Calkins, S., Nolin, T., Baumberger, T., Anderson, M., and Chadwick-Dias, A. 1990. A longitudinal study of language acquisition in autistic and Down syndrome children. *Journal of Autism and Developmental Disorders* **20,** 1–20.

Tanner, J. M. 1962. *Growth of adolescence*, 2d ed. Oxford: Blackwell Scientific Publications.

Tarnowski, K. J., Prinz, R. J., and Nay, S. M. 1986. Comparative analysis of attentional deficits in hyperactive and learning-disabled children. *Journal of Abnormal Psychology* **95,** 341–345.

Tarnowski, K. J., and Rohrbeck, C. A. 1993. Disadvantaged children and their families. In T. H. Ollendick and R. J. Prinz (eds.), *Advances in clinical child psychology*, vol. 15, pp. 41–80. New York: Plenum.

Task Force on Asian-American Students. 1991. *Report of the provost's task force on Asian American students*. Columbus, Ohio: Ohio State University.

Taylor, H. G. 1988a. Learning disabilities. In E. J. Mash and L. G. Terdal (eds.), *Behavioral assessment of childhood disorders*, 2d ed., 402–450. New York: Guilford.

Taylor, H. G. 1988b. Neuropsychological testing: Relevance of assessing children's learning disabilities. *Journal of Consulting and Clinical Psychology* **56,** 795–800.

Teuber, H. L. 1975. Recovery of function after brain injury in man: Outcome of severe damage to the central nervous system. *Ciba Foundation Symposium*, new series **34,** 159–190.

Thelen, M. H., Powell, A. L., Lawrence, C., and Kuhnert, M. E. 1992. Eating and body concerns among children. *Journal of Clinical Child Psychology* **21,** 60–69.

Thomas, A., Chess, S., and Birch, H. 1968. *Temperament and behavior disorders in children*. New York: New York University Press.

Thompson, M. C., Asarnow, J. R., Goldstein, M. J., and Miklowitz, D. J. 1990. Thought disorders and communication problems in children with schizophrenia spectrum disorders and their parents. *Journal of Clinical Child Psychology* **19,** 159–168.

Thompson, R. A. 1987. Empathy and emotional understanding. The early development of empathy. In N. Eisenberg and J. Strayer (eds.), *Empathy and its development*, pp. 119–145. Cambridge: Cambridge University Press.

Thompson, R. A., and Hoffman, M. L. 1980. Empathy and the development of guilt in children. *Developmental Psychology* **16,** 155–156.

Thompson, R. A., and Jacobs, J. E. 1991. Defining psychological maltreatment: Research and policy perspectives. *Development and Psychopathology* **3,** 103–110.

Thorne, B. 1986. Girls and boys together . . . but mostly apart: Gender arrangements in elementary schools. In W. H. Hartup and Z. Rubin (eds.), *Relationships and development*, pp. 167–184. Hillsdale, N. J.: Erlbaum.

Tienari, P., Lahti, I., Sorri, A., Naarala, M., Moring, J., Kaleva, M., Wahlberg, K., and Wynne, L. C. 1990. Adopted-away offsprings of schizophrenics and controls: The Finnish adoptive family study of schizophrenia. In L. E. Robins and M. Rutter (eds.), *Straight and devious pathways from childhood to adulthood*, pp. 365–379. Cambridge: Cambridge University Press.

Tienari, P., Sorri, A., Naarala, M., Lahti, I., Pohjola, J. 1983. The Finnish adoptive family study: Adopted-away offsprings of schizophrenic mothers. In H. Stierlin, L. C. Wynne, and M. Wirsching (eds.), *Psychosocial intervention in schizophrenia* (pp. 21–34). Berlin: Springer-Verlag.

Tinsley, B. J. 1992. Multiple influences on the acquisition and socialization of children's health attitudes and behavior: An integrative review. *Child Development* **63**, 1043–1069.

Toner, B. B., Garfinkel, P. E., and Garner, D. M. 1986. Long-term follow-up of anorexia nervosa. *Psychosomatic Medicine* **48**, 520–528.

Toner, I. J., and Smith, R. A. 1977. Age and overt verbalization in delay maintenance behavior in children. *Journal of Experimental Child Psychology* **24**, 123–128.

Torgensen, J. 1975. Problems and prospects in the study of learning disabilities. In E. M. Hetherington (ed.), *Review of child development research,* vol. 5. Chicago: University of Chicago Press.

Torgensen, J., and Morgan, S. 1990. Phonological synthesis tasks: A developmental, functional, and componental analysis. In H. L. Swanson and B. Keogh (eds.), *Learning disabilities: Theoretical and research issues,* pp. 263–276. Hillsdale, N. J.: Erlbaum.

Toth, S. L., Manly, J. T., and Cicchetti, D. 1991. Child maltreatment and vulnerability to depression. *Development and Psychopathology* **3**, 97–112.

Trankina, F. J. 1983. Clinical issues and techniques in working with Hispanic children and their families. In G. J. Powell (ed.), *The psychosocial development of minority group children,* pp. 307–329. New York: Brunner/Mazel.

Tremblay, R. E., Masse, B., Perron, D., Leblanc, M., Schwartzman, A. E., and Ledingham, J. E. 1992. Early disruptive behavior, poor school achievement, delinquent behavior, and delinquent personality: Longitudinal analyses. *Journal of Consulting and Clinical Psychology* **60**, 64–72.

Tuma, J. M. 1989. Mental health services for children: The state of the art. *American Psychologist* **44**, 188–199.

Tupper, D. E., and Cicerone, K. D. 1991. *The neuropsychology of everyday life: Issues in development and rehabilitation.* Boston: Kluwer Academic Publishers.

Ungerer, J. A. 1989. The early development of autistic children: Implications for defining primary deficits. In G. Dawson (ed.), *Autism. Nature, diagnosis and treatment,* pp. 75–90. New York: Guilford.

U. S. Advisory Board on Child Abuse and Neglect.
1990. *Child abuse and neglect: Critical first steps in response to a national emergency.* Washington, D.C.: Department of Health and Human Services, Office of Human Development Services.

U. S. Bureau of the Census. 1991. *Statistical abstract of the United States.* Washington, D.C.: U.S. Government Printing Office.

U.S. News and World Report. 1985, May 20. Stealing $200 billion dollars "the respectable way."

Urban, J., Carlson, E., Egeland, B., and Sroufe, L. A. 1991. Patterns of individual adaptation across childhood. *Development and Psychopathology* **3**, 445–460.

Vandell, D. L., and Mueller, E. C. 1980. Peer play and friendships during the first two years. In H. C. Foot, A. J. Chapman, and J. R. Smith (eds.), *Friendship and social relations in children,* pp. 181–208. New York: Wiley.

van der Meere, J., Wekking, E., and Sergeant, J. 1991. Sustained attention and pervasive hyperactivity. *Journal of Child Psychology and Psychiatry* **32**, 275–284.

van IJzendoorn, M. H., and Kroonenberg, P. M. 1988. Cross-cultural patterns of attachment: A meta-analysis of the strange situation. *Child Development* **59**, 147–156.

Vargas, L. A., and Koss-Chioino, J. D. (eds.). 1992. *Working with culture: Psychotherapeutic interventions with ethnic minority children and adolescents.* San Francisco: Jossey-Bass.

Vasey, M. W. 1993. Development and cognition in childhood anxiety. The example of worry. In T. H. Ollendick and R. J. Prinz, (eds.), *Advances in clinical child psychology,* vol. 15, pp. 1–40. New York: Plenum.

Vaughn, B. E., Kopp, C. B., and Krakow, J. B. 1984. The emergence and consolidation of self-control from eighteen to thirty months of age. Normative trends and individual differences. *Child Development* **55**, 990–1004.

Vaughn, S., and Hogan, A. 1990. Social competence and learning disabilities: A prospective study. In H. L. Swanson and B. Keogh (eds.), *Learning disabilities: Theoretical and research issues,* pp. 175–191. Hillsdale, N.J.: Erlbaum.

Vega, W. A., Hough, R. L., and Romero, A. 1983. Family life patterns of Mexican-Americans. In G. J. Powell (ed.), *The psychosocial development of mi-*

nority group children, pp. 194–215. New York: Brunner/Mazel.

Verhulst, F. C., and Koot, H. M. 1991. Longitudinal research in child and adolescent psychiatry. *Journal of the American Academy of Child and Adolescent Psychiatry* **30**, 361–368.

Vicker, B., and Monahan, M. 1988. The diagnosis of autism by state agencies. *Journal of Autism and Developmental Disorder* **26**, 55–75.

Volkmar, F. R. 1986. Compliance, noncompliance, and negativism. In E. Schopler and G. B. Mesibov (eds.), *Social behavior in autism*, pp. 171–188. New York: Plenum.

Volkmar, F. R. 1987. Social development. In D. J. Cohen, A. M. Donnellan, and R. Paul (eds.), *Handbook of autism and pervasive developmental disorder*, pp. 41–60. New York: Wiley.

Volkmar, F. R., and Cohen, D. J. 1988. Diagnosis of pervasive developmental disorders. In B. B. Lahey and A. E. Kazdin (eds.), *Advances in clinical child psychology*, vol. 11, pp. 249–284. New York: Plenum.

Volkmar, F. R., and Mayes, L. C. 1990. Gaze behavior in autism. *Development and Psychopathology* **2**, 61–69.

Volkmar, F. R., Sparrow, S. S., Rende, R. D., and Cohen, D. J. 1989. Facial perception in autism. *Journal of Child Psychology and Psychiatry* **30**, 591–598.

Vondra, J. I. 1990. Sociological and ecological factors. In R. T. Ammerman and M. Hersen (eds.), *Children at risk: An evaluation of factors contributing to child abuse and neglect*, pp. 149–169. New York: Plenum.

Vormbrock, J. K. 1993. Attachment theory as applied to wartime and job related marital separation. *Psychological Bulletin*, 114, 122–144.

Vurpillot, E. 1968. The development of scanning strategies and their relation to visual differentiation. *Journal of Experimental Child Psychology* **6**, 632–650.

Wadden, T. A., Foster, G. D., Brownell, K. D., and Finley, E. 1984. Self-concept in obese and normal weight children. *Journal of Consulting and Clinical Psychology* **52**, 1104–1105.

Wagner, S., Ganiban, J., and Cicchetti, D. 1991. Attention, memory, and perception in infants with Down syndrome: A review and commentary. In D. Cicchetti and M. Beeghly (eds.), *Children with Down syndrome: A developmental perspective*, pp. 147–179. Cambridge: Cambridge University Press.

Wahler, R. G. 1990. Who is driving the interactions? A comment on "Child and parent effects in boys' conduct disorder." *Developmental Psychology* **26**, 702–709.

Waldron, S. 1976. The significance of childhood neuroses for adult mental health. A follow-up study. *American Journal of Psychiatry* **133**, 532–538.

Waldron, S., Jr., Shrier, D. K., Stone, B., and Tobin, F. 1975. School phobia and other childhood neuroses. A systematic study of children and their families. *American Journal of Psychiatry* **132**, 802–808.

Walker, C. E., Milling, L. S., and Bonner, B. L. 1988. Incontinence disorders: Enuresis and encopresis. In D. Routh (ed.), *Handbook of pediatric psychology*, pp. 363–382. New York: Guilford.

Walker, E. F., Davis, D. M., and Gottleib, L. A. 1991. Charting the developmental trajectory of schizophrenia. In D. Cicchetti and S. L. Toth (eds.), *Models and integrations. Rochester symposium on developmental psychopathology*, vol. 3, pp. 185–205. Rochester, N.Y.: University of Rochester Press.

Walker, E. F., Davis, D. M., Gottleib, L. A., and Weinstein, J. A. 1991. Developmental trajectories in schizophrenia: Elucidating the divergent pathways. In E. F. Walker (ed.), *Schizophrenia. A life-course developmental perspective*, pp. 299–331. San Diego, Calif.: Academic Press.

Wallander, J. L., Feldman, W. S., and Varni, J. W. 1989. Physical status and psychological adjustment of children with spina bifida. *Journal of Pediatric Psychology* **14**, 89–102.

Wallander, J. L., Varni, J. W., Babani, L., Banis, H. T., and Wilcox, K. T. 1988. Children with chronic physical disorders: Maternal reports of their psychological adjustment. *Journal of Pediatric Psychology* **13**, 197–212.

Wallerstein, J. S. 1984. Children of divorce: Preliminary report of a 10-year follow-up of young children. *American Journal of Orthopsychiatry* **53**, 444–458.

Wallerstein, J. S. 1985. Children of divorce: Preliminary report of a ten-year follow-up of older children and adolescents. *Journal of the American Academy of Child Psychiatry* **24**(5), 545–553.

Wallerstein, J. S. 1991. The long-term effects of divorce on children: A review. *Journal of the American Academy of Child and Adolescent Psychiatry* **30**, 349–360.

Wallerstein, J. S., and Kelly, J. B. 1974. The effects of parental divorce. The adolescent experience. In E. J. Anthony and G. Koupernik (eds.), *The child in his family: Children at psychiatric risk,* vol. 3. New York: Wiley.

Waterman, J. 1986. Developmental considerations. In K. MacFarlane and J. Waterman (eds.), *Sexual abuse of young children: Evaluation and treatment,* pp. 15–29. New York: Guilford.

Watkins, B., and Bentovim, A. 1992. The sexual abuse of male children and adolescents: A review of current research. *Journal of Child Psychology and Psychiatry* **33**, 197–248.

Watkins, J. M., Asarnow, R. F., and Tanguay, P. E. 1988. Symptom development in childhood schizophrenia. *Journal of Child Psychology and Psychiatry* **29**, 865–878.

Watson, J. S., and Ramey, C. T. 1972. Reactions to responsive-contingent stimulation in early infancy. *Merrill-Palmer Quarterly* **18**, 219–227.

Watson, L. R., Lord, C., Schaffer, B., and Schopler, E. 1989. *Teaching spontaneous communication to autistic and developmentally handicapped children.* New York: Pro-Ed.

Watt, N. F. 1984. In a nutshell: The first two decades of high-risk research in schizophrenia. In N. F. Watt, E. J. Anthony, L. C. Wayne, and J. E. Rolf (eds.), *Children at risk for schizophrenia: A longitudinal perspective,* pp. 572–595. Cambridge: Cambridge University Press.

Watt, N. F., Anthony, E. J., Wynne, L. C., and Rolf, J. E. (eds.). 1984. *Children at risk for schizophrenia: A longitudinal perspective.* Cambridge: Cambridge University Press.

Watt, N. F., and Lubensky, A. W. 1976. Childhood roots of schizophrenia. *Journal of Consulting and Clinical Psychology* **44**, 363–375.

Watt, N. F., and Saiz, C. 1991. Longitudinal studies of premorbid development of adult schizophrenics. In E. F. Walker (ed.), *Schizophrenia. A life-course developmental perspective,* pp. 157–192. San Diego, Calif.: Academic Press.

Waxman, M., and Stunkard, A. J. 1980. Caloric intake and expenditure of obese boys. *Journal of Pediatrics* **96**, 189–193.

Webster-Stratton, C. 1991. Annotation: Strategies for helping families with conduct-disordered children. *Journal of Child Psychology and Psychiatry* **32**, 1047–1062.

Wechsler, D. 1974. *Manual for the Wechsler Intelligence Scale for Children—Revised.* New York: Psychological Corporation.

Wechsler, D. 1991. *WISC-III. Wechsler Intelligence Scale for Children—Third Edition Manual.* New York: Psychological Corporation.

Wechsler Memory Scale. 1987. Rev. ed. San Antonio, Tex.: Psychological Corporation.

Weiner, I. B. 1970. *Psychological disturbances in adolescence.* New York: Wiley.

Weiner, I. B. 1980. Psychopathology in adolescence. In J. Adelson (ed.), *Handbook of adolescent psychology.* New York: Wiley.

Weiner, I. B. 1992. *Psychological disturbances in adolescence,* 2d ed. New York: Wiley.

Weiner, P. S. 1980. Developmental language disorder. In H. E. Rie and E. D. Rie (eds.), *Handbook of minimal brain dysfunctions: A critical review.* New York: Wiley.

Weinraub, M., Clemens, L. P., Sockloff, A., Ethridge, T., Gracey, E., and Myers, B. 1984. The development of sex-role stereotypes in the third year. Relationship to gender labeling, gender identity, sex-typed toy preferences, and family characteristics. *Child Development* **55**, 1493–1503.

Weiss, B., and Weisz, J. R. 1990. The impact of methodological factors on child psychotherapy outcome research: A meta-analysis for researchers. *Journal of Abnormal Child Psychology* **18**, 639–665.

Weiss, B., Weisz, J. R., and Bromfield, R. 1986. Performance of retarded and nonretarded persons on information-processing tasks: Further tests of the similar structure hypothesis. *Psychological Bulletin* **100**, 157–175.

Weiss, G. 1980. MBD: Critical diagnostic issues. In H. E. Rie and E. D. Rie (eds.), *Handbook of minimal brain dysfunctions. A critical view.* New York: Wiley.

Weiss, S. R., and Ebert, M. H. 1983. Psychological and behavioral characteristics of normal weight bulimics and normal weight controls. *Psychosomatic Medicine* **45**, 293–303.

Weisz, J. R. 1989. Culture and the development of child psychopathology: Lessons from Thailand. In D. Cicchetti (ed.), *The emergence of a discipline.*

Rochester symposium on developmental psychopathology, vol. 1, pp. 89–118. Hillsdale, N.J.: Erlbaum.

Weisz, J. R. 1990. Cultural-familial mental retardation: A developmental perspective on cognitive performance and "helpless" behavior. In R. M. Hodapp, J. A. Burack, and E. Zigler (eds.), *Issues in the developmental approach to mental retardation*, pp. 137–168. Cambridge: Cambridge University Press.

Weisz, J. R., Rudolph, K. D., Granger, D. A., and Sweeney, L. 1992. Cognition, competence, and coping in child and adolescent depression: Research findings, developmental concerns, therapeutic implications. *Development and Psychopathology* **4**, 627–654.

Weisz, J. R., and Weiss, B. 1989. Assessing the effects of clinic-based psychotherapy with children and adolescents. *Journal of Consulting and Clinical Psychology* **57**, 741–746.

Weisz, J. R., Weiss, B., Alicke, M. D., and Klotz, M. L. 1987. Effectiveness of psychotherapy with children and adolescents: A meta-analysis. *Journal of Consulting and Clinical Psychology* **55**, 542–549.

Weisz, J. R., Weiss, B., and Donenberg, G. R. 1992. The lab versus the clinic: Effects of child and adolescent psychotherapy. *American Psychologist* **47**, 1578–1585.

Weller, R. A., Weller, E. B., Fristad, M. A., and Bowes, J. M. 1991. Depression in recently bereaved prepubertal children. *American Journal of Psychiatry* **148**, 1536–1540.

Wellman, H. M. 1988. First steps in the child's theorizing about the mind. In J. W. Astington, P. L. Harris, and D. R. Olson (eds.), *Developing theories of mind*, pp. 64–92. Cambridge: Cambridge University Press.

Wenar, C. 1971. *Personality development from infancy to adulthood*. Boston: Houghton-Mifflin.

Wenar, C. 1976. Executive competence in toddlers: A prospective, observational study. *Genetic Psychology Monographs* **93**, 189–285.

Wenar, C. 1982. On negativism. *Human Development* **25**, 1–23.

Wenar, C. 1989. Phobias. In M. Lewis and S. M. Miller (eds.), *Handbook of developmental psychopathology*. New York: Plenum.

Wenar, C., and Curtis, K. M. 1991. The validity of the Rorschach for assessing cognitive and affective changes. *Journal of Personality Assessment* **57**, 291–308.

Wenar, C., and Ruttenberg, B. A. 1976. The use of BRIACC for evaluating therapeutic effectiveness. *Journal of Autism and Childhood Schizophrenia* **6**, 175–191.

Wenar, C., Ruttenberg, B. A., Kalish-Weiss, B., and Wolf, E. G. 1986. The development of normal and autistic children: A comparative study. *Journal of Autism and Developmental Disorders* **16**, 317–333.

Werner, E. E., and Smith, R. S. 1992. *Overcoming the odds: High risk children from birth to adulthood*. Ithaca, N.Y.: Cornell University Press.

Werner, H. 1948. *Comparative psychology of mental development*. New York: International Universities Press.

Werry, J. S. 1986a. Biological factors. In H. C. Quay and J. S. Werry (eds.), *Psychopathological disorders of childhood*, 3d ed., pp. 294–331. New York: Wiley.

Werry, J. S. 1986b. Physical illness, symptoms and allied disorders. In H. C. Quay and J. S. Werry (eds.), *Psychopathological disorders of childhood*, 3d ed., pp. 232–293. New York: Wiley.

Werry, J. S. 1991. Overanxious disorder: A review of its taxonomic properties. *Journal of the American Academy of Child and Adolescent Psychiatry* **30**, 533–544.

West, D. J. 1967. *Homosexuality*. Chicago: Aldine.

Westerman, M. A. 1990. Coordination of maternal directive with preschoolers' behavior in compliance-problem and healthy dyads. *Developmental Psychology* **26**, 621–630.

Whalen, C. K. 1989. Attention deficit and hyperactivity disorders. In T. H. Ollendick, and M. Hersen (eds.). *Handbook of child psychopathology*, pp. 131–169. New York: Plenum.

Whalen, C. K., and Henker, B. 1991. Therapies for hyperactive children: Comparisons, combinations, and compromises. *Journal of Consulting and Clinical Psychology* **39**, 126–137.

Whalen, C. K., Henker, B., and Granger, D. A. 1990. Social judgment in hyperactive boys: Effects of methylphenidate and comparisons with normal peers. *Journal of Abnormal Child Psychology* **18**, 297–316.

White, C. P., and White, M. B. 1991. The Adolescent Family Life Act: Content, findings, and policy recommendations for pregnancy prevention programs. *Journal of Clinical Child Psychology* **20**, 58–70.

White, R. W. 1959. Motivation reconsidered: The concept of competence. *Psychological Review* **66**, 297–333.

Whiteside, M. F. 1979. Family therapy. In J. D. Noshpitz (ed.), *Therapeutic interventions: Basic handbook of child psychiatry*, vol. 3. New York: Basic Books.

Wicks-Nelson, R., and Israel, A. C. 1984. *Behavior disorders of childhood*. Englewood Cliffs, N. J.: Prentice-Hall.

Wicks-Nelson, R., and Israel, A. C. 1991. *Behavior disorders of childhood*, 2d ed. Englewood Cliffs, N.J.: Prentice-Hall.

Wiggins, J. S. 1981. Clinical and statistical prediction: Where are we and where do we go from here? *Clinical Psychology Review* **1**, 3–18.

Wimmer, H., Gruber, S., and Perner, J. 1984. Young children's conception of lying: Lexical realism–moral subjectivism. *Journal of Experimental Child Psychology* **37**, 1–30.

Wohl, T. H. 1980. Other assessment techniques. In H. E. Rie and E. D. Rie (eds.), *Handbook of minimal brain dysfunctions*. New York: Wiley.

Wolfe, D. A. 1987. Child abuse: Implications for child development and psychopathology. *Developmental Clinical Psychology and Psychiatry* **10**, Newbury Park, Calif.: Sage.

Wolfe, D. A. 1988. Child abuse and neglect. In E. J. Mash and L. G. Terdal (eds.), *Behavior assessment of childhood disorders*, 2d ed., pp. 627–669. New York: Guilford.

Wolfe, D. A., and St. Pierre, J. 1989. Child abuse and neglect. In T. H. Ollendick and M. Hersen (eds.), *Handbook of child psychopathology*, 2d ed. New York: Plenum.

Wolpe, J. 1973. *The practice of behavior therapy*, 2d ed. New York: Pergamon.

Woodcock Reading Mastery Tests. 1987. Rev. ed. Circle Pines, Minn.: American Guidance Service.

Woodcock-Johnson Tests of Achievement. 1989. Allen, Tex.: DLM Teaching Resources.

Wooden, W., Leon, J., and Toshima, M. 1988. Ethnic identity among Sansei and Yonsei church-affiliated youth in Los Angeles and Honolulu. *Psychological Reports* **62**, 268–270.

Woolston, J. L., and Forsyth, B. 1989. Obesity of infancy and early childhood. A diagnostic

schema. In B. B. Lahey and A. E. Kazdin (eds.), *Advances in clinical child psychology*, vol. 12, pp. 179–192. New York: Plenum.

Wright, J. C., and Vliestra, A. G. 1975. The development of selective attention: From perceptual exploration to logical search. In H. W. Reese (ed.), *Advances in child development and behavior*, vol. 10. New York: Academic Press.

Wylie, M. S. 1992. Revising the dream. *The Family Therapy Network* **16**, 10–23.

Wynne, L. C. 1984. Communication patterns and family relations of children at risk for schizophrenia. In N. F. Watt, E. J. Anthony, L. C. Wynne, and J. E. Rolf (eds.), *Children at risk for schizophrenia: A longitudinal perspective*, pp. 572–595. Cambridge: Cambridge University Press.

Wynne, L. C., Toohey, M. L., and Doane, J. 1979 Family studies. In L. Bellak (ed.), *Disorders of the schizophrenic syndrome*. New York: Basic Books.

Yager, J. 1982. Family issues in pathogenesis of anorexia nervosa. *Psychosomatic Medicine* **44**, 43–60.

Yalom, I. D. 1975. *The theory and practice of group psychotherapy*, 2d ed. New York: Basic Books.

Yamamoto, J., and Iga, M. 1983. Emotional growth of Japanese-American children. In G. J. Powell (ed.), *The psychosocial development of minority group children*, pp. 167–180. New York: Brunner/Mazel.

Yamamoto, J., and Kubota, M. 1983. The Japanese-American family. In G. J. Powell (ed.), *The psychosocial development of minority group children*, pp. 237–246. New York: Brunner/Mazel.

Yarrow, M. R. 1990. Family environments of depressed and well parents and their children: Issues of research methodology. In G. R. Patterson (ed.), *Depression and aggression in family interaction*, pp. 169–184. Hillsdale, N.J.: Erlbaum.

Yarrow, M. R., Campbell, J. D., and Burton, R. V. 1970. Recollections of childhood: A study of the retrospective method. *Monographs of the Society for Research in Child Development* **35** (5, serial no. 138).

Yates, A. 1989. Current perspectives on the eating disorders. Part I: History, psychological and biological aspects. *Journal of the American Academy of Child and Adolescent Psychiatry* **28**, 813–828.

Yates, A. 1990. Current perspectives on the eating disorders. Part II: Treatment, outcome, and research directions. *Journal of the American Academy of Child and Adolescent Psychiatry* **29**, 1–9.

Yates, A. 1991. False and mistaken allegations of

sexual abuse. In A. Tasman and S. M. Goldfinger (eds.), *Review of psychiatry,* vol. 10, pp. 320–335. Washington, D.C.: American Psychiatric Press.

Yirmiya, N., Sigman, M. D., Kasari, C., and Mundy, P. 1992. Empathy and cognition in high-functioning children with autism. *Child Development* **63,** 150–160.

Youngblade, L. M., and Belsky, J. 1990. Social and emotional consequences of child maltreatment. In R. T. Ammerman and M. Hersen (eds.), *Children at risk: An evaluation of factors contributing to child abuse and neglect,* pp. 109–148. New York: Plenum.

Yuille, J. C., and Wells, G. L. 1991. Concerns about the application of research findings: The issue of ecology validity. In J. Doris (ed.), *The suggestibility of children's recollections,* pp. 118–128. Washington, D.C.: American Psychological Association.

Yule, W., and Rutter, M. 1985. Reading and other learning difficulties. In M. Rutter and L. Hersov (eds.), *Child and adolescent psychiatry: Modern approaches,* 2d ed., pp. 444–464. Oxford: Blackwell Scientific Publications.

Yuwiler, A., Geller, E., and Ritvo, E. R. 1976. Neurobiochemical research. In E. R. Ritvo, B. Freeman, E. M. Ornitz, and P. E. Tanguay (eds.), *Autism: Diagnosis, current research, and management.* New York: Spectrum.

Zigler, E., and Hall, N. W. 1989. Physical abuse in America: Past, present, and future. In D. Cicchetti and V. Carlson (eds.), *Child maltreatment: Theory and research on the causes and consequences of child abuse and neglect,* pp. 38–77. Cambridge: Cambridge University Press.

Zucker, K. J. 1989. Gender identity disorders. In C. G. Last, and M. Hersen (eds.), *Handbook of child psychiatric diagnosis,* pp. 388–406. New York: Wiley.

Zucker, K. J., and Green, R. 1992. Psychosexual disorders in children and adolescents. *Journal of Child Psychology and Psychiatry* **33,** 107–151.

ACKNOWLEDGMENTS

Text Permissions

Figure 2.2: From "Storage and retrieval processes in long-term memory" by R. M. Shiffrin and R. C. Atkinson in *Psychological Review, 76.* Copyright © 1969 by the American Psychological Association. Adapted with permission.

Figure 3.1: From the "Youth Self-Report Profile" by T. M. Achenbach. Copyright © 1991 by T. M. Achenbach. Reprinted by permission.

Table 3.1: Adapted with permission from the DSM-IV Draft Criteria (3/1/93). Copyright 1993 American Psychiatric Association.

Table 3.2: Adapted with permission from the DSM-IV Draft Criteria (3/1/93). Copyright 1993 American Psychiatric Association.

Table 3.3: From "Convergence Between Statistically Derived Behavior Problem Syndrome and Child Psychiatric Diagnoses" by Craig Edelbrock and Anthony J. Costello, *Journal of Abnormal Child Psychology*, Vol. 16, No. 2. 1988. Reprinted by permission.

Table 4.4: Reprinted with the permission of The Free Press, a Division of Macmillan, Inc., from *The Clinical Guide to Child Psychiatry*, edited by David Shaffer, Anke A. Ehrhardt, and Laurence L. Greenhill. Copyright © 1985 by David Shaffer, Anke A. Ehrhardt, and Laurence L. Greenhill.

Figure 5.1: From "Childhood Obesity" by Foreyt and Goodrick in *Behavioral Assessment of Childhood Disorders*, 2nd Edition, by E. J. Mash and L. G. Terdal, editors. Reprinted by permission of The Guilford Press.

Figure 5.2: From "The Age of Attaining Bladder Control" by W. C. Oppel, P. A. Harper, and R. V. Rider in *Pediatrics*, Vol. 42, No. 4, October 1968. Reproduced by permission of *Pediatrics*.

Table 5.1: Reprinted with permission from the DSM-IV Draft Criteria (3/1/93). Copyright 1993 American Psychiatric Association.

Table 5.2: From "Development of children's noncompliant strategies from toddlerhood to age 5" by L. Kuczynski and G. Kochanska in *Developmental Psychology, 26.* Copyright © 1990 by the American Psychological Association. Reprinted with permission.

Figure 6.2: From "The Development of Scanning Strategies and the Relation to Visual Differentiation" by Eliane Vurpillot in *Journal of Experimental Child Psychology, 6*, 1968. Reprinted by permission.

Table 6.1: Reprinted with permission from the DSM-IV Draft Criteria (3/1/93). Copyright 1993 American Psychiatric Association.

Table 6.2: From "Therapies for Hyperactive Children: Comparisons, Combinations, and Compromises" by Carol K. Whalen and Barbara Henker in *Journal of Consulting and Clinical Psychology*, Vol. 59, No. 1. Copyright © 1991 by the American Psychological Association. Reprinted by permission.

Figure 7.1: From Patterson, C. J., and Capaldi, D. M., "A mediational model for boys' depressed mood." In J. Rolf, A. S. Masten, D. Cicchetti, K. H. Nuechterlein and S. Weintraub (Eds.), *Risk and Protective Factors in Development Psychopathology*. Cambridge: Cambridge University Press. Reprinted by permission.

Figure 7.2: From "Letter to the editor" by L. A. Fingerhut and J. C. Kleinman, 1988, *Journal of the American Medical Association, 259*, p. 356.

Figure 7.3: From Harter, S., Marold, D. B., and Whitesell, N. R., "Model of psychosocial risk factors leading to suicidal ideation in young adolescents" in *Development and Psychopathology, 1992, 4*, 167–188. Reprinted by permission of Cambridge University Press.

Table 7.1: Reprinted with permission from the DSM-IV Draft Criteria (3/1/93). Copyright 1993 American Psychiatric Association.

Figure 8.1: From "Fears of Children and Adolescents: A Cross-Sectional Australian Study Using the Revised-Fear Survey Schedule for Children" by N. J. King et al. in *Journal of Child Psychology & Psychiatry*, Vol. 30, No. 5. Copyright © 1989 Association for Child Psychology and Psychiatry. Reprinted by permission.

Table 8.3: Reprinted with permission from the DSM-IV Draft Criteria (3/1/93). Copyright 1993 American Psychiatric Association.

Figure 9.1: From "Developmental sequences in age of onset of disruptive child behaviors" by R. Loeber et al. in *Journal of Child and Family Studies, 1*, 1992. Reprinted by permission of Human Sciences Press, Inc.

Figure 9.3: Adapted from *A Social Interactional Approach*, Volume 4: *Antisocial Boys*, by G. R. Patterson, J. B. Reid, & T. J. Dishion. Copyright © 1992 by Castalia Publishing Company. Reprinted by permission.

Table 9.1: Reprinted with permission from the DSM-IV Draft Criteria (3/1/93). Copyright 1993 American Psychiatric Association.

Figure 11.1: From *Pediatric and Adolescent AIDS: Research Findings from the Social Sciences* by S. W. Henggeler, G. B. Melton and J. R. Rodrigue. Copyright © 1992 by Sage Publications, Inc. Reprinted by permission of Sage Publications, Inc.

Table 11.2: Clayton, R. R. (1992) *Transitions in Drug Use: Risk and Protective Factors*. In M. Glantz & R. Pickens, *Vulnerability to Drug Abuse*. Copyright © 1992 by the American Psychological Association. Reprinted by permission.

Table 11.3: Reprinted with permission from the DSM-IV Draft Criteria (3/1/93). Copyright 1993 American Psychiatric Association.

Figure 12.1: From *Mental Retardation: Definitions, Classification and Systems of Supports*, 9th ed., 1992. Reprinted by permission of the American Association on Mental Retardation.

Figure 12.2: From "Dimensions of adaptive behavior in institutionalized mentally retarded children and adults: Developmental perspectives" by K. Nihira, *American Journal of Mental Deficiency, 81*, 1976. Reprinted by permission of the American Association on Mental Retardation.

Figure 12.3: From "Applying the developmental perspective to Down Syndrome" by R. M. Hodapp and E. Zigler in *Children with Down Syndrome*, edited by D. Cicchetti and M. Beeghly. Cambridge: Cambridge University Press. Reprinted by permission.

Table 12.1: Reprinted by permission of the publisher from C. J. Fogelman (Ed.), *AAMD Adaptive Behavior Scale Manual*, 1974 Revision, pp. 6–7. Copyright 1974, American Association on Mental Deficiency.

Figure 13.1: Rita Wicks-Nelson and Allen C. Israel, *Behavior Disorders of Childhood*, 2nd ed., © 1991, p. 324. Reprinted by permission of Prentice Hall, Englewood Cliffs, New Jersey.

Table 13.2: From *Assessment of Children*, Revised and Updated 3rd Edition, 1992 by Jerome M. Sattler. Reprinted by permission of Jerome M. Sattler, Publisher, Inc.

Figure 14.1: From "Child Abuse: Implications for Child Development and Psychopathology" by D. A. Wolfe in *Developmental Clinical Psychology and Psychiatry, 10,* 1987. Copyright © 1987 Sage Publications, Inc. Reprinted by permission of Sage Publications, Inc.

Table 14.2: From "Impact of sexual abuse on children: A review and synthesis of recent empirical studies" by K. A. Kendall-Tackett, L. M. Williams and D. Finkelhor in *Psychological Bulletin, 113.* Copyright © 1993 by the American Psychological Association. Reprinted by permission.

Figure 15.1: Reprinted by permission of the publisher and authors from H. G. Birch and J. D. Gussow, *Disadvantaged Children: Health, Nutrition, and School Failure,* p. 268. Copyright 1970, The Psychological Corporation.

Figure 15.3: Chart by Dan Halberstein, from *A Databook of Child and Adolescent Injury* (p. 43) by Children's Safety Network, 1991. Washington, DC: National Center for Education in Maternal and Child Health. Copyright 1991 by National Center for Education in Maternal and Child Health. Data source: Fingerhut, National Center for Health Statistics, 1988. Reprinted by permission.

Table 15.1: From: *Achievement and Achievement Motives* by Janet T. Spence (ed.). Copyright © 1983 by W. H. Freeman and Company. Reprinted with permission.

Figure 16.1: From "Anxiety Disorders Interview Schedule for Children." Copyright 1991 Graywind Publications Incorporated. Reprinted with permission.

Figure 16.2: Simulated items similar to those in the Wechsler Intelligence Scale for Children—Revised. Copyright © 1974 by The Psychological Corporation. Reprinted by permission. All rights reserved.

Figure 16.3: From *Assessment of Children,* Revised and Updated 3rd Edition, 1992 by Jerome M. Sattler. Reprinted by permission of Jerome M. Sattler, Publisher, Inc.

Figure 16.4: Adapted from *The Child Behavior Checklist for Ages 4–18* by T. M. Achenbach, published by the University of Vermont. Copyright © 1991 by T. M. Achenbach.

Figure 16.5: From *Assessment of Children,* Revised and Updated 3rd Edition, 1992 by Jerome M. Sattler. Reprinted by permission of Jerome M. Sattler, Publisher, Inc.

Table 16.1: From *Assessment of Children,* Revised and Updated 3rd Edition, 1992 by Jerome M. Sattler. Reprinted by permission of Jerome M. Sattler, Publisher, Inc.

Table 16.2: Copyright by Guilford Press, 1981. Reprinted with permission from R. Barkley, "Hyperactivity." In E. Mash & L. Terdal (Eds.), *Behavioral Assessment of Childhood Disorders.* New York: Guilford Press, 1981.

Figure 17.2: From Hall, R. V. et al., 1971. "The teacher as observer and experimenter in the modification of disruptive and talking out behavior." *Journal of Applied Behavior Analysis,* 4.

Figure 17.3: From "The Lab Versus the Clinic: Effects of Child and Adolescent Psychotherapy" by John R. Weisz, Bahr Weiss, and Geri R. Donenberg in *American Psychologist,* Vol. 47, No. 12. Copyright © 1992 by the American Psychological Association. Reprinted by permission.

Photo Credits

Page 36, Elizabeth Crews/Image Works; page 45, Antman/Image Works; page 58, Peter Menzel/ Stock, Boston; page 104, Sven Martson/Comstock; page 137, Judith D. Sedwick/Picture Cube; page 156, Chuck Fishman/Woodfin Camp & Associates; page 186, Teri Leigh Stratford/Monkmeyer; page 190, Arthur Tress/Photo Researchers; page 233, Robert Houser/Comstock; page 257, Robert Houser/Comstock; page 268, Charles Gatewood/ Image Works; page 306, Arlene Collins/Monkmeyer; page 352, Meri Houtchens-Kitchens/Picture Cube; page 389, Jim Whitmer/Stock, Boston; page 424, Joel Gordon; page 433, Spencer Grant/Photo Researchers; page 495, Comstock.

NAME INDEX

SUBJECT INDEX

Abilities tests (*see* Assessment)
Abuse (*see* Physical abuse; Sexual abuse)
Achievement tests (*see* Assessment)
Acting out, antisocial (*see* Conduct disorder)
Adolescence:
  general characteristics of, 297–299
  identity in, 66–67
  (*See also specific psychopathologies and risk conditions*)
African-American children (*see* Black adolescent identity)
Aggression:
  attribution of, 52
  and conscience, 58–59
  definition of, 57
  development of, 57–59, 84
  multiple meanings of, 58, 67
  and parental discipline, 45, 46
  sex differences in, 59
  stability of, 251–252
  (*See also* Attention-deficit hyperactivity disorder; Conduct disorder; Depression; Oppositional-defiant disorder)
Anorexia nervosa:
  body image in, 299, 301–302

and bulimia nervosa, 307–308
comorbidity: depression, 300
definition and symptomatology, 87, 299–300
etiological model, 300
family characteristics in, 302, 303–304
negativism in, 299, 305–306
organic factors in, 301, 302
parental relations in, 305–306
prevalence, 300
sexual relations in, 302
and sociability, 302
societal factors in, 304–305
treatment of, 307–309
types: restricting, bulimic, 299, 302
(*See also* Bulimia nervosa)
AIDS, 311, 326, 330, 331, 427
Anxiety:
  and defense mechanisms, 53–54
  definition of, 52
  development of, 52–53
  and psychopathology, 54
  (*See also* Anxiety disorders; Depression)
Anxiety disorders:
  assessment of, 222–223
  behavioral theory of, 225–226
  classification, 86–87, 220–221

comorbidity: depression, 222
and internalization, 221–222
organic factors in, 221
parental relations in, 221
prevalence, 221
treatment of, 223
(*See also specific classifications*)
Assessment:
  achievement tests, 459–460
  clinical, art and science, 467
  cognitive aspects of, 448
  comprehensive, 444–445
  developmental dimensions of, 445
  interview, child, 448–450
  interview, parental, 447–448
  and observation, clinical, 446–447
  organic brain damage, tests for, 460–462
  rapport in, 445
  and referrals, 445–446
  standardized tests in, 445
  varieties of, 443–444
  (*See also* Behavioral assessment; Psychological tests: Intelligence; Psychological tests: Personality)
Attachment:
  cultural differences in, 67
  and exploration, 38